To Shane
with my great pleasure

Danny

Green the Capitalists

Monowar Zaman

authorHOUSE®

AuthorHouse™
1663 Liberty Drive
Bloomington, IN 47403
www.authorhouse.com
Phone: 1 (800) 839-8640

Published by AuthorHouse 05/03/2016

ISBN: 978-1-5049-6182-0 (sc)
ISBN: 978-1-5049-6183-7 (hc)
ISBN: 978-1-5049-6181-3 (e)

Library of Congress Control Number: 2016900617

Print information available on the last page.

TABLE OF CONTENTS

PREFACE

My interest in economics perhaps started when I wrote a proposal for helping rickshaw pullers to become owners of auto-rickshaw during the time of banning of rickshaws from the major roads of Dhaka city in Bangladesh titled "Rickshaw Theke Auto-rickshaw" or "Rickshaw to Auto-rickshaw" in 1993. I sent that to Muhammad Yunus, founder of Grameen Bank and later Nobel Peace laureate in 2006. The main idea here was the poor rickshaw pullers were required to build their savings first within an institutional framework instead of prompting for any micro-credit. Although my proposal was regretted since Grameen Bank did not have any operational footprint in the city as its name implies "Grameen" means "rural" or "village" but I was highly inspired by receiving a response from Mr. Yunus to continue my informal research off track of my undergraduate study in electrical engineering.

I would like to thank my friend Asrar Chowdhury, who was studying economics for introducing me with his teachers and lending me a book "Rickshaws of Bangladesh" by Robert Gallaghar, who was a former teacher of my university. There by learning the story of Ayat Ali, a rickshaw puller who pedaled equivalent to seven times around the world but at the end owned almost noting, I became a passionate thinker of economics asking the question, why he could not hold enough of his contribution for his own livelihood. I tried to explore, but most of the mainstream books of economics could not satisfy me since I was not convinced that economic growth would sustainably solve the deep rooted poverty prevailing in Bangladesh.

Inspired by J.E. Meade's concept of "machines", I wrote my first unpublished manuscript "Man's Share of Machines" in 1998 during my MBA study and job in Grameen Phone. The term "machines" were defined as accumulation of man's contribution, which should always grow but the question I raised how a man could get his share of the machines from his contribution. There I introduced my concept "Greenhouse Care Economics" that described an economic framework for workers

i

share in a way that their share would tend to dominate in a unit industry as internal dynamics and the industry would grow in numbers as its external dynamics. In another aspect, internal dynamics might create an option for employers providing support for their employees' social security and health care, education as win-win opportunity for both the employers and the workers. Eventually, workers share would spread all over the economy and counterbalance growth compulsion but fulfil the needs of workers better quality lives as far as external dynamics would go. I sent copies to Muhammad Yunus and Khalid Shams, founder and then chairman of Grammen Bank respectively. Mr.Shams responded to me on the part I argued about Grammen Bank's limitation for keeping its client at subsistence level. Now I am so glad that Mr.Yunus is the iconic promoter of workers share in the form of social business around the world. I am grateful to my teacher late professor Muzaffar Ahmed for inspiring me in writing an article on "Greenhouse Care Economics" in Dhaka University IBA Journal. I am also thankful to my classmates Towfiqul Islam and Dr. A.F.M. Ataur Rahman for sharing their views and all the discussions we had during gestation phases of these concepts.

After immigrating to Canada, my interest turned to theoretical economics and I tried to develop a theoretical model titled "Inefficient Equilibrium" to justify my previous work. I acknowledge guidance from Geoffrey M Hodgson of University of Hertfordshire, UK and editor-in-chief of the Journal of Institutional Economics through sharing his contemporary academic literatures that enhanced my knowledge about institutional economics. I believe the concept "inefficient equilibrium" bridged the gap between neoclassical economics and institutional economics. My first book "Economics of Information Biasing" was published in 2009, which was catalogued in Baker Library, Harvard Business School and Dewey Library, M.I.T.

I am greatly indebted to Miriam Kennet, the founder of the Green Economics Institute, UK who made me interested about green economics and encouraged me for publishing my articles in International Journal of Green economics (IJGE). In my first article in IJGE, the term "inefficient equilibrium" was renamed to "Biased Equilibrium". I was fully convinced by the arguments of Richard Heinberg, Jeff Rubin and many others that our growth based economic model will haunt the existence of current civilization. However, most of us are skeptical about it, puzzled by myriads of information available in digital world. Influenced by Richard Heinberg's writings, I decided to write this book by putting together right information and knowledge on this based on what I had learned in about 20 years of searching and readings thousands of pages of articles, literatures, books and videos along with my own concepts and thoughts in one single book.

The first chapter is the summary of the whole book that also defines the 'triple crunch' crises our world is facing. The next two chapters provide historical background of our industrial civilization (Chapter 2) and a brief summary of economic theories (Chapter 3) for general readers so that they better understand the fundamental concept "Biased Equilibrium" introduced in Chapter 4. The next two chapters describe how our industrial civilization now riding on financial capitalism has taken off the ground after 1990s financial deregulation (Chapter 5) for reaching to its tragic end just like a moth to a flame (Chapter 6). The next chapter "Greening Capitalism" describes how our policy makers wasted time by trying out a series of failed approaches to reduce carbon emission. To better address this situation, Chapter 8 models the fundament control structure of our economies. The next chapter (Chapter 9) formulates a fundamental strategy for adjusting our existing growth based economies with the carrying capacity of the earth. It leaves unlimited discretionary space for policy makers & leaders to set up their own version of sub-strategies. The last chapter "Greenhouse Care Economics" provides an implementation model of the strategy that would bring the existing and potential sufferers -eventually everyone under a common economic framework, while solving their economic problems in real time.

I believe this book will attract wide range of rational readers, from high school students to policy makers, leaders, activists and academics. I know how difficult it is to promote a new idea at the very beginning as I saw the same when Telenor tried to promote my award winning idea "Mobile Money Management (MMM)" in 2004. Now "Mobile Money" is a common place, even adopted by GSMA that directly benefiting hundreds of millions of poor people in the developing world.

I would like to express my gratitude to all the members of Author House who helped publish this book for their great co-operations and diligent efforts. I am grateful to Bangladesh Shilpakala Academy for granting me persimmon for using S.M. sultan's famous painting "First Plantation" on this book's cover. Very special thanks to K.M Mokbul Hossain for and Pradyut Kumar Das for helping me get the permission. Among many others, I would like to thank Richard Heinberg of Post Carbon Institute, George Fortier of Federal Reserve Bank of St. Louis, Randall Jamrok of Industrial Workers of the World, Suzanne Alavi of International Monetary Fund, Peter Harrington of Anne S.K. Brown Military Collection, Emmanuel Saez of University of California, Berkele, Library of Congress, University of Saskatchewan respective to their permissions for using figures and charts that hugely enriched this book.

I am not a prolific writer but I admire my father Makbular Rahman's passion for writing that inspired me to keep on trying. My late mother Monowara Khanam dedicated her life for others. She would be most happy person if she were able to see this book in her lifetime. I pray for her departed soul.

I would like to express my heartfelt gratitude to my wife Nasima Akter, my daughter Maisa Tamanna and my son Maisim Zaman for their tremendous sacrifice by allowing me time and holding patience since they know me. I highly appreciate my 10 year old son Maisim Zaman, who hanged around with me asked me questions like whether I am providing any solution or just describing a problem. His concern about "peak oil" or "climate change" influenced me writing about Green Coalition Z in Chapter 9.

I believe it is Generation Z who will champion making our earth a better living place for mankind. I dedicate this book to them and wish all the best for their future.

Monowar Zaman
Brampton, ON, Canada
March 2, 2016

CHAPTER 1
THE CRISES

1.1 Introduction

In 1972, the Club of Rome, a global think tank, presented their report "Limits to Growth" that predicted that economic growth could not continue indefinitely because of the limited availability of natural resources, particularly oil.[81] On the other hand, the huge amount of greenhouse gases released by burning fossil fuel, the planet's atmosphere traps more heat called "global warming", causing irreversibly shrinking of glaciers, that is, wiping out sources of fresh water on one hand and rise of sea levels on the other.

In last forty years, the global economic policies promoted consumerism under financial capitalism (Figure 1.5) instead of taking tough line on climate change that accelerated global warming. In 1992, to stabilize greenhouse gas emission, a UN Framework on Climate Change (UNFCCC) was adopted.[82] Following 2008 financial crisis, New Economics Foundation (NEF) identifies that the growth driven global economy was facing a 'triple crunch', which was a combination of a "credit-fuelled financial crisis, accelerating climate change and encroaching peak in oil production".[1]

In 2015 Paris Climate Conference, for the first time, a universal legally binding agreement is signed for holding the increase in the global average temperature 1.50C-2°C above pre-industrial levels.[83] However, none of the countries is willing to compromise their growth, while the triple crunch crises are converging and gaining potential to explode. If a financial crisis hard hits global economy, the possibility of alternate energy to take over might disappear. Do we have a hope to protect us from the looming catastrophic disaster of triple crunch?

1

1.2 Growth versus Poverty

Ever since industrial revolution, economic growth and prosperity has been thought as synonymous and a panacea for all economic problems such as poverty and distribution. The strongest selling point of growth is alleviation of poverty since the industrial revolution led to high economic growth, eliminating mass poverty in what is now considered the developed world.[84] However, much of this has been achieved not because of development of new technologies and machineries but also massive use of fossil fuel. In his recent article "Renewable Energy after COP21", Heinberg describes the impact of fossil fuel based growth on poverty as:

> "Yet globally, wealthy industrial nations have disproportionately benefitted from the fossil fuel revolution while poorer nations have disproportionately borne the costs. And a similar disparity also exists within nations, both rich and poor ones. Further, the injustice of energy wealth vs. energy poverty is increasingly magnified by climate impacts, which fall disproportionately upon energy poor societies—both because of geographical happenstance and because they do not have the same level of resources to devote toward adaptation."[100]

Now we have reached to a point where further use of fossil fuel will jeopardize the carrying capacity of our earth. On the other hand, without growth, financial industry will collapse and the existence of our industrial civilization will be jeopardized. The most severe impact is, if we continue growth and use up all economically available fossil fuel, the carrying capacity of our earth will fall quickly and suddenly by billions of population. In this case, as the poorer people will be first impacted and therefore, the transition will be extremely painful involving massacre or massive death by civil war between rich and poor either using religious banner or political banner and then famine and plague may follow. Perhaps this has already started in the Middle East and in Africa, where the resources have started to decline. According to Heinberg, although apparently, religion would provide the ostensible banner for contention in many instances but this is likely to be a secondary rather than a primary driver.[102]

Economists often argue that if we sacrifice growth, poverty will increase and poor people will suffer. In reality economic growth may temporarily mask the economic problems but because of its unsustainable nature it provides no permanent route to escaping them. Tienhaara argues

> "It goes without saying that further economic growth means something quite different in a society that has already achieved a high level of per capita income than it does in one in which the majority of the population lives on less than $2 a day."[5]

Today one third of the world poor people who earn less than 2 dollars a day live in India.[68] This means India is the biggest poverty ridden country in the world. At the same time, India is the world's third largest greenhouse gas emitting country. According to World Bank, in May 2014, the world had 872.3 million people below extreme poverty line, of which 179.6 million people lived in India. In other words, India with 17.5% of total world's population, had 20.6% share of world's poorest in 2011.[85] According to United Nation's Millennium Development Goal (MGD) program in 2011-2012, there was 270 million or 21.9% people out of 1.2 billion of Indians lived below poverty line of $1.25 per day.[86] It can be inferred that India reduced (or masked) a significant amount of poverty but that required to maintaining about 7% growth per year and burn a huge amount of fossil fuel.[87] What will happen when fossil fuel will disappear? Growth will be negative; the people will be back to severe poverty.

India is ranked world's third largest individual greenhouse gas producer or fourth largest putting European Union in the picture (Figure 1.1). However per capita emission (1.8 tons per capita) is nine (9) times lower than that of USA, about four (4) times lower than China and about 3 times lower than global average.[90] In its report "Extreme Carbon Inequality", aid group Oxfam points out that those most exposed to climate risks such as extreme weather are contributing only a fraction of the emissions. According to this report, the richest 1 per cent of the world's population on average emits 175 times more carbon than the poorest 10 per cent.[91] If we distribute Indian population in a scale considering some people maintain the same lifestyle as USA (16.5 tons per

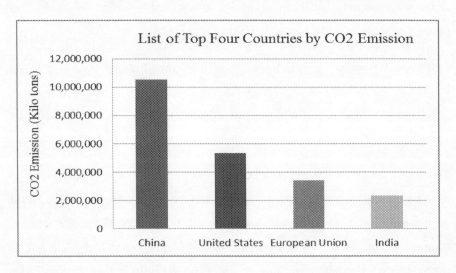

Figure 1.1: List of Top Four Countries by CO_2 Emissions[89]

capita), some like China (7.6 tons per capita), the emission from the poorest people will certainly be close to zero.[90] Since 1990 to 2014 CO_2 emission in India increased by 260% and per capita emission increased by 1.25.[90] Now pulling 179.6 million people out of poverty will not only mean add per capita emission by them but also add more proportionate emission by the riches. This means, poverty alleviation through growth is no more an efficient solution rather it is climatically suicidal.

The International Trade Union Confederation has called for the goal to be "zero carbon, zero poverty".[92] In her article "Back to the Future: Our Journey to Zero Carbon, Zero Poverty World" Sharan Burrow, its general secretary argues that there are "no jobs on a dead planet".[92] India could be world's role model, if India finds a way to alleviate its toughest poverty without increasing carbon emission.

4

According to Indian negotiator Dr. Ajay Mathur in UN Climate Conference 2015 in Paris, Denmark is the most climate responsible country. He mentions

"Even if India adopted Danish levels of sustainability, India's billion-plus population would still override the gains made unless there were advances on current technology."[93]

Looking back to history, as Figure 1.2 shows, according to economic historian Angus Maddison in his book "The World Economy: A Millennial Perspective", India was the richest country in the world and had the world's largest economy

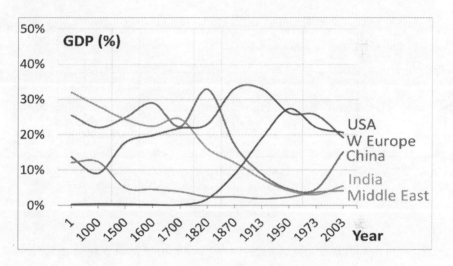

Figure 1.2: The global contribution to world's (Angus Maddison's estimates) GDP[69]

until pre-fossil fuel economy-the 17th century AD controlling between one third and one fourth of the world's wealth up to the time of the Marathas, from whence it rapidly declined during British rule.[70&71]

Bangladesh, was part of Bengal, which was one of the richest provinces of eastern India when India was the richest country of the world. For thousands of years this region attracted foreigners, invaders, mercantilists and colonists. The names "British East India Company" and "Dutch East Indian Company" reflect this claim. However, its economy ended up in deep rooted poverty, impenetrable bureaucracies, complex politics and widespread corruption, that is, full of inefficiencies. It has the similar pattern of economy as India in terms of poverty and inequality. However, as Bangladesh economy is also growing by about 6% every year, per capita carbon emission has also grown by 400%, from 0.1 in 1990 to 0.4 in 2014.[90] Now considering the political and bureaucratic complexities and linking poverty with growth, restraining CO_2 emission in Bangladesh is close to impossible even though Bangladesh is one of the most vulnerable countries to climate change in the coming decades.[101]

Let's meet Ayat Ali in Bangladesh–what he achieved in his 65 years of hard work but producing zero emission:

Ayat Ali is a 65-year-old rickshaw puller.....Nowadays his back is bent, and his eyes are glazed with age....During his lifetime he has pedaled perhaps 170,000 miles, which is equivalent to seven times around the world or three quarters the way to the moon. Yet he has little to show for his effort....The few possessions he owns are tied up into a bundle of cloth.[3]

- Robert Gallagher, "The Rickshaws of Bangladesh"

Ayat Ali is just an example of hundreds of millions of poor people in the world who absolutely (without any external energy such as fossil fuel) contribute toward growth of the economy creating zero emission but unfortunately, all they own are not enough to feed them for more than one day. He had no fault of his own, always being on right track in terms of carbon emission point of view. He had to work hard for his livelihood but fell into poverty over the generations. The rickshaws in Bangladesh provide majority of transport need serving more than one hundred million people every day.[3] According to Gallagher, with the rent Ayat Ali has paid during his lifetime, he could have purchased a rickshaw 40 times over. If Ayat Ali were able to keep that money, most probably, he

Figure 1.3 Rickshaw pullers in Dhaka city, Bangladesh[4]

would use that for his low emission living. On the other hand, as the money went up it contributed to more and more emissions.

Figure 1.2 also shows before 18th century, China and India were the two largest economies by GDP output. Now China is the second largest economy in the world (GDP $10.356 trillion) followed by USA ($17.348 trillion) but largest economy in terms of CO_2 emission (10.54 billion tons), double than USA (5.33 billion tons), next in the position.[90&94]

What does it mean to be rich? Does it mean quantitative consumptions such as big houses in big cities, driving big cars, eating more processed food etc., then it will be accompanied with corresponding emissions. As an example, an average American consumes 250g of meat per day compared to less than 10g by an average Indian. And meat production is much more energy intensive than production of vegetables. Or becoming rich is more on qualitative, a safe and clean place for living and growing food, healthy lifestyle, proper heath care and education? Economists, policymakers and rich people promote the first but we should have a choice of our own when we know that they are wrong. Unfortunately, in reality, the poor people do not have the choice of their own.

Looking back to pre-fossil fuel history again, when China was the largest economy in the world, most of the hardworking Chinese peasants were living in poverty. Carroll Quigley divides the hierarchy of Chinese society on that time into three classes, the ruling class, the gentry, and the peasants. He describes:

> "[T]he upper most group deriving its incomes as tribute and taxes from its possession of military and political power, while the middle group derived its incomes from economic sources, as interest on loans, rents from lands, and the profits of commercial enterprise, as well as from the salaries, graft, and other emoluments arising from his middle group's control of the bureaucracy. At the bottom the peasantry, which was the only really productive group in the society, derived its incomes from the sweat of its collective brows, and had to survive on what was left to it after a substantial fraction of its product had gone to the two higher groups in the form of rents, taxes, interest, customary bribes (called "squeeze"), and excessive profits on such purchased "necessities" of life as salt, iron, or opium."[72]

According to the new economic model described in this book, the relationship between the Chinese peasant class and the middle class bureaucracy can be considered as an inefficient "Biased Equilibrium" since the peasants were the only productive class supplying incomes for the upper two classes with long term stability, while they remained under poverty. According to Quigley again:

> "The inefficiency of the system was both customary and deliberate, since it allowed a large portion of the wealth which was being drained from the peasantry to be diverted and diffused among the middle class of gentry before the remnants of it reached the imperial group at the top."[73]

Quigley also defines three ages forming the central portion of the life cycle of a civilization, Age of Conflict, Age of Expansion and Age of Universal Empire. In his view a shift from an Age of Conflict to an Age of Expansion is marked by a resumption of the investment of capital and the accumulation of capital on a large scale. However, it can be argued that accumulation of capital is not an outcome of the transition between the ages, it is the reason. As an example, when more efficient, progressive Europeans went to direct conflict with inefficient and un-progressive Chinese society, it was conflict between the vested interests and sole objective was extension of European dominations on the middle group to grab the share of money produced originally by the Chinese peasants.[72] Chapter 2 provides snapshots of the capitalists' synthesis through a series of events that our civilization has come through.

The concept of capitalism is originated from Adam Smith's concept of 'invisible hand, which became popular and mainstream when the British East India Company began to bring huge wealth from India and other colonies followed by fossil fuel based industrial revolution.

New theories were developed around the degree that government does not have control over markets (laissez faire), and on property rights. The concept of capitalism tells about integrating self-interest nature of economic agents for free flow of goods and services, where government should act as a facilitator. Chapter 3 focuses on the historical context on which the capitalist concept has become dominant in our economic and political world. The historical path of our capitalist economy has been marked by many rise and fall but it has always ignored the earth's natural limit.

The politicians, policymakers of every country rely on economic growth for the "development" of world economies including the world's poorest economies, which eventually help them hold powerful positions. They think without growth, people would never achieve the consumer lifestyle enjoyed by people in the world's industrialized nations.[7] According to data published by World Bank, it shows the proportion of world population in extreme poverty 1981–2008 reduced from 40% to below 20% as the gross world product increased.[8] It supports the widespread belief among economists and policy makers that sustainable economic growth can alleviate poverty. The effect of economic growth on poverty reduction, the Growth elasticity of poverty, can also depend on the existing level of inequality.[10] This book introduces positional properties of inequalities in Chapter 4 that can be used to measure level of difficulty of poverty alleviation. As an example, income inequality in USA (Gini ratio 45%) is more than that of in India (Gini ratio 33.4%) but the positional property of Biased Equilibrium tells that, poverty in India is harder to alleviate.

The economic theories supportive to existing quantitative economic structures are based on a set of unrealistic assumptions which in reality never exist. In real picture, the world has reached to its peak in terms of resources and technologies but there are hundreds of millions of poor people are in a 'poverty trap' who may never be able to make a sustainable escape from there. This situation is explained in Chapter 4 by introducing a new concept "Biased Equilibrium".

Although our growth compulsive capitalist economy cannot solve the problems such as poverty and inequality but it has already used up the major part of our scare reserve of fossil fuel and surface water and caused ecological crisis like global warming or greenhouse effect. In its report "The Limits to Growth" Club of Rome argue that a narrow view of economic growth, combined with globalization, is creating a scenario where we could see a systemic collapse of our planet's natural resources.[11&12]

In globalized world, although many developed countries are not growing but they can leverage the products produced in sweatshops of other countries' cheap labor. Sharan Burrow, General Secretary, International Trade Union Confederation explains:

"Many communities are already devastated by poverty. Increasingly that poverty is born of the greed of a global trading system. Sixty percent of global trade now relies on production in supply chains - a model of growth that depends on massive hidden workforces with low wages, long hours, insecure work and low-cost overheads that create unsafe work and environmental damage….. When our wealthiest companies can't or won't pay $177 a month in Cambodia or $110 in Bangladesh this is just greed."[92]

Ready-Made Garment (RMG) industry is one of the big sweatshops that provide low cost clothing for developed countries and one way to keep inflation level low. Bangladesh is the second largest exporters of clothing in the world that employ mostly women who find escape from extreme rural poverty. The mushrooming sweatshops in Bangladesh have so little concern about safety of the workers that death of hundreds of workers by fire or building collapse is a commonplace. The worst among them was an eight-story sweatshop building called Rana Plaza collapsed in Bangladesh that killed over 1,129 lives.[13] The business press, economists and businessmen who put their faith with neoliberal globalization still argue for achieving growth to improve safety and lives of the workers. John Miller in his Triple Crisis blog argues:

"But their arguments distort the historical record and misrepresent the role of economic development in bringing about social improvement. Working conditions have not improved because of market-led forces alone, but due to economic growth combined with the very kind of social action that sweatshops defenders find objectionable."[15]

He refers to the 1911 Triangle Shirtwaist fire tragedy in USA, which cost 146 garment workers their lives. This incidence along with hardships of the Great Depression inspired the unionization of garment workers and led to the imposition of government regulations to improve workplace safety.[15]

The poor African nations are more unfortunate than south Asian countries like Bangladesh and India compared to their immense natural resources. The poverty situation in Africa is far more complex because as Collier explains in his book

'The Bottom Billion' that Africa suffers from one or more development traps. The African countries that are rich in natural resources are paradoxically usually worse off than countries that are not.[16] Most African nations saw inflation of approximately 10% per year of higher. An average African faced annual inflation of over 60% from 1990 until 2002 in those few countries that account for inflation. Some countries like mineral rich Angola, Congo saw triple digit inflation.[17] Despite large amounts of arable land south of the Sahara desert, small, individual land holdings are rare. In many nations, land is subject to tribal ownership and in others most of the land is often in the hands of descendants of European settlers. Widespread availability of cheap labor has often perpetuated policies that encourage inefficient agricultural and industrial practices, leaving Africa further impoverished. Unfortunately, economic growth in Africa does not reach to the poor but makes the inflation situation worse.

1.3 The Financial Frankenstein

Why the poor people do not have a choice to live their own? In the example of Ayat Ali in previous section, Ayat Ali was not able to hold the money he generated but went to the hands of the others such as his rickshaw owner, his landlord or local loan sharks except for his bare minimum livelihood. Similarly, the money generated by the garments workers of Rana Plaza was not used for their well-beings and safety but most of the money went to the others such as the owners, businessmen, bureaucrats and politicians. Eventually the money entered into a global financial and monetary market, while the governments either in developed or developing countries are starving for money to run government or support the poor people. Therefore, our capitalist world is experiencing poverty and debt crisis at the same time it is more affluent than ever.

In Africa rich natural resources have made the colonies and their aides rich but became curse for the natives. In Nigeria as David Quammen (2005) of National

Geographic described "hundreds of billions of dollars' worth of oil has poured out of Nigeria though little of that money has reached residents, Africa's rich deposits of diamonds, gold and oil have often proved a curse, fostering corruptions, coups and civil wars".[18] After 50 years of petroleum production, Nigeria has become one of the most corrupted countries in the world but the money has already entered into global financial markets, whereas most of Nigerians survive on less than a dollar a day.

The developed countries are not much different from developing nations in terms of where the money goes. The debt crisis in the U.S. and many countries in Europe tell about the crisis of funds with government and the banks, while riches are holding the money at individual levels. The dependency of the U.S. economy on debt, Russian's dependency on oil export and China's need of oil for growth all are in fact tied up with capitalist resolution of poverty prevention. If government is in short of money, the poor and elderly people in the countries will be the most affected since their healthcare, social security, pension services are directly impacted. The capitalists solution of these problems are bailout that temporarily solves banks cash flow problem but makes the governments more dependent on debts if actions are not taken addressing the root cause in economic policies. The best example of debt crisis is Greece. After more than 240 billion euros of bailout, Greece's economy has shrunk by a quarter in five years, and unemployment rose 25 percent and again it is running out of money fast.[77] According to New York Times,

"[T]he bailout money mainly goes toward paying off Greece's international loans, rather than making its way into the economy. And the government still has a staggering debt load that it cannot begin to pay down unless a recovery takes hold."[77]

Many economists, and many Greeks, blame the austerity measures for much of the country's continuing problems. Yanis Varoufakis, the finance minister of Greece, went confrontation with the creditors by saying "austerity is like trying to extract milk from a sick cow by whipping it."[78] At the height of the debt crisis, many experts worry that Greece's problems would spill over to the rest of the world[77] since many other Eurozone countries such as Portugal, Ireland, Italy and Spain are on the same line. Figure 1.4 shows public debt of different countries as

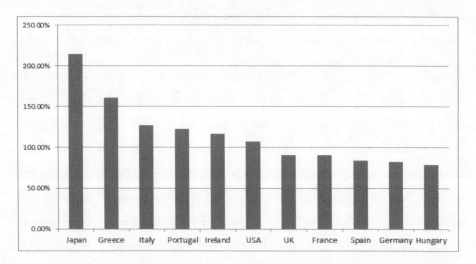

Figure 1.4: Public Debt of Different Countries as Percentage of GDP[79]

percentage of their GDPs. The graph shows governments of the world's strong economies including Japan, Germany, USA, UK and France are also now dependent on debt and therefore, much of their tax revenues are now channeled to a financial Frankenstein.

In his book, "Tragedy and Hope: A History of The World in Our Time", Carroll Quigley, defines our civilization has passed through a series of phases or ages. He defines three ages of civilization, The Age of Expansion, Age of Conflict and Age of Universal Empire.[1] Our existing phase can be treated as the Age of Universal Financial Empire under capitalism, which is only less than forty years old, whereas capitalism is about three hundred years old. He defines capitalism as "an economic system motivated by the pursuit of profits within a price system".[51] He also describes different types of capitalists as:

"The commercial capitalists sought profits from the exchange of goods, the industrial capitalists sought profits from the manufacture of goods; the financial capitalists sought profits from the manipulation of claims on money; and the monopoly capitalist sought profits from manipulation of the market to make the market price and the amount sold such that his profits would be maximized."[51]

As the economies of the world are controlled by financial capitalists, following 2008 financial crisis, a protest called Occupy Wall Street (OWS) movement began on September 17, 2011 at Liberty Square in New York's Manhattan's Financial District, which has spread to over 100 cities in the United States and over 1,500 cities globally. The protesters targeted Wall Street because of its role in the financial breakdown and economic recession began in 2008. They are against social and economic inequality, corruption and undue influence of corporations, particularly from financial services sectors on government. In turn they want, more jobs, fair distribution of income, financial sector reform and a reduction of the influence of corporations on politics. None of these agendas are new but fostered by internet campaign by the young people who see no future and vulnerable lives unless there is a reform of the capitalist economic structure. Henry Blodget summarizes the reason in his "what the Wall Street protestors are so angry about?" article as:[22]

"[T]hree years after the financial crisis, the unemployment rate in America is still at the highest level since Great Depression.....Inequality is worst around Wall Street and Oil Land. After adjusting for inflation, average hourly earnings haven't increased in 50 years...... Also, hundreds of millions of Americans are indebted up to their eyeballs, whereas the top 1% own 5% of the country's total debt."[22]

The website of Occupy Wall Street (OWS) movement (http://occupywallst.org/) describes their movement as "leaderless resistance movement" of the 99% and "will no longer tolerate the greed and corruption of the 1%".[19] In reality, nothing goes far without funding. The OWS movement failed to achieve any outcome. In

1968, James Simon Kunen wrote in his book "The Strawberry Statement: Notes of a College Revolutionary" about his firsthand experience about "The Columbia University protests of 1968", student demonstrations that spread around the world in that year. He wrote about the protestors "They have no idea that they are playing into the hands of the establishment they claim to hate."[26]

Capitalism was in need of a turning point when in United States, the post-World War II boom ended in high inflation and high unemployment called "stagflation" coupled with "peak oil" crisis that slowed down economic growth rate. In the late 1970s, inflation became as high as 10 or 11 percent that caused market interest rates to rise above the limits mandated by regulation Q of Glass-Steagall Act. Following this act, income of top 1% also fell down and became stagnant during the time of stagflation.[27] Therefore, in 1981 President Reagan reduced tax rate for the riches expecting to promote investments. The initial success of Reaganomics created a craze for consumerism all over the world at blazing rate. Figure 1.5 shows a sharp turn and exponential rise of the world GDP at an unprecedented rate since 1990s boosted capitalism as huge success. Now in USA, 70 percent of US GDP comes from consumer spending. Financial

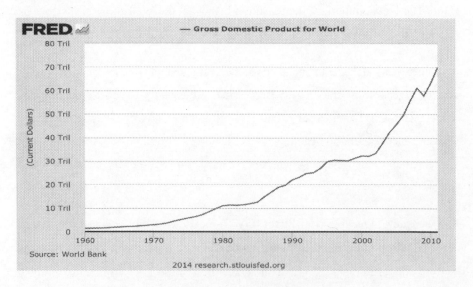

Figure 1.5: Gross Domestic Product of the World[28]

capitalism is an incentive for capitalists, which is built with the expectation of further growth by means of overconsumption.[36] This rapid growth of consumption also rapidly aggravated the amount of greenhouse gas emission, which is now hard to stop.

In 1955, economist Victor Lebow best describes how "growth" and "consumption" are synonymous:

> "Our enormously productive economy demands that we make consumption our way of life, that we convert the buying and use of goods into rituals, that we seek our spiritual satisfaction and our ego satisfaction in consumption. We need things consumed, burned up, worn out, replaced and discarded at an ever-increasing rate."[75]

Nevertheless consumption could also happen without growth. On the other hand, consumption with growth, in the long run it is physically impossible to maintain.[2] The growth based economy may bring quick prosperity but unfortunately we see prosperity on one end and poverty on the other end of our economic world and financial capitalism is largely responsible for that. The amount of carbon emission is directly related to the amount of consumption. Therefore, it can be inferred from this graph that world's carbon emission increased at unprecedented rate in last 40 years following financial liberalism.

There is no doubt that this exponential rise of GDP was accompanied with burning of fossil fuel at exponential rate. However, profit became more derived from ownership of an asset, credit, rents, and earning interest, rather than actual productive processes.[29] Heinberg explains the huge economic activities derived by financial economics as:

> "As long as the economy is growing, that means more money and credit are available, expectations are high, people buy more goods, businesses take out more loans, and interest on existing loans can be repaid."[7]

Minsky defined this as "paradox of gluttony". This paradox is explained by introducing new concepts such as Boarder Propensity of Consumption (BPC) and Market Energy Loop (MEL) in Chapter 4.

Involvement with financial markets have made wealthy Americans wealthier and influenced further deregulation. Following Margaret Thatcher's "Big Bang" change of financial market structure in England, the U.S. Federal Reserve and the U.S. governments continued deregulation of the financial markets and finally Glass-Steagall Act was officially repealed in 1999 by passing Financial Modernization Act.[29] Section 3.6 in Chapter 3 discusses more detail on financial capitalism and Chapter 5 discusses the aftermath.

The Financial Modernization Act promoted innovation of financial products by exploiting advancements in computing and information technology. The global shift toward financial capitalism has connected the global financial markets each other at the same time it has added more vulnerability to major financial crisis and recession. The meaning of the term financial capitalism goes beyond the importance of financial intermediation. It also encompasses the significant influence of the wealth holders and bankers on the political process and economic policies.

In the U.S., Quantitative Easing (QE) allows the Federal Reserve Bank create tens of billions of dollars each month out of thin air and use the money to purchase the Federal Treasury bonds.[2] This enables the federal government to borrow at low interest rates and virtually all of the money stays within financial circles that promotes speculation.[2] Susan Strange and Thomas Palley have argued that the 21st century predominance of finance capital has led to a preference for speculation "Casino Capitalism."[31]

Now finance-driven globalization is setting the stage for massive world-wide recession, while the world is more affluent than ever. The biggest category of financial instrument is derivatives. According to the Bank for International

Settlements (BIS), Over the Counter (OTC) derivatives market was $516 trillion in June 2007. The Economist reports that as of June 2011, the OTC derivatives market amounted to approximately $700 trillion and the size of the market traded on exchanges totaled an additional $83 trillion.[32] The huge OTC derivatives contracts compared to "market value" clearly indicates that we have made our entire economy a Ponzi scheme tied to speculation on continuously expanding debts much faster than economic output, which can never be repaid.[33] The Economist reported in June 2014 that U.S. student loan debt exceeded $1.2 trillion, with over 7 million debtors in default.[20]

Long before the 2008 financial crisis, in March 2003, Warren Buffet, the investment magnet and one of the top richest man in the world argued that such highly complex financial instruments are time bombs and "financial weapons of mass destruction" that could harm not only their buyers and sellers, but the whole economic system.[34] At some point of time the financial Frankenstein we have created will bring the world financial system crash to the end.

1.4 The Dead End

"What if the crisis of 2008 represents something much more fundamental than a deep recession? What if it's telling us that the whole growth model we created over the last 50 years is simply unsustainable economically and ecologically and that 2008 was when we hit the wall - when Mother Nature and the market both said: "No more.""[35]

-Thomas L Friedman, New York Times

The financial crisis of 2008 could be another wake up call, which was primarily triggered by high oil price. It was a tip of the iceberg of a much larger crisis to be caused by limits to growth. The flat oil production between the years 2004 and 2008 might have created an impression that the world has reached to its peak oil and the oil price spiked from $50 a barrel to $147 a barrel.[8] Even a falling oil price gives a wrong impression that we are moving away from the fact of peak oil but matter of fact, it is amassing the forces for triple crunch to hard hit the economy in any future time.[8] It cuts in both ways. It induces more use of oil and therefore, worsens the climate change. At the same time, it destroys the appeal of renewable energy to protect the climate change. The shale oil boom in U.S.A that created the hype of "Saudi America" is now camouflaged by low oil price. On Oct. 7, 2013, Abdalla Salem el-Badri, OPEC's secretary general, said at a conference in Kuwait that U.S. shale producers are "running out of sweet spots" and that output will peak in 2018.[116]

Whenever a recession begins, the poor people become the ultimate sufferers although they are not responsible. Although we could not solve the problems like poverty and inequality but we have already consumed the major part of our scarce reserve of fossil fuel and fresh water and caused cataclysmic ecological crisis like global warming or greenhouse effect. The era of consumerism arose from a temporary abundance of cheap concentrated, storable, and portable energy in the form of fossil fuels, which consists of millions of years' worth of stored and concentrated ancient biomass. From this perspective, the amount of poverty alleviated is also because of the temporary economic expansion driven by cheap fossil fuel.[9]

The over-consumption driven by financial economics leads to increased rate of depletion of resources such as fossil fuel, fresh water reserve, minerals and soil. This means we are led to an irreversible dead end of industrial civilization by progressively damaging the carrying capacity of the earth. As started in many parts of Africa and Middle East, the effect may be so severe that endless civil wars may gradually breakout all over the world enough to bring our civilization to the end. There were about 24 civilizations but all collapsed except the current industrial civilization.[2] Is this the time the industrial civilization come to its end?

The world fossil fuel production has followed a typical Hubbert curve, known as "Peak Oil" curve created by M. King Hubbert in 1956. He accurately predicted that United States oil production would peak between 1965 and 1970.[37] The Club of Rome[40], a global think tank founded in 1968, published a report titled "The Limits to Growth"[41] in 1972 and for the first time at the International Students' Committee (ISC) annual Management Symposium in St. Gallen, Switzerland. The report echoes some of the concerns and predictions of Thomas Malthus in "An Essay on the Principle of Population (1798)"[43] but included 'resource decline' as one of the important factors besides population growth. It predicted that economic growth could not continue indefinitely because the natural resource of energy, particularly oil and coal is similar to land that follows law of diminishing return.[41&42] This was 40 years back and we had time to be better prepared for the upcoming post-oil crisis. Colin Campbell, an eminent petroleum geologist explains his worries:

"The world's oil and gas production will start to decline within most people's lifetimes. Although this will have a dramatic effect on lifestyles and the course of civilization, vested interests have deliberately kept both policymakers and the public in the dark."[44]

Hubbert's prediction is based on conventional oil production. Recent development of new production techniques such as "horizontal drilling and hydraulic fracking" and the exploitation of unconventional supplies created a hype of "Saudi America" in Wall Street Journal.[38] In reality the decline rate of shale oil production from fracking and horizontal drilling is extremely high.[39] In his book "Afterburn: Society Beyond Fossil Fuels " Richard Heinberg explains this as:

"In the past few years, high oil prices have provided the incentive for small, highly leveraged, and risk-friendly companies to go after some of the last, worst oil and gas production prospects in North America—formations known to geologists as "source rocks," which require operators to use horizontal drilling and fracking technology to free up trapped hydrocarbons. The energy returned on energy invested in producing shale gas and tight oil from these formations is minimal. While US oil and gas production rates have temporarily spiked, all signs indicate that this will be a brief boom that will not change the overall situation significantly: society is reaching the point of diminishing returns with regard to the economic benefits of fossil fuel extraction."[2]

For the whole duration of fossil fuel burning, a huge amount of carbon dioxide gas and other greenhouse gases released in the atmosphere, which traps more heat called "global warming". Severely enough, it is causing shrinking of glaciers, that is, wiping out sources of fresh water on one hand and rise of sea levels on the other. As we are continuing using fossil fuel at high rate, the consequences are going to be cataclysmic climate impacts, serious energy shortage and fresh water scarcity. Although since the early 20th century earth's

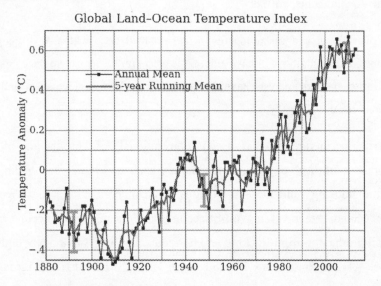

Figure 1.6: Global Annual Mean Surface Air Temperature Change (NASA)[46]

mean surface temperature has increased by about 0.8°C[45], Figure 1.6 shows about three-fourth of the increase occurring since 1970.[46] This timeline has relationship with financial deregulation and globalization promoted by economists and policy makers after economic stagflation of 1970s, which have induced consumerism at unprecedented rate. A sustained global warming of more than 2 °C (relative to pre-industrial levels) could lead to eventual sea level rise of around 1 to 4 m due to thermal expansion of sea water and the melting of glaciers and small ice caps.[47] It will be a devastating impact since not only limited to rising sea level or salinization but also once the glaciers dry out, in turn the rivers will also dry out so as the other sources of fresh water. The consequence may be as severe as famine and plague.

The Kyoto Protocol, signed on 11 December, 1997 urged the industrialized countries to cut carbon emissions by an average of 5.2 percent below 1990 levels by 2008-2012. Although there were 192 countries present at the conference, only 30 developed nations produced 90% of the world's emission.[48] This scenario is becoming worse since currently the developed nations are in competition with the emerging nations such as China, India, Brazil and Russia that put all polluting nations in dilemma taking any action to control emission. Figure 1.7 shows per capita CO_2 emission for China increased from 1.2 tons in 1970 to 7.6

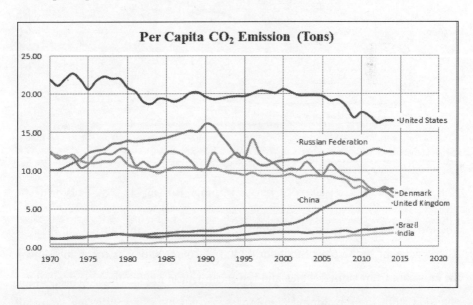

Figure 1.7: Per Capita CO2 Emission[95]

tons in 2014 (over 6 times), particularly the jump from 2.1 tons in 1990 was tremendous. For India it increased from 0.4 tons in 1970 to 1.8 tons (4.5 times) in 2014, for Brazil about 2 times. The Per capita emissions in the U.S. and in European countries remain stable or somewhat decreased because of moving most of their emission producing manufacturing such as China & India. These two countries still need to burn a huge amount of coal to lift hundreds of millions of people out of poverty. As an example, India is aiming for producing 1.5 billion metric tons of coal by 2020, up about 600 million tons in 2012.[98] Figure 1.8 shows even following Kyoto Protocol the over-all global CO_2 emission has been increasing every year despite all measures of emission control such as cap and trade system, carbon offset, carbon tax and promotion of clean energy.[49&50]

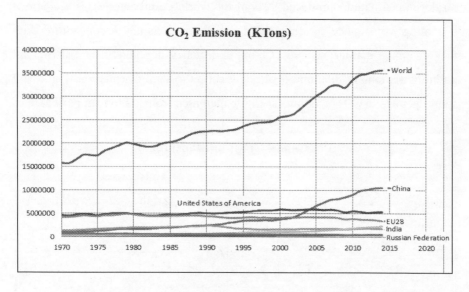

Figure 1.8: CO2 Emission of China, EU, India, Russia, USA & the World[96]

The top five (5) largest emitter countries China, USA, European Union, India & Russia account for 65.6% of the world total.[96] Among them, as the graph shows, the emission from United States and European Union remain fairly stable but the emission from the developing countries such as China and India are going up because of their exploding manufacturing and creation of new consumers in their highly growing economy. The impact of these emissions "global warming" is irreversibly accumulating every year.

Charles Hall and David Murphy show that, since 1970, high oil prices have been strongly correlated with recessions, and low oil prices with economic expansion and emission.[52&53] Past experience shows that recession tends to hit when aggregate cost of oil for the nation equals 5.5 percent of GDP.[53] However by lowering interest rate or by increasing flow of debt an economy can continue expansion even the oil price is high and shift this risk to some point in future. On the other hand, economic policies based on financial capitalism causes rapid depletion of fossil, which eventually increases the oil price. As an example, Chinese "coal fired" economy grew more than 10% annual rate from 2002 to 2010.[54] According to CNBC news, China's money supply expanded by more than threefold since 2008 and a lot of that money had gone into real estate.[55] Therefore, Chinese real estate market saw a boom by massive housing and apartment complex constructions but remaining unsold called "ghost cities of China". Although Chinese housing market is already over-blown but forecasts shows that demand for urban properties is expected to remain high over the next decade since it is estimated that another 200 million people could join China's urban areas by 2023.[56] If this happens, China's most of the domestic coal reserve will be used up and its dependency on imported oil will increase. This will further drive the oil price. If the oil price goes up coupling with sharp depletion of oil reserve, then there will be a devastating effect in the global economy.

During 2008 oil price hike, Global Research published an analysis that the price of crude oil is not made according to any traditional relation of supply to demand. It's controlled by an elaborate financial market system as well as by the four major oil companies. It estimates that as much as 60% of today's crude oil price is pure speculation driven by large trader banks and hedge funds. It writes:

"With the development of unregulated international derivatives trading in oil futures over the past decade or more, the way has opened for the present speculative bubble in oil prices. Since the advent of oil futures trading and the two major London and New York oil futures contracts, control of oil prices has left OPEC and gone to Wall Street. It is a classic case of the "tail that wags the dog."[108]

Quite contrastingly, as Figure 1.9 shows oil price has started declining since third quarter of 2014. In August 2015, New York Times writes:

"Not coincidentally, nearly all the advantages of the price swing are moving in Washington's direction. Most American consumers and industries have benefited from a sharp drop in gasoline prices and other energy costs. And abroad, the economies of oil-producing adversaries like Russia and Venezuela are reeling."[109]

As a result of oil price decline, oil-producing countries such as Russia, Venezuela, Nigeria, Ecuador and Brazil are suffering economic and perhaps

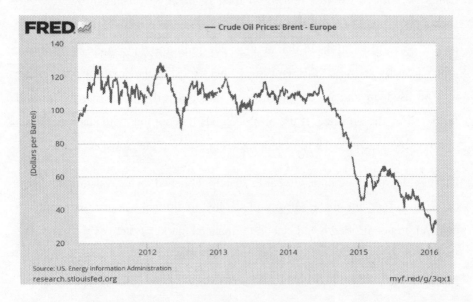

Figure 1.9: Crude Oil Price: Brent-Europe 2011-2016[110]

political crisis.[109] Russia's federal budget is based on Brent crude averaging $100 a barrel. The decline in oil prices is putting Russia into deficit budget since energy exports make up around half of Russia's budget. According to Russian President Vladimir Putin, oil price decline has been engineered by political forces. He referred to a "distinct direct link" between physical oil markets and "the financial platforms where the trade is conducted".[58] New York Times recently comments:

"There are a number of conspiracy theories floating around. Even some oil executives are quietly noting that the Saudis want to hurt Russia and Iran, and so does the United States — motivation enough for the two oil-producing nations to force down prices. Dropping oil prices in the 1980s did help bring down the Soviet Union, after all......But there is no evidence to support the conspiracy theories, and Saudi Arabia and the United States rarely coordinate smoothly."[111]

Since the oil price remains low, the financial hardships of smaller shale and non-conventional companies are increasing and many of them have gone bankrupt. There are signs, however, that production is falling because of the drop in exploration investments. Wood MacKenzie, a consulting firm has identified 68 large oil and natural gas projects worldwide, with a combined value of $380 billion, that have been put on hold around the world since prices started coming down, halting the production of 2.9 million barrels a day.[112] The big and small companies are now laying off their workers or cutting wages but the smaller companies are selling their assets to big companies. The large companies are now take advantage of bargain basement prices to gobble up the assets of weaker companies.[111] The shale oil or fracking companies that are surviving now, either they have future contracts or insurance coverage for minimum price (say, $90 per barrel), which are now expiring.[113&114] This means they will have to survive based on borrowing and scale up their production. Similarly, the oil exporting countries small to big are now enduring budget deficits are heading toward full-scale sovereign-debt crises. The International Monetary Fund estimates that the revenues of Saudi Arabia and its Persian Gulf allies of OPEC will slip by $300 billion this year.[111] This means, when the oil price will rebound, much of their earnings will be channeled to the big oil companies and the banks, more precisely to the financial power houses or to the core capitalists who run them. Eventually once the oil price will rise too high or cross its economic limit, a big financial crisis will follow to crash the banks.

On the other hand, the worst thing about low oil price is that they encourage more consumption. This means our earth is now warming faster, which is irreversibly depleting glaciers and fresh water. For oil, either price goes up or down or we go to North Pole or deserts in the Middle East, the impact on climate will be devastating. On the other hand, renewable energies are not yet or never will be an independent source of energy. Its machineries, accessories require fossil fuel to produce and to transport. If we continue using fossil fuel at existing rate, fossil fuel will disappear suddenly by reaching its economic limit but before destroy the environment–leaving transition to renewable energy stranded. Regarsless of price, oil or fossil fuel is the price-most precious substance for keeping our earth sustainable along side renewable energy. We still need them to produce or to build renewable energy materials and infrastructures. The remaining fossil fuels are not for burning for growth but for our survival.

In its World Oil Outlook, OPEC says that oil demand to hit 111m barrels by 2040 despite its impact on climate change.[61] World's leading oil producing group sees crude remaining as the world's economy life blood through to 2040 as Asian demand grows. Oil prices will average $177 per barrel by 2040 and the world will need to find an additional 21m barrels per day (bpd) of crude over the next 25 years to meet demand from rising global populations and rapid economic growth in Asia.[61] This will have definitely a catastrophic blow on global warming. On the other hand, higher oil price in the event of depletion will bring down the economies of oil importing countries. Therefore, governments that borrowed heavily during the time of cheap oil with the expectation that further economic growth would swell tax revenues and make it easy to repay debts, but according to Heinberg, with declining revenue and higher borrowing cost after oil price rise will be a "sure formula for default".[2]

As an oil exporting country, Russia will get a turn when oil price will come back to its favor to recover its budget deficits occurred during oil price downturn. Once that happens, if again Russia hits the Achilles' heel of us economy by dumping the U.S. dollars again and that cascades to the other parts of the world, the debt infested U.S. economy will face the biggest financial and monetary challenges ever. This is just one way of possible financial crisis. Heinberg highlights the causes of financial crises are looming around the world as:

"Financial and monetary systems can crash suddenly and completely. This almost happened in September 2008 as the result of a combination of a decline in the housing market, reliance on overly complex and in many cases fraudulent financial instruments, and skyrocketing energy prices. Another sovereign debt crisis in Europe could bring the world to a similar precipice. Indeed, there is a line-up of actors waiting to take center stage in the years ahead, each capable of bringing the curtain down on the global banking system or one of the world's major currencies. Each derives its destructive potency from its ability to strangle growth, thus setting off chain reactions of default, bankruptcy, and currency failure."[33]

If this chain reaction begins, it effects will be increasingly severe that will spread throughout the world. Many of the technological advancements and huge infrastructures will be useless to most of the people in both developed and developing countries. As an example, only super rich people would be able to drive cars and live in warm houses. Due to shortage of power and raw materials, industries would be closed down, banking system and international trade would collapse and all the economies will fall in the deepest recession. As a result, inequalities between various people in a country and between the regions of the world may become further worse. In developing countries, the most severe impact would be on food supply, which is largely dependent on fertilizers and chemical pesticides directly or indirectly rely on oil products. Increased food price would cause mass starvation and famine.

The cities and urban areas that are the drivers and growth centers of our consumption based economies are nothing but "cages for rats racing"[118]. Ironically, we are trapped in cages of concretes. Imagine that if there is no oil, there will be no job, no heating, no water and no food and no escape since all of the country sides and farmlands will be guarded with weapons.

The depletion of this water resource can be shown by a similar Hubbert curve since like "Peak oil", the usable fresh water is also harvested faster than it can be replaced. The impact of fresh water scarcity might be more severe on mankind since about 80 percent of the world's population (5.6 billion in 2011) lives in areas with threats to water scarcity. In 2000, the world population was 6.2 billion. The UN estimates that by 2050 there will be an additional 3.5 billion and most of them will be born in countries already experiencing water shortages.[62] This will impact almost all big cities in the world where water table has already dropped hundreds of feet because of extensive overdraft. As an example, a 2007 study by the Asian Development Bank showed that in 20 cities in India the average duration of supply was only 4.3 hours per day.[63] None of the 35 Indian cities with a population of more than one million distribute water for more than a few hours per day, despite generally sufficient infrastructure.[63] Now if urbanization continues, how these cities will sustain with more population and depleted ground water at the same time?

An increase in global temperature will cause sea levels to rise and a probable expansion of subtropical deserts. This would displace millions of people. Already the severity of storms such as hurricanes and cyclones is increasing like the one recently hit Japan and the subsequent nuclear crisis has demonstrated the devastating impact of global warming. The climate change would also be responsible for massive crop failures and diminish fresh water supply. It may cause more violent swings between floods and droughts. According to research published in Nature, by 2050, rising temperatures could lead to the extinction of species and damage ecosystems.[64] As suggested, with warmth comes disease and may cause outbreaks of deadly diseases.[65] As the overall impact summarized by Simmons in his article "20 Deadliest Effects of Global Warming" as:

"With greatly reduced rainfall, more severe droughts and loss of soil fertility, food and water supplies would soon diminish, resulting in higher prices, famine, disease, malnutrition, starvation and, ultimately, death. Politically unstable countries or badly affected areas might descend into various degrees of anarchy, with governmental collapses and shifts in authority as those in control of resources become more powerful. Countries that still retain good food and water resources might be unwilling to part with these vital commodities or accept the millions of refugees that would seek new homes. Ultimately these consequences would be catastrophic."[66]

Like the first human footstep, Africa is already demonstrating the disastrous era would begin in the post-oil world. National Geography reports on its special issue on Africa that "today with competition for resources on the rise, convergence has become collision, fueling war, disease and extinction."[18] The magazine reports, oil in poor African countries has been called the "devil's excrement"-a curse as "hundreds of billions of dollars' worth of oil has poured out of Nigeria though little of that money has reached residents, Africa's rich deposits of diamonds, gold and oil have often proved a curse, fostering corruptions, coups and civil wars"[18] Some parts of Arica already have reached to the dead end of their economic lives. The rest of the world would follow them as we cannot ignore that we are part of the same world.

According to Quigley's concept 'Ages of Civilization", if we continue existing path of growth, despite all the expensive efforts of "fracking" and oil sand mining, we will reach to an endless 'age of conflict', which will take us to the dead end of carrying capacity of the earth. By that time not only our existing economic system will collapse but also we will lose the most vital resources such as the glaciers–the origin of the fresh water and much of the surface water at disastrous level for all living human beings and species in the earth. For the remaining of the resources, there will be seven to eight billion of people on earth to fight with each other with all their deadly weapons. As happened in the past that each big episode of war or invasion was followed by malnutrition, plagues and famines until World War I. This time one single episode may lead to end of industrial civilization. And if it is coupled with nuclear weapon, it may extinct our civilization itself. As John F. Kennedy highlights in his "A Strategy of Peace" speech in American University in Washington (1963)

"It makes no sense in an age where a single nuclear weapon contains almost ten times the explosive force delivered by all the allied air forces in the Second World War. It makes no sense in an age when the deadly poisons produced by a nuclear exchange would be carried by wind and water and soil and seed to the far corners of the globe and to generations yet unborn."[107]

Bulletin of Atomic Scientists maintains a virtual clock called "Doomsday Clock" that conveys how close we are to destroying our civilization with dangerous technologies of our own making. In 2015 it is set only three minutes to the impending doomsday and explains:

"Unchecked climate change, global nuclear weapons modernizations, and outsized nuclear weapons arsenals pose extraordinary and undeniable threats to the continued existence of humanity, and world leaders have failed to act with the speed or on the scale required to protect citizens from potential catastrophe. These failures of political leadership endanger every person on Earth......The clock ticks now at just three minutes to midnight because international leaders are failing to perform their most important duty—ensuring and preserving the health and vitality of human civilization."[97]

1.5 Switching the Trajectory

"Our problems are manmade—therefore, they can be solved by man. And man can be as big as he wants. No problem of human destiny is beyond human beings. Man's reason and spirit have often solved the seemingly unsolvable—and we believe they can do it again."[107]

–John F. Kennedy "A Strategy of Peace (1963)"

The current trajectory of growth based economy is taking us toward its dead end. In his recent book "Afterburn" Richard Heinberg summarizes the trajectory:

[W]e have already reached the point of diminishing returns for investments in world oil production.....the same time, burning Earth's vast storehouses of ancient sunlight releases carbon dioxide into the atmosphere, resulting in global warming and ocean acidification.....Climate change is contributing to a mass extinction of species, extreme weather, and rising sea levels—which, taken together, could undermine the viability of civilization itself.....If civilization fails, then we will have no need for cars, trucks, aircraft, ships, power plants, or furnaces—or for the oil, coal, and gas that fuel them.[2]

Figure 1.10 below summarizes our history of industrial civilization (not on scale) with respect to capital accumulation. The capital accumulation here is symbolic of what we piled up in terms of money, assets or infrastructures in our fossil fuel based globalized way of life. The more we have moved on along the trajectory, we have added complexity and helped consolidate the financial powers. The figure shows the sequence of ages mentioned by Carroll Quigley in his book "Tragedy and Hope" that capital accumulation continued as we moved from the Age of Conflicts (the World Wars) and an Age of Expansion (during Cold Wars) until finally reached to the existing Age of Universal Financial Empire, mostly after financial deregulations (for details, please see Chapter 3) in dominating countries, where the capital accumulations have happened. However, a monstrous growth of financial derivatives–way bigger than the total world GDP,

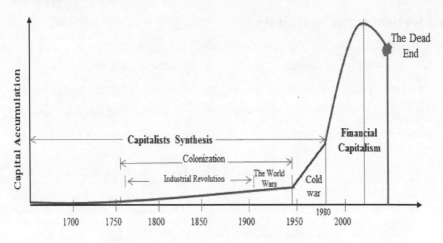

Figure 1.10: Current Economic Trajectory (Example only, not drawn in scale)

which have gained enough potential to bring the whole financial system down to the dead end of the carrying capacity of the earth.

Now the challenge of climate change is seen as $10 trillion wealth creation opportunity.[104] Jigar Shah, the founder of the U.S. based world's largest renewable company SunEdision argues that this opportunity can be harvested based on the world's existing technology.[104] By foreseeing this huge growth opportunity, the renewable energy companies borrowed aggressively from financial industry but not yet able to generate enough cash flow due to slower market response compared to high investments. The lenders are also taking advantage of the industry's need of short-term liquidity. As an example, SunEdision's total outstanding debt rose to about $11.7 billion at the end of third-quarter 2015 from $6.3 billion a year ago.[105] Following a temporary rise of its stock price after 2015 Paris Climate Change Agreement, SunEdision has signed an onerous debt restructuring deal to finance its recently committed billion dollar mega projects. The clean energy giant has been facing a series of lawsuits over the past year.[115] As a result, SunEdision's stock price fell down by 99.4% in six months from $32.13 to $0.195 in April, 2016.[106] The fate of renewable energy industry or in turn, saving our earth from the impact of climate change also depends on the blessing and vulnerability of the financial industry. Kevin Brehm and Joseph Goodman of Rocky Mountain Institute comments:

"The U.S. solar industry has enjoyed impressive growth of late, with strong forecasts for 2016, but it's been an at-times bumpy ride as the industry has faced unfavorable rulings and stock-market troubles."[117]

It does not matter where the growths are happening in context of finite resources since once the resources will be used up, the impact will spread all over the world. China's economy has been growing at eight percent or more per year; that means it is more than doubling in size every ten years.[73] Indeed China now consumes more than twice as much coal as it did a decade ago and the same with iron ore and oil. The nation now has four times as many highways as it had, and almost five times as many cars.[73]

Historically neoliberal economists and policy makers used crisis as opportunities to promote privatization and globalization, which is now accelerating the dooms day. On the other hand, the recent increase in global oil production from unconventional sources is actually shifting the oil crisis by some time but deteriorating climate change. Richard Heinberg calls this opportunity as "living on borrowed time". And he recommends:

"Somehow, the opportunities presented by crisis need to be seized first by citizens and communities to build local, low-carbon production and support infrastructure."[74]

That is, we need to re-build local economies, enough renewable energy infrastructure at the same time adapt ourselves with minimum fraction of the amount of energy that industrial nations and urban people currently use. According to Bulletin of the Atomic Scientists to avoid the severe, widespread and irreversible impact of climate change we should decrease carbon emission quickly.[80] They warned that waiting for new technological innovations for a solution will be high-risk:

"Many technological innovations touted in the past have failed to achieve practical success. Even successful technologies will do little good if they mature too late to help avert climate disaster."[80]

There are question raised by climate experts and scientists in climate conference 2015 regarding what extent we can depend on technological innovation:

"To what extent can the world depend on technological innovation to address climate change? And what promising technologies—in generating, storing, and saving energy, and in storing greenhouse gases or removing them from the atmosphere—show most potential to help the world come to terms with global warming?"[80]

Figure 1.11 below shows that an alternative trajectory bypassing the dead-end, discussed in the last two chapters of this book (Chapter 9 & 10). If we think technology or innovation will change our trajectory, it will be pipedream until

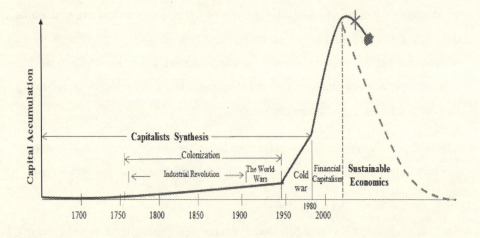

Figure 1.11: Switching the Trajectory (Example only, not drawn in scale)

and unless we make a pathway for technology to reach to us. Since CO_2 emission is accumulating in atmosphere at higher rate every year, we will have to reduce greenhouse gas emissions at much higher rate than that. As Richard Smith (2011) points out:

"Capitalist economic system is inherently eco-suicidal, that endless growth can only end in catastrophic global eco-collapse that no amount of tinkering can alter the market system's suicidal trajectory, and that, therefore, like it or not, humanity has no choice but to try to find a way to replace capitalism with a post-capitalist ecologically sustainable economy."[49]

However, either the solution is technological or political, these are not pragmatic and close to impossible to implement or enforce in real world dominated by financial power. This is true for the Paris Agreement on climate change to contain the increase in the global average temperature 1.5^0C-$2°C$ above pre-industrial levels, even it is legally binding for all 195 participating countries.[83] The agreement is criticized for imposing no sanctions on countries that fail to reduce emissions.[83] Schmidt-Traub, Executive Director of the UN Sustainable Development Solutions Network comments on why 1.5^0C matters:

"The bottom line is that 2^0C requires all countries to decarbonize their economy at a very rapid rate, but in our analysis there is some wiggle room......If you go to 1.5^0C, it becomes very hard to have any wiggle room left."[99]

The concept of Capitalists Dilemma (CD) introduced in Chapter 7 tells that if one country fails to meet this agreement, the others will get excuses to fail. The failing of J. F. Kennedy's "strategy of peace" is an important example, where he declared to reposition United States toward peace as:

"The United States, as the world knows, will never start a war. We do not want a war. We do not now expect a war. This generation of Americans has already had enough—more than enough—of war and hate and oppression. We shall be prepared if others wish it. We shall be alert to try to stop it. But we shall also do our part to build a world of peace where the weak are safe and the strong are just. We are not helpless before that task or hopeless of its success. Confident and unafraid, we labor on—not towards a strategy of annihilation but toward a strategy of peace."[107]

When all big and powerful one fail, no penalty will be enforceable in reality. The first year of implementation is very important. If heavy user countries such as China & India fall behind at the beginning, it will be much harder to compensate and eventually this agreement will fail in the same way as carbon tax failed or "strategy of peace" failed.

Although IPCC's Synthesis Report, no more than 1,000 billion tonnes (1,000 Gt) of CO2 can be emitted between 2011 and 2100 for a 66% chance (or better) of remaining below 2 °C of warming (over preindustrial level), we have only 19 years of window left to make a complete transition to renewable energy.[103] Therefore, if we focus on the emission reduction or limiting temperature only we will be in the middle of the sea on the course of sustainable economy. If another financial crisis hit the global economy, which is very likely, the climate concern will be moved to back seat again.

As per definition of sustainable economy we should reach to a boiling point–the changes are to be seen everywhere in an economy from a small village community to downtown financial industry. Like J.F. Kennedy's definition of peace[107], "sustainability" is also "sum of many acts", "dynamic, not static" and a process—a way of solving problems."

The next chapter travels through history of our industrial civilization followed by a brief summary of mainstream economic theories for general readers so that they better understand the fundamental concept of "Biased Equilibrium" introduced in Chapter 4 and discussed in the rest of the book. The last two Chapters discuss a break-through strategy for counteracting the universal financial empire (the Core Capitalists) through an Unbiased Vertical Learning Process (UVLP), while dynamically solving problems like poverty, inequality and climate change locally and in real time. Nevertheless, there is a catch; we have to act fast before it is too late since the time between the choices 'to live' or 'to die' is getting shorter.

CHAPTER 2

A BRIEF HISTORY OF CAPITALIST SYNTHESIS

2.1 Introduction

This chapter focuses on the historical context on which the capitalist concept was born and become dominant in our economic and political world. Historically wealth accumulation was one of the reasons for war and invasion that integrated different regions and countries ruled by monarchies. Slavery, moneylending, usury and poverty were always prevailing. Although all religions were against usury and slavery but war and wealth accumulation continued using religious banner. As monarchies and governments were engaged in war with each other, their lenders gradually became powerful. The historical path of capitalism was marked by many rise and fall of military and political powers but streamlined the resources flowing to the dominating powers.

The Industrial Revolution marks a major turning point in history of capitalism; almost every aspect of daily life was influenced in some way. The industrial revolution and high production in Europe geared entirely towards the war economies.[2] It merged into "The Age of Synergy", where many new science based technologies were developed that gave a way to financial capitalism. The ultimate control and direction of large industries came into the hands of financiers. Several major challenges to capitalism appeared in the early 20th century. The Russian revolution in 1917 established the first communist state in the world. The Great Depression triggered increasing criticism of the existing capitalist system. Nevertheless capitalism reinforced amid reshuffling the powers in response to the conflicts and crisis arose.

2.2 The Road to Capitalism

In ancient times, although there was no such thing called 'capitalism' but there was practice of money lending. The excessive interests on the loans were called "usury, which was considered sinful, unethical and immoral in all religious beliefs. At times, many nations from ancient China to ancient Greece to ancient Rome have illegalized loans with any interest.[3] Some of the earliest known condemnations of usury come from the Vedic texts of India.[3] Similar condemnations are found in religious texts from Buddhism, Judaism, Christianity, and Islam.[3] In practice, Israelites were forbidden to charge interest on loans made to other Israelites, but allowed to charge interest on transactions with non-Israelites.[3] Moneylending during this period was largely a matter of private deals with high interests and were almost entirely unrestricted by law. Banking was of the small, back-street variety, run by the urban lower-middle class of petty shop-keepers.[3]

Many Indian economists[4] consider that historically, the first book on economics ever written was "Arthashastra" written by Kautilya (also called Chanakya) in 4th century BC in India. "The book advocates protection of private property rights. It also discusses the legal basis on loans, bank deposits, mortgages, labor contracts, partnerships, and the sale of property. Kautilya was even aware of problems involving the separation of ownership and control in large businesses.[5] He was a key advisor to Chandragupta Maurya (317-293 BC), who stopped the advance of Alexander the Great's successors, and was the first ruler to unite the Indian subcontinent. Chandragupta's famous grandson Ashoka (268-232 BC) converted to Buddhism and raised the religion to official status in his northern Indian empire. He was later dedicated to the propagation of Buddhism across Asia and patronized develop intellectual hubs in Nalanda in India, close to Nepal, the birthplace of Gautama Buddha. Later Nalanda Univeristy (427AD-1197AD) became the first university in recorded history in the world.[6]

Buddhism spread through Silk Road, a 6,437 kilometers long trade route, got the name for lucrative Chinese silk trade to the Romans that began during Han Dynasty in China (206 BC–220 AD).[7] China had very long history of prosperity and self-sufficiency. It was the richest country in the world for thousands of years. During Han Dynasty (206 BCE – 220 AD) China's industries was based on salt or iron. They knew drilling techniques that allowed drilling up to 4800 feet were developed, allowing Chinese to extract salt and even natural gas for use in fuel and lighting.[8] The support of Ashoka and his descendants also led to spread Buddhism into neighboring lands-particularly to the Iranian-speaking regions of Afghanistan and Central Asia and further into two opposite directions, in the first case into China, and in the second case, to the coastal lands of Southeast Asia. The Parthians Dynasty in Iran took control of the early Silk Road. Merchants found the moral and ethical teachings of Buddhism to be an appealing and therefore, they spread Buddhism as they traveled. As a result, Merchants supported Buddhist Monasteries along the Silk Roads and in return the Buddhists gave the Merchants somewhere to stay as they traveled from city to city. Because of this, these communities became centers of literacy and culture with well-organized marketplaces, lodging, and storage. The Silk Road transmission of Buddhism essentially ended around the 7th century with the rise of Islam in Central Asia.[9&10]

In ancient Greece, the city-states after the Persian Wars in 323 BC produced a government and culture sufficiently organized for the birth of a private citizenship. Therefore it can be considered as embryonic capitalist society, allowing for the separation of wealth from exclusive state ownership to the possibility of ownership by the individual.[11] The Roman urbanized economy produced more rich people who became money lenders and most banking activities were conducted by private individuals.[12] Rich Romans farmers were dependent on slave laborers. Slavery was a legally accepted institution long before Romans and Greek civilization. In historical perspective a slave is legally the property of his master who can be bought or sold, is not allowed to escape and must work for his owner without any choice involved. Therefore, they were considered as economic means not as human beings. As the Roman Republic expanded outward, it enslaved entire populations, thus ensuring an ample supply of laborers to work in Rome's farms and households.[13]

Arnold J. Toynbee describe that the Romans had no budgetary system and thus wasted whatever resources they had available rather than producing anything new.[14&15] The empire relied on riches from conquered territories, which was ending with the end of territorial expansion and on taxes collected from small-scale farmers. The Roman elites were exempt from taxation that required even more exactions upon those who could not escape taxation.[15] The money lenders took advantage of the ever-increasing tax demands and when in the last declining days of the Empire crippled and eventually destroyed the peasant class by reducing tenant-farmers to serfdom.[16] The nutritional state of the common people degraded and therefore, when severe Antonine Plague spread starting around 165 AD that killed half of the roman population in twenty years. When Emperor Constantine had re-conquered Rome under the banner of the cross in 312, he soon afterwards issued the Edict of Milan in 313, declaring the legality of Christianity in the Roman Empire.[16] In order to maintain control and improve administration, in 285 AD, Roman Emperor was divided into east and west. The main capital moved from Rome to Byzantium.

Constantine became the first emperor to convert to Christianity, and who established Constantinople as the new capital of the eastern empire. Egypt was part of the empire. On that time, the Royal Library of Alexandria in Alexandria, Egypt, was one of the largest and most significant libraries of the ancient world. The library was but one part of the Musaeum of Alexandria, which functioned as a sort of research institute. The classical thinkers who studied, wrote, and experimented at the Musaeum include the mothers and fathers of mathematics, astronomy, physics, geometry, engineering, geography, physiology and medicine.[456] These included notable thinkers such as Euclid, Archimedes, Eratosthenes, Herophilus, Erasistratus, Hipparchus, Aedesia, Pappus, Theon, Hypatia, and Aristarchus of Samos.[456]

Theodosius I (379–395 AD), the last emperor to rule over both the eastern and the western halves of the Roman Empire adopted Christianity as official state religion instead of previous Roman polytheism. He made paganism illegal by an edict in AD 391. Library of Alexandria was burnt and destroyed by a decree from the bishop of Alexandria using this edict. Later in 415 AD, Hypatia a female mathematician, philosopher astronomer and the head of the Neoplatonic School at Alexandria and the last member of Musaeum of Alexandria was killed by the religious fanatics in Egypt.[456] Her killing and destruction of the library left not only the Roman Empire but also the world one thousand years behind in terms of knowledge and sprit.[457] After Theodosius's death, Roman Empire was divided into the Eastern Roman Empire (later to be referred to as the Byzantine Empire) centered in Constantinople and Western Roman Empire centered in Ravenna and never again re-united. In the end, due to economic failure and severe fall in population, military defense became too large for the population to support that the empire became exposed to outside invasion.[15] During the 4th and 5th centuries, the Germanic peoples of northern Europe grew in strength and repeated attacks led to the Fall of the Western Roman Empire in 476 AD (This eastern part of the empire, known as the Byzantine Empire remained for thousand more years), a date which traditionally marks the end of the classical period and the start of the Middle Ages.[17]

In Western Europe, a political structure was emerging: in the power vacuum left in the wake of Rome's collapse, de-urbanization led to commerce and trade ceasing and economies became centered around agricultural manors, warrior-landlords or the medieval nobility where localized hierarchies were based on the bond of common people to the land on which they worked.[18] The landlord manors collected rent from their serfs in the form of their produce and the lord owed duties to the regional prince that were used to pay for the state and wars. After the decline of the Roman Empire, In Western Europe, Germanic peoples moved into positions of power in the remnants of the former Western Roman Empire and established kingdoms and empires of their own. Of all of the Germanic peoples, the Franks would rise to a position of hegemony over Western Europe, the Frankish Empire reaching its peak around 800 AD. This empire was later divided into several parts; West Francia would evolve into the Kingdom of France, while East Francia would evolve into the Holy Roman Empire, a precursor to modern Germany. Charlemagne became the king of the Franks who was crowned by the pope as emperor. The pope was officially a vassal of the Byzantine Empire.[19] The British Isles were the site of several large-scale migrations. Native Celtic peoples had been marginalized during the period of Roman Britain, and when the Romans abandoned the British Isles during the 400s, waves of Germanic Anglo-Saxons migrated to southern Britain and established a series of petty kingdoms in what would eventually develop into the Kingdom of England by 927 AD. During this period, the kingdoms of Poland and Hungary were organized as well.[17] Within the tenth century independent kingdoms were established in Central Europe, for instance, Belgium and Kingdom of Hungary. The following period, ending around 1000, saw the further development of feudalism, which weakened the Holy Roman Empire.[17]

The Viking Age, a period of migrations of Scandinavian peoples, dominated the period from the late 700s to the middle 1000s. The Scandinavian population was too large for the peninsula and there was not enough good farmland for everyone. This led to a hunt for more land. The Vikings raided across Europe, but took the most slaves in raids of the British Isles and Eastern Europe and sold most captives in the Byzantine or Islamic markets.[20&21] In the West their target populations were primarily English, Irish, and Scottish, while in the East they were mainly Slavs, from where the term "slavery" coined. Chief among the Viking states was the Empire of Cnut the Great, a Danish leader who would become king of England, Denmark, and Norway. The Normans, a Viking people who settled in Northern France and founded the Duchy of Normandy, would have a significant impact on many parts of Europe, from the Norman conquest of England to Southern Italy and Sicily. Another Scandinavian people, the Rus' people, founded Kievan Rus', an early state which was a precursor for the modern country of Russia.[17]

According Karl Marx, before capitalist societies, the mode of production was based on slavery (e.g. in ancient Rome) before moving to feudal serfdom (e.g. in mediaeval Europe). Aristotle examined ideas about the "art" of wealth acquisition and questioned whether property is best left in private or public funds.[22] Romans developed a legal system that allowed the smooth functioning of capitalism, particularly important was protection of property rights, freedom of contract and limited liability.[23] The feudal lords in coalition with catholic churches were positioned in an upper layer of social structure and it was not a choice of the serfs who they belong. This was the dominant economic system until trade began to return in the late Middle Ages leading to the rise of the merchant class. According to some historians, the modern capitalist system has its origin in the crisis of the fourteenth century, a conflict between the land-owning aristocracy and the agricultural producers, the serfs. On that time, serfs were forced to produce for their land-lords and to sustain their lives. Neither the landlords nor the serfs had interests in technological innovations.[24&25]

There were a series of wars between Islamic Arabs and the Byzantine Empire started in the 7th century after death of Prophet Muhammad in 632. According to Islamic historians many Christians were disaffected from the Christian Orthodoxy which deemed them heretics and Jews in the Byzantine territories welcomed the Arab invaders.[26] Within only a decade, Muslims conquered Mesopotamia, Persia, Byzantine Syria, and Byzantine Egypt,[27] and established the Rashidun Caliphate. In April 637, the Arabs, after a long siege, captured Jerusalem and conquered Gaza under leadership of Islamic Caliph Umar ibn

Khattab. During his time the Islamic empire expanded at an unprecedented rate ruling the whole Sassanid Persian Empire and more than two thirds of the Byzantine Empire.[28] He set aside the Christian ban on Jews and allowed Jews into Jerusalem and to worship.[29] He lived in a simple mud hut without doors and walked the streets every evening to be close to the poor.[30] He established the first welfare state for the Muslim and non-Muslim poor, needy, elderly, orphans, widows, and the disabled. He built canals to support irrigation encourage agricultural production and supply of drinking water. Due to his prudent management, millions of people were saved from famine during severe drought in 638 AD. He established free trade. In Islam trade is not taxed, wealth is taxed. The Jews and the Christians continued to use their own laws in the Islamic State and had their own judges and therefore they only paid for policing for the protection of their property, which was far lower as compared to Sassanid Persian Empire and Byzantine Empire. Their local administration was kept un-touched and several of the former Byzantine and Persian official were retained on their services under Umar's governors.[30] A social transformation and an agricultural revolution continued in the Islamic territories under the Islamic Caliphate. The Caliphate provided incentives for increasing productivity and wealth and thus enhances tax revenues. Individuals of any gender, ethnic or religious background were given the right to buy, sell, mortgage, and inherit land for farming or any other purpose. Islamic jurists argued that privatization of the origin of water, agricultural land, and fire-producing fuels were forbidden. Aside this view early form of prototype capitalism were present in the Caliphate.[31]

Later, after assassination of Caliph Ali by a Kharijite (Islamic fundamentalist) in 661AD and the Islamic Caliphate was changed to Umayyad dynasty and sustained until 750 AD. The Umayyads continued the Muslim conquests, and at its greatest extent, the Umayyad Caliphate covered 15 million square kilometers making it the largest empire on that time.[32] The Byzantine and Sassanid Empires relied on money economies before the Muslim conquest, and that system remained in effect during the Umayyad period in the conquered territories. In addition to this, the Umayyad government began to mint its own coins in Damascus. Gold coins were called dinars while silver coins were called dirhams. Many of the various business techniques and forms were introduced during this time included early contracts, bills of exchange, limited partnerships, capital accumulation, cheques, promissory notes,[33] trusts, startup companies[34], exchange rates, bankers, money changers and so on.[35&36] The concept of corporations independent from the state also existed in the medieval Islamic world and the concepts of welfare and pension were introduced in early Islamic law.[34] Many of these concepts were adopted and further advanced in medieval Europe from the 13th century onwards.[37]

After the Muslim conquests of North Africa and most of the Iberian Peninsula, the Islamic world became a huge importer of slaves from central and eastern Europe.[38] According to historian Robert Davis (2004) Islamic law forbade Muslims to enslave fellow Muslims or so-called People of the Book: Christians, Jews, Sabians and Magians, but the slave traders made an exception if they were captured in battle. If they converted to Islam, their master was expected to free them as an act of piety, and if they did not, the master had to teach them.[39] On the other hand, the focus of the Byzantine Empire shifted from the western re-conquests to a primarily defensive position, against the Islamic armies on its eastern borders. In absence of Byzantine interference in the emerging Christian states of Western Europe, the situation gave a huge stimulus to feudalism and economic self-sufficiency.[40]

There was a powerful buffer between Byzantine Empire and Umayyad empire called Khazaria founded by were a semi-nomadic Turkic people called Khazars during around 618 AD.[41] It became one of the foremost trading emporia of the medieval world, commanding the western marches of the Silk Road and played a key commercial role as a crossroad between China, the Middle East, and European Russia.[42] During 740AD the Khazar court embraced Judaism as its official faith, a decision which clearly owed a great deal to the determination of the Khazars to avoid assimilation by and emphasize their independence from the Christian Byzantine and the Muslim Arab empires.[32]

In 750 AD, the Umayyad dynasty was overthrown from all but the al-Andalus region (what are today Spain, Portugal, Andorra, and part of southern France) by Abbasid dynasty, who built their capital in Baghdad moving from Damascus. Umayyads in Spain proclaimed themselves caliphs in 929.[43] During this period, cultural exchange and cooperation between Muslims and Christians rose under Abbasid and considered the Islamic Golden Age. An revolution in science, literatures, commerce, industry and agriculture happened during this time.[44] Abbasid Caliph Harun al-Rashid established an alliance with China. The Abbasids were influenced by the Qur'anic injunctions and hadith such as "the ink of a scholar is more holy than the blood of a martyr" stressing the value of knowledge.[45] During this period the Muslim world became an intellectual center for science, philosophy, medicine and education as the Abbasids championed the cause of knowledge and established the House of Wisdom in Baghdad; where both Muslim and non-Muslim scholars sought to translate and gather all the world's knowledge into Arabic.[46] Many classic works of antiquity that would otherwise have been lost were translated into Arabic and Persian and later in turn translated into Turkish, Hebrew and Latin. During this period the Muslim world was a cauldron of cultures which collected, synthesized and significantly advanced the knowledge gained from the ancient Roman, Chinese, Indian, Persian, Egyptian, North African, Greek and Byzantine civilizations.[46]

In the year 750, Abu al-'Abbas al-Saffah, the founder of the Abbasid Caliphate, sent his forces to consolidate his caliphate, including Central Asia, where his forces confronted many regional powers, including those of China's Tang Dynasty. The Chinese Tang Dynasty's western expansion of their territory ended with the Arab victory of the Battle of Talas in 751AD. The battle of Talas and the rise of Islam marked the end of Buddhist Central Asia. Chinese cultural influence in Central Asia declined with the deterioration of the Tang Dynasty, and would not reappear until after the Qing conquests of the 18th century.[47] The Chinese prisoners captured as the result of the battle allowed for the transference of paper-making technology to the Middle East and eventually Europe. The technology of paper making was thus transmitted to and revolutionized the Islamic world, and later the European West.[48] In the 8th and 9th centuries woodblock printing began in China that allowed the rapid production of books. The first book to be printed in this manner, with a production date, was the Jin Gang Jin, a Buddhist text printed in 868 AD.[49]

Song Dynasty (960–1279 AD) reunified most of China. This was one of the most prosperous periods in Chinese history. Unlike its predecessors, the monarchy and aristocracy weakened under the Song, allowing a class of non-aristocratic gentry to gain power.[50] The central government withdrew from managing the economy, provoking drastic economic and technological changes. The so-called Four Great Inventions: gunpowder, woodblock printing, and the compass, were invented or perfected during this era. There were heavy industries such as shipbuilding and textiles as well as prosperous cottage industries including porcelain during that time. By the mid-11th century the central government introduced its paper money, produced using woodblock printing and backed by bronze coins.[50]

A number of medieval thinkers and scientists living under Islamic rule played a role in transmitting Islamic science to the Christian West. They contributed to making Aristotle known in Christian Europe.[51] The rediscovery of Aristotle's works - more than 3000 pages fuelled a spirit of inquiry into natural processes that had already begun to emerge in the 12th century.[52] In addition, the period saw the recovery of much of the Alexandrian mathematical, geometric and astronomical knowledge, such as that of Euclid and Claudius Ptolemy. These recovered mathematical methods were later enhanced and developed by other Islamic scholars.[51] Throughout the Europe, the High Middle Ages produced many different forms of intellectual, spiritual and artistic works. At that time, the

Caliphate of Córdoba, Al-Andalus under Umayyad was a beacon of learning, and the city of Córdoba became one of the leading cultural and economic centers. With the fall of Córdoba in 1236, the Emirate of Granada was the only Muslim territory in Europe what is now Spain. In 1238, the Emirate of Granada officially became a tributary state to the Kingdom of Castile.[53]

The eleventh century marked a significant boom in Italy's Lombard region's economy, due to improved trading and, mostly, agricultural conditions. In a similar way to other areas of Italy, this led to a growing self-acknowledgement of the cities, whose increasing richness made them able to defy the traditional feudal supreme power. As Lombardy merchants and bankers grew in stature based on the strength of the Lombard plains cereal crops, many displaced Jews fleeing Spanish persecution were attracted to the trade and introduced merchant banking.[54] The Jewish newcomers who were not permitted to own any land, lend to farmers against crops in the field. They then began to advance payment against the future delivery of grain shipped to distant ports. In both cases they made their profit from the present discount against the future price. This two-handed trade was time-consuming and soon there arose a class of merchants who were trading grain debt instead of grain. Across Europe, prohibited from nearly every other trade, the Court Jew emerged as someone who handled finances for European royalty and nobility.[55]

In the late Middle Ages, from 1100 to 1500, the European slave trade continued, though with a shift from being centered among the Western Mediterranean Islamic nations to the Eastern Christian and Muslim states. The city states of Venice and Genoa controlled the Eastern Mediterranean from the 12th century and the Black Sea from the 13th century. They sold both Slavic and Baltic slaves, as well as Georgians, Turks, and other ethnic groups of the Black Sea and Caucasus, to the Muslim nations of the Middle East. The sale of European slaves by Europeans slowly ended as the Slavic and Baltic ethnic groups Christianized by the Late Middle Ages.[39]

The beginning of eleventh century there were major religious conflicts, called Crusades under sanction of the Latin Catholic Church. There were nine major crusades lasted about 200 years from 1095 to 1291 along with numerous minor ones and then followed by several other minor crusades until fifteenth century. Pope Urban II proclaimed the first crusade in 1095 with the stated goal of restoring Christian access to the holy places in and near Jerusalem.[56] It reunited Christian churches all over Europe under his leadership with new vigor and power against expansion of Islam after loss of Anatolia by the Byzantine's defeated by Seljuk Turks in 1071. The majority of the crusader numbers were the poor trying to escape the economic hardships of medieval life in an armed pilgrimage leading to Apotheosis at Jerusalem.[56] In the first Crusade (1095–1099) Jews and Muslims fought together to defend Jerusalem.[57]

After the First Crusade recaptured Jerusalem in 1099, many Christian pilgrims travelled to visit what they referred to as the Holy Places. In the 12th century, the need to transfer large sums of money to finance the Crusades stimulated the re-emergence of banking in Western Europe.[58] A nobleman who was interested in participating in the Crusades might place all his assets under a Templar management while he was away. Accumulating wealth in this manner throughout Christendom, the Order in 1150 began generating letters of credit for pilgrims journeying to the Holy Land: pilgrims deposited their valuables with a local Templar preceptory before embarking, received a document indicating the value of their deposit, then used that document upon arrival in the Holy Land to retrieve their funds. This innovative arrangement was an early form of banking, and may have been the first formal system to support the use of cheques in medieval Christian world. It improved the safety of pilgrims by making them less attractive targets for thieves, and also contributed to the Templar coffers.[59] In 1162, Henry II of England levied a tax to support the crusades. The Templars acted as Henry's bankers in the Holy Land. The Templars' wide flung, large land holdings across Europe also emerged as the beginning of Europe-wide banking.

Their practice was to take in local currency, for which a demand note would be given that would be good at any of their castles across Europe, allowing movement of money without the usual risk of robbery while traveling.[58] In his book "Human Progress Amid Resistance to Change" Joseph E. Pluta describes the impact of the Crusades as:

> "Even more important, crusaders in the Middle East were introduced to a generally more advanced standard of living and more sophisticated tastes in consumer goods....Those who safely returned home sought change from the drab manorial or village way of life. Ultimately, the Church-led Crusades helped to create an economic transformation based on money-making principles that the Church opposed."[23]

As a result of the Crusaders experience in the Middle Ease contributed inevitable change in European social and economic system. As a result, the feudalism collapsed and at the same time, the rise of Christianity brought new organized charitable activities and institutions, including hospices, hospitals, and shelters for the poor.[108] Joseph Pluta further argues:

> "The somewhat surprising refusal of Western scholars to acknowledge the contribution of Middle Eastern thought to the history of economic ideas may well have been more intentional than accidental."[23]

Sultan Saladin, founder of the Muslim Ayyubid dynasty, led the Muslim opposition against the European Crusaders in the Levant. His army defeated the Crusaders at the decisive Battle of Hattin in 1187, leading the way to the Muslims' re-capture of Palestine from the Crusaders who had conquered it 88 years earlier.[60] After the fifth crusade declared by Pope Innocent III, there was a treaty between the crusaders and Sultan Al-Kamil. This treaty allowed Christians to rule over most of Jerusalem, while the Muslims were given control of their sacred areas in Jerusalem.[61] Crusades also spread within Europe and became political as crusades were declared against political opponents. The need to raise, transport and supply large armies led to a flourishing of trade throughout Europe and then it established "Europe Overseas" dominating trade in Mediterranean Crusader states.[62] The major attempt to take the Holy Land ended when Louis IX died in the ninth crusade (1270–1272).[63]

All over Europe, with Christian dominancy, Jews were ostracized from most professions by local rulers, the church and the guilds, they were pushed into marginal occupations considered socially inferior, such as tax and rent collecting and moneylending.[64] In England, the departing Crusaders were joined by crowds of debtors in the massacres of Jews at London and York in 1189–1190. In 1275, Edward I of England passed the Statute of Jewry which made usury illegal and linked it to blasphemy, in order to seize the assets of the violators.[65] In 1290, all Jews were expelled from England and their property became the Crown's. Many other crowned heads of Europe followed the same.[65]

Though Pope Leo the Great forbade charging interest on loans by canon law, it was not forbidden to take collateral on loans. Pawn shops thus operate on the basis of a contract that may structure a sale-repurchase by the 'borrower' where the interest is implicit in the repurchase price. Similar conventions exist in modern Islamic banking. Various ways around the prohibition were devised, so that the lowly pawnshop contractors could bundle their risk and investment for larger undertakings. Christianity and Judaism generally ban usury, but allow usury towards heretics. Thus Christians could lend to Jews and vice versa. It was the interpretation that interest could be charged to non-Israelites that would be used in the 14th century for Jews living within Christian societies in Europe to justify lending money for profit. The methods used for bookkeeping were carefully kept within families and slowly spread along trade routes. Therefore, this knowledge was available most readily to Jesuits and Jews, who consequently played a major role in European finance. This explains the disproportionately large share of Jews in the goldsmith trade and early diamond market.[66]

In the middle of the 13th century, groups of Italian Christians, particularly the Cahorsins and Lombards, invented legal fictions to get around the ban on Christian usury and reduced the importance of the Jews to European monarchs. As an example, one method of effecting a loan with interest was to offer money without interest, but also require that the loan is insured against possible loss or injury, and or delays in repayment.[58&66] In Islam, interest of any kind is forbidden. Islam prohibit an increase in capital with no services provided and commodity exchanges in unequal quantities and trade in promissory notes (e.g. fiat money and derivatives) is forbidden. In an Islamic banking model banks would still operate for profit. This would be done through charging for loans in different ways such as through fees and using method of risk sharing and different ownership models such as leasing.[58]

A Mongolian tribe leader Temüjin, upon receiving his title in 1206 as Chinggis Khan, thought to mean Universal Ruler or, Oceanic Ruler or Firm, Resolute Ruler.[67] He united many of the nomadic tribes of northeast Asia and invaded central Asia to Eastern Europe via Silk Road often accompanied by wholesale massacres of the civilian populations, especially in the Khwarezmian controlled lands in Greater Iran.[68] The Mongol conquest caused 30 million human lives.[69&70] The Mongols established a decentralized empire that at its height, extended from China in the east to the Black and Baltic seas in Europe. The Kievan Rus' state had broken up, replaced by several small warring states. In the face of the Mongol conquests, many of these states paid tribute to the Mongols, becoming effective vassals. The center of the Islamic Empire at the time was Baghdad, which had held power for 500 years but was suffering internal divisions. Mongols besieged and captured Baghdad in 1258, an event considered as one of the most catastrophic events in the history of Islam.[71]

The Mongols launched a series of attacks on the prosperous Chinese Song Dynasty. By the 1270s, the Song economy had collapsed from the burden of taxes and inflation which the Song government used to finance its war against the Mongols.[72] In their conquest of China the forces carried out massacres in cities they captured. Under Mongol rule, approximately 65 million people were registered in 1290 AD reduced from between 110 and 120 million during Song Dynasty in 1215 AD.[50] Kublai Khan, after becoming ruler of China enhanced Beijing's status from a peripheral city to capital city. He extended the Grand Canal, connecting the Yellow and Yangtze rivers, to the capital, Beijing. This eased transportation between the south, now the hub of economic activity, and Beijing. The Mongol Yuan government introduced paper currency as the predominant circulating medium that was guaranteed by the state and not by the private merchant or private banker but later issuing large amounts of notes which caused hyperinflation.[50] These policies greatly conflicted with Confucian ideals of frugal government and light taxation.[73]

During Mongol rule Marco Polo, an Italian merchant traveler from the Republic of Venice, who travelled 24,000 km to China through Silk Road and apparently met Kublai Khan, the Mongol Emperor in China and returned to Venice after 24 years in 1295 AD. His travels are recorded in his book which did much to introduce Europeans to Central Asia, India, China and Japan.[77] His pioneering journey inspired Christopher Columbus[78] and many other travelers. There is a substantial literature based on his writings. Polo influenced European cartography, leading to the introduction of the Fra Mauro map.[77]

During the 1340s AD, frequent famines, droughts, and plagues encouraged unrest among the Chinese. In 1351 AD, a peasant rebel leader, who claimed he was the descendant of the Song Emperor Huizong, sought to restore the Song by driving out the Mongols.[74] Later founded the Ming Dynasty (1368–1644 AD), whose reign is considered one of China's Golden Ages.[75] He enacted a series of policies designed to favor agriculture at the expense of other industries. The state gave aid to farmers, providing land and agricultural equipment and revising the taxation system. Overseas trade brought great prosperity to China, as Japanese and European importers paid for Chinese products with silver, thus monetizing

China's economy. The state's control of the economy diminished, allowing private merchants to prosper and a large increase in investment and profit.[50] Despite disruptions during the Mongol conquest of 1279, the population much increased under the Ming Dynasty and following Qing Dynasty, but its GDP per capita remained static since then.[76]

The 13th century also saw attempts at a Franco-Mongol alliance attempts at military collaboration in the Holy Land during the latter Crusades.[79] However, eventually the Mongols after they had destroyed the Abbasid and Ayyubid dynasties, themselves converted to Islam, and signed the 1323 Treaty of Aleppo with the surviving Muslim power.[80] The descendants of Chinggis Khan later invaded north India and later established Moghul Empire in the whole Indian subcontinent. Zahir-ud-din Muhammad Babur was the first Moghul emperor in India. Culturally, he was greatly influenced by the Persian culture and this affected both his own actions and those of his successors, giving rise to a significant expansion of the Persianate ethos in the Indian subcontinent.[81]

The root of the Middle age conflicts not only in religious rivalry but also in political interests or disagreements of the ruling class such as Kings and Churches. William the Conqueror, a Duke of Normandy invaded England in 1066. The Norman Conquest was a pivotal event in English history for several reasons. This linked England more closely with continental Europe through the introduction of a Norman aristocracy, thereby lessening Scandinavian influence. Over the course of King John's reign a combination of higher taxes, unsuccessful wars that resulted in the loss of English barons' titled possessions in Normandy following the Battle of Bouvines (1214), and the conflict with Pope Innocent III had made King John unpopular with many of his feudal barons.[17] In 1215 some of the most important barons engaged in open rebellion against him and made him sign an agreement called Magna Carta which stated the right of the barons to consult with and advise the king in his Great Council in an attempt to limit his powers by law and protect their privileges. In 1295 a model parliament was made up of nobles and bishops, and two representatives for each county and for each town - the model for future Parliaments. It created England one of the most powerful monarchies in Europe and engendered a sophisticated governmental system.[17] Being based on an island, moreover, England was to develop a powerful navy and trade relationships that would come to constitute a vast part of the world.[17]

The reestablished Silk Routes was not only used for trading silks and various other trade items, technologies, religions and philosophies, as well as the bubonic plague (the "Black Death"), also traveled along this routes. In early 14th century, bad weather led to the Great Famine of 1315–1317 followed by the Black Death in 1348–1350 led to a population crash.[24] The Great Famine caused millions of deaths in Europe. The wheat prices increased couple of times due to scarcity that peasants could no longer afford and grains were stored for lords and nobles. Therefore, following Great Famine, most of the Europeans were suffering from malnutrition, which increased susceptibility to infections due to weakened immunity.[82&83] In China, the 13th century Mongol conquest caused a decline in farming and trading and resulted in similar malnutrition. Following this, a devastating plague in China killed an estimated 25 million Chinese and other Asians during the 15 years before it entered Constantinople in 1347 by travelling along the Silk Road. From there, it was most likely carried by Oriental rat fleas living on the black rats that were regular passengers on merchant ships. Spreading throughout the Mediterranean and Europe, the Black Death is estimated to have killed 30–60% of Europe's total population.[84&85] Mediterranean Europe was the most affected such as Italy, the south of France and Spain, where plague stayed for about four consecutive years, the death toll was probably closer to 75–80% of the population. In Germany and England the death toll was probably closer to 20% .[86]

In 1328, when the King of France Charles IV died leaving only daughters, the nearest male relative was Edward III of England. But instead, the assemblies of the French barons and prelates and the University of Paris decided the dead king's cousin, Philip VI, to be crowned King of France in accordance with Salic law, which disqualified the succession of males descended through female lines. This dynastic disagreement eventually caused in the Hundred Years' War from 1337 to 1453 between England and France.[87] In France, there was about 17 million people but after the Black Death and the Hundred Years' War the population had declined by at least one-half to two third or more, while the Black Death killed between a fifth and a third of the English population.[87&88]

Although the Salic law not only undermines female but also female successor lines, after hundred years the English occupation of the French territories was challenged by a 17 year old peasant girl Joan of Arc in 1429. She boosted up moral power of French people after long sufferings from the plague and war devastations and led them toward several important victories. Tragically, she was captured and burned at the stake by English for heresy when she was 19 years old.[89] The war has very big significance in both the nations. It stimulated nationalistic sentiments on both sides. It accelerated the process of transforming France from a feudal monarchy to a centralized state. The war basically confirmed the fall of the French language in England, which had served as the language of the ruling classes and commerce.[90]

During the end of thirteenth century (1299 AD), Osman Bey a Turkish tribe leader, from whom the name "Ottoman" is derived, declared himself a Sultan in some border areas of Seljuq with the Byzantine Empire. In 1453, with the conquest of Constantinople by Mehmet II, the Ottoman state was transformed into an empire. He allowed the Orthodox Church to maintain its autonomy and land in exchange for accepting Ottoman authority.[91] Because of bad relations between the states of Western Europe and the latter Byzantine Empire, the majority of the Orthodox population accepted Ottoman rule.[91] Mehmed and his successors also encouraged and welcomed migration of the persecuted Jews from different parts of Europe. In the 16th century, Marrano Jews fleeing from

Iberia introduced the techniques of banking and even the mercantilist concept of state economy to the Ottoman empire.[92] They soon acquired a dominating position in the state finances of the Ottoman Empire and in commerce with Europe.[93] The economic structure of the Empire was defined by its geopolitical structure as the Ottoman Empire stood between the West and the East, thus blocking the land route eastward and forcing Spanish and Portuguese navigators to set sail in search of a new route to the Orient. The Empire controlled the spice route that Marco Polo once used.[94] During Ottoman Empire, Muslim pirates, primarily Algerians continued salve trade with the support of the Empire, raided European coasts and shipping from the 16th to the 19th centuries, and took thousands of captives, whom they sold or enslaved. They gradually ended their attacks with the naval decline of the Ottoman Empire in the late 16th and 17th centuries, as well as the European conquest of North Africa.[39]

In 1492, when Ottoman Empire was at its zenith, the Umayyad Emir Muhammad XII surrendered the Emirate of Granada to Queen Isabella I of Castile.[53] As Ottoman Empire restricted the trade route through Silk route, the Western Europe was forced to discover new trading routes through sea in the contest for the lucrative spice trade with Asia. Italian navigator Christopher Columbus' voyages with financing from Queen Isabella I of Spain intended to reach India sailing through West but reached at the Bahamas, the first entry point to Americas, the New World in 1492. Following him but sailing to the East, Portuguese navigator Vasco da Gamma was succeeded reaching to India in 1498. They were the first states to set up colonies in America and trading posts and factories along the shores of Africa and Asia, establishing the first direct European diplomatic contacts with Southeast Asian states in 1511, China in 1513 and Japan in 1542.[17]

In 1411, Pope John XXIII proclaimed a crusade against King Ladislaus of Naples, the protector of rival Pope Gregory XII. John XXIII also authorized the sale of indulgences to raise money for the war, and priests selling indulgences urged people to crowd the churches and give their offerings. This traffic in indulgences was to some a sign of the corruption of the church. Jan Hus spoke out against these indulgences. He asserted that no Pope or bishop had the right to take up the sword in the name of the Church; he should pray for his enemies and bless those that curse him; man obtains forgiveness of sins by true repentance, not money. He was prosecuted by the Church and eventually, he was burned at the stake for heresy in 1415 AD. After his death, followers of Hus's religious teachings rebelled against their Roman Catholic rulers and defeated five consecutive papal crusades in what became known as the Hussite Wars. Hus is considered the first Church reformer.[95]

Following the Islamic Golden Age, the 15th century was also a time of great progress in Europe within the arts and sciences. It was a renewed interest in ancient Greek and Roman texts led to what has later been termed the Renaissance. The Renaissance was a cultural movement that profoundly affected European intellectual life in the early modern period. It began in Italy, and later spread to the north, west and middle Europe influencing literature, philosophy, art, politics, science, history, religion, and other aspects of intellectual enquiry.[96] The most prominent intellectual during Renaissance was Leonardo Da Vinci who was an Italian Renaissance polymath: painter, sculptor, architect, musician, mathematician, engineer, inventor, anatomist, geologist, cartographer, botanist, and writer. He conceptualized flying machines, concentrated solar power, an adding machine, the double hull, also outlining a rudimentary theory of plate tectonics.[97] Relatively few of his designs were constructed or were even feasible during his lifetime. "In all, the Renaissance could be viewed as an attempt by intellectuals to study and improve the secular and worldly, both through the revival of ideas from antiquity, and through novel approaches to thought".[96]

The rapid economic and socio-cultural development during Renaissance in Europe created favorable intellectual and technological conditions for invention of printing press by Germany's Gutenberg.[98] With this invention, knowledge spread throughout Europe challenging traditional doctrines in science and theology. Martin Luther, a German Catholic priest and professor of theology and a follower of John Huss strongly disputed the claim that freedom from God's punishment for sin could be purchased with money.[99] This time, his position eventually embarked Protestant Reformation. He consistently rejected the idea of a Holy War.[100] It gained many followers especially among princes and kings seeking a stronger state by ending the influence of the Catholic Church.[99]

The Protestant Reformation also led to a strong reform movement in the Catholic Church called the Counter-Reformation, which aimed to reduce corruption as well as to improve and strengthen Catholic Dogma. Another important development in this period was the growth of pan-European sentiments. In the 15th century, at the end of the Middle Ages, powerful sovereign states were appearing, built by the New Monarchs who were centralizing power in France, England, and Spain. The Protestant Reformation against the Catholic Church caused the northern states became Protestant, while the southern states remained Catholic. The two parts of the empire clashed in the Thirty Years' War (1618–1648), which caused casualties of eight million civilians.[101] The effective end of the Holy Roman Empire in 1648 and the beginning of the modern nation-state system, with Germany divided into numerous independent states, such as Prussia, Bavaria and Saxony.[102]

The 15th-century Portuguese exploration of the African coast is commonly regarded as the harbinger of European colonialism. In 1452, Pope Nicholas V issued a papal bull regarding the right to reduce any "Saracens, pagans and any other unbelievers" to hereditary slavery which legitimized slave trade under Catholic beliefs of that time, which came to serve as a justification for the subsequent era of slave trade and European colonialism. The followers of the Church of England and Protestants did not use the papal bull as a justification. Later the position of the church was to condemn the slavery of Christians, but slavery was regarded as an old established and necessary institution which supplied Europe with the necessary workforce.[20] In the 15th century, one third of the imported slaves were resold to the African market in exchange of gold.[103]

Britain played a prominent role in the Atlantic slave trade, especially after 1600.[103] At that time, new opportunities for trade with America and Asia were opening; mercantile theorists thought international trade could not benefit all countries at the same time. Because money and gold were the only source of riches, there was a limited quantity of resources to be shared between countries. Therefore, tariffs could be used to encourage exports (meaning more money comes into the country) and discourage imports (sending wealth abroad). In other words a positive balance of trade ought to be maintained, with a surplus of exports. New powerful monarchies wanted a powerful state to boost their status by using of the state's military power to ensure local markets and supply sources were protected. Mercantilists argued that a state should export more goods than it imported so that foreigners would have to pay the difference in precious metals. Although they asserted that only raw materials that could not be extracted at home should be imported; and promoted government subsides, such as the granting of monopolies and protective tariffs, were necessary to encourage home production of manufactured goods. They further emphasized state power and overseas conquest as the principal aim of economic policy that encouraged colonialism. If a state could not supply its own raw materials, according to the mercantilists, it should acquire colonies from which they could be extracted.[24]

In the late 16th century, England, France, Spain and the Netherlands launched major colonization programs in eastern North America. In 1553, the first joint-stock company, the Company of Merchant Adventurers to New Lands, was chartered in London. During this time, the spice trade was dominated by the Portuguese but unable to increase supply to satisfy growing demand, in particular the demand for pepper. Demand for spices was relatively inelastic, and therefore each lag in the supply of pepper caused a sharp rise in pepper prices.[104]

Portugal had been united with the Spanish crown in 1580, with which the Dutch Republic was at war. Philip II of Spain had been co-monarch of England until the death of his wife, Mary I, in 1558. A devout Roman Catholic, he deemed his Protestant sister-in-law and successor, Elizabeth I, a heretic and illegitimate ruler of England. On the other hand, Elizabeth, who sought to advance the cause of Protestantism where possible, had supported the Dutch Revolt against Spain. Philip planned an expedition to invade England and overthrow the Protestant regime of Elizabeth by sending a big fleet of battle ships, called "The Spanish Armada" against England in 1588.[105] In this war, Spain eventually suffered a decisive defeat, accomplished nothing but fall in debt default four times- in 1557, 1560, 1575 and 1596 and became the first nation in history to declare sovereign default.[106]

Soon after the defeat of the Spanish Armada in 1588, London merchants presented a petition to Queen Elizabeth I for permission to sail to the Indian Ocean. The permission was granted in 1591 but several attempts to reach India failed and the ships were lost. Finally, the Queen granted a Royal Charter to form a company called "Governor and Company of Merchants of London trading with the East Indies" on 31 December 1600 with a period of fifteen years monopoly on trade.[107] Shares of the company were owned by wealthy merchants and aristocrats and later the named changed as East India Company (EIC). Dutch merchants also entered the intercontinental spice trade themselves. Some Dutchmen already obtained first-hand knowledge of the "secret" Portuguese trade routes. The Dutch East India Company (VOC) was a chartered company established in 1602.[104] In the same year The Amsterdam Stock Exchange was established by the Dutch East India Company for dealings in its printed stocks and bonds. Initially the East India Company struggled in the spice trade due to the competition with its already well-established Dutch counterpart. After landing in India in the Bay of Bengal, the high profits reported by the EIC initially prompted King James I to renew the charter given to the Company for an indefinite period with a clause which specified that the charter would cease to be in force if the trade turned unprofitable for three consecutive years.[107]

The Portuguese first arrived in Japan and started trading Chinese goods (silk, porcelain) with Japan. Japan was also perceived as a sophisticated feudal society with a high culture and advanced pre-industrial technology, craftsmanship and metalsmithing. Since Japan has been poor in natural resources, Japanese were famously frugal with their consumable resources; what little they had they used with expert skill.[109] In 1609 Jacques Specx, a Dutch merchant arrived in Japan, who later founded European trade with Japan and Korea.[110] The Dutch also engaged in piracy and naval combat to weaken Portuguese and Spanish shipping in the Pacific. They ultimately became the only westerners to be allowed access to Japan from the small enclave of Dejima after 1638 and for the next two centuries.[109] It is at the beginning of the Edo period that Japan built her first ocean-going Western-style warships. During the period, Japan progressively studied Western sciences and techniques through the information and books received through the Dutch traders in Dejima. The main areas that were studied included geography, medicine, natural sciences, astronomy, art, languages, physical sciences, and mechanical sciences. However, in order to eradicate the influence of Christianization, Japan entered in a period of isolation called sakoku, during which its economy enjoyed stability and mild progress.[109]

Before the colonization of the Americas, Russia was a major supplier of fur pelts to Western Europe and parts of Asia. Russia was the world's largest supplier of fur developed in the Early Middle Ages. The fur trade played a vital role in the development of Siberia, the Russian Far East and later the Russian colonization of the Alaska.[111] French explorer Jacques Cartier in his three voyages into the Gulf of St. Lawrence in the 1530s and 1540s conducted some of the earliest fur trading between European and First Nations in North America.[112] During the same time, April 10, 1606, James I of England also issued a royal charter for privately funded ventures in North America to Plymouth and London

64

Companies, intended to claim land for England, trade, and return a profit. In 1620, Plymouth in Massachusetts was settled by Pilgrims from the Mayflower, beginning the history of permanent European settlement in North America.[113] Although there was British colonies in America (New England) but the they were not interested in fur trade at the beginning until two Frenchmen Radisson and Groseilliers approached English investors in London about the huge opportunities in fur trading in the north and west part in the Hudson Bay areas. The Hudson's Bay Company was established by London merchants that granted a monopoly to trade into all the rivers that fall into Hudson Bay. From 1670 onwards it was a major player in the fur trade for the next two centuries. As soon as English colonies were established, it was discovered that furs provided the best way for the colonists to remit value back to the mother country. The era from roughly 1660 through 1763 saw a fierce rivalry grow between France and Great Britain as each European power struggled to expand their fur-trading territories.[112]

After England's crushing defeat by France, the dominant naval power, in Battle of Beachy Head in 1690, England had no choice but to build a powerful navy. No public funds were available and William III's government wanted to borrow £1.2 million at 8% interest.[114] To solve this problem, parliamentarian Charles Montagu devised establishment of privately owned Governor and Company of the Bank of England, later Bank of England according to proposal of Scottish tradesman William Paterson. In order to induce subscription to the loan to the government, the subscribers were to be incorporated by the name of the Bank. It was given exclusive possession of the government's balances and was the only limited-liability corporation allowed to issue bank notes.[115] Thus privately owned Bank of England became the central bank of the United Kingdom and the model on which most modern central banks have been based. The Bank was nationalized in 1946 after World War II.[114]

2.3 The Bengal Origin of Capital

India during the Mughal period in the 16th century was the second richest country in the world after the Manchu China.[120] The gross domestic product of India was estimated at about 25.1% of the world economy. Emperor Akbar's treasury in 1600 at £17.5 million (in contrast to the entire treasury of Great Britain two hundred years later in 1800, which totaled £16 million).[120] The richness of India attracted Europeans sail for India rounding half of the world.

Although Portugal discovered the route to India, the Portuguese traders faced tough competition with their Dutch and English counterparts in the Indian Ocean. They were defeated by British East India Company in 1612. Then the company took a clever step to gain a territorial foothold in India with official

Figure 2.1 Sir Thomas Roe to the court of Jahangir at Agra from 1615-18[117]

sanction of both countries by launching a diplomatic mission.[116] In 1612, King James of England sent Sir Thomas Roe to visit the Mughal Emperor Jahangir (1605 – 1627) to arrange for a commercial treaty that would give the company exclusive rights to reside and build factories. This mission was highly successful as Jahangir sent a letter to James through Sir Thomas Roe and wrote:

> "I have commanded all my governors and captains to give them freedom answerable to their own desires; to sell, buy, and to transport into their country at their pleasure."[118&119]

In 1634, the Mughal emperor Jahangir extended his hospitality to the English traders to the region of Bengal. The company settled down to a trade in cotton and silk piece goods, indigo, and saltpetre, with spices from South India. It extended its activities to the Persian Gulf, Southeast Asia, and East Asia.[121] Later the Mughal Prince Shah Shuja, grandson of emperor Jahangir gave the town of Calcutta of Bengal to East India Company as grant thus making the Company effectively another tributary power of the Mughal in that city. The British East India Company, benefiting from the imperial patronage, soon expanded its commercial trading operations establishing 23 factories by 1647.[107]

As mercantilism was generating huge profit from the businesses with Indian and eastern part of Indian Ocean, the three nations the English, The Dutch and the Portuguese were engaged in wars to take control over the maritime routes. The Dutch took over most of Portugal's trade posts in the East Indies, gained control over the hugely profitable trade in spices. From January 1631 Charles I of England engaged in a number of secret agreements with Spain, directed against Dutch sea power. After Oliver Cromwell united England following the English Civil War into the Commonwealth of England and created a powerful navy to challenge Dutch trade dominance. There were three wars, known as Anglo-Dutch wars fought between the English and the Dutch in between 1652 and 1674 for control over the seas and trade routes. For their long voyages to India, both Dutch & English East India Companies were looking for a favorable place for provisions to stock passing their ships. In 1652, Dutch East India Company established a refreshment station at the Cape of Good Hope in Africa, at what would become Cape Town. The Dutch transported slaves from Indonesia, Madagascar and India as labor for the colonists in Cape Town.[458] The Indian subcontinent was the main source of slaves in South Africa during the early part of the 18th century. Approximately 80% of slaves came from India during this period.[459] Dutch maritime trade recovered from 1666 onward, but English commercial interests were badly hurt and King Charles faced virtual bankruptcy.[121]

Following the second Anglo-Dutch war, during his financial hardship, King Charles II tried to strengthening the power of the East India Company (EIC) in a series of five acts around 1670 with the rights to autonomous territorial acquisitions, to mint money, to command fortresses and troops and form alliances, to make war and peace, and to exercise both civil and criminal jurisdiction over the acquired areas.[122] Subsequently EIC set up a new base in Calcutta in Bengal called Fort William in 1690.

The fortune of EIC was halted when English pirates led by Henry Every attacked the Mughal convoy included the treasure-laden Ganj-i-Sawai belonging to the Mughal emperor Aurangzeb, reported to be the greatest in the Mughal fleet and the largest ship operational in the Indian Ocean and looted between £325,000 and £600,000, including 500,000 gold and silver pieces, and has become known as the richest ship ever taken by pirates.[107&122] In 1700 the exchequer of the Emperor Aurangzeb reported annual revenue of more than £100 million. In 1697, land revenue alone was £39 million from 24 provinces.[123]

After the incidence of pirating, in 1698, a new "parallel" East India Company officially titled the "English Company Trading to the East Indies" was founded under a state-backed indemnity of £2 million, dominated by the powerful stockholders of the old company. However, in practice, the original Company faced scarcely any measurable competition. The companies merged in 1708 and the merged company lent to the Treasury a sum of £3,200,000, in return for exclusive privileges for the next three years.[107] During the reign Mogul Emperor Farrukhsiyar (1713-1719), in 1717, that the British East India Company received duty-free trading rights in all of Bengal for a mere three thousand rupees a year. It is said that the Company's surgeon, William Hamilton, cured the Emperor and therefore, he was moved to grant trading rights to the Company.[124] In the same year, as Master of the Mint in 1717 in the "Law of Queen Anne" Sir Isaac Newton moved the Pound Sterling de facto from the silver standard to the gold standard by setting the bimetallic relationship between gold coins and the silver penny in favor of gold. Thus while exports were paid for in gold, effectively moving Britain from the silver standard to its first gold standard.[125] These two changes together have increased gold inflow and made Britain the most influential economic power.

In 1711, before EIC granted duty-free privilege from Mogul Empire, a joint-stock company named South Sea Company formed in London with a capital stock of more than £9 million as a public–private partnership to consolidate and reduce the cost of national debt. The idea was tried that it was granted a monopoly to trade with South America and would attempt to convert the entire British short term national debt into South Sea shares along with East India Company and Bank of England.[126] However, Their most significant trade was slaves. On that time it was thought that Spanish America would be a more promising trade area than was India and the Far East, as it was more accessible and the customers were more likely to purchase traditional English exports such as cloth and iron goods because of the European origin of the settlers.[126] This never happened and the company never realized any significant profit from its monopoly. On the other hand, British East India Company prospered and brought gold inflow from its trade with India centered at Calcutta in Bengal.[127]

French had huge land in possession of their colonies in North America. The outbreak of the Seven Years' War in Europe resulted in a renewal of the long running conflict between French and British trading companies in Indian subcontinent for influence. The French had also established an East India Company under Louis XIV. Although they were a late comer in India trade, but they quickly established themselves in India and were poised to overtake the English.[131] The rivalry between the English and the French turned into battle between British East India Company and Siraj-ud-daulah, the Nawab of Bengal (an independent rulers of the Principality of Bengal) and his French allies. The Nawab was betrayed by his general Mir Jafar, which caused his defeat on 23 June 1757.[132] The East India Company subsequently gained administrative authority over Bengal, which eventually spread to the entire Indian subcontinent. The Bengal region would serve as a lifeline for the British Empire, with its raw materials, textiles and shipbuilding industries supplying the Industrial revolution and funding the expansion of the empire.[134]

Following the Battle of Plassey the British East India Company plundered the

Figure 2.2: Lord Clive meeting with Mir Jafar after the Battle of Plassey[133]

Bengali treasury. The victory was consolidated in 1764 at the Battle of Buxar, when they defeated Mughal emperor, Shah Alam II, who granted the Company the right for "collection of Revenue" in the provinces of Bengal, Bihar, and Odisha known as "Diwani".[135] As a trading body, the company was to maximize its profits and with taxation rights, the profits to be obtained from Bengal came from land tax as well as trade tariffs. As lands came under company control, the land tax was typically raised fivefold what it had been – from 10% to up to 50% of the value of the agricultural produce.[136] In the first years of the rule of the British East India Company, the total land tax income was doubled and most of this revenue flowed out of the country to finance the ongoing Seven Years' War or protection of other British colonies.[137] During that time, a shortfall in crops in 1768 followed by severe droughts in 1769 was ignored by the British company and caused a catastrophic famine between 1769 and 1773 that caused the deaths of 10 million people, reducing the population to thirty million in Bengal, which included Bihar and parts of Odisha. As the famine approached its height in April 1770, the Company announced that the land tax for the following year was to be increased by a further 10%.[137]

After the occupation of British East India Company, the common people in Bengal fell into poverty and famine but growth had actually begun in Britain as a result of colonialism in Bengal.[6] However it was at a comparatively slow pace until industrial revolution when it jumped by adopting coal-fired machinery in the late 18th century. The industrial revolution required capital intensification, division of labor and more and more energy. The history of capital intensification is marked with many wars and conflicts among the industrialized nations and continued following war time peak production, destruction and reconstruction cycle but always required to burn fossil fuel.

The Portuguese began direct maritime trade between Europe and China in the 16th century competing with Arab, Chinese, Indian, and Japanese traders. They leased an outpost at Macau starting from 1557.[138] British ships began to appear

71

infrequently around the coasts of China from 1635 without establishing formal relations through the tributary system using their trade positions in India. Low Chinese demand for European goods, and high European demand for Chinese goods, including tea, silk, and porcelain, forced European merchants to purchase these goods with silver, the only commodity the Chinese would accept. It became increasingly difficult for the British trading in silver after introduction of gold standard in Britain; they began importing opium from India cultivated under British control, particularly in Bengal. The cultivation of opium by destructing of food crops in Bengal for export in China reduced food availability and exacerbate the Bengal famine.[139]

Opium has been known in China since the 7th century since for centuries it was used for medicinal purposes. It was not until the 17th century that the practice of mixing opium with tobacco for smoking was introduced into China by Europeans.[140] The introduction of opium into China was caused by Britain's need to send something back to China in return for their highly consumed Chinese tea.[141] Now the flow of silver was reversed by addicting thousands of Chinese addicted in opium. Recognizing the growing number of addicts, the Chinese Emperor prohibited the sale and smoking of opium in 1729 except only allowed a small amount for medicinal purposes.[142] Despite the embargo, British exports of opium to China grew from an estimated 15 tons in 1730 to 75 tons in 1773.[143]

The East India Company continued its monopoly on opium smuggling recognized by the British government, which itself wanted silver. By the 1820s 900 tons of opium annually from the poppy fields in fertile Ganges basin in Bengal, India under British control was supplied to China.[144] After the loss of the American colonies in 1776, Britain built a "Second British Empire", based in colonies in India, Asia, Australia and Canada. However, the crown jewel was India.[145] The huge money earned by the East India Company from Bengal either by exacting taxes or cultivating opium gifted the first industrial revolution in Britain,[134] new colonization, establishment of Singapore and Hong Kong, British victory in Napoleonic War and fortunes of the many early capitalists such as Rothschild Family. The Rothschild financial houses later financed establishment of the European central banks, the Manhattan banks including the First Bank of United States and the Second Bank of United States, the Federal Reserve Banks and the Wall Street banks.

2.4 The First Industrial Revolution

The First Industrial Revolution began in the 18th century in United Kingdom, when the colonies either in India, Africa or America were captive markets for British industry, and the goal was to enrich the mother country.[145] Many historians such argue that the profits that Britain received from its sugar colonies, or from the slave trade between Africa and the Caribbean, was a major factor in financing Britain's industrial revolution.[460] Earlier Portuguese, Dutch, French and British were engaged in slave trade, which is well-known as Atlantic triangular slave trades that were making a profit at every stop. The first side of the triangle was the export of goods from Europe to Africa. These included guns, ammunition and other factory made goods. The second leg of the triangle exported enslaved Africans across the Atlantic Ocean to the Americas and the Caribbean Islands, who were sold to the agricultural investors. The third and final part of the triangle was the return of goods to Europe from the Americas. The goods were the products of slave-labor plantations and included cotton, sugar, tobacco, molasses and rum.[461] It was estimated that 75% of all sugar produced in the plantations was sent to London as West Indian sugar became ubiquitous as an additive to Indian tea, and much of it was consumed in the highly lucrative coffee houses there.[478]

Karl Marx in his influential economic history of capitalism Das Kapital wrote that "...the turning of Africa into a warren for the commercial hunting of black-skins, signaled the rosy dawn of the era of capitalist production." He argued that

73

the slave trade was part of what he termed the "primitive accumulation" of capital.[462] Other researchers and historians have strongly contested this view. David Richardson has concluded that the profits from the slave trade amounted to less than 1% of domestic investment in Britain.[463] Economic historian Stanley Engerman finds that even without subtracting the associated costs of the slave trade (e.g., shipping costs, slave mortality, mortality of British people in Africa, defense costs) or reinvestment of profits back into the slave trade, the total profits from the slave trade and of West Indian plantations amounted to less than 5% of the British economy during any year of the Industrial Revolution.[464]

Nevertheless the First Industrial Revolution was driven by technological innovations in textile, steam power and in iron making. As the revolution in industry progressed a succession of machines became available which increased food production with ever fewer labourers.[147] The first real attempt at industrial use of steam power was due to Thomas Savery in 1698. Savery's pump was economical in small horsepower ranges, but was prone to boiler explosions in larger sizes. The improved steam engine invented by James Watt was patented in 1775 and first commercially launched in 1776. The introduction of steam power, wider utilization of water wheels and powered machinery (mainly in textile manufacturing) underpinned the dramatic increases in production capacity.[148] The application of steam power stimulated the demand for coal. In textile sector, the use of cotton spinning using Richard Arkwright's water frame, James Hargreaves's spinning jenny etc. increased productivity to the extent that manufactured cotton goods became the dominant British export by displacing India. An improvement was made in the production of steel. Benjamin Huntsman developed his crucible steel technique in the 1740s. The supply of cheaper iron and steel aided the development of boilers and steam engines, and eventually railways. The demand for machinery and rails stimulated the iron industry. The demand for transportation to move raw material and finished products out stimulated the growth of the canal and the railway system.[147]

There were two main values, self interest and an entrepreneurial spirit that really drove the industrial revolution in Britain.[149] Greater liberalizations of trade from a large merchant base may have allowed Britain to produce and use emerging scientific and technological developments more effectively than any other countries. The stable political situation in Britain from around 1688 and British society's greater receptiveness to change can also be said to be factors favoring the industrial advances resulted in a huge increase in personal wealth. Many other countries around the world started to recognize the changes and advancements in Britain and use them as an example to begin their own industrial revolutions.[149] The huge natural or financial resources that Britain received from India, particularly from Bengal and from its many overseas colonies and slave trade between Africa and the Caribbean helped fuel industrial investment and gain massive lead over other countries.

After gaining the right to collect revenue in Bengal in 1765 following the battle of Battle of Plassey, the land revenue collected in the Bengal Presidency and money from opium trade with China helped finance the East India Company's wars in other part of India.[150] The money collected by the company from India also went to the British government to spread its colonies and business world-wide. During the period, 1780–1860, India changed from being an exporter of processed goods for which it received payment in bullion, to being an exporter of raw materials and a buyer of manufactured goods.[150] As an example, in the 1750s, mostly fine cotton and silk was exported from India to markets in Europe, Asia, and Africa. In the 17th and 18th centuries, the eastern part of Bengal, currently known as Bangladesh used to produce the most beautiful, loosely-woven cotton fabric in the world called Muslin and export to Europe.[151] It became very popular to the elites in France and England. The British cotton mill industry began to lobby the government to both tax Indian imports and allow them access to markets in India from the late 18th century.[152]

British cotton exports reach 3 per cent of the Indian market by 1825. Starting in the 1830s, British textiles began to appear in—and soon to inundate—the Indian markets, with the value of the textile imports growing from £5.2 million 1850 to £18.4 million in 1896.[153] British cotton exports reach 30 per cent of the Indian market by 1850. Industrial revolution did little for India as the world was moving from agriculture toward industrialization. Investment in Indian industries was limited since it was a colony. The infrastructure the British created was mainly geared towards the exploitation of resources in the world.[154]

Figure 2.3 shows exponential growth of GDP per capita of United Kingdom after their presence in India. On the other hand, it shows stagnation in India's per capita GDP and income during the colonial era. In India as the industrial development stalled, agriculture alone was unable to feed a rapidly accelerating population.[154] The people in India were subject to frequent famines, had one of the world's lowest life expectancies, suffered from pervasive malnutrition and were largely illiterate. China was the world's largest economy followed by India and France. Even under British control, the Gross Domestic Product (GDP) of

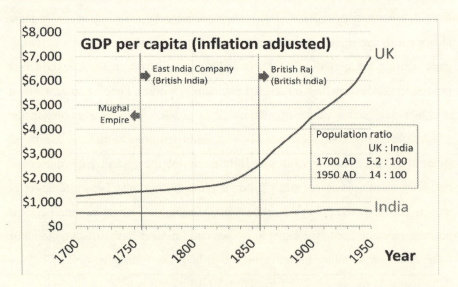

Figure 2.3: GDP of United Kingdom and India during the Colonial Era[155]

India in 1825 was estimated at about 50 per cent that of China (Figure 1.2).

The Industrial Revolution led to a population increase, but the chances of surviving childhood did not improve throughout the Industrial Revolution.[156] There was still limited opportunity for education, and children were expected to work. Employers could pay a child less than an adult even though their productivity was comparable; there was no need for strength to operate an industrial machine, and since the industrial system was completely new there were no experienced adult laborers. This made child labor the labor of choice for manufacturing in the early phases of the Industrial Revolution between the 18th and 19th centuries. In England and Scotland in 1788, two-thirds of the workers in 143 water-powered cotton mills were described as children.[157] Many children were forced to work in relatively bad conditions for much lower pay than their elders, 10-20% of an adult male's wage.[158] Children as young as four were employed. Beatings and long hours were common, with some child coal miners working from 4 am until 5 pm. Many children developed lung cancer while they were working in cotton industries and other diseases and died before the age of 25.[158] Workhouses would sell orphans and abandoned children as "pauper apprentices", working without wages for board and lodging. The mining works used young people, called a "drawer" who had to crawl on his hands and knees because the gallery was so small to pull coal tubs along a mine gallery.[159] Those who ran away would be whipped and returned to their masters, with some masters shackling them to prevent escape. Children employed as mule scavenger by cotton mills would crawl under machinery to pick up cotton, working 14 hours a day, and six days a week. Some lost hands or limbs, others were crushed under the machines, and some were decapitated. Children employed at glassworks were regularly burned and blinded, and those working at potteries were vulnerable to poisonous clay dust.[160]

Politicians and the government tried to limit child labor by law, but factory owners resisted; some felt that they were aiding the poor by giving their children money to buy food to avoid starvation, and others simply welcomed the cheap labor.[147] In 1833 and 1844, the first general laws against child labor, the Factory Acts, were passed in England: Children younger than nine were not allowed to work, children were not permitted to work at night, and the work day of youth under the age of 18 was limited to twelve hours. Factory inspectors supervised the execution of the law, however, their scarcity made enforcement difficult.[160] About ten years later, the employment of children and women in mining was forbidden. These laws decreased the number of child laborers; however, child labor remained in Europe up to the 20th century.

The rapid industrialization cost many craft workers their jobs. Many weavers also found themselves suddenly unemployed since they could no longer compete with machines which only required relatively limited (and unskilled) labor to produce more cloth than a single weaver. Many such unemployed workers, weavers and others, turned their animosity towards the machines that had taken their jobs and began destroying factories and machinery. In England, these attackers became known as Luddites, supposedly followers of Ned Ludd, a folklore figure. The first attacks of the Luddite movement began in 1811. The Luddites rapidly gained popularity, and the British government took drastic measures, using the militia or army to protect industry. Those rioters who were caught were tried and hanged, or transported for life.[147] To subdue labor unrest, many leaders of labor organizations were also transported for life to Australia.

Industrial revolution in the UK raised the nation to the top league of Europe for the first time ever. During this period, British foreign and economic policies began treating India as an unequal partner for the first time.[161] After 1850, Britain replaced France as European top. China was still the world's largest economy followed by the UK and India. The decline of Indian economy actually started in the mid-1820s.[154]

Spinning evolved from twisting the fibers by hand, to using a drop spindle, to using a spinning wheel were invented in India between 500 and 1000 AD.[162] Bengal industries were globally dominant on the eve of the industrial revolution. In early 17th century, India had a superior cotton manufacturing industry with dye technology, mechanical devices and division of labor among specialized craftspeople.[163] Indian cotton was so popular among British women that English silk and wool weavers felt threatened. Therefore, in 1725, British government banned Indian textiles but the demand for Indian fabrics continued. This situation stimulated the mechanization of Britain's textile industry.[134] Although textiles have been identified as the catalyst in technological change in Britain, the working conditions in the textile factories were substandard and the workers had to put in 70 hour weeks on a regular basis.[164]

The East India Company deindustrialization Bengal as it was the first Indian region British targeted selling its products.[134] Ray estimates that the Indian industry shrank by about 28% by 1850. However, it survived in the high-end and low-end domestic markets. Ray agrees that British discriminatory policies undoubtedly depressed the industry's export outlet, but suggests its decay is better explained by technological innovations in Britain.[165] British economist, Angus Maddison (2006) argues that India's share of the world income went down from 27% in 1700 (compared to Europe's share of 23%) to 3% in 1950.[166]

Some have stressed the importance of natural or financial resources that Britain received from its many overseas colonies or profits from the British slave trade between Africa and the Caribbean helped fuel industrial investment.[145] The Industrial Revolution saw a rapid transformation in the British economy and society. These new factories proved far more efficient at producing goods than the cottage industry of a previous era. These manufactured goods were sold around the world, and raw materials and luxury goods were imported to Britain. There began devastating contentions among newly industrial European nations to retain or extend their acquired territories so that they have a granted export market for their products. Much of the money earned from rapid industrial growth in local economies burned in military ventures among the economically expanding European countries.

The industrial revolution came along with intellectual revolution called the "Age of Enlightenment" that not only include scientific innovations but also cultural movements in the late 17th- and 18th-century Europe emphasizing reason and individualism rather than tradition. It opposed superstition and intolerance. The ideas of the Enlightenment have had a long-term major impact on the culture, politics, and governments of the Western world. Originating about 1650 to 1700, it was sparked by philosophers Baruch Spinoza, John Locke, Pierre Bayle, Voltaire, Rousseau and Montesquieu and physicist Isaac Newton. The Scientific discoveries overturned many traditional concepts and introduced new perspectives on nature and man's place within it.[167] The music of Haydn and Mozart, later Beethoven were usually regarded as being the most in line with the Enlightenment ideals. The new intellectual forces spread to urban centers across Europe and then jumped the Atlantic into the European colonies, where it influenced George Washington, Benjamin Franklin and Thomas Jefferson, among many others, and played a major role in the American Revolution. The political ideals of the Enlightenment influenced the American Declaration of Independence, the United States Bill of Rights, the French Declaration of the Rights of Man and of the Citizen.[167]

2.5 Revolution, War and Accumulation

There was already heated colonial struggle between the British Empire and French Empire for control of colonial possessions followed by Seven Years' War between 1756 and 1763. It was a continuation of the War of the Austrian Succession and eventually involved most of the great powers of the time and affected Europe, North America, Central America, the West African coast, India, and the Philippines involving Austria, France, Russia, Sweden and Spain on one side and Prussia, Great Britain and Portugal on another side. There was big monetary consequence of Seven Years' War.[130] The East India Companies were the sources of the money of the colonialist countries such as Britain, France, Spain and Portugal. And military conscription and economy in Russia, Prussia and Austria continued to depend on serfdom and the looted wealth and treasuries of the acquired states during the war. On that time, British had suffered defeats in North America by French armies at the beginning. The Seven Years' War ended when long British naval blockade of French ports had declined the morale of the French populace in 1762.[130] And In Russia, Emperor Peter III had been overthrown by his wife Catherine the Great who now switched Russian support back to Austria and launched fresh attacks on Prussia. Austria, however, had been weakened from the war and, like most participants, was facing a severe financial crisis. In 1763 a peace settlement was reached at the Treaty of Hubertusburg ending the war in central Europe. In North America, the French forces were eventually defeated by British troops at the Battle of Signal Hill. This was the final battle of the war in North America, and it forced the French to surrender to the British.[130]

The British victory in the Seven Years' War (1756–1763) had been won only at a great financial cost. During the war, the British national debt nearly doubled, rising from £72 million in 1755 to almost £130 million by 1764.[168] Post-war expenses were expected to remain high because stationing 10,000 regular British soldiers in North America made strategic sense because Great Britain had acquired the vast territory of New France in the 1763 peace treaty, and troops would be needed to maintain control of the new empire. To help offset this cost, the British Parliament passed two acts, the Currency Act of 1764 and the Townshend Revenue Act of 1767.

The British American colonies had issued paper money known as "bills of credit" to help pay for military expenses during the French and Indian Wars. The first currency act, the Currency Act of 1751 allowed the colonies of New England use the existing bills as legal tender for public debts (i.e. paying taxes), but disallowed their use for private debts (e.g. for paying merchants). This Act was in response to the over-issuance of bills by Rhode Island, eventually reducing their value to 1/27 of the issuing value.[169] The Currency Act of 1764 extended the 1751 Act 1764 but completely banned the issuance of Bills of Credit in the colonies and the making of such bills legal tender because their depreciation allowed the discharge of debts with depreciated paper money. However, after objection from the colonies 1770, Parliament gave permission for New York to issue £120,000 in paper currency for public but not private debts and extended these concessions to the other colonies in 1773 by amending the Currency Act of 1764. However, psychological controversies remained in the colonies that Parliament did not understand or care about the their problems.[170]

The Townshend Revenue Act levied new taxes, including one on tea, in the colonies but exempted East India Company from 25% duty on tea that was re-exported to the colonies.[171] When this tax indemnity expired in 1772, the Parliament passed a new act that reduced this refund but left in place the three

Figure 2.4: The Destruction of Tea at Boston Harbor[173]

pence Townshend duty in the colonies. With this new tax burden driving up the price of British tea, sales plummeted and by late 1772 the East India Company was in a serious financial crisis. In this situation, a new Tea Act in 1773 restored the East India Company's full refund on the duty for importing tea into Britain, and also permitted the company, for the first time, to export tea to the colonies on its own account by eliminating the middlemen who bought the tea at wholesale auctions in London.[172] This Act renewed controversy in American colonies about Parliament's right to tax the colonies. Americans objected to the Tea Act because they believed that it violated their rights as Englishmen to "No taxation without representation".[174] In an event they destroyed the entire supply of tea sent by the East India Company into Boston Harbor, known as Boston tea party (Figure 2.4). The British government responded harshly and the episode escalated into the American Revolution.

The thirteen British colonies in America demanded their rights as Englishmen, to select their own representatives to govern and tax them. This was refused by Britain and finally resulted in a new sovereign nation external to the British Empire, the United States of America, on July 4, 1776.[175] The British tried to crush the American economy with a blockade of all ports, but with 90% of the people in farming, and only 10% in cities, the American economy proved resilient and able to support a sustained war, which lasted 1775–1783.[176] France, Spain and the Dutch Republic all secretly provided supplies, ammunition and weapons to the revolutionaries starting early in 1776. The British spent about £80 million and ended with a national debt of £250 million, which it easily financed at about £9.5 million a year in interest from the stream of money started to flow after British East India Company captured Bengal, India in 1757. The French spent about £56 million and their total national debt was £187 million, which they could not easily finance; over half the French national revenue went to debt service in the 1780s. The debt crisis became a major enabling factor of the French Revolution as the government could not raise taxes without public approval.[177] The United States spent $37 million at the national level plus $114 million by the states. This was mostly covered by loans from France and the Netherlands, loans from Americans, and issuance of paper money.

The U.S. finally solved its debt and currency problems in the 1790s after establishment of the First Bank of the United States in 1791 by the first United States Secretary of the Treasury Alexander Hamilton.[178] It was a national bank, chartered for a term of twenty years by the United States Congress and signed by the first U.S. President George Washington.[179] As Secretary of the Treasury, Alexander Hamilton was the primary author of the economic policies of the George Washington administration, especially the funding of the state debts by the Federal government along with the establishment of the First Bank, a system of tariffs, and friendly trade relations with Britain. He gathered the ideas from Adam Smith, extensive studies on the Bank of England and his experience in establishing the Bank of New York. Accordingly, Hamilton suggested only one-fifth of the total $10 million capitalization was to be handled by the Government and the rest was to be available to individual investors.[180] Since the Government did not have the money, it would borrow the money from the bank itself, and repay the loan in ten even annual installments. Much of the national debt was in the form of bonds issued to continental veterans, in place of wages the Continental Congress did not have the money to pay. As the bonds continued to go unpaid, many had been pawned for a small fraction of their value.[181] Hamilton's bank model had many similarities to that of the Bank of England, except Hamilton wanted to exclude the government from being involved in public debt, but provide a large, firm elastic money supply for the functioning of normal businesses and usual economic development, among other differences. In his Report on Manufactures, he quoted from Adam Smith's Wealth of Nations that being a dominant agrarian country would be at a disadvantage in dealing with Europe.[180] On the other hand, he opposed the ideas of free trade, which he believed skewed benefits to colonial and imperial powers rather he favored protectionism, which he believed would help develop the fledgling nation's emerging economy. Later many countries such as Japan's Meiji, Taiwan, Korea embraced Hamilton's words and work as being applicable to their own need to modernize. They used Hamilton's report on credit to establish their own modern financial systems.[181]

Following the Seven Years' War and the American Revolutionary War, the French government was deeply in debt and attempted to restore its financial status through unpopular taxation schemes although it was hard to raise taxes for the riches who acquired wealth through mercantilism. Although many land-owning peasants and enterprising merchants had been able to grow rich during the boom, the standard of living fell greatly for rural peasants or the Third Estate or positioned at the bottom of the French social class, who were forced to deal with bad harvests at the same time.[183] As affordability was increasing in urban classes, the rising prices, particularly for agricultural products, were extremely

Figure 2.5: The Third Estate carrying the Clergy and the Nobility on its back[182]

profitable for large landholders. Artisans and tenant farmers also saw wage increases, but on the whole, they benefited less from the growing economy. Figure 2.5 shows a caricature that the third estate carrying the clergy and the nobility-The First and the Second Estates on its back. While the Seven Years' War, 1756–1763, led to an increase in the royal debt in France and the loss of nearly all of France's North American possessions but the government could not implement effective taxes from rich elites due to protest from parliament and clergy. The agricultural and climatic problems of the 1770s and 1780s led to an important increase in poverty: in some cities in the north, historians have estimated the poor as reaching upwards of 20% of the urban population. The discrimination between the elites and the poor led to French Revolution. The French Revolution began in 1789 was a period of radical social and political upheaval in France that had a major impact on France and indeed all of Europe. Following French Revolution, the society underwent an epic transformation as feudal, aristocratic and religious privileges disappeared. The next few years featured political struggles between various liberal assemblies and right-wing supporters of the monarchy intent on thwarting major reforms. Eventually, the Republic was proclaimed in September 1792 and Louis XVI was executed in January 1793.[183]

Mayer Amschel Rothschild (1744-1812) son of a goldsmith and money changer in Frankfurt, Germany founded Rothschild banking dynasty, which is believed to have become the wealthiest family in human history. He discovered that although loans to farmers and small businesses could be profitable, the real profits lay in making loans to governments. He helped King George III of England hire 16,800 sturdy young Hessian soldiers to fight against American Revolutionists from which he made an advantageous fortune. Mayer developed a finance house and spread his empire by installing each of his five sons in the five main European financial centers to conduct business. The eldest, Anselm, was placed in charge of the Frankfurt bank. The second son, Salomon, was sent to

Vienna, where he soon took over the banking monopoly. The third son, Nathan, founded the London branch. Karl, the fourth son, went to Naples. The youngest son, James, founded the French branch of the House of Rothschild in Paris. They have been keeping control of their banks in family hands, allowing them to maintain full secrecy about the size of their fortunes.[184]

The French Revolution of 1789 had a significant impact throughout Europe monarchies. The first attempt to crush the French Republic came in 1793 when Austria, the Kingdom of Sardinia, the Kingdom of Naples, Prussia, Spain and the Kingdom of Great Britain formed the First Coalition. French measures, including general conscription, military reform, and total war, contributed to the defeat of the First Coalition, despite the civil war occurring in France. The war ended when France led by Napoleon forced the Austrians to accept his terms in the Treaty of Campo Formio. He established hegemony over most of continental Europe and sought to spread the ideals of the French Revolution. The Second Coalition was formed in 1798 by Austria, Great Britain, the Kingdom of Naples, the Ottoman Empire, the Papal States, Portugal, Russia, Sweden and other states when Napoleon was in Egypt. On that time, France also lacked funds to finance the war. On the other hand, Britain had influx of money from Bengal by East India Company. British financial support brought back the new coalition into the war.[185] Britain had a large navy but a small army deployed in Europe. However, as a wealthy commercial power, they were able to pay out millions of pounds to Allied nations, who could field much larger armies against the French.[185]

British East India Company took over the Cape of Good Hope area in 1795, to prevent it from falling under control of the French First Republic, which had invaded the Dutch Republic. The Dutch East India Company became bankrupt by 1795.[458] Given its standing interests in Australia and India, Great Britain wanted to use Cape Town as an interim port for its merchants' long voyages. After Napoleon's return from Egypt, he took over full control of French government, replacing the Directory with the Consulate led by him. Each place he went to, he found his opposition being financed by the bankers, making huge profits as Prussia, Austria and finally Russia all went heavily into debt trying to stop him.[186] Under his command, French army defeated the Second Coalition, even though an incomplete one as Britain continued to finance France's continental enemies and encourage hostility towards France. Napoleon realized that without either defeating the British or signing a treaty with them he could not achieve complete peace.[185] In 1800 financial power in France was in the hands of about ten to fifteen banking houses. These bankers, all Protestant, were deeply involved in the agitations leading up to the French Revolution. When the revolutionary violence got out of hand, they orchestrated the rise of Napoleon, whom they regarded as the restorer of order. As a reward for their support, Napoleon gave these bankers a monopoly over French finance by founding Bank of France in 1800 and giving them control of the bank.[187]

France controlled a vast 828,000 square miles (2,140,000 km^2) area in North America outside the thirteen British colonies called territory of Louisiana from 1699 until 1762, the year it gave the territory to its ally Spain. Under Napoleon, France took back the Louisiana territory in 1800 in the hope of building an empire in North America. However, a slave revolt in Haiti and an impending war with Britain, led France to abandon these plans and sell the entire territory to the newly formed United States for a total sum of 15 million dollars in 1803 instead of borrowing the war money from the bank.[188] The constant "war-footing" of the Napoleonic Era, between 1795 and 1815, stimulated production at the cost of investment and growth. Production of armaments and other military supplies, fortifications, and the general channeling of the society toward the establishment and maintenance of massed armies, temporarily increased economic activity after several years of revolution.[183] Napoleon, lead French victory against five of seven coalitions. These great victories gave the French Army a sense of invulnerability, especially when it approached Moscow. But after the retreat from Russia, in spite of incomplete victories, France was defeated by the sixth coalition at Leipzig, in the Peninsular War at Vitoria and at the hands of the seventh coalition at Waterloo.[185]

The Rothschilds already possessed a significant fortune before the start of the Napoleonic Wars, and the family had gained preeminence in the bullion trade by this time.[189] The third son of Mayer Amschel Rothschild, Nathan Mayer Rothschild (1777–1836) founded N. M. Rothschild & Sons Limited, a multinational investment banking company in the City of London in 1811 who made his fortune from the event of Napoleonic War.[190] At the time the main French army in Russia, Nathan financed Wellington, a British army general to attack from south. General Wellington is also known as General Arthur Wellesley who led the British victory against Tipu Sultan in India.[191] His attack and other defeats eventually forced Napoleon into exile. Now Napoleon borrowed money from Banking House of Paris to equip again an army to fight back. The British national debt also increased dramatically during and after the Napoleonic Wars, rising to around 200% of GDP.[192]

The origins of the British national debt can be found during the reign of William III, who engaged a syndicate of City traders and merchants to offer for sale an issue of government debt. This syndicate soon evolved into the Bank of England, eventually financing the wars of the Duke of Marlborough and later Imperial conquests.[192] Nathan Rothschild, the most prominent among the syndicate during Napoleonic Wars, poised a plan to take control of the British stock market, the bond market, and possibly even the Bank of England.[186] As Jewish encyclopedia describes Nathan's role "The elector's money had been sent to Nathan in London, who in 1808 utilized it to purchase £800,000 worth of gold from the East India Company, knowing that it would be needed for Wellington's Peninsular campaign. He made no less than four profits on this: (1) on the sale of Wellington's paper, (2) on the sale of the gold to Wellington, (3) on its repurchase, and (4) on forwarding it to Portugal.[193] This was the beginning of the great fortunes of the Rothschilds and eventually Rothschild family banking houses controlled the financial empire of the world.

Nathan's four brothers helped co-ordinate the activities across the continent, and the family developed a network of agents, shippers and couriers to transport gold and information across Europe. This private intelligence service enabled Nathan to receive in London the news of Wellington's victory at the Battle of Waterloo a full day ahead of the government's official messengers.[190&194] Therefore he was able to manipulate the bond market by creating an opposite impression that Napoleon has own so everyone in Britain started to sell their bonds. "Meanwhile Nathan began to secretly buy up all the hugely devalued bonds at a fraction of what they were worth a few hours before and took control of the bond market and captured more in one afternoon than the combined forces of Napoleon and Wellington had captured in their entire lifetime."[186]

When France and Britain went to war in early 1793, all four members of Washington's cabinet including secretary of state Thomas Jefferson, secretary of the treasury Alexander Hamilton were consulted on what to do. They unanimously agreed to remain neutral. To avoid war, Washington sent Chief Justice John Jay to negotiate with the British; Hamilton largely wrote Jay's instructions. The result was Jay's Treaty, which resolved issues remaining from the Revolution, averted war, and made possible ten years of peaceful trade between the United States and Britain.[195] Thus Britain was the largest trading partner, receiving 80% of U.S. cotton and 50% of other U.S. exports. However, in 1807, Britain introduced a series of trade restrictions via a series of Orders in Council to impede American trade with France. The United States contested these restrictions as illegal under international law.[195]

The Northwest Territory, comprising the modern states of Ohio, Indiana, Illinois, Michigan, and Wisconsin, was the battleground for conflict between the Indian Nations and the United States.[196] The British Empire had ceded the area to the

United States in the Treaty of Paris in 1783, both sides ignoring the fact that the land was already inhabited by various Indian nations. The British saw the Indian nations as valuable allies led by native leader Tecumseh and a buffer to its Canadian colonies and provided arms. All these resulted a war declaration by President James Madison on June 1, 1812. It was a 32-month military conflict between the United States of America and the United Kingdom, its North American colonies and its Indian allies. In 1814, during the War of 1812, the White House was set ablaze by British troops during the Burning of Washington, in retaliation for burning Upper Canada's Parliament Buildings in the Battle of York. After death of Tecumseh and growing opposition to wartime taxation and the demands of British merchants to reopen trade with America, the new British Prime Minister Lord Liverpool, dropped its demand for an independent Indian state. The outcome resolved many issues which remained from the American War of Independence, but involved no boundary changes between the United States and British North American territory (part of modern day Canada).[197]

At the beginning of the 19th century, banking in Britain was an affair for clubs of very wealthy families. However, after collapse of the threat from Napoleon, a new sort of banking emerged, owned by anonymous stockholders, run by professional managers, and the recipient of the deposits of a growing body of small savers.[24] After the settlement of the war of 1812, the British government effectively relinquished its mercantilist policies towards the United States, preparing the way for the development of free trade and the opening of America's vast western frontier.[198] Europe was undergoing a period of readjusted to peacetime production and commerce in the aftermath of the Napoleonic Wars. Britain had advanced its industrial capacity to fully meet its wartime demands, but post-war continental Europe was temporarily too devastated to absorb Britain's surplus manufactured goods. Moreover, European agriculture production, exhausted by years of warfare, was unable to feed its own population. While the US markets swamped with British products, continental

Europe, offered new markets for American staple crops, particularly cotton, wheat, corn and tobacco.[198] As prices soared for agricultural goods, a speculative agrarian land boom ensued in the South and West United States.[199] The land based boom compounded by excessive speculation and fueled by the unrestrained issue of paper money from state banks and business concerns called for revival of a national banking system. Thus the Second Bank of the United States was chartered from February 1817 to January 1836, for 20 years. Likewise the First Bank of United States, it was a private corporation with public duties. Twenty percent of its capital was owned by from federal government and the bank handled all fiscal transactions for the US Government, and was accountable to Congress and the US Treasury.[200]

In 1832 presidential re-election, the efforts to renew the Second Bank of United States' charter was at the center of the campaign. Right before the election, when the American congress voted to renew the Bank's charter, President Andrew Jackson exercised his veto power to prevent the renewal bill from passing. This is what he had to say:

> "It is not our own citizens only who are to receive the bounty of our government. More than eight millions of the stock of this bank are held by foreigners... is there no danger to our liberty and independence in a bank that in its nature has so little to bind it to our country?......Controlling our currency, receiving our public moneys, and holding thousands of our citizens in dependence... would be more formidable and dangerous than a military power of the enemy."[201]

In reaction of this, to promote sympathy for the institution's survival, President of the Bank, Nicholas Biddle retaliated by contracting Bank credit, inducing a serious and protracted financial downturn.[202] The struggle over the issue of re-chartering the Bank is called the Bank War. In his presidential race Jackson skillfully reduced the issue to a choice between Jackson and "the People" versus Biddle and "the Aristocracy". A reaction set in throughout America's financial and business centers against Biddle's economic warfare[202] compelling the Bank to reverse its tight money policies.[204] By the close of 1834, re-charter was a "lost

Figure 2.6: A cartoon depicts President Andrew Jackson battling the many-headed monster of the Second Bank of United States[203]

cause."[202] The federal charter expired in March 1836. This episode of the Bank's ended in 1841 with liquidation of the institution. Jackson's campaign against the Bank had triumphed for the time.[205]

There were several results of this action—one was an increase in the importance of the London banks to the U.S. economy, and another was an expansion of the state banking systems, amongst which the federal treasury was now splitting its deposits. The U.S. government also sold huge amounts of public land in Jackson's second term, lands acquired at the cost of dispossessing their inhabitants. It deposited the proceeds from these sales in the state banks. As the money supply expanded, asset prices rose, increasing the appetite of Europe's investors, creating a bubble. Between 1830 and 1837, the US trade deficit was $140 million. By 1839 this bubble burst. The Union Bank of Mississippi collapsed. As credit conditions worsened, a wave of defaults resulted in many of the American states that had borrowed from London banks.[24]

The addition of the Americas to the world trading network provided Europe with new agricultural goods such as tobacco, and greatly increased the availability of products such as sugar and fur. America became a ready source for precious metals, especially silver.[206] Britain introduced free trade in 1840s and its overseas trade was protected by the overwhelming power of the Royal Navy that created an economic empire has been called "The Imperialism of Free Trade."[207] Numerous independent entrepreneurs expanded the Empire, such as Stamford Raffles of the East India Company who founded the port of Singapore in 1819. Businessmen eager to sell Indian opium in the vast China market led to the Opium War and the establishment of British colonies at Hong Kong.[145] However GDP of China reduced drastically after Chinese defeat in the Opium wars.

After the British settlement in North America from 1620s it was used for penal transportation from of convicts from United Kingdom to America until American Revolution of 1776.[208] The American Revolutionary War brought that to an end and, since the remaining British colonies in what is now Canada were close to the new United States of America, prisoners sent there might become hostile to British authorities. Thus, the British Government was forced to look elsewhere. Then from 1788 onward the British settlement is Australia began through penal transportation to the colony of New South Wales. They also brought boats providing food and animals from London. The ships and boats would help discover the coast of Australia better by sailing all around Australia looking for suitable farming land and resources. The sentence was imposed for life or for a set period of years. If imposed for a period of years, the offender was permitted to return home after serving out his time, but had to make his own way back. Until the massive influx of immigrants during the Australian gold rushes of the 1850s, the settler population had been dominated by English and Irish convicts and their descendants. However, compared to America, Australia received a significantly higher number of English prisoners.[208&209]

China had very low demand for European goods and there was very high European demand for Chinese goods such as tea, silk, and porcelain, forced European merchants to purchase these goods with silver. From the mid-17th century around 28 million kilograms of silver were received by China, principally from European powers, in exchange for Chinese goods.[210] Britain was able to reverse the flow of silver by exporting opium to India in huge quantity. It created strong mass addiction in all over China that made Qianlong Emperor ban opium trading. The British tried several times to persuade the Chinese to ease the ban, sending an ambassador to the court of the Qianlong Emperor. When they were rejected, the East India Company started smuggling opium into China. The result was disastrous for the Chinese. It is estimated that between 1821 and 1840, as much as one-fifth of the silver circulating in China was used to purchase opium, the abuse of which incapacitated able men throughout the country.[211] When the Qing government tried to stop opium trade, the result was the Opium Wars, in which the Qing government was defeated. In 1842, the Qing authorities sued for peace, which concluded with the Treaty of Nanking ratified in 1843. In the treaty, China was forced to pay an indemnity to Britain, open four ports to Britain, and cede Hong Kong to Queen Victoria.[210] The treaty also unilaterally fixed Chinese tariffs at a low rate, granted extraterritorial rights to foreigners in China and diplomatic representation. When the court still refused to accept foreign ambassadors and obstructed the trade clauses of the treaties, disputes over the treatment of British merchants in Chinese ports and on the seas led to the Second Opium War from 1856 to 1860 and the Treaty of Tientsin.[212]

The Opium Wars began a pattern of war, defeat, concessions, and silver payments to foreign powers, which further weakened the Chinese government and economy through outflow of silver.[210] These treaties, soon followed by similar arrangements with the United States and France, later became known as the Unequal Treaties, and the Opium Wars represented the start of China's "Century of humiliation". Anger at the Qing rulers grew after the Opium Wars, in 1851, there was a revolt against the Qing Dynasty. The rebels called the Taipings, quickly took control of much of southern China. The Qing defeated the rebels with aid from the British and French, but the rebellion claimed over 20 million lives. The Taiping Rebellion was one of the bloodiest wars in history lasted until 1871 and it devastated the Qing economy.[214]

In India the East India Company soon expanded its territories around its bases in Bombay and Madras; the Anglo-Mysore Wars (1766–1799) and the Anglo-Maratha Wars (1772–1818) led to control of the vast region of India. After the turn of the 19th century, Governor-General Wellesley, brother of General Wellington began what became two decades of accelerated expansion of Company territories.[214] This was achieved either by subsidiary alliances between the company and local rulers or by direct military annexation. The subsidiary alliances created the princely states or native states of the Hindu maharajas and the Muslim nawabs. Punjab, North-West Frontier Province, and Kashmir were annexed after the Second Anglo-Sikh War in 1849. However, Kashmir was immediately sold under the Treaty of AmriCzar (1850) to the Dogra Dynasty of Jammu and thereby became a princely state.[214&215]

The border dispute between Nepal and British India, which sharpened after 1801, had caused the Anglo-Nepalese War of 1814–16 and brought the defeated Gurkhas under British influence. Thus the privately owned company extended its rule across India after expelling the Dutch, French and Portuguese until the Indian Rebellion of 1857. The rebellion 1857 began as a mutiny of armies of the East India Company's army, in the cantonment of the town of Meerut and soon escalated into other mutinies and civilian rebellions. It was previously triggered by a revolt of a 29-year-old soldier Mangal Pandey on 29 March 1857 at a parade ground, near Calcutta. The rebellion led to the dissolution of the East

India Company in 1858.[216] The last Mogul emperor Bahadur Shah was exiled to Rangoon, Burma (currently Myanmar) and brought Mughal dynasty to an end. In 1877 Queen Victoria took the title of Empress of India. India was thereafter directly governed by the crown as the new British Raj until independence in 1947.[217] Essentially the old East India Company bureaucracy remained, though there was a major shift in attitudes. In looking for the causes of the mutiny the authorities highlighted two things: religion and the economy. On religion it was felt that there had been too much interference with indigenous traditions, both Hindu and Muslim. On the economy it was now believed that the previous attempts by the Company to introduce free market competition had undermined traditional power structures and bonds of loyalty placing the peasantry at the mercy of merchants and money-lenders. In consequence the new British Raj army, financial system and administration was constructed in part around a conservative agenda, based on a preservation of local tradition and hierarchy.[216]

Slave trade perhaps was the second most profitable business next to opium trade of the privately owned European trading system. The use of slaves made huge profits possible within both the plantation and mining endeavors. In 1663 the Company of Royal Adventurers to Africa was given the monopoly of the slave trade to the English colonies in America. In 1672 it was replaced by the 'Royal African Company'. The previously discussed South Sea Company had arranged contracts with the Royal African Company to supply the necessary African slaves to Jamaica. £10 was paid for a slave aged over 16 and £8 for one over 10. The Royal African Company transported around 100,000 slaves between 1672 and 1689. Its profits made a major contribution to the increase in the financial power of those who controlled London.[218]

The slave trade increased because it was considered to be more profitable to buy adult slaves than to allow or encourage slaves in America to have children. It was calculated that it would cost twice as much to raise a child to a suitable age for work than it cost to buy an adult slave.[219] Britain shipped about 2.5 million

Africans across the Atlantic, equaling 41% of the total transport of 6.1 million slaves.[220] Portugal controlled one third, and France controlled one fifth. One-third of the slaves went to Brazil, a quarter each went to the French colonies and the British colonies in the West Indies, and 5% went to the northern American mainland. Estimates by Patrick Manning are that about 12 million slaves entered the Atlantic trade between the 16th and 19th century, but about 1.5 million died on board ship. About 10.5 million slaves arrived in the Americas. Besides the slaves who died on the Middle Passage, more Africans likely died during the slave raids in Africa and forced marches to ports. Manning estimates that 4 million died inside Africa after capture, and many more died young. Manning's estimate covers the 12 million who were originally destined for the Atlantic, as well as the 6 million destined for Asian slave markets and the 8 million destined for African markets.[479] In "Encyclopedia of Human Rights, Volume 1", David P. Forsythe wrote:

"The fact remained that at the beginning of the nineteenth century an estimated three-quarters of all people alive were trapped in bondage against their will either in some form of slavery or serfdom."[221]

Great Britain played a prominent role in the Atlantic slave trade, especially after 1600. Slavery was a legal institution in all of the 13 American colonies and Canada. In 1785, English poet William Cowper wrote:

"We have no slaves at home – Then why abroad? Slaves cannot breathe in England; if their lungs receive our air, that moment they are free. They touch our country, and their shackles fall. That's noble, and bespeaks a nation proud. And jealous of the blessing. Spread it then, And let it circulate through every vein."[474]

In 1807, following many years of lobbying by the abolitionist movement, led primarily by William Wilberforce, the British Parliament voted to make the slave trade illegal anywhere in the Empire with the Slave Trade Act 1807. The act imposed a fine of £100 for every slave found aboard a British ship. The intention was to outlaw entirely the Atlantic slave trade within the whole British Empire. This act impacted the global trade of slaves.[220] The Slavery Abolition Act, passed on 23 August 1833, out lawed slavery itself in the British colonies. Meanwhile, many of the early capitalists in Europe and in the colonies have made their fortunes from opium and slave trade until the second industrial revolution added more products in the trade lines. Later, many of them such as JPMorgan, Lehman Brothers apologized for their predecessors' link with slave trading.[222] Nathan Meyer Rothschild was known for his role in the abolition of the slave trade through his part-financing of the 20 million pound British government buyout of the plantation industry's slaves.[223] However in 2009 it was claimed that as part of banking dealings with a slave owner, Rothschild used slaves as collateral. The Rothschild bank denied the claims.[190&222] On 24 August 2007, Ken Livingstone, Mayor of London, apologized publicly for London's role in the slave trade. "You can look across there to see the institutions that still have the benefit of the wealth they created from slavery", he said pointing towards the financial district, before breaking down in tears. He claimed that London was still tainted by the horrors of slavery.[475]

In 1820, Moses Austin, a banker from Missouri, was granted a large tract of land in Texas, but died before he could bring his plan of recruiting American settlers for the land to fruition. Mexico got independence from Spain in 1821 but fraught with internal struggles that verged on civil war. However it was relatively united in refusing to recognize the independence of Texas and threatened war with the U.S. if it annexed Texas. In 1842 the American minister in Mexico, Waddy Thompson, Jr., suggested Mexico might be willing to cede California to settle Mexican debts incurred during its civil war saying: "As to Texas, I regard it as of very little value compared with California."[224] Texas consolidated its status as an independent republic and received official recognition from Britain, France, and the U.S., which all advised Mexico not to try to reconquer the new nation. Most Texians wanted to join the U.S. but annexation of Texas was contentious in the

U.S. Congress. In 1845 Texas agreed to the offer of annexation by the U.S. Congress. Texas became the 28th state on December 29, 1845.[224] However, this annexation caused the Mexican–American War from 1846 to 1848. Mexico accepted the loss of Texas. The Treaty of Guadalupe Hidalgo specified the major consequence of the war: the forced Mexican Cession of the territories of Alta California and New Mexico to the United States in exchange for $15 million. In addition, the United States assumed $3.25 million of debt owed by the Mexican government to U.S. citizens. However, the war was highly controversial in the United States, with the Whig Party, anti-imperialists and anti-slavery elements strongly opposed. Heavy American casualties and high monetary cost were also criticized. The political aftermath of the war raised the slavery issue in the United States, leading to intense debates that pointed to civil war.[224] However, with annexation of Texas and California, the concept of an American Empire was first popularized during the presidency of James K. Polk who led the United States into the Mexican–American War.[225]

The North part of the United States phased slavery out of existence, industrialized, urbanized and built prosperous farms, while the South concentrated on plantation agriculture based on slave labor. The North and South became divided in the issue of slavery. In 1857, the Supreme Court Chief justice issued an opinion that blacks were not citizens, and derived no rights from the Constitution. Republican Abraham Lincoln denounced the decision and argued, "The authors of the Declaration of Independence never intended 'to say all were equal in color, size, intellect, moral developments, or social capacity', but they 'did consider all men created equal—equal in certain inalienable rights, among which are life, liberty, and the pursuit of happiness'."[226] After the state Republican party convention nominated him for the U.S. Senate in 1858, Lincoln delivered his House Divided Speech,

> "A house divided against itself cannot stand. I believe this government cannot
> endure permanently half slave and half free. I do not expect the Union to be

dissolved—I do not expect the house to fall—but I do expect it will cease to be divided. It will become all one thing, or all the other."[227]

In the 1860 presidential election, Republicans, led by Lincoln won but before his inauguration, seven slave states with cotton-based economies formed a Confederacy. The states that remained were known as the "Union" or the "North". The secession of South from North turned into a Civil War fought from 1861 to 1865 that left over 600,000 soldiers died, the Confederacy collapsed and slavery was abolished.[228]

Confronted with the expenses of war, the Lincoln Administration sought loans from New York bankers, most of whom were fronts for, or connected to, European banks dominated by Rothschild family.[229] Given the very high interest rates of 24 to 36 percent, Lincoln decided to print the government's own money instead of leading the country into perpetual debt at the hand of European banks.[230] After the union victory at the Gettysburg battlefield cemetery on November 19, 1863, in his three minute speech, Lincoln declared that the deaths of so many brave soldiers would not be in vain, that slavery would end as a result of the losses, and the future of democracy in the world would be assured, that "government of the people, by the people, for the people, shall not perish from the earth"[231] Lincoln was assassinated in April 15, 1865 at the beginning of the second term of his Presidency.

2.6 The Second Industrial Revolution

The First Industrial Revolution, which began in the 18th century, merged into the Second Industrial Revolution around 1850, when technological and economic progress gained momentum with the development of steam-powered ships, railways, and later in the 19th century with the internal combustion engine and electrical power generation. Industrialization allowed cheap production of household items using economies of scale, while rapid population growth created sustained demand. Some industry and industrial technique developed for the wars was carried over, converted to peacetime purposes. The first industrial revolution was centered on textiles, iron and steam engine technologies, while

Figure 2.7: An 'Industrial Workers of the World' poster, 1911.[236]

the second industrial revolution revolved around steel, railroads, petroleum and chemicals and, finally, electricity.[232]

From 1815 to 1870 Britain reaped the benefits of being the world's first modern, industrialized nation. It was the 'workshop of the world', meaning that its finished goods were produced so efficiently and cheaply. Karl Marx (1859) views the system of capitalization through industrialization in Britain as inherently exploitative.[233] The period from 1870 to 1890 saw the greatest increase in economic growth in such a short period as ever in previous history. Living standards improved significantly in the newly industrialized countries as the prices of goods fell dramatically due to the increases in productivity. This also caused unemployment and great upheavals in commerce and industry, with many laborers being displaced by machines and many factories, ships and other forms of fixed capital becoming obsolete in a very short time span.[234] Many families where having economic problems because they were getting paid too little, and they felt that it was unfair that they work for so long with only a little bit of money. Many people were not able to feed their kids everyday which sent them to sleep on empty stomachs until they got to work the next day. During the industrial revolution, factories were criticized for long work hours, deplorable conditions, and low wages. Children as young as 5 and 6 could be forced to work a 12-16 hour day and earn as little as 4 shillings per week.[235] Living conditions during the Industrial Revolution varied from the splendor of the homes of the owners to the squalor of the lives of the workers. Poor people lived in very small houses in cramped streets. These homes would share toilet facilities, have open sewers and would be at risk of developing pathologies associated with persistent dampness. Disease was spread through a contaminated water supply. Conditions did improve during the 19th century as public health acts were introduced covering things such as sewage, hygiene and making some boundaries upon the construction of homes.[235]

The Industrial Revolution created a larger middle class of professionals such as lawyers and doctors. The famines that troubled rural areas did not happen in industrial areas. However, urban people especially small children died due to diseases spreading through the cramped living conditions. The diseases such as tuberculosis (spread in congested dwellings), lung diseases from the mines, cholera from polluted water and typhoid were also common. A description of housing of the mill workers in England in 1844 was given by Friedrich Engels, the founder of Communism. However, in the 1892 edition of the same book he notes that the most of the conditions had been greatly improved.[237]

The British invented the modern railway system and exported it to the world. Britain had a superior financial system based in London that funded both the railways in Britain and also in many other parts of the world, including the United States. The boom years were 1836 and 1845–47, when Parliament authorized 8,000 miles of railways.[238] By 1850 Britain had a well-integrated, well-engineered railroad system that provided fast, on-time, inexpensive movement of freight and people to every city and most rural districts. Freight rates had plunged to a penny a ton mile for coal.[238] The system directly or indirectly generated employments, bringing a new level of business sophistication that could be applied to many other industries, and helping many small and large businesses to expand their role in the industrial revolution. Thus railways had a tremendous impact on industrialization. They reduced costs for all industries moving supplies and finished goods, and they increased demand for the production of all the inputs needed for the industrial revolution.[238]

At the time of the second industrial revolution Russia and the Ottoman Empire went to war called Crimean War in October 1853 led by Nicholas I over Russia's claim to protect Orthodox Christians. It lasted until February 1856 in which Russia lost to an alliance of France, Britain and the Ottoman Empire. Austria was neutral but played a role in stopping the Russians. Earlier Nicholas I defeated the Ottoman Empire in the Russo-Turkish war 1828-1829. Thus he was a key player in the ascendency of Russia as a world power and helped hasten the disintegration of the aging Ottoman Empire. When he died in 1855, the Russian Empire reached over 20 million square kilometers. The Crimean War was one of the first "modern" wars because it saw the first use of major technologies, such as railways and telegraphs.[239] This war is notorious for logistical, medical and tactical failure on both sides. It is also famous for the work of Florence Nightingale who pioneered nursing practices while caring for wounded British soldiers. Part of the Russian resistance was credited to the deployment of newly created blockade mines for the navy by a civil engineer Immanuel Nobel, the father of Alfred Nobel. The Crimean War was one of the first wars to be documented extensively in written reports and photographs. After the French extended the telegraph to the coast of the Black Sea during the winter of 1854, the news reached London in two days. When the British laid an underwater cable to the Crimean peninsula in April 1855, news reached London in a few hours.[240]

Russia had incurred so large a war debt from the Crimean War. The new Russian Emperor Alexander II tried to recover Russia from the loss of the war by making radical reforms of his policies and administrations, including an attempt to not depend on a landed aristocracy controlling the poor, a move to developing Russia's natural resources. He built a great network of railways, partly for the purpose of developing the natural resources of the country, and partly for the purpose of increasing its power for defense and attack. His most important achievement was the emancipation of serfs in 1861, for which he became known as Alexander the Liberator. Following this emancipation, he sought to repay money to its landowners and borrowed 15 million pounds sterling from Rothschilds at 5% annually.[241] After realizing difficulty of defending Alaska ($1,518,800 \ km^2$) from British, he decided to sell it to a third party, the United States, in 1867 at $7.2 million, or about 2 cents per acre ($4.74/km2).[241] The valuable minerals including gold and oil were discovered in Alaska beginning from 1880, thirteen years after the sale.

Japan went through two periods of economic development after 1854, when the country first opened the country to Western commerce and influence. However, Japanese Westernization began completely during Meiji period began in 1868. The word "Meiji" means "enlightened rule" and the goal was to combine "western advances" with the traditional, "eastern" values.[242] The industrial revolution first appeared in textiles, including cotton and especially silk, which was based in home workshops in rural areas. By the 1890s, Japanese textiles dominated the home markets and competed successfully with British products in China and India, as well. Japanese shippers were competing with European traders to carry these goods across Asia and even to Europe. The Meiji period brought the end of the feudal system. More importantly based on Western-based education system and implementing Western ideal of capitalism, Japan's industrial sector and military grew significantly.[243]

The Imperial Japanese Navy was modeled after the British Royal Navy, which at the time was the foremost naval power in the world. The Meiji government built railroads, improved roads, and inaugurated a land reform program to prepare the country for further development. The government emerged as chief promoter of private enterprise, enacting a series of pro-business policies.[243&244] Japan became an economic powerhouse by the beginning of the 20th century, which led to its rise as a military power by the year 1905, under the slogan of "Enrich the country, strengthen the military" to strengthen Japan against the threat represented by the colonial powers of the day.[245] Japan won in the First Sino-Japanese War fought with Qing Dynasty China primarily over control of Korea from 1 August 1894 – 17 April 1895. After that for the first time, regional dominance in East Asia shifted from China to Japan.[246]

In Europe, after the French Revolution and the Napoleonic Wars, feudalism fell away and liberalism and nationalism clashed with reaction. The Prussian economy under Bismarck was rapidly growing during the second industrial revolution gave her an advantage in the Austro-Prussian War reflecting long term struggle between Austria & Prussia for economic supremacy.[247] The Seven Weeks War between Austria and Prussia broke out in June 1866 involving half a million men and then merged into Franco-Prussian war. The causes of the Franco-Prussian War are deeply rooted in the events surrounding the balance of power in Europe after the Napoleonic Wars. Now the French faced an increasingly strong Prussia.[248] The war left Prussia dominant in Germany, and German nationalism would compel the remaining independent states to ally with Prussia in the Franco-Prussian War in 1870.[247]

The end of the Franco-Prussian War in 1871 yielded a new political order in Germany. The Prussian Chancellor Otto von Bismarck united Germany and led to form German Empire. After 1870, European conflict was averted largely through a carefully planned network of treaties between the German Empire and the remainder of Europe orchestrated by Bismarck. The £200 million reparations imposed on France led to an inflationary investment boom in Germany and central Europe.[248] New technologies were being rapidly applied, railroads were booming. The Industrial Revolution modernized the German economy, led to the rapid growth of cities and to the emergence of the Socialist movement in Germany. Prussia, with its capital Berlin, grew in power. Bismarck introduced social insurance programs to head off support for socialism in the 1880s, the first in the world and became the model for other countries and the basis of the modern welfare state.[249] He introduced old age pensions, accident insurance, medical care and unemployment insurance. His paternalistic programs won the support of German industry because its goals were to win the support of the working classes for the Empire and reduce the outflow of immigrants to America, where wages were higher but welfare did not exist.[250&251] German universities became world-class centers for science and the humanities, while music and the arts flourished.[248] The optimism that had been driving booming stock prices in central Europe had reached a fever pitch, and fears of a bubble culminated in a panic in Vienna beginning in April 1873 and spread heavily in Europe and the United States.[252]

Following the Civil War, particularly following the panic in Europe and Depression of 1873–79 in the United States, there was a rapid expansion of industrial production in the United States. Chicago was a major industrial center dominated by German immigrants workers employed at about $1.50 a day and worked on average slightly over 60 hours, during a six-day work week.[253] The city became a center for many attempts to organize labor's demands for better working conditions. Employers responded with anti-union measures, such as firing and blacklisting union members, locking out workers, recruiting strikebreakers; employing spies, thugs, and private security forces and exacerbating ethnic tensions in order to divide the workers.[254] Mainstream newspapers supported business interests, and were opposed by the labor and immigrant press.[255] During the economic slowdown between 1882 and 1886, socialist and anarchist organizations were active. In October 1884, a convention held by the Federation of Organized Trades and Labor Unions unanimously set May 1, 1886, as the date by which the eight-hour work day would become standard. On May 4, 1886 a bombing took place at a labor demonstration at Haymarket Square in Chicago. It began as a peaceful rally but an unknown person threw a dynamite bomb at police. The bomb blast and ensuing gunfire resulted in the deaths of seven police officers and at least four civilians. Later in a trial, seven organizers were sentenced to death. Among them four were hanged on November 11, 1887. According to witnesses, in the moments before hanged, August Spies, the editor of German-language newspaper Arbeiter-Zeitung ("Workers' Times"), shouted,

"The time will come when our silence will be more powerful than the voices you strangle today!"[256]

In 1893, Illinois' new governor pardoned the remaining defendants and criticized the trial.[256]

2.7 The Age of Synergy

During later stage of the second industrial revolution, the new science based technologies such as electricity, the internal combustion engine, new materials and substances, including alloys and chemicals, and communication technologies such as the telegraph, telephone and radio were developed. Vaclav Smill called the period 1867–1914 "The Age of Synergy" during which most of the great innovations was developed.[257] These new inventions created a big prospect of industrial capitalism that gave way to financial capitalism and the ultimate control and direction of large industry came into the hands of financiers.

The financial houses or big banks in Britain were able to exert a great deal of control over the British economy and politics by creating of super corporations and conglomerates. Britain had built up a vast reserve of overseas credits in its formal Empire, as well as in its informal empire in Latin America and other nations.[145&257] Through their investments in the new technology based industrial revolution, the British financial houses had huge financial holdings in the United States. This contributed to increasing concerns among policymakers over the protection of British investments overseas, particularly those in the securities of foreign governments and in foreign-government-backed development activities, such as railways. At the end of the Victorian era, the service sectors (banking, insurance and shipping, for example) began to gain prominence at the expense of manufacturing. Britain ranked as the world's largest trading nation in 1860, but by 1913 it had lost ground to both the United States and Germany.[145&259]

The Americans closely followed and copied British railroad technology. The Pacific Railway Acts were passed in 1862, allowing the first transcontinental railroad to be completed in 1869, making possible a six-day trip from New York to San Francisco.[260] Other transcontinental were built in the South and along the Canadian border (Northern Pacific, Great Northern), accelerating the settlement of the West by offering inexpensive farms and ranches on credit, carrying pioneers and supplies westward, and cattle, wheat and minerals eastward. New

York financier J.P. Morgan played an increasingly dominant role in consolidating the rail system in the late 19th century.[260] He raised large sums in Europe using his ties with European bankers built when he worked for his father's partnership merchant banking firm, Peabody, Morgan & Co. with George Peabody in London. American born banker George Peabody was the largest trader of American securities in the world. He has a statue in London, just opposite the Bank of England.[261]

In his visit to Egypt, Napoleon Bonaparte became interest in finding the remnants of an ancient waterway passage that connected Nile River from Old Cairo and Red Sea.[262] In 1854 and 1856 Ferdinand de Lesseps of France obtained a concession from Sa'id Pasha, the Khedive of Egypt and Sudan, to create a Suez Canal, which was opened to shipping on 17 November 1869 after 10 years of construction work.[263] Although numerous technical, political, and financial problems had been overcome, the final cost was more than double the original estimate. After the opening of the canal, the Suez Canal Company was in financial difficulties. Britain bought the Egyptian share of the canal for £4,000,000 in 1875 with funding from the Rothschilds as Egypt was suffering from debt.[264] French shareholders still held the majority. The canal has been a vital economic and military link. To protect the canal Britain expanded again and again, taking control of Egypt, the Sudan, Uganda, Kenya, Cyprus, Palestine, Aden, and British Somaliland.[145]

Another big canal, the Panama Canal, a 77.1-kilometre ship canal was built in Panama that connects the Atlantic Ocean to the Pacific Ocean. There are locks at each end to lift ships up to Gatun Lake, an artificial lake created to reduce the amount of excavation work required for the canal, 26 meters above sea level. The first attempt to construct the canal began on January 1, 1881. The project, designed as a sea-level canal (i.e., without locks) by France, was under the leadership of Ferdinand de Lesseps, builder of the Suez Canal, with substantial financing and support from Paris.[265] However, the French effort eventually went bankrupt after reportedly spending US$287 million because of engineering problems and high mortality of the workers due to disease. The United States took over the project in 1904, and took a decade to complete the canal, which was officially opened on August 15, 1914. American Society of Civil Engineers has named the Panama Canal one of the seven wonders of the modern world.[265]

J. P. Morgan worked with closed ties with European banking houses and made his banking and financial company "J. P. Morgan & Company" as one of the most powerful banking houses of the world. He also became wealthy through railroad ownerships by creating monopoly. In 1893 the largest economic depression in U.S. history at that time called "The Panic of 1893" was the result of railroad overbuilding, which set off a series of bank failures. One-quarter of U.S. railroads had failed by mid-1894. Acquisitions of the bankrupt companies led to further consolidation of ownership. In 1895, at the depths of the Panic of 1893, the Federal Treasury was nearly out of gold.[267] President Grover Cleveland accepted Morgan's offer to join with the Rothschilds and supply the U.S. Treasury with 3.5 million ounces of gold.[268]

The railroads not only enabled flow of goods and people from one place to another but also created the need of flow of information without changing any physical position. The earlier form of this type of communication was telegraphy, which started in 1792 during French Revolution by sending messages to a distant observer through line-of-sight signals. The commercial electrical telegraphs were introduced from 1837. Incidentally, the great inventor Thomas Alva Edison was a telegraph operator at Stratford Junction, Ontario, on the Grand Trunk Railway.[269] He developed many devices that greatly influenced life around the world, especially contributed to mass communication, including the phonograph, the motion picture camera and improvement of telecommunications such as carbon telephone transmitter. He is also the inventor of long-lasting, practical electric light bulb and a system of electric-power generation and distribution–a crucial development in the modern industrialized world. He founded the first electrical power distribution company Edison Illuminating Company, Edison General Electric, which later became General Electric.[270] In 1892 J.P. Morgan arranged the merger of Edison General Electric and Thomson-Houston Electric Company to form General Electric.[268]

The businesses and research centers Edison established not only pioneered American technology base industries but also created many genius inventors such Nikola Tesla and Henry Ford. Nikola Tesla gained experience in telephony and electrical engineering in Continental Edison Company in France before immigrating to the United States in 1884 to work for Machine Works in New York City ending in a disagreement over pay. After leaving Edison, in 1886, Tesla formed his own company, Tesla Electric Light & Manufacturing. His invention of AC induction motor and transformer pioneered power system using alternating current by Westinghouse.[271] However Thomas Edison and George Westinghouse became adversaries due to Edison's promotion of direct current (DC) for electric power distribution over alternating current (AC) advocated by several European companies in the late 1880s. As a result of the "War of Currents," Edison and Westinghouse went nearly bankrupt. Edison had lost control of his company to J.P. Morgan, and Morgan was refusing to loan more money to Westinghouse due to the financial strain of the Tesla AC patents.[272] In 1900, Tesla was granted patents for a "system of transmitting electrical energy" and "an electrical transmitter". The Italian inventor Marconi's famous transatlantic radio transmission in 1901 was equipped with 17 Tesla patents.[271]

J. C. Bose from Bengal, India demonstrated remote wireless signaling or radio transmitter which has priority over Marconi.[310] In May 1897, two years after Bose's public demonstration in Kolkata, Marconi conducted his wireless signaling experiment.[273] The Institute of Electrical and Electronics Engineers (IEEE) named him one of the fathers of radio science or wireless telecommunication.[274] He was the first to use a semiconductor junction to detect radio waves, and he invented various now commonplace microwave components.[273] Sir Nevill Mott, Nobel Laureate in 1977 for his own contributions to solid-state electronics, remarked that "J.C. Bose was at least 60 years ahead of his time."[274] In contrast to American contemporary inventors such as Edison, Tesla or Marconi, he was not interested in patenting his inventions and later declined an offer from a wireless apparatus manufacturer for signing a remunerative agreement. In his Friday Evening Discourse at the Royal Institution, London, he made public his construction of the Coherer. Thus the Electric Engineer expressed:

"surprise that no secret was at any time made as to its construction, so that it has been open to the entire world to adopt it for practical and possibly moneymaking purposes."[275]

Henry Ford, was an American industrialist, the founder of the Ford Motor Company, and sponsor of the development of the assembly line technique of mass production was an engineer with the Edison Illuminating Company. After his promotion to Chief Engineer in 1893, he had enough time and money to devote attention to his personal experiments on gasoline engines.[276] These experiments culminated in 1896 with the completion of a self-propelled vehicle which he named the Ford Quadricycle. He founded Ford Motor Company. His introduction of the Model T model revolutionized transportation and American industry. He was a pioneer of "welfare capitalism", designed to improve the lot of his workers and especially to reduce the heavy turnover. Henry Ford turned the presidency of Ford Motor Company over to his son Edsel Ford in December 1918. Henry started another company, Henry Ford and Son, and made a show of taking himself and his best employees to the new company; the goal was to scare the remaining holdout stockholders of the Ford Motor Company to sell their stakes to him before they lost most of their value. The ruse worked and Henry and his son purchased all remaining stock from the other investors, thus giving the family sole ownership of the company.[277] Henry Ford became one of the richest and best-known entrepreneur in the world.[276]

Two American brothers Wilbur Wright and Orville Wright brothers invented the world's first practical fixed-wing aircraft in 1903. It was built using their preferred material for construction, spruce, a strong and lightweight wood, and Pride of the West muslin (is a loosely woven cotton fabric. Originating in Bengal, India) for surface coverings. Their first successful flying machine traveled only 120 ft (36.6 m) in 12 seconds on December 17, 1903.[278] From 1905 to 1907, the brothers developed their flying machine into the first practical fixed-wing aircraft. They were granted U.S. Patent for "new and useful improvements in flying machines", a system of aerodynamic control that manipulated a flying machine's surfaces, including lateral flight control in 1906. The U.S. government or the newspapers were unreceptive to the claims of two unknown bicycle makers from Ohio. Dayton Daily published a small article on page 9, with agriculture and business news on October 6, 1905.[278]

Although Wright Brothers got their patent for inventing aircraft but they refused to participate in the first ever Scientific American Cup trophy and $25,000 in cash prize for making a public flight of over 1 kilometer on July 4, 1908 on the American independent day. The prize was won by Glenn Curtiss of Aerial Experiment Association (A.E.A), who was a motorcycle manufacturer, using an

Figure 2.8: First flight of the Wright Flyer I, December 17, 1903[279]

aircraft called "AEA June Bug".[280] In fact, none of the AEA's aircraft used a wing-warping system like the Wrights' for control, relying instead on triangular ailerons designed by Alexander Graham Bell, who also invented the first telephone in 1876.[281] Bell successfully patented his aircraft design in December 1911. However, in 1913 a court ruled that this technique was an infringement of the Wright's 1906 patent.[280] Among many others Alexander Graham Bell invented photophone, which allowed for the transmission of both sounds and normal human conversations on a beam of light. It presaged later the ground breaking invention fiber optical telecommunications. In 1888, Bell became one of the founding members of the National Geographic Society.[281]

The invention of telephone by Alexander Graham Bell rooted in his research on elocution and speech as both his mother and wife were deaf, profoundly influencing Bell's life's work. His research on hearing and speech further led him to experiment with hearing devices which eventually culminated in invention of telephone, the first ever patented in 1876.[281] While Bell was working as a private tutor, one of his most famous pupils was Helen Keller, who was deaf and blind from her childhood but earned a Bachelor of Arts degree and became an author, political activist, and lecturer with continuous support of her teacher Anne Sullivan for 49 years.[282] Helen was later to say that Bell dedicated his life to the penetration of that "inhuman silence which separates and estranges."[283]

The story of railroads, automobile and airplane is tied up with the story of oil. John Davison Rockefeller co-founded Standard Oil Company, the largest oil company in the world until the United States Supreme Court ordered to break the company from its monopoly in 1911.[284] He along with chemist Samuel Andrews and Clark brothers founded a refinery when Whale oil had become too expensive for the masses, and a cheaper, general-purpose lighting fuel was needed.[285] His wealth continued to grow significantly, in line with U.S. economic growth as the demand for gasoline soared, including significant interests in banking, shipping, mining, railroads, and other industries. The railroads were fighting fiercely for traffic and, in an attempt to create a cartel to control freight rates, formed the South Improvement Company in collusion with Standard oil and other oil men outside the main oil centers, which enabled him to crush his competitors through volume rebates. In 1911, with the dissolution of the Standard Oil trust into 33 smaller companies, Rockefeller became the richest man in the world.[284]

The second richest person in the world was Andrew Carnegie, behind only John D. Rockefeller of Standard Oil. He was born in Scotland, and immigrated to the United States with his very poor parents in 1848. Carnegie started as a telegrapher and by the 1860s had investments in railroads, railroad sleeping cars, bridges and oil derricks. He built further wealth as a bond salesman raising money for American enterprise in Europe. He built Pittsburgh's Carnegie Steel Company, which he sold to J.P. Morgan in 1901 for $480 million and devoted the remainder of his life to large-scale philanthropy. In his 1889 article "The Gospel of Wealth" Carnegie proposed that the best way of dealing with the new phenomenon of wealth inequality was for the wealthy to redistribute their surplus means in a responsible and thoughtful manner.[286]

The philanthropic proposal of Andrew Carnegie contrasted with traditional patrimonial preservation of wealth, where wealth is handed down to heirs. The traditional practices of the wealthy businessmen were consolidation of wealth and businesses and kill any competition on the way. J.P. Morgan founded U.S. Steel Company in 1901 by merging with the Carnegie Steel Company and several other steel and iron. It was the first billion-dollar company in the world, having an authorized capitalization of $1.4 billion, which was much larger than any other industrial firm and comparable in size to the largest railroads. The U.S. Congress enacted antitrust legislation to prohibit railroad monopolies the Sherman Antitrust Act in 1890. However, for the most part, politicians were unwilling to refer to and enforce this law until Theodore Roosevelt's Presidency (1901–1909) and beyond.[266]

As the whale oil was becoming expensive, shale-oil became one of the first sources of mineral oil used by humans since 14th century.[287] The British Crown granted a patent in 1694 to three persons who had "found a way to extract and make great quantities of pitch, tar and oil out of a sort of stone."[288] Modern shale oil extraction industries were established in France during the 1830s and in Scotland during the 1840s.[289] The Industrial Revolution had created additional demand for lighting as a substitute for the increasingly scarce and expensive whale oil.[288] During the late 19th century, shale oil extraction plants were built in many countries including the United States, Australia, Brazil, China. The discovery of crude oil in the Middle East during mid-century brought most of these industries to a halt, although Estonia and Northeast China maintained their extraction industries into the early 21st century.[289]

Abraham Pineo Gesner, a Canadian geologist developed a process to refine a liquid fuel from coal, bitumen and oil shale. His new discovery, which he named kerosene, burned more cleanly and was less expensive than competing products, such as whale oil. In 1850, Gesner created the Kerosene Gaslight Company and began installing lighting in the streets in Halifax and other cities. By 1854, he had expanded to the United States where he created the North American Kerosene Gas Light Company at Long Island, New York.[290] In 1854, Benjamin Silliman, a science professor at Yale University in New Haven, was the first person to fractionate petroleum by distillation. These discoveries rapidly spread around the world, and Meerzoeff built the first modern Russian refinery in the mature oil fields at Baku in 1861. At that time Baku produced about 90% of the world's oil. Edwin Drake's 1859 well near Titusville, Pennsylvania, discussed more fully below, is popularly considered the first modern well. Drake's well is probably singled out because it was drilled.[290] The modern US petroleum industry is considered to have begun with Edwin Drake's drilling of a 69-foot (21 m) oil well in 1859, on Oil Creek near Titusville, Pennsylvania.[291]

Royal Dutch Petroleum Company was a Dutch company founded in 1890 when a Royal charter was granted to a small oil exploration and production company known as "Royal Dutch Company for the Working of Petroleum Wells in the Dutch East Indies". The "Shell" Transport and Trading Company was a British company, founded in 1897 for importing and selling sea-shells.[292] These two companies merged and formed Royal Dutch Shell Group in February 1907 to compete with then dominant American petroleum company Standard Oil, having 60% Dutch ownership and 40% British ownership.[292] In May 1908 a group of British geologists discovered a large amount of oil at Masjid-i-Suleiman county in Khuzestan Province in Iran. It was the first commercially significant find of oil in the Middle East. In the following year, the Anglo-Persian Oil Company (APOC) was incorporated.[293] In 1913, the British Government acquired a controlling interest in the company and at the suggestion of Winston Churchill, the British navy switched from coal to oil. The Royal Navy, which projected British power all over the world, came to be run 100% on oil from Iran. In 1919, the company became a shale-oil producer by establishing a subsidiary named Scottish Oils which merged remaining Scottish oil-shale industries.[294]

During the Panic of 1907, when major New York banks were on the verge of bankruptcy, a private conglomerate led by J. P. Morgan stepped in and set themselves up as "lenders of last resort".[268] This event led to the passage of the Aldrich–Vreeland Act in 1908, which established the National Monetary Commission, sponsored and headed by Republican leader Nelson Aldrich.[295] He worked with several key bankers and economists to design a plan for an American central bank following the models of privately owned European central banks. One of them was Paul Warburg, a German immigrant banker from who masterminded the plan for Federal Reserve System. In 1913 Woodrow Wilson signed the Federal Reserve Act into law. This act established a privately owned Federal Reserve System. The new system began operations in 1915 and played a major role in financing the American war effort in Europe.[296]

2.8 The World Wars

The Age of Synergy began to consolidate the economic power in the hand of few with financial power led extension of geopolitical power to meet the financial investment needs of the political economy of capitalism.[297] In his book "Imperialism, the Highest Stage of Capitalism" by Vladimir Lenin, describes the function of financial capital in generating profits from imperial colonialism, as the final stage of capitalist development to ensure greater profits. He describes that in order for capitalism to generate greater profits than the home market can yield, the merging of banks and industrial cartels produces finance capitalism— the exportation and investment of capital to countries with underdeveloped economies. In turn, such financial behavior leads to the division of the world among monopolist business companies and the great powers. [298]

The rapid industrialization of Russia also resulted in urban overcrowding and poor conditions for urban industrial workers. Between 1890 and 1910, the population of the capital, Saint Petersburg, swelled from 1.03 million to 1.91 million, with Moscow experiencing similar growth. This created a new 'proletariat' which, due to being crowded together in the cities, was much more likely to protest and go on strike than the peasantry had been in previous times. In one 1904 survey, it was found that an average of sixteen people shared each apartment in Saint Petersburg, with six people per room. There was also no running water, and piles of human waste were a threat to the health of the workers.[299] The poor conditions aggravated with the number of strikes and incidents of public disorder.

On the other hand, the Czar of Russia, Nicolas II personally owned 150 million acres of land. He had enormous cash reserves in European and American banks. Between 1905 and 1910 the Czar had sent more than $900 million in six leading New York banks: Chase, National City Bank, Guaranty Trust, J.P. Morgan, Hanover, and Manufacturers Trust.[300] These were also the six New York banks which bought the controlling stock in the Federal Reserve Bank of New York in

1914. They have held control of the stock ever since.[300] He also had hundreds of million dollars in four European banks. Dissatisfied with the Czar, a huge national upheaval that followed the Bloody Sunday massacre of January 1905 in which hundreds of unarmed protesters were shot by the Czar's troops. Workers responded to the massacre with a crippling general strike, forcing Nicholas to put forth the October Manifesto, which established a democratically elected parliament (the State Duma). The Czar undermined this promise of reform but a year later with Article 87 of the 1906 Fundamental State Laws, and subsequently dismissed the first two Dumas when they proved uncooperative. Unfulfilled hopes of democracy fueled revolutionary ideas and violent outbursts targeted at the monarchy.[299]

The rapidly industrialized countries in Europe eventually engaged in geopolitical conflict over the economic exploitation of large portions of the geographic world and its populaces.[298] Thus a resurgence of imperialism was an underlying cause of the World War I.[301] After unification and the foundation of the Empire in 1871 by Bismarck, German industrial and economic power had grown greatly. From the mid-1890s on, the government of Wilhelm II used this base to devote significant economic resources for building up the Imperial German Navy, in rivalry with the British Royal Navy for world naval supremacy.[302] The arms race between Britain and Germany eventually extended to the rest of Europe, with all the major powers devoting their industrial base to producing the equipment and weapons necessary for a pan-European conflict[303] between 1908 and 1913, the military spending of the European powers increased by 50 percent and catered World War I 1914–1918.[304]

The World War I was triggered on the assassination of Archduke Franz Ferdinand of Austria, heir to the throne of Austria-Hungary on 28 June 1914.[301] After one month, on 28 July, invasion of Serbia by Austro-Hungarians army mobilized Russia in the war. Germany invaded neutral Belgium and Luxembourg before moving towards France, leading Britain to declare war on

Germany. The war drew in all the world's economic great powers, which were assembled in two opposing alliances: the Allies (based on the Triple Entente of the United Kingdom, France and the Russian Empire) and the Central Powers of Germany and Austria-Hungary. In November 1914, the Ottoman Empire joined the war, opening fronts in the Caucasus, Mesopotamia and the Sinai. Although Italy had also been a member of the Triple Alliance alongside Germany and Austria-Hungary, it did not join the Central Powers. Italy, Japan and the United States joined the Allies. Italy and Bulgaria went to war in 1915 and Romania in 1916. More than 70 million military personnel, including 60 million Europeans, were mobilized in one of the largest wars in history.[301]

The engagement of Russia in World War I only added to the already existing internal chaos in its newly developing industrial economy. Conscription swept up the unwilling in all parts of Russia. The vast demand for factory production of war supplies and workers caused many more labor riots and strikes. Conscription stripped skilled workers from the cities, who had to be replaced with unskilled peasants, and then, when famine began to hit due to the poor railway system, workers abandoned the cities in droves to look for food. Finally, the soldiers themselves, who suffered from a lack of equipment and protection from the elements, began to turn against the Czar.[314] This was mainly because, as the war progressed, many of the officers who were loyal to the Czar were killed, and were replaced by discontented conscripts from the major cities, who had little loyalty to the Czar. There were 3.3 million people killed in this revolution. The situation turned against capitalism led by Vladimir Lenin and was based upon Lenin's writing on the ideas of Karl Marx, a political ideology often known as Marxism-Leninism. It marked the beginning of the spread of communism in the 20th century.[315] Nicholas II, his wife their children all were executed. At the time of his death, his net worth was $900 million, which is the inflation adjusted equivalent to $300 billion in 2012 dollars, thus making him one of the richest monarchs in human history.[316] None of the Czar's money deposited in European and American banks ever been disbursed.[300] Lenin died in 1924. At the end, he wrote, "The state does not function as we desired. A man is at the wheel and seems to lead it, but the car does not drive in the desired direction. It moves as another force wishes."[317]

The U.S. President Woodrow Wilson spent 1914 through to the beginning of 1917 trying to keep America out of the war in Europe. He offered to be a mediator, but neither the Allies nor the Central Powers took his requests seriously. Republicans, led by Theodore Roosevelt, strongly criticized Wilson's refusal to build up the U.S. Army in anticipation of the threat of war. Wilson argued that an army buildup would provoke war.[318] In his 1916 election, Wilson used as a major campaign slogan "He kept us out of war". He promoted a minimum wage, an eight-hour day and six-day workweek, health and safety measures, the prohibition of child labor, and safeguards for female workers and a retirement program.[319] After winning for the second term, in 1917, Wilson found it increasingly difficult to maintain U.S. neutrality after Germany as it was revealed that Germany attempting to provoke Mexico as an ally against the U.S. He took America into World War I stating "war to end war" and to make "the world safe for democracy", otherwise, "the western civilization itself could be destroyed".[318] The U.S. did not sign a formal alliance with the United Kingdom or France but operated as an "associated" power.[318]

The war approached a resolution after the Russian Czar's government collapsed in March 1917 and a subsequent revolution in November brought the Russians to terms with the Central Powers. After Russia left World War I following the Bolshevik Revolution of 1917, the Allies sent troops there to prevent a German or Bolshevik takeover of allied-provided weapons, munitions and other supplies previously shipped as aid to the pre-revolutionary government.[320] After the October Revolution, the Russian Empire lost much of its western frontier as the newly independent nations of Estonia, Finland, Latvia, Lithuania, and Poland were carved from it. After a 1918 German offensive along the western front, the

Allies drove back the Germans in a series of successful offensives and American forces began entering the trenches. Though not sent to engage the Bolsheviks, the U.S. forces engaged in several armed conflicts against forces of the new Russian government. Revolutionaries in Russia resented the American intrusion. As Robert Maddox puts it, "The immediate effect of the intervention was to prolong a bloody civil war, thereby costing thousands of additional lives and wreaking enormous destruction on an already battered society."[321] Germany, which had its own trouble with revolutionaries following the Russian revolution, agreed to an armistice on 11 November 1918, ending the war in victory for the Allies. The war had profound economic consequences. Of the 60 million European soldiers who were mobilized from 1914 to 1918, 8 million were killed, 7 million were permanently disabled, and 15 million were seriously injured.[301] Germany lost 15.1% of its active male population, Austria-Hungary lost 17.1%, and France lost 10.5%.[322] The war time diseases and post war diseases such as typhus, malaria and flu epidemics killed millions of people. Some speculate the soldiers' immune systems were weakened by malnourishment, as well as the stresses of combat and chemical attacks, increasing their susceptibility.[323] A major influenza epidemic spread around the world in 1918 killed at least 50 million people.[324]

On 8 January 1918, the U.S. President Woodrow Wilson issued a statement, known as the Fourteen Points intended as a means toward ending the war and achieving an equitable peace for all the nations.[325] He spent six months in Paris for the Peace Conference. He worked tirelessly to promote his plan. The charter of the proposed League of Nations was incorporated into the conference's Treaty of Versailles. It included a policy the withdrawal of the central powers from occupied territories, the creation of a Polish state, the redrawing of Europe's borders along ethnic lines. Japan proposed to include a racial equality clause. After the conference, Wilson said that "at last the world knows America as the savior of the world!"[326]

After signing the armistice, it took couple of months of negotiations at the Paris Peace Conference to conclude the peace treaty. The Treaty of Versailles, signed on 28 June 1919 was one of the peace treaties at the end of World War I, ended the state of war between Germany and the Allied Powers.[327] The other Central Powers on the German side of World War I were dealt with in separate treaties. The treaty required Germany to accept the responsibility causing all the loss and damages during the war and forced Germany to disarm, make substantial territorial concessions, and pay reparations to certain countries that had formed the Entente powers. In 1921 the total cost of these reparations was assessed at 132 billion Marks. However, "Allied experts knew that Germany could not pay" this sum. The treaty was registered by the Secretariat of the League of Nations on 21 October 1919.[328]

At the time economists, notably John Maynard Keynes predicted that the treaty was too harsh, and said the figure was excessive and counterproductive.[327] The World War I however produced an economic outcome disastrous for all parties, not just for the German losers. As predicted by Keynes in his bitter post-Versailles Conference book "The Economic Consequences of the Peace", the heavy war reparations imposed upon Germany not only were insufficient to fuel French economic recovery, they greatly damaged a Germany which might have become France's leading trade and industrial development partner, thereby seriously damaging France as well.[329] In the United Kingdom, funding the war had a severe economic cost. From being the world's largest overseas investor, it became one of its biggest debtors with interest payments forming around 40% of all government spending. Inflation more than doubled between 1914 and its peak in 1920, while the value of the Pound Sterling fell by 61.2%. In all nations, the government's share of GDP increased, surpassing 50% in both Germany and France and nearly reaching that level in Britain.[330] The European inflations were more severe than America's. This meant that the costs of American goods decreased relative to those in Europe. Between August 1914 and spring of 1915, the dollar value of US exports tripled and its trade surplus exceeded $1 billion for the first time.[331] To pay for purchases in the United States, Britain cashed in its extensive investments in American railroads and then began borrowing heavily on Wall Street. President Wilson was on the verge of cutting off the loans in late 1916, but allowed a great increase in U.S. government lending to the Allies.[301]

As a result of World War I the United States, which had been a net debtor country, had become a net creditor by 1919.[333] The US did not suspend the gold standard during the war. The newly created Federal Reserve intervened in currency markets and sold bonds to "sterilize" some of the gold imports that would have otherwise increased the stock of money. By 1927 many countries had returned to the gold standard.[333] After 1919, the US demanded repayment of these loans. The repayments were, in part, funded by German reparations which, in turn, were supported by American loans to Germany. This circular system collapsed in 1931 and the loans were never repaid. Britain still owed the United States $4.4 billion debt in 1934, and this money was never repaid.[301&332] In 1932 the payment of reparations was suspended by the international community, by which point Germany had only paid the equivalent of 20.598 billon gold marks in reparations.[301]

The German Empire was dissolved in the German Revolution of 1918–1919, and a democratic government, later known as the Weimar Republic, was created.[335] In order to pay the large costs of World War I, Germany suspended the convertibility of its currency into gold when that war broke out. Unlike France, which imposed its first income tax to pay for the war, the German Kaiser and Parliament decided without opposition to fund the war entirely by borrowing.[336] The Treaty of Versailles imposed a huge reparation load on Germany that could be paid only in gold or foreign currency. With its gold depleted to pay off the international bankers, the German government attempted to buy foreign currency with German currency, but this caused the German Mark to fall rapidly in value, which greatly increased the number of Marks needed to buy more foreign currency. This caused German prices of goods to rise rapidly which increased the cost of operating the German government which could not be financed by raising taxes. The resulting budget deficit increased rapidly and was financed by the central bank creating more money.[337] When the German people realized that their money was rapidly losing value, they tried to spend it quickly. This increase in monetary velocity caused still more rapid increase in prices which created a vicious cycle.[338] John Maynard Keynes described the situation in The Economic Consequences of the Peace:

"The inflationism of the currency systems of Europe has proceeded to extraordinary lengths. The various belligerent Governments, unable, or too timid or too short-sighted to secure from loans or taxes the resources they required, have printed notes for the balance."[329]

During the first half of 1922, the Mark stabilized at about 320 Marks per Dollar. This was accompanied by international reparations conferences, including one in June 1922 organized by U.S. investment banker J. P. Morgan, Jr.[339] When these meetings produced no workable solution, the inflation changed to hyperinflation and the Mark fell to 800 Marks per Dollar by December 1922. In January 1923 French and Belgian troops occupied the Ruhr, the industrial region of Germany to ensure that the reparations were paid in goods, such as coal from the Ruhr since the Mark was practically worthless. Inflation was exacerbated when workers in the Ruhr went on a general strike, and the German government printed more money in order to continue paying them for "passively resisting."[341] The hyperinflation reached its peak by November 1923 as shown in Figur introduced backed by mortgage bonds indexed to market prices of gold and setting up a new bank, the Rentenbank on November 16, 1923 controlled by new Finance Minister Hans Luther.[337]

At the outbreak of World War I in August 1914, the Italian political left became severely split over its position on the war. The Italian Socialist Party (PSI) opposed the war on the grounds of internationalism. Another group of revolutionary syndicalist led by Benito Mussolini, the expelled chief editor of the e 2.9.The hyperinflation ended when a new currency, the Rentenmark was

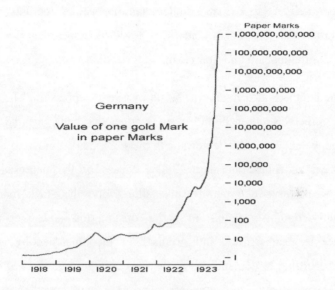

Figure 2.9: Hyperinflation in Weimar Republic (Germany)[340]

PSI's newspaper Avanti who supported intervention against the Central Power on the grounds that their reactionary regimes needed to be defeated to ensure the success of socialism.[381] He promoted fascism, which the promotes nationalism and establishment of a totalitarian. The Doctrine of Fascism states,

"The Fascist conception of the State is all-embracing; outside of it no human or spiritual values can exist, much less have value. Thus understood, Fascism is totalitarian, and the Fascist State—a synthesis and a unit inclusive of all values—interprets, develops, and potentiates the whole life of a people."[342]

In fascism economic planning the prosperity of private enterprise depended on its acceptance of synchronizing itself with the fascist state's economic goals, where industries must uphold the national interest as superior to private profit.[343] It promotes economics as a "third position" alternative to capitalism and

Marxism, as fascism declares both as being obsolete.[344] Similar political ideas arose in Germany after the outbreak of the war. German sociologist Johann Plenge spoke of the rise of a "National Socialism" in Germany within what he termed the "ideas of 1914" that included "German values" of duty, discipline, law, and order and rejected the "ideas of 1789" that included rights of man, democracy, individualism and liberalism.[345]

In 1929, the United States economy was hit by Great Depression. The depression originated in the U.S., after the fall in stock prices that began around September 4, 1929, and became worldwide news with the stock market crash of October 29, 1929 (known as Black Tuesday).[346] The causes of the depression include structural weaknesses like major bank failures and the stock market crash. Institutional economists points to under-consumption and over-investment, malfeasance by bankers and industrialists, or incompetence by government officials. According to demand-driven theories, a large-scale loss of confidence led to a sudden reduction in consumption and investment spending exacerbating the drop in demand. Monetarist economists (such as Milton Friedman and Peter Temin) point to monetary factors such as actions by the US Federal Reserve that contracted the money supply, as well as Britain's decision to return to the gold standard at pre–World War I parities (US$4.86:£1) caused the Great Depression. The Great Depression had devastating effects in countries rich and poor. Personal income, tax revenue, profits and prices dropped, while international trade plunged by more than 50%. Unemployment in the U.S. rose to 25%, and in some countries rose as high as 33%.[347] Many economists believe that government spending on the war caused or at least accelerated recovery since it did help in reducing unemployment. The rearmament policies leading up to World War II helped stimulate the economies of Europe in 1937–39. By 1937, unemployment in Britain had fallen to 1.5 million. The mobilization of manpower following the outbreak of war in 1939 ended unemployment. America's entry into the war in 1941 finally eliminated the last effects from the

Great Depression and brought the U.S. unemployment rate down below 10% and doubled economic growth rates, either masking the effects of the Depression or essentially ending the Depression.[348]

During the time of the Great Depression, there was a need to establish a dedicated institution to facilitate reparations imposed on Germany by the Treaty of Versailles after World War I. Thus the Bank for International Settlements (BIS), the international organization of central banks was established on May 17, 1930 based in Basel, Switzerland by an intergovernmental agreement by Germany, Belgium, France, Great Britain and Northern Ireland, Italy, Japan, United States and Switzerland at a conference at The Hague.[349] According to the charter, shares in the bank could be held by individuals and non-governmental entities. As an international institution, it is not accountable to any single national government. Professor Carroll Quigley writes in his book "Tragedy and Hope" about this bank:

"The powers of financial capitalism had another far reaching aim, nothing less than to create a world system of financial control in private hands able to dominate the political system of each country and the economy of the world as a whole. This system was to be controlled in a feudalist fashion by the central banks of the world acting in concert, by secret agreements arrived at in frequent meetings and conferences.

The apex of the system was to be the Bank for International Settlements in Basel, Switzerland, a private bank owned and controlled by the world's central banks which were themselves private corporations.

Each central bank ... sought to dominate its government by its ability to control treasury loans, to manipulate foreign exchanges, to influence the level of economic activity in the Country, and to influence cooperative politicians by subsequent economic rewards in the business world."[350]

After establishment of the Bank for International Settlements (BIS), the gold standard in Britain lasted until September 19, 1931, when speculative attacks on the pound forced Britain entirely off the gold standard. Loans from American and French Central Banks of £50 million were insufficient and exhausted in a matter of weeks, due to large gold outflows across the Atlantic.[351] The partially backed gold standard was inherently unstable, because of the conflict between the expansion of liabilities to foreign central banks and the resulting deterioration in the Bank of England's reserve ratio. France was then attempting to make Paris a world class financial center, and it received large gold flows as well.[333] On the other hand, Germany's reparation payments was reduced to 112 billion Gold Marks, equivalent to US $8 billion in 1929 (US$ 109 billion in 2013) over a period of 59 years, which would end in 1988.[352] In addition, the Young Plan divided the annual payment, set at two billion Gold Marks, US $473 million, into two components: one unconditional part, equal to one third of the sum, and a postponable part, equal to the remaining two-thirds, which would incur interest and be financed by a consortium of American investment banks coordinated by the J.P. Morgan's Morgan Guaranty Trust Company.[353]

Germany's Weimar Republic was hit hard by the depression, as American loans to help rebuild the German economy now stopped. This forced the government take austerity program as a result the economy suffered from massive deflation, unemployment soared, especially in larger cities, and the political system veered toward extremism. The unemployment rate reached nearly 30% in 1932, bolstering support for the Nazi (NSDAP) and Communist (KPD) parties. Repayments of the war reparations due by Germany were suspended in 1932 following the Lausanne Conference of 1932.[355] By that time, Germany had repaid one eighth of the reparations. Hitler and the Nazi Party came to power in January 1933, establishing a totalitarian single-party state within months. Adolf Hitler himself in his book, Mein Kampf, makes many references to the German debt and the negative consequences that brought about the inevitability of "national socialism".[337] The Nazis rose to power while unemployment was very high but achieved full employment following massive rearmament. Inspired by Italian Fascists March on Rome in 1935 led by Benito Mussolini, less than a month after the March, Hitler had begun to model himself and the Nazi Party upon Mussolini and the Fascists[355] and initiated the path towards World War II, the most devastating conflict in world history.

China had one of the world's largest and most advanced economies prior to the nineteenth century and then declined in absolute terms in the nineteenth and much of the twentieth century. After defeat by the Japanese in 1894 AD in the First Sino-Japanese War, China lost Korea as a vassal state. This defeat sparked an unprecedented public outcry and it was a catalyst for a series of revolutions and political changes. These trends would later manifest in the 1911 Xinhai Revolution that overthrew Manchu rule and established the Republic of China.[356] After the fall of the Qing Dynasty in 1912, China underwent a period of instability and disrupted economic activity.[356] The Republican era was a period of turmoil. From 1913 to 1927, China disintegrated into regional warlords, fighting for authority and causing misery and disrupting growth. Too weak to resist Japan, China appealed to the League of Nations for help.[335] Japan withdrew from the League of Nations after being condemned for its incursion into Manchuria. After 1927, Chiang Kai-shek managed to reunify China. During the Nanjing decade (1927–1937), China advanced in a number of industrial sectors, in particular those related to the military, in an effort to catch up with the west and prepare for war with Japan. China was largely unaffected by the Depression, mainly by having stuck to the Silver standard. However, the US silver purchase act of 1934 created an intolerable demand on China's silver coins, and so in the end the silver standard was officially abandoned in 1935 in favor of the four Chinese national banks' "legal note" issues. In addition, the Nationalist Government also acted energetically to modernize the legal and penal systems, stabilize prices, amortize debts, reform the banking and currency systems, build railroads and highways, improve public health facilities, legislate against traffic in narcotics and augment industrial and agricultural production. During Nanjing decade, China developed a modern industrial sector, which stimulated modest but significant economic growth but again was impacted by the collapse of international trade that followed the onset of the Great Depression. The level of China's share of world trade and its ratio of foreign trade to GDP achieved during 1930s were not regained for over sixty years.[357]

Nazis under leadership of Adolf Hitler mobilized the country for war by deliberately promoting social Darwinism following Völkisch nationalism that denounce soulless materialism, individualism, and secularized urban industrial society, while advocating a "superior" society based on ethnic German "folk" culture and German "blood".[358] It denounced foreigners, foreign ideas and declared that Jews, national minorities, Catholics, and Freemasons were "traitors to the nation" and unworthy of inclusion.[359] It viewed societies as organic, extolling the virtues of rural life, condemning the neglect of tradition and decay of morals, denounced the destruction of the natural environment, and condemned "cosmopolitan" cultures such as Jews and Romani.[360] In 1934 Hitler accused Jews as "The economic system of our day is the creation of the Jews."[361] He argued that capitalism damages nations due to international finance, the economic dominance of big business, and Jewish influences.[362] The concept of the Aryan race, which the Nazis promoted, stems from racial theories asserting that Europeans are the descendants of Indo-Iranian settlers, people of ancient India and ancient Persia who possess a great capacity for wisdom, nobility, restraint, and science.[363]

In March 1935, under the government of Adolf Hitler, Germany violated the Treaty of Versailles by introducing compulsory military conscription in Germany and rebuilding the armed forces. And in March 1936, Germany violated the treaty by reoccupying the demilitarized zone in the Rhineland. In July 1937, Japan captured the former Chinese imperial capital of Beijing, which culminated in the Japanese campaign to invade all of China.[364] In the following year, Japan invaded Soviet Union and Mongolia but defeated by the Soviet army. The World War II officially began on 1 September 1939 with the invasion of Poland by Germany and subsequent declarations of war on Germany by France and the United Kingdom. This war involved all of the great powers, 30 different countries eventually forming two opposing military alliances: the Allies and the Axis. Germany formed the Axis alliance with Italy, conquering or subduing much of continental Europe at the beginning of the war. In December 1941, Japan joined the Axis and thus the Sino-Japanese War merged with the war in Europe and its colonies. Japan attacked the United States and European territories in the Pacific Ocean, and quickly conquered much of the Western Pacific. In a state of "total war", the major participants threw their entire economic, industrial, and scientific capabilities behind the war effort, erasing the distinction between civilian and military resources.[335]

The World War II is the deadliest conflict in human history, resulted in an estimated 50 million to 85 million fatalities. An estimated 11to 17 million civilians died as a direct or indirect result of Nazi ideological policies, including the systematic genocide of around six million Jews in Holocaust along with a further five million ethnic Poles and other Slavs, notably Ukrainians and Belarusians, Roma, who were deemed "unworthy of life" as part of a program of deliberate extermination.[365] Approximately two-thirds of the nine million Jews including children who had resided in Europe before the Holocaust were killed.[366] In her book "Children of the Holocaust", Stephanie Fitzgerald writes:

> "At the start of World War II, about 1.6 million Jewish children were living in Europe. Fewer than one in 10 of them survived Hitler's reign of terror. More than 100,000 did survive, however-through a combination of strength, cleverness, the help of others, and-more often than not-simple good luck."[450]

In Germany, tremendous scientific and technological changes during the late 19th and early 20th centuries, together with the growth of the welfare state, created widespread hopes that utopia was at hand and that soon all social problems could be solved.[367] At the same time a racist, social Darwinist, and eugenicist world-view which declared some people to be more biologically valuable than others was common. After the First World War, the pre-war mood of optimism gave way to disillusionment as German bureaucrats found social problems to be more insoluble than previously thought, which in turn led them to place increasing emphasis on saving the biologically "fit" while the biologically "unfit" were to be written off.[367] The economic strains of the Great Depression led many in the German medical establishment to advocate the idea of euthanisation of the "incurable" mentally and physically disabled as a cost-saving measure to free up money to care for the curable.[368] By the time the Nazis came to power in 1933, a tendency already existed in German social policy to save the racially "valuable" while seeking to rid society of the racially "undesirable".[367] Israeli historian and scholar Yehuda Bauer argues that:[369]

> "The basic motivation [of the Holocaust] was purely ideological, rooted in an illusionary world of Nazi imagination, where an international Jewish conspiracy to control the world was opposed to a parallel Aryan quest. No genocide to date had been based so completely on myths, on hallucinations, on abstract, nonpragmatic ideology—which was then executed by very rational, pragmatic means."[369]

When Jews were exterminated in Germany and Europe, Saul Friedländer highlights:

> "Not one social group, not one religious community, not one scholarly institution or professional association in Germany and throughout Europe declared its solidarity with the Jews."[370]

The Japanese military during the 1930s and 1940s is often compared to the military of Nazi Germany during 1933–45 because of the sheer scale of suffering. The best-known Japanese atrocity was the Nanking Massacre, in which several hundred thousand Chinese civilians were raped and murdered. Between 3 million to more than 10 million civilians, mostly Chinese, were killed by the Japanese occupation forces.[371] Much of the controversy regarding Japan's role in World War II revolves around the death rates of prisoners of war (POW) and civilians. Historian Chalmers Johnson has written that: [372]

"It may be pointless to try to establish which World War Two Axis aggressor, Germany or Japan, was the more brutal to the peoples it victimised. The Germans killed six million Jews and 20 million Russians (i.e. Soviet citizens); the Japanese slaughtered as many as 30 million Filipinos, Malays, Vietnamese, Cambodians, Indonesians and Burmese, at least 23 million of them ethnic Chinese. …If you were a Nazi prisoner of war from Britain, America, Australia, New Zealand or Canada (but not the Soviet Union) you faced a 4% chance of not surviving the war; (by comparison) the death rate for Allied POWs held by the Japanese was nearly 30%."[372]

On 22 June 1941, Germany and Romania invaded the Soviet Union accusing the Soviets of plotting against them. They were joined shortly by Finland and Hungary after Soviet aircraft bombed their territory. In June 1941, the European Axis launched an invasion of the Soviet Union, giving a start to the largest land theatre of war in history, which tied down the major part of the Axis' military forces for the rest of the war. The Soviet Union lost around 27 million people during the war, including 8.7 million military and 19 million civilian deaths.[373] In 1943, during the heavy winter, Soviet army fought back and Germany was defeated at Stalingrad in Russia. After this a series of German defeats in Eastern Europe followed. With Italy's surrender to the Allied and American victories in the Pacific, the Axis lost the initiative and undertook strategic retreat on all fronts. In November 1943, Franklin D. Roosevelt and Winston Churchill met with Chiang Kai-shek in Cairo and then with Joseph Stalin in Tehran to decide the remaining war strategy.[374] In 1944, the Western Allies invaded France, while the Soviet Union regained all of its territorial losses and invaded Germany and its allies. During 1944 and 1945 the United States defeated the Japanese Navy and captured key Western Pacific islands. The war in Europe ended with an invasion of Germany by the Western Allies and the Soviet Union culminating in the capture of Berlin by Soviet and Polish troops and the subsequent German unconditional surrender on 8 May 1945. Following the Potsdam Declaration by the Allies on 26 July 1945, the United States dropped atomic bombs on the Japanese cities of Hiroshima and Nagasaki on 6 August and 9 August respectively. Between the two bombings, the Soviets invaded Japanese-held Manchuria, and quickly defeated the Kwantung Army, the largest Japanese force. Japan surrendered on 15 August 1945, ending the war in Asia and cementing the total victory of the Allies over the Axis.[335]

Vietnam was a French colony since 1884. During World War II, the French were defeated by the Germans in 1940. For French Indochina, this meant that the colonial authorities became Vichy French, allies of the German-Italian Axis powers. In turn this meant that the French collaborated with the Japanese forces after their invasion of French Indochina during 1940. The French continued to run affairs in the colony, but ultimate power resided in the hands of the Japanese.[375] Following Japanese occupation, during 1944–1945, a deep famine struck northern Vietnam due to a combination of bad weather and French/Japanese exploitation (French Indochina had to supply grains to Japan). Northern Vietnam was mostly affected and between 400,000 and 2 million people are estimated to have starved to death during this time. Exploiting the administrative gap that the internment of the French had created, the communist national independence coalition Viet Minh urged the population to ransack rice warehouses and refuse to pay their taxes in March 1945. This rebellion against the effects of the famine and the authorities that were partially responsible for it bolstered the Viet Minh's popularity and they recruited many members during this period.[376] During August the Japanese forces remained inactive as the Viet Minh and other nationalist groups took over public buildings and weapons, which began the August Revolution led by Ho Chi Minh. After Japanese surrender in World War II, he declared the independent Democratic Republic of Vietnam before a crowd of 500,000 in Hanoi on September 2, 1945.[375] In an overture to the Americans, he began his speech by paraphrasing the United States Declaration of Independence:

"All men are created equal. The Creator has given us certain inviolable Rights: the right to Life, the right to be Free, and the right to achieve Happiness."[375]

In January 1946, the Viet Minh won elections across central and northern Vietnam. The French landed in Hanoi by March 1946 and in November of that year they ousted the Viet Minh from the city.[375] British forces departed on 26 March 1946, leaving Vietnam in the hands of the French.[377] Soon thereafter, the Viet Minh began a guerrilla war against the French Union forces.

During World War II, another famine also struck in Bengal, India in 1943.[412] The Bengal famine of 1943 struck the Bengal province of pre-partition British India during World War II following the Japanese occupation of Burma. In the Bengal famine, estimates are that between 1.5 and 4 million people died of starvation, malnutrition and disease.[379] According to Amartya Sen, approximately 3 million people died due to famine.[378] In response to an urgent request by the Viceroy of India, Wavell, to release food stocks for India, then British Prime Minister Winston Churchill responded with a telegram to Wavell asking, "if food was so scarce, why Gandhi hadn't died yet."[380]

The greatest politician of all time Mohandas Karamchand Gandhi, led India to independence on August 15, 1947 and inspired non-violent movements for civil rights and freedom across the world. Gandhi was greatly influenced by Leo Tolstoy's ideas on nonviolent resistance, expressed in such works as "The Kingdom of God Is Within You".[465] In this book he explains that he considered Church's doctrine of war a "perversion" of Christ's teachings. Tolstoy believed being a Christian required him to be a pacifist and this was the reason why he is

137

considered a philosophical anarchist. He also believed that the aristocracy was a burden on the poor. He wrote A Letter to a Hindu outlining his belief in non-violence as a means for India to gain independence from British colonial rule. In 1909, a copy of the letter was read by Gandhi, who was working as a lawyer in South Africa at the time and just becoming an activist.[466] Gandhi first employed nonviolent civil disobedience, in the resident Indian community's struggle for civil rights. After his return to India in 1915, he set about organizing peasants, farmers, and urban laborers to protest against excessive land-tax and discrimination. Assuming leadership of the Indian National Congress in 1921, Gandhi led nationwide campaigns for easing poverty, expanding women's rights, building religious and ethnic amity, but above all for achieving Swaraj or self-rule.[467] Gandhi dedicated his life to the wider purpose of discovering truth, or Satyagraha (devotion to the truth).[468]

Although Gandhi's vision of an independent India based on religious pluralism, but India was partitioned into two separate countries, India and Pakistan based on two religions, Hindus and Muslims. The Dominion of Pakistan comprised two geographically and culturally separate areas to the west and the east with India in between, namely West Pakistan and East Pakistan respectively. The Bengal province was divided into West Bengal and East Bengal, where the latter got the name East Pakistan. The Partition was a highly controversial and caused a complete breakdown of law and order during the transition and migration of the people the Hindus and Sikhs to India and Muslims to Pakistan—one of the largest population movements in recorded history. Many died in riots, massacre, or just from the hardships of their flight to safety. According to Richard Symonds: At the lowest estimate, half a million people perished and twelve million became homeless.[381] The partition of India to be the moment that the British Empire ceased to be a world power, following Lord Curzon's dictum:

"[T]he loss of India would mean that Britain drop straight away to a third rate power."[382]

2.9 Reshuffling the Powers

The discovery of oil in the Middle East in 1908 and strategic importance of Suez Canal to the British, the Middle East became an extended front of World War I. It started with an Ottoman attempt at raiding the Suez Canal in 1915, Arab bureau of the British Foreign Office instigated Arab Revolt by destabilizing sections of the Ottoman Empire through which the Hejaz Railway ran north to south, from Istanbul to Damascus and on to Amman, Medina and to Mecca. The Ottoman army was defeated in June 1916 at the Battle of Mecca, led by Sherif Hussein of Mecca and ended with the Ottoman surrender of Damascus. At the end, the Ottoman Empire was partitioned of which France won the mandate for Syria and Lebanon and the British won the mandates for Mesopotamia (currently Iraq) and Palestine.[305] The dissolution of the Ottoman Empire at the end of World War I was pivotal in contributing to the current political situation of the Middle East, including the Arab-Israeli conflict.[306]

In Iran, the discovery of oil in 1908 by the British spawned intense renewed interest in Persia by the British Empire. Control of Persia remained contested between the United Kingdom and Russia, in what became known as The Great Game, and codified in the Anglo-Russian Convention of 1907, which divided Persia into spheres of influence, regardless of her national sovereignty.[307] The British Anglo-Persian Oil Company (APOC) and the Armenian businessman Calouste Gulbenkian were the driving forces behind the creation of Turkish Petroleum Company (TPC) in 1912 to explore oil in Mesopotamia (now Iraq); and by 1914, APOC held 50% of TPC shares.[308] During World War I, the country was occupied by British, Ottoman and Russian forces but was essentially neutral. In 1919, after the Russian revolution and their withdrawal, Britain attempted to establish a protectorate in Iran, which was unsuccessful.[307] In 1921, a military coup established Reza Khan, a Persian officer of the Persian Cossack Brigade, as the dominant figure for the next 20 years. In 1923, Winston Churchill was employed as a paid consultant to lobby the British government to allow Anglo-Persian Oil Company (APOC) have exclusive rights to Persian oil resources, which were subsequently granted by the Iranian monarchy.[309]

In 1925, after being prime minister for a couple of years, Reza Shah became the king of Iran and established the Pahlavi dynasty. In 1925, TPC received concession in the Mesopotamian oil resources from the Iraqi government under British mandate. After fall of Ottoman Empire, all of the partners in the TPC signed an agreement called "Red Line Agreement" on July 31, 1928 to formalize the corporate structure of TPC that prohibited any of its shareholders from independently seeking oil interests in the ex-Ottoman territory.[310] It marked the creation of an oil monopoly, or cartel, of immense influence, spanning a vast territory. The cartel preceded easily by three decades the birth of another cartel, the Organization of Petroleum Exporting Countries (OPEC), which was formed in 1960. After the Read Line agreement, TPC was changed to Iraq Petroleum Company (IPC) and APOC's shareholding was reduced to 23.75%. During the 1928–68 time period, IPC monopolized oil exploration inside the Red Line; excluding Saudi Arabia and Bahrain.[311] In 1934, APOC and Gulf Oil founded the Kuwait Oil Company as an equally owned partnership. In 1935, Reza Shah requested the international community to refer to Persia as 'Iran', which was reflected in the name change of APOC to the Anglo-Iranian Oil Company (AIOC).[312] In 1937, AIOC and Royal Dutch Shell formed the Shell/D'Arcy Exploration Partners partnership to explore for oil in Nigeria. The partnership was equally owned but operated by Shell. It was later replaced by Shell-D'Arcy Petroleum Development Company and Shell-BP Petroleum Development Company (now Shell Petroleum Development Company).[313]

In the last stages of the World War II, at the Bretton Woods Conference, from 1 to 22 July, 1944 Norwegian delegation put forth allegation with evidence against the Bank for International Settlements (BIS) that BIS had helped transfer the Germans loot assets from occupied countries during World War II. Therefore, they demanded "liquidation of the Bank for International Settlements at the earliest possible moment."[383] The Americans, specifically the then U.S. President Franklin Delano Roosevelt and Henry Morgenthau, the U.S. Secretary of the Treasury and other European countries except British delegation, headed by John Maynard Keynes and Chase Bank representative Dean Acheson supported this motion. The dissolution of the BIS was approved in the conference. The British delegation did not give up, however, and the dissolution of the bank was still not accomplished when Roosevelt died. In April 1945, the new President Harry S. Truman and the British suspended the dissolution and the decision to liquidate the BIS was officially reversed in 1948.[384]

Apart from the BIS issue, a system similar to a gold standard and sometimes described as a "gold exchange standard" was established by the Bretton Woods Agreements. Under this system, many countries fixed their exchange rates relative to the U.S. dollar and central banks could exchange dollar holdings into gold at the official exchange rate of $35 per ounce; this option was not available to firms or individuals. All currencies pegged to the dollar thereby had a fixed value in terms of gold.[385] In England, the Bank of England made deliberate efforts to move away from commercial banking and become a central bank during the governorship of Montagu Norman, from 1920 to 1944. After 1945 the Bank pursued the multiple goals of Keynesian economics, especially "easy money" and low interest rates to support aggregate demand. It tried to keep a fixed exchange rate, and attempted to deal with inflation and sterling weakness by credit and exchange controls.[386] In 1946, shortly after the end of Norman's tenure, the bank was nationalized by the Labor government.

Nevertheless the seminal idea behind the Bretton Woods Conference was the notion of open markets. This would require that the foremost industrial democratic nations must lower barriers to trade and the movement of capital, in addition to their responsibility to govern the system. Therefore, in that conference the General Agreement on Tariffs and Trade (GATT) was signed and agreements were executed that later established the International Bank for

Reconstruction and Development (IBRD, which is part of today's World Bank Group) and the International Monetary Fund (IMF). In Henry Morgenthau's farewell remarks at the conference, he stated that the establishment of the IMF and the World Bank marked the end of economic nationalism.[387] This meant that the countries would maintain their national interest, but trade blocks and economic spheres of influence would no longer be their means. At the beginning IMF began to loan for post-war reconstruction of the European countries. However, when the Marshall Plan went into effect in 1947, many European countries began receiving aid from other sources. Faced with this competition, the World Bank shifted its focus to non-European countries.[388]

After World War II the Allies established occupation administrations in Austria and Germany. Austria became a neutral state, non-aligned with any political bloc. Germany was divided into western and eastern occupation zones controlled by the Western Allies and the Soviet Union, accordingly. Germany lost a quarter of its pre-war (1937) territory, followed by the expulsion of the 9 million Germans from these territories, as well as of 3 million Germans from the Sudetenland in Czechoslovakia, to Germany. Allies formed the United Nations, which officially came into existence on 24 October 1945, and adopted the Universal Declaration of Human Rights in 1948, as a common standard for all member nations.[389] The great powers that were the victors of the war, the United States, Soviet Union, China, Britain, and France formed the permanent members of the UN's Security Council. Germany was divided. West Germany and East Germany were created within the borders of Allied and Soviet occupation zones, accordingly. The whole Europe was also divided onto Western and Soviet spheres of influence. Most eastern and central European countries fell into the Soviet sphere, which led to establishment of Communist led regimes, with full or partial support of the Soviet occupation authorities. As a result, Poland, Hungary, East Germany, Czechoslovakia, Romania, and Albania became Soviet Satellite states. Communist Yugoslavia conducted a fully independent policy, causing tension with the Soviet Union.[390] Korea, formerly under Japanese rule, was divided and occupied by the US in the South and the Soviet Union in the North between 1945 and 1948. Separate republics emerged on both sides of the 38th parallel in 1948, each claiming to be the legitimate government for all of Korea, which led ultimately to the Korean War.[391] In China, nationalist and communist forces resumed the civil war in June 1946. Communist forces were victorious and established the People's Republic of China on the mainland, while nationalist forces retreated to Taiwan in 1949.[392] In the Middle East, the Arab rejection of the United Nations Partition Plan for Palestine and the creation of Israel as Jewish homeland in 1948 escalated the Arab-Israeli conflict.

In January 1947, Truman appointed retired General George Marshall as Secretary of State. The Marshall Plan for reconstruction of the European countries was established on June 5, 1947. The Marshall Plan (officially the European Recovery Program, ERP) was the American initiative to aid Europe, in which the United States gave economic support to help rebuild European economies by various means such as investment, technology transfers after the end of World War II in order to prevent the spread of Soviet Communism.[393] However, the ERP offered the same aid to the Soviet Union and its allies, but they did not accept it, as to do so would be to allow a degree of US control over the Communist economies.[394] During the four years that the plan was operational, US $15 billion in economic and technical assistance was given to help the recovery of the European countries that had joined in the Organization for European Economic Co-operation. The best part of this plan was it looked to the future, and did not focus on the destruction caused by the war. Therefore, efforts were given to modernize European industrial and business practices using high-efficiency American models, reducing artificial trade barriers, and instilling a sense of hope and self-reliance.[395] By 1952, as the funding ended, the economy of every participant state had surpassed pre-war levels; for all Marshall Plan recipients, output in 1951 was at least 35% higher than in 1938.[396] Marshall Plan was one of the first elements of European integration, as it erased trade barriers and set up institutions to coordinate the economy on a continental level.[397]

The German Democratic Republic (East Germany) was declared on 7 October 1949. The West Germany became Federal Republic of Germany and its economy began to recover with the mid-1948 currency reform, and was sped up by the liberalization of European economic policy that the Marshall plan (1948–1951). The post 1948 West German recovery has been called the German economic miracle.[398] Following huge economic recovery, in 1953, Germany agreed to resume interest on its bonds issued to pay World War I reparation. On 3 October 2010, Germany made the final interest payment on these bonds.[399] Ironically, now Germany has become a rescuer of European Sovereign debt crisis. Also the Italian and French economies rebounded. By contrast, the United Kingdom was in a state of economic ruin,[400] and although it received a quarter of the total Marshall Plan assistance, more than any other European country,[401] continued relative economic decline for decades. The Soviet Union, despite enormous human and material losses, also experienced rapid increase in production in the immediate post-war era.[402] Japan experienced incredibly rapid economic growth, becoming one of the most powerful economies in the world by the 1980s. China returned to its pre-war industrial production by 1952.[403]

The German "economic miracle" or "Wirtschaftswunder" describes the rapid reconstruction and development of the economies of West Germany and Austria after World War II adopting an Ordoliberalism based social market economy.[404] The post war rebuilding of the German economy was overseen by the government led by German Chancellor Konrad Adenauer and his Minister of Economics, Ludwig Erhard, who went down in history as the "father of the German economic miracle". West Germany had a skilled workforce and a high technological level in 1946, but its capital stock had largely been destroyed during and after the war. This small capital stock as well as production conversion back to civilian goods, monetary and regulatory problems led to an unusually low economic output during the first post-war years. These initial problems were overcome by the time of the currency reform of 1948, which replaced the Reichsmark with the Deutsche Mark as legal tender, halting rampant inflation. The U.S. then the U.S. secretary of states, George Marshall scrapped Joint Chiefs of Staff Directive 1067 (JCS 1067) implemented as part of the Morgenthau Plan under the personal supervision of Roosevelt's treasury secretary Henry Morgenthau, Jr., which had decreed "take no steps looking toward the economic rehabilitation of Germany designed to maintain or strengthen the German economy."[405] At the same time, the government, following Erhard's advice, cut individual income taxes sharply. The amount of monetary aid (which was in the form of loans) received by Germany through the Marshall Plan (about $1.65 billion in total) was far overshadowed by the amount the Germans had to pay back as war reparations and by the charges the Allies made on the Germans for the ongoing cost of occupation. At the founding of the European Common Market in 1957 Germany's economic growth stood in contrast to the struggling conditions at the time in the United Kingdom.[406]

Following World War II, nationalistic sentiments were on the rise in the Middle East; most notable being Iranian nationalism and Arab Nationalism. In Iran, the Anglo-Iranian Oil Company (AIOC) and the pro-western Iranian government led by Prime Minister Ali Razmara resisted nationalist calls to revise AIOC's concession terms in Iran's favor. In March 1951, Razmara was assassinated and Mohammed Mossadeq, a nationalist, was elected as the new Prime Minister.[407] In April 1951, the Iranian government nationalized the Iranian oil industry by unanimous vote, and the National Iranian Oil Company (NIOC) was formed, displacing the AIOC. The AIOC withdrew its management from Iran, and Britain organized an effective worldwide embargo of Iranian oil. The British government, which owned the AIOC, contested the nationalization at the International Court of Justice at The Hague, but its complaint was dismissed.[408] Prime Minister Churchill asked President Eisenhower for help in overthrowing

Mossadeq. The anti-Mossadeq plan was orchestrated under code-name 'Operation Ajax' by CIA, and 'Operation Boot' by SIS (MI6).[293] The CIA and the British helped stage a coup in August 1953, the 1953 Iranian coup d'état, which established pro-Western government and greatly strengthened the political power of Shah Mohammad Reza Pahlavi. The AIOC was able to return to Iran.[293] In 1954, the AIOC became the British Petroleum (BP) Company.

On 29 May 1933, the Saudi Arabian government granted a concession to Standard Oil of California (SoCal) in preference to a rival bid from the Iraq Petroleum Co.[454] However, when there was no success at locating oil, it sold it 50% share to Texas Oil Co. (Texaco).[409] After four years of fruitless exploration, the first success came with the seventh drill site in Dhahran in 1938, a well referred to as Dammam No. 7. This well immediately produced over 1,500 barrels per day, giving the company confidence to continue. On 31 January 1944, the company name was changed from California-Arabian Standard Oil Co. to Arabian-American Oil Company (ARAMCO), a consortium comprising Standard Oil of California (SoCal), Standard Oil of New Jersey (Exxon), Standard Oil of New York (Mobil) and Texaco. In 1950, Saudi King Ibn Saud threatened to nationalize his country's oil facilities, thus pressuring Aramco to agree to share profits 50/50.[410] King Ibn Saud was being influenced by Juan Pablo Pérez Alfonso of Venezuela who cut a similar 50/50 deal with New Jersey Standard Oil and Royal Dutch Shell. This 50/50 deal called the Golden Gimmick agreed by the US Government under President Harry Truman that accorded the American oil companies a tax break equivalent to 50% of their profits on oil sales, the other 50% was diverted to King Ibn Saud via the US Treasury.[410] This deal also created an interest of the Saudi government in the U.S. dollar.

Venezuela eventually led the effort in forming Organization of the Petroleum Exporting Countries (OPEC). The major oil producing countries in non-Western regions, Iraq, Kuwait, Iran, Saudi Arabia and Venezuela created a cartel called OPEC at the Baghdad Conference on September 10–14, 1960 with a mission is to coordinate the policies of the oil-producing countries. Later it was joined by nine more governments: Libya, United Arab Emirates, Qatar, Indonesia, Algeria, Nigeria, Ecuador, Angola, and Gabon. OPEC was headquartered in Geneva, Switzerland before moving to Vienna, Austria, on September 1, 1965. Since launching, the OPEC preferred currency is the U.S. dollar which allows USA to export its securities (treasury bonds) in turn the OPEC nations direct their accumulated dollars into U.S. markets.[411]

The Group of Ten or G-10 refers to the group of countries that have agreed to participate in the General Arrangements to Borrow (GAB). The GAB was established in 1962, when the governments of eight International Monetary Fund (IMF) members—Belgium, Canada, France, Italy, Japan, the Netherlands, the United Kingdom, and the United States—and the central banks of two others, Germany and Sweden, agreed to make resources available to the IMF for drawings by participants, and, under certain circumstances, for drawings by nonparticipants. The GAB was strengthened in 1964 by the association of Switzerland. Bank for International Settlements (BIS), European Commission, International Monetary Fund, and Organization for Economic Co-operation and Development are official observers of the activities of the G10. France during the time of President Charles de Gaulle reduced its dollar reserves, exchanging them for gold at the official exchange rate, reducing the US economic influence starting in the 1959 until 1970. This, along with the fiscal strain of federal expenditures for the Vietnam War and persistent balance of payments deficits, led US President Richard Nixon to end international convertibility of the dollar to gold on August 15, 1971.[333] However, until October 1976, the U.S. government did not officially removed the references to gold from statutes. From this point, the international monetary system was made of pure fiat money.[333]

In October 1973, OPEC declared an oil embargo in response to the United States' and Western Europe's support of Israel in the Yom Kippur War of 1973. The result was a rise in oil prices from $3 per barrel to $12 and the commencement of gas rationing. Other factors in the rise in gasoline prices was the peak of oil production in the United States around 1970 and the devaluation of the U.S. dollar.[412&413] During the embargo the total consumption of oil in the U.S. dropped twenty percent. The U.S. government had to limit on the amount of gasoline that could be dispensed, a 55 mph speed limit, introduced incentives for development of alternate energy such as solar and wind power, fuel efficient vehicles and so on.[414] One of the most lasting effects of the 1973 oil embargo was a global economic recession. Unemployment rose to the highest percentage on record while inflation also spiked. Although the embargo only lasted a year, during that time oil prices had quadrupled and OPEC nations discovered that their oil could be used as both a political and economic weapon against other nations.[414] In 1974 the U.S. President Nixon negotiated a formal agreement with the Saudi Arabian government that created a basis that Saudi Arabian Monetary Agency (SAMA) would purchase new issues of marketable U.S. Treasury bonds involving the Federal Reserve Bank of New York.[415] Finally Saudi government took full control of Aramco by 1980 by acquiring a 100% percent stake in the company.[416] In November 1988, a royal decree changed its name from Arabian American Oil Co. to Saudi Arabian Oil Co. (or Saudi Aramco). It was the world's largest and most valuable non-publically listed company.[417] Nevertheless as Saudi government continues to buy the U.S. Treasury since 1974 the U.S. dollar has been backed by oil, "a commodity of far greater utility than gold".[418]

During Shah's time, Iran had become the world's fourth largest oil producer, supplying 18% of both Japan's and West Germany's oil, 50% of Israel's oil although the average Iranian worker languished in poverty.[419] In 1978, leftist Tudeh Party launched strike in the British Petroleum oilfields of Khuzestan. When Shah's deployed his secret police SAVAK to quell the strikers, it only inflamed the situation.[420] Eventually, the leftist, nationalist and Islamist groups attacked the government for violating the Iranian constitution, political corruption, and the political oppression by the SAVAK and turned into a revolution that overthrew the Pahlavi dynasty in February 1979. After a national referendum Iran became an Islamic Republic on April 1, 1979 and Ayatollah Khomeini became Supreme Leader of the country.[421] In July 1979 Saddam Hussein in Iraq assumed the offices of both President and Chairman of the Revolutionary Command Council. In the following year (September 1980) Iraq invaded Iran following a long history of border disputes, and fears of Shia insurgency among Iraq's long-suppressed Shia majority influenced by the Iranian Revolution. This led to an inconclusive and costly eight-year war, the Iran–Iraq War (1980–1988), which devastated both the countries—half a million Iraqi and Iranian soldiers as well as civilians are believed to have died in the war with many more injured but it brought neither reparations nor change in borders.[422]

The Chinese economy was heavily disrupted by the war against Japan and the Chinese Civil War from 1937 to 1949, after which the victorious Communists installed a planned economy. By the completion of the first five Year Economic Plan in 1957, Mao Zedong, Chairman the Communist Party of China had come to doubt that the path to socialism that had been taken by the Soviet Union was appropriate for China. Mao had become convinced that China should follow its own path to communism. In 1957 he invited free speech and criticism under the Hundred Flowers Campaign, which he viewed: "The policy of letting a hundred flowers bloom and a hundred schools of thought contend is designed to promote the flourishing of the arts and the progress of science".[423&424] After this brief period of liberalization, Mao Zedong abruptly changed course. Some claim that Mao simply swung to the side of the hard-liners once his policies gained strong opposition. Those who publicly criticized his policies were condemned to prison labor camps. Mao remarked at the time that he had "enticed the snakes out of their caves."[425]

In the First Indochina War, the Viet Minh fight was hampered by a lack of weapons; this situation changed by 1949 when the Chinese Communists had largely won the Chinese Civil War and were free to provide arms to their

Vietnamese allies.[375] In January 1950, the People's Republic of China and the Soviet Union recognized Viet Minh's Democratic Republic of Vietnam, based in Hanoi, as the legitimate government of Vietnam. The following month the United States and Great Britain recognized the French-backed State of Vietnam in Saigon, led by former Emperor Bao Dại, as the legitimate Vietnamese government.[426] The outbreak of the Korean War in June 1950 convinced many Washington policymakers that the war in Indochina was an example of communist expansionism directed by the Soviet Union.[427] By 1954, the United States had supplied 300,000 small arms and spent US$1 billion in support of the French military effort, shouldering 80 percent of the cost of the war.[428] However, the French were defeated by Viet Minh led by commander Vo Nguyen Giap's and on 7 May 1954, the French Union garrison surrendered. At the Geneva Conference, the French negotiated a ceasefire agreement with the Viet Minh, and independence was granted to Cambodia, Laos, and Vietnam.[429]

The ideological differences between capitalism and socialism demonstrated post-war mutual distrust and suspicion between the Western powers and the Soviet Union. This division of the world was formalized by two international military alliances, the United States-led NATO and the Soviet-led Warsaw Pact.[430] The long period of political tensions and military competition between them, the Cold War, was accompanied by an unprecedented arms race and proxy wars.[431] Therefore, arms businesses flourished in the bi-polar world created by the Cold War allegedly financed by the international bankers.[420] As West Germany's economy grew, and its standard of living steadily improved, many East Germans wanted to move to West Germany. In 1961, to protect this defection, the Berlin Wall was built by East Germany that completely cut off (by land) West Berlin from surrounding East Germany and from East Berlin. The Cold War split the temporary wartime alliance against Nazi Germany, leaving the Soviet Union and the US as two arms superpowers.[430] On June 26, 1963 in his public speech in

West Berlin, the U.S. President John F. Kennedy criticized the construction of the Berlin Wall as an example of the failures of communism:

"Freedom has many difficulties, and democracy is not perfect. But we have never had to put a wall up to keep our people in, to prevent them from leaving us."[473]

A leftist movement led Fidel Castro led the Cuban Revolution of 1949 to 1959 and ousted the president Fulgencio Batista. Fidel Castro severed the country's formerly strong links with the U.S. and developing links with the Soviet Union, with whom the U.S. was then embroiled in the Cold War.[432] Eisenhower allocated $13.1 million to the CIA in order to plan Castro's overthrow. On April 17, 1961, the new U.S. President John F. Kennedy ordered CIA proceeded to organize the operation called Operation Bay of Pigs Invasion[433] although Kennedy primarily focused on the political repercussions of the plan rather than military considerations.[469] The invading force was defeated within three days by the Cuban armed forces, under the direct command of Fidel Castro. The failed invasion strengthened the position of Castro's administration, who proceeded to openly proclaim their intention to adopt socialism and strengthen ties with the Soviet Union. Although the invasion was a major embarrassment for U.S. foreign policy, across much of Latin America, it was celebrated as evidence of the fallibility of U.S. imperialism.[433]

The two superpowers never engaged directly in full-scale armed combat but they each armed heavily in preparation of an all-out nuclear war. Aside from the development of the two sides' nuclear arsenals, and deployment of conventional military forces, the struggle for dominance was expressed via proxy wars around the globe, psychological warfare, propaganda and espionage, and technological competitions such as the Space Race.[430] In November 1960, John F. Kennedy was elected president after a campaign that promised American superiority over the Soviet Union in the fields of space exploration and missile defense. On April 12, 1961, Soviet cosmonaut Yuri Gagarin became the first person to fly in space, reinforcing American fears about being left behind in cold-war technological competition.[434] Kennedy proposed a manned Moon landing project Apollo that eventually required the most sudden burst of technological creativity, and the largest commitment of resources (USD$24 billion) ever made by any nation in peacetime. At its peak, the Apollo program employed 400,000 people and required the support of over 20,000 industrial firms and universities.[435]

On October 14, 1962, the U.S. spy planes took photographs of intermediate-range ballistic missile sites being built in Cuba by the Soviets an overreaction in light of U.S. missiles that had been placed in Turkey by Eisenhower, which posed an immediate nuclear threat to USA. Kennedy faced a dilemma: if the U.S. attacked the sites, it might lead to nuclear war with the U.S.S.R., but if the U.S. did nothing, it would be faced with the increased threat from close-range nuclear weapons. The U.S. would also appear to the world as less committed to the defense of the hemisphere.[476] Although more than a third of the members of the National Security Council (NSC) favored an unannounced air assault on the missile sites, Kennedy favored on a naval quarantine. The U.S. Navy would stop and inspect all Soviet ships arriving off Cuba, beginning October24.On October 28 Khrushchev agreed to dismantle the missile sites.[476] The U.S. publicly promised never to invade Cuba and privately agreed to remove its missiles in Turkey. After the Cuban Missile Crisis in October 1962, Kennedy was determined to construct a better relationship with the Soviet Union to discourage another threat of nuclear war. In his "A Strategy of Peace" speech in American University, Washington, Kennedy said:

"We must, therefore, persevere in the search for peace in the hope that constructive changes within the Communist bloc might bring within reach solutions which now seem beyond us. We must conduct our affairs in such a way that it becomes in the Communists' interest to agree on a genuine peace. Above all, while defending our own vital interests, nuclear powers must avert those confrontations which bring an adversary to a choice of either a humiliating retreat or a nuclear war. To adopt that kind of course in the nuclear age would be evidence only of the bankruptcy of our policy--or of a collective death-wish for the world."[477]

Kennedy's speech was made in its wholeness available in Soviet press[472] so that the people in the Soviet Union could read it without hindrance. Khrushchev was deeply moved and impressed by Kennedy's speech. After 12 days of negotiations and less than two months after the president's speech the Partial Nuclear Test Ban Treaty was completed at Moscow on August 5, 1963.[472] US ratification occurred by the U.S. Senate on September 24, 1963 and the treaty was signed into law by Kennedy on October 7, 1963.[472]

In the following month after signing the treaty, on November 22, 1963, President Kennedy was assassinated. However, almost six years after Kennedy's death, his dream of moon landing by Americans was successful. On July 20, 1969, Apollo 11 landed the first manned spacecraft on the Moon. According to The Economist, Apollo succeeded in accomplishing President Kennedy's goal of taking on the Soviet Union in the Space Race, and beat it by accomplishing a singular and significant achievement, and thereby showcased the superiority of the capitalistic, free-market system as represented by the US.[436] The publication noted, however, the irony that in order to achieve the goal, the program required the organization of tremendous public resources within a vast, centralized government bureaucracy. It wrote:

"In other words, it mimicked aspects of the very command economy it was designed to repudiate". [436]

Vietnam was temporarily partitioned at the 17th parallel, and under the terms of the Geneva Accords. Between 1953 and 1956, the North Vietnamese government instituted various agrarian reforms, including "rent reduction" and "land reform". This was a campaign against land owners. The landlords were arbitrarily classified as 5.68% of the population and many of them (Official records suggest that 172,008 "landlords") were executed during the "land reform".[437] South Vietnam declared to be an independent state under the name Republic of Vietnam (ROV), with himself as president.[438] Likewise, Ho Chi Minh and other communist officials always won at least 99% of the vote in North Vietnamese "elections". According to then U.S. secretary of defense, Robert McNamara "The domino theory, which argued that if one country fell to communism, then all of the surrounding countries would follow, was first proposed as policy by the Eisenhower administration."[426] The North Vietnamese government and the communist party Viet Cong in South Vietnam fought against South Vietnam government, which it regarded as a U.S. puppet state to reunify Vietnam under communist rule. Ngo Dinh Diem, the President of South Vietnam was killed in the 1963 coup just few days before Kennedy's assassination. After this incidence, United States became involved in the war, Regular U.S. combat units were deployed beginning in 1965 under President Johnson.[470] Later in an interview Secretary of Defense McNamara and vice President Lyndon Johnson admitted that Kennedy was strongly considering pulling out of Vietnam after the 1964 election.[471]

The U.S. operations in Vietnam crossed international borders, with Laos and Cambodia heavily bombed by the U.S. American involvement in the war peaked in 1968. Among heavy casualties of the U.S. soldiers and protest at home, direct U.S. military involvement ended on 15 August 1973.[439] The capture of Saigon by the North Vietnamese Army in April 1975 marked the end of the war, and North and South Vietnam were reunified the following year. The war exacted a huge human cost in terms of fatalities civilians killed vary from 800,000[440] to 3.1 million.[441] Robert McNamara, the architect of the Vietnam War and then the U.S. sectary of defense concluded that the war was 'futile' and later took a stand against his own conduct of the war confessing in a memoir that it was 'wrong, terribly wrong.'" In return, he faced a "firestorm of scorn" at that time.[442]

During the Cold War, in 1957, the 40th anniversary of Russian October revolution, Mao Zedong was inspired by the presentation of Khrushchev, the first secretary of Russian communist party set target to catch up and exceed the U.S. in next 15 years. Chairman Mao targeted to surpass the UK in next 15 years by introducing 'The Great Leap Forward' campaign.[443] This campaign aimed to transform China from an agrarian economy into a modern communist society through the process of rapid industrialization and collectivization. Mao encouraged the establishment of small backyard steel furnaces in every commune and in each urban neighborhood. Huge efforts on the part of peasants and other workers were made to produce steel out of scrap metal. Millions of Chinese became state workers as a consequence of this industrial investment: in 1958, 21 million were added to non-agricultural state payrolls, and total state employment reached a peak of 50.44 million in 1960, more than doubling the 1957 level; the urban population swelled by 31.24 million people. These new workers placed major stress on China's food-rationing system, which led to increased and unsustainable demands on rural food production.[444]

The weather in 1958 was very favorable and the harvest promised to be good. Unfortunately, the amount of labor diverted to steel production and construction projects meant that much of the harvest was left to rot uncollected in some areas. This problem was exacerbated by a devastating locust swarm, which was caused when their natural predators were killed as part of the Great Sparrow Campaign. Although actual harvests were reduced, local officials competed with each other to announce increasingly exaggerated results. These were used as a basis for determining the amount of grain to be taken by the state to supply the towns and cities, and to export. This left barely enough for the peasants, and in some areas, starvation set in.[445] During 1958–1960 China continued to be a substantial net exporter of grain, despite the widespread famine experienced in the countryside, as Mao sought to maintain face and convince the outside world of the success of his plans. Foreign aid was refused. The failure of agricultural policies, the movement of farmers from agricultural to industrial work, and possibly weather conditions led to severe famine, which killed between 30 and 40 million people.[445] The Great Leap also led to the greatest destruction of real estate in human history, approximately 30 to 40 per cent of all houses were turned to rubble.[446] In subsequent conferences in 1960 and 1962, Mao was criticized in the party conferences. One of the party members, Liu Shaoqi made a speech in 1962 criticizing that "The economic disaster was 30% fault of nature, 70% human error." Moderate Party members like Liu Shaoqi and Deng Xiaoping rose to power, and Mao was marginalized within the party, leading him to initiate the Cultural Revolution in 1966.[357]

After independence from Britain, Indian leaders were influenced by the progress achieved by the planned economy of the Soviet Union.[447] Jawaharlal Nehru, the first prime minister of India, formulated an economic policy tended towards protectionism, with a strong emphasis on import substitution industrialization, economic interventionism, a large public sector, business regulation, and central planning.[448] The socialist policies of Nehru favored support for agricultural innovation programs and extra government support launched in the 1960s finally transformed India's chronic food shortages into surplus production of wheat, rice, cotton and milk. The use of genetically modified high-yielding varieties of seeds introduced to India in 1963 by Dr. Norman Borlaug, increased fertilizers and improved irrigation facilities collectively contributed Green Revolution. After Nehru, Prime Minister Lal Bahadur Shastri promoted the White Revolution-a national campaign to increase the production and supply of milk.

Nehru's daughter Indira Gandhi became the Prime Minister of India in 1966, following her father, she took pro-Soviet left-wing economic policies and continued support for Green Revolution that increased agricultural productivity and strengthened forward and backward linkages between agriculture and industry. However, it has also been criticized as an unsustainable effort to change the indigent lives of the marginal farmers, resulting in the growth of capitalistic farming, ignoring institutional reforms and widening income disparities.[449] On the other hand, there was so much government control on business that capital investment was difficult.

In Pakistan, although the population of the two zones was close to equal, political power was concentrated in West Pakistan and it was widely perceived that East Pakistan was being exploited economically, leading to many grievances.[451] On 25 March 1971, after an election won by an East Pakistani political party was ignored by the ruling (West Pakistani) establishment, rising political discontent and cultural nationalism in East Pakistan was met by brutal suppressive force from the ruling elite of the West Pakistan establishment.[452] The violent crackdown by West Pakistan forces led to the wining party leader Sheikh Mujibur Rahman declaring East Pakistan's independence as Bangladesh on 26 March 1971.[451] The Pakistan Army, in collusion with religious extremist militias (the Razakars, Al-Badr and Al-Shams), engaged in the systematic genocide and forced millions more to flee their homes during the war.[453] Indira Gandhi government in India provided economic, military and diplomatic support to Bengali nationalists, and the Bangladesh government-in-exile was set up in Calcutta, India led by Tajuddin Ahmad as the Prime Minister.[451] India entered the war on 3 December 1971, after Pakistan launched pre-emptive air strikes on northern India. The United States supported Pakistan as President Nixon and Henry Kissinger feared Soviet expansion into South and Southeast Asia. And when Pakistan's defeat seemed certain, Nixon sent the aircraft carrier USS Enterprise to the Bay of Bengal,[452&454] a move deemed by the Indians as a nuclear threat. On 6 and 13 December, the Soviet Navy dispatched two groups of ships, armed with nuclear missiles, from Vladivostok; they trailed US Task Force 74 in the Indian Ocean.[455] On 16 December, the Allied Forces of Bangladesh and India defeated Pakistan in the east and Bangladesh got independence. The subsequent surrender resulted in the largest number of prisoners-of-war since World War II.[451]

<u>CHAPTER 3</u>

ECONOMIC THEORIES AND PRACTICES

3.1 Introduction

This chapter describes mainstream economic theories and practices related to capitalism with their historical basis. The first modern school of thoughts in economics began as political economics with the publication of his book "The Wealth of Nations" in 1776 by Adam Smith. He introduced the vision of a free market economy or "invisible hand" of the market, through which the pursuit of individual self-interest produces a collective good for society that causes an economy to grow.[11] The concept like Say's law "supply creates own demand" and David Ricardo's 'principle of diminishing returns" was introduced after half a century. It took about a hundred year to formulate the concepts of demand and supply as a function of price. And then it took another half century to show the concept of equilibrium at the intersection of demand and supply curve.

Efforts were made to refine classical ideas more theoretically precise but since then whole view has been narrowed down to consumerism. They considered inflation is good since it will create more production and more employments. Contrarily during Great Depression, price dropped suddenly but unemployment became high. Keynes (1883–1946) advised that when the economy falls into a recession government should spend more in order to restart growth.[3] However, when government spending ended up in "stagflation" during 1970s, economists advised government should cut taxes on the rich that would ultimately benefit everyone.[4] At the same time, deregulation of financial sector integrated the global economy under dominance and vulnerability of financial powers.

3.2 Classical Economics

In Europe, the Great Famine and Black Death in early 14th century led to a decline in agricultural production. In response feudal lords sought to expand agricultural production by expanding their domains through warfare; they therefore demanded more tribute from their serfs to pay for military expenses.[5] In England, many serfs rebelled. The collapse of the manorial system in England created a class of tenant-farmers with more freedom to market their goods and thus more incentive to invest in new technologies. Lords who did not want to rely on rents could buy out or evict tenant farmers, but then had to hire free-labor to work their estates.[6&7] According to Karl Marx (1867), the rise of the contractual relationship is inextricably bound to the end of the obligatory relationship between serfs and lords. He characterizes this transformation as "the historical process of divorcing the producer from the means of production."[6&7] It was this "divorcing" that turned the serf's land into the lord's capital. As he describes this rearrangement led to a new division of classes:[8]

> "two very different kinds of commodity owners; on the one hand, the owners of money, means of production…on the other hand, free workers, the sellers of their own labor-power, and therefore the sellers of labour. Free workers, in the double sense that they neither form part of the means of production themselves … nor do they own the means of production" that transformed land and even money into what we now call "capital."[8]

With the waning feudal lords, new national economic frameworks particularly mercantilism began to be strengthened. The Chinese innovations like gun powder used for entertainment and compass used for divination in China brought by Mongols to the Europeans contributed mercantilism. Although the Roman Empire developed more advanced forms of merchant capitalism, and similarly widespread networks existed in Islamic capitalism, but the modern form took shape in Europe in the late Middle Ages.[6]

The birth of the discipline economics was more specifically called 'political economics' is from the dissent against mercantilism, which overemphasized the importance of precious metal as a measure of national wealth.[9] In the mercantilist era, countries that encouraged inflow of bullions experienced inflation since the inflow did nothing to increase the real resources of the economy or promote technological advancement.[9] The term mercantilism was popularized by Adam Smith, who vigorously opposed its ideas. The first modern school of thoughts, classical economics began with the publication of his legendary book "The Wealth of Nations" in 1776. He is also considered as the father of modern economics and modern capitalism.[11]

The ideas of Adam Smith are built upon a considerable body of work from predecessors in the eighteenth century particularly the Physiocrats.[12] The Physiocrats are a group of economists who believed that the wealth of nations was derived solely from the value of "land agriculture" or "land development". Physiocrat Boisguilbert (1646-1714) asserted that wealth came from self-interest and markets are connected by money flows. Thus he realized that lowering prices in times of shortage was dangerous economically as it served as a disincentive to production. He advocated less government interference in the grain market, as any activity by the government would give birth to "anticipations" which would prevent the policy from working.[13]

Adam Smith's legendary book "The Wealth of Nations" was published in 1776 on the time of the first industrial revolution and coincidently in the same year of American independence. He himself never used the term "capitalism".[9] He described his own preferred economic system as "the system of natural liberty."[11] A major difference between Adam Smith's view of economics and that of present day capitalist theory is that he viewed value as a product of labor, and thus operated under the Labor Theory of Value. According to Smith (1776) and his followers, the growth and distribution of wealth is based on division of labor. He devised a set of concepts that remain strongly associated with capitalism

161

today, particularly his theory of the "invisible hand" of the market, through which the pursuit of individual self-interest unintentionally produces a collective good for society that causes an economy to grow.[11] He first used the metaphor of an "invisible hand" in his book "The Theory of Moral Sentiments" to describe the unintentional effects of economic self-organization from economic self-interest.[14] Some have characterized this metaphor as one for laissez-faire, but Smith never actually used the term himself.[15]

Miriam Kennet (2006) of "Green Economics Institute" argues about classical economics as:

"[T]he classical economic approach from Adam Smith was more often than not broad, diverse and philosophical in nature. Basic fundamental principles have been developed out of it to form the narrower and more conservative foundation of economics as a new science."[16]

The classical foundation of economics 'division of labor' views division and specialization of labor led to increased labor productivity, greater output, higher wages to reward that productivity, higher per capita incomes, higher levels of consumptions, and greater wealth of the nation. Although Adam Smith's had the vision of a free market economy but since then whole view of political economics has been narrowed down to accumulation of capital.[17]

Although Adam Smith is famous for his 'invisible hand' proposition but he also precisely defined role of government in certain areas. According to him government must address "three duties of great importance."[11] These include national defense, the administration of justice, and those goods that would not be provided under the profit motive. This last area includes education and basic public works such as roads and bridges. He argues that the state has a role in providing roads, canals, schools and bridges that cannot be efficiently implemented by private entities.[9] Despite some specific essential areas, overall, the values of classical political economy are strongly associated with the classical liberal doctrine of minimal government intervention in the economy.

The concepts of capitalism and free markets were active during the Islamic Golden Age and Muslim Agricultural Revolution, where an early market economy and form of merchant capitalism took root between the 8th–12th centuries.[18] The concept of organizational enterprises independent from the state also existed in the medieval Islamic world, while the agency institution was also introduced.[19] These early capitalist concepts were adopted and further advanced in medieval Europe from the 13th century onwards.[20] Many Arab-American economists today believe that Ibn Khaldun (1332-1406), rather than Adam Smith, deserves the title "Father of Economics".[10&21] Ibn Khaldun believed that profit is a reward for taking risk. In his book "The Muqaddimah" he discouraged government interference to alter market prices, such as through subsidies.[21] Pluta (2011) mentions:

"It is the contention of some economists today that Smith was influenced by both Ibn Khaldun (1332-1406) and Al-Ghazali (1058-1111). When Smith explained the division of labor in 1776, he used the now-famous example of a pin theory. Writing some seven centuries earlier, Al-Ghazali's strikingly similar division of labor concept is explained using the example of a needle factory!"[10&22]

In Europe, the concept division of labor and specialization was used by Dudley North (1641-1691), about 100 years before Smith as a concept to increase flow of wealth.[12] Adam Smith used this concept as an important driver of market efficiency, yet it is limited to the widening process of markets. He emphasized on accumulation of capital for widening of market by more production and thought distribution of income will happen in three forms, wages, rent and profit. On the other hand, Jeremy Bentham (1748–1832) was perhaps the most radical thinker of his time, and developed the concept of utilitarianism. He proposed that the aim of legal policy must be to decrease misery and suffering so far as possible while producing the greatest happiness for the greatest number.[23]

Bentham argued that all goods were subject to the principle of diminishing marginal utility. Bentham's idea has many policy implications. As Pluta (2011) explains

"Since the marginal utility of a dollar to a rich man was smaller than the marginal utility of a dollar to a poor man, one could argue that money should be redistributed from rich to poor".[174]

Following Smith, Jean-Baptiste Say (1767–1832) developed Say's law that supply always equals demand, or in other words "supply creates own demand" which was unchallenged until the 20th century. According to his law, overproduction and unemployment is impossible.[9] The classical economists emphasized on production and on the factors that influence the supply of goods. Pluta (2011) explains

"[E]ven if savings temporarily reduced demand, flexible interest rates guaranteed that savings would automatically be transformed into investment. Even if the demand for some products and demand for labor needed to produce them both fell, flexible prices and wages guaranteed that full employment would be maintained and Say's law upheld."[9]

The classical economists believe that expansion of money supply increases in aggregate demand and price level, however, has no effect on output. Economic growth occurs only because of changes in aggregate supply. Four factors influence aggregate supply: technology, capital stock, employment and the level of natural resources. Economic growth of a country benefits all segments of the population, the entrepreneurs, the workers and the consumers.

Thomas Malthus (1766–1834), a British minister believed that strict government abstention from social ills. He is more known however for his work "An Essay on the Principle of Population", where he wrote that the human race would reproduce faster than its ability to feed itself. He showed that population grows in a geometric progression but the food supply increases in an arithmetic progression.[24] Malthus realized, of course, that high death rates during certain periods reduced the impact of his geometric progression. As an example, half the population of Europe died during a five-year period in the mid-1300s because of bubonic plague. Malthus proposed that to prevent worldwide catastrophe, the poor should not be encouraged to have large families, but should instead be encouraged to have smaller families, through direct or indirect means.[25] However, Malthus was challenged as despite population growth, average income rose, while acute food shortages was not materialize. In his book "Principles of Political Economy (1820)", he refuted Say's law as argued that the economy could stagnate with a lack of "effectual demand".[12] In other words, wages if less than the total costs of production cannot purchase the total output of industry and that this would cause prices to fall. Price fall decrease incentives to investment and the spiral could continue indefinitely. To Malthus, new jobs were created due to demand of weapons and military supply for the series of wars in Europe. The causes of the wars can also be explained by Say's supply side economics. In both ways, capitalist economy works as long as there is capital accumulation. The views of Malthus became popular again in the 20th century with the advent of Keynesian economics.[26]

Friedrich Hegel (1770 – 1831) was a German philosopher, and a major figure in German Idealism. His triad thesis, antithesis, synthesis and idealist account of reality revolutionized European philosophy and was an important precursor to Continental philosophy and Marxism. The triad is usually described in the following way:[27]

1. The thesis is an intellectual proposition.

2. The antithesis is simply the negation of the thesis, a reaction to the proposition.

3. The synthesis solves the conflict between the thesis and antithesis by reconciling their common truths and forming a new thesis, starting the process over.

In summary, a thesis, giving rise to its reaction, an antithesis, this contradicts or negates the thesis, and the tension between the two being resolved by means of a synthesis. Although this model is often named after Hegel, he himself never used that specific formulation. Hegel ascribed that terminology to Immanuel Kant (1724 – 1804), a German philosopher who is considered to be a central figure of modern philosophy.[28] He argued that human concepts and categories structure our view of the world and its laws, and that reason is the source of morality.[29]

David Ricardo (1772–1823), British economists who also became Parliamentarian placed greater emphasis on the question of income distribution. He put more attention to the potential conflict of interest between landowners, business owners, and workers and defined the efforts of each group for 'shares of the economic pie'.[9] Wages were received by workers, profits by business owners, and rent by landowners. He was against the infamous Corn Lawn in 1815 passed in British Parliament to protect the landowners from competition after possible postwar fall in agricultural prices during Napoleonic wars. This law imposed tariffs on the import of all grains and made easier for landlords to raise rents by virtually doing nothing but just owning lands. To analyze this issue, Ricardo introduced the 'principle of diminishing returns'. This principle explains the wages tend toward a basic subsistence level. As population grows, the demand for food and the price of food both rise and therefore the wagers must now increase just to maintain subsistence. As land becomes increasingly scarce, landlords charge higher rents, which drive food prices still higher. The high rents squeeze profits while the higher food prices squeeze wages and eventually make an economy stagnant or 'standstill'.[12]

The business owners and workers normally at odds were influenced by Ricardo and united against landlords in opposition to the Corn Laws, which were eventually repealed after 31 years in 1846. This was a turning point in British economy as Pluta (2011) explains

"By repealing the Corn Laws, free trade became a cornerstone of British policy and free market capitalism officially replaced mercantilism. The stage was now set for the development of British manufacturing whose export possibilities were enhanced by reduced trade restrictions. Mutual benefits of free trade were soon to be realized."[9]

Ricardo encouraged free trade, guided by comparative advantage that would enable nations to grow and standards of living. The idea of comparative advantage suggests that even if one country is inferior at producing all of its goods than another, it may still benefit from opening its borders since the inflow of goods produced more cheaply than at home, produces a gain for domestic consumers. This concept would lead to a shift in prices, so that eventually England would be producing goods in which its comparative advantages were the highest. He was a supporter of Say's Law and held the view that full employment is the normal equilibrium for a competitive economy.[31] He also argued that inflation is closely related to changes in quantity of money.

John Stuart Mill (1806–1873) was the dominant figure of political economic thought of his time, was heavily influenced by David Ricardo. He is credited with being the first person to speak of supply and demand as a relationship and the concept of opportunity cost and real income. He thought that if technology advanced faster than population and capital stock increased, the result would be a prospering economy.[12] Mill was an advocate of social reform, especially on such issues as rights of workers and consumers, redistribution of wealth, and the economic position of women. When the economy stopped growing, Ricardo argued it had reached a stationary state that in his view was cause for concern. Mill reasoned that the stationary state was not necessarily bad. As long as a certain level of affluence was at this point, government could now take steps to redistribute wealth and create opportunities for those with modest incomes.[9]

Mill's contemporary French philosopher and mathematician Augustin Cournot (1801–1877), introduced the ideas of functions and probability into economic analysis and derived the first formula for the rule of supply and demand as a function of price. In fact, he was the first to draw supply and demand curves on a graph, anticipating the work of Alfred Marshall by roughly thirty years. His books "Researches on the Mathematical Principles" of the "Theory of Wealth" was published in 1838.[32] The Cournot duopoly model developed in his book also introduced the concept of a strategic decision making model in his theory of oligopoly which later known as a pure strategy 'Nash equilibrium'.[12] The Nash equilibrium was named after John Forbes Nash Jr., an American mathematician. In Cournot's theory firms choose how much output to produce to maximize their own profit. However, the best output for one firm depends on the outputs of others. A Cournot equilibrium occurs when each firm's output maximizes its profits given the output of the other firms, which is a pure strategy Nash Equilibrium. Cournot also introduced the concept of best response dynamics in his analysis of the stability of equilibrium.[33]

Just as the term "mercantilism" had been coined and popularized by its critics, like Adam Smith, so was the term "capitalism" used by its dissidents, primarily Karl Marx (1818–1883). His famous book "Das Kapital" is yet sold many copies in almost all languages in the world. Although its Volume I sold only 1000 copies, made him to comment that his royalties did not cover all the cigars he had smoked while writing the book.[34] According to Marx, industrialization polarized society into the bourgeoisie (those who own the means of production) and the much larger proletariat (the working class). Marx was influenced by the German philosopher Georg W. F. Hegel (1770-1831) who viewed society as governed by dialectic. When an idea gains acceptance (a thesis), it is destined to be challenged by an antithesis. From this conflict emerges a new idea (a synthesis).[34] Marx applied the dialectic to economic concerns and called his version "dialectical materialism".[30] He saw the industrialization process as the logical dialectical progression of feudal economic modes (thesis) was countered by the market (antithesis) and the outcome of this clash was capitalism (synthesis), which he saw as in itself a necessary precursor to the development of socialism (antithesis) and eventually communism (synthesis).[34]

Classical economic theories explain the social phenomena in terms of methodological holism by dividing the people of an economy into three major classes: capitalists, landlords, and workers. Marx explained the booms and busts, like the Panic of 1873, as part of an inherent instability in capitalist economies.[12] Employers are constantly under pressure from market competition to drive their workers harder, and at the limits invest in labour displacing technology (e.g. an assembly line). This raises profits and expands growth, but for the sole benefit of those who have private property in these means of production. The working classes meanwhile face progressive misery like having been fired from their jobs for machines, they end unemployed. Marx believed that a reserve army of the unemployed would grow and grow, fuelling a downward pressure on wages as desperate people accept work for less. But this would produce a deficit of demand as the people's power to purchase products lagged. There would be a glut in unsold products, production would be cut back, and profits would decline until capital accumulation halts in an economic depression. When the glut clears, the economy again starts to boom before the next cyclical bust begin. With every boom and bust, with every capitalist crisis, thought Marx, tension and conflict between the increasingly polarized classes of capitalists and workers heightens. Moreover smaller firms are being gobbled by larger ones in every business cycle, as power is concentrated in the hands of the few and away from the many. Ultimately, Marx envisaged a revolution and the creation of a classless society.[12] Quigley argues

"By 1900 social developments took a direction so different from that expected by Marx that his analysis became almost worthless, and his system had to be imposed by force in a most backward industrial country (Russia) instead of occurring inevitable in the most advanced industrial country as he had expected. The social developments which made Marx's theories obsolete were the result of technological and economic developments which Marx had not foreseen. The energy for production was derived more and more from inanimate sources of power and less and less from human power. The spread of corporate form of industrial enterprise allowed control to be separated from ownership."[35]

Marx used Friedrich Hegel (1770 – 1831)'s theory of "The law of the negation of the negation" to describe how capitalism is evolved and how eventually it will end up in a classless society or communism. Although Hegel coined the term, it gained its fame from Marx's using it in Capital. There Marx wrote this:[30]

"The [death] knell of capitalist private property sounds. The expropriators [capitalists] are expropriated. The capitalist mode of appropriation, the result of the capitalist mode of production, produces capitalist private property. This is the first negation [antithesis] of individual private property. [The "first negation," or antithesis, negates the thesis, which in this instance is feudalism, the economic system that preceded capitalism.] . . . But capitalist production begets, with the inexorability of a law of Nature, its own negation. It [final communism, the synthesis] is the negation of [the] negation."[36]

In the latter half of nineteenth century the scientific inventions and supporting economic policies caused an industrial boom in Europe and in the United States. The living standards of a growing number of people in the industrialized nations are generally seen as Marx's predictive failure or it has moved away. Encouraged by new scientific inventions and ideas, some enthusiastic philosophers tried to apply the methods of physical science to explain social and economic matters. In 1859, biologists Charles Darwin published his book "Origin of Species". In his thesis, man evolved from a lower animal forms but survive to become dominant because he adapted best to changing conditions. After reading this book Herbert Spencer (1820-1903) invented the concept "survival of the fittest". Darwin never used this term.[34] He wrote "which I have here sought to express in mechanical terms, is that which Mr. Darwin has called 'natural selection', or the preservation of favored races in the struggle for life.""[37]

Spencer opposed public health measures such as sanitation because it offered unnecessary protection to weaker members of the societies. For similar reasons, he also objected to public education, relief for the poor, and regulation of business.[34&38]

The phrase "survival of the fittest" became a new ideology called Social Darwinism, which eventually motivated extremist ideas of eugenics, scientific racism, imperialism,[39] fascism, Nazism and struggle between national or racial groups.[40] After the First World War, the pre-war mood of optimism gave way to disillusionment as German bureaucrats found social problems to be more insoluble than previously thought, which in turn led them to place increasing emphasis on saving the biologically "fit" while the biologically "unfit" were to be written off.[41] The economic strains caused by the Great Depression had led to many in the German medical establishment to advocate with increasing vigor the idea of selective killings of the "incurable" as a cost-saving measure in order to free up money to care for the curable.[42] Thus by the time the Nazis had come to power in 1933, a huge boost was given to the already existing tendency in German social policy to save the racially "valuable" while seeking to rid society of the racially "undesirable".[41] Nazism killed approximately six million Jews in Nazi occupied Europe during World War II, [42]

In summary, in the nineteenth and early twentieth centuries either progress or atrocities, the social, political and economic philosophies played an influential role. However, 'inequality' remained as the major economic question as the theories supporting wealth accumulation remained strong.[34]

3.3 Neoclassical Economics

Pluta (2011) identified, by the 1870s, there were three approaches defined the mainstream classical economics. Some European nations embraced the socialism of Marx or some variant thereof. Others promoted the union movement in its effort to secure better wages and working conditions. A third response called for government regulation and social programs to redistribute income.[34] She argues "Therefore, the policy prescriptions of classical economics were increasingly questioned."[34]

Neoclassical economics is frequently dated from William Stanley Jevons's Theory of Political Economy (1871), Carl Menger's Principles of Economics (1871), and Leon Walras's Elements of Pure Economics (1874–1877). They began "the Marginal Revolution".[43] The marginalists were attracted to the rigorous analytical approach of David Ricardo and his principle of diminishing returns. They were also similarly influenced by Jeremy Bentham's concept of diminishing marginal utility. Pluta (2011) describes:

"Its leaders would ultimately resurrect and refine classical ideas, make them more theoretically precise, and provide ideological arguments that rejected socialism and fit nicely with the increasingly popular Social Darwinism."[34]

He elaborates the real world practice of "Social Darwinism" as:

"A manager of a firm should be paid more than a worker on the assembly line because the manager presumably adds more to output than his or her subordinate. Hard-working, highly productive workers were paid more than lazy, incompetent workers. The Social Darwinists could not have said it better."[34]

Jevons saw his economics as an application and development of Jeremy Bentham's utilitarianism.[44] In classical economics, value was considered as a property inherent in an object, gradually gave way to a perspective in which value was associated with the relationship between the object and the person obtaining the object, which is called utility perspective of value (Weintraub, 2007).[43] The concept of marginal utility led to the replacement of the labor theory of value by neoclassical value theory in which the relative prices of goods and services are simultaneously determined by marginal rates of substitution in consumption and marginal rates of transformation in production, which are equal in economic equilibrium.

Stanley Jevons emphasized that at the margin, the satisfaction of goods and services decreases, called the theory of diminishing returns.[44] Then Leon Walras (1834–1910), again working independently, generalized marginal theory across the economy as describing small changes in people's preferences.[45] Early marginalists used Bentham's diminishing marginal utility principle to explain why price and quantity demanded were inversely related. Later marginalists used Ricardo's law of diminishing returns to argue that workers were paid exactly what they deserved based on productivity.[34]

The classical economics defines factors of production as land, labor and capital. Adam Smith and David Ricardo referred 'land' as land or natural resource, which is naturally-occurring goods like water, air, soil, minerals. In neoclassical economics increased importance of land ownership in economics reduced the meaning of land from natural resource to capital. As Heinberg describes:

"A key to this transformation was the gradual deletion by economists of land from the theoretical primary ingredients of the economy (increasingly, only labor and capital really mattered, land having been demoted to a sub-category of capital). This was one of the refinements that turned classical economic theory into neoclassical economics."[16]

Vilfredo Pareto (1848–1923) was an Italian engineer and economist, best known for developing the concept of Pareto efficiency and helped develop the field of microeconomics. The Pareto principle was named after him and built on observations of his such as that 80% of the land in Italy was owned by 20% of the population. The industrial revolution in the 19th century allowed 'better off the poor people through employment without worse off the riches'-the term called Pareto improvement. He also was the first to discover that income follows a Pareto distribution, which is a power law probability distribution. An allocation is defined as "Pareto efficient" or "Pareto optimal" when no further Pareto improvements can be made as shown in Figure 3.1. Pareto devised mathematical representations for such a resource allocation, notable in abstracting from institutional arrangements and monetary measures of wealth or income distribution.[46] Pareto efficiency is an important criterion for evaluating economic

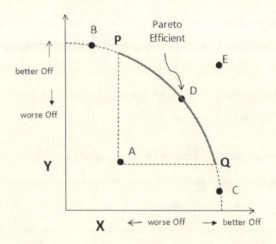

Figure 3.1: Pareto Efficient Allocation

The above figure (Figure 3.1) shows a Pareto Efficient Allocation for two individuals X & Y. Point A is their initial allocation. Any allocation moving from A to D (any point between P and Q) enables make one person better off without making anyone else worse off (Pareto improvement). Moving to point C from point A, however, is not Pareto improvement, as it makes Y worse off. Likewise, moving to point B from point A is not Pareto improvement, as it makes X worse off. The curve PQ shows Pareto efficient allocation since no more Pareto improvement possible moving along the curve. Point "E" lies outside the curve, representing an impossible allocation in existing conditions.

174

system and public policies since the outcomes that are not Pareto efficient are to be avoided. Under certain idealized conditions, it can be shown that a system of free markets will lead to a Pareto efficient outcome. This is called the first welfare theorem. It was first demonstrated mathematically by economists Kenneth Arrow and Gerard Debreu. However, the result does not rigorously establish welfare results for real economies because of the restrictive assumptions necessary for the proof (markets exist for all possible goods, all markets are in full equilibrium, markets are perfectly competitive, transaction costs are negligible, there must be no externalities, and market participants must have perfect information).

Weintraub (2002) views neoclassical economics as a scientific research program that generates economic theories. As he lists down those fundamental assumptions including the following that are not open to discussion:[43]

1. People have rational preferences among outcomes.

2. Individuals maximize utility and firms maximize profits.

3. People act independently on the basis of full and relevant information.

Alfred Marshall (1842-1924) is also credited with an attempt to put economics on a more mathematical footing. He was the first Professor of Economics at the University of Cambridge and his work, "Principles of Economics"[47] coincided with the transition of the subject from "political economy" to his favored term, "economics". He popularized the use of supply and demand functions as tools of price determination (previously discovered independently by Augustin Cournot). He insisted it is the intersection of both supply and demand that produce equilibrium of price in a competitive market. Over the long run, argued Marshall, the costs of production and the price of goods and services tend towards the lowest point consistent with continued production. The Supply and demand model is a partial equilibrium model where the clearance on the market of some specific goods is obtained independently from prices and quantities in other markets. In other words, the prices of all substitutes and complements, as well as income levels of consumers are constant. This makes analysis much simpler than in a general equilibrium model which includes an entire economy.[48] This classification of costs into fixed and variable and the emphasis given to the element of time probably represent one of Marshall's chief contributions to economic theory. He was committed to partial equilibrium models over general equilibrium on the grounds that the inherently dynamical nature of economics made the former more practically useful. John Maynard Keynes and Arthur Cecil Pigou were the Marshall's most famous students.[49]

Arthur Cecil Pigou in Wealth and Welfare (1920), insisted on the existence of market failures. Markets are inefficient in case of economic externalities, and the State must interfere. However, Pigou retained free-market beliefs, and in 1933, in the face of the economic crisis, he explained in "The Theory of Unemployment"[50] that the excessive intervention of the state in the labor market was the real cause of massive unemployment, because the governments had established a minimal wage, which prevented the wages from adjusting automatically. This was to be the focus of attack from Keynes.[51]

The marginal revolution also changed the methodology aspect of economic theories from methodological holism in classical economics to methodological individualism. As Arrow says, it is a touchstone of accepted economics that all explanations must run in terms of actions and reactions of individuals (Arrow, 1994).[52] The term 'methodological individualism' was first coined by Joseph Schumpeter (1883–1950), an Austrian economist and political scientist. According to Schumpeter, the concept of methodological individualism explains social phenomena as being meaningful from the point of view of acting individuals. The objective is to explain the operation of the price system, which is a social phenomenon. As he (Schumpeter, 1908) explains "Total demand and total supply are concepts which rest on entirely individualistic principals."[53] Accordingly, methodological individualism does not allow non-individualist decision makers such as institutions. Institutions, which might be considered as prior to and conditioning individual behavior, are de-emphasized. Schumpeter emphasized the "creative destruction" of capitalism—the facts that market economies undergo constant change.[54] He is most known for his works on business cycles and innovation. According to him, capitalism necessarily goes through long-term cycles, because it is entirely based upon scientific inventions and innovations. A phase of expansion is made possible by innovations, because they bring productivity gains and encourage entrepreneurs to invest. However, when investors have no more opportunities to invest, the economy goes into recession, several firms collapse, closures and bankruptcy occur. This phase lasts until new innovations bring a creative destruction process, i.e. they destroy old products, reduce the employment, but they allow the economy to start a new phase of growth, based upon new products and new factors of production.[55]

The other remarkable Austrian economists Ludwig von Mises and Friedrich Hayek were among the leading defenders of market economy against 20th century proponents of socialist planned economies.[56] They argue that only market capitalism can manage a complex, modern economy since a modern economy produces such a large array of distinct goods and services, and consists of such a large array of consumers and enterprises. The information problems facing any other form of economic organization other than market capitalism would exceed its capacity to handle information.[56] Capitalism, to this school, is defined by lack of state restraint on the decisions of producers. Austrian economics has been a major influence on some forms of libertarianism, in which laissez-faire capitalism is considered to be the ideal economic system.[57]

Neoclassical economics emphasizes equilibria, where equilibria are the solutions of agent maximization problems. The first attempt in neoclassical economics to model prices for a whole economy was made by Léon Walras (1834–1910). In formation of general equilibrium, More than one variable or economy as a whole is taken into consideration. It is based on the assumption that various sectors are mutually interdependent. There is an effect on other sectors due to change in one. Prices of goods are determined simultaneously and mutually. Hence all product and factor markets are simultaneously in equilibrium.[45]

The modern conception of general equilibrium is provided by a model developed jointly by Kenneth Arrow, Gerard Debreu and Lionel W. McKenzie in the 1950s. Basic questions in general equilibrium analysis are concerned with the conditions under which an equilibrium will be efficient, which efficient equilibria can be achieved, when an equilibrium is guaranteed to exist and when the equilibrium will be unique and stable.[55] The First Fundamental Welfare Theorem asserts that market equilibria are Pareto efficient. In a pure exchange economy, a sufficient condition for the first welfare theorem to hold is that preferences be locally non-satiated. Implicitly, the theorem assumes complete markets and perfect information. In an economy with externalities, for example, it is possible for equilibria to arise that are not efficient. As Wittman Donald (2004) describes:

"Now there is a fallback position. Instead of unrealistically comparing the outcome to a world of perfect information, one can construct models where the outcome of competition is on average best given asymmetric information. So we still have something that approximates the results rely on a whole host of assumptions. For example, there may be many (possibly a continuum of) competitive equilibrium, with one being efficient. We do not have a general welfare theorem, but rather a particular model where an efficient competitive outcome may arise."[58]

The first welfare theorem is informative in the sense that it points to the sources of inefficiency in markets. Under the assumptions above, any market equilibrium is tautologically efficient. Therefore, when equilibria arise that are not efficient, the market system itself is not to blame, but rather some sort of market failure. While every equilibrium is efficient, it is clearly not true that every efficient allocation of resources will be an equilibrium.

The second theorem tells that all that is required to reach a particular outcome is a redistribution of initial endowments of the agents after which the market can be left alone to do its work. In other words, every efficient allocation can be supported by some set of prices. This suggests that the issues of efficiency and equity can be separated and need not involve a trade-off. The conditions for the second theorem are stronger than those for the first, as consumers' preferences now need to be convex (convexity roughly corresponds to the idea of diminishing rates of marginal substitution, or to preferences where "averages are better than extrema").[55]

The reason of widespread popularity of neoclassical economics is that as Weintraub (2007) described "The rules of theory development and assessment are clear in neoclassical economics, and that clarity is taken to be beneficial to the community of economists."[43] Some of the recent work in general equilibrium has in fact explored the implications of incomplete markets, which is to say an intertemporal economy with uncertainty, where there does not exist sufficiently detailed contracts that would allow agents to fully allocate their consumption and resources through time. While it has been shown that such economies will generally still have equilibrium, the outcome may no longer be Pareto optimal.[55] Pluta (2011) argues that introduction of the concept of equilibrium brings the broad economic challenges to an increasingly narrow mainstream. He describes this as:

"Marshall and the marginalists who immediately preceded him narrowed the scope of economics and made the discipline more specialized. Their preoccupation with microeconomic matters guaranteed that macroeconomics remained largely unchanged between 1850 and the 1930s. Most economists during this period were more concerned with establishing economic laws than with offering policy recommendations."[34]

3.4 Keynesian Economics and Beyond

The simple Marshallian theory suggests that equilibrium ought to be at the intersection of demand and supply. Here prices represent a market at micro level that carry information between consumers and producers, and allocate resources.[59] In this theory, inflation is good since if price increases, the firms will be motivated to increase supply by increasing production, in turn which will create more employments. According to this theory, there cannot be any supply glut as market will clear that out as price falls. However, during Great Depression in 1930 price dropped suddenly but market did not responded, investment reduced and unemployment became high. John Maynard Keynes, a student of Marshall looked into this problem differently. According to him as price dropped, holding money became profitable as lower and a given amount of money bought ever more goods, exacerbating the drop in demand. Once panic and deflation set in, many people believed they could avoid further losses by keeping clear of the markets. Keynes argued in "General Theory of Employment Interest and Money"[60] that lower aggregate expenditures in the economy contributed to a massive decline in income and to employment that was well below the average. In such a situation, the economy reached equilibrium at low levels of economic activity and high unemployment.

Keynes argued that the solution to the Great Depression was to stimulate the economy through some combination of two approaches:[61]

1. A reduction in interest rates (monetary policy), and

2. Government investment in infrastructure (fiscal policy).

By reducing the interest rate at which the central bank lends money to commercial banks, the government sends a signal to commercial banks that they should do the same for their customers. And the second idea is simple: to keep people fully employed, governments have to run deficits when the economy is slowing, as the private sector would not invest enough to keep production at the normal level and bring the economy out of recession. Keynesian economists called on governments during times of economic crisis to pick up the slack by increasing government spending and or cutting taxes.[62]

The classical approach of economics treat unemployment as a temporary deviance of market forces that should correct if left to the markets. Adherence to this approach by the contemporary economists came under attack by Keynes and many others particularly during Great Depression due to massive unemployment of capital and labor. He argued that limited government intervention could solve it.[59] Once unemployment was reduced, the classical vision of the efficient market could be restored. Samuelson dubbed this the Neoclassical Synthesis.[59] Stiglitz and Greenwald identified the following four insights of Keynesian economics as essential to the explanation of unemployment and business fluctuations:[59]

1. A general theory must account for the persistence of unemployment

2. A general theory must account for the fluctuations in unemployment

3. Savings and investment must be carefully distinguished

4. Disturbances in demand, not supply, underlie the cyclical behavior of macroeconomic aggregates.

In his General Theory, Keynes attributed the persistence of unemployment to the failure of wages to adjust with sufficient speed to clear labor markets.[59] During the Great Depression, the classical theory attributed mass unemployment to high and rigid real wages. Therefore, they advocated abolishing minimum wages, unions, and long-term contracts, increasing labor market flexibility.[61] Keynes argued that it is not real but nominal wages that are set in negotiations between employers and workers—any reduction of wage will be resisted by people. Keynes rejected the idea that cutting wages would cure recessions. He concluded that such wage cutting would be more likely to make recessions worse since if wages and prices were falling, people would start to expect them to fall. As Irving Fisher argued in 1933, in his Debt-Deflation Theory of Great Depressions, deflation (falling prices) can make a depression deeper as falling prices and wages made pre-existing nominal debts more valuable in real terms.[63]

Regarding the third case, in his General Theory, Keynes distinctly defines savings and investment as:[60]

"Those who think (that an act of individual saving leads to a parallel act of investment) ... are deceived.... They are fallaciously supposing that there is a nexus which unites decisions to abstain from present consumption with decisions to provide for future consumption; whereas the motives which determine the latter are not linked in any simple way with the motives which determine the former"[60] (General Theory, p. 21)

As shown in Figure 3.2, the classical economists argue that interest rates falls due to the excess supply of "loanable funds". According to Keynes, excessive saving results if investment falls, perhaps due to falling consumer demand,

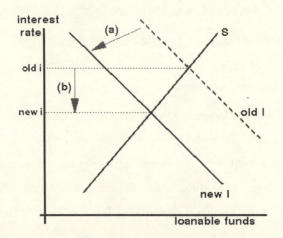

Figure 3.2: Classical economics view of Saving & Investment[64]

overinvestment in earlier years, or pessimistic business expectations, and if saving does not immediately fall in step, the economy would decline. However, saving does not fall much as interest rates fall and planned fixed investment in plant and equipment is based mostly on long-term expectations of future profitability, that spending does not rise much as interest rates fall.[61] Therefore, Figure 3.3 shows this as savings (S) lines are drawn as perfectly inelastic and investment (I) lines are drawn as inelastic with interest change. Given the inelasticity of both demand and supply, a large interest-rate fall is needed to

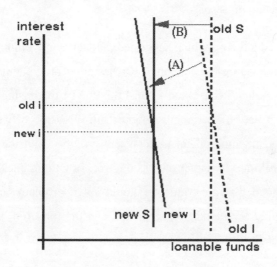

Figure 3.3: The Keynesian view of Saving & Investment[65]

close the saving/investment gap. As drawn, this requires a negative interest rate at equilibrium (where the new I line would intersect the old S line).[61] Therefore, Keynes argued that saving and investment are not the main determinants of interest rates, especially in the short run.

Finally, Keynes suggested that, because of fear of capital losses on assets besides money, there may be a "liquidity trap" setting a floor under which interest rates cannot fall.[61] In Figure 3.3, the equilibrium suggested by the new "I" line and the "old S" line cannot be reached, so that excess saving persists. Some economists (such as Paul Krugman) see this latter kind of liquidity trap as prevailing in Japan in the 1990s. Saving involves not spending all of one's income and excessive saving corresponds to an unwanted accumulation of inventories, or what classical economists called a general glut.[61] This pile-up of unsold goods and materials encourages businesses to decrease both production and employment. This in turn lowers people's incomes – and saving, causing a leftward shift in the S line in the diagram (step B). For Keynes, the fall in income did most of the job by ending excessive saving and allowing the loanable funds market to attain equilibrium. Instead of interest-rate adjustment solving the problem, a recession does so.[61]

Keynes developed a theory which suggested that active government policy could be effective in managing the economy. Keynes advocated countercyclical fiscal policies, that is, policies that acted against the tide of the business cycle: deficit spending when a nation's economy suffers from recession or when recovery is long-delayed and unemployment is persistently high – and the suppression of inflation in boom times by either increasing taxes or cutting back on government outlays. He argued that governments should solve problems in the short run rather than waiting for market forces to do it in the long run, because, "in the long run, we are all dead."[66]

In summary, there are two aspects of Keynes's model has implications for policy. First, there is the "Keynesian multiplier", first developed by Richard F. Kahn in 1931. Exogenous increases in spending, such as an increase in government outlays, increases total spending by a multiple of that increase. A government could stimulate a great deal of new production with a modest outlay if:

1. The people who receive this money then spend most on consumption goods and save the rest that is, who have very high marginal propensity of consumptions.

2. This extra spending allows businesses to hire more people and pay them, which in turn allows a further increase in consumer spending.[61]

Second, Keynes re-analyzed the effect of the interest rate on investment. In the classical model, the supply of funds (saving) determines the amount of fixed business investment. That is, under the classical model, since all savings are placed in banks, and all business investors in need of borrowed funds go to banks, the amount of savings determines the amount that is available to invest. Under Keynes's model, the amount of investment is determined independently by long-term profit expectations and, to a lesser extent, the interest rate. The latter opens the possibility of regulating the economy through money supply changes, via monetary policy. Under conditions such as the Great Depression, Keynes argued that this approach would be relatively ineffective compared to fiscal policy. But, during more "normal" times, monetary expansion can stimulate the economy.[61]

Keynes's ideas influenced Franklin D. Roosevelt's policies during Great Depression. He took a job building program for the unemployed (the Works Progress Administration, WPA) and increased public spending for building infrastructures and increased farm subsidies. As the depression wore on, he tried public works, farm subsidies, and other devices to restart the US economy, but never completely gave up trying to balance the budget. The common view among mainstream economists is that Roosevelt's New Deal policies either caused or accelerated the recovery, although his policies were never aggressive enough to bring the economy completely out of recession until the start of World War II.[67] Many economists believe that government spending on the war caused or at least accelerated recovery since it did help in reducing unemployment. The rearmament policies leading up to World War II helped stimulate the economies of Europe in 1937–39. The mobilization of manpower following the outbreak of war in 1939 ended unemployment. America's entry into the war in 1941 finally eliminated the last effects from the Great Depression and brought the U.S. unemployment rate down below 10% and doubled economic growth rates, either masking the effects of the Depression or essentially ending the Depression.[68] Keynesian ideas of fiscal and monetary policies became almost official in social-democratic Europe after the war and in the U.S. in the 1960s.[61]

There are some other views, often called heterodox views of the causes and recoveries of Great Depression that needs to be discussed here. The causes for the first downturn in 1929 include the structural weaknesses and specific events that turned it into a major depression and the manner in which the downturn spread from country to country. In relation to the 1929 downturn, historians emphasize structural factors like major bank failures and the stock market crash. In contrast, economists such as Milton Friedman and Peter Temin point to monetary factors such as actions by the US Federal Reserve that contracted the money supply, as well as Britain's decision to return to the Gold Standard at pre–World War I parities (US$4.86:£1).[62] The monetarists believe that the Great Depression started as an ordinary recession, but that significant policy mistakes by monetary authorities (especially the Federal Reserve), caused a shrinking of the money supply which greatly exacerbated the economic situation, causing a recession to descend into the Great Depression.[62]

The Austrian school of economics focuses on the macroeconomic effects of money supply, and how central banking decisions can lead to over-investment (economic bubble). Two economists of the 1920s, Waddill Catchings and William Trufant Foster, popularized a theory that influenced many policy makers, including Herbert Hoover, Henry A. Wallace, Paul Douglas, and Marriner Eccles. It held the economy produced more than it consumed, because the consumers did not have enough income. Thus the unequal distribution of wealth throughout the 1920s caused the Great Depression.[71] According to this view, the root cause of the Great Depression was a global over-investment in heavy industry capacity compared to wages and earnings from independent businesses, such as farms. The solution was the government must pump money into consumers' pockets. That is, it must redistribute purchasing power, maintain the industrial base, but re-inflate prices and wages to force as much of the inflationary increase in purchasing power into consumer spending. The economy was overbuilt, and new factories were not needed.

According to Christina Romer, the money supply growth caused by huge international gold inflows was a crucial source of the recovery of the United States economy, and that the economy showed little sign of self-correction. The gold inflows were partly due to devaluation of the U.S. dollar and partly due to deterioration of the political situation in Europe.[68] Economic studies have indicated that just as the downturn was spread worldwide by the rigidities of the gold standard, it was suspending gold convertibility (or devaluing the currency in gold terms) that did most to make recovery possible.[72]

After death of Keynes in 1946, the post-war economics profession began to synthesize much of Keynes' work with mathematical representations. A new school of thought called Keynesian economics developed by extending the basic ideas of Keynes. Introductory university economics courses began to present economic theory as a unified whole in what is referred to as the neoclassical synthesis. "Positive economics" became the term created to describe certain trends and "laws" of economics that could be objectively observed and described in a value free way, separate from "normative economic" evaluations and judgments. Paul Samuelson (1915–2009) extended the mathematics to describe equilibrating behavior of economic systems, including that of the then new macroeconomic theory of Keynes.

A new correlative relationship between inflation and unemployment called "Phillips Curve" (described in next chapter) was discovered by A. W. Phillips, which reasserted economics as a hard science. The workable policy conclusion was that securing full employment could be traded-off against higher inflation.[73] In his paper "Relation between Unemployment and the Rate of Change of Money Wage Rates in the United Kingdom, 1861-1957", William Phillips (1958) describes how he observed an inverse relationship between money wage changes and unemployment.[73] In 1960, Paul Samuelson and Robert Solow also observed similar patterns in other countries and they took Phillips' work to make explicit link between inflation and unemployment: when inflation was high, unemployment was low, and vice-versa.[74&75] That is, governments could control unemployment and inflation with a Keynesian policy. However, in the 1970s, much the U.S. economy experienced high levels of both inflation and unemployment also known as stagflation. Milton Friedman famously described this situation as "too much money chasing too few goods".[76]

Later Keynes, theories, such as rational expectations and the NAIRU (Non-Accelerating Inflation Rate of Unemployment) developed by Edmund Phelps explain how stagflation could occur. It argues that in the long run, monetary policy cannot affect unemployment, which adjusts back to its "natural rate", also called the NAIRU or "long-run Phillips curve" as shown in Figure 3.4 but by increasing permanent inflation.[77] It explains that policymakers can therefore reduce the unemployment rate temporarily, moving from point A to point B through expansionary policy. However, according to the NAIRU, exploiting this short-run tradeoff will raise inflation expectations, shifting the short-run curve rightward to the "New Short-Run Phillips Curve" and moving the point of

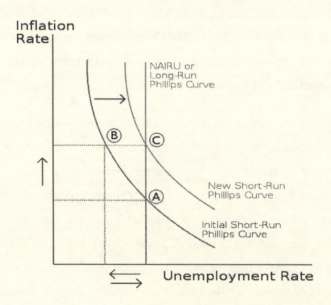

Figure 3.4: Long-Run Phillips Curve (NAIRU)[78]

equilibrium from B to C. Thus the reduction in unemployment below the "Natural Rate" will be temporary, and lead only to higher inflation in the long-run. The name "NAIRU" arises because with actual unemployment below it, inflation accelerates, while with unemployment above it, inflation decelerates.[74] With the actual rate equal to it, inflation is stable, neither accelerating nor decelerating. Edmund Phelps won the Nobel Prize in Economics in 2006 for this. There are total seven Nobel Prizes have been given for work critical of the Phillips curve since 1974.[79]

According to Keynesian economics, fiscal stimulus could actuate production during economic downturn. But, to classical and neoclassical economics, the efforts to stimulate the economy would be self-defeating.[61] The Keynesian response is that such fiscal policy is appropriate only when unemployment is persistently high, above the non-accelerating inflation rate of unemployment (NAIRU). In that case, crowding out is minimal. Further, private investment can be "crowded in": Fiscal stimulus raises the market for business output, raising cash flow and profitability, spurring business optimism. To Keynesian, this accelerator effect meant that government and business could be complements rather than substitutes in this situation.[61] Contrary to some critical characterizations of it, Keynesianism does not consist solely of deficit spending. Keynesianism recommends counter-cyclical policies.[61&80] An example of a counter-cyclical policy is raising taxes to cool the economy and to prevent inflation when there is abundant demand-side growth, and engaging in deficit spending on labor-intensive infrastructure projects to stimulate employment and stabilize wages during economic downturns. Classical economics, on the other hand, argues that one should cut taxes when there are budget surpluses, and cut spending – or, less likely, increase taxes – during economic downturns. Contrary to some critical characterizations of it, Keynesianism does not consist solely of deficit spending. Keynesianism recommends counter-cyclical policies.[80] Keynesian economists believe that adding to profits and incomes during boom cycles through tax cuts, and removing income and profits from the economy through cuts in spending during downturns, tends to exacerbate the negative effects of the business cycle. This effect is especially pronounced when the government controls a large fraction of the economy, as increased tax revenue may aid investment in state enterprises in downturns, and decreased state revenue and investment harm those enterprises.[61]

From the 1970s onwards Friedman's monetarist critique of Keynesian macroeconomics formed the starting point for a number of trends in macroeconomic theory opposed to the idea that government intervention can or should stabilize the economy. Robert Lucas criticized Keynesian thought for its inconsistency with microeconomic theory. Lucas's critique set the stage for a neoclassical school of macroeconomics, New Classical economics based on the foundation of classical economics. Lucas also popularized the idea of rational expectations, which was used as the basis for several new classical theories.[81] Kennet (2006) argues "whether they really related to the Keynesian economic policies needs to be debated – the opportunity arose to destroy the Keynesian economic logic with the intention to reinstate the old normative conventions, now named 'monetarism'." An adjusted monetarism called neo-liberal, which was itself a version of the classical economic mainstream, emerged to fill the gap after the decline of monetarism. Contrary to textbook economics theory, as Kennet & Heinemann (2006) concludes "the radical application of neo-liberal logic appears to be making matters worse for the world's poor."[82]

Keynesian economics made a comeback among mainstream economists with the advent of New Keynesian macroeconomics. Stiglitz describers this as:

"The New Keynesian Economics begins with Keynes' basic insights. But it recognizes the need for a more radical departure from the neoclassical framework, and for a much deeper study of the consequences of imperfections in capital markets, imperfections which can be explained by the costs of information."[59]

As an example Efficiency wage model, this is based on the hypothesis that there is imperfect information about the characteristics of workers.[59] The first model of 'efficiency wage hypothesis' was introduced by Alfred Marshall in 1920 argues that wages, at least in some markets, could be more than the market clearing wage in order to increase productivity or efficiency.[83] This increased labor productivity pays for the higher wages.

The graph in Figure 3.5 represents the Shapiro-Stiglitz model (1984) of efficiency wages.[84] The model proposes a Non-Shirking Condition (NSC) which once satisfied avoid workers to incur in shirking.[86] It shows that workers are paid

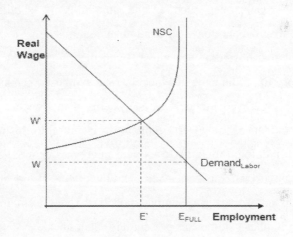

Figure 3.5: Efficiency wage chart based on Shapiro and Stiglitz (1984)[85]

at a level that dissuades shirking. This prevents wages from dropping to market clearing levels. Full employment cannot be achieved because workers would shirk if they were not threatened with the possibility of unemployment. If there is unemployment, then there will be a high opportunity cost for shirking. Therefore, for equilibrium there has to be unemployment. The curve for the NSC goes to infinity at full employment. This means in case of full employment, high wage provides no incentive.[84] Efficiency wages are therefore a market failure explanation of unemployment in contrast to theories which emphasize government intervention (such as minimum wages).[87] Stiglitz summarizes this as

> "[T]he efficiency wage models further show why the wages of firms are interdependent: the optimal wage for any one firm depends on the wages paid by all other firms. This interdependence may lead to multiple equilibria, in which no firm changes its wage even in the face of changes in its demand."[59]

The central theme of new Keynesianism was the provision of a microeconomic foundation for Keynesian macroeconomics, obtained by identifying minimal deviations from the standard microeconomic assumptions which yield Keynesian macroeconomic conclusions, such as the possibility of significant welfare benefits from macroeconomic stabilization. Economists have combined the methodology of real business cycle theory with theoretical elements from new Keynesian theory to produce the new neoclassical synthesis. Dynamic stochastic general equilibrium (DSGE) models, large systems of microeconomic equations combined into models of the general economy, are central to this new synthesis. The DSGE methodology attempts to explain aggregate economic phenomena, such as economic growth, business cycles, and the effects of monetary and fiscal policy, on the basis of macroeconomic models derived from microeconomic principles. The synthesis dominates present day economics.[88]

3.5 Supply-side Economics

Keynesian economics holds that the government should stimulate economic growth by increasing demand through increased credit and public spending. During 1970s Keynesian economics resulted in low growth and high inflation, called stagflation. In response to this situation, the Western economies, particularly, the United States and United Kingdom a new range of non-Keynesian thoughts, particularly the Chicago School and Neo-Classical School got ground again. Bruce Bartlett, an advocate of supply-side economics, traced the school of thought's intellectual descent from the philosophers Ibn Khaldun and David Hume, political economist Adam Smith, and even Founding Father of United States Alexander Hamilton.[89]

As in classical economics, supply-side economics proposed that production or supply is the key to economic prosperity and that consumption or demand is merely a secondary consequence.[90] In early eighteenth century Say's Law of economics states:

"A product is no sooner created, than it, from that instant, affords a market for other products to the full extent of its own value."

John Maynard Keynes, the founder of Keynesianism, summarized Say's Law as "supply creates its own demand."[90] He turned Say's Law on its head in the 1930s by declaring that demand creates its own supply.[91]

According to David Harper, supply-side theory has three pillars: tax policy, regulatory policy and monetary policy. However, the single idea behind all three pillars is that more production and more consumption is most important in determining economic growth.[92] In regard to a tax and capital, supply-siders believe that lower capital-gains tax induce investors to deploy capital productively. They further argue that the government would not lose total tax revenue because lower rates would be more than offset by a higher tax revenue base - due to greater employment and productivity. On the question of regulatory policy, supply-siders prefer a smaller government and less intervention in the free market. The government should intervene only to create a free market by lowering taxes, privatizing state industries and increasing restraints on trade unionism. The third pillar, monetary policy, refers to the process by which the monetary authority of a country manages the supply of money, often targeting a rate of interest for the purpose of promoting economic growth and stability. However, the official goals usually include relatively stable prices and low unemployment.[93] Economists often overlook that without technical innovation with marketing techniques such as advertisements, particularly radio and television commercials, widespread use of credit cards, e-commerce and now a days mobile banking, supply-side economics might not outpace Keynesian economics. Therefore, technological innovation can be considered as fourth pillar of supply-side economics.

The monetary policy involves setting banking-system lending or interest rates. A central bank conducts monetary policy by raising or lowering its interest rate target for the interbank interest rate. If the nominal interest rate is at or very near zero, the central bank cannot lower it further. Such a situation, called a liquidity trap. In the U.S., managing money supply mainly involves buying government bonds (expanding the money supply) or selling them (contracting the money supply). In the Federal Reserve System, these are known as open market operations, because the central bank buys and sells government bonds in public markets. Monetarist economists such as Milton Friedman advocated that government budget deficits during recessions be financed in equal amount by money creation to help to stimulate aggregate demand for output.[94] Later he advocated simply increasing the monetary supply at a low, constant rate, as the best way of maintaining low inflation and stable output growth.[95] However, when then U.S. Federal Reserve at the time Chairman Paul Volcker tried this policy, starting in October 1979, it was found to be impractical, because of the highly unstable relationship between monetary aggregates and other macroeconomic variables.[96] In this context, the first pillar "tax policy" has become the preferred policy tool for supply side economics. In her book The Shock Doctrine: The Rise of Disaster Capitalism, Naomi Klein describes how Friedman and other neoliberal economists used crisis after crisis, beginning in the 1970s, as opportunities to undermine democracy and privatize institutions and infrastructure across the world.[109]

Figure 3.6 shows an example of typical monetary and fiscal policy intervention strategies under different conditions recession, boom, stagflation and deflation based on historical scenarios in U.S. economy. Recently, Charles L. Evans, President and CEO of the Chicago Federal Reserve Bank, described several scenarios for intervention in monetary policy during a September 2014 speech.[69]

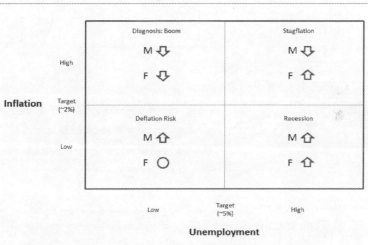

Figure 3.6: Economic Policy - Intervention Strategy Matrix[70]

The idea of lower tax is influenced strongly by the idea of the Laffer curve, which states that tax rates and tax revenues were distinct—that tax rates too high (100%) or too low (0%) will not maximize tax revenues as shown in Figure 3.7 (a). Nevertheless, the curve need not be single peaked nor symmetrical at 50%. The term "Laffer curve" was reportedly coined by Jude Wanniski (a writer for The Wall Street Journal) after a 1974 dinner meeting at the Two Continents Restaurant in the Washington Hotel with Arthur Laffer, Wanniski, Donald Rumsfeld (Chief of Staff to President Gerald Ford), and Dick Cheney (Rumsfeld's deputy and Laffer's former classmate at Yale).[97] Laffer presented the curve as a pedagogical device to show that, in some circumstances, a reduction in tax rates will actually increase government revenue and no need to

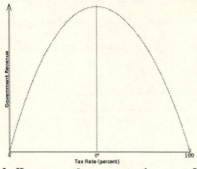

Laffer curve: t* represents the rate of taxation at which maximal revenue is generated. However, the curve need not be single peaked nor symmetrical.

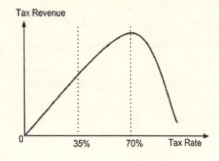

A possible non-symmetric Laffer Curve with a maximum revenue point at around a 70% tax rate, based on "How Far Are We From The Slippery Slope?"[98]

Figure 3.7: A Typical Laffer Curve a) Symmetrical b) Non-symmetrical[99]

be offset by decreased government spending or increased borrowing. He describes (as shown in Figure 3.7.a):

"While discussing President Ford's "WIN" (Whip Inflation Now) proposal for tax increases, I supposedly grabbed my napkin and a pen and sketched a curve on the napkin illustrating the trade-off between tax rates and tax revenues."[97]

The Laffer Curve reflects the hypothesis that only cutting tax rates to the right of peak economic performance rate will increase revenues, and that cutting tax rates to the left of the peak rate will decrease revenues. A 1981 paper published in the Journal of Political Economy presented a model integrating empirical data that indicated that the point of maximum tax revenue in Sweden in the 1970s would have been 70% (Figure 3.7 (b)).[100] A paper by Trabandt and Uhlig of the NBER from 2009 presented a model that predicted that the US and most European economies were on the left of the curve, where raising taxes would raise further revenue.[98]

According to Arthur Laffer, the Laffer Curve itself does not say whether a tax cut will raise or lower revenues. If the existing tax rate is too high, then a tax-rate cut would result in increased tax revenues.[97] The economic effect of the tax cut would outweigh the arithmetic effect of the tax cut. He explains this as:

"Revenue responses to a tax rate change will depend upon the tax system in place, the time period being considered, the ease of movement into underground activities, the level of tax rates already in place, the prevalence of legal and accounting-driven tax loopholes, and the proclivities of the productive factors."[97]

Laffer himself does not claim to have invented the concept, attributing it to 14th-century Arab scholar Ibn Khaldun and, more recently, to John Maynard Keynes. As he describes Ibn Khaldun's work the Muqaddimah:

"It should be known that at the beginning of the dynasty, taxation yields a large revenue from small assessments. At the end of the dynasty, taxation yields a small revenue from large assessments."[97]

An argument along similar lines has also been advocated by Ali ibn Abi Talib, the fourth Caliph of the Islamic empire (Between 656 to 661); in his letter to the Governor of Egypt, Malik al-Ashtar. It implies that revenues might rise in time because of this reduction of taxes. Ali wrote the followings:

"If the tax-payers complain to you of the heavy incidence to taxation, of any accidental calamity, of the vagaries of the monsoons, of the recession of the means of irrigation, of floods, or destruction of their crops on account of excessive rainfall and if their complaints are true, then reduce their taxes. This reduction should be such that it provides them opportunities to improve their conditions and eases them of their troubles. Decrease in state income due to such reasons should not depress you because the best investment for a ruler is to help his subjects at the time of their difficulties. They are the real wealth of a country and any investment on them even in the form of reduction of taxes, will be returned to the State in the shape of the prosperity of its cities and improvement of the country at large. At the same time you will be in a position to command and secure their love, respect and praises along with the revenues."[101]

On the contrary, following industrial revolution, when industrial productivities increased, it led to series of wars in Europe to cater supply-side economics. The war rapidly enhanced industrial production capacities, mining of coal and steel but most of the produces were burnt. After completion of capitalist synthesis as described in the previous chapter, the concept of supply-side economics changed focus from market expansion by war to by reducing trade barriers or tariff. It views that higher taxation leads to lower levels of specialization and lower economic efficiency. The operation of supply-side theory is the expansion of free trade and free movement of capital. It is argued that free capital movement, in addition to the classical reasoning of comparative advantage, frequently allows an economic expansion.[90]

Although it was expected that the government revenue would be sufficient

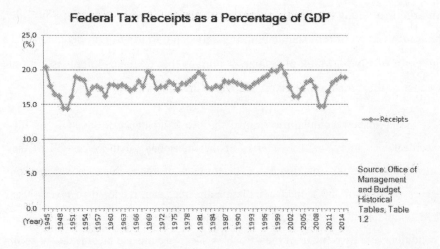

Figure 3.8: Federal Tax Receipts as a Percentage of GDP 1945–2015[103]

enough to compensate completely for the short-term costs of a tax cut, and that tax cuts could, in fact, cause overall revenue to increase. President Kennedy's fiscal policy stance made it clear that he believed in pro-growth, supply-side tax measures in his Tax Message to Congress on January 24, 1963.[102] The Kennedy tax cut set the example that President Ronald Reagan followed some 17 years later. Figure 3.8 shows U.S. federal government tax receipts as a percentage of GDP from 1945 to 2015 (the data for years 2010 to 2015 are statistical projections) is more or less below 20% of GDP and any claim of increased revenue is disputable. Some contemporary economists do not consider supply - side economics a tenable economic theory, with Alan Blinder calling it an "ill-fated" and perhaps "silly" school on the pages of a 2006 textbook.[104] In a 1992 article for the Harvard International Review, James Tobin wrote,

"[The] idea that tax cuts would actually increase revenues turned out to deserve the ridicule"[106]

Case and Fair writes in their book "Principles of Economics":

"The extreme promises of supply-side economics did not materialize. President Reagan argued that because of the effect depicted in the Laffer curve, the government could maintain expenditures, cut tax rates, and balance the budget. This was not the case. Government revenues fell sharply from levels that would have been realized without the tax cuts."[107]

Mundell in his Nobel Memorial Prize in Economic Sciences acceptance lecture (awarded for unrelated work in optimum currency area) countered that the success of price stability was proof that the supply-side revolution had worked. The continuing debate over supply-side policies tends to focus on the massive federal and current account deficits, increased income inequality and its failure to promote growth.[108 & 109] In 1986, a tax overhaul, described by Mundell as "the completion of the supply-side revolution" was drafted. It included increases in payroll taxes, decreases in top marginal rates, and increases in capital gains taxes. Combined with the mortgage interest deduction and the regressive effects of state taxation, it produces closer to a flat-tax effect. Supply-side advocates claim that revenues increased, but that spending increased faster. However, they typically point to total revenues even though it was only income taxes rates that were cut while other taxes, notably payroll taxes were raised. That table also does not account for inflation. For example, of the increase from $600.6 billion in 1983 to $666.5 billion in 1984, $26 billion is due to inflation, $18.3 billion to corporate taxes and $21.4 billion to social insurance revenues as per Federal Insurance Contributions Act (FICA) taxes.[110] According to Mundell,

> "Fiscal discipline is a learned behavior." Therefore, to put it another way, eventually the unfavorable effects of running persistent budget deficits will force governments to reduce spending in line with their levels of revenue."[90]

The relationship between tax rate and tax revenue is likely to vary from one economy to another and depends on the elasticity of supply for labor and various other factors. Even in the same economy, the characteristics of the curve could vary over time. Complexities such as progressive taxation and possible differences in the incentive to work for different income groups complicate the task of estimation. The structure of the curve may also be changed by policy decisions. For example, if tax loopholes and off-shore tax shelters are made more readily available by legislation, the point at which revenue begins to decrease with increased taxation is likely to become lower.[99]

In 2005, the U.S. Congressional Budget Office (CBO) released a paper called "Analyzing the Economic and Budgetary Effects of a 10 Percent Cut in Income Tax Rates". This paper considered the impact of a stylized reduction of 10% in the then existing marginal rate of federal income tax in the US (for example, if those facing a 25% marginal federal income tax rate had it lowered to 22.5%). In other words, deficits would increase by nearly the same amount as the tax cut in the first five years, with limited feedback revenue thereafter. Through increased budget deficits, the tax cuts primarily benefiting the wealthy.[111] It also points out that the projected revenue shortfalls would have to be made up by borrowing.[111]

Cutting marginal tax rates can also be perceived as primarily beneficial to the wealthy, which commentators such as Paul Krugman see as politically rather than economically motivated.[112] The economist John Kenneth Galbraith notes that supply-side economics was merely a cover for the trickle-down approach to economic policy, which is also called the horse and sparrow theory: If you feed the horse enough oats, some will pass through to the road for the sparrows.[113]

3.6 Welfare Capitalism

Welfare capitalism refers to capitalist economies that include comprehensive social welfare policies. It also refers to the practice of businesses providing welfare services to their employees. The 19th century German economist, Gustav von Schmoller, defined welfare capitalism as government provision for the welfare of workers and the public via social legislation. In the late 19th and early 20th centuries, Germany and Britain created "safety nets" for their citizens, including public welfare and unemployment insurance. Western Europe, Scandinavia, Canada and Australasia are regions noted for their welfare state provisions, though other countries have publicly financed universal healthcare and other elements of the welfare state as well.[114]

The concept of welfare was introduced during Islamic Caliphate of Umar bin al-Khattab (577-644) in the 7th century. The taxes collected in the treasury of an Islamic government were used to provide income for the poor, elderly, orphans, widows, and the disabled. According to the Islamic jurist Al-Ghazali (1058–1111), the government was also expected to stockpile food supplies in every region in case a disaster or famine occurred. The Caliphate can thus be considered the world's first major welfare state.[115] In Europe first change of feudal system toward welfare came after exposure of the Crusaders to advanced cultures and social system in the Middle East. As Pluta describes:

"A series of forces eroded feudal institutions and eventually led to collapse of the system. The Crusades sent people of different social classes to the Middle East, where they observed more advanced cultures and sought change when they returned to their drab manors and villages...Cities were reborn as improved safety in travel encouraged international trade, women worked with men in several industries, and a new middle class emerged"[10]

In France, During mercantilism agriculture remained as backbone of the French economy since industries did not prosper because of web of regulations resulting from mercantilists policies.[10] However, the French peasantry called the Third Estate had high tax burden, while the First Estate (clergy) and the Second Estate (nobility) were mostly exempted from taxes in the same way as Roman elites. The French engagement in Seven Years' War for dominance of colonial possessions and their support in the American Revolutionary War ended up in a deep financial crisis. The French government failed to solve this crisis by taxing the elites and churches but tried to exact more taxes to the peasants and working class. Dissatisfied with government's position fueled by enlightened writings such as Voltaire destabilized the positions of clergies and monarchy and eventually turned into a revolution called French Revolution took place during 1789-1799. The French revolution abolished the highly inefficient system of tax farming and totally restructured the government to provide an annual stream of revenue for hospitals, poor relief, and education and thereby creating a foundation of welfare economics in Europe.[117]

Under industrial capitalism, one of the first attempts at offering philanthropic welfare to workers was made at the New Lanark mills in Scotland by the social reformer Robert Owen. He became manager and part owner of the mills in 1810, and encouraged by his success in the management of cotton mills in Manchester, he hoped to conduct New Lanark on higher principles and focus less on commercial profit. Owen opened a store where the people could buy goods of sound quality at little more than wholesale cost, and he placed the sale of alcohol under strict supervision. He sold quality goods and passed on the savings from the bulk purchase of goods to the workers. These principles became the basis for the cooperative stores in Britain that continue to trade today. Owen's schemes involved considerable expense, which displeased his partners. Tired of the restrictions on his actions, Owen bought them out in 1813. New Lanark soon became celebrated throughout Europe, with many leading royals, statesmen and reformers visiting the mills. They were astonished to find a clean, healthy industrial environment with a content, vibrant workforce and a prosperous, viable business venture all rolled into one. Owen's philosophy was contrary to contemporary thinking, but he was able to demonstrate that it was not necessary for an industrial enterprise to treat its workers badly to be profitable. Owen was able to show visitors the village's excellent housing and amenities, and the accounts showing the profitability of the mills.[119]

Owen and the French socialist Henri de Saint-Simon were the fathers of the utopian socialist movement. Esping-Andersen categorized three different traditions of welfare provision in his 1990 book 'The Three Worlds of Welfare Capitalism'; Social Democracy, Christian Democracy (conservatism) and Liberalism. The ideal Social-Democratic welfare state is based on the principle of universalism granting access to benefits and services based on citizenship, limiting the reliance of family and market (Ferragina and Seeleib-Kaiser 2011).[120] Example of Social Democratic welfare states are: Denmark, Finland, the Netherlands, Norway and Sweden.[120] Christian-democratic welfare states are based on the principle of subsidiarity and the dominance of social insurance schemes, offering a medium level of de-commodification and a high degree of social stratification. Examples: Austria, Belgium, France, Germany and Italy.[120] The liberal regime is based on the notion of market dominance and private provision. Ideally, the state only interferes to ameliorate poverty and provide for basic needs, largely on a means-tested basis. Hence, the de-commodification potential of state benefits is assumed to be low and social stratification high. Example: Australia, Canada, Japan, Switzerland and the United States.[120] Though increasingly criticized, these classifications remain the most commonly used in distinguishing types of modern welfare states, and offer a solid starting point in such analysis.[114]

Social capitalism as a theory or political or philosophical stance, challenges the idea that the capitalist system is inherently antagonistic to the goals of socialism.[124] The essence of social capitalism is that private markets are the most effective allocation mechanism, and output is maximized through sound state macroeconomic management of the economy. Social capitalism posits that a strong social support network for the poor enhances capital output. By decreasing poverty, capital market participation is enlarged. It also tells that government regulation, and even sponsorship of markets, can lead to superior economic outcomes, as evidenced in government sponsorship of the internet or basic securities regulation.[125] Australian Prime Minister for the period 2007-2010, Kevin Rudd called for a new economic approach that he termed "social capitalism" which includes "a system of open markets, unambiguously regulated by an activist state, and one in which the state intervenes to reduce the greater inequalities that competitive markets will inevitably generate."[126] The scholarly roots of social capitalism seem to be in Kees van Kersbergen's landmark study of European economies, entitled "Social Capitalism: A Study of Christian Democracy and the Welfare State".[127] Van Kersbergen identifies social capitalism as the "common kernel" of the European welfare state and situates social capitalism as a "middle way" between socialist collectivism and neo-liberal individualism. Another exposition of social capitalism is Robert Corfe's three volume set entitled Social Capitalism: In Theory and Practice.[128] He views a core value of social capitalism "to realize the full potential of those from every background according to their ability and inclination." He therefore "repudiates any measures influenced by class bias."[128]

In Germany, after the collapse of the totalitarian Third Reich, a group of economists and academics at the University of Freiburg im Breisgau advocated a neo-liberal or new liberal and socio-economic order, from where the concept Ordoliberalism was opted for the economic-rebuild following World War II. According to this concept, the state must solely create a proper legal environment, a proper institutional framework or 'ordo' for the economy and maintain a healthy level of competition through measures that follow market principles.[129] The ordoliberal competitive order was further developed by the Cologne School around the economist and anthropologist Alfred Müller-Armack, who therefore coined the term 'Soziale Marktwirtschaft' (Social Market Economy) in a publication in December 1946.[130]

Social Market Economy is a form of market capitalism combined with a social policy favoring union bargaining and social insurance, and is sometimes classified as a coordinated market economy.[131] It is considered as an extension of ordo-liberal thought but 'an adjustable holistic conception pursuing a complete humanistic societal order as a synthesis of seemingly conflicting objectives, namely economic freedom and social security'.[132] In the early twentieth century, the Frankfurt sociologist and economist Franz Oppenheimer postulated a so-called "Liberal Socialism", i.e. socialism achieved via liberalism, as the pursuit of a societal order, in which economic self-interest preserves its power and persists in free competition.[133] Ludwig Erhard, one of Oppenheimer's student implemented this idea into practice and led the German postwar economic reform and economic recovery as Minister of Economics under Chancellor Konrad Adenauer in 1949.[135]

In Japan, social welfare assistance for the elderly, ill or disabled and for the, has long been provided by both the government and private companies. Beginning in the 1920s, the government enacted a series of welfare programs, based mainly on European models, to provide medical care and financial support. Following Germany, the Post-World War II economic miracle of Japan was also result of social market economy or coordinated market economy.[136] It occurred partly due to the aid and assistance of the United States to slow the expansion of Soviet influence in the Pacific during Cold War but chiefly due to the economic interventionism of the Japanese government. The United States was also concerned with the growth of the economy of Japan because there was a risk after World War II that an unhappy and poor Japanese population would turn to communism. The distinguishing characteristics of the Japanese economy during the "economic miracle" years included: the cooperation of manufacturers, suppliers, distributors, and banks in closely knit groups called keiretsu; the powerful enterprise unions and good relations with government bureaucrats, and the guarantee of lifetime employment in big corporations and highly unionized blue-collar factories.[136] The Japanese government under Prime Minister Hayato Ikeda contributed to the post-war Japanese economic miracle by stimulating private sector growth. , first by instituting regulations and protectionism that effectively managed economic crises and later by concentrating on trade expansion.[137] Under his leadership, the Japanese government undertook an ambitious "income-doubling plan" by lowering interest rates and taxes to private players to motivate spending. He established a comprehensive system of social security in combination of public and private funding. However, Japanese older tradition calls for support within the family and the local community.

By the time Ikeda left office in 1964, the GNP was growing at a phenomenal rate of 13.9 percent that has made Japan the third biggest economy in the world.[136] GDP Growth Rate in Japan averaged 0.49 Percent from 1980 until 2014.[137] Following the concept of John Stuart Mill (1806–1873) it can be said that the low growth is not necessarily bad, as long as a certain level of affluence has been met at this point.[9] Although Japanese economy is not growing, the futures of

Japan's health and welfare systems are being shaped by the rapid aging of the population. As elderly people are living longer, cost of pensions also increasing, which requires more contributions from the people who are employed, while Japanese government is indebted over 200% of GDP.

The United States introduced Medicare, Medicaid and Social Security provisions for elderly and low income people but it is not generally considered to have enough of a social safety net to properly be called a welfare-state since businesses provide more of these services. French economist Michel Albert compared the so-called "neo-American model" based on the ideas of Friedrich von Hayek and Milton Friedman of a capitalistic market economy with the German model and found the latter model as more equitable and efficient. However, according to Albert, complex psychological phenomena and the functioning of the press lets the American model appear more attractive and dynamic to the general public.[138]

3.7 Institutional Economics

After World War II, the economy of United States continued to grow and it had become the leading global economic power. A new American group of economists emerged in America, called "the institutional economists" had been largely critical of the "American Way" of life, especially regarding conspicuous consumption of the "Roaring Twenties" before the Wall Street Crash of 1929. As explained in last section that investment continued to grow but sudden fall in consumption level ended up in the Great Depression. In his book "The Theory of the Leisure Class", Thorsten Veblen (1857–1929) asserted that there exists a fundamental split in society between those who work and those who exploit the work of others; as societies evolve, the latter come to constitute a "leisure class" that engages in "conspicuous consumption." He saw mass production as a way to universalize the trappings of leisure so the owning class could engage workers in

207

an endless pursuit of status symbols, thus deflecting their attention from society's increasingly unequal distribution of wealth and from their own political impotence.[109] He argued that profit focused businesses protect their existing capital investments and employ excessive credit, leading to depressions and increasing military expenditure and war through business control of political power. He argued that economics is not an evolutionary science as any evolutionary science is a close knit body of theory but economics cannot satisfy its critics that its credentials are good.[139] He coined the term "neoclassical economics" just as Marx was the first to use the term "capitalism" before offering his critique of it.[9]

In 1911 Veblen predicted a political revolution in Russia and a major war in Europe. During the 1020s, he also forecast a major depression, but he died just weeks before the 1929 stock market crash. Pluta explains this as:

> "The reform impulse advocated by Veblen influenced Franklin D. Roosevelt's New Deal. Because several of Veblen's former students actually advised Roosevelt at this time, many considered their role in the design of programs to combat the Great Depression to be the ultimate triumph of institutionalism in the policy area."[9]

His criticism to neoclassic economists proposing theories without supporting data has prompted the profession to collect and analyze statistics on economic performance. Ultimately, the macroeconomics of Keynes overshadowed the institutionalist contribution. Veblen died 17 years before Keynes. Pluta points out:

> "This gave Keynes the opportunity to influence government policy for a longer period, during the troubled years of Depression and war."[140]

Later on, John R. Commons (1862–1945) consolidated his ideas in Institutional Economics that the economy is a web of relationships between people with diverging interests. There are monopolies, large corporations, labour disputes and fluctuating business cycles. They do however have an interest in resolving these disputes. Government, thought Commons, ought to be the mediator between the conflicting groups.[141] The ideas of the institutionalists helped to draft legislation in the areas of government regulations to the utility companies, unemployment compensation, factory safety laws, child labor and eventually social security.[140] As Brown (2005) argues "it is questionable after the "golden age (1945-1972) expansion of output and productive capacity could have been achieved without the ameliorative effects of the minimum wage, unionism and collective bargaining, progressive taxation and income transfers."[142]

The Great Depression was a time of significant upheaval in the States. One of the most original contributions to understanding what had gone wrong came from a Harvard University lawyer, named Adolf Berle (1895–1971). He along with Gardiner Means was a foundational figure of modern corporate governance. In their book "The Modern Corporation and Private Property"[143], they argued that those who controlled big firms should be better held to account like directors of companies are held to account to the shareholders of companies, or not, by the rules found in company law statutes. This might include rights to elect and fire the management, require for regular general meetings, accounting standards, and so on. After the war, John Kenneth Galbraith (1908–2006) became one of the standard bearers for pro-active government and liberal-democrat politics. According to him it is unrealistic to think of markets of the classical kind. They set prices and use advertising to create artificial demand for their own products, distorting people's real preferences. Consumer preferences actually come to reflect those of corporations—a "dependence effect"—and the economy as a whole is geared to irrational goals.[144]

Ronald Coase (born 1910) is the most prominent economic analyst of law and the 1991 Nobel Prize winner, who introduced the concept of transaction cost and set up a link between neoclassical economics and institutional economics. His first major article, "The Nature of the Firm" (1937)[145], argued that the reason for the existence of firms (companies, partnerships, etc.) is the existence of transaction costs. Rational individuals trade through bilateral contracts on open markets until the costs of transactions mean that using corporations to produce things is more cost-effective. His second major article, "The Problem of Social Cost" (1960), argued that if we lived in a world without transaction costs, people would bargain with one another to create the same allocation of resources, regardless of the way a court might rule in property disputes.[146]

One of the most eminent institutional economists of recent time, Douglass North in his Nobel Prize lecture in 1993 described that neoclassical economics missing an analytical understanding of the way economies evolve through time.[147] He criticizes neoclassical economics as:

"Neo-classical theory is concerned with the operation of markets, not with how markets develop." He argues "In the analysis of economic performance through time it contained two erroneous assumptions: one that institutions do not matter and two that time does not matter."[147]

According to him neoclassical economics gave it mathematical precision and elegance modeled a 'frictionless' and 'static world' but ignored the incentive structure embodied in institutions that determined the extent of societal investment in those factors.[147]

Douglass North asserts that the analytical framework from institutional economics perspective is a modification of neo-classical theory. As he compares these two theories:

"What it retains is the fundamental assumption of scarcity and hence competition and the analytical tools of micro-economic theory. What it modifies is the rationality assumption. What it adds is the dimension of time."[147]

However, he asserts that institutional economics does not have a theory like general equilibrium. Rather it provides an analytical framework of Institutions as humanly devised constraints that structure human interaction. They are made up of formal constraints (rules, laws, constitutions), informal constraints (norms of behavior, conventions, and self imposed codes of conduct), and their enforcement characteristics. Using Ronald Coase's concept of transaction costs, he describes that the neo-classical result of efficient markets only obtains when it is costless to transact.[147] Wallis and North (1986) demonstrated in an empirical study that 45 percent of U.S. GNP was devoted to the transaction sector in 1970.[148] Efficient markets are created in the real world when competition is strong enough via arbitrage and efficient information feedback to approximate the Coase zero transaction cost conditions and the parties can realize the gains from trade inherent in the neo-classical argument.[148]

3.8 Neocolonialism

In the aftermath of the Second World War (1939–45) although the colonial powers had to release all or most of their colonies, they found another way to exercise their political and financial powers to other countries having natural or human resources and not limited to economic colonization but extended to social and cultural colonization. Kwame Nkrumah, president of Ghana (1960–66), coined the term "neo-colonialisms" in the book "Neo-Colonialism, the Last Stage of Imperialism" (1965).[149] As a political scientist, Nkrumah theoretically developed and extended, to the post–War 20th century, the socio-economic and political arguments presented by Lenin in the pamphlet "Imperialism, the Highest Stage of Capitalism" (1917), about 19th-century imperialism as the logical extension of geopolitical power to meet the financial investment needs of the political economy of capitalism.[150] In "Neo-Colonialism, the Last Stage of Imperialism", Kwame Nkrumah writes:

"In place of colonialism, as the main instrument of imperialism, we have today neo-colonialism....[which] like colonialism, is an attempt to export the social conflicts of the capitalist countries...

The result of neocolonialism is that foreign capital is used for the exploitation rather than for the development of the less developed parts of the world. Investment, under neo-colonialism, increases, rather than decreases, the gap between the rich and the poor countries of the world. The struggle against neo-colonialism is not aimed at excluding the capital of the developed world from operating in less developed countries. It is aimed at preventing the financial power of the developed countries being used in such a way as to impoverish the less developed."[149]

Now the question is why the neocolonial powers want the other countries impoverished? One reason can be explained by "Dependency Theory", which is the theoretic basis of economic neo-colonialism. It proposes that the global economic system comprises wealthy countries at the center, and poor countries at the periphery. Economic neo-colonialism extracts the human and the natural resources of a peripheral (poor) country to flow to the economies of the wealthy countries at the center of the global economic system. This means the poverty of the peripheral countries is the result of how they are integrated in the global economic system. Dependency theory derives from the Marxist analysis of economic inequalities within the world's system of economies, thus, the under-development of the Global South is a direct result of the development in the Global North; the theories of the semi-colony from the late 19th century.[151] The Marxist perspective of the "Theory of Colonial Dependency" is contrasted with the capitalist economics of the free market, which propose that such poverty is a development stage in the poor country's progress towards full, economic integration to the global economic system. Proponents of Dependency Theory, such as Venezuelan historian Federico Brito Figueroa, who has investigated the socio-economic bases of neo-colonial dependency, have influenced the thinking of the former President of Venezuela, Hugo Chávez.[152]

During the mid-to-late 20th century, in the course of the Cold War (1945–91) ideological conflict between the U.S. and the Soviet Union., each country and its satellite states accused each other of practicing neo-colonialism in their imperial and hegemonic pursuits.[153] The term "neocolonialism" is now used to describe the role of changing the world order. Dean Henderson argues that the international bankers have a different way of using Hegel's 'synthesis' theory. The states that subscribes to the geopolitical interests of the international bankers are in fact markets of the colonial powers ('thesis'). This causes anarchies, political unrests and civil war that accuse the colonial power sponsoring anti-democratic governments, whose regimes do not represent the interests of the majority of the populace ('antithesis').[154] At the end Henderson infers the 'synthesis' as

"The ensuing conflict, which manifest in the Cold War produced a huge market for arms and oil which their trusts manufactured."[154]

President Richard Nixon unilaterally ordered the cancellation of the direct convertibility of the USD to gold in 1971 mostly to facilitate unbridled oil import after reaching peak oil in 1970. On his State of the Union address on January 30, 1974 proclaimed "We will break the back of the energy crisis. We will lay the foundation for our energy capacity to meet America's energy needs from America's own sources"[155] when United States already reached its 'peak oil'. Nixon really solved the U.S. energy crisis but not discovering new oil and gas reserves but by inventing a new resource 'Petrodollar'. As discussed in Chapter 2 that the agreement Saudi Arabia signed with President Nixon's government in 1974 opened the channel that the Saudi Arabian Monetary Authority could privately transfer large amounts of their dollars in exchange for

U.S. government securities, all without disruptions to the public debt or equities markets.[156] Riley (2011) comments

> "This successful private negotiations between the U.S. and Saudi Kingdom ensured that one of the largest and most important commodity pools in the world, Saudi Arabian oil, was a commodity that could only be purchased by using another commodity that the U.S. solely controlled and could produce at will–the U.S. dollar."[156]

Afterwards the U.S. government was successfully able to convince the OPEC nations to direct their accumulated dollars into U.S. markets thereby recycling the Petrodollar.[157] This is how USA has founded a form of neo-colonization to meet its energy needs by exchanging dollars with oil and then exporting Treasury securities to recycle back the accumulated dollars to make up its trillion dollar deficit budget. Since USA can print dollar as per its wish, the value of dollar devaluates over time but because of Oil-Dollar market structure, Oil prices goes up. This Oil-Dollar relationship helped the Middle East countries achieve huge infrastructural development because of their prudent decision of keeping most of the shares of the oil with themselves. As an example, Saudi economy grew 52 times bigger from 1970 to 2005 and from 2005 to 2012 it grew more than double.[158] However, when the oil money will begin to deplete, Saudi government may demand liquidation of the U.S. Treasury securities it holds so will the other countries prompting the bond market to crash–the effect of neo-colonization will be visible.

After 1968, 'loans' from developed countries to the conflict ridden Third World countries has become another weapon of colonization. This mainly started when the former U.S. secretary of defense Robert McNamara took position as President of World Bank from 1968 to 1981.[159] McNamara shifted bank policy toward measures such as building schools and hospitals, improving literacy and agricultural reform. He created a new system of gathering information from potential borrower nations that enabled the bank to process loan applications much faster. To finance more loans, World Bank used the global bond market to increase the capital available to the bank outside of the northern banks that had been the primary sources of bank funding. One consequence of the period of poverty alleviation lending was the rapid rise of third world debt. From 1976 to 1980 developing world debt rose at an average annual rate of 20%.[159]

During the 1980s, World Bank emphasized lending to service Third-World debt, and structural adjustment policies designed to streamline the economies of developing nations. UNICEF reported in the late 1980s that the structural adjustment programs of the World Bank had been responsible for "reduced health, nutritional and educational levels for tens of millions of children in Asia, Latin America, and Africa"[160] however, dependency on debt increased. Even the United States Senate Committee on Foreign Relations report criticized the World Bank and other international financial institutions for focusing too much "on issuing loans rather than on achieving concrete development results within a finite period of time" and called on the institution to "strengthen anti-corruption efforts".[161] Making the Third World countries dependent on loans is a big reason for spreading corruptions, especially among bureaucrats in those countries. Once a country is corrupted, it is easier to recycle back multiple of the aid money, while the country still be paying the loan interests.

In 1999, the World Bank and the IMF introduced the Poverty Reduction Strategy Paper approach to replace structural adjustment loans. However, it has been interpreted as an extension of structural adjustment policies as it continues to reinforce and legitimize global inequities. Neither approach has addressed the inherent flaws within the global economy that contribute to economic and social inequities within developing countries.[162] By reinforcing the relationship between lending and client states, many believe that the World Bank has usurped indebted countries' power to impose their own economic agenda.[163]

In his book "Confessions of an Economic Hit Man" John Perkins, a former chief economist at a Boston based strategic consulting firm, claims that World Bank needlessly plunge poor nations like Indonesia and Panama into debt. In the preface he writes "Economic hit men (EHMs) are highly paid professionals who cheat countries around the globe out of trillions of dollars. They funnel money from the World Bank, the U.S. Agency for International Development (USAID), and other foreign "aid" organizations into the coffers of huge corporations and the pockets of a few wealthy families who control the planet's natural resources."[164] Perkins tells how he used purposefully over-optimistic economic projections to persuade foreign governments to accept billions of dollars in loans from the World Bank and other institutions in order to build dams, airports, electric grids, and other infrastructure that he knew they couldn't afford and didn't need. Construction and engineering contracts were routed to US companies, with bribes to top foreign officials smoothing the way. However, the resulting debts ultimately had to be shouldered of the people of the countries. When payments couldn't be made, the World Bank or International Monetary Fund would dictate the country's economic and political policies. Perkins contends that this all amounted to a clever way for the US to expand its global influence at the expense of citizens in poor.[164&165]

The effect of neo-colonization is brutally visible in African resource rich countries such as Nigeria, Angola, Congo or Ghana destitute, damaged and corrupted. As an example, after 50 years of petroleum production, Nigeria has become one of the most corrupted countries in the world, whereas most of Nigerians survive on less than a dollar a day. As David Quammen (2005) of National Geographic described "Hundreds of billions of dollars' worth of oil has poured out of Nigeria though little of that money has reached residents, Africa's rich deposits of diamonds, gold and oil have often proved a curse, fostering corruptions, coups and civil wars".[166] As of 2000, oil and gas exports accounted for more than 98% of export earnings and about 83% of federal government revenue, as well as generating more than 14% of its GDP. It also provides 95% of foreign exchange earnings, and about 65% of government budgetary revenues. The U.S. remains the largest importer of Nigeria's crude oil, accounting for 40% of the country's total oil exports. Nigeria provides about 10% of overall U.S. oil imports and ranks as the fifth-largest source for oil imports in the U.S. However, petroleum products are unavailable to most Nigerians and are quite costly, because almost all of the oil extracted by the multinational oil companies is refined overseas, while only a limited quantity is supplied to Nigerians themselves.[167]

During oil boom of the 1970s that the political economy of petroleum in Nigeria truly became characterized by endemic patronage and corruption by the political elites supported by the oil companies, which plagues the nation to this day. At both state and federal government levels, power and therefore wealth has typically been monopolized by select lobby groups who maintain a strong tendency to 'look after their own' by financially rewarding their political supporters. Nigeria had been saddled with a crushingly large international debt at this point. This was because, despite over 101 billion US dollars having been generated by the oil industry between 1958 and 1983,[168] nearly all of these funds had been siphoned into the private bank accounts and the state sponsored pet projects maintained by the succession of Nigerian governmental elites. The country's history following the oil discovery is full with military coups and political turmoil is viewed by some as having been orchestrated by international oil and banking interests. In 1985, when general Ibrahim Babangidathe took the power, International Monetary Fund was exerting increasingly acute pressure on the Nigerian government to repay its massive debts, of which 44% of all federal revenue was already servicing.[168] Therefore, it was not a surprise when he implemented the IMF's Structural Adjustment Program (SAP) in order to facilitate debt repayment. The SAP caused massive unemployment and reversing SAP caused high inflation and in turn the middle class of Nigeria almost annihilated. On the other hand, billions of dollars are siphoned off into private accounts or expenditures, "clandestinely undertaken while the country was openly reeling with a crushing external debt".[168] Undoubtedly, much of this money laundered to outside Nigeria. The oil rich Niger Delta is now facing a big ecological challenge– water is now poisoned, vegetation and agricultural land is damaged by oil spills. Large tracts of the mangrove forests have been destroyed. Nigeria is now the most corrupted country in the world. Most of Nigerian live in deepest poverty. About 20% of children die before the age of five.[169] And it is the second largest HIV/AIDS epidemic country in the world.[170]

The situation in Nigeria is just an example of corruptions, political turmoil and eventually resource drain of many developing countries that had or having resources either natural resources or reservoirs of cheap labor and raw materials. The modern capitalists businesses of the developed nations are continued through multinational corporations to exploit the natural resources of the former colony or developing countries. Critics of neo-colonialism also argue that investment by multinational corporations enriches few elites and middle class in underdeveloped countries, but causes humanitarian, environmental and ecological devastation to the populations which inhabit the neo-colonies whose "development" and economy is now dependent on foreign markets and large scale trade agreements.[152 & 171] As an example, Bangladesh, the world's second-leading apparel exporter after China, keep costs down by paying garment workers the lowest wages in the world about $38, a month (2013).[172] Although Bangladesh government is pressuring for minimum wage $68 per month, the factory owners say that to stay competitive they must keep wages from rising too high. They demand that the global brands to pay higher prices for the goods they order otherwise the proposed wage increase could bankrupt many factories, especially smaller ones.[172] It is hard for the global brand to buck the trend of cheap clothes or to change the comfort level of the western consumers.[173] In the same way, the owners of the garments industry are also not willing to sacrifice their comfort level.[172] On the other hand, much of the export money is fleeing offshore. In this way, the developed countries are getting a big margin of their money back except the little wage paid to the workers.

In summary, neocolonialism now works in many forms for the benefit of rich and influential countries over the poor developing countries. In reality, a few rich countries can exploit and control the natural and human resources of poor countries through neocolonialism. On the other hand, a few super rich people virtually control the world financial institutions, in turn the fate of the world economies through financial capitalism.

3.9 Financial Capitalism

The term "Financial Capitalism" was coined by Karl Marx who saw it as being exploitative by supplying income to non-laborers.[174] In Marxist perspective, finance capitalism is seen as a dialectical outgrowth of industrial capitalism, and part of the process by which the whole capitalist phase of history comes to an end.[175] It is characterized by a predominance of the pursuit of profit from the investment in currencies and financial products such as bonds, stocks, futures and other derivatives. Rudolf Hilferding (1910) studied of the links between German trusts, banks, and monopolies before World War I – a study subsumed by Lenin into his wartime analysis of the imperialist relations of the great world powers.[175&176] Lenin concluded of the banks at that time that they were "the chief nerve centers of the whole capitalist system of national economy".[177] With the rise of financial capitalism, profit becomes more derived from ownership of an asset, credit, rents, and earning interest, rather than actual productive processes.[70] The global shift toward financial capitalism has connected the global financial markets each other at the same time it has added more vulnerability to major financial crisis and recession.

The meaning of the term financial capitalism goes beyond the importance of financial intermediation. It also encompasses the significant influence of the wealth holders and bankers on the political process and the aims of economic policy. Looking back to history, the experience of the Great Depression changed attitudes of the policy makers regarding the regulation of financial markets. In 1933, the U.S. Congress fundamentally reformed banking with the Glass-Steagall Act. One provision of the act, named Regulation Q, placed limits on the interest rates banks could offer on deposits. Savings accounts were capped at 5.25 percent, and time deposits were limited to between 5.75 and 7.75 percent, depending on maturity.[178]

In the late 1970s, inflation became as high as 10 or 11 percent that caused market interest rates to rise above the limits mandated by Regulation Q. Investors began to seek out and find alternatives to traditional deposit accounts. In the commercial paper market, investors could lend directly to borrowers, bypassing banks as intermediaries and operated without reserve requirements or restrictions on rates of return. Brokerage firms and other financial institutions began to create money market mutual funds, which pooled small investors' funds to purchase commercial paper. They quickly became popular among small investors who shifted their money out of the regulated accounts in depositary institutions. Then in 1980 President Carter signed into law the Depository Institutions Deregulation and Monetary Control Act (DIDMCA) with the aim of allowing banks and savings and loans to compete with money market mutual funds. The legislation established a committee to oversee the complete phase-out of interest rate ceilings within six years.[178]

Financial deregulation in the U.S. and many Western countries was aimed to allow more competition and lower borrowing costs for consumers and firms. London had been a global center of finance but it had been surpassed by New York and was in danger of falling still further behind. Margaret Thatcher's government claimed that the two problems behind the decline of London banking was overregulation and the dominance of "elitist old boy networks".[179] The once-dominant financial institutions of the City of London were failing to compete with foreign banking. On 27 October, 1986, a sudden big financial deregulation called "Big Bang" fundamentally changed the structure of the financial markets in London. The changes saw many of the old firms being taken over by large banks both foreign and domestic.[179]

Following the "Big Bang" in U.K., in December of 1986, for the first time, the U.S. Federal Reserve reinterpreted the Glass-Steagall restrictions and ruled that a bank could derive up to 5 percent of gross revenues in investment banking business. Matthew Sherman describes:

> "This seemed to conflict with the letter of the law, but the Fed argued that since Glass-Steagall did not precisely define the meaning of "engaged principally," the regulation was open to reinterpretation."[178]

Susan Strange describes the 21st century predominance of finance capital has led to a preference for speculation "Casino Capitalism"[180] that results in bank failures, financial fraud, political corruption, money laundering, and general volatility in world financial markets.[180 & 181]

In August 1987, Alan Greenspan, a student of Ayn Rand's "objectivist" thinking and an outspoken advocate of deregulation was appointed as Chairman of the Federal Reserve.[178] He served five terms, stretching three decades and four Presidencies, becoming the second-longest serving Fed Chairman in history.[178] Early in his tenure, the Federal Reserve reinterpreted Glass-Steagall to allow banks to deal in certain debt and equity securities, so long as it did not exceed the 10 percent limit rule. Later, in 1996, the Federal Reserve issued an audacious ruling, allowing bank holding companies to own investment banking operations that accounted for as much as 25 percent of their revenues. The decision rendered Glass-Steagall effectively obsolete, since virtually any institution would be able to stay within the 25 percent level.[178 & 182]

Officially in 1999 Glass-Steagall Act was repealed by the U.S. congress by passing Financial Modernization Act. A year before the law was passed, Citicorp, a commercial bank holding company, merged with the insurance company Travelers Group in 1998 to form the conglomerate Citigroup. This merger violation of the Glass–Steagall Act and the Bank Holding Company Act of 1956, the Federal Reserve gave Citigroup a temporary waiver in September 1998.[182] Less than a year later, the Act was passed to legalize these types of mergers on a permanent basis. Sherman writes:[178]

> "The crumbling walls of Glass-Steagall received a final blow in 1999 when Congress passed the Financial Modernization Act, also known as the Gramm-Leach-Bliley Act. The act repealed all restrictions against the combination of banking, securities and insurance operations for financial institutions. The deregulation was a boon for national commercial banks, allowing for the formation of "mega-banks." The Gramm-Leach-Bliley Act was the crowning achievement of decades and millions of dollars worth of lobbying efforts on behalf of the finance industry. The repeal of Glass-Steagall was a monumental piece of deregulation, but in many ways it ratified the status quo of the time."[178&184]

Many argue that consolidation in banking was an inevitable evolution and championed it as financial "modernization," but the changes posed challenges for market regulators to keep pace with the innovations in financial markets.[178] The widespread use of computers and information technology facilitated the financial innovations and rapid growth of new types of derivative instruments that posed problems for regulators. Wallace C. Turbeville writes in Demos:

> "The 35-year experiment in deregulation of the financial markets created an environment in which innovative instruments and structures could be rapidly distributed around the world by their inventors (primarily, the largest banks) with little or no consideration of consequences, aside from potential profits. Information technology and the use of advanced valuation algorithms and

statistics enabled the banking industry to create and market hundreds of financial products, many of which are so complicated that understanding them challenges even the most sophisticated market participants."[185]

Derivatives are one of the three main categories of financial instruments, the other two being equities (i.e. stocks) and debt (i.e. bonds and mortgages). Derivatives are financial instruments that derive their value on their claim to another asset, such as an option to purchase wheat or a futures contract on oil.[178] They can be used to hedge against risk, protecting against a decline in value of the underlying asset. Alternatively, they can be used for simple speculation, to profit off an expected change in value. Derivatives do not involve the actual transfer of assets, so a buyer often does not own the underlying asset. There are two groups of derivative contracts: the privately traded over-the-counter (OTC) derivatives such as swaps that do not go through an exchange or other intermediary, and exchange-traded derivatives (ETD) that are traded through specialized derivatives exchanges or other exchanges. OTC derivatives are not traded on an exchange but directly between two parties without going through an exchange or other intermediary. Therefore, they are subject to counterparty risk, like an ordinary contract, since each counter-party relies on the other to perform. Now OTC derivative market is the largest market for derivatives, and is largely unregulated with respect to disclosure of information between the parties, since the OTC market is made up of banks and other highly sophisticated parties, such as hedge funds. Reporting of OTC amounts is difficult because trades can occur in private, without activity being visible on any exchange.

According to Matthew Sherman in the late 1990s, Brooksley Born, the chairwoman of the Commodity Futures Trading Commission (CFTC), raised concerns about the potential risks of the unregulated market in many derivative instruments. Her opposition left her politically isolated, and she left the CFTC in mid-1999. Later that year, Greenspan and the U.S. Treasury Secretary Robert Rubin issued a report along with Born's successor at CFTC that recommended no regulation on derivatives.[186] Afterwards the U.S. congress passed Commodity Futures Modernization Act of 2000, just the day after the Supreme Court effectively decided the fate of the 2000 Presidential election, attached as a rider to an 11,000-page spending bill. The legislation, passed without debate or review, exempted derivatives from regulation and made a special exemption for energy derivative trading that would gain notoriety as the "Enron loophole."[187]

In U.K., Nigel Lawson, Thatcher's Chancellor of the Exchequer during 2007-2012 global financial crisis, appeared on the Analysis program to discuss banking reform, explaining that the financial crisis was an unintended consequence of the "Big Bang".[188] In 2011, Speaking at the Institute for "New Economic Thinking's" annual conference in Bretton Woods New Hampshire, Chancellor of the Exchequer from 1997-2007 and also ex-British Prime Minister Gordon Brown, reviewed his changes:

"We know in retrospect what we missed. We set up the Financial Services Authority (FSA) believing that the problem would come from the failure of an individual institution," he said. "So we created a monitoring system which was looking at individual institutions. That was the big mistake. We didn't understand how risk was spread across the system, we didn't understand the entanglements of different institutions with the other and we didn't understand even though we talked about it just how global things were, including a shadow banking system as well as a banking system. That was our mistake, but I'm afraid it was a mistake made by just about everybody who was in the regulatory business."[189]

In a completely unregulated market, derivatives trading expanded quickly, increasing from a total outstanding nominal value of $106 trillion in 2001, to a value of $531 trillion in 2008.[190] According to the Bank for International Settlements (BIS), Over the Counter (OTC) derivatives market was $516 trillion at the end of June 2007 (Figure 3.9).[191] As of June 2007, the total outstanding notional amount is US$708 trillion.[192] Of this total notional amount, 67% are interest rate contracts, 8% are credit default swaps (CDS), 9% are foreign exchange contracts, 2% are commodity contracts, 1% are equity contracts, and 12% are other.[193&194] CDS are effectively a form of bond insurance, where the issuer would pay the loss in the event that a bond defaulted.[177] Another type of derivative is called Exchange-traded derivatives (ETD) are those derivatives instruments that are traded via specialized derivatives exchanges or other exchanges. According to Bank for International Settlements (BIS), the combined turnover in the world's derivatives exchanges totaled USD $681 trillion by December 2007.[194] In 2010, while the aggregate of OTC derivatives exceeded $600 trillion, however, the value of the market was estimated much lower, at $21

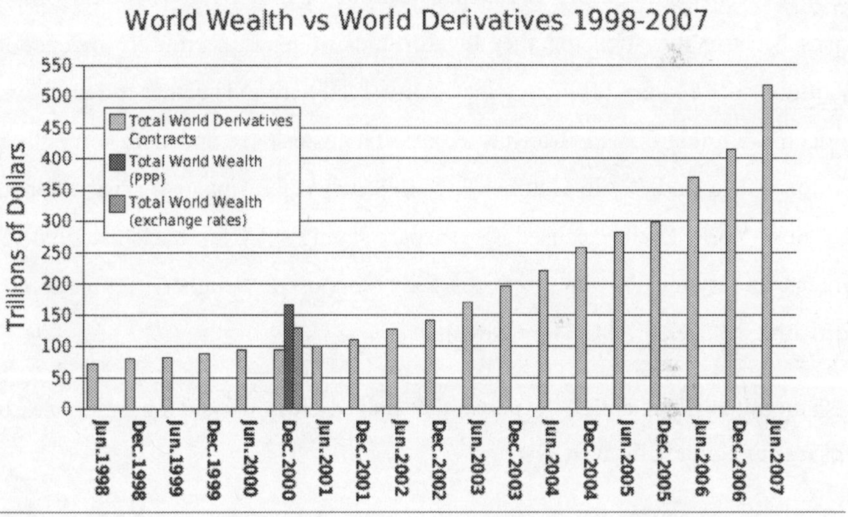

World Wealth vs World Derivatives 1998-2007

Figure 3.9: Total world wealth vs. total value in derivatives contracts, 1998-2007 (compared to total world wealth in the year 2000)[191]

trillion.[195] In 2007 the global GDP was around USD $54.35 trillion (in 2013 around US$75.59 trillion) which was chasing over USD $700 trillion OTC derivatives in nominal value.[196] Gabriel O'Hara comments:

"The highly volatile derivatives market is worth noting in true economic sense of economic production because it dwarfs the entire world's GDP and total financial assets combined."[197]

In March 2003, Warren Buffet, the investment magnet and one of the top richest man in the world argued that such highly complex financial instruments are time bombs and "financial weapons of mass destruction" that could harm not only their buyers and sellers, but the whole economic system."[198]

Although Warren Buffet warned us about derivatives, the New York Times reports on May 9, 2003 that the longtime U.S. Federal Reserve chairman Alan Greenspan praised derivatives, saying "their benefits materially outweighed the risks and had insulated the financial system from the stock market crash and economic downturn."[199] However, during onset of the 2008 financial crisis New York Times reports: "Mr. Greenspan warned that derivatives could amplify crises because they tied together the fortunes of many seemingly independent institutions. 'The very efficiency that is involved here means that if a crisis were to occur, that that crisis is transmitted at a far faster pace and with some greater virulence,' he said."[200] In October 23, 2008, when the financial crisis happened the New York Times accused Greenspan saying "As far back as 1994, Mr. Greenspan staunchly and successfully opposed tougher regulation on derivatives".[201] Gabriel O'Hara laments

"Quite often the qualified "experts" that helped crash a system are the ones in charge of building the next system."[197]

3.10 The Other Contemporary Economic Thoughts

Information Economics is another branch of microeconomic theory that studies how information affects an economy and economic decisions. Much of the literature in information economics was originally inspired by Friedrich Hayek's "The Use of Knowledge in Society" on the uses of the price mechanism in allowing information decentralization to order the effective use of resources.[202] Joseph Stiglitz argues that information economics is not just about the cost of acquiring information could be viewed as fixed costs. He shared the Nobel

Memorial Prize in Economics in 2001 "for laying the foundations for the theory of markets with asymmetric information" with George A. Akerlof and A. Michael Spence. As Stiglitz describes Information Economics as:

> "while early work in the economics of information dealt with how markets overcame problems of information asymmetries, and information imperfections more generally, later worked turned to how markets create information problems, partly in an attempt to exploit market power."[203]

A brand new theoretical framework called 'Biased Equilibrium" based on "Information Economics" is explained on the next chapter.

In recent times, due to the effects of global warming and fossil fuel depletion, another paradigm of economics is promoted by progressive societies called 'Green Economics'. It positions economics within a very long-term, earth-wide, holistic context of reality as a part of nature. Its philosophy is to manage economics for nature as usual, rather than to manage the environment for business as usual.[82] Green Economics calls for a 'no growth' steady state economy that is completely opposite to mainstream economics. The institutional economists argue that the development of green power has only taken place when it was required by state law.[9] Although there are few governments who realize the urgency of green policies, the measures so far have been taken by them are too little.

CHAPTER 4

NEW CONCEPT "BIASED EQUILIBRIUM"[*]

4.1 Introduction

The mainstream economic theories ignore information concerns as that might alter their comfortable conclusion about efficiency of markets.[1] The other stream of thoughts is known as "heterodox economics" such as institutional economics and information economics that throws away the entire mainstream and starts all over new paradigms.[2] This chapter introduces a new concept 'Biased Equilibrium'[3] based on information economics and consolidates much of the strength of the two theoretical streams aiming to find out solutions of our economic and ecological challenges as discussed in the rest of this book.

The concept "Biased Equilibrium" fundamentally defines how our society is structured and most importantly, its wealth accumulation process. It tells that the probability of achieving Pareto efficiency for a subset of the population is much higher than that for the whole population and our markets are distributed in layers of energy states. The history of capitalist synthesis is nothing but streamlining the process of wealth accumulation toward an ultimate biasing source. A market dynamics contributes distributive growth that tends to bring market equilibrium. In reality, imbalanced money and market dynamics create growth and debt pressure on the economy, essentially burning more energy from fossil fuel, while adding vulnerability to financial and ecological crisis.

[*] Much of the contents of this chapter is reproduced from the author's article "**A Consolidated Economic Model Based on a New Concept of Biased Equilibrium**", International. Journal of Green Economics, Vol. 6, No. 1, 2012, pp.55-72 upon permission from Inderscience Enterprises Ltd.

4.2 The Concept of Biased Equilibrium

The starting point of economic analysis is the observation that information has economic value because it allows individuals to make choices that yield higher expected payoffs or expected utility than they would obtain from choices made in absence of information.[4] In this new model, the fundamental assumption is that information is no longer a given parameter but a strategic tool that individual economic agent uses with others in his or her economic or social matters.[4] Although the path of capitalists synthesis is marked with many adjustments of disequilibrium of wars and revolutions, at very molecular level there exists equilibrium between information sharing strategies of individual economic agents and their payoff functions. Any economic achievement and challenge are fundamentally rooted in this information sharing equilibrium.

There could be two types of scenarios of information sharing strategies be used to analyze an equilibrium. One is perfect information sharing strategy and the other is imperfect or asymmetric information sharing strategy. The concept of perfect information between two individuals X and Y is explained in Figure 4.1 in a simple Game Theory model.[3] Let f is the payoff profiles of respective

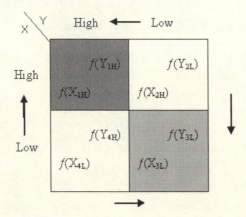

Figure 4.1: equilibrium in case of equal sharing of information

strategies. If X takes 'High' strategy to share information with Y and on the other hand, Y takes conservative ('Low') strategy, then the corresponding payoffs of X and Y will be $f(X_H)$ and $f(Y_L)$ respectively. If we assume that both of them have perfect information about the all possibilities of the game, then one will expect that that his opponent will follow the same strategy and the game will produce a win-win outcome. The outcome of this game is two Nash Equilibriums (Nash, 1951)[6] where they choose the same combinations of strategies either (high, high) or (low, low) and no unilateral deviation in strategy is profitable. In this situation, theoretically the payoffs are the same for X and Y like either $f(X_H) = f(Y_H)$ or $f(X_L) = f(Y_L)$.

We may apply this outcome to our real world, where X is an employer and Y represents a worker. If the employer and the worker share information equally with each other, the worker will have to be paid equal to his marginal contribution for whatever output he or she produces. However, the marginal contribution is calculated in the other way around. The amount the employers pay the worker, we consider that equals to his marginal contribution for simplification our math. At this point, if we consider that everyone wants to maximize his or her payoffs, then this game will reach to equilibrium at (high, high) or $(f(X_{1H}), f(Y_{1H}))$. In this way we cannot explain how the capitalists are created in the world or how they have gathered their capitals from their once zero ownership (technology is not considered). Similarly the "perfect information" concept fails to explain the empirical behaviors of an economy as a whole. In our real world, although individuals share information in any combinations, the outcome of information sharing can be either 'win-win' or 'win-lose'. In case of win-win outcome for a group of individuals among many individuals in an economic game, we may abstract them as a 'virtual coalition' relative to the others (Zaman, 2009).[5] The individuals in the coalition are assumed to share the same level of information with their peers and hold the same level of rationality or preferences.

The term information asymmetry used in micro-economics that explains a situation of a transaction where one party has superior information compared to another. At micro level, informational asymmetries impair labor mobility; partially lock an employee into his employer, or a borrower into his creditor. If the job market creates asymmetric information, then it may be locally efficient for an employee to be stick with his employer otherwise he would be less paid or unemployed (which may be zero, if there is unemployment).[7] If the information sharing is imperfect, one will try to dominate over the other. This happens when two or more individuals actively or passively form a 'virtual coalition' relative to the other and try to dominate.

In our previous example, it can be considered that X and Y constitute a virtual coalition A1 to achieve higher payoff than any other individual outside their coalition as shown in Figure 4.2 below. If there is another individual Z (pay-off function f (Z)) who is in outside the virtual coalition A1, there will be two

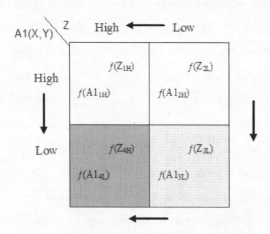

Figure 4.2: Biased Equilibrium[8]

possibilities for him. He may either merge with A1 or he may compete with X and Y. The possibility of merging depends on whether the win-win characteristic of coalition A1 will be undistorted after the merging or not. Therefore, merging decision largely depends on coalition A1 and requires equal sharing of information that eventually leads to an efficient equilibrium. In the other case, as a member of a virtual coalition, X and Y may share information with Z in a way whatever strategy Z takes (high or low) X or Y receives higher payoff than that of Z. That is $f(X_{4L})$ or $f(Y_{4L}) > f(Z_{4H})$ and $f(X_{3L})$ or $f(Y_{3L}) > f(Z_{3L})$. If the payoff of Z is locally efficient, as $f(Z_{4H})$ is always greater than $f(Z_{3L})$, this game will reach equilibrium at A1= 'Low' and Z= 'High' position where ($f(X_{4L})$ or $f(Y_{4L}) > f(Z_{4H})$). We may call this situation as **"Biased Equilibrium (BE)"**[5].

Let us further assume X, Y and Z have started with equal amount of property rights or capital. They would therefore have an equal amount of payoff, say 'M' in case of efficient equilibrium. However, in this particular case here, Z receives less payoff than that he would receive in case of efficient equilibrium and the difference goes to A1 that is to be distributed between X and Y. That is, $f(Z_H) <$ M and $f(X_L)$ or $f(Y_L) > M$. The difference M-$f(Z_H)$ goes to the coalition A1, which is to be distributed between X and Y. This difference of payoff value can be called as Money (M) or Kinetic Money (KM).

In this game model, Z represents one of the many individuals who have to compete with a virtual coalition for their economic needs. Ideally, X and Y do not allow many individuals to share their gains but will continue to play the game with more and more individuals on the other side. Here the concept of Biased Equilibrium introduces directional property with every unit of money created in an economy, while traditional economic concepts talks about only quantitative aspect of money (or growth). This is how capitalism works and resources are agglomerated in the hand of few people.

Thus, this concept of "Biased Equilibrium" can be used as a fundamental building block of the 'capitalist synthesis' (see Chapter 2). Under Biased Equilibrium, by applying Hegel's 'synthesis' at this molecular (individual) level, we may compare the "low" sharing of information as "thesis".[8] The opposite of this—the "high" sharing of information as "anti-thesis", then the synthesis is the reinforcement of "Biased Equilibrium", whose outcome is the more differential payoff $(M\text{-}f(Z_H))$ accumulated by coalition A1(X, Y).

The term capitalism, in its modern sense, is often attributed to Karl Marx.[9] As Marx (1859) explains, in work-wage bargains derives from the fact that employers pay their workers less in "exchange value" than the workers produce in "use value". The difference makes up the capitalist's profit, or in Marx's terminology, "surplus value". "Therefore" says Marx, "capitalism is a system of exploitation".[10] Although we described in section 2.7 ("Age of Synergy") that at the same time, capitalism is also a system of progress.

The above example has similarity with the example of 'sharecropping described as principal-agent problem' by Greenwald and Stiglitz (1974, 1986).[11] They showed sharecropping was locally efficient equilibrium and quite different from the general equilibrium model although the workers had to surrender 50% or more of their income to landlords. Stiglitz (2002) argued "it was equivalent to a 50% tax on workers' labor."[1] However, in Principal-Agent problem, the agents and the principals complement each other. The agents are given incentives and they are motivated to comply with the principals' objectives. On the other hand, in this model of biased equilibrium, every individual is substitute to each other to achieve the same set of objectives. As per definition, "Principal Agent Problem" is institutional. On the other hand, the concept of Biased Equilibrium is the fundamental concept of formation of institutions.

The above example also shows that the problem of information asymmetry has evolved from the time dimension that economists often ignore. We have assumed that X and Y have superior information compared to that of Z since Z appears late to play the game. The individuals who are already positioned in a virtual coalition are also probabilistically apart from each other in time and context perspective. If Z had appeared earlier than Y, then Z would have taken the position of Y and vice versa. It is hard to break an existing coalition since it consolidates more as the game continues. This is why the initial capitalists Rothschild and J.P. Morgan banking houses still dominate the financial world. This also explains why most of the European central banks or the U.S. Federal Reserve is owned by private coalitions.

The definition of 'biased equilibrium' is not only limited to 'better off (or worse off)' in monetary values rather broadened to 'better off' in human values. It is up to an analyst to decide whether to choose narrow view or broad view of this concept based on the real life economic problem he or she analyzes. Although all major religions promote humanitarian values such equal rights of people but in reality, they are reduced to rituals by the biasing forces. The biasing forces are in fact, established through information biasing, which we call institutions.

This concept incorporates Amartya Sen's (Sen, 1999) 'capability approach' of poverty and inequality and explains why poor people suffer from "capability deprivation", which tells that when a person's capabilities are lowered, they are in some way deprived of earning as much income or enjoying as much freedom as they would do otherwise.[12] The concept of 'biased equilibrium' can be applied to the cases of any number of individuals even for the population of a country or for the population of the whole world, especially wherever information sharing strategies of less number of individuals shapes and limits actions, as well as opportunities and behavior of many individuals.

4.3 Pareto Coalition

Following the second industrial revolution, the "Age of Synergy" (See Section 2.7) in the 20th century created an opportunity to 'better off the poor people through employment without worse off the riches'-the term called Pareto improvement, introduced by Vilfredo Pareto (1848 – 1923).[13] The ultimate goal of Pareto improvement is Pareto efficiency, the concept applied in Fundamental Theorems of Welfare Economics formalized by Arrow (1964)1 and Debreu (1959).[14] The theorem contains some restrictive assumptions such as complete set of markets, no enforcement problems and perfect competition. This is now the prevailing paradigm of neoclassical economics on which the economists can be divided into two groups. One group of the economists circles around the restrictive assumptions of the welfare theorems. The other group is skeptical about the neoclassical approach for its normative bias and unrealistic set of assumptions. The first group may be called as the optimists and the second group as the pessimists (Zaman 2009).[5] The optimists find a way of workaround the assumptions as they are induced by Adam Smith's 'invisible hand' proposition.[15] On the other hand, the pessimistic assumptions negate the optimistic assumptions arguing that markets are incomplete and/or information is imperfect, which are true in virtually all economies. Accordingly, among pessimist economists, we find such eminent figures as Joseph Stiglitz, Ronald Coase and Douglass North, all of whom have won Nobel Prizes for their contributions to economic theory.

The Fundamental Welfare Theorem contains a number of implicit assumptions, the most important being that there is no imperfect and asymmetric information. Wittman (an optimist) argues "And if asymmetric information exists, the theorem only holds under very stringent assumptions."[16] On the other hand, Stiglitz argues that the perfect information assumption was so ingrained in neoclassical economics it did not have to be explicitly stated.[1] I would like to take position between the pessimists and the optimists. Stiglitz won Nobel Prize for his contribution in Information Economic in 2001. Information economics provides a larger perspective of analysis of the economic problems than that of neoclassical economics. As an example, recessions and depressions, accompanied by massive unemployment were explained in neoclassical economics as symptomatic of massive market failures (Stiglitz, 2002)[1]. Stiglitz argues "massive unemployment was just the tip of the iceberg". He explains "If markets seemed to function so badly some of the time, certainly they must be malperforming in more subtle ways much of the time."[1] In reality, we see that the more global market is liberalized by means of free trade or open market, the chances of recessions or unemployment are spread but more money is concentrated in hands of fewer people.

The first welfare theorem states that 'under certain conditions any competitive equilibrium is Pareto efficient'. This was first demonstrated graphically by economist Abba Lerner and mathematically by economists Harold Hotelling, Oskar Lange, Maurice Allais, Kenneth Arrow and Gerard Debreu.[17] The important assumptions include here complete market and price-taking behavior of market. In a pure exchange economy, a sufficient condition for the first welfare theorem to hold is that preferences be locally non-satiated. In particular, no convexity assumptions are needed. Unfortunately, our real world does not meet the any of the stringent assumptions. According to Wittman:

"Now there is a fallback position. Instead of unrealistically comparing the outcome to a world of perfect information, one can construct models where the outcome of competition is on average best given asymmetric information. So we still have something that approximates the results rely on a whole host of assumptions. For example, there may be many (possibly a continuum of) competitive equilibrium, with one being efficient. We do not have a general welfare theorem, but rather a particular model where an efficient competitive outcome may arise."[16]

The first theorem is considered as analytical confirmation of Adam Smith's invisible hand hypothesis.[18] Feldman pointed out "the first theorem ignored the basic distributional questions: how should unfair distributions of goods be made fair?"[19] The underlying price assumption of the welfare theorems persuades the neoclassical economists to become much concerned about the efficiency properties of market. In other words, the first welfare theorem states that any

Pareto allocation depends on the initial allocation of resources and the preferences possessed by economic agents. Poverty in this theory is explained by the existence of inequality in initial allocation of resources. This theory provides a benchmark framework to identify the effects of introducing the imperfections that we observe in the real world on welfare and economic efficiency. However, it does not explain how the inequality of initial allocation of resources is created in an economy. Here the concept of biased equilibrium may address this gap as it conceptualizes agglomeration of resources out of a molecular equilibrium between two or more individual economic agents in terms of their preferred payoff functions and information sharing strategies.

As an example, suppose that there are two goods in the economy: A and B, which have the same value in monetary terms ($1). Now consider a rich person, say **P** has 200 units of good A and 100 units of good B (i.e. his wealth is $300), that is **P**(200, 100). In contrast, a poor person, say **Q** who has 10 units of good A and 20 units of good B (i.e. his wealth is $30), that is **Q**(10, 20). The first welfare theorem says that both individuals can be better off by exchanging these units in a beneficial way that is consistent with their self-interest preferences. In the example, if **Q** prefers having 20 units of good A and 10 units of good B, and P prefers 100 units of good A and 200 units of good B, then they both can be better off by interchanging their initial allocation of goods. A better allocation would be **Q**(20, 10) and **P**(190, 110). In this example, **P** still has a wealth of $300 and Q has a wealth of $30, but they are better off because both have a more desirable allocation of good after the exchange. A further re-allocation from this point to better off **P** will worse off **Q**. This means this economy is Pareto efficient at this point until the preference functions or their wealth allocation remains unchanged. The concept of using information as strategic tool explains why the preference functions of **P** and **Q** are essentially different. If **P** and **Q** had the same level of information, then **Q**'s preference function would become the same as **P**'s. The concept of biased equilibrium explains that then they would be treated as a potential coalition or a virtual coalition by assuming there are more other players involved.

Now let me little modify the preference functions of the above example. **P**'s strict preference is at least 200 units of good B but he is flexible between 200-100 units of good A. Similarly, **Q**'s strict preference is 20 units of good A but (20-10) units of good B. If another person **R** is introduced in this economy whose preference function is the same as that of **P**, then no more Pareto improvement will be possible between them. However, this will impact their strategy of information sharing with **Q** since **R** and **P** likely to form a potential coalition. Say, **R** has 100 units of good A and 50 units of good B, that is **R**(100, 50) however he prefers to have 100 units of good B and (100–50) units of good A. If there are 15 people like **Q**, then **P** and **R** will create a biased equilibrium with all **Q**s to fulfill their optimum preferences. A better allocation of **P** will be **P**(190, 200), gain \$90 and **R** will be **R**(95, 100), gain \$45 but will cost each **Q** lose \$9 to achieve their preferred allocations **Q**(11, 10). This explains how the rich people have more resources than the poor people, that is, it explains accumulation perspective of capital. In this example, although **P** and **R** have reached their preferred allocations but **Q**s are yet to reach to their preferred levels. Here **P** and **R** hold the control of any further equilibrium when the technology or the environment that influence the preference functions changes.

Following the first theorem, while every equilibrium is efficient, it is clearly not true that every efficient allocation of resources will be an equilibrium.[20] The second fundamental welfare theorem says that every Pareto-optimal allocation can be sustainable by a competitive equilibrium after a suitable redistribution of initial endowments of the agents after which the market can be left alone to do its work'.[20] The conditions for the second theorem are stronger than those for the first, as consumers' preferences now need to be convex. Although in reality, the convexity assumption of the fundamental welfare theorems which corresponds to long standing principles of diminishing rates of marginal substitution is not valid for wealth accumulation[20], the fundamental preference of every capitalist. In the above example, if **P** and **R** follow non-convex preference functions, the above game will be able to accommodate more and more poor people at their equilibrium level **Q**(11, 10). The second theorem says that every efficient allocation can be supported by some set of prices.[20] It also says that instead of focusing lots of externalities and factors, only limited government intervention by means of redistributive policies can restore market failure and uphold market power. This suggests that the issues of efficiency and equity can be separated and need not involve a trade-off although in real life we cannot.[20] It ignores the history of market formation and institutional involvement where 'invisible hand' was crippled (Stiglitz, 1991).[21] The fundamental theorems allow reforms that increase efficiency, regardless of their impact on distribution. If society does not like the distributional consequences, it should simply redistribute income although in reality, redistributions seemingly developed resistance and does not work. For example, we see few wealthy individuals have got control of the market and they also influence the government to protect and uphold their interest, which is the toughest challenge of our capitalist world.

Yew-Kwang Ng (1984) defined the term 'quasi-Pareto improvement', 'in which for all levels of income, the average households were made better off but the average households at any given level of income might be worse off'.[22] This proposed model here assumes the 'quasi-Pareto improvement' exists in every economic activity in various extents. It can explain the controversy of the first fundamental welfare theorem that why our resources are agglomerated somewhere while market has become more liberalized and more competitive. This has happened when our economy has become energy driven after industrial revolution. As explained in previous chapter that the production structure of industrial economy is controlled by a virtual coalition of 'capitalists'.[10] After discovery of huge oil fields in the early twentieth centuries, the more the economy is liberalized, the more output it produces using cheap energy, the more 'surplus value' for the capitalists. According to Heinberg "Energy is what moves the economy; money is just a means of keeping track of wealth."[85]

Here the concept of biased equilibrium tells that a virtual coalition is locally Pareto efficient since no one in the coalition can be made better off without making someone else worse off; everyone should be better off at the same time. In economic literatures, the concept of coalition only involves active individuals who cooperate each other to achieve a common goal. At micro-level, the origin of the virtual coalition is described in section 4.2 that essentially involves active people only who wants to better off themselves without caring the others are worse off or not. Following the path of 'capitalist synthesis' described in Chapter 2, particularly with the "surplus value" created after industrial revolution and availability of cheap energy, the equilibrium may have been extended and sustained by establishing institutions at the macro level and involved passive individuals who have rational interest to better off themselves but no deliberate intention to worse off the others. Thus instead of looking for possibilities of a continuum of equilibrium[16], the concept of biased equilibrium tells that the probability of achieving Pareto efficiency is high for a subset of population instead of the whole population. In a Pareto inefficient economy, from the discussion of section 4.2 it can be said that this subset establishes a 'biased equilibrium' with the remaining population. The first part can be called as **Pareto Coalition (PC)** and the second part can be called as **Pareto Space (PS)**.[3] This means the concept Pareto Coalition and Pareto Space have relative existence in presence of a biased equilibrium.

The term **Pareto Coalition (PC)** can be defined as the subset of population of an economy among whom no further individual Pareto improvement is possible but their collective presence biases the economy to better off themselves while worse off the others. And the remaining population can be defined as a **Pareto Space** for whom individual Pareto improvement is possible.[3] This does not mean competition is absent within a PC but we may assume that the competition or rivalry always produces a discretionary win-win outcome for them. As an example, breaking up Standard Oil into 33 smaller oil companies in the United States promoted competition among them, while they together acted like a virtual coalition relative to the whole economy so that they produced win-win outcomes for their individual shareholders. In case, if there is a win-lose outcome, we may break the coalition into further discretionary PC and PS until there is an ultimate unbreakable 'core' Pareto Coalition, which produces win-win outcome for its members (see Chapter 8). Contrarily competition in a Pareto Space (PS) ultimately produce lose-lose outcome for the individuals in the PS since under biased equilibrium it reduces their incomes, in turn, cause more gains for corresponding Pareto Coalition. This tells that probability of achieving Pareto efficiency is high toward the core and vice versa.

The individuals of a PC are actively involved in creating, running and controlling the institutions while the individuals of a PS have mostly passive involvement. Therefore, in real life, the institutional structure establishes and protects 'claims' of a PC over a PS. As an example, regarding the May 4, 1886 labor demonstration event at Haymarket Square in Chicago, the government, the mainstream newspapers, the police and even the judges supported business interests but did not support the labors' demand of eight hour a day working hours. Although it was not stated that the businesses, the government body or the media formed a coalition but they acted like a virtual coalition. In a capitalist economy, likelihood of manufacturing workers is to be in a PS even during full employment and oppositely, the likelihood of financial workers is to be in a PC.

In most of the ancient agrarian societies, peasants were the only productive class but lived a mere subsistence life. As an example when China was the richest country in the world, Chinese peasants were living in poverty. Chinese agrarian society in early nineteenth century had three classes, the peasants, the gentry and the imperial class. Quigley describes

"In China, at the bottom the peasantry, which was the only really productive group in the society, derived its incomes from the sweat of collective brows, and had to survive on what was left to it after a substantial fraction of its product had gone to the two higher groups in the form of rents, taxes, interest, customary bribes (called "squeeze"), and excessive profits on such purchased "necessities" of life as salt, iron, or opium."[23]

He further explains this:

"This society was based on an inefficient agricultural system in which the political, military, legal and economic claims of the upper classes drained from the peasantry such a large proportion of their agricultural produce that the peasants were kept pressed down to the subsistence level."[23]

The other members of the society such as the rulers, soldiers, bureaucrats, traders, priests, and scholars none of whom produced the food, clothing, or shelter they were consuming.[23] Figure 4.3 shows the old Chinese economic

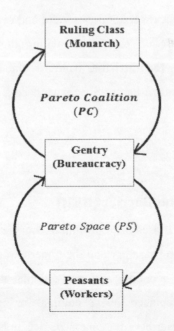

Figure 4.3: Pre-industrial Chinese Economic Structure

structure, where gentry and the imperial classes together can be considered as Pareto Coalition (PC) and the peasants could be considered as Pareto Space (PS). In fact, the similar economic structure could be found in all feudal societies, monarchy, and industrial societies. As an example, in late Roman Empire and middle-age Europe, the ruling class can be represented by monarchs and the churches, the gentry can be represented by the elites and businessmen and the peasants were the common working people, who actually were the productive class. As described by Quigley, the ruling class and gentry (here, the PC) used to collect tax and interest in such a high rate that the peasants had to live at subsistence level. This means the PC creates a compulsion for the PS to keep on producing and generate money for the PC.

By following Ng (1984), it can be derived from this model that in a 'quasi-Pareto improvement' economic action, the segment of population that is made better off is a PC, while the others who are worse off can be positioned in a PS. The Pareto Coalition (PC) is an analytical abstraction where the concept of methodological individualism of neoclassical economics is valid and every individual shares the benefits of development with each other within the coalition in a defined manner. In other words, the 'invisible hand' is already working in a Pareto Coalition. However, outside a Pareto Space, we need a 'visible hand' for Pareto improvement.

4.4 Biased Equilibrium Barrier (BEB)

In an agrarian society, Biased Equilibrium is quite stable since bureaucracy works as a buffer between peasantry and the imperial regime. The same has been continued in a colonial economy and post-colonial agrarian economy where imperial regime was replaced by a colonial or independent government respectively. Quigley describers bureaucracy in Chinese agrarian economy of nineteenth century:

"This buffer followed a pattern of deliberate amorphous inefficiency. ..The inefficiency of the system was both customary and deliberate, since it allowed a large portion of the wealth which was being drained from the peasantry to be diverted and diffused among the middle class of gentry before the remnants of it reached the imperial group at the top......The bureaucracy did not desire efficiency because this would have reduced its ability to divert the funds flowing upward from the peasantry."[23]

In fact, this middle layer creates a Biased Equilibrium (BE) between peasantry and the rest of the economy. It supports a network of vested interests so that the larger part is being diverted by the gentry and bureaucracy for themselves on its upward flow leaving only a small subsistence amount to the peasant class.

In industrial society, the extent of biasing can be measured based on the extent of social mobility. If the social mobility is high, the biasing is less. The following graph in Figure 4.4 shows how the social mobility in the United States between

Figure 4.4: Social Mobility in US Economy [25]

This graph shows the probability of improving the economic conditions of the bottom 40% to the upper 60% and vice versa became hard and the social mobility trend stabilized at a certain low level (below 4%), which reflects the concept of Biased Equilibrium.[25]

bottom 40% and upper 60% income groups has reached to equilibrium since 1970s. It shows, social mobility was high immediately after the Great Depression due to 'pro-poor' new deal.[24] These data are also supported by the Gini coefficient (a measure of inequality) of the U.S. economy. Since 2000, the Gini coefficients of the US have been stabilized between 0.46 and 0.47 (except for 0.45 in 2010). During the economic expansion between 2002 and 2007, the income of the top 1% of Americans grew 10 times faster than the income of the bottom 90%.[22] It is also shown in Figure 4.5. In this period, 66% of total income gains of the US economy went to the top 1%. The year before the financial

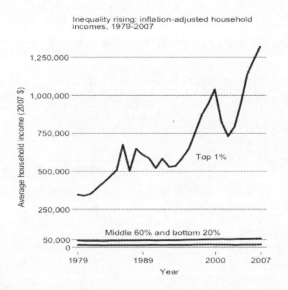

Figure 4.5: The income inequality of US economy from 1979 and 2007[26]

The above illustration shows changes in real incomes in top 1%, middle 60%, and bottom 20% after inflation adjustment. The years listed on the horizontal axis are business-cycle peaks. (Source: Inequality-by-Kenworthy)[26]

breakdown, in 2007, the richest 1% of Americans owned 34.6% of the country's wealth and the next 19% owned 50.5%, thus the top 20% owned 85% of the country's wealth. This means the bottom 80% of the population owned 15%. However, after the financial crisis in 2008, the share of total wealth owned by the top 1% Americans grew from 34.6% to 37.1%, and that owned by the top 20% of Americans grew from 85% to 87.7% (Deborah, 2011).[27] This means there is a clear demarcation above which rich Americans are in a virtual Pareto Coalition so that their income levels are maintained and protected from any economic downturn, whereas the others (the PS) are not. However, an economic analyst may apply his discretion to define the fine line. The imaginary fine line can be defined as **Biased Equilibrium Barrier (BEB)** that separates a Pareto Space (PS) from a Pareto Coalition (PC) as shown in Figure 4.6.[3] The concept of

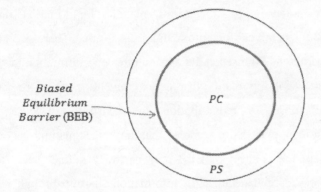

Figure 4.6: Biased Equilibrium Barrier

biased equilibrium is also a meeting point of neoclassical economics and institutional economics since within a PC, institutions do not matter much. However, when a PC interacts with a PS the institutions do matter. In view of institutional economics, for simplicity, it can be said that BEB imposes virtual transaction cost (Coase, 1960)[28] on a PS. As Coase (1960) argues

"If we lived in a world without transaction costs, people would bargain with one another to create the same allocation of resources, regardless of the way a court might rule in property disputes."[28]

Here the transaction cost may be assumed as cost of acquiring information. However, it is neither measurable in terms of money nor redeemable in real economy but tells about a cost that causes a market not to convey proper information through price.

There have been debates within the domain of neoclassical economics around one key issue: the efficiency of the market economy and the appropriate relationship between the market and the government.[1] Stiglitz analyzes that the incentives and constraints facing government different from those facing the private sector, so that even when government faces exactly the same informational constraints, welfare could be improved upon.[29] Stiglitz identifies two important results of policy imports toward information. "First, markets do not provide appropriate incentives for information disclosure. There is, in principle a role for government. And secondly, expenditures on information may be too great."[1] If we accept the reality that a government is no more an independent, impartial entity for redistribution, the constraints faced by government are multifarious, even more complex than any other institutions or the private sectors. Here the concept of BEB may narrowly define where a government should work for enhancement of information sharing through its policy tools. This means, similar to neoclassical economics, we may build a micro-like macroeconomics based on scarce resources by using the concept of biased equilibrium to address macroeconomic problems such as poverty, inequality, financial crisis, recession, corruption, fossil fuel depletion and so on.

The concept of biased equilibrium is a market failure approach of economic analysis. Before the advent of models of imperfect and asymmetric information, the traditional neoclassical economics literature had assumed that markets are efficient except for some limited and well defined market failures. More recent work by Stiglitz and others reversed that presumption. They assert that it is only under exceptional circumstances that markets are efficient and under the imperfect information paradigm, markets are almost never Pareto efficient (Stiglitz, 2002).[1] The concept 'biased equilibrium' supports Stiglitz's proposition that market failure is inherent in every economy since the market structure cannot change the institutions as a whole because of their slow responses. An economic analyst may use the concept of BEB to simplify the complex problem of market and the institutional failures.

The neoclassical basis of perfect information and complete market were never in existence in real world, nor will they ever exist in future but may be considered as expected characteristics of a market. Stiglitz (1991) describes that imperfect information and incomplete markets alter the standard micro-economic results in fundamental ways.[30] However, the extents of imperfections have differential existences in different markets in different time frames. Neoclassical economists believe in market power and ignore the role of institutions since they assume that the market has ability to override the institutions. On the other hand, the institutional economists believe in the other way around, the dominance of institutions over market. As North (1994) argues,

"It is the polity that defines and enforces property rights and in consequence it is not surprising that efficient economic markets are so exceptional".[31]

It can be said that the institutions are there to energize, facilitate and guide the market. Combining both the approaches, we may define that the BEB is the result of institutional failure to empower the market and also market failure to bring Pareto efficiency in the economy. Therefore, BEB is the demarcation where both the market and the institutions fail.

The concept of PC and PS can be used to explain income inequality in a country. Amartya Sen (Sen, 1999) explains income inequality and poverty as form of "capability deprivation"[32], where economic growth and income are considered a means to an end rather than the end itself.[33] Its goal is to "widen people's choices and the level of their achieved well-being"[34] through increasing functioning (the things a person values doing), capabilities (the freedom to enjoy functioning) and agency (the ability to pursue valued goals).[32] The concept of 'biased equilibrium' sees that poor people have restricted capabilities and therefore, it can also be seen from the broad perspective Sen's 'capability deprivation'. In case of poverty, it makes sense considering poor people as Pareto Space (PS) separated from the non-poor people (as Pareto coalition) by a Biased Equilibrium Barrier (BEB). Amartya Sen (1999) argues that it becomes more difficult to reduce inequality, the gap between poor and non-poor, without additional aid. To prevent such inequality, he suggests having political freedom, economic facilities, social opportunities, transparency guarantees, and protective security to ensure that people aren't denied their functioning, capabilities, and agency and can thus work towards a better relevant income.[32] This proposed model of 'biased equilibrium' sees Sen' s model from one step up, which implies that an ideal government should enhance information sharing between PC and PS so that Sen's capabilities objectives can be achieved. Enhancement of information sharing weakens BEB and therefore, not only unlocks market competition but also unlocks the social and economic freedom of PS.

Although Smith (1776) argued for enhancing market power but also on the same book Wealth of Nations he precisely defined the role of government. As Pluta (2011) mentions,

> "Smith begins his discussion of this issue by stating that government must address three duties of great importance. These include national defense, the administration of justice and those goods that would not be provided under the profit motive. This last area includes education and basic public works such as roads and bridges."[35]

Apart from this role we may conclude that government should act as information enhancer where competition is to be reinforced in the market not a mere regulator or deregulator. This will require right policies, practices, systems, norms, motivation, laws and orders and so on. As an example, government should promote physical fitness and sports, while promoting competition among pharmaceutical companies.

There is of course no guarantee that government intervention will have positive effects, as it is just as likely to reinforce market inefficiency as it is to reduce it. There is a chance that the government is part of a PC and therefore, redistribution may not pass beyond the PC. As an example, in many Third World countries in Africa and Asia, World Bank development loan programs such as building schools and hospitals, improving literacy and agricultural reform or Structural Adjustment Programs (SAPs) or Millennium Development Goals (MDGs) achieve small compared to the money invested. This proposed model of 'Biased Equilibrium' does not support 'trickle-down theory', which tells that tax breaks or other economic benefits provided by government to businesses and the wealthy will benefit poorer members of society by improving the economy as a whole.[30] Rather it supports progressive taxation for a PC and welfare for a PS.

Ideally, involvement of government in financial transaction is not a focus but if economy slows down and needs a boost, government may take the big steps like infrastructure development or job building. Similarly, government supported welfare like healthcare should focus the poor people who cannot afford otherwise. Any government support for uniform education minimize information gap between PC & PS. Stiglitz identifies "there are strong forces on the part of those in government to reduce transparency".[1] Therefore, he emphasizes for laws such as right-to-know, which is part of governance in Sweden for the last two hundred years.[1] On the Contrary, if government policies reduce transparency, it will reinforce BEB and as a result, benefits of economic development will be concentrated within the Pareto Coalition (PC).

There is no question of competition within a Pareto Coalition (PC), since a PC is already Pareto efficient with respect to Pareto Space (PS). On the other hand, under biasing, a perfect competition within a PS does not make it Pareto efficient, it remains as a PS. Therefore, under biased equilibrium, a PC is where the first welfare theorem is already achieved and PS is where the first welfare theorem always fails. However, considering the whole economy, if specific conditions infer there is no biased equilibrium, the fundamental welfare theorems are valid. In other words, the line of Biased Equilibrium or the Biased Equilibrium Barrier (BEB) is the place where competition should happen to annul the biasing. And the position of BEB is discretionary depending on the economic problem an analyst is trying to address.

4.5 Differential Market Model (DMM)

Every economy has started from a reference position and the position of Biased Equilibrium Barrier (BEB) has moved to its existing position through the capitalists' synthesis (Chapter 2) process over time. The individuals in a Pareto Space (PS) can be made better off without making the individuals of a Pareto Coalition (PC) worse off. However, it is not possible to distribute the resources already piled up with a PC since the BEB prevents that from happen. We may say that a PC has an optimum size under certain conditions such as certain technological state, motivational state or availability of natural resources.

According to the definition of Biased Equilibrium, the individuals in a PS and the individuals in a PC are substitutes and therefore, the capacity of the PC will expand with technological advancements backed by fossil fuel. In other words, it creates more opportunities in the economy and some individuals from the PS may move to the PC. As a result, the economy reaches to another Biased Equilibrium. This is how technological advancement shifts the position of BEB further down into a PS but it does not necessarily weaken the BEB. However, a combination of government policy intervention and technology does both. As an example, deregulation in telecommunication sector raises competitiveness to weaken BEB, that is it breaks the monopolistic capital accumulation. And the development of telecommunication technology pushes BEB down, that is more and more people now access to this. A BEB is specific to what economic or social problem you are trying to solve. In other words, an analyst should focus on the BEB that best suits the problem he is analyzing.

A market is a place to produce commodities and also to provide wages to the workers to buy the commodities. In the real world, following Amartya Sen's "capabilities approach" (Sen, 1995)[12], it can be said that the individuals who have better opportunities to acquire better skill and better job opportunities are also more capable of fulfilling their demands than others. According to this approach formulations of capability have two parts: functionings and opportunity freedom, the substantive freedom to pursue different functioning combinations.[36] The market equilibrium is the price at which demand equals supply. The average capability of a market to fulfill the demands of an individual can be defined as '*market energy*'. Using the concept of "capabilities", 'market energy' can be broadly defined as the opportunity freedom offered by a market for functionings a person is feasibly able to achieve. In this chapter we will work on the narrower definition of market energy practiced under capitalism.

The term 'market energy' is to be distinguished from the term 'market potential'. In economic literatures the term market potential corresponds to a geographic location. For example Krugman (1992)[37] defined market potential in terms of the weighted sum of purchasing power of all the regions under the market. A Pareto efficient economy has the same level of market energy across the economy. Similarly a Pareto Coalition (PC) represents the same level of market energy for every individual in the coalition. In an incomplete or imperfect market, market energy varies among different coalitions or among the individuals who have different levels of information sharing. However, market potential is independent of information sharing since that is calculated by aggregating the purchasing powers of different individuals.[37]

According to the first theorem of welfare economics, competition leads to an efficient allocation of resources. In other words, competition distributes market energy throughout an economy by weakening the BEB. As North (1994) describes, "efficient markets are created in the real word when competition is strong enough via arbitrage".[31] That is, theoretically, a competitive market can be attained through favorable institutional processes and on the other hand, it may counteract the unfavorable institutions (unfavorable agreements and enforcement practice) and force them to change. In the real world, institutions changes through a stubborn learning process and therefore, they are quite slow to change and impede competition. As far the economic theories goes, if there were perfect competition in an economy, the BEB would disappear, the economy would contain one single classical market that eventually would become Pareto efficient as described in the first fundamental theorem of welfare economics.

Here we may imagine a compatible market with own equilibrium corresponding to each side of BEB. The market on Pareto Coalition (PC) side is more powerful than the market on Pareto Space (PS) since PC accumulates the resources produced in the economy. This is how BEB splits an economy into a multiple equilibriums economy under biasing. In the standard neoclassical model, there is a universal equilibrium mediated by prices. The only way to converge this multiple equilibrium economy to the universal equilibrium economy is to completely eliminate the biasing.

The abstraction of BEB is absolutely subjective and therefore can be discretionally defined by an analyst in the view of the problem he analyzes. The smaller the PC is, the more the market energy and vice versa. Now by further partitioning the PC, we will get a more powerful PC separated by a BEB from the remaining population. If we assume there is compatible market energy in each case, we may imagine that the whole economy can be distributed in layers of '**Market Energy States (MES)**' as shown in Figure 4.7. This model can be called as **Differential Market Model (DMM)**.[3] The concept of DMM tells about the fact that every individual has a relative position in the market that he or she does not want to lose but to gain. This model defines that the probability of

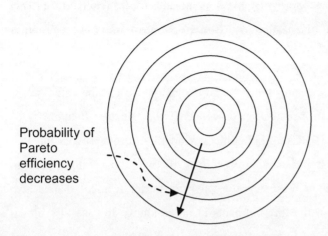

Probability of
Pareto
efficiency
decreases

Figure 4.7: Differential Market Model (DMM)[5]

achieving Pareto efficiency is the highest at the center of a DMM and it decreases downward the MESs. Similarly, market energy is the highest at the center of a DMM and it gradually declines away from the center. This means an economy reserves most of its energy potential at the center of a DMM.

The concept of Biased Equilibrium tells that interaction between two MESs is such that Money (M) goes up from a lower MES to an upper MES. A MES contains disposable income plus accumulated capital. The propensities of consumption for non-durable goods are higher in the lower MES and for durable goods like property rights and financial assets are higher in upper MESs. The micro-economic equilibrium of the lowest MES is limited by the money remaining in there that is money generated minus the money goes to the upper MES. The price equilibrium of a middle MES is determined by the money generated in there plus the money comes from the lower MES minus the money goes to the upper MES. Essentially when we talk about 'market energy states', we do not consider the same set of products. However, we may assume the following two things about product set:

1. The product set for lower MES is a subset of higher MES. This proposition can be called as 'Subset Proposition of Consumption (SPC)'.

2. The individuals around the boundary of BEB vie for the same set of products. This propensity can be called as the **'Border Propensity of Consumption (BPC)'**. Marketing is kind of information biasing that induces BPC. It has a radiating effect all over the economy. As an example, we see increase in real estate price in rich residential areas also increase price of the tiny hutments in urban slums. In case of a global DMM, Chinese coal fired economy and Indian booming middle class are nothing but global scale BPC.

In this case if we talk about the same set of products, there will be only one price equilibrium as shown in Figure 4.8. As an example, let us imagine that there are three MES in a DMM. Figure 4.8 shows demand curves D_1D_1', D_2D_2' and D_3D_3' for the three MESs, 1, 2 and 3, respectively. Although, we are taking about a single set of products for three different MESs but elasticity of demand may vary. The below figure also shows supply curves S_1S_1', S_2S_2' and S_3S_3' for the product set (the same elasticity of supply) in three MESs, 1, 2 and 3 respectively.

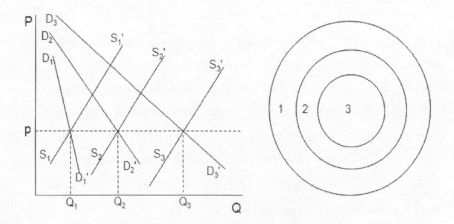

Figure 4.8: Price Equilibrium in DMM[5]

256

In real life, the same product sells for the same price everywhere as shown as equilibrium price 'p'. This means there is more undisposed incomes (savings) in the higher MESs, which we call capital accumulation. The accumulation of capital enhances market potentials and therefore, energy differential between the upper and lower market energy state increases.

It can be inferred that the farther the distance from the center of a DMM, the bigger the boarder, the more people are affected by the adverse effect of "Biased Equilibrium (BE)". As an example, if a robust BEB is assumed close to the center of a DMM such as in USA between 1% super-rich and 99% of the population, less number of people is affected compared to India. Since in India, a robust BEB can be positioned between its huge middle class and its huge poor class. In a DMM, the difference in market energy levels is the fundamental of capital flow and businesses. As an example, farmers in lower MES can sell their produce in higher MES in a greater price. If there is a stable BEB, middlemen will surface around it. In an impoverished country one big reason of poverty is an inefficient middle layer, where the money created from the difference in market energy levels is diffused among the people on the middle layer, can be called as middlemen. If differential of market energy levels of a country reduces, the economy will reach close to saturation and growth will slow down.

4.6 Money Market Dynamics (MMD)

The difference in market energy levels in different countries in the world is the reason for promoting international trade. Thus globalization represents a global Differential Market Model (DMM) that has integrated the economies of different countries. As discussed in section 4.2, the concept of biased equilibrium adds directional property with the net amount of money is being accumulated by this integration. The competition among the global capitalists at the upper Market

Energy States (MESs) to increase labor productivity and boost up capital accumulation is underlying reason for technological advancement.

A simplified way of showing technological advancement can be explained by Production Possibility Frontier (PPF)[38] curve shown in Figure 4.9. For theoretical simplification, a PPF represents a two-goods world (e.g., in this case 'gun' and 'butter') that shows all possible combinations of the two goods that can be produced simultaneously during a given period of time. It compares the production rates of two commodities that use the same fixed total of the factors of production. Therefore, to increase the quantity of one good produced, production of the other good must be sacrificed (opportunity cost). It can be noticed that the PPF curve XY in Figure 4.9 is similar to Figure 3.1 'Pareto Efficient Allocation', where all points on or within the curve are part of the production set. The points on the curve are points of maximum productive efficiency. All points inside the frontier (such as A) can be produced but productively inefficient; If production is efficient, the economy can choose

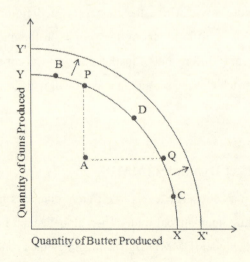

Figure 4.9: Production Possibility Frontier Curve and Technological Progress

between combinations on the curve B if guns are of interest, C if more butter is needed.[38] Similar to Figure 3.1, not all points on the curve are Pareto efficient.

More guns and more butter can be produced between P & Q, without sacrificing the other. All points outside the curve cannot be produced with the existing resources and technology. However, an outward shift of the PPF (X'Y') results from growth of the availability of inputs such as physical capital or labor or technological progress.[38] If all other factors of production remains the same, the right shift of the PPF curve represents technological progress. We may call this shift as change in positive change of technological state of an economy. The shift in the opposite direction is negative change of technological state of an economy. The last two centuries technological advancement is firmly rooted in supply of easy energy from fossil fuel. Once in future, if cheap energy is no more available, technological state may change negatively.

The concept of DMM explains that a realistic economy accumulates capital and it does not mean that it helps more production of goods and services unless there is a technological progress. Richard Smith (2010) explains:

"Producers must constantly strive to increase the efficiency of their units of production by cutting the cost of inputs, seeking cheaper sources of raw materials and labor, by bringing in more advanced labor-saving machinery and technology to boost productivity, or by increasing their scale of production to take advantage of economies of scale, and in other ways, to develop the forces of production."[39]

In other words, as theoretically, the accumulated money is re-invested for production of more of the goods and services and creating new opportunities. It means, in a perfectly competitive economy Money (M) is converted into Market Energy (ME), that is into new entitlements and opportunities using technology (as shown as right shift of the PPF curve in Figure 4.9) that tends to create universal market equilibrium.

One of the objectives of technological advancement is to improve a product by making it more elastic with respect to price. The supply curves shown in the previous example (Figure 4.8) can be modified by making them more elastic to price due to advancement of technology as shown in Figure 4.10 as S_1S_1'', S_2S_2'' and S_3S_3'' for three MESs, 1, 2 & 3 respectively. Here the new equilibrium price for all markets will be "p_T", significantly lower than "p". As an example, three decades ago, the Internet was an obscure network, mostly for researchers; today almost 2 billion people worldwide are connected almost free or at very low costs, with nearly \$8 trillion traded through e-commerce (Farrell, 2011).[40] Nowadays

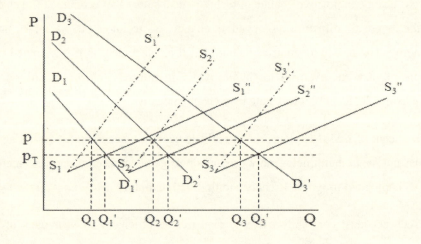

Figure 4.10: Price Equilibrium after Technological Advancement[8]

technology such a consumer electronics has reduced the gap of lifestyles between rich and poor countries although those are developed in developed and rich countries.

This is to be noted that although conversion from Money (M) to Market Energy (ME) and vice versa happens at every single point of a DMM but for simplicity we may consider that a certain Market Energy State (MES) has the same level of Market Energy at its every point. However, under "Biased Equilibrium" there are two opposing forces, accumulation property of capital and distribution property of market. The accumulation property of capital tells that Money (M) goes up centripetally from lower MESs to the uppermost MES. From there the market centrifugal force powered by technology and consumption of energy and other resources spread down with new and better products and services with resized prices. If this mechanism works perfectly as matching with mainstream economic theories, any small disturbance will be automatically counteracted and corrected by the system itself.

In reality, money is created at every point of economic activity (market energy). The more Money (M) goes up, the more it is accumulated in the upper Market Energy States (MESs). The accumulated money can be called as **Potential Market Energy (PME)** or wealth. Examples of PME are ownership of capital or property rights. A part of the money from PME is actually the Money (M) applied to production of goods and services. The Market Energy (ME) created through production system by applying M (capital) along with labor, energy and natural resources and technology can be called as **Kinetic Market Energy (KME)**. The upper the MES is, the higher the PME. Similarly, the lower the MES is, the more the competition and therefore, the more the KME but lower the PME. Here KME also represents distributive growth since according to the First Theorem of Welfare Economics, more production in a competitive environment leads to a Pareto efficient allocation of resources.

The technological advancement and competition creates more combinations of products for more rapid returns on their capital. According to the definition of Potential Market Energy (PME), we may interpret that there is process where Money (M) is being accumulated toward an imaginary center of a Differential Market Model (DMM) from where it is converted into Market Energy (ME) and gains potential to centrifugally spread down creating new opportunities, better skill, jobs and products and services with resized prices and better qualities over time. This dynamics can be called as **Money Market Dynamics (MMD)**.[3] As the concept of Biased Equilibrium introduces the directional property of money, MMD describes cyclic relationship between M and ME. Theoretically, accumulation of money and Pareto efficient distribution happens on the same cycle of MMD, however, in reality and historically this is not the case.

The concept MMD also tells how an economy is achieving prosperity over the time by using technology and consumption of energy. As an example, when someone is buying a product, he is not only paying for that particular item but may also indirectly sharing any cost of research for a medicine of a disease or for a new technology or for a deadly weapon. The Say's Law "supply creates its own demand" can be elaborated here as production creates a demand for the product itself and a demand for "other products to the full extent of its own value." A better formulation of the law is that the supply of one good constitutes demand for one or more other goods.[41]

For simplicity, we may imagine a two Market Energy State (MES) economy as shown in Figure 4.11. Let us consider the two types of market energies, PME and KME are the two demand centers and sources of money for the economy. According to the definition, we may imagine that PME is at the central MES (MES_0), whereas KME is in any MES (MES_N) and between them there is a clockwise flow of money. The kinetic money (M_{KME}) flows toward *KME* and then generates more money (*M*) by applying labor, energy and technology that flows to PME. A part of this money (M_{PME}) contributes PME and the rest is

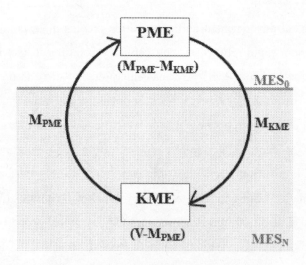

Figure 4.11 Money Market Dynamics (MMD)

again re-invested. The concept Market Energy State (MES) plays very important role for consumption of any overproduction in the economy. Here supply side economics assumption is valid that if a surplus of goods or services exists, they would naturally drop in price to reach to lower MES, where they would be consumed. The circular flow of money represents Money Market Dynamics (MMD). It represents the relationship between Money and Market Energy without any explicit economic policy–similar to the concept of neoclassical economics. Theoretically, it can be seen as the ultimate outcome of capitalist synthesis particularly after industrial revolution. Without MMD we would not have big investment, big research or the level of comfort what we have now in developed societies. The use of fossil fuel speeded up MMD. Let's use some mathematical expressions to better understand MMD in following three steps:

Step1: Kinetic Money: This is the money produces actual products or values and opportunities through investment. Ideally, the amount of money is invested is primarily driven by demand or in this case, Kinetic Market Energy (KME). In Figure 4.11, kinetic money is represented as M_{KME}. Accordingly,

$$M_{KME} = f(KME) \text{ ceteris paribus} \dots\dots\dots\dots\dots\dots\dots\dots\dots\dots\dots 4.1$$

Step 2: Creation of money (or values): An economy creates additional money or value, products, buildings, or machinery by using the factors of production capital, labor, energy or natural resources. We may assume kinetic money (M_{KME}) is the capital invested in an economy. By using the concept factors of production, if the other factors labor can be represented as L and natural resources and energy as E then the economy will create more value (V) as:

$$V = f(M_{KME}, L, E), \text{ ceteris paribus}, \dots\dots\dots\dots\dots\dots\dots\dots\dots 4.2$$

Step 3: Accumulation of wealth: According to the definition of MMD, a part of money created in an economy (M) is accumulated in upper Market Energy States (MESs). This part can be denoted as M_{PME}. As per definition of "Biased

Equilibrium", M_{PME} is a function of the money created in the economy (V) and the level of information biasing. Let "$\tilde{I}_B$" denotes information biasing. Accordingly, M_{PME} can be expressed as:

$$M_{PME} = f(V, \tilde{I}_B) \text{ ceteris paribus}, \dots\dots\dots\dots\dots\dots\dots\dots\dots\dots\dots.4.3$$

The opposite of information biasing is information sharing ($\tilde{I}_S$). Here information biasing ($\tilde{I}_B$) abstracts institutional structure of the economy. If institutional structure has more information biasing component, it will increase M_{PME}. Similarly, if institutional structure has more information sharing component, it will decreases M_{PME}.

According to the definition of Potential Market Energy (*PME*), the money accumulated in the upper MESs in terms of property right or financial assets (wealth) can be expressed as:

$$\Delta PME = f(M_{PME} - M_{KME}) \text{ ceteris paribus} \dots\dots\dots\dots\dots\dots\dots\dots.4.4$$

From equations 4.3 & 4.4, it can be concluded that information biasing increases wealth accumulation. Oppositely, information sharing increases distribution.

The growth of Kinetic Market Energy (*KME*) means better distribution, new employments, better products, new technologies and new opportunities. It can be expressed as:

$$\Delta KME = f(V - M_{PME}) \text{ ceteris paribus}, \dots\dots\dots\dots\dots\dots\dots\dots\dots.4.5$$

In normal operation of MMD, ΔKME is always positive. However, in combination with equation 4.3, it can be inferred that by improving institutions to share more information among the market energy states, the economy can create more opportunities and more distribution of wealth by more investment for common benefits. Information sharing has a qualitative aspect too. If the economy shares more information, there will be more use of clean energy or reduction of greenhouse gas, healthy living and more competition.

If we consider M_{KME} in two consecutive cycles are M_{KME1} and M_{KME2} respectively, then the growth of investment can be shown as:

$$\Delta M_{KME} = M_{KME2} - M_{KME1} \dots\dots\dots\dots\dots\dots\dots\dots\dots\dots\dots 4.6$$

In normal operation of MMD, if ΔM_{KME} is positive, then the economy will grow and validate the assumption that future economy will be bigger than existing.

$$\Delta M_{KME} > 0 \dots\dots\dots\dots\dots\dots\dots\dots\dots\dots\dots\dots\dots\dots 4.7$$

Similarly, for a normal operation of MMD, in consecutive cycles if ΔM_{PME} is positive, then the economy will provide incentives to the capitalists (e.g., Reagan's tax cut). That is,

$$\Delta M_{PME} > 0 \dots\dots\dots\dots\dots\dots\dots\dots\dots\dots\dots\dots\dots\dots 4.8$$

A normal operation of Money Market Dynamics (MMD) is expected to satisfy equations 4.7 & 4.8. If equation 4.7 is valid but equation 4.8 is not, then the economy is going to face liquidity (cash-flow) problems—an onset of recession. If both of them are not satisfied, then the economy will fall in depression or in a deeper economic crisis. There is more discussion on "Economic Crisis" is in section 4.11.

In an economy, a perfect distribution can be achieved if economic policies aim no capital growth on the same cycle in Figure 4.11, that is M_{KME} is close to M_{PME} and all money accumulated is re-invested, ΔPME will be close to *0* (equation 4.4). This concept helps us differentiate between growth and prosperity. A perfect distributive growth means prosperity is achieved but not necessarily any capital growth is needed. An economy having distributive growth or prosperity without any capital growth is much like healthy life is maintained without gaining weight or fat but consuming and burning the same amount of calories. The mainstream economists assume growth equals prosperity and therefore emphasize on growth to achieve prosperity. Martenson argues "growth alone does not bring prosperity, and, worse, growth can steal from prosperity if there aren't enough resources to support both."[42]

In a Differential Market Model (DMM), each MES has its own demand and supply pattern. However, as per definition of MMD, part of the money accumulated in the economy must be converted into market energy for development and prosperity. A technological shift produces products for a larger market each time, stretching from upper MES toward lower MES. This attribute of a specific technology can be called as 'Transformation Potential of a Technology (TPT)'. A technology with high TPT causes more production and consumption of the products (e.g., electronics, plastic, aluminum and glass products), which eventually corresponds to more use of energy and more accumulation of capital toward the upper MESs. Therefore, availability of cheap energy has direct impact on TPT.

In Figure 4.9, Guns have more TPT value than that of Butter. The present digital revolution is firmly rooted in silicon technology which has a high TPT value. The PPF models in Figure 4.12 represents how a technological state more favors production possibilities of one of the goods, say Guns, shifts the PPF outwards more along the Guns axis, "biasing" production possibilities in that direction.[38]

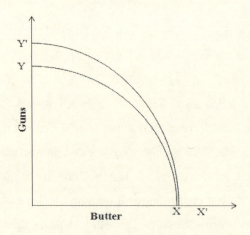

Figure 4.12: Technology Effect of Production Possibilities[78]

Similarly, if one product makes more use of capital and if capital grows faster than other factors, growth possibilities might be biased in favor of the capital-intensive good. Thus Guns may become the product of choice over Butter to the core capitalists since more Guns can be sold by creating information asymmetries as an attempt to exploit market power under institutional biasing. Ideally, MMD considers global economy as single economy. In global context, the concept of MMD substantiates Krugman's "Dynamic Spatial Model"[37] of economic geography where he described how economic geography exhibit a tension between two kinds of forces: "centripetal" forces that tend to pull economic activity into agglomerations, and "centrifugal" forces that tend to break such agglomerations up or limit their size. In other words, if these two forces are not balanced on both directions, the resources and benefits will be concentrated on some upper MESs. In reality accumulation property of capital is based on imperfect information. On the other hand, perfect sharing of information is required to achieve Pareto efficient distribution. The first half cycle of MMD is driven by imperfect information sharing tendencies between upper and lower MESs. And the second half depends on policies and their enforce performances to make the imperfect information perfect.

The global economy can be assumed as a single MMD that works on top of a global DMM allowing free flow of goods and services leveraging maximum use of 'easy' energy from fossil fuel. In context of global DMM, the poorer countries can be positioned on the outer MESs and the richer countries can be positioned on the inner (core) MESs. Now the concept of MMD also explains how resources are agglomerated to the richer countries. Similarly, poor people in a developing country are to be positioned on the outermost MESs in a DMM for that country. This model says globalization does not bring benefits for all but more for the upper MESs and less or negative for the lower MESs. Considering the fact of finite energy, poverty in the lower MESs of global DMM may never pass the development stage of free market economy.

There are few more points to be noted about real life MMD. Firstly, MMD represents a full employment economy. Secondly, in an ideal economy having local market only, entrepreneurs take the challenge to bear high wages and at the same time achieve good profit. Therefore, they diversify their investments and adopt new technologies, which create new jobs and increases productivity per labor. Thirdly, in a global MMD, the global entrepreneurs exploit low wage wages of developing countries to generate high profit. Fourthly, a complete cycle of MMD results in accumulation of capital in the form of profit or surplus payroll for employees, which is also the source of income of a government in the form of tax. Fifthly, it supports Minsky's (1992) statement that money is connected with market through time.[44] In case technological state is changed, the money an individual spends and the products and services he or she receives are not exactly "goods for goods". MMD tells that ideally he or she should receive better values over time because of technological advancement. Sixthly, conversion of Money (M) to Market Energy (ME) also depends on institutional complexities of our world.

4.7 Market Energy Loop (MEL)

The process of integration of global economy under capitalism was never easy. We have seen our history is marked with conflicts or wars over grabbing or controlling the markets among the nations. Ironically, the post-war reconstruction speeds up MMD and brings fortunes for some nations or more precisely to say, for some people of those nations. Even after war, the investors or the policy makers are not happy with the capital accumulation at normal pace of Money Market Dynamics (MMD).

The concept of capitalism tells that any new capital created in an economy should be distributed in accordance to the ownership of existing capital. In other words, capital is accumulated to the owners of existing capital. Therefore, a capitalist economy is born with economic inequality and follows the process of wealth accumulation over time for the wealthy people. In his book "Anarchy, State, and Utopia", Robert Nozick defines entitlement theory that would imply "a distribution is just if everyone is entitled to the holdings they possess under the distribution".[45]

Amartya Sen's "capability approach" defines when a person's capabilities are lowered, they are in some way deprived of earning as much income as they would otherwise. As a result, income and economic inequality increases.[12] He describes famine occur not only a lack of food but when ownership entitlement and exchange entitlements of the people of a region are not enough to get food because of inequalities built into mechanisms for distributing food.[46]

We cannot change the history. This model abstracts the history and any unjust distribution into the concept of "Biased Equilibrium". The history of capitalist synthesis (Chapter 2) shows before industrial revolution, the economics of different countries were driven by only one objective, wealth accumulation. Then after industrial revolution the concept of distribution appeared in the mainstream. Therefore, historically agglomeration and distribution of money never happened on the same cycle. Similarly, in reality, the first half and the second half of MMD are not balanced.

At any point of time, total Market Energy (*ME*) of a Market Energy State (MES) can be expressed as vector sum of PME and KME:

$$\overline{ME} = \overline{PME} + \overline{KME} \dots\dots\dots\dots\dots\dots\dots\dots\dots\dots\dots\dots\dots 4.9$$

In Figure 4.13, KME is shown in horizontal direction and PME is shown in vertical direction. Ideally, without any Potential Market Energy (PME), all money would be converted into KME, while *PME* = 0. In presence of PME, it can be assumed that there is a phase shift $\angle\alpha$ of Market Energy (ME) from its ideal horizontal position. This phase difference $\angle\alpha$ can be called as **Market**

Skewness Factor (MSF) of a Market Energy State (MES). In a Differential Market Model (DMM), the higher the position of a MES, the more the MSF is

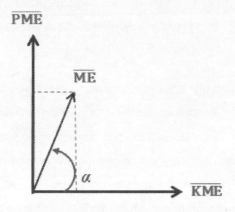

Figure 4.13 Market Skewness Factor (MSF)

tilted toward PME and the lower the position of a MES, the more the MSF is tilted toward KME. That is,

$$\alpha_0 > \alpha_1 > \alpha_2 > \ldots\ldots\ldots \alpha_{N-1} > \alpha_N \ldots\ldots\ldots \ldots\ldots\ldots\ldots 4.10$$

Economic policies such as monetary and fiscal policies are required to reduce MSF and to increase KME. In Figure 4.14, $\angle\theta$ denotes the effect of economic policies for reduction of MSF. As a result, PME is reduced by ΔPME and KME is increased by ΔKME. Here $\angle\theta$ can be called as **Economic Policy Factor (EPF)**. EPF may also increase PME and reduce KME as happened after Reagan's tax cut in 1981.

Here, if $\angle\theta$ is the EPF, then

$$\theta = f(P), \text{ ceteris paribus} \ldots\ldots\ldots\ldots\ldots\ldots\ldots\ldots\ldots\ldots\ldots 4.11$$

Where, P = Economic policy.

The relationship 4.11 is true by assuming that all of the factors of production, labor, technology, energy and institutions are constant.

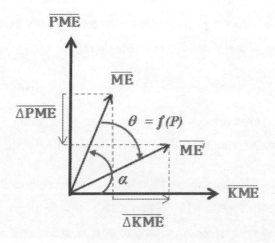

Figure 4.14 Economic Policy Factor (EPF)

The solution to the Great Depression by Keynesian economics was combination of two approaches:[61]

3. A reduction in interest rates (monetary policy), and

4. Government investment in infrastructure (fiscal policy).

Since the economy was slowing in consumption, which Keynes called "Paradox of Thrift", the objective was to bring consumption level back on track either by lowering interest rate or by spending more to keep people fully employed even though governments run deficits.

To explain the concept of consumerism in this model, a new type of market energy can be introduced between Potential Market Energy (PME) and Kinetic Market Energy (KME). It can be called as **Inductive Kinetic Market Energy (IKE)** as shown in Figure 4.15.

Similar to previous section, let us formulate some simple mathematical equations for better illustration of the concept of IKE. Let M_{IKE} is the "inductive money" induced by IKE. This may be expressed as function of the money (or value) produced in the economy (V), Border Propensity of Consumption (γ), information biasing through marketing promotion ($\tilde{I}_{BM}$):

$$M_{IKE} = f\ (V_{KME},\ \gamma,\ \tilde{I}_{BM})\ \text{ceteris paribus} \dots\dots\dots\dots\dots\dots\text{......}4.12$$

Where, V_{KME} =the total value is produced in an economy using M_{KME}, γ=Border Propensity of Consumption, $\tilde{I}_{BM}$=Information Biasing through marketing.

As per equation 4.11, financial and monetary policies control the money flow from PME to KME. Figure 4.15 illustrates two separate flows of money from PME to Economy. First, M_{KME}, as already discussed in Section 4.6. According to

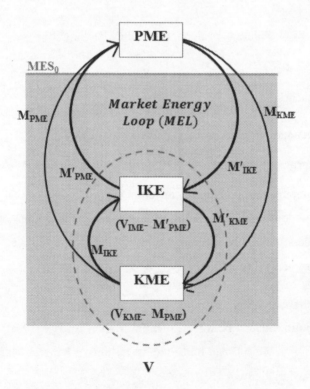

Figure 4.15 Market Energy Loop (MEL)

272

the concept of MMD and equation 4.1, M_{KME} is primarily demand driven. The second, flow of money that is policy driven goes to enhance consumption in the economy in addition to M_{KME}. It includes debt and other government expenditure to build infrastructure or welfare such as pension and social security. Its basic idea was to keep an economy fully employed, a government had to run deficits when the economy was slowing, as the private sector would not invest enough to keep production at the normal level and bring the economy out of recession. This money can be considered as "financial incentive" for the economy. Mathematically this money can be expressed as:

$$M'_{IKE} = f\ (PME,\ P_{FM})\ ceteris\ paribus\ \dots\dots\dots\dots\dots\dots\dots\dots\dots.4.13$$

Where P_{FM} = Financial and Monetary policy. The objective is to promote consumption.

If an economy achieves better distribution, then Border Propensity of Consumption (ɤ) will reduce and therefore, less money will flow toward upper MESs to cater IKE, that is $\Delta M_{IKE} < 0$ and therefore, $\Delta M_{KME} < 0$ and $\Delta M_{PME} < 0$ or MMD will slow down. This is the situation when people are almost paying off their mortgages, companies see no more sales of electronics because most people have one or they not more need or attracted to have more. To balance this out, IKE may be kept higher by increasing money supply (M'_{IKE}) by central bank, which may cause inflation. However, up to the 1960s historical experience suggested that high inflation was good for an economy since it encouraged more investments and therefore, reduced unemployment and vice versa. This relationship is called the Phillips curve and discussed in section 4.9.

For immediate effect if an economy slows down, its central bank can enhance M'_{IKE} by its elastic monetary policy such as lowering down interest rate or printing money called "Quantitative Easing (QE)" to maintain consumption level but that also create inflation.

The value created by IKE (V_{IKE}) is separate from the one an economy ordinarily creates by using the traditional factors of production that is, Land, Labor and Capital (V_{KME}). We may consider IKE is absolutely technology driven and is a function of capital and technology.

$$V_{IKE} = f\ (M_{IKE},\ M'_{IKE},\ \check{T})\ \text{ceteris paribus} \dots\dots\dots\dots\dots.4.14$$

Where, V_{IKE}=the total inductive value produced in an economy using M_{ME}, M_{IKE} =Inductive money, M'_{IKE} = Debt attributes to IKE. $\check{T}$=Technological innovation.

The higher you go to the Market Energy State (MES), the higher is the value of V_{KME} and V_{IKE}. This is also true for *IKE*. In other words, more consumption happens, more economic benefits and capabilities concentrate within certain upper Market Energy States (MESs). The bottommost MES has them all the lowest. If a capability of the bottommost MES is below a certain minimum level, the upper MESs can be merged together and called as **"Market Energy Loop (MEL)"**.[5] In this model, the people who have entitlements and capabilities below a certain low level can be positioned outside MEL and may be called as **Residual Market Energy State (RMS).** On the other hand, the corresponding market energy for the people who have entitlements and capabilities above that

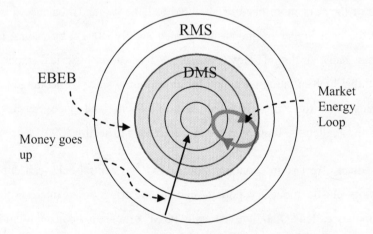

Figure 4.16 Effective Biased Equilibrium Barrier (EBEB)[8]

certain level can be can be merged together and called as **Dominating Market Energy State (DMS)**. The positioning of the boundary between DMS and RMS is up to discretion of an analyst since MEL exists within DMS in varying strengths. As shown in Figure 4.16, the concept of DMM is also valid within a MEL. A DMS can also be called an Effective Pareto Coalition (EPC) and RMS can also be called as Effective Pareto Space (EPS). Between them the boundary between EPC and EPS can be called as Effective Biased Equilibrium Barrier (EBEB). As per definition, a MEL internalizes benefits within DMS and externalizes costs to RMS. This means RMS needs special support such as social security, welfare, job building etc. from external bodies such as government and non-profit organizations.

The Residual Market Energy State (RMS) represents the vulnerable part of an economy. As shown in Figure 4.15, if RMS is positioned on MES_N, then MEL

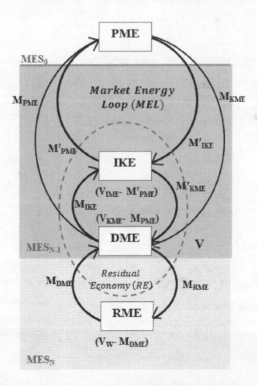

Figure 4.17 Market Energy Loop & Residual Market Energy State

will be comprised of MES_0 to MES_{N-1}. If economic growth stops or an economy does not perform well, more and more people will move from DMS to RMS and vice versa. In this model whatever the people in RMS do, the people in DMS or MEL are benefited. The more money goes to MEL, the less remains in RMS. The corresponding Kinetic Market Energy (KME) of DMS can be called as **Dominant Market Energy (DME)** and of RMS can be called as **Residual Market Energy (RME)**. Accordingly, Figure 4.15 is modified as Figure 4.17 by positioning RME on MES_N and DME on MES_{N-1}. For simplicity of understanding we may assume that absolute labor power as the only entitlement to RMS. Thus here we may distinguish the people whose income absolutely comes from their labor power from the others whose incomes mostly come from their 'rights'. RME is fed from DME (M_{RME}) such as wage, lease, loans and always adds more values (M_W) for the MEL, where part of M_W goes to DME (M_{DME}) in form of profit, rent, tithe or interest but staying outside of MEL. The more money goes to DMS, the less remains in RMS.

Accordingly, money toward *RME* can be expressed as a function of *MEL* and economic policy toward labor (P_R) of the economy:

$$M_{RME} = f\,(MEL,\ P_R)\ \text{ceteris paribus} \ldots\ldots\ldots\ldots\ldots\ldots\ldots\ldots 4.15$$

If we differentiate the money or value produced by absolute labor as V_W who do not have any other entitlement such as property right or intellectual right, then similar to equation 4.2, V_W can be expressed as:

$$V_W = f(M_{RME},\ L),\ \text{ceteris paribus,} \ldots\ldots\ldots\ldots\ldots\ldots\ldots 4.16$$

As per definition of "Biased Equilibrium" and equation 4.3, the money goes to MEL by exploiting absolute labor power, M_{DME} is a function of the money created in the economy by labor force (V_W) and the level of information biasing by the socio-economic institutions of the economy:

$$M_{DME} = f\,(V_W,\ \tilde{I}_B),\ \text{ceteris paribus,} \ldots\ldots\ldots\ldots\ldots\ldots\ldots 4.17$$

Similar to equation 4.4, RME can be expressed as function of money remains (V_W-M_{DME}) in RMS:

$$\Delta RME = f(V_W-M_{DME}) \text{ ceteris paribus} \ldots\ldots\ldots\ldots\ldots 4.18$$

According to the equations 4.17 & 4.18, distributional growth or values (*RME*) can also be improved by sharing more information (inverse $\tilde{I}_B$) between MEL and RMS, while M_{DME} impacts negatively on distribution. As discussed earlier that information sharing also improve qualitative aspect of life.

As discussed in earlier section, if equation 4.7 is valid but equation 4.8 is not, then the economy faces liquidity problem and private sector does not want to invest as they have already over-invested, that is equation 4.8 also become invalid. In that case, the economy falls into depression. To solve this problem, Keynes suggested that government should investment more to build infrastructure and welfare by running deficit budget. Equation 4.2 can be modified in view of Figure 4.15 as:

$$V_{KME} = f(M_{KME}, M'_{KME}, L, E) \text{ ceteris paribus} \ldots\ldots\ldots\ldots 4.19$$

The money invested to promote consumption revitalized the demand. Equation 4.5 can be modified in view of Figure 4.15 as:

$$\Delta KME = f(V_{KME}-M_{PME}) \text{ ceteris paribus} \ldots\ldots\ldots\ldots\ldots 4.20$$

The total value created in the economy, V is the summation of V_{KME} and V_{IKE}. For simplicity, as shown in Figure 4.15, total value created in the economy based on equations 4.2 and 4.14 can be expressed as:

$$V = f(M_{KME}, M'_{IKE}, L, E, \check{T}) \text{ ceteris paribus} \ldots\ldots\ldots\ldots 4.21$$

Where, V_{KME} =kinetic money, M'_{IKE} = Debt attributes to IKE. L =Labor, E =Natural resource and energy and $\check{T}$ =Technological innovation.

If we assume, the amount of labor employed in the economy remains the same ($\Delta f(L)=0$) or there is no change in absolute labor efficiency ($\Delta(V_W-M_{RME})/\Delta M_{RME})=0$) the following relationship can be derived (simplified):

$$\delta(V - M_{KME} - M'_{IKE}) = \delta f(E, \check{T}), \text{ ceteris paribus} \quad \ldots\ldots\ldots\ldots 4.22$$

Where, δV= gross earning in a year, δM_{KME} = interest cost for investment M_{KME}, M'_{IKE} = interest cost for debt for consumption and tax to government. That is, rapid growth of an economy is dependent on its ability to use "cheap" energy and technological innovation. As long as there is enough supply of energy, the future economy will be larger than existing and consumption potential of people of an economy will always increase. This is what Minsky called "paradox of gluttony".[44] Smith (2011) further points out:

> "Indeed, most jobs in industrialized countries critically depend not just on consumerism but on ever-increasing overconsumption. We "need" this ever-increasing consumption and waste production because, without growth, capitalist economies collapse."[75]

In a crisis situation, central bank can still intervene either by printing money or converting private debts into public debts to prop up the economy ($\Delta M'_{IKE} > 0$) against any abrupt downfall as long as there is enough supply of energy. However, there is a limit of the supply of energy, in the long-run, it creates a bigger risk by adding more vulnerability to the economy.

At certain high level of inequality, Market Energy Loop (MEL) creates a **Price Pressure (PP)** on Residual Market Energy State (RMS). It is technically different from 'inflation'. Inflation is a rise in the general level of prices of goods and services in an economy over a period of time. It is attributed to changes in real demand for goods and services, or changes in available supplies such as during scarcities, as well as to growth in the money supply for overall economy.[50] The term **"Price Pressure (PP)"** can be defined as reduction of affordability of RMS because of price increase of the same or similar goods and services in DMS due to MEL. As an example, according to Amartya Sen, Bengal famine was caused by an urban economic boom that raised food prices, thereby causing millions of rural workers to starve to death when their wages did not keep up.[51] Price Pressure (PP) is a negative externality. The term negative externality is a negative effect on a party not directly involved in a transaction, which results in a market failure.[52]

The reason for inflation can be explained in this model by slowing down capital to market energy conversion process, which increases the money supply in the economy. Therefore, according to this model, inflation and increase in money supply both are effects of the same cause. However, the early monetarists suggested increasing money supply to boost up consumption but that actually aggravated the inflation situation. On the other hand, reducing money supply to combat inflation has negative impact on economic growth. As an example, GDP of British economy reduced after Margaret Thatcher increased interest rates to slow the money supply and thus to lower inflation at the beginning of her government.[55] However, fiscal policies such as reducing marginal tax rate and tariff, deregulation and privatization have worked to control unemployment and inflation in cases where capital to market energy conversion was backed by digital and semiconductor technology (T) revolutions along with increased supply of energy (E).

Corruption has similar effect of Price Pressure (PP) in the economy. Similarly, 'deflation' can be explained if there is enormous capital investments but business cannot generate enough cash flow (money) in the economy. An economy can have both inflation and PP at the same time. The role of government is to reduce income inequality and control inflation. However, if there exists a PP and government officials are paid low salaries, the concept Border Proposition of Consumption (BPC) tells that corruptions will increase. In this case, government policies and enforcements are biased to the capitalists and government expenditures are mishandled. The end result, inequality rises, capability deprivation increases, government officials become rich but cripple the government.

By referring to equation 4.12, the more is M_{IKE}, the more is the Price Pressure on RMS but it requires the workers work harder for their livings. Since Price Pressure is inflation in DMS, it motivates the investors for more investment that should generate more employments, provided that the goods produced are sold in the market. Nevertheless Price Pressure (PP) also exists within DMS with varying strengths since DMS is composed of many MESs with more labor components downward. Price Pressure after a certain point may cause the goods produced in the economy remain unsold, economic growth may slow down and therefore, unemployment rate may remain high. This situation may be reflected as expanding RMS and contracting DMS.

4.8 Money Loop (ML)

Following the Great Compression, this situation happened in the U.S. economy during 1970s, called "stagflation".[43] In response to stagflation, the U.S. Federal Reserve increased interest rate but unemployment problem remained and the U.S. economy dipped into recession. To overcome the recession, then the U.S. President Ronald Reagan implemented fiscal stimulus by reducing taxes for the wealthy, expecting that this will increase investment and wages and therefore more money as payroll taxes for the government.

Following Reagan's tax cut and financial deregulation there was huge investments in consumer goods based on high TPT technological innovations–especially with digital transformation, high use of silicon and aluminum materials expedited with globalization. This became a big opportunity for innovations of the financial industry to exploit Border Propensity of

Consumptions (BPC) of individual economic agents. Let's imagine there are two types of BPCs. The first one is BPC for real goods and services. The second one is BPC for financial products and services. Let's also imagine another Market Energy called **Inductive Potential Market Energy (IPE)** that is dependent on the second type of BPC within a Market Energy Loop (MEL). As shown in Figure 4.18 that now money from Inductive KME (IKE) to PME goes via IPE. The separation of IPE and PME help create a positive feedback loop of money for the riches, can be named as **Money Loop (ML)**[3] to promote investment as shown in Figure 4.18.

A ML constitutes a primary market of values and rights such as oil price, real estate or other property rights. A secondary market works on top of it based on financial innovations that may reinforce existing Money Loop (ML). This reinforcement may be called a Bulling Money Loop (BML). We see a small change in oil price has large change in oil stock markets. As long an economy was holding gold standard, expansion of money supply (here, M_{IKE}) was limited. After abandonment of gold standard and introduction of petro-dollar, central bank of an economy can supply more money than that can be converted into market energy as long as the country can afford dollar to buy oil. The deregulation of the financial sectors during 1990s in the U.S. followed by many other countries created credit boom that contributed to BML.

Similar to previous section, let us formulate some simple mathematical equations for better illustration of the concept of IPE. Let M_{IPE} is the "inductive money" induced by IPE. This may be expressed as function of the money (or value) produced in IKE (V_{IKE}), Border Propensity of Consumption for financial products (γ_F), information biasing through marketing promotion for financial products and services ($\tilde{I}_{BF}$):

$$M_{IPE} = f\ (V_{IKE},\ \gamma_F,\ \tilde{I}_{BF})\ \text{ceteris paribus} \dots\dots\dots\dots\dots\dots 4.23$$

M_{IPE} keeps alive the Money Loop (ML), where a ML is analogous to human heart that circulates money by drawing from lower MESs to the center of a DMM. However, in reality a ML creates growth and debt pressure on the economy and promotes speculative interaction between PME and IME, essentially by burning more energy from fossil fuel, while adding vulnerability to financial and ecological crisis. Speculation and financial innovation works on

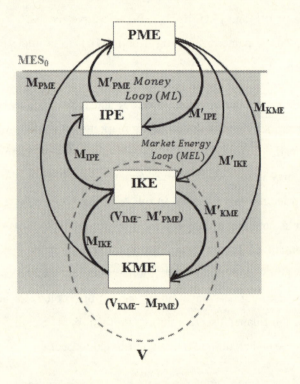

Figure 4.18 Money Loop (ML)

top of a ML in the form financial instruments or IOUs ("I Owe You"), which is now multiples of a ML of an economy. As Richard Heinberg explains our overwhelming financial claims:

"We have accumulated too many financial- monetary claims on real assets–consisting of energy, food, labor, manufactured products, built

282

infrastructure, and natural resources. Those claims, essentially IOUs, exist in the forms of debt and derivatives."[47]

The money that leverages financial industry is compounded in the financial market. Financial deregulation in 1990s in U.K., in USA and then eventually all over the world virtually unlocked the limit of compounding. This money can be called as "compounding money" for the economy. Mathematically this money can be expressed as:

$$M'_{IPE} = f(PME, P_F) \text{ ceteris paribus} \ldots\ldots\ldots\ldots\ldots 4.24$$

Where P_F = Financial policy for promoting financial market such as financial deregulation.

The "compounding money", M'_{IPE} includes the inflated component of real estate, stocks, IOUs etc. In other words, this is the risk bearing component of money.

In fact, a ML does not produce any value in the economy but enhance investment through innovations of financial products. Accordingly, Inductive PME (IPE) can be expressed as:

$$IPE = f(M_{IPE}, M'_{IPE}, \text{F}) \text{ ceteris paribus} \ldots\ldots\ldots\ldots\ldots 4.25$$

Where, F = Financial innovations.

A positive flow of "compounding money" by means of credit or bailout keeps IPE higher, provided that technological state is accompanied with high Transformation Potential of Technology (TPT). Speculative financing reinforces a pre-existing ML. Before 1990s financial market deregulation, IPE was constrained. However, after the financial deregulation and advancement of digital technologies, IPE has become virtually unlocked. Lowering down interest rate on consumer credit enhances consumption (MEL) that contributes to GDP but does not control Money Loop (ML) since propensity of consumption is low for upper MESs.

As shown in Figure 4.18, the market energy or resources created in presence of a ML concentrates within a Market Energy Loop (MEL). A MEL and a ML always involves the core MES of a DMM. A ML transmits the financial and political power toward the core MES through internalization of wealth. Similarly a MEL internalizes purchasing power within upper MESs and externalizes costs to RMS. Financial innovations such as shadow banking system and derivatives market works on top of ML and it can bring the whole economic system down.

In normal operation of an economy, Money Loop is inflated ($+ML$) because of positive feedback loop. And in case of an economic crisis, ML is deflated ($-ML$). In the first case it reinforces M'_{PME} and in the second case, it lessens M'_{PME}. Similarly, in normal case, a positive ML increases the productive and supplementary money flows ($\Delta M_{KME} > 0$ and $\Delta M'_{IKE} > 0$). On the other hand, during economic crisis, a negative Money Loop ($-ML$) will roll back those ($\Delta M_{KME} < 0$ and $\Delta M'_{IKE} < 0$).

A ML is also created or reinforced when cash money enters in a market from an outside source, bypassing production system. The products that are driver of ML are financial products, durable assets like property and gold etc. The concept of ML can be used to analyze inflation, corruption and financial crisis of an economy. The concepts of ML and 'savings glut' are significantly different. If marginal propensity of savings (MPS) of a country is very high, there will be a 'savings glut'. "On the other hand, if only a small subset of the population of a country holds most of the savings, there will be a potential ML. To prevent this government lowers interest rate for deposit and therefore, people are discouraged to save money in their home country.

The financial capitalism allows individuals and firms to uplift their position from lower MES to upper MES driven by IKE through debts and thus translate 'Price Pressure' from upper MES into debt pressure. The debt pressure will not immediately be realized if there is a continuous flow of debt. It helps the politicians and government in two ways. Firstly, it preserve status quo of the citizens' living standard and lifestyle that keeps them happy. And secondly, it creates a growth pressure on the economy. However, at the same time it accumulates vulnerability of the economy to collapse.

Let us imagine a Differential Market Model (DMM) of two 'market energy states (MES)', MES_N & MES_{N-1} as shown in Figure 4.19. For a single product the demand and supply curves of MES_N are D_ND_N' and S_NS_N' respectively and for MES_{N-1} are $D_{N-1}D_{N-1}'$ and $S_{N-1}S_{N-1}'$ respectively. They are in equilibrium at price '**P**'. It assumes one product world that the product has demand in all possible MESs (MES_0 to MES_{N-1}) but with varying Boundary Proposition of Consumption (BPC) and Subset Proposition of Consumption (SPC). In presence of pre-existing Market Energy Loop (MEL), the demand and supply curves in

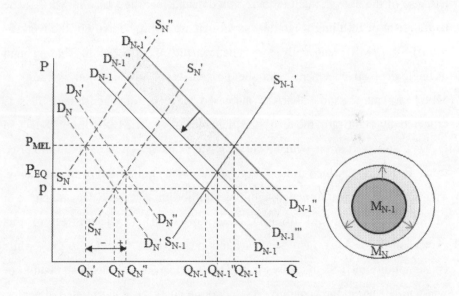

Figure 4.19: Effect of Market Energy Loop in Price Equilibrium

MES_{N-1} are in a higher position than those of in MES_N. Let MES_N is the Residual Market Energy State (RMS). Now the effect of further reinforcement of MEL in MES_{N-1} is shown as rightward shift of the demand curve from $D_{N-1}D_{N-1}'$ to D_{N-}

$_1$'D_{N-1}". Due to the MEL reinforcement, the equilibrium price would potentially move up to 'P_{MEL}'. This inflates consumption potential of MES_{N-1} from Q_{N-1} to Q_{N-1}'. If we imagine MES_{N-1} is composed of all higher MESs between MES_{N-1} to MES_0, the quantity of consumption will vary for each of higher MESs according to their strengths. As an example, if the product is 'land' and the individuals in MES_{N-1} invest all their money to buy lands, there will be big hike of the land prices and in turn, will contribute Border Propensities of Consumptions (BPC). On the other hand, to comply with 'P_{MEL}', the supply curve of MES_N would shift leftward from $S_N S_N$' to S_N'S_N" (the demand curve is stable) and therefore, consumption in MES_N (RMS) would decrease from Q_N to Q_N'. This means in case of land, people in MES_N would be impacted because of potential "Price Pressure" from MES_{N-1} by paying much more money toward real estates.

Because of the above situation there is a demand for wage raise in MES_N. The requirement of fulfilling wage raise is to increase of productivity of the workers in MES_N (RMS) that calls for enhancement of information sharing and technological advancements. As the propensity of consumption is more in MES_N, we may assume that the increased wage is fully consumed. This is reflected by rightward move of the demand curve in MES_N from $D_N D_N$' to D_N'D_N". This shift of the demand curve in MES_N moves up the equilibrium price from 'P' to 'P_{EQ}', which indicates the actual price equilibrium of the economy. The figure shows that to match with this equilibrium price, the demand curve in MES_{N-1} shifts rightward from $D_{N-1} D_{N-1}$' to D_{N-1}"D_{N-1}"'. The effect of this expansion of the MEL increases consumption in MES_N from Q_N to Q_N", while consumption in MES_{N-1} increases from Q_{N-1} to Q_{N-1}". This reflects a situation of win-win change in the economy. As economic energy is concentrated at center, 'progress' in the capitalist world is synonymous to centrifugal expansion of MEL. On the other hand, as the economy reaches its price equilibrium at 'P_{EQ}', its impact on MES_{N-1} can be seen as virtual shift of the demand curve from its virtual position D_{N-1}'D_{N-1}" to actual D_{N-1}"D_{N-1}"'. Here the price equilibrium 'P_{EQ}'

is much lower than 'P_{MEL}'. This gap represents an equivalent non-dispensed income in MES_{N-1}. The excess money in MES_{N-1}, shown as the shaded area in Figure 4.19 is actually the Money Loop (ML) contributes toward PME, in descending strengths among different MESs between MES_0 to MES_{N-1} that promotes non-productive and speculative use of money.

From micro-perspective, although Money Loop (ML) contributes non-productive use of money but the investors owe interests to the bank to be paid from the income produced by the "compounding money". By adding together all the interest cost and taxes owned by the economy should be covered by the income the investments produce. That is, from micro-economic credit perspective, as shown in Figure 4.20, there are three cost components of credit an individual

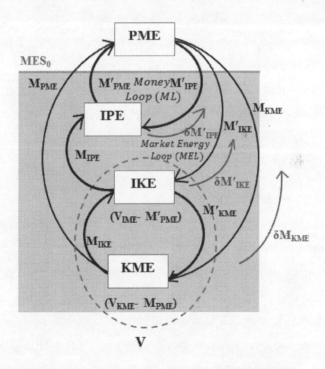

Figure 4.20: Credit Perspective of Money Loop (ML)

economic agent has to bear. 1. Real cost component of investment (δM_{KME}), 2. Inductive cost component for financial leverage of MEL ($\delta M'_{IKE}$) and 3. Inductive cost component for financial leverage of ML ($\delta M'_{IPE}$). If (δV) is the income that should be able to cover the three cost components, then

$$\delta V \geq \delta M_{KME} + \delta M'_{IKE} + \delta M'_{IPE.} \text{ ceteris paribus} \dots\dots\dots\dots 4.26$$

Or, $\Delta(V - \delta M_{KME} - \delta M'_{IKE}) \geq \delta M'_{IPE.}$ ceteris paribus $\dots\dots\dots\dots 4.27$

From equations 4.22 & 4.27, the following relationship can be derived for a sustainable economy:

$$\delta f(E, \check{T}) \geq \delta M'_{IPE.} \text{ ceteris paribus} \dots\dots\dots\dots\dots\dots 4.28$$

As $\delta M'_{IPE}$ compounds in a Money Loop (ML), consumption of an economy should also compound by using more energy and technological innovations to leverage the debt caused by it. A capitalist economy is sustaiable as long as equation 4.28 is valid or in other words, it is supported by enough supply of energy and technology (keeping aside the climate change concerns). Another way to reach to sustainable economy is to unwind the ML and switch to renewable energy, while fossil fuel is declining.

Theoretically, a capitalist economy assumes unlimited supply of energy and ever changing technological state. There are two aspects of technology. One is capital aspect and the other is energy aspect. There must be a limit of the maximum amount of capital that can be converted into market energy under certain technological state in a moment of time without creating or reinforcing existing Money Loop (ML), provided that all other causes of ML such as economic policies or money supply remain constant. This limit can be defined as **Optimal Capital for a Technological State (OCT)**. An economy with macro-economic MSF $\angle\alpha > 45^0$, operates beyond OCT to cater BPC and as a result, MEL is reinforced. And a ML is a situation where technological state does not change fast enough to convert PME into KME but using cheap 'energy' it multiplies wealth of the riches. If the technology is used for benefits of mankind at large, technological advancement will enhance OCT (in this case, MSF $\angle\alpha < 45^0$), which is synonymous to prosperity. Therefore, objective of an economic policy should be carefully planned for enhancement of OCT. The concept of OCT separates out prosperity from growth and tells that prosperity can be achieved without capital growth.

According to the definition of OCT, if capital investment exceeds OCT, MMD becomes imbalanced and therefore, existing MEL and ML are reinforced. In both cases, whether OCT is enhanced or operates beyond OCT, it needs more consumption of energy and other resources. Therefore, each technological state has a requirement for a specific amount of consumption of energy and other resources. This consumption of energy can be defined as **Energy Cost for a Technological State (ECT)**. In case of a balanced MMD, conversion to market energy should enhance through technological progress. If technology stays at certain state, then more investment exceeds OCT. If an economy were operated within OCT from the beginning, there would be no MEL and therefore, no incentives for capitalists. Capital is energy intensive but the opposite is not true in the long-run considering the fact that we have limited reserve of fossil fuel. However, in the short-run, the more we are moving from conventional oil (cheap oil) to non-conventional oil, the more capital intensive is the energy. It can be inferred that if an economy operates within OCT, ECT will be the lowest. This level of ECT can be defined as **Optimal Energy for a Technological State (OET)**. Enhancement of OCT calls for reduction of ECT and therefore enhancement of OET. Since ECT is increasing, if a supply side economy operates beyond OCT, it will also operate beyond OET. The energies burnt and wasted in wars following industrial revolution until now all are beyond OET.

If Money Market Dynamics (MMD) cannot enhance Optimal Capital for Technological State (OCT) due to institutional constraints or constraint in technology itself other than energy constraint, it will become imbalanced and reinforce MEL and ML. The concept of ML describes a situation where law of diminishing marginal utility fails (say, for financial assets) but law of diminishing return is valid in context of energy behind the capital growth. As described in the example of Figure 4.19, capital growth also creates a price-wage spiral in a certain part of an economy, which is an instance of ML.

The capital aspect of technology is firmly rooted in easily available minerals such as silicon and aluminum, which are the second (28%) and the third (8%) most abundant substances of earth surface respectively. The technologies based on these materials have high 'Transformation Potential of Technology (TPT)' value. On the other hand, the energy aspect of technology uses scarce and vital resources on earth, the fossil fuel. Too much emphasis on capital growth is hiding the second aspect of technology from our attention. Moore's law (1965) is applicable for the first aspect, which predicts that over the history of computing hardware, the number of transistors on integrated circuits doubles in approximately every two years.[55] Moore's law supports the idea that technology will continue to improve dramatically. Heinberg (2011) comments that if Moore's law were applicable for energy and transportation, a new car would cost $750 and get 2000 miles to the gallon by now.[56]

In reality, there is no limit of capital accumulation but the world's reserve of fossil fuel is limited that has formed in millions of years and now we are running out of it. Heinberg (2011) argues

"Our basic energy, water, and transport infrastructure shows signs of senescence, and of vulnerability to Murphy's law–the maxim that anything that can go wrong, will go wrong."[56]

At present world, information biasing can be defined as capitalist biasing that promotes consumerism and growth. While MMD conceptualizes prosperity over time, a Market Energy Loop (MEL) describes consumerism and Money Loop (ML) describes the reason for exponential growth. All economic growth is dependent on 'the master resource-energy'.[57] That is, the growth of an economy based on ML is absorbing physical mineral resources and fossil fuel reserves. Following the industrial revolution, the prosperity of the world driven by growth accompanied with exponential use of fossil fuel. Martenson (2011) describes this as "the inconvenient truth about growth" as:

> "because there was always sufficient surplus energy that we could have both growth and prosperity at the same time. But that was largely an artifact of a fossil fuel bonanza, not an intrinsic attribute of growth."[42]

Unfortunately, when the oil bonanza will end, whatever prosperities we have achieved by the name of 'growth' will be just scraps.

4.9 Horizontal and Vertical Growth

A capitalist economy is only concerned about capital growth and therefore it operates beyond Optimal Capital for a Technological State (OCT). In an economy, 'Market Energy (ME)' is the highest at the center of its MEL and descends down toward the EBEB. The capitalists are positioned at and around the center of the MEL and our capitalist economic policies focus on giving them incentives to stimulate growth, with the expectation that Kinetic Market Energy (KME) should improve 'consumerism' in Residual Market Energy State (RMS). This type of growth can be called as 'Horizontal Growth (HG)' as shown in Figure 4.21 as centrifugal expansion of MEL in a three layer DMM, where the three MESs–M3 at the core and the M2 in the middle and M1in the bottom. A HG can also be considered as win-win market expansion since it creates a win-win effect on the individuals inside the Dominant Market Energy State (DMS) and the individuals in RMS (EPS) around the boundary of the MEL, which is positive for an economy. In an economy whenever MEL centrifugally extends or rolls, it creates new job and income opportunities for the people outside the MEL, mostly those positioned around the boundary of the DMS. At macro level,

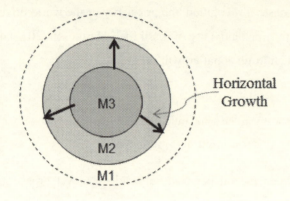

Figure 4.21: Horizontal Growth (HG)

'Horizontal Growth (HG)' is the summation of all micro level expansions Kinetic Market Energy State (KME) and Inductive KME (IKE).

$$HG > \Sigma(\Delta KME + \Delta IKE) \text{ ceteris paribus } ....4.29$$

Contrarily, if the MEL squeezes then the people around the boundary will lose more opportunities than people at the bottom MESs. Horizontal Growth (HG) represents the true growth such as new employments, poverty reduction, new infrastructures, welfare etc.

There is another type of growth in the capitalist world. If EBEB is strengthened at certain position, it will prevent the MEL from expanding. This means growth will still happen without extending the MEL, in the vertical direction. This type of growth can be called as 'Vertical Growth (VG)'. High Market Skewness Factor (MSF) is the reason for VG. At macro level, VG is the summation of all micro level expansions of Potential Market Energy State (PME) and Inductive PME (IPE) expansions.

$$VG > \Sigma(\Delta PME + \Delta IPE) \text{ ceteris paribus } ....4.30$$

Figure 4.22 shows three dimensional model of "Vertical Growth (VG)" and "Horizontal Growth (HG)". MEL of on upper MESs reduces consumption potential on the lower MESs, while it inflates consumption potential in the upper MESs. If the resultant ME tilts toward vertical direction, there will be negative

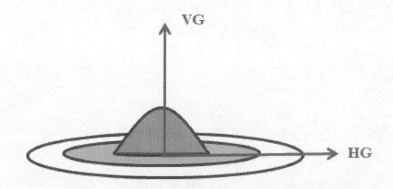

Figure 4.22 Three Dimensional Market Energy Model

impact of ME on the economy since it puts implicit 'Price Pressure (PP)' on RMS. On the other hand, if the resultant ME tilts toward horizontal direction, then there will be positive impact of ME on the economy.

According to this model, both types of growth HG & VG are backed by technological advancements and consumption of energy and other resources. Government policy incentives should be intended to HG by reducing the MSF. However, in reality growth always has both components and should be seen from both perspectives. As an example, the upward trend of house price as shown in Figure 4.23 provides incentives for more development of new houses followed by many new economic activities such as new utilities and infrastructures, markets and services, employments and businesses that can be translated as HG in that area. The Figure shows that around 1990 the upward trend in housing market became saturated for a short period of time. This situation can be interpreted as at that point, a Biased Equilibrium Barrier (BEB) was preventing HG in the economy. The people outside the DMS were impacted by the housing market beyond their affordability and the housing market virtually stopped growing. This is where the U.S. Federal Reserve Bank further slashed the interest rate, reflected as downward trend in mortgage interest rate (to

Figure 4.23: Price of New House vs. Mortgage Interest Rate in USA[58]

increase PME) in Figure 4.23. As a result, the housing market soared but mass people in the middle (M2) and at the bottom (M1) MESs (Figure 4.21) fell in deep debt due to price hike. The increased debt and soaring housing market together clearly indicates VG along with HG. What will happen if a recession hits the economy? Like previous, we will see lots of foreclosures, both HG & VG will squeeze and a lot of people will fall down from DMS to RMS.

Let's take a look at the cost distribution of "iPhone 5" in Figure 4.24. It is sold at $749 without contract. The material cost is $209, 28% of the total value and labor cost is only $8, which is 1% of the total value.[59] If iPhone 5 were manufactured in USA, the labor cost would contribute to HG of the U.S. economy. The rest of the costs imply to shipping, marketing warranty and profit, which accounts for 71% of the value[59], contributes mostly toward VG that eventually goes to the upper ML of the U.S. economy. In other words, if there

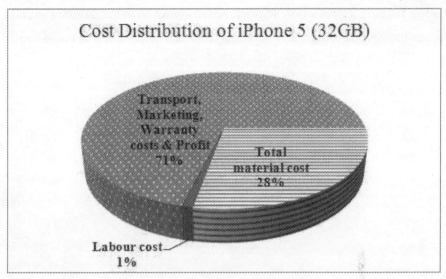

Figure 4.24: Cost Distribution of iPhone 5

were no VG or otherwise, the upper ML had sacrificed few dollars, the cost of iPhone 5 would be cheaper even by manufacturing in the United States.

The concept of DMM tells that difference between the market energy levels is the very fundamental reason of capital flow in an economy. It is important to note that ideally, MMD represents a market economy without any policy intervention. In presence of MEL, if economic policies are influenced from center of DMM, it will be the same as 'supply side economics' (Figure 4.25). The supply siders focus on more private investment for more production and more profit since they claim that private sectors are more efficient and capable in increasing productivities. They urge for lowering marginal tax rate and trade barriers by claiming that consumers will be benefited from a greater supply of goods and services at lower prices.[60]

According to above illustration, supply side economic policy reducing marginal taxes and trade barriers to enhance economic activities may potentially create an economic bubble. In case of demand-side economics, government may increase tax from wealthy and spend to create new demands especially in lower Market

Energy States (Figure 4.25) to stipulate KME. However, the opposite might also happen by imprudent and corrupted bureaucrats and politicians wasting money

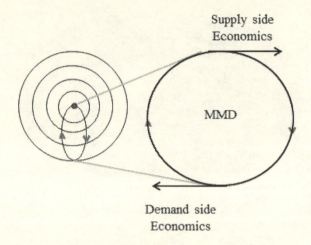

Figure 4.25: Supply side and Demand side Economic Policies

and energies building unnecessary infrastructures and later wasting again by replacing or fixing them. Thus again, corrupted bureaucrats and politicians become wealthy and the investors follow them. Recently economists and politicians urge for big financial stimulus package to the big corporate and financial companies targeting to jump-start a slow economy feeding again BPC, which eventually bounce back reinforcing the pre-existing Money Loop (ML).

At the beginning of a new technological state, an economic expansion happens since technological advancement triggers Minsky's self-reinforcing debt dependent cycle of economic expansion.[44] This relationship of technology and financial capitalism explains why a capitalist economy operates beyond Optimum Capital for a Technological State (OCT). If an economy operates beyond OCT and OET, economy will be caught in a Money Loop (ML). As explained in Figure 4.26 that because of ML, Market Energy increases from *ME* to *ME′* and Market Energy Factor (MSF) increases from α to α′ but KME remains the same. In this situation, economic policy intervention increases

Market Energy from *ME′* to *ME″* toward horizontal direction that is toward more KME. The main idea is to bring money out of the Money Loop (ML) to the

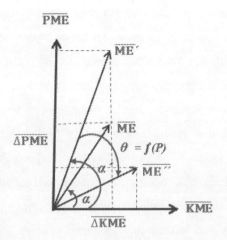

Figure 4.26 Market Energy Perspective of Growth

production system so that the people in DMS and in RMS are also benefited. However, in real world economic capitalists policies are either supply-side or demand side, they reinforce the pre-existing ML. As an example, if in case the Economic Policy Factor EPF, $\angle\theta$ is less than the increase of MSF ($\alpha′$-α), the economic progress will be nothing but Vertical Growth (VG), showing high figures in stock market and economic indicators.

According to this model, the best way to reduce MSF is to focus on information sharing between DMS and RMS in economic policies. If government policies do not support this objective, the monetary and financial policies whether seen as supply-side economic policies or demand-side economic policies cannot be synchronized. As an example, supply-side economic policies such as lowering the barriers for production of more goods and services must be synchronized with increased tax rates for the riches (capitalists) to build infrastructures, social security for the poor in RMS. In real life we see supply-side economics is implemented by lowering tax rates for the riches, which leaves the government dependent on debt largely to be paid by the employed poor and middle class people from their payroll.

Here the concept of MMD tells us that VG is the result of supply side economics which is more of a capitalist interest. Therefore, we see supply-side policy advocates generally lower marginal income tax and capital gains tax rates claiming to increase the supply of labor and capital in addition to smaller government and a lower regulatory burden on enterprises to lower costs.[60] In this model, it can be said that the high right peak of Laffer Curve described in the previous chapter (Figure 3.7b) reflects economic progress is backed by a technology with high Transformation Potential for a Technological state (TPT) such as silicon products, where cutting tax rates may increase revenues. Similarly, left of the peak of economic progress (Figure 3.7b) reflects that the TPT of the technologies reduces, where cutting tax rates will decrease revenues. However, as Paul Krugman contended that supply-side adherents did not fully believe that the United States income tax rate was on the "backwards-sloping" side of the curve and yet they still advocated lowering taxes to encourage investment of personal savings.[61]

As we have seen in the past that the supply side economics led to wars for market expansion such as series of wars following industrial revolution in Europe or depression such as the Great Depression. One big cause of the Great Depression was a global over-investment in heavy industry capacity compared to wages and earnings. It was solved by Keynes's 'demand-side economics' where in the U.S. Roosevelt government took initiatives to increase purchasing power and wages for consumer spending.

The demand side economics argues that increased infrastructure spending and cuts in taxes results in an increase in the nominal wages of those who tend to spend the greatest portion of their income on consumables.[62] Keynes viewed excessive saving and investment as a potential harm to the economy, since giving additional income to the rich gives them a low marginal incentive to spend[62], whereas giving additional incomes to the poor and middle class in the Residual Market Energy State (RMS) provide a high marginal incentive for additional spending, which results in improved business income and grows the economy. It is important to note that capitalists are part of MMD cycle but ideally, a government is not. Therefore, it can be said that in case of demand-side economics, the policy intervention from government is external to MMD.

After Great Depression, economic growths of most economies have been a combination of supply-side and demand-side economies. As indicated in Figure 4.25 that MMD may run more smoothly in if both are synchronized. Nevertheless, once markets are integrated and expanded, enough infrastructures are built, a smother operation of MMD is possible through monetary policies[63] by expanding or controlling money supply in the economy. The demand-side economists think that monetary policy is an important tool for tweaking the economy and dealing with business cycles, whereas a supply-sider does not think that monetary policy can create economic value.[64] However increasing money supply by lowering interest rate does the same as 'supply-side' economics but on the other hand, lower interest on consumer loans may also make poor and middle class people dependent on debt. The objective of increasing money supply is more growth, which brings more VG than HG, which makes MMD imbalanced. Then the whole effort of the economy is dedicated to deal with impacts of the imbalanced MMD such as poverty, corruptions, unemployment and the other economic and financial crisis.

The supply-side economics tells that a greater marginal tax cut provides incentives to invest and produce economic benefits for the overall economy. It argues that the government would not lose total tax revenue because lower rates would be more than offset by economic growth a higher tax revenue base due to greater employment and productivity.[64] By assuming a certain percentage of economic output is government revenue but economic policy alone cannot decide how much the government revenue will be, rather it largely depends on technology and energy consumptions. In the U.S., income tax rates were cut several times in the 1920s, totaling the average tax rate down by less than half. Although it was claimed that the cuts would increase tax revenue, this did not occur.[65] We know that technology and energy availability was significantly limited on that time. Income tax revenue did not reach even close to 1920 levels until tax rates were returned to 1920 levels in 1941.[65&66] We often forget that much of this pressure is under control because of technological progress and cheap supply of energy and not solely on policy alone.

Arthur B. Laffer after whom Laffer curve is named (Section 3.5) explains that by 1965 President Kennedy had cut the highest federal marginal tax rate to 70% from 91%. Thus, a person in the highest tax bracket would have received a 233 percent increase from what he earned when the tax rate was 91 percent, which clearly indicates VG. Laffer argues "The lessons here are simple: The higher tax rates are, the greater will be the economic impact of a given percentage reduction in tax rates."[67] In contrary to Mundell and Laffer's arguments, the ideal role of stock market should be reducing MSF, which requires availability of right technology. If MSF is not reduced then VG may become unrestrained that will cause a Bulling Money Loop (BML). They point to the dramatic rise in the stock market as a sign that the tax cut for the investors was effective, although they note that the hike in capital gains may be more trouble than it was worth.[66]

There is another big implication of Vertical Growth (VG) is corruption. In a developing country filled with corruption, a corrupted government official normally does not take bribes from a poor farmer or a worker directly but from a middle layer such as rich middlemen or businessmen. There PME and Inductive PME (IPE) are very high and a huge amount of free money circulates in the upper layers as a Money Loop (ML), which again gives birth of more money grabbers. Whatever the way to gather money in the upper layer is, the money mostly circulates among the grabbers. They try to hold control of the institutions so that they can establish monopolistic decision making process to dictate the economy according to their interests and wishes. Moreover, the individuals who are not corrupted but are supportive to this structure are also indirect stakeholders of the money. As an example, they get indirect raises in their salaries or excessive profits in their businesses. Consequently, the net result is that the rich people become richer and the costs of property ownership become high, increasingly unreachable to the poor people.

In summary, Vertical Growth (VG) has many negative implications as some of them are mentioned below:

1. Increases 'Price Pressure (PP)' and inflation.
2. Causes inequality and poverty.
3. Spreads corruption.
4. Creates monetary supremacy over humanity, culture, environment etc.
5. Finally, causes economic and financial crisis.

4.10 Unemployment under Biased Equilibrium

The concept of biased equilibrium is a market failure approach of economic analysis. Information about scarcity explains the situation why employed workers receive high wages while identical individuals are unemployed (Stiglitz, 2000).[68] Using this model, we may conclude that the employed workers are in a Pareto Coalition and establish a biased equilibrium with the unemployed individuals since the economy has certain capacity of employment under certain conditions. When the conditions change, the employment capacity of the economy also changes.

The short-run Phillips curve (see Figure 3.4 in Chapter 3) can also be explained by using the concept of 'Biased Equilibrium (BE)'. It explains that if there exists a BE in an economy, increase of money wage or Keynesian transfer expands the MEL and therefore, it will create new jobs and opportunities for RMS around the boundary of the EBEB. Figure 4.27 shows a Differential Market Model (DMM) consists of two MESs M1 and M2. Figure 4.27a initial position of an economy in accordance with point A on the initial short run Phillips curve shown in Figure 3.4 of Chapter 3. M1 represents unemployed people or poor people in RMS, whereas M2 represents employed or rich people in DML. Figure 4.27b represents reduction of unemployment but creation of inflation in accordance with point B in Figure 3.4. It expands M2 and squeezes M1. If new economic policy reinforces Money Loop (ML) when reducing unemployment, it will spread inflation within the extended MEL and increase 'price pressure' on those who are still unemployed in M1 and therefore, inflation in overall economy will increase. This is what happens at point B in Figure 3.4. Edmound Phelps and Milton Friedman explains the short-run trade off will raise inflation expectation that shifts the short-run Phillips curve rightward and moves the point of equilibrium from B to C, where it will sustain as NAIRU representing stagflation. In our model, the definition of MEL tells that M2 is already in a price-wage spiral, which is a sub-set of Money Loop (ML). Now the rational

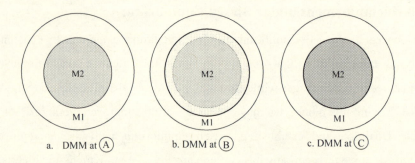

a. DMM at (A)   b. DMM at (B)   c. DMM at (C)

Figure 4.27: Differential Market Structure corresponds to Figure 3.4

expectation of the newly recruited individuals will increase. According to the concept of Border Propensity of Consumption (BPC), they will vie for the same set of products that of the individuals at the boundary of the EBEB between the original and extended M2. As every economy has certain capacity of employment under certain conditions, the one-time wage raise do not create a sustainable employment capacity to accommodate the extended price-wage spiral. Therefore, it squeeze back to its 'natural rate' as shown in Figure 4.27c but the inflation level prevails at point C.

Economists such as Milton Friedman and Edmund Phelps further argue that rational workers would only react to real wages, that is, inflation adjusted wages. However, one of the characteristics of a modern industrial economy is that workers do not encounter their employers in an atomized and perfect market. In many cases, they may lack the bargaining power to act on their expectations, no matter how rational they are, or their perceptions, no matter how free of money illusion they are. It is not that high inflation cause low unemployment as much as vice-versa: Low unemployment raises worker bargaining power, allowing them to successfully push for higher nominal wages. To protect profits, employers raise prices."[69] This is how inflation rises. Our model argues that due to Biased Equilibrium (BE), after the price rise, the money goes to the MEL at much higher rate than the wage raise. That is why we see in Figure 4.28 that in the U.S. economy, wages as a percent of the economy have been falling down

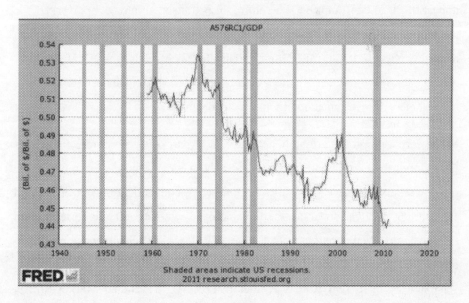

Figure 4.28: Wages as a percent of the economy (USA)[70]

regardless there was any recession or not. Eventually, the money causing extended inflation will be trapped in the original MEL keeping the inflation level and corresponding 'Price Pressure' high. Edmund Phelps's definition of NAIRU thus justifies presence of BEB in the U.S. economy. Another model called 'Efficiency Wage Hypothesis' introduced by Alfred Marshall in 1920 argues that wages, at least in some markets, could be more than the market clearing wage in order to increase productivity or efficiency.[71] This increased labor productivity pays for the higher wages.

As discussed in Chapter 3 Shapiro-Stiglitz model (1984) of efficiency wages, the workers are paid at a level that dissuades shirking..[72] The model proposes a Non-Shirking Condition (NSC) which once satisfied avoid workers to incur in shirking.[73] Efficiency wages theory is a market failure explanation of unemployment in contrast to theories which emphasize government intervention such as minimum wages.[74] Alternatively, whenever there is a demand for wage raise among the people in the lower MES (RMS) due to 'price pressure (PP)', central bank may reduce interest rates for consumer credit market to offset the impact of PP in consumption. Therefore, PP is translated into 'debt pressure' for the individuals who are in the weaker MES. Lowering down interest rate has many benefits: 1. It can be centrally controlled 2. It reduces wage pressure. 3. Simultaneously, it reduces PP and controls inflation, 4. It enhances consumption. Nevertheless, it leads an economy toward debt spiral.

When corporate profits are high, certainly all or part of the corporate employees get share of the pie as bonus or salary raise. However, at the same time there are many workers whose wages fall over time. Here comes the concept of 'Biased Equilibrium' that can separates out the employees who are not able to shirk from those who do when a market fails. Figure 4.29 shows 'efficiency wage model' in a two MES DMM, where M2 represents the MES where NSC is applicable. It is separated by an EBEB from the other market M1 a Residual Market Energy State (RMS), where NSC is not applicable since the workers have to work otherwise they will have to starve. In this case, the NSC curve is perfectly wage elastic, as shown in Figure 4.29 as a horizontal line at certain low wage. It shows that the wage in M1, W_{M1} is lower than the wage in M2, W_{M2} but it solves the stagflation problem of the economy by crossing the full employment point of M2. By summing these two NSC together with their elasticity vectors, the resultant NSC curve is positioned between the two NSC curves shown as NSC'

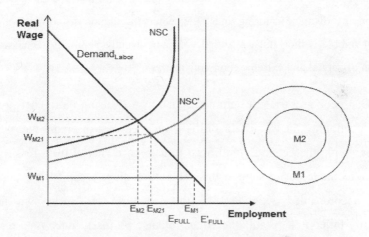

Figure 4.29: Efficiency wage under Biased Equilibrium

(Modified Shapiro-Stiglitz[58] Model)

in Figure 4.29, which shows the economy may achieve a new full employment (E'_{FULL}). This model has an important policy implication. As an example, if an economy becomes stagnant, it may invite immigrant workers who will not shirk for lower wage, as the second best option for them is to go back to their own country. This explains the reason of the new immigrant law in 1965 to stimulate the American economy. Many Middle East and developed countries have been able to boost their economy based on immigrant workers from developing countries. Similarly, many developing countries are able to achieve high growth by employing migrant workers from rural areas.

4.11 Economic Crises

In last few decades, the availability of cheap energy has been an incentive for large-scale trade, which requires money, and so economic growth has required an ongoing expansion of currency, credit, and debt, which eventually translates into Bulling Money Loop (BML). In his book "Afterburn" Heinberg explains this bubble as:

> "It is possible, however, for credit and debt to expand faster than the energy-fed "real" economy of manufacturing and trade; when this happens, the result is a credit/debt bubble, which must eventually deflate–usually resulting in massive destruction of capital and extreme economic distress."[85]

As a capitalist economy tries to optimize equation 4.28 using more energy and improving technology for its sustainability, if induced cost of credit due to ML ($\delta M'_{IPE}$) rises high, the economy will need to use more energy from fossil fuel and improve technologies to support this. Therefore, since a capitalist economy is always accompanied with a ML, this equation tells why we have fundamentally failed to substantially reduce reliance on fossil fuels. As a result, we are experiencing climate change, which is contributing meltdown of the glaciers, drying out rivers and water reservoirs, scarcity of surface water, mass extinction of species, extreme weather, and rising sea levels–all together undermine the viability of civilization. As we are failing to reduce the use of fossil fuel or consumption, the environmental impacts are worsening every moment. Equation 4.28 also explains the reason why we have almost used up all easily accessible, that is "cheap" fossil-fuel resources.

Now we have reached to the point of diminishing return for fossil fuel investment. However, this situation can be temporarily masked by increasing flow of credit, which eventually creates a BML (section 4.9) or vertical growth. A BML is a temporary problem as long as we have energy to back up or to revitalize the economy. At this point if price of energy rises due to declined supply, $\delta f(E, T)$ may tend to become smaller than $\delta M'_{IPE}$, then a severe economic or financial crisis will begin with massive contraction (or destruction) of capital. On the other hand, if energy price falls, the stock price will also fall and the oil industries will become more dependent on credit, as a result, their interest on credit ($\delta M'_{IPE}$) will rise. Nevertheless, it will take us toward a bigger crisis faster since it will drive sharper rise of oil price in future and cause the non-oil industries to broow more, while by all means oils are declining.

Although there are many theories on financial crisis, there is little consensus among the economists on how financial crisis develop and how they could be prevented. One of them, the 'learning model' explains that the investors behave similarly as because they learn from each other. These theories try to explain 'up' and 'down' of asset prices from psychological view point of the investors as 'true asset value is high when they observe others buying' and vice versa.[78] In our proposed model, the concept of 'information biasing' argues that information is no longer a given parameter but a strategic tool of individual economic agents. However, the concept of Pareto Coalition (PC) explains that the investors always follow their peers for holding their position in the wining coalition leaving others behind in a Pareto Space (PS). From outside, we see that when asset market is 'up', the Dominant Market Energy State (DMS) expands and when the market is 'down' DMS squeezes.

Going back to the history, Keynes defined a situation "Paradox of Thrift" when consumer spending in the U.S. economy reduced ($\Delta M_{IKE} < 0$) compared to the investment growth (ΔM_{KME}). In turn, unemployment increased, IKE was still low and therefore, the economy further went down and caused the Great Depression (1929-1930). At that time Keynes recommended government should spend generously in order to revive growth. In reference to Figure 4.18, when private sector was not willing to invest ($\Delta M_{KME} < 0$) Keynes suggested government for investing generously to keep people fully employed. Following Roosevelt's Keynesian economic policy, the economy focused on enhancing demand or

Monowar Zaman

Kinetic Market Energy (KME) by government spending, unionization etc. Also afterwards, promotion of products through advertising enhanced "Inductive KME (IKE)". At that point, Federal Reserve's monetary policy to increase money supply allowed government to borrow. Although it might have caused inflation but it reduced unemployment and because of the cyclic relationship of Money Market Dynamics (MMD), the economy began to roll, $\Delta V_{KME} > 0$ (equation 4.2 & 4.19), $\Delta IKE > 0$ (equation 4.20) then $\Delta M_{KME} > 0$ (equation 4.1). As Heinberg describes:

> "The next few decades saw a three-way contest between Keynesian social liberals, the followers of Marx, and temporarily marginalized neoclassical or neoliberal economists who insisted that social reform and government borrowing or meddling with interest rates merely impeded the ultimate efficiency of the free Market."[79]

As Keynesian economic measures caused better distribution, the Border Propensity of Consumption (BPC) reduced and MMD of the U.S. economy gradually slowed down. Federal Reserve bank increased money supply but there was not enough demand for investment ($\Delta M_{KME} < 0$) since previous huge investments failed to enhance inductive spending (M_{IPE}), the economy turned to a stagflation. Up to the 1960s many Keynesian economists ignored the possibility of stagflation because historical experience and widely accepted Phillips curve suggested that high unemployment was typically associated with low inflation, and vice versa. The idea is that high demand for goods drives up prices, and also encourages firms to hire more; and likewise high employment raises demand.[80] However, in the 1970s and 1980s, when stagflation occurred, the relationship between inflation and employment levels was not necessarily stable: that is, the Phillips relationship could shift (Figure 3.4).[81]

Another reason many economist provide for stagflation is that unfavorable supply shock, particularly oil tends to raise prices at the same time that it slows

308

the economy down by making production more costly and less profitable.[82&83] If supply of Energy (E) reduces, oil price will go up. The high oil prices impose costs on government purchases and also undermine the purchasing power of consumers. This situation can be described as ($\Delta M_{KME} > 0$ but & $\Delta V < 0$, $\Delta M_{IKE} < 0$ & $\Delta IKE < 0$). In this situation, financial and monetary policies of central bank of the country may increase money supply to enhance "Inductive KME (IKE)" but it may create or reinforce Price Pressure on Residual Market Energy State (RMS) or a cost-push inflation that may end up in a runaway price/wage spiral.[84] Neoclassical economics expresses this situation little differently that when some adverse changes in real factors such as economic output and unemployment are shifting the aggregate supply curve left at the same time that unwise monetary policies are shifting the aggregate demand curve right, the result is stagflation.[80]

A capitalist economy having a Market Energy Loop (MEL) must always create money through more production and more consumption. If money supply in financial market reaches to a stage that cannot expand or the volume of financial transaction contracts compared to the money invested in previously inflated assets such as real estate, the economy will fall into a financial crisis. An economic contraction at the beginning may relatively be contained. If it sustains then it may spread to a greater worldwide economic crisis.

Looking from microeconomics perspective and adding them up at macro-level, by referring to Figure 4.18, if net speculative values of financial assets goes up ($\Delta M'_{PME}$) compared to the money demand in production system (ΔM_{KME} & $\Delta M'_{IKE}$), it will lead to a financial bubble. In his "theory of reflexivity" George Soros' described that where price changes are driven by a positive feedback process whereby investors' expectations are influenced by price movements so their behavior acts to reinforce movement in that direction until it becomes unsustainable, whereupon the feedback drives prices in the opposite direction.[86]

Hyman Minsky (1992) theorizes that high speculation of financial economics leads to a higher risk of financial crisis. At micro-level, he defines three approaches of financing firms may choose, according to their tolerance of risk. They are hedge finance, speculative finance, and Ponzi finance. Ponzi finance leads to the most fragility.[44&78] For hedge finance, income flows are expected to meet financial obligations in every period, including both the principal and the interest on loans. Therefore, it has the lowest amount of risks and more capital component.[44] For speculative finance, a firm must roll over debt because income flows are expected to only cover interest costs, none of the principal is paid off.[44] And for Ponzi finance, expected income flows will not even cover interest cost.[44]

Here in Table 4.1, Minsky's model is explained reducing the concept of Money Loop (ML) to a micro-level. A ML reflects the contractual value not the real value of inflated financial assets or real estates or increase of the costs such as salaries, raw materials etc. due to the ML. Let imagine Figure 4.20 at micro-level, $\delta M'_{IPE}$ is the interest cost absolutely due to ML such as inflated assets and property rights (M'_{IPE}). $\delta M'_{IKE}$ is the interest cost and government tax absolutely

Income flow	δV	δV	δV
Interest cost	$\delta M_{KME} + \delta M'_{IKE} + \delta M'_{IPE}$	$\delta M_{KME} + \delta M'_{IKE} + \delta M'_{IPE}$	$\delta M_{KME} + \delta M'_{IKE} + \delta M'_{IPE}$
Relationship	$\delta V > \delta M_{KME} + \delta M'_{IKE} + \delta M'_{IPE}$	$\delta V = \delta M_{KME} + \delta M'_{IKE} + \delta M'_{IPE}$	$\delta V < \delta M_{KME} + \delta M'_{IKE} + \delta M'_{IPE}$

Table 4.1: Minsky's Three Phases of Financial Expansion (Illustration)

due to MEL. A ML expands the money and makes more money available for further investment. δM_{KME} the interest cost of the money invested to the economic process (production system). δV is net income generated by the firm at present time. A ML is an incentive for capitalists for more investments (M_{KME} +

M'_{IKE}) and in turn, more consumption (IKE) that reinforces the MEL. This explains Minsky's concept "paradox of gluttony".[44&87]

According to Minsky, financial expansion happens in three phases[44] that leads to a self-reinforcing cycle of economic expansion through debt creation.[87] In reference to Figure 4.20 these phases can be explained as below:

1. **Hedge finance:** At micro-level, at the beginning, a firm borrows money (M_{KME}) since it has more income (δV) to pay off the loan. Minsky explains that after a recession firms choose hedge financing. If we assume, after a recession, Money Loop (ML) is dormant or under control, then the net income of the firm (δV) can cover more than the interest costs and taxes as shown below:

$$\delta V > \delta M_{KME} + \delta M'_{IKE} + \delta M'_{IPE} \dots\dots\dots\dots\dots\dots 4.31$$

Or, from equation 4.22, the following relationship can be derived:

$$\delta f(E, \check{T}) > \delta M'_{IPE} \dots\dots\dots\dots\dots\dots\dots 4.32$$

The above equation shows hedge finance is sustainable (equation 4.28) as long as there is enough energy and technology to support the economy.

2. **Speculative finance:** As the economy grows and expected profit rise, firms move to speculative financing that adds more M'_{IPE} component as long as they are able to roll over debt. Since the firm's ability for borrowing increases with increased income (δV), a Money Loop (ML) will gradually reinforce again soon after recovery from the recession. Now to chase its inductive interest costs ($\delta M'_{IPE}$), income of the firm will also have to increase. According to Minsky's 'paradox of gluttony' hypothesis, higher income will allow the firm to borrow more for more

production (M_{KME}) but now the income flow (δV) can roll over debt by paying the interest cost and taxes only.

$$\delta V = \delta M_{KME} + \delta M'_{IKE} + \delta M'_{IPE} \ldots\ldots\ldots\ldots\ldots\ldots 4.33$$

Or, from equations 4.22, the following relationship can be derived:

$$\delta f(E, T) = \delta M'_{IPE} \ldots\ldots\ldots\ldots\ldots\ldots\ldots\ldots 4.34$$

Equations 4.34 explains a growth compulsion since as long as a Money Loop (ML) inflates the economy, to keep pace with its inductive interest costs ($\delta M'_{IPE}$), the firm has to use more energy resources, which is a serious concern considering the fact of depletion of energy resources. In this situation, as more money enters into the ML, if central bank continues to reduce interest rate, borrowing will increase but much of the borrowings are to cover $\delta M'_{IPE}$. Therefore, both borrowing and energy use increase.

Ponzi finance: Minsky describes that a long periods of prosperity and increasing value of investments lead to increasing speculation using borrowed money. More loans lead to more investment, and the economy grows further. Since the end point is not known, that provokes the firms and the lenders taking more risks beyond their ability. This means future economy is wagered to be much bigger than existing economy, which at some point is impossible. Financial innovations of very high degree allow the firm to continue borrowing but the income of the firm (δV) fall behind the interest claim and taxes.

$$\delta V < \delta M_{KME} + \delta M'_{IKE} + \delta M'_{IPE} \ldots\ldots\ldots\ldots\ldots\ldots 4.35$$

Or, from equation 4.22, the following relationship can be derived:

$$\delta f(E, \check{T}) < \delta M'_{IPE} \ldots\ldots\ldots\ldots\ldots\ldots\ldots\ldots 4.36$$

Clearly, equation 4.36 violates equation 4.28. This information can be kept camouflaged in two ways. First, the funds from new investors are used to pay out unusually high returns, which in turn attract more new investors, causing rapid growth toward a collapse. Second, if oil price goes down or the rate of oil production increases.

Minsky (1992) predicts that over periods of prolonged prosperity, an economy faces financial instability when investors fall in cash flow problems for investors since the cash generated by their assets is no longer sufficient to pay off the original debt.[37] Most of the cash or money goes to feed the inductive interest cost ($\delta M'_{IPE}$), which is actually part of the ML itself. Losses on such speculative assets prompt lenders to call in their loans, the Money Loop (ML) now moves to opposite direction as shown in Figure 4.30. This is likely to lead to a sudden collapse of the economy, which is defined as "Minsky Moment".[88] The term was

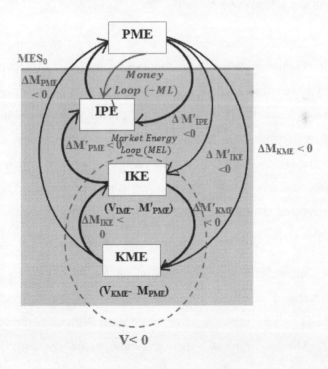

Figure 4.30: Economic Crisis

coined by Paul McCulley in 1998, to describe the 1998 Russian financial crisis.[89] According to Minsky, the collapse of asset values is part of the credit cycle or business cycle.[88] After reaching Minsky Moment, both investment to production (M_{KME}+ M_{IKE}) and financial industry (M'_{IPE}) continues to unwind and the firms actually defaults in debt. Refinancing becomes impossible for many, and more firms default. If less or no new money comes into the economy ($\Delta M_{KME} < 0$) to allow the refinancing process from outside, a real economic or financial crisis begins. Minsky (1992) describes the financial crisis as:

> "if an economy with a sizeable body of speculative financial units is in an inflationary state, and the authorities attempt to exorcise inflation by monetary constraint, then speculative units will become Ponzi units and the net worth of previously Ponzi units will quickly evaporate. Consequently, units with cash flow shortfalls will be forced to try to make position by selling out position. This is likely to lead to a collapse of asset values."[44]

An economic bubble is described as trade in values when happened in high volume with inductive price with or without speculation.[90&91] In this model, it is nothing but self-amplifying ML with inflated or compounded price level until it reaches Minsky Moment. Here any abnormal growth of M'_{IPE} with respect to $M_{KME} + M_{IKE}$ is the onset of an economic bubble but at the moment $\Delta M_{KME} < 0$, $\Delta M_{IKE} < 0$ and $\Delta M'_{IPE} < 0$, the economy begins to fall into crisis. However many mainstream economists believe that bubbles cannot be identified in advance, cannot be prevented from forming and any attempt to "prick" the bubble would cause financial crises.[90]

As we have seen in 2008, sudden rise of oil price triggered the recession. For some time increased supply of oil or coal still creates new demand for more consumption. However, increased oil or coal price may cause cost-push inflation and trigger "Minsky Moment" after a certain value. Bottom line, in an unregulated and camouflaged Ponzi market, either oil price goes up or down, bothways economic crises converge and gain potential to explode.

CHAPTER 5
THE TAKE OFF

5.1 Introduction

There is an important turning point in the U.S. economy toward financial capitalism that was followed by all major economies in the world that has accelerated consumerism. The point President Reagan reduced taxes for the riches followed by deregulation of financial markets GDP of the U.S. economy took off the ground and caused "The Great Divergence."[1&2] It attracted the other parts of the world. The breakdown of Soviet Union and demise of socialism in Europe are seen as apparent success of capitalism. Russia's wish for transition from planned economy to market economy attracted top American economists who prescribed a "shock therapy" that ended up creating a Money Loop (ML) of "oligarchs" and a Market Energy Loop (MEL) of privileged. Although the Great Divergence generated more income for the wealthy Americans, since then we see an exponential growth of public debt in the U.S. economy that is massing forces toward collapse of the American Empire. Following the same path, the European Union and many other countries are also facing sovereign debt crisis as their prime challenges.

On the other hand, the differential gap created by Reaganomics and financial capitalism to promote Money Market Dynamics (MMD) eventually created a big MEL. China immediately grabbed this opportunity and began to chase the U.S. economy with unprecedented growth. India began chasing too, behind China but often loosing pace as something inevitably holding it back. Now in a globalized world, all coming together—every single economy is under a growth compulsion under biasing of a Global Pareto Coalition (GPC), which is costing huge energy from fossil fuel, while each of them are holding their individual challenges.

5.2 The Great Divergence

Looking back to American history, as shown in Figure 5.1 that the top income display a U-shaped pattern over the century.[3&4] Although the figure shows the top 1% income share, the other top income shares also have the same U-shaped pattern. The figure shows that there was high inequality in the U.S. economy sometime around 1937 and then from about 1937 to 1947 the income inequality fell dramatically. Krugman (2007) identified "highly progressive New Deal taxation, the strengthening of unions, and regulation of the National War Labor Board during World War II raised the income of the poor and working class and lowered that of top earners."[1&5] It remained roughly stable through the postwar

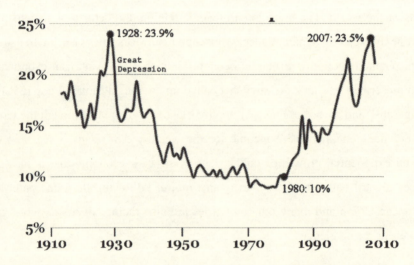

Figure 5.1: Top 1% income share during the periods from 1910-2010[4]

economic boom of the 1950s and 1960s.[2] Economic historians Claudia Goldin and Robert Margo have termed this midcentury era as the "Great Compression."[6] The Great Compression ended in the 1970s. The inequality returned again in the late 1980s what Krugman referred as the "Great Divergence."[1&2] The Great Divergence is marked by unprecedented sharp rise in corporate profit after tax (Figure 5.7) and exponential growth of public debt while social mobility is stagnant (Figure 4.4) and wage as a percent of the economy started falling

(Figure 4.29). Krugman (2007) estimated that between 1980 and 2005, more than 80 percent of total increase in the Americans' income had gone to the top 1 percent.[1] All these shows a clear Market Energy Loop (MEL) in American economy during the period Great Divergence. How did that begin?

After post-war baby boom between 1946 and 1964, the birth rate fell down by half, the new Immigration and Nationality Act of 1965 allowed non-European immigrations to the U.S. From 1970 to 2007, the foreign-born proportion of America's population grew from 5% to 11%, most of whom had lower education levels and incomes than native-born Americans.[5] However, the U.S. economy, which experienced post-war economic boom of the 1950s and 1960s got competitive source of labor. "By keeping labor supply down," Samuelson wrote in his best-selling economics textbook, a restrictive immigration policy "tends to keep wages high."[7] After the 1965 immigration law reopened the spigot, the income trend reversed itself and income inequality grew.[2&7] In fact this is how American economy re-established the 'Biased Equilibrium (BE)'.[8] As Noah argues "But when economists look at actual labor markets, most find little evidence that immigration harms the economic interests of native-born Americans, and much evidence that it stimulates the economy."[7] Therefore, in our analytical model, we may position the native-Americans on the Pareto Coalition side and the low-paid new immigrants on the Pareto Space (PS) side of the 'Biased Equilibrium Barrier (BEB)'.

Further in the 1970s, integrated circuit technology and the subsequent creation of microprocessors, many products contained dedicated computers called microcontrollers, and they started to appear as a replacement to mechanical controls in domestic appliances such as washing machines. The shift in technology or computerization everywhere, which should have a high "Transformation Possibility of a Technology (TPT)"[8] value, increased relative productivity and relative demand. Noah (2011) argues although computers as a transformative technology was not responsible for "Great Divergence',

317

computerization eliminated many moderately-skilled jobs, and it increased demand for workers with a college or graduate-level education.[2] American education system was not able to keep pace with the sudden new demand of educated and skill workers. Therefore, the scarcity of highly skilled knowledge based workers increased salaries of the skilled people and consequently those Americans and immigrants who do not possess those skill sets lost their incomes. Noah estimated various failures in American education system to support the 'skill-biased technology change'[15] are responsible for 30% of the 'Great Divergence'.[2]

The impact of the 'skill-biased technology change' on our 'Biased Equilibrium (BE)' model is shown in Figure 5.2. There was a renewed Biased Equilibrium, where the gainers, that is, the high paid skilled workers and wealthy Americans can be positioned on the 'Pareto Coalition (PC)' side. And the losers, that is, the low paid workers and unemployed people can be positioned on the 'Pareto Space (PS)' side. Of course there exists a BE between the wealthy Americans and the high skilled workers. Therefore, by further splitting the PC, we may develop the three layer 'Differential Market Model (DMM)'[8] model in the U.S. economy during the 'Great Divergence' as shown in the Figure 5.2, where (1) The wealthy Americans are on the center, say, M3 MES, (2) The high paid skilled workers

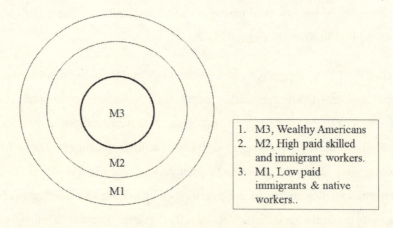

1. M3, Wealthy Americans
2. M2, High paid skilled and immigrant workers.
3. M1, Low paid immigrants & native workers..

Figure 5.2: DMM Model in the U.S. during the 'Great Divergence'

workers, native and immigrants are on the middle, say M2 MES and (3) The low paid native and immigrant workers are on the bottom, say M1 MES.

According to this model, the increased productivity is a joint effort of all three groups of the people shown in three layers of MESs, however, the effort of the low paid works are not recognized in exiting system. Let's put in this way, if a cleaner in a software company did not do his job, then the computer programmers would have to clean their offices by themselves by taking some time from their working hours. In other words, the cleaner is sacrificing the opportunity to go to college for a computer education by doing the cleaning job. Anyway, whether he got paid or not, his contribution is being absorbed in the economic system for increasing productivity. The amount unpaid to him goes to the programmers and their employers and every other person in the middle and upper market layers. Similarly, the net amount unpaid to the computer programmers goes to their employer and the every other person in the upper market layer. To further explain, consider a case well recognized in the developed world that a housewife gets equal share of her husband's income and wealth. Although if she stays at home for taking care of their children and she has no direct contribution of what her husband has done at his office, she has sacrificed any other opportunities to earn by herself. Her unpaid contributions go to the economy together with her husband's contributions for the economy.

Here Figure 5.3 describes effect of immigration and technology 'efficiency wage model' following the modified Shapiro-Stiglitz[9] 'efficiency wage model' in Figure 4.30 for the U.S. job market. The effect of technological transformation is shown by rightward shift of the 'demand for labor' curve as shown in the figure from D_{Labor} to D'_{Labor}. Here the core MES, M3 consists of wealthy native Americans and the high paid employees whose incomes or wages are not impacted by immigration and rise from W_{M3} to W'_{M3} with specific technological advancement (digital transformation) and economic growth. The effect of immigration (as M1) on employment in the U.S. economy is shown by combined

NSC (No-Shirking Condition) curve, NSC_{M21} for M1 and M2, a rightward shift from NSC_{M2}, which may reach the full employment line of M2, E'_{FULL} (see section 4.9 for detail). As described in section 4.9 that immigration reduces stagflation by enhancement of employment (here from E_{M2} to E_{M21}), while the

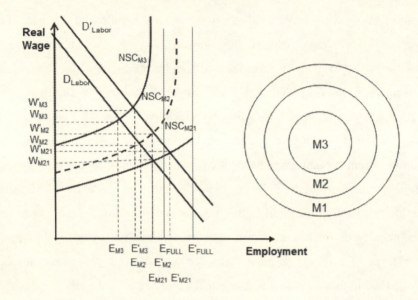

Figure 5.3: Technology Effect on Modified Shapiro-Stiglitz[9] 'Efficiency Wage Model' (Reference Figure 4.30)

average inflation adjusted wage for M2 and M1 are reduced (from W_{M2} to W_{M21}). However, the average wage rises for the M2 and M1 (from W_{M21} to W'_{M21}) due to technological advancements but still below the level of before immigration (W_{M2}). Therefore, in the U.S. we see in Figure 4.29 that wages as a percent of the economy have been falling down since 1970.

Figure 5.1 shows that the income distribution remained roughly stable through the postwar economic boom of the 1950s and 1960s, when firms were growing rapidly and the economy was booming.[2] Frydman and Saks were especially struck by the considerable stability during the 1950s and 1960s.[10] In the 1950s and the early 1960s, the top marginal tax bracket exceeded 90 percent and more importantly, inflation was under control. As Brown argues

"It is questionable whether the "golden age" (1945-1972) expansion of output and productive capacity could have been achieved without the ameliorative effects of the minimum wage, unionism and collective bargaining, progressive taxation, and income transfers."[11]

The post-World War II boom ended in the "stagflation" of the 1970s led laissez-faire capitalism. The U.S. production peak of oil reached in 1971 that caused 1973 energy crisis that led to stagnant economic growth as oil prices climbed peak in 1980.[12] Though there were genuine issues with supply, part of the run-up in prices resulted from the perception of a crisis. The combination of stagnant growth, unemployment and price inflation during this era led to the coinage of the term stagflation.[13] It raises a dilemma for economic policy since actions designed to lower inflation may exacerbate unemployment, and vice versa.[14] The oil supply crisis was solved when then Secretary of State Henry Kissinger and the Saudi government worked out a deal. In 1974 the U.S. President Nixon negotiated a formal agreement with the Saudi Arabian government that would purchase new issues of marketable U.S. Treasury bonds involving the Federal Reserve Bank of New York.[15] On the other hand, Saudi Arabia would price oil in dollars. It secured the role of the dollar as the global reserve currency.

Although 'stagflation' affects inflation and unemployment but Figure 5.1 shows share of income of top 1% also fell down and became stagnant during this time. Even after the oil deal with Saudi Arabia, 'stagflation' lasted for a decade prior to Ronald Reagan took over the White House. Political pressure favored stimulus resulting in an expansion of the money supply. Inflation reached to 13.5% in 1981, while the top marginal tax bracket was at or above 70 percent.[2] During the early years of Reagan's administration, the unemployment rate reached highs of 10.8% in 1982 and 10.4% in 1983, averaging 7.5% over the eight years.[16] During the boom years of the 1950s and 1960s, every dollar of debt that was created (selling Treasury Bonds), the U.S. economy got \$2.41 worth of economic growth. During the "stagflation" of the late 1970s that relationship dropped to \$.41 in growth.[17]

The inflation in this model (see Chapter 4) can be explained as slowing down MMD, which is because of reduced capital investment. In the contrary, following Milton Friedman's (the recipient of the 1976 Nobel Memorial Prize in Economic Sciences) concept, then the U.S. Federal Reserve Chairman Paul Volcker raised the federal funds rate, from 11.2% in 1979 to a peak of 20% in June 1981.[19] Previously, Paul Volcker played an important role in President Nixon's decision leading to the suspension of gold convertibility as under-secretary of the Treasury. As an effect, the prime rate rose to 21.5% in 1981 as well and unemployment rate climbed up over 10%. Eventually, Paul Volcker found this policy to be impractical because of the highly unstable relationship between monetary aggregates and other macroeconomic variables.[19] Even Milton Friedman acknowledged that money supply targeting was less successful than he had hoped.[20] According to William Silber,

> "His policy of preemptive restraint during the economic upturn after 1983 increased real interest rates and pushed Congress and the president to adopt a plan to balance the budget. The combination of sound monetary and fiscal integrity sustained the goal of price stability."[21]

Regarding the fiscal policy, President Ronald Reagan was very much influenced by Arthur Laffer's theoretical taxation model based on the elasticity of tax rates, known as the Laffer curve (see Section 3.5, Chapter 3) as a supply-side economic policy to counteract the stagflation allegedly caused by Keynesian demand-side economic policy. On Aug. 13, 1981, matching with his previous career as Hollywood film actor, he dramatically dropped the top marginal tax bracket from 70 percent to 50 percent ('The Economic Recovery Tax Act of 1981') and eventually pushed it all the way down to 28 percent (Tax Reform Act of 1986).[22] This caused a very sharp drop of the average tax rate percentages for the highest-income U.S. taxpayers as shown in Figure 5.4. As explained in Section 4.8 that supply-side economics works (enhance Kinetic Market Energy, ΔKME) as long as the capital supplied to the wealthy is reinvested and backed

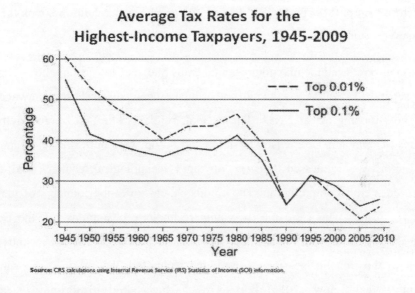

Figure 5.4: The U.S. Average Tax Rates for Wealthy, 1945-2009[23]

(CRS calculations using Internal Revenue Service (IRS) Statics of Income (SOI) Information)

by technology and physical energy. Before Reagan's Presidency, federal oil reserves were created to ease any future short term shocks. President Jimmy Carter had begun phasing out price controls on petroleum, while he created the Department of Energy.

Technology also played an important role here. At the beginning of the "Great Divergence", already a new shift in digital transformation technology was in the pipeline in need of huge investment.[8] Michael J. Mandel (2004) of Bloomberg BusinessWeek reports this:

"Just the previous day, with far less attention and fanfare, IBM (IBM) announced the introduction of its first personal computer, the IBM PC, powered by a microprocessor from Intel Corp. (INTC), which then had revenues of less than $1 billion, and sporting an operating system by a virtually unknown company called Microsoft Corp. (MSFT) the IBM PC, and the machines that followed, took the country by storm."[24]

Reagan also reduced the maximum capital gains rate to as low as only 20%[25] and later set at the same level as the rates on ordinary income like salaries and wages, with both topping out at 28%.[26] The technology giants like Sun Microsystems, Compaq Computer, Dell, Cisco Systems and so on were born during Regan's first term. We witnessed 'an era of rapid technological change' and an unprecedented economic boom. The credits should go to the founders of these new companies who were mostly young technology champions not the rich businessmen. In a bigger timeframe, it is hard to prove that the tax incentives given to the rich businessmen contributed technology boom since the same incentives exist now (2014) but seems to be neutral to technology and innovation. However, it is much easier to deduce the relationship of the tax incentives and the financial innovation that caused economic bubble and onward multiple recessions including the ongoing longest one. As explained in Chapter 4 that at the beginning of a new technological transformation 'Optimal Capital for a Technological State (OCT)' and 'Optimal Energy for Technology (OET)' are very high that they require capital and energy inflow respectively into the economy, which contributes to 'Horizontal Growth (HG)'. As soon as they reach optimal level, any further investment becomes over investment that contributes to 'Vertical Growth (VG)' and eventually economic bubble (see Chapter 4).

Some economists, such as Nobel Prize winners Milton Friedman and Robert A. Mundell, argue that Reagan's tax policies invigorated America's economy and contributed to the economic boom of the 1990s.[24] The missing piece here is that none of those theories distinguish between positive effect of growth due to HG and negative effect of growth due to VG.[8] President Reagan and his economic policies called as "Reaganomics" got all the credit for repositioning USA on the tip of global economy followed by peaceful end of cold war.

President Reagan implemented policies based on supply-side economics and advocated a classical liberal and laissez-faire philosophy, seeking to stimulate employment and growth with large tax cuts for riches.[27] As shown in the Figure 5.5 below that although corporate tax dropped drastically, the payroll tax increased sharply. By comparing to our model in Figure 5.2, it can be said that the middle layer MES, the new big chunk of technology people became the new big source of the tax revenue for the U.S. government. Mandel (2004) comments

"Reagan's 1986 tax-reform bill helped support "idea-based" industries such as software and financial services."[24]

Economist Paul Krugman contends that supply-side adherents did not fully believe that the United States income tax rate was on the "backwards-sloping" side of the Laffer curve and yet they still advocated lowering taxes to encourage investment of personal savings[28]

Figure 5.5 shows mostly due to payroll tax, the net effect of all Reagan-era tax

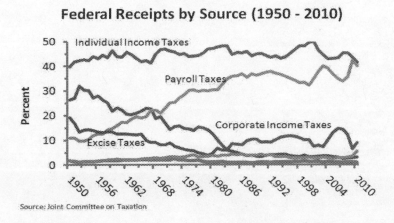

Figure 5.5: The U.S. Federal receipts by Source Historical 1950-2010[31]

bills was only 1% decrease in government revenues when it is compared to Treasury Department's initial revenue estimate.[29] The Federal income tax receipts increased from $308.7 billion to $549 billion between 1980 and 1989.[30] billion.[32] Eventually this middle and the bottom layer MES in the DMM have become dependent on debt as their after tax income with respect to the economy has gone down over the years. The middle MES, which is basically dependent on payroll, was more attractive segment to the lenders as their consumption set expanded (according to the concept "Boundary Proposition of Consumption (BPC)" in Chapter 4) when they move closer to the boundary of the EBEB.

Unfortunately, there was no policy on place during Reagan's regime that could favor the poor people. It was in the assumption of his tax reforms that favoring the riches would spur investments and create employments and raise wages instead. In fact, he did the opposite by freezing the minimum wage at $3.35 an hour, slashing federal assistance to local governments by 60%, cutting the budget for public housing and rent subsidies and so on.[33] Figure 5.6 shows

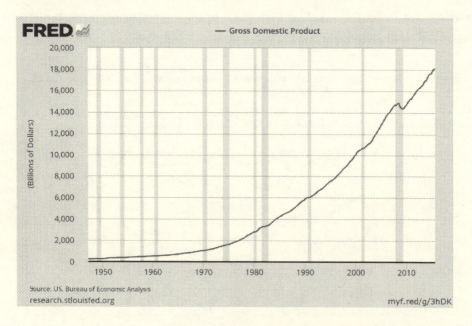

Figure 5.6: Gross Domestic Product of USA 1947-2015[34]

exponential rise of the U.S GDP since the Reagan years. The income of the top 1% nearly doubling during this time, while income for other income levels increased only marginally; income actually decreased for the bottom quintile.[36] Figure 5.7 shows that in the U.S., corporate profits are rising high since President Reagan reduced marginal taxes for the corporates, although they dropped during financial crisis in 2008 but recovered quickly and reached all-time high.[35] This means Reagan's less-government intervention views created a

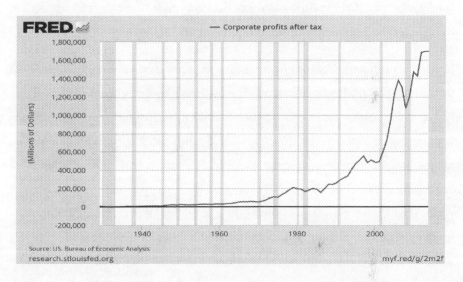

Figure 5.7: Corporate Profits after Tax (U.S.A.)[35]

solid foundation for corporate coalition, a form of Pareto Coalition (PC). The corporates such as big oil companies, banking houses and their investors who can consolidate their positions following a financial crisis are in fact financial power houses.

On the other hand, Reagan cut the budgets of non-military research, including Medicaid, food stamps, federal education programs[36] and the environmental protection[37].The real value of the minimum wage sank 27% during his administration and he turned a blind eye to workers.[24] Although Reaganomics is given credit for a tech-driven, high-productivity economy, Regan cut spending on nondefense research and development-a critical component for long-term growth and increased spending on military research and development.[29] Although corporate profits are rising while social mobility is stagnant or stuck (see Figure 4.4) and wages as a percentage of the economy consistently going down (see Figure 4.29) during the Great Divergence. Neoclassical economics justifies workers lower pay by the law of diminishing return and the corresponding lower marginal contribution of a worker, which is not the case here since marginal contribution of workers must have increased due to technological advancements such as digital revolutions.

In 1996, President Clinton implemented a new method for calculation of inflation based on Boskin Commission findings[38] to bring the inflation figure down. This method uses three new statistical tools-substitution, weighting, and hedonics. The 'substitution effect' tells that when the price of something rises, people will switch to something cheaper. Therefore, any time the price of something goes up too rapidly, it's replaced by a cheaper item in the basket of goods used for the calculation. Similar to substitution, if price of something goes up rapidly, people will use less. As an example, if health care costs go up, it will get a reduced weight. In 2009, the U.S. total expenditure on healthcare was $2.5 trillion, $8,047 per person. This amount represented 17.3% of the GDP, up from 16.2% in 2008. [39] In our model, the rising health insurance cost can be explained by the concept of Money Loop (ML). Although the health insurance costs are rising faster than wages or inflation, the inflation figure does not capture that. Martenson (2011) explains

> "Because health care costs have been rising extremely rapidly, reducing health care weighing has had a dramatic reduction in reported inflation."[38]

Figure 5.8 shows a sharp rise of personal health care expenditure in USA due to presence of a Market Energy Loop (MEL) in U.S. economy. The third adjustment is called 'hedonics'. It tells that new features are always beneficial and these features can be thought of as synonymous with falling prices.[38] This adjustment makes sense if it were only limited to the silicon products, where Transformation Potential of the Technology (TPT) is high (see Chapter 3). Martenson (2011) explains this adjustment as if a new version of TV set has an

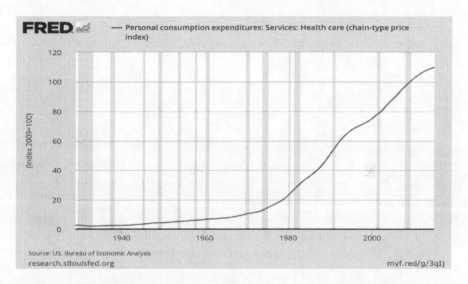

Figure 5.8: Personal Consumption Expenditure-Health Care USA 1947-2015[40]

additional nice button, a value will be deducted from the older TV price.[38] Figure 5.9 shows personal consumption expenditures of both durable and non-durable goods (consumer goods) took a sharp turn since 1980s. Although the price of the non-durable goods reduced as per the definition of "hedonics", expenditure increased more rapidly than durable goods. There is a big difference between the expenditure on health care and expenditure on consumer goods. In the first case, much of the expenditure covers the rise of price level (due to Money Loop) and the second case much of the expenditure is due 'hedonics' as price level falls (due to Money Market Dynamics).

Producing in China and selling in America help government show lower inflation by applying substitution and hedonics effects. All together does it mean that the money saved (?) by Americans by using 'made in China' products might be used for health care! This is how the U.S. government has been showing low inflation in last twenty years. Martenson argues that the U.S. government wants

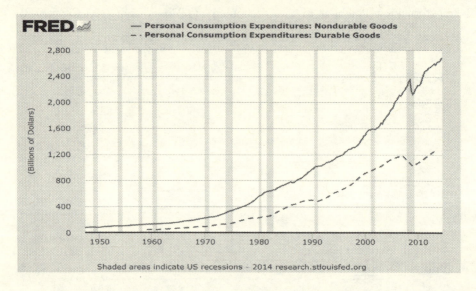

Figure 5.9: Personal Consumption Expenditure-Non Durable vs. Durable Goods[41] Source: St. Louis Fed (http://research.stlouisfed.org/)

to show low inflation because it amplifies GDP growth rate. He explains, that if inflation is shown as 1% and the nominal GDP grows by 5.9%, the real growth rate of the economy can be shown as such high as 4.9%.[38] What if the actual inflation were shown to public and it were higher than nominal GDP growth rate? There would be a big negative impact on the US currency and so will on all others, investments, wages, employments, stock prices, welfare and so on. However, showing low inflation allows low interest for mortgage, consumer credits, which mean high real estate prices, debt and consumption–good for the banking houses, retail businesses and politics but bad for pay raise, savings, employment and environment.

5.3 The Great Breakdown

During Reaganomics, while U.S. economy was back on growth track from stagflation, Soviet Union under Brezhnev (in office 1964–1982) was suffering from "Era of Stagnation"–The term coined by Mikhail Gorbachev when he took his office in 1985.[42] During the 1973 oil crisis, economic growth in the rest of the world plummeted but the Soviet hard currency earnings grew as a result of oil exports. Following the crisis, overall economic activity decreased and began to lag behind that of the West. One of the big reasons was high-level of expenditure on the armed forces, heavy and defense industry but too little spending on light industry and non-durable consumer goods such as electronics, grocery items, computers etc. The economy, especially the agricultural sector, began to fall apart.

During the time of World War II, Soviet leaders introduced central planning system to marshal resources quickly in times of crisis and to reindustrialize the country during the postwar period. The rapid development of its defense and industrial base after the war permitted the Soviet Union to become a superpower. Before the "Era of Stagnation", by the early 1970s, the Soviet Union had the world's second largest industrial capacity and expanding at a rate faster, by a small margin, than that of the United States. Robert Service claims that during stagnation, worker discipline decreased, which the Soviet government could not counter effectively because of the full employment policy.[43]

The country lacked technological advancements afterwards and used inefficient factories, while consumers were buying low-quality products. This situation can be explained by nonexistence of a Money Market Dynamics (MMD). As explained in Chapter 4 that the foundation of MMD is a "biased equilibrium", which was not possible in state ownership or centrally controlled collective production structure. Under Brezhnev, private plots yielded 30% of the national agricultural production when they only cultivated four percent of the land.[44] This was seen by some as proof that de-collectivization was necessary to prevent

Soviet agriculture from collapsing. However, leading Soviet politicians averted from supporting such drastic measures due to ideological and political interests, who did not want any economic reform that resembles market economy.

Another cause of stagnation was the increased military expenditure over consumer goods and other economic spheres.[45] By the 1970s both sides of the Cold War had become interested in accommodations to create a more stable and predictable international system, inaugurating a period of détente that saw Strategic Arms Limitation Talks (SALT I & II) towards actual limits in the nuclear capabilities of the two superpowers. USA also opened relations with the People's Republic of China as a strategic counterweight to the Soviet Union. Détente collapsed at the end of the decade with the Soviet war in Afghanistan beginning in 1979.[46] The United States increased diplomatic, military, and economic pressures on the Soviet Union, at a time when the communist state was already suffering from economic stagnation.

One of the most prominent critics of Brezhnev's economic policies was Mikhail Gorbachev who called the economy under Brezhnev's rule "the lowest stage of socialism".[45] Soviet GNP growth rates began to decrease in the 1970s from the level it held in the 1950s and 1960s. In the mid-1980s, the new Soviet leader Mikhail Gorbachev introduced the liberalizing reforms of glasnost ("openness", 1985) and perestroika ("reorganization", 1987) and ended Soviet involvement in Afghanistan.[46] He attempted to address economic problems by moving towards a market-oriented socialist economy. In June 1987, the most significant of Gorbachev's reforms in the foreign economic sector allowed foreigners to invest in the Soviet Union in the form of joint ventures with Soviet ministries, state enterprises, and cooperatives.[47] The law permitted private ownership of businesses in the services, manufacturing, and foreign-trade sectors. The law initially imposed high taxes and employment restrictions, but it later revised these to avoid discouraging private-sector activity. The reforms decentralized things to some extent, although price controls remained, as did the ruble's inconvertibility and most government controls over the means of production. Tax revenues declined because republic and local governments withheld tax revenues from the central government under the growing spirit of regional autonomy. The elimination of central control over production decisions, especially in the consumer goods sector could not establish a traditional market based supply demand relationships. Thus, instead of streamlining the system, Gorbachev's decentralization caused new production bottlenecks.[47]

On the other hand, pressures for national independence grew stronger in Eastern Europe, especially Poland by Solidarity movement. Gorbachev meanwhile refused to use Soviet troops to bolster the faltering Warsaw Pact regimes as had occurred in the past.[46] In August, 1989 Residents in the Baltic States formed a human chain that stretched unbroken across hundreds of kilometers and passed through the three republics' capital cities as a demonstration of support for Baltic independence.[48] The tidal wave of change culminated with the fall of the Berlin Wall in November 1989, which symbolized the collapse of European Communist governments. The 1989 revolutionary wave swept across Central and Eastern Europe peacefully overthrew all the Soviet-style communist states: East Germany, Poland, Hungary, Czechoslovakia and Bulgaria. Romania was the only Eastern-bloc country to topple its communist regime violently and execute its head of state.[49] The Communist Party of the Soviet Union itself lost control and was banned following an abortive coup attempt in August 1991. This in turn led to the formal dissolution of the USSR in December 1991 and the collapse of Communist regimes.[46] Boris Yeltsin who appeared climbing onto a tank to make a defiant statement denouncing the plotters later became the next Russian President.[50] After the breakdown, the Russia reduced from superpower to a state of anarchy with hyper inflation, unemployment, crime and destitution spreading rapidly. United States remained as the world's only superpower.

Following the collapse of the Soviet Union, Russia had undergone a radical transformation, moving from a centrally planned economy to a globally integrated market economy. Yeltsin choice of man was Yegos Gaidar, then 35 year old economist to run the economic reform. The president personally presented the government's privatization program on national TV, promising everyone a share in what was once state property and stressing that the country needed "millions of proprietors rather than a handful of millionaires."[51] In an attempt at "people's capitalism," virtually every Russian was issued vouchers worth 10,000 rubles each, good for shares in a soon-to-be-private enterprise. Initially 50 million vouchers were issued, one for every person in Russia. That figure was decided upon by taking a ballpark estimate of the book value of a third of Russia's large industries as of Jan. 1, 1992.[52] However, price liberalization and the consequent rate of inflation rapidly devalued the vouchers. Figure 5.10 shows hyperinflation at the beginning of "shock therapy". In 1992, the first year of economic reform, retail prices in Russia increased by 2,520% (not shown).[53] By the end of 1993 it had become worthless: 10,000 robles could now buy just three or four bottles of vodka.[55] The vouchers were bought out by a small group of investors through their 'tin-pot' banks by offering cash in exchange for equity. This so called radical market-oriented reform came to be

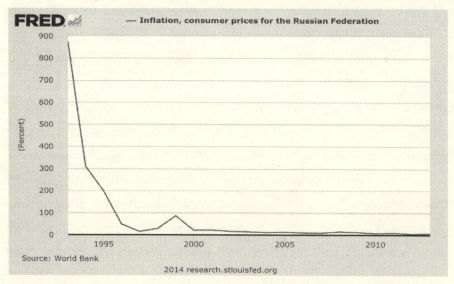

Figure 5.10: Inflation of the Russian Federation since Fall of Soviet Union[54]

known as a "shock therapy" based on the recommendations of the IMF and a group of top American economists, including Larry Summers.[56&57] Does not matter how hard the Russian collapse was in terms of rubles, in his book "Reinventing Collapse", Dmitry Orlov shows, Soviet Union provided more collapse preparedness than does the US today.[56] Richard Heinberg explains referring this book as:

> "No one became homeless when the Soviet system disintegrated, since no one had a mortgage to be foreclosed upon; when the economy crashed, people simply stayed where they were."[18&56]

Eventually, Corrupt and haphazard privatization process turned over major state-owned firms to politically connected "oligarchs", which has left equity ownership highly concentrated. The largest state enterprises were controversially privatized to insiders[59] for far less than they were worth. Through their immense wealth, the oligarchs wielded significant political influence. Stocks of the state-owned enterprises were issued, and these new publicly traded companies were quickly handed to the members of Nomenklatura or known criminal bosses.[60] During the same period, violent criminal groups often took over state enterprises, clearing the way by assassinations or extortion.[61] Hyperinflation which wiped out personal savings, crime and destitution spreading rapidly.[61] Corruption of government officials became an everyday rule of life. Under the government's cover, outrageous financial manipulations were performed that enriched the narrow group of individuals at key positions of the business and government.[62&63] Many took billions in cash and assets outside of the country in an enormous capital flight.[60] In late 1992, deteriorating economic conditions and a sharp conflict with the parliament led Yeltsin to dismiss neoliberal reform advocate Yegor Gaidar as prime minister.

Gaidar's successor was Viktor Chernomyrdin, a former head of the State Natural Gas Company (Gazprom), who was considered less favorable to neoliberal reform.[61] He formed a new government with Boris Fedorov, an economic reformer, as deputy prime minister and finance minister. Fedorov considered macroeconomic stabilization a primary goal of Russian economic policy. In January 1993, he announced a so-called anti-crisis program to control inflation through tight monetary and fiscal policies. The printing of money and domestic credit expansion moderated somewhat in 1993. However, stabilization was undermined by the Central Bank, which issued credits to enterprises at subsidized rates, and by strong pressure from industrial and agricultural lobbies seeking additional credits.[61]

In late 1994, Yeltsin replaced Viktor Gerashchenko, head of the Central Bank, and nominating Tatyana Paramonova as his replacement. She was able to implement a tight monetary policy that ended cheap credits and restrained interest rates. Furthermore, the parliament passed restrictions on the use of monetary policy to finance the state debt, and the Ministry of Finance began to issue government bonds at market rates to finance the deficits.[61] From July 1992, when the ruble first could be legally exchanged for United States dollars, to October 1995, the rate of exchange between the ruble and the dollar declined from 144 rubles per US$1 to around 5,000 per US$1.[61] By the end of October 1995, the ruble had stabilized and actually appreciated in inflation-adjusted terms. However, a 1996 government report quantified so-called "shadow economy" which yields no taxes or difficulties in collecting government revenues amid the collapsing economy and a dependence on short-term borrowing to finance budget deficits led to a 1998 Russian financial crisis.[61]

Russian economy saw little growth in 1991, by an officially estimated 6.4%, regaining 4.6% drop of 1998.[61] This increase was achieved with a great help of doubling of international oil prices in the second half of 1999, raising the export surplus to $29 billion.[61] During 1994-2008 international oil price rose sharply and crossed $100 per barrel in 2008. However, inflation rose to an average 85% in 1998, compared with an 11% average in 1997. Ordinary persons found their wages falling by roughly 30% and their pensions by 45%. After resignation of President Boris Yeltsin in the New Year's Eve in 1999, the new president Vladimir Putin government has given high priority to supplementing low incomes by paying down wage and pension arrears.[61] The Russian under the presidency of Vladimir Putin saw the nominal Gross Domestic Product (GDP) double, of President Boris Yeltsin in the New Year's Eve in 1999, the new president climbing from 22nd to 11th largest in the world. Figure 5.11 show Russian GDP (PPP) since fall of Soviet Union. During Putin's eight years in office, industry grew by 75%, investments increased by only 125%,[65] and agricultural production and construction increased as well. Real incomes more than doubled and the average salary increased eightfold from $80 to $640.[66] However, the volume of consumer credit between 2000–2006 increased 45 times,[63] and during that same time period, the middle class grew from 8 million

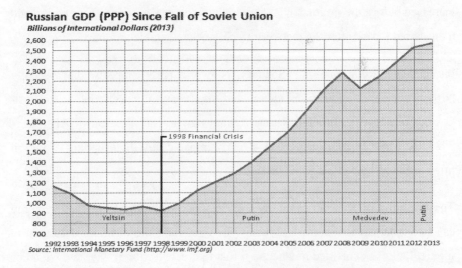

Russian GDP (PPP) Since Fall of Soviet Union
Billions of International Dollars (2013)

Source: International Monetary Fund (http://www.imf.org)

Figure 5.11: Russian GDP (PPP) Since 1992[69]

to 55 million, an increase of 7 times. The number of people living below the poverty line also decreased from 30% in 2000 to 14% in 2008.[67] Undoubtedly all these achievements cost additional huge amount of oil extraction. As of 2012 oil and gas sector accounted for 16% of the GDP, 52% of federal budget revenues and over 70% of total exports.[68] Figure 5.12 shows the rise and fall of Russian

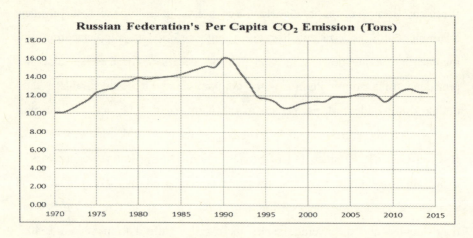

Figure 5.12: Per Capita CO2 Emission of Russia[64]

economy is reflected in its per capita CO_2 emission. The per capita emission increased before the fall of Soviet Union, then decreased during crisis period and then started to rise after the recovery since 1999 and stable around 1975 level.

International Relations and Security Network (ISN) reports that recently "Russia's defense industry is slowly but surely pulling itself out of its post-Soviet doldrums"[58] although Russia's State Armaments Program (SAP) 2011-2020, 20.7 trillion ruble budget is severely impacted by the dropping of the oil price following the crisis with Ukraine.[58]

The transition of Russian economy from planned economy to market economy can be explained in Figure 5.13 below by extending the example described in Figure 4.20. As explained in Chapter 4 that to create a Money Market Dynamics (MMD), Russia was needed to create a "Differential Market". To begin with, let us assume that Russia could have only one MES, M0 as a reference market (Figure 5.13.a). We may further assume that hypothetically, the equilibrium price level without any inflation as P_R, where D_0D_0' and S_0S_0' would represent corresponding demand and supply curves. However, what the "shock therapy" did actually created hyperinflation as shown in Figure 5.13 as P_{ST}. For simplicity, we may assume that the hyperinflation divided Russian economy into three Market Energy States (MESs). The Russian oligarchs who took the ownership of enterprises are shown as M3. And those who were also benefited by the new took over either by salary raise as a skilled worker or as businessmen

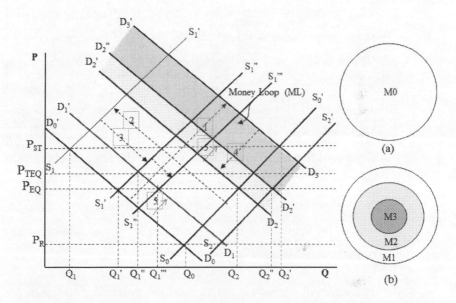

Figure 5.13: Equilibrium Analysis of Russia's transition to Market Economy

are shown as M2. Lastly M1, the common Russian who fall in cheap labor class by losing all they have during hyperinflation (Figure 5.13.b). This example assumes one product world that the product has demand in all three 'MESs' but with varying Boundary Proposition of Consumption (BPC) and Subset Proposition of Consumption (SPC). Let P_{ST} is the hyper inflated price after the "shock therapy". The subsequent impacts are explained below:

1. The hyperinflation allowed all the money and equity both concentrated in the hands of few in M3. This is shown as the new

virtual demand curve for M3 as D_3D_3'. Much of this money flew out of Russia through newly established "tin-pot" banks.

2. The impact of the hyperinflation on M1 is shown as new supply S_1S_1'. This would cause a big reduction of consumption from Q_0 to Q_1 reflecting a potential negative impact triggered by "shock therapy".

3. After breaking of Soviet Union, GDP reduced drastically since most of the people were in M1 who could not afford basic needs. Figure 5.13 shows that after the 'shock therapy', there was only one way to increase output—to reduce the price level so that mass population can afford it. However, to reduce price the firms had to increase production, shown as moving the supply curve rightward and downward from S_1S_1' to $S_1'S_1''$. Therefore, the price level fell from 'P_{ST}' to 'P_{EQ}' and the quantity consumption increased from Q_1 to Q_1'. To increase supply, the industrial and agricultural firms had to depend on credits that they were trying to get at subsidized rate from the banks using their political lobbies.

4. The effort of increasing output required generating entrepreneurs, businessmen, creating employments, hiring skilled workers, and executives etc who also contributed reaching price equilibrium. They can be positioned on a new middle layer Market Energy State, M2 as shown in Figure 5.13. This middle layer can be seen as Effective Pareto Coalition (EPC) or Market Energy Loop (MEL) together with M3. In this way, it can be imagined that the demand curve of M2 is created by splitting D_3D_3' and moving downward and leftward to D_2D_2'. Accordingly, if we imagine the economy reaches to a realistic price equilibrium at "P_{EQ}", the shaded area between the two demand curves D_3D_3' and D_2D_2' represents a

Money Loop (ML) that promotes non-productive and speculative use of money.

5. The effect of the Money Loop (ML) impacted M1, the low income people. Therefore, Russian economy was not stabilized until Vladimir Putin has given supplements to low income people. The impact of this supplement can be seen as moving the demand curve of M1 upward and rightward from D_0D_0' to D_1D_1'. M2 will match the price by moving its demand curve upward and rightward from D_2D_2' to $D_2'D_2''$. The figure also shows that this supplements also allows additional consumption from Q_1' to Q_1'' in M1 at new temporary equilibrium price P_{TEQ}.

6. The increase of this price level can be considered as moderate inflation around 1999 (see Figure 5.10) but may have been offset as the Russian economy continued to produce more consumer products from this reference point. Figure 5.13 reflects this as moving supply curve for M1 rightward from $S_1'S_1''$ to $S_1''S_1'''$ and similarly, for M2 rightward from S_0S_0' and S_2S_2' keeping the price level down again to P_{EQ}. Figure 5.10 shows a pretty stable inflation since 2000.

Now Russia's economy is back on growth track. It took 17 years until 2007 to reach that of 1990. Russia is world's second oil exporting country, second in the in sale of weapons. Its Information Technology (IT) industry has achieved a record year of growth concentrating on high end niches like algorithm design and microelectronics, making Russia the world's third biggest destination for outsourcing software behind India and China. The space launch industry is now the world's second largest.[61]

Russia is the biggest supplier of oil and gas in Europe. In other words, European economies are largely dependent on Russian energy supplies. On the other hand, oil and gas account for half of its revenue. Figure 5.14 shows that during high oil price Russia attempted to pay off its debts. Russia needs an oil price of $100 per barrel to have a balanced budget.[71] Now global crude oil prices have dropped almost half to $60.59 per barrel recently (December, 2014) after peaking above $115 in June, 2014.[72] Low oil price is now pulling Russia into debt territory again amid economic sanctions imposed on Russia following Russia's annexation of Crimea and Russian military intervention in Ukraine.[73] Economic sanctions have also contributed to the decline of the ruble since Russian companies have been prevented from rolling over debt, forcing companies to exchange their rubles for U.S. dollars or other foreign currencies on the open market to meet their interest payment obligations on their existing

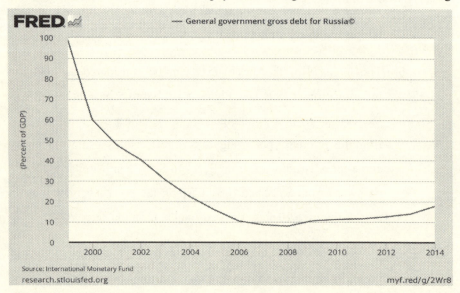

Figure 5.14: Russian Government Gross Debt 1999-1014[70]

debt. Russian economy needs to be diversified. This option will be challenging as long as prices remain low. Bloomberg reports Russia will unseal its $88 billion Reserve Fund to mitigate the country's worst currency crisis in almost 17 years.[74] Russian President Vladimir Putin accused the Western nations of engineering the Russian economic crisis and called them "an Empire".[75] On the other hand, he is declared world's most powerful for third year in a row.[274]

5.4 The Debt Driven Economy

Following the 'Great divergence', the high GDP growth of the U.S. economy (Figure 5.6) would not happen without high consumption of oil. After reaching "peak oil" around 1970 (Figure 1.5), the U.S. economy became very much dependent on oil import. And following 1974 deal of then President Nixon with Saudi Arabia of pricing oil in US dollars, USA have been enjoying both easy access to oil and the same time easy access to debt by selling Federal Reserve Treasury bonds. Figure 5.15 shows that there is a relationship between the U.S. oil import and the federal public debt.[76] As discussed in Chapter 4 (Section 4.7) that a Money Loop (ML) has reinforced following financial deregulation and that might have increased the price level such as health care expense, value of real estates. Afterwards the cost to cover the rising cost, federal debt and consumption of oil both increased (equation 4.28) as reflected in Figure 5.15. The fact is that the U.S. economy has entered in a situation that its dependency

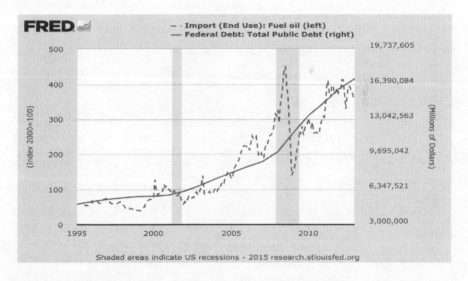

Figure 5.15: The US Federal Debt and Import: Fuel Oil[76]

on debt is hard to reduce. The recent boom of shale oil may temporarily reduce the accumulation rate of debt but as Figure 5.15 shows that the total debt is rising. It will not become better as long as the oil price is falling and the future contracts or insurance coverage for minimum oil prices are expiring.

Who actually own the debt burden? As Blodget (2011) comments that hundreds of millions of Americans are indebted up to their eyeballs, whereas the top 1% own 5% of the country's total debt. The next 9% has 21% and the remaining 90% has 73% of the debt.[77] The aggregate tax rate for the top 1% is lower than for the next 9% and not much higher than it is for pretty much everyone else.[77] Whereas the top 1% of Americans own 42% of the financial wealth, in this country and the top 5% own nearly 70%.[27]

There is an important difference between the debt of the top 1% and that of the bottom 90%. In the first case, the debt is an investment debt with an intention of "money making" that provides the means to pay itself back.[38] In the latter case, for the others, the bottom 90%, the debt is mostly consumptive in nature or 'non-self-liquidating debts'. Reagan's tax policy made the lower MES weaker by reducing their disposable incomes. On the other hand, more money on the upper MES (the capitalists) cannot enhance kinetics of market energy or Kinetic Market Energy (KME) as law of marginal utility saturates and therefore, creates a 'Bulling Money Loop (BML)'.

Pluta (2011) explains 'money making' as "top-level executives award themselves sizable bonuses when the firm's profit level as well as stock price drop and assembly-line workers are either laid off or asked to take salary cuts. Performance measures, in other words, indicate a lack of productivity on the part of management, which is then rewarded for its ineptness."[14] In case of debt, the 'money markers' are in a better situation than who make goods as the former have savings and assets and the later has all debts. Martenson argues c As we know now this is absolutely opposite for the middle and bottom layer MESs (see Figure 5.2) as their real wages are going down (Figure 4.29), while unemployment remains high. The level of consumption of an economy with constant reduction of real wage does not reflect the proper condition of the economy as the individuals can easily smooth their consumption by borrowing, which they have to pay back out of their finite pool of incomes. Unfortunately here is what Reagan failed to distinguish. He targeted finite incomes as a source of his tax base (see Payroll tax in Figure 5.5) by reducing taxes on the infinite incomes. The 'infinite income' contributes mostly to 'Vertical Growth (VG)' favored by capitalists that may mislead an economy toward economic 'bubble'. Whereas the former, 'finite income' contributes to "Horizontal Growth (HG)', which brings economic progress but unfortunately bears the debt burden.

The relationship between employment, consumption and debt in the U.S. economy is very close. Let us use the two MES model, M3 & M2 again for analysis of this situation as shown in Figure 5.16. By comparing with Figure 5.2, M2 here represents M1 and M2 combined. This example assumes one product world that the product has demand in both the 'MESs'. Here increase in income is reflected by upward and rightward shift of demand curve for the product and vice versa. The MESs are in equilibrium at price level "p", where D_3D_3' and

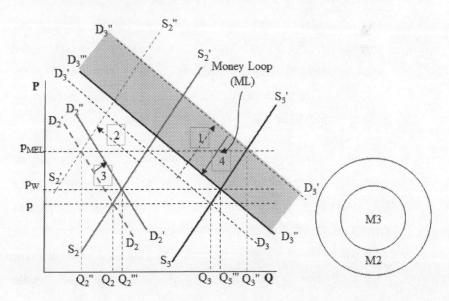

Figure 5.16: Equilibrium Analysis of the U.S. Economy

S_3S_3' represents demand and supply curves for M3 respectively and D_2D_2' and S_2S_2' represents demand and supply curves for M2 respectively. After Reagan's tax incentive for the riches, M3 certainly gained more energy and reinforced the pre-existing 'Money Loop (ML)' and 'Market Energy Loop (MEL)'. Let M3 represents the original MEL, if expands horizontally, it will accommodate part of M2 and vice versa. The subsequent impacts are explained in few steps below:

1. As shown in Figure 5.1 that Reagan's tax policy in 1981, the income of the top 1% Americans rose dramatically. They are positioned in M3 and can be considered as the heart of the MEL of the U.S. economy. In Figure 5.16 the reinforcement of the MEL in M3 is reflected by the virtual upward and rightward shift of the demand curve from D_3D_3' to $D_3'D_3''$ and the corresponding upward shift of the potential equilibrium price from 'p' to 'p_{MEL}'.

2. If wages in M2 did not change or Shapiro-Stiglitz's NSC (No-Shirking Condition) did not hold due to the Biased Equilibrium between M3 and M2, then to comply with the potential equilibrium price 'P_{MEL}', the supply curve of M2 would move leftward and upward from S_2S_2' to $S_2'S_2''$ as shown in Figure 5.16. Thus, the corresponding consumption in M2 would virtually reduce from Q_2 to Q_2''. This is a potential negative impact on M2 triggered by growth of the Market Energy Loop (MEL).

3. The above situation increases inflationary expectation in the economy. In this case, if Shapiro-Stiglitz NSC holds to some extent for M2, wages in M2 will increase. To raise wages, employers expect increased productivity of the workers that calls for adoption and enhancement of new technologies (digital transformation). Figure 5.3 shows wage raise from W_{M2} to W'_{M2} at the level that the

workers do not shirk as they are gaining more skills for the new technology.

In Figure 5.16, the wage raise (also includes new opportunities) is reflected by upward and rightward movement of the demand curve of M2 from D_2D_2' to $D_2'D_2''$. The corresponding increase in consumption is from Q_2 to Q_2'''. Accordingly, the economy reaches to a realistic price equilibrium "p_W" little over the original price "p" and far down from 'P_{ML}', matching the income capacity (wage) of the individuals in M2 for whom Shapiro-Stiglitz's NSC holds.

4. Fortunately, there were new technologies and ideas in the pipeline to create new job and enhance productivity. The U.S. economy has achieved progress mostly because the digital transformation that created millions of jobs over the past two-three decades. Therefore, we may assume, the equilibrium piece is "p_W". To comply with this price, the demand curve in M3 actually moves downward and leftward from its virtual position $D_3'D_3''$ to $D_3''D_3'''$. The shaded area between the two demand curves for M3 represents the 'vertical' component of the MEL or represents a Money Loop (ML). The Horizontal component of MEL that accommodates Border Propensity of Consumption (BPC) puts implicit 'Price Pressure (PP)' on M2. As the price equilibrium 'p' is much lower than 'p_{ML}', there is more non-dispensable income in M3. The excess money in M3 promotes non-productive and speculative use of money in a ML and causes a Bulling Money Loop (BML).

The virtual moving of the demand curve from $D_3'D_3''$ to $D_3''D_3'''$ can eventually be seen as moving upward and rightward from D_3D_3' to $D_3''D_3'''$. Accordingly, consumption in M3 actually increases from Q_3 to Q_3''', while consumption in M2 also increases from Q_2 to Q_2'''.

> This is how MEL expands or the U.S. economy achieves progress–the 'Kinetic Market Energy (KME)" (see Chapter4, section 4.7) and creates opportunities for the people around the boundary of the MEL.

There are millions of job created during the economic boom of technically demanding work in the U.S. economy-software, communication, information technology and corresponding industrial transformation increased productivity and created more opportunities that expanded Kinetic Market Energy. The increase in productivity following the specific technological advancement (digital transformation) and corresponding capital investment increases further cash flow to M3 at much higher rate than increase of wages in M2 because of the Reagan's cut in marginal tax rates. This explains the situation of declination of the wages as a percentage of the economy (see Figure 4.29), while productivity of the manufacturing workers has increased.

If the policy intervention strengthens ML, it may create a bubble. And then if the bubble bursts, the economy will degenerate unless counteracted by policy intervention such as lowering down interest rate. Lowering down interest rate is

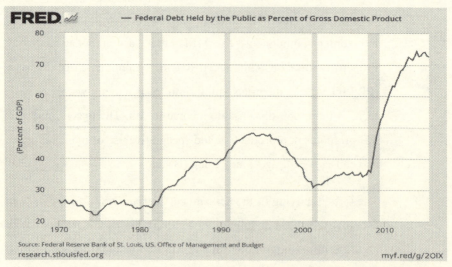

Figure 5.17: The U.S. Public Debt as Percent of GDP from 1970 to 2015.[78]

a temporary solution that enhances "Boundary Propensity of Consumption (BPC)" (see section 4.5). If M2 is under continuous 'Price Pressure' (official inflation is still low), the end result will be increased debt (Figure 5.17) and declination of savings (Figure 5.18) in M2 as observed in the U.S. economy since 1990s. Ideally, if there were no ML in M3, the cost of real estate and the

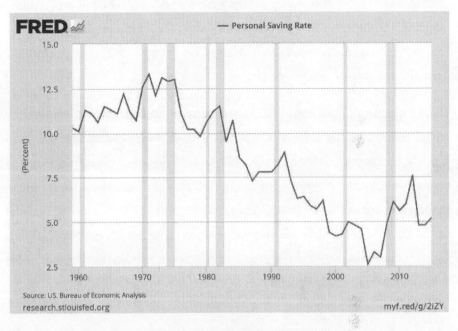

Figure 5.18: The U.S. Personal Savings Rate 1960-2015[80]

services such as health cares, or higher education would be much lower and so would the debt pressure be on M2.

Currently not only the working people are severely drowned in debt, recently, on March 22, 2012, Bloomberg reports that U.S. student-loan debt reached the US$1-trillion mark.[79] Rohit Chopra from Consumer Financial Protection Bureau comments "Young consumers are shouldering much of the punishment in the form of substantial student-loan bills for doing exactly what they were told would be the key to a better life."[79] Joachim Hagopian of Global Research writes about the death of American dream for your generations as:

"The forsaken American population finds itself more in poverty (46.2 million people) as well as more in debt ($57 trillion) now than ever before in history. Young generations of the college educated are having to pay off mounting college loan debts ($1.2 trillion and rising) that without jobs they can never even hope to repay. Rather than marry, have kids and buy homes like generations before them, they worry how to pay the light bill and avoid eviction. Sometime when we weren't looking, the American dream died in the last century. Foreclosures and unpaid debts are now sucking the lifeblood out of Americans."[122]

The U.S. federal government has some sorts of welfare and social security programs available for low income people such as such as Medicare, Medicaid and Social Security. Although the skill based technology people are in the middle who are the major contributor of the economic growth after the Great Divergence, are now left out in a debt spiral. Figure 5.17 shows the exponential rise of the U.S. public debt after implementation of Reagan's tax policy in 1981. On the other hand, as shown in Figure 5.18 that the personal saving rate of the U.S. citizens has sharply come down to nearly zero[2] (in 2005) as opposed to the debt that has been climbing up to infinity. It increased a little after some measures taken by Obama government but still pretty low and seems to be unsustainable.[81] Robert Samuelson of Washington Post accuses foreign funds for American's low saving habit as

"Foreign funds poured into U.S. bonds and mortgages, keeping interest rates down. Low interest rates on mortgages increase housing demand and prices, making Americans (again) feel wealthier. People borrow against the inflated values of their homes. That reduces U.S. saving and increases consumption. Americans' low saving and high consumption offset foreigners' high saving and low consumption."[82]

In 2011, the credit rating agency Standard & Poor's (S&P) downgraded the credit rating of the U.S. federal government from AAA to AA+, while it is still remaining as dollar super power. As the U.S. government continues to run deficits in other parts of the budget, it has to issue debt held by the public to fund the unfunded Social Security Trust Fund, in effect exchanging one type of debt for the other, which make the U.S. a debt driven economy.[83]

5.5 Is American Empire Falling?

Although rapid industrial transformation due to digital revolution in the U.S. has increased incomes for the middle layer people, soon they became target of booming credit market. As a result, their personal savings as a percent of national income have come down (Figure 5.18) and they have been caught in a debt spiral.[38] This is where Wall Street applied lots of innovations that eventually turned into big return to the financial investors as economic indicators were showing healthy. Economic bubble is created when the economy shows good sign in its financial indicators but not in the wage indicators. After a business cycle when the bubble bursts, we see sudden rise in unemployment rate. In the worst case, massive unemployment raises debt defaulters, which lead to bankruptcy and eventually to an economic depression.

As discussed earlier that the 'Great Divergence' eventually accelerated wealth accumulation but for certain upper MESs. The wealth accumulation process reinforced Money Loop (PME) which was a breeding ground of financial businesses called 'financialization'. According to the "'Biased Equilibrium' model" described in Chapter 4, government policy should enhance information sharing between both sides of its 'Effective Biased Equilibrium Barrier (EBEB)'. Unfortunately, the U.S. Government policy from the 1970s onward has emphasized deregulation to encourage business in a way which resulted in less oversight of activities and less disclosure of information about new activities undertaken by banks and other evolving financial institutions.[84]

Monowar Zaman

In the U.S. the upper layer market is inflated not only because of internal economic imbalances originated from biased equilibrium, but also because of a flood of funds (capital or liquidity) reached the U.S. financial markets as neocolonial superpower after the 'Great Divergence'. The balance of payments identity requires that a country (such as the U.S.) running a current account deficit also have a capital account (investment) surplus of the same amount.[84] Foreign investors had these funds to lend either because they had very high personal savings rates (as high as 40% in China) or because of excessive profits from high oil prices (as from Middle-East).[85]

How do savings from foreign countries come to the United States? This is because of the status of the U.S. dollar as the world's reserve currency since 1970 as long as dollar is backed by oil. Much of this is explained in section 3.8 and enhanced in the next section. The oil-dollar relationship, for every 1% of dollar devaluation, the price of oil increases by 1.95%.[86] The high oil prices impose costs on government purchases and also undermines the purchasing power of U.S. consumers. This is why the U.S. budget in last decades falling behind expectation. Kevin Riley (2011) describes the impact of oil-dollar relationship on the U.S. consumer spending as:

"This new era for the dollar had far-ranging policy implications and allowed the United States to not only delay fiscal restraint but unleash spending on an unprecedented scale, while shielding it from the costs of empire....By avoiding market forces through use of its hegemony, the U.S. has been able to print dollars at will and maintain military and domestic spending that would have been quickly exhausted otherwise."[87]

This relationship between oil and dollar resulted in the U.S. receiving a double-loan, as David E. Spiro describes:

"The first part of the loan was for oil. The government could print dollars to pay for oil, and the American economy did not have to produce goods and services in exchange for the oil until OPEC used the dollars for goods and services. Obviously, the strategy could not work if dollars were not a means of exchange for oil. The second part of the loan was from all other economies that had to pay dollars for oil but could not print currency. Those economies had to trade their goods and services for dollars in order to pay OPEC. Again, so long as OPEC held the dollars rather than spending them, the United States received a loan. It was, therefore, important to keep OPEC oil priced in dollars at the same time that government officials continued to recruit Arab funds."[88]

Economist Paul Krugman's view is different from this. According to him, American investors are actually benefited from the claims of foreigners on U.S. dollar. As he argues:

"It's true that foreigners now hold large claims on the United States, including a fair amount of government debt. But every dollar's worth of foreign claims on America is matched by 89 cents' worth of U.S. claims on foreigners. And because foreigners tend to put their U.S. investments into safe, low-yield assets, America actually earns more from its assets abroad than it pays to foreign investors."[89]

Here Paul Krugman is looking at the wealthy American investors (say, M3 in Figure 5.16), while the other Americans (say, M2 in Figure 5.16) hold the double liabilities that David Spiro has mentioned.

Although Reagan gave tax benefit to the rich Americans expecting that it would stimulate the investors create employments, instead they were stimulated in trading, buying foreign securities and outsourcing wealth-creating and software jobs. Between 1980 (before Reagan's tax cut) and 2007 the U.S. private ownership of foreign securities increased 106 times (from $62.5billion to $1.478 trillion) and foreign corporate stock increased 273 times (from $18.9billion to $5.171 trillion), whereas the U.S. direct investment in foreign country increased only 9 times (from \$388 billion to \$3.33 trillion).[90] On the other hand, foreign investment in the U.S. securities on government ownership increased 18 times

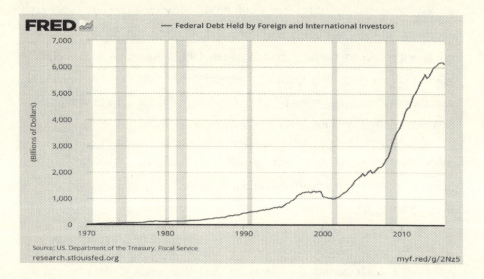

Figure 5.19: The U.S. Federal Debt Held by Foreign Investors 1970-2015[91]

(from \$230 billion to \$4.21 trillion). However, foreign investment in US corporate bonds skyrocketed to 346 times (from \$64 billion to \$3.3 trillion) between 1980 and 2007.[90] This means foreign countries own increasingly more assets in USA than USA own in the foreign countries. Figure 5.19 shows the U.S. Federal debt held by foreign & international investors as percent of GDP, which is growing more rapidly after 2008 financial crisis, recognizing U.S. dollar more trustworthy than any other currency in the world and the dependency of global economy on oil.

Among the foreign countries, Figure 5.20 shows Japan and China hold most of the U.S. treasury bonds. However, as on May 2012 Japan holds \$1,105.2 trillion of USD Treasury Securities, next to China (\$1.169.6 trillion). Any country holding US Treasury Bonds is a major exporter to USA. As long as these countries hold the USD, the U.S. economy will be leveraged by them. Although trades are mutually beneficial, here USA has this absolute advantage over the others. Japan allowed a very large appreciation in the mid-1980s that led to an asset bubble, its subsequent collapse, and ten years of lost growth. Japan once

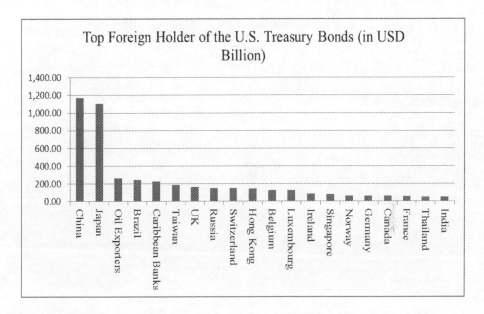

Figure 5.20: Top Foreign Holder of the U.S. Treasury Bonds (in USD Billion)[92]

having a 'savings glut' is now close to collapse under its debt burden roughly 200% of GDP[93] (Figure 5.27). The household savings rate in Japan has declined from a peak 44% in 1990 to existing 2%.[93]

The above analysis explains why the U.S. government so keen to uplift its political hegemony in the dollar centric world and involvement in the multi-trillion dollar war in the Middle East. Although this explains the survivability of dollar lie outside the U.S., it does not explain internal flaw of the American economic system that has failed to keep the economy on track. Now the U.S. economy is in such a debt spiral that, the Federal interest rate has reached so close to zero that it cannot go any lower. The value of dollar falls with every time the Federal Reserve applies Quantitative Easing (QE), in other words, print money.[94&95] Here it buys up the innovatively inflated assets like long-term Treasury Securities or mortgage-backed securities from commercial banks to pump money into the economy.[95] Figure 5.21 shows that after the economic crisis of 2008, the Federal Reserve has purchased hundreds of billions of dollars

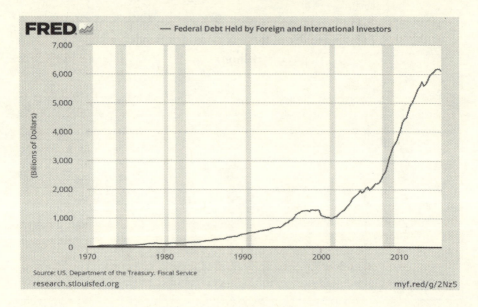

Figure 5.21: Federal Debt Held by Federal Reserve Banks (USA)[96]

in U.S. Treasury debt, effectively printing money to keep the U.S. government and economy afloat.[87] In his book "Afterburn", Heinberg summarizes the effect of Quantitative Easing (QE) as:

"The Fed's Quantitative Easing (QE) program props up the banks, the auto companies, the housing market, and the Treasury. But, with overall consumer spending still anemic, the trillions of dollars the Fed has created have generally not been loaned out to households and small businesses; instead, they've simply pooled up in the big banks. This is money that's constantly prowling for significant financial returns, nearly all of which go to the "one percenters." Fed policy has thus generated a stock market bubble, as well as a bubble of investments in emerging markets, and these can only continue to inflate for as long as QE persists."[18]

The inflow to the U.S. financial market also includes money from third world countries earned by either exploiting cheap natural resources such as oil or cheap labor or by corruption. After another peak of high inflation and a high interest rate that reached over 20% in 1980s, the steadily decreasing interest rates backed by the U.S Federal Reserve from 1982 onward raised demand for house and therefore, the house price exponentially went up. The concept of 'Money Market Dynamics (MMD)' and 'Market Loop' at global level explains the reason why the U.S. financial market has become the one of the global financial agglomeration centers and also why the poor financial decisions of a few investors and managers have impacted the global market and lead to a global recession. It supports "Dependency Theory" that resources flow from a "periphery" of poor and underdeveloped states to a "core" of wealthy states, enriching the latter at the expense of the former.[97] The large inflows of foreign funds created easy credit conditions for a number of years prior to the crisis (2001-2005), fueling a housing construction boom and encouraging debt-financed consumption by the growing middle class.[98]

This housing bubble resulted in many homeowners refinancing their homes at lower interest rates, or financing consumer spending by taking out second mortgages secured by the price appreciation.[84] Paul Krugman (2010) argues "all this borrowing took place both because banks had abandoned any notion of sound lending and because everyone assumed that house prices would never fall. And then the bubble burst."[99] An 'economic bubble' is another vulnerability of an economy that inclined to Potential Market Energy (PME) or Vertical Growth (VG). An economic bubble is "trade in high volumes at prices that are considerably at variance with intrinsic values".[100] In case of a PME, it is often difficult to observe intrinsic values of products and services in real-life markets. Therefore, bubbles are often conclusively identified only in retrospect, when a sudden drop in prices appears. Such a drop is known as a bubble burst.[101]

Monowar Zaman

According to Minsky (1992) the starting point of economic bubble could be at the point of business cycle when an economy is turning from speculative finance to Ponzi finance since expected income will not even cover interest cost but hoping that the market value of the assets will rise enough in future.[102] Minsky describes "In particular, over a protracted period of good times, capitalist economies tend to move from a financial structure dominated by hedge finance units to a structure in which there is large weight to units engaged in speculative and Ponzi finance. Furthermore, if an economy with a sizeable body of speculative financial units is in an inflationary state, and the authorities attempt to exorcise inflation by monetary constraint, then speculative units will become Ponzi units and the net worth of previously Ponzi units will quickly evaporate. Consequently, units with cash flow shortfalls will be forced to try to make position by selling out position. This is likely to lead to a collapse of asset values."[103] In Chapter 4 it is described that a Ponzi scheme actually inflates Money Loop (ML) whose obvious effect is rise of the price levels of real estate that exercise Price Pressure (PP) on those who are outside the corresponding Market Energy Loop (MEL). The concerned authorities (Central Bank) may mistakenly consider Price Pressure (PP) as inflation. As a dilemma, if the authorities do not take any action, the bubble will continue to blow until it is overblown and bursts or it is pricked by any event such as "oil price hike" or reduced throughput of cash inflow.

Although some article shows that bubbles may appear even when speculation is not possible.[103] In the 'Biased Equilibrium' model in previous Chapter, section 4.7 and 4.8 it was shown, a bubble might be created when PME strengthen at much higher rate than KME. PME could expand with or without speculation such as excessive cash flow from outside the country or spread of corruption throughout the economy. None of these increase KME but PME. The U.S. economy has a huge inflow of foreign funds in various forms such as investment in treasury bonds or in private stocks or in real-estate. These funds can easily create an illusion of healthy economy to mislead the common people taking risks and eventually lose money.

Where does the money go when a bubble burst? In 2007, just before the crash, the top 1% American owned 42% of the country's financial wealth but only 5% of the national debt. On the other hand, the bottom 90% owned less than 5% of the financial wealth but 73% of the national debt.[77] When U.S. economy was recovering from 2008 recession, in 2010, average real income per family grew by 2.3% but the gains were very uneven. Top 1% incomes grew by 11.6% while bottom 99% incomes grew only by 0.2%. Saez (2012) calculated, the top 1% captured 93% of the income gains in the first year of recovery.[104] Although this recovery is symptomatic not hitting the origin at all, it can be concluded that when a bubble booms, the money that the people save come to the financial market and when the bubble bursts, all go to a smaller sub set of wealthy people.

After a full cycle of economic bubble and burst, we will see lots of merging and accusations, as opposed to the expansion and competition–the very objectives of the government policy. If economic bubble is a periodical phenomenon of an economy, it can be said that the economy has 'money grabbing engine' that pump bulk volume of money to the wealthy from the middle class without producing any value. This not only impairs sustainability of existing businesses but also hinder any future business potential. As shown in Figure 5.22 that the economic recession started in 2008, the excess reserves of depository institutions in US Federal Reserve Bank is sky rocketing, while the US debt surpassed 100% of gross domestic product. Although, after the recession, the Fed has slashed interest rates to basically zero.[106] The banks are able to borrow money for almost free and the banks have slashed the rates they pay on deposits to basically zero. At the beginning of global economic recession in 2008, the US government bailed out $700 billion to the financial companies hoping that the banks could keep lending so that the companies can create new jobs.[107] In reality, as Henry Blodget (2011) describes that by refuting supply-side dream economics of

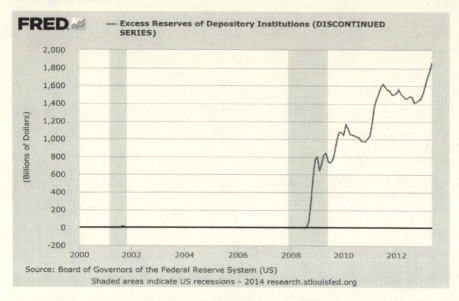

Figure 5.22: Excess Reserves of Depository Institutions (USA)[105]

Reaganomics bank lending to businesses sharply dropped and bank increased lending to the government by buying risk free treasury bonds and other government securities.[77]

As described in the previous section that the 'Bulling Money Loop (BML)' created in the U.S. economy after the 'Great Divergence' put 'Price Pressure (PP)' on the real estate market for the growing middle class people, which was reflected as sharp rise in the housing price. This is where financial innovations came into play to let them buy houses amid PP by taking mortgages that fit to their individual specific abilities. The term financial innovation refers to the ongoing development of financial products designed to achieve particular client objectives, such as offsetting a particular risk exposure (such as the default of a borrower) or to assist with obtaining financing.[84] However, since the lenders act as a Pareto Coalition to innovate products in a way that persuade people to buy the products beyond their abilities, it can be considered as 'information biasing'. The short-run equilibrium achieved in this way should be considered as 'Biased Equilibrium (BE)'. The investment banks and hedge funds used financial innovation to enable large wagers to be made, far beyond the actual value of the underlying mortgage loans, using derivatives.[84] In the U.S., derivatives have special legal exemptions that make them a particularly attractive legal form to extend credit.[108] However, the strong creditor protections afforded to derivatives counterparties, in combination with their complexity and lack of transparency, can cause capital markets to underprice credit risk. This can contribute to credit booms, and increase systemic risks.[108] Indeed, the use of derivatives to mask credit risk from third parties while protecting derivative counterparties contributed to the financial crisis of 2008.[81&108]

Financial deregulation within the US, particularly repealing Glass-Steagall Act., have served only to reinforce special protections for derivatives, including greater access to government guarantees, while minimizing disclosure to broader financial markets.[109] The largest derivative market is the Over-the-counter (OTC) derivative contracts, which is privately negotiated derivative contracts that are transacted off organized futures exchanges. This is largely unregulated with respect to disclosure of information between the parties, since the OTC market is made up of banks and other highly sophisticated parties, such as hedge funds. Reporting of OTC amounts are difficult because trades can occur in private, without activity being visible on any exchange. According to the Bank for International Settlements (BIS), the total outstanding notional amount was US$500 trillion in June 2007 and US$708 trillion as of June 2011[110], which is couple of times of whole world economy.

Figure 5.23 shows Federal budget deficit (or surplus) since 1970. The only two years balance sheet was positive was 2000 ($236,241 million) and 2001 ($128236 million) that encouraged George W. Bush administration project a $1.288 trillion surplus from 2001 through 2004.[111] Likewise, series of war efforts during industrial revolution in Europe, these positive figures may also have made him confident about the war effort with Iraq and Afghanistan. However, in the 2005 mid-session review this had changed to a projected four- year deficit of

$851 billion, a swing of $2.138 trillion.[112] Figure 5.23 shows that since then (2002) until 2010 the U.S. government was unable to control the budget deficit

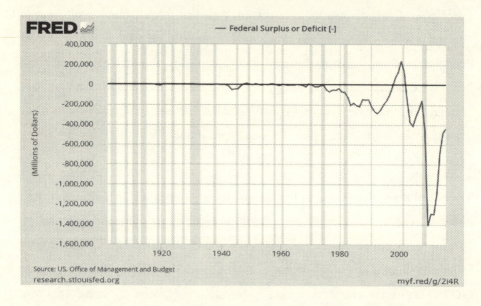

Figure 5.23: The U.S. Federal Budget Surplus or Deficit 2000-2015[115]

and so was the public debt growing faster than its GDP (Figure 5.17). In 2001 estimate was $5.6 trillion surplus for 2002-2011 period, whereas it ended up in accumulated $6.1 trillion debt increase.[113&114] During this time frame, the loss of revenue due to Bush tax cut was 1.6 trillion, war spending 1.4 trillion and interest spending was 1.4 trillion dollars. Medicare/Medicaid spending increased by 2.0% GDP and individual income tax revenues fell by 2.4% GDP.[114] Much of the increase in price of Medicare can be attributed to the underlying MEL or ML in the U.S. economy. As an example, between 2008 and 2009, the health care expense increased by 16.2%.[38] Much of the loss of revenue could be recovered by taxing directly to the wealthy (M3 in Figure 5.16) instead of taxing from the middle class (M2 in Figure 5.16).

To reduce budget deficit, Obama government passed the Budget Control Act of 2011 that mandates caps on discretionary spending, which is about $1.2 trillion of spending over the ten years.[116] The U.S. Secretary of Defense Leon Panetta estimated that this Act would reduce the base military budget by 23% from the funding levels expected by the Defense Department.[117] The automatic cuts to domestic programs would include cuts of up to 11% to science research and development agencies such as the National Institutes of Health, NASA, and the U. S. National Laboratories run by the Department of Energy. The cuts could also endanger research such as climate change research programs in NASA and National Oceanic and Atmospheric Administration.[118&119]

Recently, tech billionaires such as Bill Gates, Mark Zuckerberg, Richard Branson, Jeff Bezos have announced that they are forming a partnership called the "Breakthrough Energy Coalition" to invest a substantial portion of their money in early stage clean energy companies.[275] In a recent interview Bill Gates have mentioned his interest as:

"If you look at where we've had huge success in the past, the government's been there to fund the basic research.....We need the basic research, but we have to pair that with people who are willing to fund high-risk breakthrough energy companies."[275]

This is good but we cannot wait for a breakthrough technology since it is already late to deal with impacts of climate change. As the Bulletin of Atomic Scientists points out:

"If the world is to avoid "severe, widespread, and irreversible [climate] impacts," carbon emissions must decrease quickly—and achieving such cuts, according to the Intergovernmental Panel on Climate Change, depends in part on the availability of "key technologies." But arguments abound against faith in technological solutions to the climate problem. Electricity grids may be ill equipped to accommodate renewable energy produced on a massive scale."[277]

Bill Gates have also indicated these investments as high-risk since unlike internet or mobile phone these clean technologies may not be driven by globalized market and not in-line with American Empire objectives.

Despite huge privilege of the U.S. economy, poverty and vulnerable people are growing fast in the country. Whatever is the risk, the outermost MES of a country is the most vulnerable. In November 2012 the U.S. Census Bureau said more than 16% of the population lived in poverty, including almost 20% of American children,[120] up from 14.3% (approximately 43.6 million) in 2009 and to its highest level since 1993. In 2008, 13.2% (39.8 million) Americans lived in poverty.[121] Starting in the 1980s, relative poverty rates have consistently exceeded those of other wealthy nations. California, the technology and oil state has a poverty rate of 23.5%, the highest of any state in the country.[123] In 2011, child poverty reached record high levels, with 16.7 million children living in food insecure households, about 35% more than 2007 levels.[124] A 2013 UNICEF report ranked the U.S. as having the second highest relative child poverty rates in the developed world.[125] While the American welfare state effectively reduces poverty among the elderly, it provides relatively little assistance to the working-age poor.[126] The U.S. has the weakest social safety net of all developed nations.[127] The more people fall below poverty line, the more liability on the U.S. government to support Medicare and social security.

In 2011 the U.S. Federal spending budget ($3,598 Billion), the Medicare spending was 23% ($835 Billion) and social security spending was 20% ($725 Billion).[114] On the other hand, the revenue receipt was $2,303 Billion (deficit $1,295 Billion) of which 47% ($1,092 Billion) was from individual income tax (payroll), and 36% ($819 Billion) was from social security contribution, whereas corporate income tax was 8% ($181 Billion) only (Figure 5.24).[114] However, the figure shows that the U.S. government is more dependent on personal income tax than corporate income tax since introduction of supply-side Economics in 1980s. Again, if the 'Price Pressure (PP)' for Medicare and social security were kept

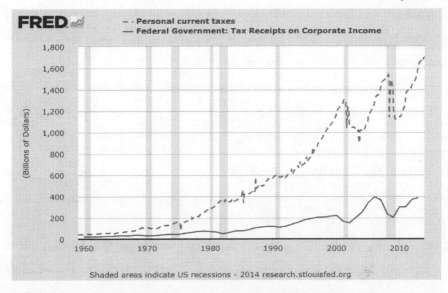

Figure 5.24: The Federal Tax Receipt, Personal and Corporate Income Tax[128]

down by controlling the Money Loop (ML) in M3 and by taxing the corporates (M3) the budget deficit certainly would be low. Unfortunately, the payroll taxes dedicated to Social Security were credited to the Trust Fund upon receipt, but spent for other purposes.[38]

The Government Accountability Office (GAO) projects that payouts for Medicare/Medicaid and social security will exceed government income by over $40 trillion tax revenues over the next 75 years.[272] The Medicare Part A (hospital insurance) payouts already exceed program tax revenues, and social security payouts exceeded payroll taxes in fiscal 2010. These deficits require funding from other tax sources or borrowing.[129] The present value of the national debt and other federal obligations such as Medicare, Medicaid, Social Security, student loans, Fannie Mae, Freddie Mac, FHA would bring total to nearly $127 trillion of unfunded liability.[17] Apart from this, President Obama's 2015 "Clean Power Plan (CPP)" declaration will more likely further indebt the federal government since private investors are less likely interested in investment in national grid system. The national grid system will require a big overhaul and upgrade and onward maintenance to accommodate highly intermittent solar and wind energy sources. At the same time, the energy cost for the end users will also jump, which will again be a burden to the ninety-nine percenters-the common Americans on top of the tax they are paying. Whereas the tax privileged will again be virtually exempted as they can offset their cost by laying off their workers or demanding further tax reduction from the government.

David Friedman (2002) of New America Foundation argues "Currently, growth in service jobs appears to be increasingly dependent on government spending, a connection not normally correlated with sustainable wealth creation."[130] The foreign purchase of the U.S. Treasury Bonds is spent by the U.S. government to support jobs in health care, education, social security, and other government services and then collect payroll taxes from the employees to pay off interests. Any new long-term investment of maintenance or repair of many old highways, roads, bridges-many are about hundred year old, the U.S. government will have to depend on foreign borrowing and all interest burdens will go to the tax payers, mostly from their payrolls. This is why keeping unemployment rate down is very important to the U.S. policy makers.

The idea keeping marginal tax low for riches and corporates can lower down unemployment rate is no longer valid without any technological boom such as digital revolution. The beginning of a new technology requires increased capital investment, MMD moves fast that reduces inflation but capitalization increase productivity and therefore, creates demand for wage raise.[8] As soon as the industry capitalization saturates, MMD slows down and therefore, inflation comes back. And again wage pressure increases in all sectors. Due to the wage pressure, the U.S. investors prefer to import manufactured products from the countries of cheap labor such as like China, India, Mexico or Brazil instead of investing in manufacturing. David Friedman (2005) of New America Foundation argues that wealth-producing primary sector jobs in the U.S. such as those in manufacturing and computer software have often been replaced by much lower

366

paying wealth-consuming jobs such as those in retail and government in the service sector when the economy recovered from recessions.[130&131]

China, the world's largest holder of US debt, condemned the high trade deficit of USA with China and their political "short-sightedness". China also threatened that the world needed a new and stable global reserve currency.[132] China along with Brazil, Russia, India and South Africa formed a new bank called BRICS Development Bank[133], as an alternative to the existing US-dominated World Bank and International Monetary Fund.[134], which will start lending in 2016. Earlier the BRIC nations announced the need for a new global reserve currency, which would have to be "diversified, stable and predictable".[135] In July 2014, the Governor of the Russian Central Bank, Elvira Nabiullina, claimed that the

"BRICS partners the establishment of a system of multilateral swaps that will allow to transfer resources to one or another country, if needed" in an article which concluded that "If the current trend continues, soon the dollar will be abandoned by most of the significant global economies and it will be kicked out of the global trade finance."[136]

As the bail out money is circled back costing the government more money and not helping the real need of the U.S. economy, President Obama proposed the new tax plan for the wealthiest called the "Buffett Rule" a proposal that would see the country's wealthiest pay at least 30% of their income in taxes, which would impact 0.3 percent of taxpayers.[137] The legislation is named after America's second richest person, Warren Buffett as he no more wants to pay a lower tax rate than his secretary.[138] Obama proposed this bill during July 2012 allowing the Bush tax cuts to expire for individual taxpayers earning over $200,000 and couples earning over $250,000, which represents the top 2% of income earners. Reverting to Clinton-era tax rates for these taxpayers would mean increases in the top rates to 36% and 39.6% from 33% and 35% respectively. This would raise approximately $850 billion in revenue over a decade. Not much compared to over USD 18 trillion debts.[139] Ultimately the bill was stopped by a Republican filibuster and did not proceed to debate and a vote.[140] Joachim Hagopian of Global Research expresses his resentment:

"The disparity between the rich and poor in this nation–never worse since the Great Depression–like an evil cancer. Tax burdens continue plaguing the disappearing middle class while the superrich got bailed out, only to make obscene record profits while still enjoying Bush-era tax cuts milking trickle-down Reaganomics for all the scam it is worth."[122]

The similar situation caused declination of Roman Empire when the Empire needed more money to maintain its huge military for keeping the vast territories it conquered but landed elites were exempt from taxation and therefore, the Empire required even more exactions upon those who could not escape taxation.[141&142] Figure 5.24 shows the same situation, when it is hard to raise taxes from corporate elites, dependency of government on payroll tax or debt to maintain its liabilities are getting huge, especially with weak economic situation. Imagine the situation if the foreign banks and governments stop buying the U.S. Treasury securities or start selling them heavily. Economist Rubin (2012) explains his worry

"Everything from the price a bank charges for a car loan to mortgage rates are benchmarked to the Treasury's borrowing rate. If China decides it's better off with a stronger Yuan that rate will inevitably rise–and the consequence will touch every American who holds any debt."[143]

In other words, this will hit in the heart of American economy since American middle class who hold the most debt also bear the most tax burden deducted from their payrolls. Ironically, a big part of the revenue from their taxes goes for debt servicing owned by American government. This means more exactions on those Americans who cannot escape taxes whereas the wealthy Americans are exempted by political shields of reduced marginal tax rates. Doesn't it mean that likewise the fall of the Roman Empire the American Empire is at risk?

5.6 The European Deep Debt Trap

The post-war (World War II) British economy ended up with resentment of the inflation, and taxation. In 1976 the British Government led by James Callaghan faced a Sterling crisis during which the value of the pound tumbled and the government found it difficult to raise sufficient funds to maintain its spending commitments. The Prime Minister was forced to apply to the International Monetary Fund for a £2.3 billion rescue package; the largest-ever call on IMF resources up to that point.[145] In November 1976 the IMF announced its conditions for a loan, including deep cuts in public expenditure, in effect taking control of UK domestic policy.[146] The crisis was seen as a national humiliation, with Callaghan being forced to go "cap in hand" to the IMF.[147]

When Margaret Thatcher became the Prime Minister in 1979 general election, her initial economic policies policy was influenced by monetarist thinking of the economists such as Milton Friedman and Alan Walters.[148] According to monetarist theory, inflation is the result of there being too much money in the economy. She started out in her economic policy by increasing interest rates to slow the growth of the money supply and thus lower inflation.[149] However by 1979 it was not only she and the supporters of her monetary policies who were arguing for stricter control of inflation. The Labour Chancellor of the Exchequer Denis Healey had already adopted some monetarist policies, such as reducing public spending and selling off the government's shares in British Petroleum. Figure 5.25 shows that the outcome was highly negative on the economic growth. In 1981, as unemployment soared, exceeded 2.5 million by the summer.[149] Over two million manufacturing jobs were ultimately lost in the recession of 1979–81.[150] Unemployment continued to rise, passing 3 million by January 1982. By 1983, manufacturing output had dropped by 30% from 1978, although economic growth had been re-established the previous year. According to Middleton this labor-shedding helped firms deal with long-standing inefficiency from over-manning, enabling the British economy to catch up to the productivity levels of other advanced capitalist countries.[150] This means that

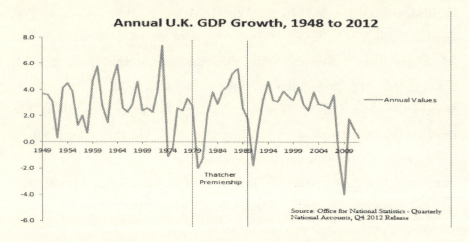

Figure 5.25: Post-war GDP Growth of United Kingdom[151]

reduction of labor forces enabled the factories to adopt technologies to convert more capital into market energy as a result, inflation rate had dropped back to 8.6% from earlier highs of 18%.[152] Then interest rate was allowed to fall to increase money supply that enhanced growth. By 1983 overall economic growth was stronger and inflation and mortgage rates were at their lowest levels since 1970, although unemployment remained high, peaking at 3.3 million in 1984. Middleton describes this situation as prove for the link between the money supply and inflation without taking technological state into consideration.[150] As discussed in Chapter 4, if technology reaches to a certain state and Optimal Capital for the Technological state (OCT) remains constant, increased money supply will cause inflation.

Following President Reagan in USA, Thatcher's political philosophy and economic policies emphasized supply-side economics, lowering the marginal tax rate, deregulation (particularly of the financial sector), flexible labor markets, the privatization of state-owned companies, and reducing the power and influence of trade unions.[153] The policy of privatization has been called "a crucial ingredient of Thatcherism".[154] After the 1983 election the sale of state utilities accelerated;[155] more than £29 billion was raised from the sale of nationalized industries, and another £18 billion from the sale of council houses.[156] Although she reduced direct taxes on income but increased indirect taxes. She introduced cash limits on public spending, and reduced expenditure on social services such as education and housing. By 1987, unemployment was falling, the economy was stable and strong, and inflation was low.[149] The privatization of public assets was combined with financial deregulation in an attempt to fuel economic growth. The Big Bang of 1986 (Chapter 3) removed many restrictions on the London Stock Exchange that enhanced Vertical Growth (VG). The GDP growth shown in Figure 5.25 combines both Horizontal Growth (HG) and Vertical Growth. Since supply-side economics reinforces VG, similar to the U.S. economy, the British economy had to run with deficit budget and therefore, gradually debt increased. In 1990 when Thatcher resigned, the budget deficit was £3.9 Billion.[157] Figure 5.26 the U.K. government Debt as percent of GDP. The figure shows that in the late 1990s and early 2000s the national debt again dropped in relative terms, falling to 40% of GDP by 2001. After that it began to increase,

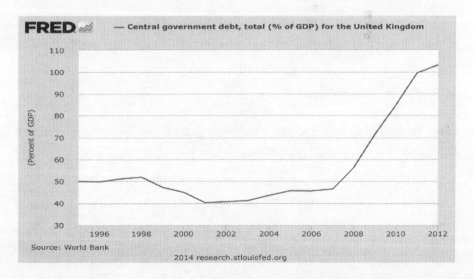

Figure 5.26: Government Debt as % of GDP of United Kingdom[158]

despite sustained economic growth. By 2007 the national debt had increased to 46% of GDP.[159] The deficit continued to grow and, following the Great Recession beginning in early 2008, both government borrowing and the national debt rose dramatically. Despite all these, the British Pound Sterling is also the third most held reserve currency in global reserves (about 4%) after US Dollar and Euro. Following the global financial crisis in late 2008, however, the pound has since depreciated at one of the fastest rates in history, reaching $1.38 per £1 on 23 January 2009 and falling below €1.25 against the euro in April 2008.[160] On 5 March 2009, the Bank of England pumped £75 billion through a process of quantitative easing (printing money), for the first time. By November, 2009 some £175 billion had been injected using quantitative easing.[161]

The European Union introduced Euro by the provisions in the 1992 Maastricht Treaty to compete with USD as the world's reserve currency. Currently about 60% of the global currency reserves have been invested in the USD, while 24% have been invested in the Euro.[162] According to Simon Johnson of M.I.T., a former chief economist at the International Fund "The U.S. has high debt but we are the presumed safe haven, so capital would flood into the U.S. if the euro zone goes really badly".[163] The Eurozone countries particularly Portugal, Italy, Ireland, Greece and Spain, sometimes called as (PIIGS) are in deep debt trap and dragging all the others down but this time might be propping up American debt driven Empire from falling.

There were strict criteria such as a budget deficit of less than three per cent of their GDP, a debt ratio of less than sixty per cent of GDP, low inflation, and interest rates close to the EU average to participate in the monetary union which resulted in introduction of Euro.[164] In the Maastricht Treaty, the United Kingdom and Denmark were granted exemptions per their request. In the early 2000s, a number of EU member states were failing to stay within the confines of the Maastricht criteria and turned to securitizing future government revenues to reduce their debts and/or deficits. Many European countries sold rights to receive future cash flows, allowing governments to raise funds without violating debt and deficit targets, but sidestepping best practice and ignoring internationally agreed standards.[165] This allowed the sovereigns to mask their deficit and debt levels through a combination of innovative techniques of complex currency and credit derivatives structures.[165] At the same time globalization of finance, easy credit conditions during the 2002–2008 period that encouraged high-risk lending and borrowing practices that caused real estate bubbles ("Bulling Money Loop (BML)").

As shown in Figure 1.3 in Chapter 1, Greece's total debt is running over 150 percent of GDP following Japan's twice as large as its annual GDP. Italy, Portugal and Ireland's debt is roughly 120 percent of GDP more than that of USA followed by United Kingdom, France, Spain, Germany and Hungary and so on, all are rising. Rubin explains the situation of Greece:

"Prior to adopting the euro, if Greece found itself in a fiscal mess, it would invariably devalue its exchange rate... A plunging drachma would breathe new life into tourism, Greece's most important industry. Over time, a pickup in tourism spending would send more tax dollars to Greece's government, helping the country back into its feet....Now Greece has no choice but to look to its European partners for a bailout. In practice, that means German taxpayers end up sending welfare checks to Athens. In the old days of a plunging drachma, Germans would pay less money and get a holiday in Santorini for the trouble of helping Greece out"[167]

The similar situations all around Europe but now might be suppressed because of low oil price. In late 2007, global oil prices reacted strongly as OPEC members spoke openly about potentially converting their cash reserves to the Euro and away from the US dollar.[168] High oil price caused economic recession throughout the world Then following the U.S. financial crisis of 2007-08, the bubble also burst in Europe. A financial crisis that combines government debt crisis, a banking crisis and a growth and competitiveness crisis became visible in late 2009 that made it difficult or impossible for many European states to repay or refinance their government debts. As Rubin emphasizes "The problem is servicing debt is very energy intensive."[167] Therefore, pulling off such a recovery will take huge amount of energy. On the other hand, any austerity measures and budget restraints will reduce budget deficit but will impact the whole economy, specially the public services such as reduced health care spending, school closures, cuts to social security for seniors. New York Times reports that Greece got it hard as its GDP was lost by 26 percent of its G.D.P. from the pre-crisis peak, while Portugal, Ireland and Spain lost no more than 7 percent each.[166] Since Greece government has failed to increase taxes or revenues, much of the bailout money bailout money mainly goes toward paying off Greece's international loans. Recently a third bailout of €7.16bn in emergency funding has been arranged for Greece to let the economy roll again but following the referendum the bailout has been widely criticized.[169] Greece is first on the line and staying in Eurozone for time being but Greece's economy will never reach to the scale that would save her from the debt trap. Many others in Eurozone are no different in the long run, especially with shift of the center of gravity of the world economy and delineation of the world's energy resources.

Now European economies are apparently recovering for the first time since 2007 because of low oil prices and the European Central Bank (ECB)'s €1.1trillion quantitative easing (QE). The European Commission forecasted 1.7 percent growth in 2015 and 2.1 percent in next year across the EU. The Telegraph comments on this report as:

> "Commission officials are concerned that a short term boost to economies from falling oil prices will allow euro area countries, such Italy, France and Spain, to dodge economic reforms."[273]

5.7 China is Chasing

China has become the world's second largest economy after the U.S[171] and would become the world's largest economy (by nominal GDP) sometime as early as 2020.[172] The Great Divergence in the U.S. economy and the 'Great' 'upsurge' in Chinese economy began during the same time. In 1978 there was an economic reform by Deng Xiaoping, successor of Mao Zedong introduced various market reforms called "Gai ge kai fang" meaning 'reforms and openness'. Deng emphasized that "socialism does not mean shared poverty". He liberalized trade that opened up direct foreign investment, but not opening the capital account more generally to portfolio flows.[173] Following the economic reform, China joined World Trade Organization (WTO) in 2001. Since then as Figure 5.28 shows that GDP of Chinese economy saw exponential growth, on average 10% for decades. The trade increased from under 10% of GDP to 64% of GDP.[177] This benefitted every household significantly in the economy. The poverty rate

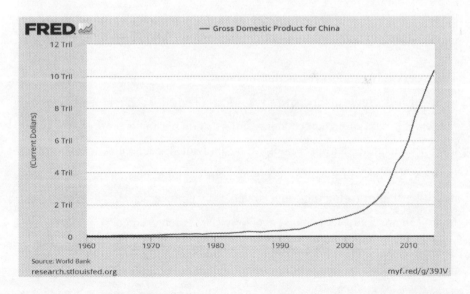

Figure 5.28: People's Republic of China's GDP between years 1960 to 2014[174]

decreased from 65% in 1981 to 10% in 2004.[173] The return to capital was high in investing in China compared to USA, the U.S. investors and the fund managers, including those who already benefited by Reagan's tax cut, preferred to invest in multinational companies operating or producing in China.

As the Chinese economy is growing, the trade deficit of the U.S with China every year is setting a new record $295 billion in 2011, climbing from $315.1 billion in 2012 to $318.4 in 2013[175] and up from $304 million in 1983.[176] During Mao's regime, the Chinese economy was riddled with huge inefficiencies and mal-investments. After his death, Deng Xiaoping came into the power of the Communist Party of China (CPC) who introduced market-oriented economy within a planned economic framework to salvage the failing economy.[177] His reform is often characterized by his famous slogan: "Who cares if a cat is black or white, as long as it catches the mice."[173] The economic reforms introducing capitalist market principles began in 1978 and were carried out in two stages. The first stage, in the late 1970s and early 1980s, involved the decollectivization of agriculture, the opening up of the country to foreign investment, and permission for entrepreneurs to startup businesses. However, most industry remained state-owned at the beginning.[178]

The concept of information biasing described in Chapter 4 has to be distinguished from the perspectives of a planned economy and a market economy. In case of market economy, information biasing is originated in micro-level information sharing strategies of individual economic agents. On the contrary, in case of planned economy, information biasing is originated at macro-level information imposing strategies by political leaders. In the following figure (Figure 5.29) the planned economy (F0) is represented by perfectly price elastic demand curve D_0D_0' and perfectly price inelastic supply curve S_0S_0', however it shows a fixed price P_F set by government. Let us focus on the market economy introduced by Deng began in agriculture, a sector long neglected by the Communist Party during the Great Leap Forward. In the late 1970s and early 1980s he de-collectivized agriculture, which divided the land of the People's communes into private plots. Farmers were able to keep the land's output after

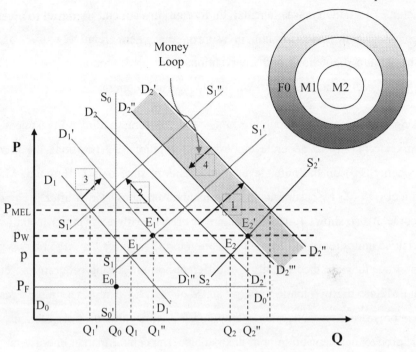

Figure 5.29: Equilibrium Analysis of Chinese Economy

paying a share to the state. This move increased agricultural production, increased the living standards of hundreds of millions of farmers and stimulated rural industry.[177] Reforms were also implemented in urban industry to increase productivity. Analytically speaking, if both state government and private sectors compete in the same market, the set price (say, 'p_F') is to be equal to the market price (say, 'p'), where state government is likely to lose due to inefficiency. Deng introduced a dual price system, in which state-owned industries were allowed to sell any production above the plan quota, and commodities were sold at both plan and market prices, allowing citizens to avoid the shortages of the Maoist era. Private businesses were allowed to operate for the first time since the Communist takeover, and they gradually began to make up a greater percentage of industrial output. Price flexibility was also increased, expanding the service

377

sector. The country was opened to foreign investment. A series of special economic zones for foreign investment that were relatively free of the bureaucratic regulations and interventions hampered economic growth. These regions became engines of growth for the national economy.[178]

Deng created special economic zones for the foreign direct investment and market economy to generate employments. Figure 5.29 positions the planned economy (F0) on the outer layer market energy state of a Differential Market Model (DMM) by assuming that the planned economy looks after the poorest people. It also shows a market economy is created within a planned economy but no price interference as there is no relation to the set price "p_F" and market price "p" since they are theoretically two different non-interfering economies. Let M1 and M2 are the two market energy states of the DMM representing the market economy. Like previous, this example also assumes one product economy that the product has demand in both the markets. The central market energy state M2 represents the rich and higher middle class Chinese people who have surplus income more than a certain level. They are separated by a Biased Equilibrium Barrier (BEB) from the remaining people under the market economy positioned on market energy state M1. The reference demand and supply curves for M2 market energy state are D_2D_2' and S_2S_2' respectively. Similarly, the reference demand and supply curves for M1 market energy state are D_1D_1' and S_1S_1' respectively. The both markets are in equilibrium at reference price 'p' completely separate from the set price 'p_F' of the planned economy F0. The planned economy F0 represents any economy outside M1 & M2 within China. The market economy outside the planned economy F0 is represented by the two market energy states M1 & M2.

China took a little different approach. The first phase was privatization of agriculture and industries and creation of special economic zone for generation of employments. In other words, the first phase was building a process of forming a 'Market Energy Loop (MEL)' in a gradual manner as opposed to

Russia's "shock therapy", where the state-owned sector was rapidly privatized that ultimately went to some influential "oligarchs" now known as Russian oligarchic capitalism (see section 5.3). The financial sector reform happened in a much slower pace.[179] At the beginning of the reform, the Chinese banking system was weak and therefore, companies raise most of their capital through an informal, nonstandard financial sector developed during the 1980s and 1990s, consisting largely of underground businesses and private banks.[180] In the second phase, incentives were given to the new capitalists and foreign investors to establish export oriented industries focusing global economy. Let us walk through the steps:

1. Let the core MES, M2 is the heart of the MEL of Chinese economy. As shown in Figure 5.29, the MEL in M2 shifts the demand curve upward and rightward from D_2D_2' to $D_2'D_2''$. Then corresponding equilibrium price moves to 'p_{MEL}'. Without the export market, 'p_{MEL}' would be much higher, similar to Russia's transformation to market economy at the beginning.

This is what happened after the first stage of implementation of market-oriented policy in China. Inflation and corruption caused discontent among younger people and students. Naughton (2008) argues increased discontent (because of corruption and inflation) contributed to the Tiananmen Square protests of 1989 and a conservative backlash after that event which ousted several key reformers and threatened to reverse many of Deng's reforms.[181] However, Deng stood by his reform.[181] The inflation came under control as privatization and capitalization of the industries accelerated. He also reopened the Shanghai Stock Exchange for that after 40 years of its closing by Mao to facilitate rapid market capitalization. It is now the world's 5th largest stock market by market capitalization at US$2.3 trillion as of December 2011. Unlike the Hong Kong Stock Exchange, the Shanghai Stock Exchange is still not entirely open to foreign investors due to tight capital account controls exercised by the Chinese mainland authorities.[182]

2. If wages in M1 did not change or Shapiro-Stiglitz NSC (No-Shirking Condition) did not hold for M1, then the supply curve for M1 would move upward and leftward from S_1S_1' to $S_1'S_1''$ to comply with potential equilibrium price 'P_{MEL}' as shown in Figure 5.29 . Accordingly, the output would not increase and the corresponding consumption would reduce from Q_1 to Q_1'. Like any other market economy, this would be the negative impact triggered by the growth of the Market Energy Loop (MEL).

The above steps 1-2 describes what could happen in Chinese economy at the beginning of the reform as happened in Russia and in Eastern Europe during their transition from socialism to socialist market economy.[178] The Eastern bloc economies saw decline of 13 to 65% in GDP and 200 to 1000% hyperinflation at the beginning of reforms.[183] On the other hand, in China, this success is attributed Deng's gradualist and decentralized approach also in contrast with President Reagan's dramatic approach of tax cut, which allowed market institutions to develop to the point where they could replace state planning.[178] China slowly and carefully expanded recognition of private sector first as a "complement" to the state sector (1988) and then as an "important component" (1999) of the socialist market economy.[177]

Although Deng placed industries in the front line of the Chinese economy, simultaneously he made reform in agriculture to increase productivity. He implemented the household responsibility system, agricultural output increased by 8.2 percent a year. Food prices fell nearly 50%, while agricultural incomes rose. Increases in agricultural productivity allowed workers to be released for work in industry and services, while simultaneously increasing agricultural production.[184] Deng's careful handling of the agricultural productivity, transition, control of labor migration and consistent rapid growth created high employment demand and therefore, the Shapiro-Stiglitz 'efficiency wage theory' can be applied to explain the cause of wage increase along with increase of per capital production. China's manufacturing wages have risen sharply in recent years, at double-digit rates. As Dollar argues "It is hard to imagine that manufacturing wages would have risen so rapidly if there had not been such controls on labor migration."[185] The second stage of reform, in the late 1980s and 1990s, involved privatization and contracting out of much state-owned industry and the lifting of price controls, protectionist policies, and regulations except state monopolies in few sectors such as banking and petroleum remained.[178] The analysis of Figure 5.29 continues:

3. On the other hand, if Shapiro-Stiglitz NSC does hold for M1, wages will increase. To do that the employers expect increase of productivity of the workers that is achieved by introduction of new technologies based on Foreign Direct Investment and export led growth.

In China, average wages rose six fold between 1978 and 2005,[186] while absolute poverty declined from 41% of the population to 5% from 1978 to 2001[177] following exponential GDP growth rate on average 9% per year. Figure 5.29 shows the reflection of wage increment in M1 by moving the demand curve upward and rightward from D_1D_1' to $D_1'D_1''$. The corresponding increase in consumption from Q_1 to Q_1'' is met mostly by local output. Accordingly, Chinese economy reaches to a realistic price equilibrium "p_W".

In the past decade Chinese economy has achieved unimaginable growth over 9%. Patrick (2009) reports that when China adopted a loose monetary policy, it led to the formation of a U.S.-style property bubble in which property prices tripled.[187] The average hospital visit in China is paid 60% out-of-pocket by the patient, compared to zero before the reform. Poor households either forego treatment or face devastating financial consequences. In the 2003 National

Monowar Zaman

Health Survey, 30% of poor households identified a large health care expenditure as the reason that they were in poverty.[185] Although inflation under control, in recent times, the Economist reports that food price also increased dramatically. For example, the CPI increased by 4.8% and 5.9% in 2007 and 2008, respectively, but food prices increased by 12.3% and 14.3%.[188] Let's go back to our analysis again (Figure 5.29):

4. Now the equilibrium piece is "p_W". To comply with this price, the new M2 demand curve is shown as $D_2''D_2'''$, originally moves from D_2D_2'. Accordingly, consumption in M2 actually increases from Q_2 to Q_2'', while consumption in M1 also increases from Q_1 to Q_1''. This is how MEL in Chinese economy extends (KME) with high growth (see Chapter 4, section 4.8). This shows how the economic progress has been achieved in China based on market economy.

    The shaded area between the two demand curves $D_2'D_2''$ and $D_2''D_2'''$ in M2 represents a Money Loop (ML) in Chinese economy that puts implicit 'Price Pressure (PP)' on M1. Unlike the U.S. economy, the impact of PP is not translated to 'debt pressure' as long as Potential Market Energy (PME) is controlled and Kinetic Market Energy (KME) is strengthened by a certain level of wage growth, collecting taxes and new employments in pace with the growth of the economy.

As Chniese economy is growing, inequality is also growing. The Gini coefficient of inequality in China increased from 0.31 at the beginning of reform to 0.48 in 2011, passed the U.S. economy (.468).[189] Chinese people has high marginal propensity of savings (MPS) and that makes a 'savings glut'.[190]

Although savings in China occurred in all levels, certainly the majority occurred in boarder between M2 and M1. This is the reason that China's developers are building houses for them. The Economists call them as "speculators" and reports

382

"Instead of accommodating China's overcrowded urban masses".[192] Now the developers have become crazy, they are building cities instead of houses. As an example, they were building a replica of New York City outside the Northern Chinese city of Tianjin. Marketplace reports

"Workers were constructing dozens of skyscrapers on a piece of swampland inside a bend in the river, giving it an uncanny resemblance to the island of Manhattan. There were plans for a Lincoln Center, a Rockefeller center, and much more."[192]

Then it reports

"A year later, construction on this city, named Yujiapu, has all but grinded to a halt. Investors have pulled out. And a cluster of skyscrapers sit, half-finished – Manhattan on hold."[192]

Gao Fei, an investment consultant explains the reason for so huge project

"Tianjin's government has always been a high GDP rate. That means the government has to spend a lot of money on huge projects like this one. In China, these kinds of wasteful projects are everywhere."[192]

These 21st century projects in different parts of China run by borrowing giving big business for banks and stock markets. David Stockman in this website "Contra Corner" argues that in last two decades the huge "borrow & build" in China erected a "monumental Ponzi economy" that is "economically rotten to the core". As he explains as:

"It has 1.5 billion tons of steel capacity, but "sell-through" demand of less than half that amount.........The same is true for its cement industry, ship-building, solar and aluminum industries–to say nothing of 70 million empty luxury apartments and vast stretches of over-built highways, fast rail, airports, shopping malls and new cities......Effectively, the country-side pig sties have been piled high with copper inventories and the urban neighborhoods with glass, cement and rebar erections that can't possibly earn an economic return, but all of which has become "collateral" for even more "loans" under the Chinese Ponzi."[170]

On the other hand, the Economists reports:

"China's building boom has left some parts of the country with too much floorspace and other parts with too little. Nearly half of all migrant workers still live in dormitories or on worksites. Where housing is oversupplied, prices will have to fall, inflicting losses on homeowners. But where housing needs remain unmet, scope remains for further construction to fill the gap."[193]

Now all the huge construction works including the above mention types of ghost cities, spreading consumerism all across the world and within China are hapening primarily by burning huge amount of coal. That's why China's economy is called "Coal Fired Economy". Figure 5.30 shows a similar pattern of

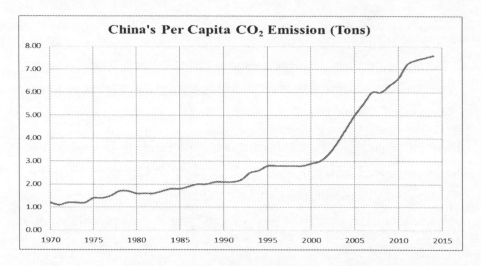

Figure 5.30: China's Per Capita CO2 Emission[196]

China's per capita CO_2 gas emission as its GDP (Figure 5.28). Now China is the largest producer of greenhouse gas (10,540,750 kilo tons) and it produces twice as much as USA (5,334,530 kilo tons). It is the largest consumer of coal in the world[194&195] and is about to become the largest user of coal-derived electricity, generating 1.95 trillion kilowatt-hours per year, or 68.7% of its electricity from coal as of 2006.[195] It has approximately 13 percent of the world's proven reserves, there is debate as to how many years these reserves will last at current levels of consumption.[197] According to the U.S. Energy Information Administration (EIA), China is now the world's largest net importer of petroleum and other liquid fuels now.[198]

This model recommends the best option for China to reduce China's economic bubble or Bulling Money Loop (BML), Chinese government should collect tax from the surplus money and spend for renewable energy infrastructures and welfare of F0, the rural and poor people who are isolated from the market economy and discourage rural migration. This will also increase wage of the already migrated people (M1). In this way, China may reach 'Lewisian turning point". There is another benefit of public spending in rural and less developed areas (F0 market) on services like health care and education. It increases opportunity cost of the rural people for migration to the urban areas and therefore, the urban economy reaches high up in employment. On the other hand, the bulk of the migrants, 60% or more, have only nine years of education and lack of technical skill.[199] These are the reason that the wages of the existing workers (in M1) rise, while requirement of skilled workers increasing.

The Nobel-prize-winning economist Sir Arthur Lewis (1954) noted that "development must be inegalitarian because it does not start in every part of the economy at the same time".[206] Many research papers indicates that China is approaching the 'Lewisian Turning Point'[207] as the economy is moving from labor intensive economy to capital intensive machine based heavy industries such as automobile and steels.[208] Dollar (2007) argues "China classically manifests two of the characteristics of development that Lewis had in mind: rising return to education and rural-urban migration."[185] He explains "As an underdeveloped country, China began its reform with relatively few highly educated people, and with a small minority of the population (20%) living in cities, where labor productivity was about twice the level as in the countryside."[185] However, Yao (2010) from the Economist comments "this conclusion may be too hasty because it does not fit into the large picture of demography in China."[199]

The Economists reports that the Chinese government has said it will spend more than 1 trillion Yuan this year renovating 'shoddy housing' that is, housing for M1, the urban poor people. This will help keep homebuilders busy and prevent the economy from slowing down so that the Economists writes "For China's property Cassandras are often believed, but have yet to come true".[193] In the past 35 years the population of urban China has grown by more than 500 million people.[200] Three fifth of them, about 300 million people are still carrying rural 'hukou', who are often classified as "second-class citizens" since they get far less access to government-funded health care and education than the others who carry urban 'hukou'.[200] The Guardian reports that demand for urban properties is expected to remain high over the next decade since it is estimated that another 200 million people could join China's urban areas by 2023.[201]

If the economic growth slows down, M1 will become weaker and fall under debt pressure in the same way as the U.S. economy. Therefore, M1 is the most vulnerable part of Chinese economy. This model explains, by obtaining urban hukou vulnerability of M1 will reduce but Chinese government will still be in growth pressure for funding their urban welfare while health care and education are becoming expensive. The Chinese government is planning 100 million migrants are to obtain urban hukou by 2020.[200]

Nevertheless, whether China has or will ever reach "Lewisian turning point", Chinese economy cannot stop growing, which is only possible by burning fossil fuel. This is the reason China signed a memorandum for a gas route from Russia to China for as long as 30 years and planning to develop its own shale gas resources, believed to be world's largest.[209]

In summary, all China is doing just chasing America–the American gluttony of consumerism translated into energy and debt (equation 4.28). The U.S. total credit market debt is now $59 trillion that is "America has been burying itself in debt at nearly a 7% annual rate".[170] As Stockman describes:

"But move over America! As the 21st century dawned, China had about $1 trillion of credit market debt outstanding, but after a blistering pace of "borrow and build" for 14 years it now carries nearly $25 trillion."[170]

As a lot of money has moved to Money Loop (ML), the same overinvestment or market capitalization is also reflected in stock market as Bulling Market Loop (BML). Bloomberg recently analyzes Chinese stock market as:

"Fueled by record margin debt and unprecedented numbers of novice investors, China's market capitalization has tripled in the past year to $9.8 trillion. At 84 times projected earnings, the average stock on mainland exchanges is now almost twice as expensive as it was when the benchmark Shanghai Composite Index peaked in October 2007."[177]

Therefore, Bloomberg concludes

"It's no longer a question of whether China's stock-market rally is a bubble, but when the bubble will burst."[177]

5.8 What is Holding India Back?

If Chinese economy approaches to 'Lewisian Turning Point', will this open opportunity for another country to compete with China in labor intensive manufacturing? Chris Barth (2012) of Forbes magazine argues that western investors love to compare India with China as if they were identical economies at different points on the same timeline.[210] He comments this

"After all, both are growth powerhouses."[210] Unlike China, the 'Lewisian Turning Point' is far reaching for India, because 'poverty' remains the toughest challenge for Indian economy. Roy argues "that the structural change in employment in India that results from the exclusionary nature of the growth process hardly approximates the Lewisian trajectory."[211]

United Nations Research Institute for Social Development (UNRISD)'s 2010 report comes to conclusion that reducing poverty through growth is difficult when inequality is rampant; wealth and land tends to concentrate in small groups, which in turn excludes the poor from economic participation.[212] We have two types of scenario. In one scenario, as we have seen in the previous section (section 5.7) that in China poverty dramatically reduced while inequality increased. In another scenario, the countries such as India & Bangladesh substantiate the UNRISD finding that poverty reduced in a very slow pace but inequality increased rapidly. Indian poverty is one of the toughest in the world to alleviate although Gini ratio of India is lower (36.8) than that of U.S.A (46.8). In 2013, the Indian government stated 21.9% of its population is below its official poverty limit.[213] The World Bank estimated that 68.7% of India's 1.21 billion people (832 million) live on less than $2 a day and 32.7% Indians (400 million) lives below the International Poverty Line on less than $1.25 a day in 2010.[214] According to United Nations Development Programme, an estimated 29.8% of Indians lived below poverty line in 2009-2010.[215] However, London based McKinsey Global Institute use 'empowerment line' approach that reveals that 56 percent of Indians, some 680 million, lack the means to meet their basic needs. Just above the official poverty line, some 413 million are "vulnerable." Richard Dobbs of McKinsey Institute explains

"They have only a tenuous grip on a better standard of living, and shocks such as illness or a lost job can easily push them back into desperate circumstances."[216]

On the other hand, India is the ninth-largest economy in the world by nominal GDP, $2.047 trillion (2014) and the third-largest by purchasing power parity

(PPP).[217] It imported a total of $616.7 billion worth of merchandise (19th largest in the world) and services (6th largest in the world) in 2013. It has one of the youngest populations among emerging-market nations, nearly half its citizens are under 25.[210] India's economic growth slowed to 4.7% for the 2013–14 fiscal year, in contrast to higher economic growth rates in 2000s.[218] As an example, it was growing at GDP growth rate in 2010-11 of 8.5% and inflation rate 9.44%.

Going back to history, India had the world's largest economy during the years 1 AD and 1000 AD.[219] During the Mughal period in the 16th century, the gross domestic product of India was estimated at about 25.1% of the world economy, the second largest in the world after the Manchu China.[220] Economist and then Indian Prime Minister Manmohan Singh commented

"There is no doubt that our grievances against the British Empire had a sound basis. As the painstaking statistical work of the Cambridge historian Angus Maddison has shown, India's share of world income collapsed from 22.6% in 1700, almost equal to Europe's share of 23.3% at that time, to as low as 3.8% in 1952. Indeed, at the beginning of the 20th century, "the brightest jewel in the British Crown" was the poorest country in the world in terms of per capita income."[221]

The socialist biased economic policies adopted by Indira Gandhi, split her party, the Indian National Congress in two factions, the socialists led by Gandhi, and the conservatives led by Morarji Desai. In the same year, in July 1969 she nationalized banks.[222] The inflation suddenly went up in 23.81% in 1973 and 25.40% in 1974 mostly because of stagnancy in capital investment, unionism and plague of bureaucracy in every sector of the economy. The hyper inflation figures imply there were enough reasons for political contention and turmoil and further economic problems. This situation became worsen by Allahabad High Court's conviction against her for using corrupt electoral practices in her constituency held four years earlier (in 1971), and ended up in an national emergency. During the Emergency, Indira Gandhi implemented a 20-point program of economic reforms that resulted in greater economic growth, aided by the absence of strikes and trade union conflicts.[224] Inflation impressively went down at -6.18% in 1975 and 0% in 1976 and the economy started to grow.[223] However, in the following election in 1977 she lost the power to her estranged colleague Morarji Desai.

As a reformer Morarji Desai introduced many pro-business measures to bring the economy out of socialist mode set by Prime Minister Jawaharlal Nehru. He eased restrictions on capacity expansion for incumbent companies, removed price controls, reduced corporate taxes and promoted the creation of small scale industries in large numbers.[225] However, his government was short lived and the subsequent government policy of socialism and political turmoil hampered the benefits of the economy. Indira Gandhi regained her position as Prime Minister in 1980 for her fourth term. During this time the economy continued high inflation and slow growth since her government was mostly engaged in handling political agitations. She was assassinated in 1984 in the aftermath of a political decision.[222]

Indira Gandhi's son Rajiv Gandhi became the Prime Minister of India after her assassination. Rajiv Gandhi set the goal of visionary India. As he commented in a speech in the US Congress

"I dream of an India, strong, independent, self-reliant and in the forefront of the front ranks of the nations of the world in the service of mankind."[226]

He increased government support for science and technology and associated industries, and reduced import quotas, taxes and tariffs on technology-based industries, especially computers, airlines, defense and telecommunications.[227] Coincidently, Rajiv Gandhi's policy complemented Reagan's policy of tax cut for the investors in the U.S. by supplying the huge work force of computer professionals from India. As a result, we experienced the revolution in Information Technology and computerization in the U.S and also in the other part of the world. He also introduced measures significantly reducing the 'License Raj', allowing businesses and individuals to purchase capital, consumer goods and import without bureaucratic restrictions.[226] License Raj refers to the elaborate licenses, regulations and accompanying red tape that were required to set up and run businesses in India introduced as part of the planned economy. While internal reform was going on and India was struggling for its political stability, Indian economy remained vulnerable to external shocks. Arunabha (2006) analyzes

"From 1979 onwards the second oil shock, agricultural subsidies, and consumption-driven growth had pushed up the fiscal deficit. It further increased in the mid-1980s as defense expenditure was substantially increased and direct taxes were progressively reduced. The result was that from 1985 onwards the deficit ballooned to an annual average of 9 percent and by 1991 it was 9.4 percent of GDP."[228]

The collapse of the Soviet Union, which was India's major trading partner, and the Gulf War, which caused a spike in oil prices, resulted in a major balance-of-payments crisis for India, which found itself facing the prospect of defaulting on its loans.[228] India asked for a $1.8 billion bailout loan from the International Monetary Fund (IMF), which in return demanded reforms.[229] In response, Prime Minister Narasimha Rao, along with his finance minister Manmohan Singh, initiated the economic liberalization of 1991. The Licence Raj is considered to have been significantly reduced in 1991 when India had only two weeks of dollars left. After the IMF bailout, the government abolished industrial licensing regulations except few sectors such as alcohol, tobacco, pharmaceuticals, and hazardous chemicals. The government lowered tariffs, duties and taxes, opened up to international trade and investment.[229] Figure 5.31 shows how Indian economy responded to all these liberalization measures. However, it does not tell severe disparities exist among people in different states terms of income, literacy rates, life expectancy and living conditions. The number of wealthy individuals

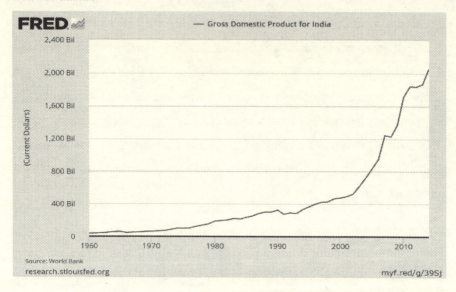

Figure 5.31: GDP Growth of Indian Economy 1960 to 2014[231]

in India surged by 23% from 2006-2007, which is the highest growth rate in the world.[230] Renowned journalist Kuldip Nayar writes "Indian black money in Swiss banks, according to Swiss Banking Association report, 2006, was the highest—as much as $1456 billion."[232] This worth more than three times the country's gross external debt of $440 billion in 2014.[233]

Our analysis on Indian economy begins here as shown in Figure 5.32. Let us imagine that the Differential Market Model (DMM) of Indian economy constitute with three market energy states M1, M2 & M3. The figure also shows the corresponding Shapiro-Stiglitz 'Efficiency Wage Model'[9] for Indian Economy. Similar to Figure 5.3, the effect of technology (includes educational reform) and liberalization policy is shown by rightward shift of the 'demand for labor' curve from D_{Labor} to D'_{Labor}. The core MES, M3 represents wealthy Indians who have surplus money more than a certain level. Their incomes or wages rise from W_{M3} to W'_{M3} due to shift of the demand curve. The next level MES, M2 consists of skilled workers that matches with specific technological advancement (digital transformation) or who have high disposable income but insignificant

392

amount of surplus money. The individuals in M2 are able to shirk with wage reduction and their wages rise from W_{M2} to W'_{M2} due to shift of the demand curve. Lastly, M1 represents the poorest Indians who has very low disposable

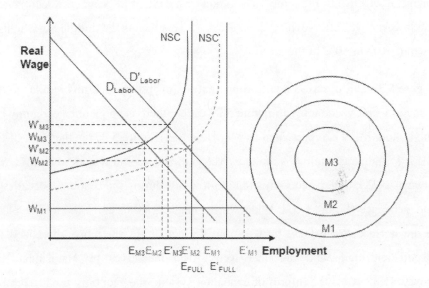

Figure 5.32: Shapiro-Stiglitz 'Efficiency Wage Model'[55] for Indian Economy

incomes and of course, no surplus. They, whether skilled (e.g., workers in small factories or garments industry) or unskilled, cannot shirk with wage reduction or they have no bargaining ability for their wage raise. As shown in Figure 5.32, their wages are indifferent to the specific technological advancement (digital transformation). Figure 5.33 shows that the three MESs are in equilibrium at price level "p", where D_3D_3' and S_3S_3' represents demand and supply curves respectively for M3, D_2D_2' and S_2S_2' represents demand and supply curves respectively for M2 and D_1D_1' and S_1S_1' represents demand and supply curves respectively for M1. Unlike President Reagan's favor to the riches for boosting up the U.S. economy, Rajiv Gandhi tried to uplift the middle class (M2) to boost up the Indian economy and then it was followed by all other governments. As mentioned earlier that the Gini coefficient exhibit India in a better position than U.S.A. in terms of income inequality.[234] It tells. that the wealth of America is

393

skewed toward riches, whereas the wealth of India is skewed toward its huge middle class base. In U.S.A., top 1% American own 35% of country's net wealth (and 43% of financial wealth) and top 10% own 73% of net wealth (93% of financial wealth). In India top 10% Indian own 31% of the country's income and the lowest 10% suffers with merely 3.6%.[235] This means the middle 80% Indians own more than 60% of the income.

Figure 5.33 below shows equilibrium analysis of Indian economy similar to the same of Chinese economy in Figure 5.29 except there is no planned economy but the bottom MES is represented as M1. Here M3 (Figure 5.32) is the heart of the MEL of Indian economy. As long as M2 in Indian economy was weak (M1 was always weak), Indian economy did not grow fast during the first three decades of independence (Figure 5.31). When Rajiv Gandhi tried to uplift the middle class, it did not accelerate GDP growth until the economy was more liberalized for export and trade and investors were given incentives by Narasimha Rao government. After the reform of education system, the economy produced a big supply of skilled workers for internal and external markets. And after liberalization for export and foreign direct investment, huge demand of skilled workers was created in certain fields, particularly in Information Technology industries. According to Shapiro and Stiglitz (1984) 'efficiency wage' model,[9] as soon as the industry approaches high up in employment, the wages or incomes of the skilled workers increases.

Here the outermost layer market M1 has no active contribution on the price equilibrium for the entire economy. The impact of 'P_{ML}' on M1 is not discussed here as there is no boundary between M3 & M1. Therefore, individuals in M 1 and the individuals in M3 do not vie for the same set of products but may vie for a subset component of the products. As a result M1 will be impacted by the new equilibrium price 'P_W' that causes inflation. As shown in Figure 5.33, the supply curve of M1 moves leftward and upward and from S1S1' to S1"S1"' to comply with the new equilibrium price 'P$_W$', whereas the demand curve D$_1$D$_1$' remains steady. Accordingly, their consumption reduces from Q$_1$ to Q$_1$' that indicates

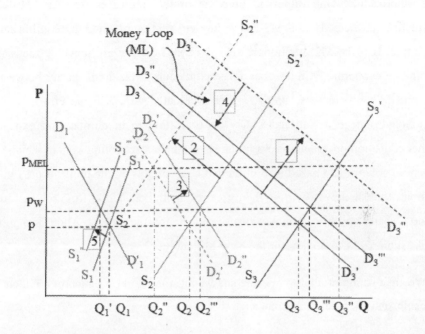

Figure 5.33: Equilibrium Analysis of Indian Economy (A Micro-perspective)

they become further poor in real income even though their nominal wage remains the same and the economy generates more employments (Figure 5.32). The impact of implicit Price Pressure due the Market Loop spreads all over the Indian economy. As an example, although the rich or middle class people do not live in slums but high land price in the surrounding area increases in price of the tiny hutments in urban slums.[236] This situation continues and makes the marginal poor people further poor. As an example, the farmers may become dependent on the debts from rural loan sharks with high interests and eventually may sell their little lands and are forced to migrate to urban slums. Although life standard of Indian middle class increased, in 2007 40% of Indians were landless and 23% were in abject poverty.[237]

India is a land of more than 1.21 billion people, at least half of the population can be positioned on M1 based on McKinsey Global Institute's 'empowerment line' approach.[216] One important outcome of this model is that for M1 the inequality between M1 and M2 has to be very minimum since the equilibrium price 'p_W' is set by M2 that impact M1 directly. Therefore, if the whole focus of the Indian economic policies goes for strengthening M2, the disparity between M1 and M2 will increase and M1 will eventually suffer. In his effort, Rajiv Gandhi introduced a National Policy on Education to modernize and expand higher education programs across India. He founded a schooling system which is a Central government based institution that concentrates on the uplift of the rural section of the society providing them free residential education from 6th to 12th grade.[238] Later on, this urgency was also reflected in the A. P. J. Abdul Kalam's book "India 2020: A Vision for the New Millennium" as

"We are a nation of a billion people and we must think like a nation of a billion people, only then can we become big."[239]

India to some extent over achieving much of its Vision 2020 target for the middle class people, such as growth in IT industry, Foreign Direct Investment, GDP growth etc. Indian IT industry has already achieved $100 billion landmark, FDI $47 billion in 2011-2012 year and growing 13% every year[240] and 2 trillion dollar GDP landmark in 2014. On the other hand India has hundreds of million people under hardcore poverty and living miserable lives.

According to a recent Times report, to lift hundreds of millions of Indians out of poverty India needs to use a huge amount of coal, the dirtiest type of fossil fuel for climate change. For electricity generation, as its economy grows. India is planning is to produce 1.5 billion metric tons of the fossil fuel by 2020, up about 600 million tons in 2012.[276] According to International Energy Agency, one in five of India's 1.3 billion people continue to live without access to electricity.

The excessive use of coal leaving India is in contest with China on CO_2 emission. As India's power minister Piyush Goyal justifies

"Ultimately, coal-based power is cheaper.....It provides the base load. It can be used to bundle with and to use more expensive renewable power with cheaper power and provides energy access which is the need of the hour."[276]

On the other hand, Indian government put forward a major initiative for a massive deployment of solar energy, called The Jawaharlal Nehru National Solar

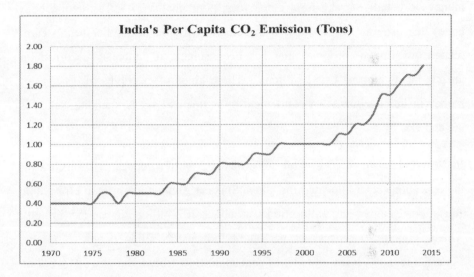

Figure 5.34: Per Capita CO_2 Emission of India

Mission by former Prime Minister of India, Dr. Manmohan Singh in 2010. Initially it targeted 20GW by 2022 which was later increased to 100 GW in 2015 Union budget of India in three phases.[282]

Still about 53 percent of Indian do not have sanitation or drainage facilities on premises, 33 percent of the households have no access to electricity. India has about 61 million children under the age of 5 who are chronically malnourished.[241] A critical problem facing India's economy is the sharp and growing regional variations among India's different states and territories in terms of poverty, availability of infrastructure and socio-economic development.[242] Most part of all Public spending for the welfare of the poor people have failed and money has gone to the non-poor due to waste, corruption, or simple ineffectiveness.[216] Example includes Examples include Mahatma Gandhi National Rural Employment Guarantee Act (MGNREGA) and National Rural Health Mission (NRHM). After 5 years of implementation of the MGNREGA project the outlay of US$7.24 billion for welfare of the poor people is criticized no more effective. It is beset with controversy about corrupt officials pocketing money on behalf of fake rural employees, poor quality of infrastructure built under this program.[243] National Rural Health Mission is another health care-related government program that has been subject to large scale corruption allegations as high as US$2 billion.[244] These kinds of examples of wastage of money in India by name of entitlement programs and social spending schemes are endless.

In 2011-2012 year budget, about 50% of 520.5 billion rupees ($10 billion) for the education sector allocated for 'Sarva Shiksha Abhiyan', a program for public education. Health sector allocation was about 267 billion rupees ($5 billion), which is mere 20 rupees per person of Indian 1.2 billion people.[245] Global Financial Integrity (GFI) the illicit financial outflow from India was $94.8 billion in 2012 alone. This huge some is equivalent to at least six years spending for health and education sectors or twenty years of health services of Indian 1.2 billion people. The cumulative figure for India between 2003 and 2012 was $439.6 billion, equivalent to total cumulative external debt ($440 billion in 2014) of Indian government.[246] In both ways Indian hardworking poor people are deprived and much of the money spent for protection of them are flowing out of India leaving debt and emission burden to them.

5.9 Globalization-All Coming Together

The globalized world we are living now every country wants to increase their revenues though a free flow of goods and services, technology and capital across the world. It allows free flow of goods and service professionals across different countries in the world to enhance capitalization and growth in each respective country. As this happens, on one hand, it multiplies the global production and consumption (economic growth) and on the other hand, it makes part of the population well off. Here economic progress under globalization can be best described as centrifugal expansion of the MEL (see chapter 4). The concept of MEL also describes that the growth based on free trade is unsustainable since it is contingent on certain comparative advantages and availability of certain resources and energy (fossil fuel). Rubin (2012) argues "Oil is the fuel of growth". As he explains:

"You can draw a straight line between oil consumption and GDP growth. The more oil we burn, the faster the global economy grows. On average over the last four decades, a 1 percent bump in world oil consumption has led to a 2 percent increase in global GDP."[247]

Although free trade and economic globalization were attempted since 1900s, it was disrupted by World War I. Globalization of the economy didn't fully resume until the 1970s[248] after gold standard was suspended by President Richard Nixon mostly to facilitate unbridled oil import after reaching peak oil in 1970. Since then international economic and financial organizations are under the control of the United States and its allied western countries. According to Gao Shangquan (2000) of United Nations, globalization eventually benefited less than 20 developing countries that the average trade deficit of developing countries in 1990's increased by 3% as compared with that in 1970s, whereas it expanded gap between North and South. In globalized world, over 80% of the capital is flowing among US, Western European and East Asian countries.[248]

In chapter 4, the concept Money Market Dynamics (MMD) describes the centripetal flow of money (capital) to a central point where it essentially converts into technology and from where market gains potential to centrifugally spread down by means of new opportunities, and products and services with resized prices and better qualities over time. As Shangquan (2000) describes

"The advancement of science and technologies has greatly reduced the cost of transportation and communication, making economic globalization possible. Today's ocean shipping cost is only a half of that in the year 1930, the current airfreight 1/6, and telecommunication cost 1%. The price level of computers in 1990 was only about 1/125 of that in 1960, and this price level in 1998 reduced again by about 80%. This kind of 'time and space compression effect' of technological advancement (digital transformation) greatly reduced the cost of international trade and investment, thus making it possible to organize and coordinate global production."[248]

As mentioned previously (Chapter 4) that in one aspect, all these technological innovations that has powered the globalization is firmly rooted in abundant minerals on earth such as silicon and aluminum. And in another aspect, the growth is powered by energy resource, which is depleting and therefore, any time soon the growth should turn down. Figure 1.3 shows the Gross World Product (GWP). The GWP in 2013 was about US$75.59 trillion 84% up in a decade from $41 trillion in 2000. The U.S. economy alone led the $17.4 trillion GWP expansion between 2000 and 2006 by contributing 20%, China 9%, Germany 6%, United Kingdom on 6% and France 5%. During this time 176 markets expanded ($17.4 trillion), while the economic output of 4 markets contracted by $94.2 billion. Since 2007 China leads the expansion, which accounts for 12%, while the United States accounted for 10% of the global output expansion.[249]

It is important to note that China is not investing directly to the U.S. industries and USA is also not a major investor in Chinese industries. In 2010, 84% of

$194 billion FDI in the U.S. came from or through eight countries mostly in manufacturing: Switzerland, the United Kingdom, Japan, France, Germany, Luxembourg, the Netherlands, and Canada.[250] The growth of over-productive export industries in China has created trade deficit with almost all countries in the world. In 2011, the U.S. trade deficit with China alone was $295 billion,[251] a new record and up from $304 million in 1983.[252] Figure 5.35 shows the U.S. trade deficit 1970-2013.253 This shows that contrarily Reagan's tax cut in 1981

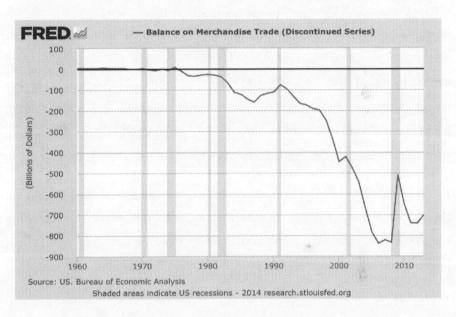

Figure 5.35: United States Balance of Trade, 1970–2013[253]

for the investors to boost supply-side economics ended up in falling trade balance. The trade deficit increased since 1997 when large scale privatization occurred in China and again almost free fall in 2001, the year China joined WTO. The graph also indicates that deficit slackened during recessions (2008-2009) and grew during periods of expansion.[254]

Paul Krugman (1995) argues that trade liberalization has a measurable effect on the rising inequality in the United States.[255] He attributes this trend to the increased trade with poor countries like China, resulting in low skilled jobs becoming more tradable.[256] Economists use historical data, which at the national level is often five to ten years old. We know by now, China no more dependent on low-skilled job, now China leads the world in hi-tech industries such as electronics, telecommunication products, machinery, ships, rail cars, automobiles and so on. In 2009, China surpassed the United States as the world's largest automobile producer by volume.[257] China is now the world's biggest producer of concrete, steel, fastest trains, ships and textiles, and has the world's largest automobile market. Chinese steel output is one-third of global production, with productivity exceeds Western productivity.[258] From 1975 to 2008, China's automobile production rose from 139,800 to 9.35 million.[259] China's Textiles exports increased from 4.6% of world exports in 1980 to 24.1% in 2005. Textile output increased 18-fold over the same period.[258] All these big things have happened in China in an unimaginably short timeframe because of economic reform and pressure from international competition due to globalization.

David Dollar (2007) of World Bank assures that the integration of China into the global economy benefits the Chinese economies as well as the U.S. economy since both economies have grown well although there are individual winners and losers.[185] In Figure 5.36, the winners are positioned in the core 'market energy

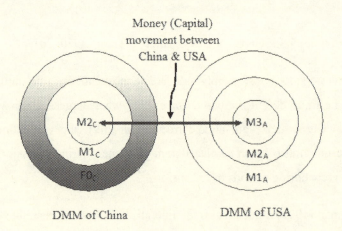

Figure 5.36: A Capitalist Partnership between USA & China

states (MESs)', $M2_C$ and $M3_A$ of China and USA respectively. The figure shows that the globalization directly connects the core MESs, while keeping separated the others, $M1_C$ and $M2_A$ respectively by respective BEBs. In the United States, despite globalization, millions of people are plunged into poverty.[260] They are positioned in a separate MES, $M1_A$ as shown in Figure 5.36. The rural Chinese people who are not yet part of market economy are shown as F0c.

Who are actually gaining by the integration of these two countries? One may answer 'everyone' as long as growth continues at existing pace. The concept of MEL tells that growth has negative impact on those who are outside the MEL and positive impact on those who are within the MEL. There is a mutual interest for both USA and any other country holding US Dollar to keep its value up. As an example, if the value of U.S. dollar falls with respect to Chinese Yuan, the Chinese manufacturing people in $M1_C$ (Figure 5.36) will be the most affected. Firstly, they will lose jobs at the very first place as the demand of Chinese products in U.S. market will fall. Secondly, inflation or Money Loop (ML) in $M2_C$ and therefore 'Price Pressure' on $M1_C$ will increase and eventually the economy will become stagnant as happened in Japan in mid-1980s. It will impact more seriously in the U.S. economy. Americans in $M2_A$ will lose jobs at the very first place as China will intend to sell the U.S. treasury bonds so will the others and therefore the service sectors employments will be catastrophically impacted. And also, inflation will increase as the prices of the manufacturing goods that are exported from China will increase. This inflation can be considered as cost-push inflation, which surfaces the whole economy that is essentially different from the inflation causing 'Price Pressure (PP)'. In his book "The Death of Money", Jim Rickards warns that this threat will take USA into the darkest economic period in the U.S. history– stock market could plunge overnight and may last as long as 25 years or more.

Although the free flow of goods refers the tradable items mostly manufactured products and raw materials, consumption in every developed society is primarily composed real estate and services.[185] The differences between the tradable goods and services is that the later one produced locally by professional people. Therefore, with free trade, we see real estate prices and income of the professional services people such as doctors, lawyers, bankers, financial consultants increase. This is how capitalization in the core MSE extends the MEL toward the non-capitalists professional people. However, when the two core MESs of two different countries are integrated one has trade surplus with the other, it creates an opportunity for the first to balance out its Money Loop (ML) and reduce the Price Pressure (PP) by moving money to the later. On the other hand, the PP in the later country having trade deficit is translated into 'debt pressure'. This explains why the export-led economies like China and Japan hold large sums of U.S debt that has funded the consumptions. David Dollar (2007) of World Bank explains the reason of China's investment in US Treasury Bond as "China's trade account is so stimulative of the economy that it then has to reign in demand elsewhere."[185] China is balancing out its MEL in two different ways. Firstly, it has moved money outside China. China's investment for low-return U.S. treasury bonds reaches to about $1.3 trillion in 2014.[261] Secondly, by halting appreciation of Chinese Yuan with respect to USD.

Ideally, globalization is based on David Ricardo's principle of comparative advantage. It refers to the ability of a country to produce a particular good or service at a lower marginal and opportunity cost over another.[262] Economist Paul Craig Roberts notes that the comparative advantage principles do not hold where the factors of production such as capital and technology are internationally mobile.[263] He explains that a Chinese worker working with U.S. capital and technology is just as productive as an American however he is paid a small fraction of his American counterpart. An iPhone worker in China makes $1.78 an hour that would cost $30 in USA. Labor costs are still a small part of the overall cost structure at between 2 percent and 5 percent of sales price.[264] Eric Mack a freelancer blogger writes

"In other words, when you spend hundreds on an iPhone, it's possible that more of those dollars are going toward a promise on paper you probably won't use (the warranty) than to the people who actually put the thing together."[264]

Since to save labor costs, the developed countries prefer to buy from low-wage countries such as China, India or Bangladesh, there have been exploding growths of low-wage manufacturing industries. These countries are now able to lift hundreds of millions of people out of poverty, who now consume much more than before as reflected on their per-capita emission growth in Figure 5.30 and Figure 5.34. On the other hand per capita emission remains pretty much stable in the developed countries. In both cases, consumptions both in developed and in developing countries have gone up but in developing countries it happened at exponential rate. Figure 5.37 shows the growth of total emission of the world, which is accumulating every year and call for more drastic reduction of greenhouse gases. Now China has become the planet's largest emitter of greenhouse gases and India is the third. Since their policy makers link growth with their poverty reduction, they cannot easily promise to limit their emission. Before 2002, China was accounted 7% of global emission, EU accounted for 26

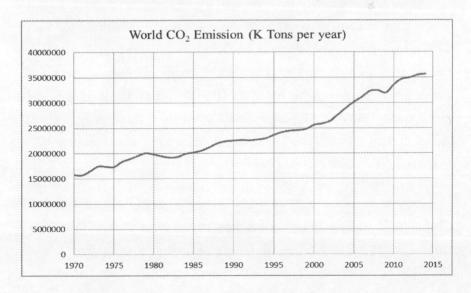

Figure 5.37: World CO_2 Emission per Year 1970-2014[278]

percent and the United States 29 percent. Now China accounts for 30% of global emission and together with India produces about 40% of the global emission. A recent study suggests that this will cause about 5,500 glaciers of Mount Everest region of the Himalayas to disappear or drastically retreat (70%-99%) by the end of this century. This will have drastic consequences for farming and fresh water for about 1.3 billion people living on this basin and for food, and energy to more than 3 billion people. [281]

Although poverty reduction is used as an excuse for growth and emission, by using the concept of Differential Market Model (DMS), it can be inferred that the consumption increased for upper layer Market Energy States (MES) more than lower layer MESs. In China the real wage increased significantly from the pre-globalization bare minimum, the Chinese capitalists gained much more than the non-capitalists. As an example, the rapid industrialization in China certainly has helped the rich people accumulated huge private capital. Since the return to capital is high in China, so that Americans who own shares in multinational companies are also benefited. Gao Shangquan (2000) elaborates this as:

"Compared with commodity and labor markets, the financial market is the only one that has realized globalization in the true sense of 'globalization'. Since 1970's, cross-border flow of capital has been rapidly expanding. ....this figure had far surpassed 100% in 1995. The value of the average daily transactions of foreign exchanges have grown from US$ 200 billion in the middle of economic globalization 1980's to the present US$ 1,200 billion, which is 85% of the foreign exchange reserves of all the countries in the world and 70 times as large as the value of the daily export of commodities and services."[248]

These figures are certainly much higher in recent times. In summary, due to globalization there is more money accumulating in paper contract than actually used in wealth creation. This is how globalization has created a global partnership of capitalists—a big "Global Pareto Coalition (GPC)" as shown in Figure 5.38, while most governments are gradually drowning into debt. As long as the governments can collect substantial tax revenue, the GPC is secured. This figure is an extension of Figure 5.36. Although the GPC connects the Effective Pareto Coalitions (EPCs) of each country, the respective Effective Pareto Spaces

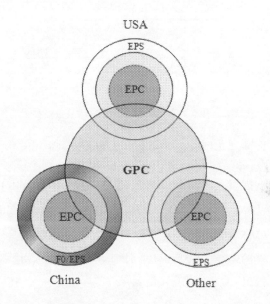

Figure 5.38: Global Pareto Coalition (GPC)

(EPSs) are locally separated by respective Effective Biased Equilibrium Barriers (EBEBs). Following Great Divergence there has been a big change in global private assets of GPC as shown in Table 5.1 from the perspective of the U.S. investment in foreign country. The change in the net international investment position of USA between 1980 and 2012 arises from a large increase in U.S. private assets owned abroad as a result of a large upward revaluation in corporate stocks values. Private asset holdings are comprised primarily of direct investment in businesses and real estate, purchases of publicly traded government securities, and corporate stocks and bonds. The U.S. private assets in foreign country were valued at $17.4 trillion or about 80% of the total $21.63 trillion U.S. investment in foreign countries.[265] The rightmost column of the table shows huge Vertical Growth (VG) of global private assets since 1980 as

US Investment in Foreign Country			
	1980 (Billion $)	2012 (Billion $)	Multiplied
US Investment abroad	930	21,638	23
US government asset	237	666	3
US Private assets	693	17,352	25
Direct Investment at current cost	388	5,250	14
Foreign securities	62	7,531	121
Bonds	44	2,141	49
Corporate Stock	19	5,391	285

Table 5.1 U.S. Investment in Foreign Country[265]

the values of corporate stocks, bond and securities multiplied, which has established big Global Money Loop (GML). In other words, during this period the global economy created huge "Potential Market Energy (PME)" which is set to grow except conversion to Kinetic Market Energy (KME) at huge cost of physical energy.

A similar table (Table 5.2) shows that foreigners own substantially larger shares of U.S. financial assets than USA has in other countries. Here private investment is 60% of total $25.5 trillion foreign investment in USA.[265] The foreign investment position in the United States continues to increase as foreigners acquire additional U.S. assets and as the value of existing assets appreciates. The United States Congressional Research Service promotes the US Treasury securities as safe heaven investment to the Global Pareto Coalition (GPC) that has been proven during troubled or unsettled economic conditions, including during the 2008-2009 financial crisis. As per definition of Pareto Coalition in Chapter 4, unilateral withdrawal of foreign capital highly unlikely, particularly since the vast majority of the investors is private entities that presumably would find it difficult to coordinate a withdrawal. This unique advantage of US economy attracts the private investors based their business in USA and allow us

Foreign Investment in USA			
	1980 (Billion $)	2012 (Billion $)	Multiplied
Foreign Investment in USA	564	25,502	45
US government securities (inc. bond)	230	5,692	25
Private Assets	335	16,247	48
Direct Investment at current cost	127	3,057	24
US Treasury Securities	16	1,542	96
US Other securities	74	6,904	93
US currency	19	454	23
Corporate Stock	65	3,842	60
Corporate Bond	10	3,062	321

Table 5.2 Foreign Investment in USA[265]

position USA at the core of a global Differential Market Model. The rightmost column of the table shows huge Vertical Growth (VG) of foreign capital in the U.S. market.

The VG represents a Global Money Loop (GML) between USA and the investing country that boosts Border Propensity of Consumption (BPC) in U.S. economy and eventually translated into a debt pressure on the citizens. Since debt servicing is energy intensive, USA needs more energy to reduce its debt pressure, which would be possible through its shale oil boom. Since the output of shale wells declines rapidly, by 60-70% in their first year, within a couple of years this oil will stop flowing. The Economists reports that the shale oil industries already have dodgy balance sheets (defined as debt of more than three times gross operating profits).[266] Total debt for listed American exploration and production firms has almost doubled since 2009 to $260 billion (see chart), according to Bloomberg; it now makes up 17% of all America's high-yield (junk) bonds.[266] Now with dropping oil price these firms will have to cut their investment budgets until the oil price rebounds again.

The Economists also reports that the greatest pain of declining oil price is in countries such as Russia where the governments are dependent on a high oil price to pay for expensive social programs. According to Global Financial Integrity (GFI) report 2014, Russia is listed as the second highest among the countries with illicit financial out-flow, accounts for about $1.0 trillion dollar outflow between 2003 and 2012.[246] The report says that a total about $6.6 trillion out-flown from 145 developing countries to developed countries. The figure shows only top 15 countries among them, which includes oil exporting and oil importing countries. The developed countries that are receiving the money are apparently benefited in both ways. As an example, a part of the money that they are paying for oil or cheap products is coming back to them. But unfortunately this money in the receiving countries create Money Loops (ML) and Price Pressures (PP) such as on real estate markets, medical expenses, constructions, corporate expenses and living standards. Nevertheless the concerned governments are not benefited but becoming losers since governments in the source countries are losing taxes that could be used for welfare or the countries infrastructural developments. On the other hand, the governments of the destination or receiving countries are spending more on the welfare or infrastructural development due to the Price Pressure.

The figures in Table 5.1 and 5.2 do not show the hundreds of trillion dollars IOUs owned by the wealthiest members of the GPC. On the other hand, the 2008-2009 debt crises tells that almost in all cases the corresponding governments have failed to collect taxes to offset their mounting debts. Tax Justice Network, (TJN) reports the rich people of the world are hiding more than $21 trillion in offshore tax havens, an amount roughly equal to the combined GDP of the United States and Japan.[267] The report states that this estimate is conservative since it does not count any physical properties purchased by the hidden money. It could be as large as $32 trillion, and represents a massive black hole in the world's economy.[268] It also says this

"The hidden money is enough to make a significant difference to the finances of many countries...that are now struggling to replace lost aid dollars and pay for climate change. Indeed, once we take these hidden offshore assets and the earnings they produce, 'debtor countries' are in fact revealed to be wealthy."[267]

The oil price has been plunging and now in November, 2015 price of a barrel of oil is roughly half since June 2014. According to New York Times, due to temporary shale oil boom, the U.S. reduced its oil import and the oil producing countries are now competing for the growing Asian market, the price of oil is falling.[270] Since the price is falling, the biggest "cheap" oil producer in the world, Saudi Arabia increased its oil production to manage its budget deficit, 80% of which is dependent on oil export. The International Monetary Fund (IMF) warned that the biggest Arab economy may run out of financial assets needed to support spending within five years if the government maintains current policies.[271] Following the plunge in crude oil price, Saudi Arabia is planning to launch "Vision for the Kingdom of Saudi Arabia" to transform Saudi Aramco from an oil company into an energy and industrial conglomerate to reduce the country's reliance on oil. According to Bloomberg,

> "Saudi authorities are weighing measures that include more steps to restructure subsidies, imposing a value-added tax, and a levy on energy and sugary drinks as well as luxury items. The National Transformation Program will also focus on ways to boost economic growth, create jobs, attract investors and hold government offices more accountable."[283]

The bottom line, Saudi Arabia is planning for becoming an user of fossil fuel, which will require more extraction of oil, in other words, more rapid depletion of its reserve. In other words, with declining oil price if the oil dependent countries want to stay the same economic standing, they will run like the Red Queen of Alice in Wonderland[284]. If this is the case, their accelerated oil production will accelerate declination of the world's cheap oil. But before that happens, our only earth will lose much of its carrying strength.

CHAPTER 6

TOWARD FOSSIL CIVILIZATION

6.1 Introduction

Carroll Quigley's legendary book "Tragedy and Hope: A History of The World in Our Time" published in 1966 gives deep insight into social science, economics, sociology and psychology behind the history of civilization. He points out the following, the most serious question ever posed to mankind:

> "One of these persistent questions is typical of twentieth century rather than of earlier times: Can our way of life survive? Is our civilization doomed to vanish?"[1]

In 1956, M. King Hubbert almost accurately predicted that United States oil production would peak between 1965 and 1970. Matthew Simmons one of the key advisors in Bush Administration's 2001 Energy Task Force and the Council on Foreign Relations (CFR) commented:

> "[T]hen time was on the side of preparing Plan B. They like Dr. Hubbert got to be seen as Chicken Little or the Boy Who Cried Wolf...."[2]

The burning of fossil fuel accelerated with globalization, we see the rising level of carbon dioxide trapping more heat and melting the glaciers at cataclysmic rate, potentially leading to conditions in which our civilization cannot persist. Our civilization is also challenged since fossil fuel is running out its economic limit with all the burning and even faster with lower oil price.

The Nobel peace prize winner of 2006 Mohammad Yunus dreamed that one day "poverty will be in museum".[4] Ironically, the reality is going to be opposite that the 'our existing civilization will be in museum' instead.

413

6.2 The End of Fossil Fuel

"It takes all the running you can do, to keep in the same place."

- Lewis Carroll, "Alice in Wonder Land"[149]

As of November 23, 2015, oil is trading $45 a barrel, have fallen about 50 percent since the organization declined to cut production at a 2014 meeting in Vienna.[153] Saudi Arabia, the number one exporter of crude oil in the world, is running on deficit and now going to borrow from the international capital markets.[153] As the oil price deteriorating, Standard and Poor downgraded its credit rating one level down to A+, as it said the biggest OPEC producer's deficit will increase to 16-20 percent of gross domestic product this year.[154] Now to keep the budget deficit within limit, OPEC led by Saudi Arabia has increased oil production just like the Red Queen's run in "Alice in Wonder Land". There is no good news that oil price has fallen down, rather we should be worried the declination is accelerated with OPEC's increased production of crude oil.

There is no question that the present day prosperities are empowered by fossil fuel–the blessing we have been enjoying as granted for about last two centuries and something we cannot live without. Martenson describes the prosperities we have achieved using fossil-fuel as

> "[T]hat nearly every citizen of any developed country today lives at a level of prosperity and comfort that is equivalent to a level enjoyed only by the wealthy in the not-too-distant past."[5]

The world fossil fuel production has followed a typical Hubbert curve, popularly known as "Peak Oil" curve created by M. King Hubbert in 1956 (Figure 1.5) to accurately predict that United States oil production would peak between 1965 and 1970 (Figure 6.1).[6] The world's fossil fuel or hydrocarbon supply is fixed because petroleum is naturally formed in many millions of years. Heinberg (2011) explains the formation of oil or fossil fuel:

414

"Oil was produced over the course of tens millions of years without need for any human work. Ancient sunlight energy was chemically gathered and stored by vast numbers of microscopic aquatic plants, which fell to the bottoms of seas and were buried under sediment and slowly transformed into energy-dense hydro-carbons."[7]

The economy we are living is dependent on a finite supply of fossil fuel that we are close to peak if not already there. Although there may be a vast amount of

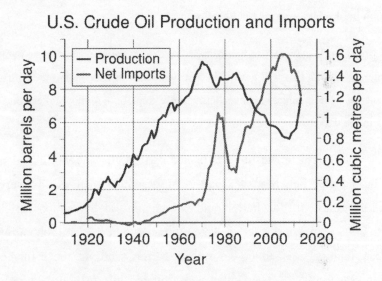

Figure 6.1: US Crude Oil Production and Imports[6]

stored resource of fossil fuel, after the "peak", there will higher level of investment and effort be required to extract the remaining much riskier and dirtier deposit of fossil fuels. In his book "Afterburn" Richard Heinberg argues:

"We'll never run out of any fossil fuel, in the sense of extracting every last molecule of coal, oil, or gas. Long before we get to that point, we will confront the dreaded double line in the diagram, labeled "energy in = energy out."[147]

The Club of Rome, a global think tank founded in 1968, published a report titled "The Limits to Growth" in 1972 and for the first time at the International

Students' Committee (ISC) annual Management Symposium in St. Gallen, Switzerland.[7] The report echoes some of the concerns and predictions of Thomas Malthus in An "Essay on the Principle of Population (1798)" but included 'resource decline' as one of the important factors besides population growth.[8] It predicted that economic growth could not continue indefinitely because the natural resource of energy, particularly oil and coal is similar to land that follows law of diminishing return.[9] This was 40 years back and we had time to be better prepared for the upcoming post-oil crisis. Colin Campbell (2003), an eminent petroleum geologist explains his worries as:

"The world's oil and gas production will start to decline within most people's lifetimes. Although this will have a dramatic effect on lifestyles and the course of civilization, vested interests have deliberately kept both policymakers and the public in the dark."[10]

The American Petroleum Institute estimated in 1999 that the world's oil supply would be depleted between 1962 and 2094, assuming total world reserves at between 1.4 and 2 trillion barrels and consumption at 80 million barrels per day.[12] In 2004 total world reserves were estimated to be 1.25 trillion barrels and daily consumption was about 85 million barrels, shifting the estimated oil depletion year to 2057.[13] The United States Energy Information Administration predicted in 2006 that world consumption of oil will increase to 98.3 million barrels in 2015 and 118 million barrels in 2030 to keep pace with demand from growing countries like China, India and Brazil. In 10 years between 1995 and 2005, US oil consumption increased from 17.7 million barrels per day to 20.7 billion barrels per day, which is now relatively stable. Whereas China's oil consumption increased from 3.4 million barrels per day to 10.58 million barrels per day.[14] In a recent report, International Energy Agency (IEA) forecasts that by 2040, China's oil imports to be five times those of the U.S., while India's will "easily exceed" the European Union's.[155]

Recently China signed $400 billion deal to receive natural gas from Russia after more than a decade of negotiations under which China will receive 38 billion cubic meters (bcm) of gas annually in a 30 year arrangement that is slated to start in 2018. Similar to oil demand, China's gas demand tripled from 56 bcm to 169 bcm, and imports jumped from less than 1bcm to 53bcm between 2006 and 2013.[15] As the US is importing a substantial proportion of its consumer goods from China; China is burning the oils for the US consumers. This keeps the US oil consumption relatively stable but borrowing continues to fill out the trade deficit close to $17 billion per month. India's oil imports are expected to more than triple from 2005 levels by 2020 rising to 5 million barrels per day.[14] By adding them up, it can be concluded that world oil reserve will deplete before the estimate by 2057. And the era of cheap oil will end any time before that.

Martenson (2011) points out that although between the years 2004 and 2008, the conventional crude oil production was almost flat (Figure 6.2), prices spiked

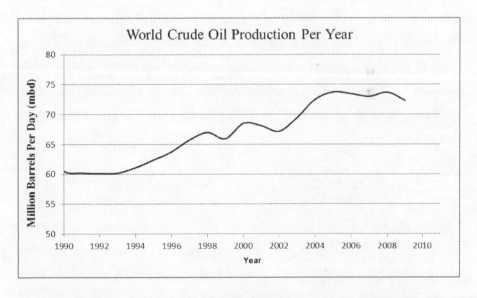

Figure 6.2: World Crude Oil Production per Year, 1990-2009[17]

from $50 a barrel to $147 a barrel.[5] However, from 2003 to 2011, the inflation adjusted oil price increased average of $35 per barrel in 2003 to a yearly average of $110 per barrel in 2011. During this time, the average crude oil production did not increase much. However demand increased from 73.8 million barrels per day in 2003 to 75 million barrels per day in 2012, less than 1.5 million barrels in seven years. The average annual growth rate was 0.3 percent, which is one tenth of the demand forecast by the oil industries.[16] However, as Figure 6.2 shows the oil price spike in 2008 might be reflection of perceived 'peak oil' because of four years of consecutive flat production (approximate) between 2004 to 2008. The high oil price in 2008 caused a global recession. Martenson (2011) argues:

"If there ever was a strong incentive to get oil out of ground and off to market, a near tripling of the price of oil would be it. Yet oil production did not rise in response to these market signals."[5]

As he indicates there is perfect similarity of the 40 year time gap between the U.S. peak oil discovery (1930) and production peak (1970) and world oil peak discovery in1964 and apparently production peak in 2004. Peak Oil has a severe impact on transport networks, food system, global trade and all industries, chemicals, plastics and pharmaceuticals. As an example, by realizing that the world might have reached "peak oil" (Figure 6.2) between 2006 and mid-2008 investors worldwide "fled toward futures contracts in oil, metals, and food, driving up commodities prices".[18] In many poor countries, for a brief period food riots erupted, where the cost of wheat and rice doubled or tripled.[18]

If there is no oil, global trade will stop. Almost all of the largest oilfields 'super-giants', containing billions of barrels of crude oils were identified or discovered between 1930s-1960s are already depleted or close to depletion. The other oil fields are far smaller, less accessible and therefore, more expensive and environmentally risky. The big oil companies are trying their best effort to delay the inevitable peak by using advanced technologies to increase the amount of oil that can be obtained from each well drilled, deep sea drilling farthest below sea level and extracting from alternative hydrocarbon resources principally tar sands and oil shale. In reality, the oil-producing countries are seeing their extraction rates peaking and beginning to decline despite efforts to maintain production growth using high-tech, expensive secondary and tertiary extraction methods like the injection of water, nitrogen, or CO_2 to force more oil out of the ground.

The increase of domestic demand in the oil exporter countries, the oil importer countries may fall in oil crisis far before peak oil is reached. As an example, Kuwait parliament refused permission to expand production, arguing that the nation might need to conserve resources for use domestically in building the national economy. Before the embargo, Iran's domestic demand was growing at up to 10 per cent per year.[20] Similarly, the domestic demands of oil in Saudi Arabia and all over Middle East are also increasing.

On the other hand, as the easy and cheap fossil fuel are depleting, the energy extraction process is also becoming too much energy-intensive. The term used to define net energy is called EROEI (Energy Returned on Energy Invested) or simply EROI (Energy Returned on Investment). According to Chris Martenson (2011), in 1930, EROEI was 100:1. That is, for every barrel of oil used to find oil, it's estimated that 100 were produced. On the other hand, he estimates that new oil resources found after the year 2010 will return a much lower net energy, perhaps as low as 3:1."[5]

Tar sands have a EROEI around 5:1[21] and tar shales are thought to be even worse, in the vicinity of 2:1 or less, when self-energy is counted as a cost. Self-energy is energy released by the oil shale conversion process that is used to power that operation.[22] This means the advanced extraction technologies we are relying on for continuing growth is becoming economically unviable. Rubin explains economic extraction limit as:

"Every year, the world loses about 4 million barrels a day to flagging production in depleting fields....In 2010, global production notched a net increase of 2 million barrels a day, but to achieve that increase the oil industry actually had to add 6 million barrels of new production"[23]

He concludes "The bad news is that the oil we're losing to depletion is the low cost stuff we can afford to burn."[23] As an example, between 2005 and 2013, the oil and gas industry spent $4 trillion on exploration and production, yet this more-than-doubled investment produced only 4 million barrels per day in added production compared to 8.6 million barrels per day after $1.5 trillion investment between 1998 and 2005.[148]

The oil produced between 2005 to 2013 are mostly from unconventional sources such as shale oil, tar sands, tight oil etc. In the past few years, high oil prices have provided the incentive for horizontal drilling and fracking technology to free up trapped hydrocarbons from "source rocks," which is known as shale oil. Although because of this fracking technology, the U.S. shale oil and gas production rates have temporarily spiked, the declination rate is so high that it cannot stop diminishing return on oil and gas investment.[147] Now the oil and gas companies are increasingly searching for those source rocks, operating in ultra-deep water, or in arctic regions, and need to use sophisticated technologies like hydro-fracturing, horizontal drilling, and water or nitrogen injection.[147] In his book "Afterburn", Heinbeg further analyzes:

> "It gets worse: all net new production during the 2005-2013 period was from unconventional sources (primarily tight oil from the US and tar sands from Canada); of the $4 trillion spent since 2005, it took $350 billion to achieve a bump in their production. Subtracting unconventionals from the total, world oil production actually fell by about a million barrels a day during these years. That means the oil industry spent over $3.5 trillion to achieve a decline in overall conventional production."[147]

Similarly, we are losing the highest grades of coal such as anthracite and bituminous since we are using them more and therefore, costs of production are rising. As an example, Figure 6.3 shows that in China, use of anthracite has increased sharply mainly for industrial use. Another high category coal bituminous already reached its peak because of its high demand in electricity generation. China relies on coal for 70 percent of its energy. Its installed coal-based electrical capacity was 484 GW, or 77% of the total electrical capacity, in

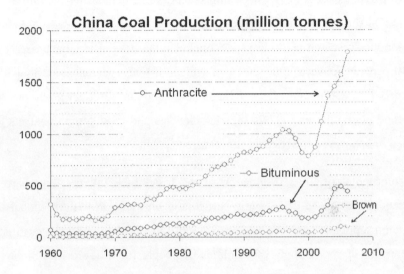

Figure 6.3: Production of coal within China by type[24]

2006[25] about 20% on hydro-electricity and 4% on nuclear power. Therefore, Chinese economy is sometimes called 'coal-fired' economy. It has 13 percent world's proven reserves[26] but it is the largest user of coal in the world, investment in the coal industry rising at an annual rate of 50 percent in recent years. In 2013, China built approximately one large coal plant every week.[27] Every year twenty million Chinese move from the countryside to cities each year. They are buying around 13 million automobiles per year, versus 11 million annually in the US.[29] According to a forecast by Energy Watch Group of Germany in 2007 a peak of production of Chinese coal will be in 2015 with a rapid production decline commencing in 2020.[30] Another forecast in 2010 by Patzek and Croft shows China's coal peak also occurring essentially now.[31]

Ethanol made from corn was thought to be the one to reduce our dependence on the fossil fuel. It takes huge land area to produce a substantial amount of ethanol that reduces the amount of cropland available for growing food and resulted in global higher food price in 2007-2008. Lester R. Brown, a prominent environmental analyst, in his testimony before U.S. Senate Committee on Environment and Public Works claimed that, since converting the entire grain harvest of the US would only produce 16% of its auto fuel needs.[32] A World Bank policy research working paper concluded that food prices have risen by 35 to 40 percent between 2002–2008, of which 70 to 75 percent is attributable to biofuels.[33] It also increases water use, soil erosion and fertilizer pollution. After the food price hike in 2007-2008, soil scientists and food system analysts were united in opposing further ethanol expansion.[34]

At some point of time, declination of the fossil fuel will be very sharp and consequences will be devastating, particularly on transport system, global trade and food supply. It might be so severe that driving a car for a kilometer might be in expense of food supply of hundreds of people for a day or health care for thousands of people.

6.3 Global Warming-Getting Worse

There are two other severe impacts of growth, the global warming and fresh water scarcity alongside depletion of fossil fuel. The fossil fuel we have used so far has released so much carbon dioxide (CO2) and other greenhouse gases that our planet's atmosphere is now much thicker heat-trapping greenhouse than used to be causing global warming.[36] As we are continuing using fossil fuel at high rate, the consequences are going to be devastating climate impacts, serious energy shortage and fresh water scarcity.

The solar radiation at the frequencies of visible light largely passes through the atmosphere to warm the planetary surface, which then emits this energy at the lower frequencies of infrared thermal radiation. The infrared radiation is absorbed by greenhouse gases such as water vapor (36–70%), CO2 (9–26%), methane (4–9%), ozone (3–7%) which in turn re-radiate much of the energy to the surface and lower atmosphere and keep our earth warm and makes life on earth possible.[37] The mechanism is called 'greenhouse effect' although the way it retains heat is fundamentally different from greenhouse used to grow plants during winter as a greenhouse works by reducing airflow, isolating the warm air inside the structure so that heat is not lost by convection.[38 & 39] However, human activities, primarily the CO2 by burning of fossil fuels and clearing of forests, have over-intensified the natural greenhouse effect, causing global warming.[40]

Human activity since the Industrial Revolution has increased the amount of greenhouse gases in the atmosphere. Figure 6.4 shows atmospheric CO2 concentration from 650,000 years ago to near present, using ice core proxy data

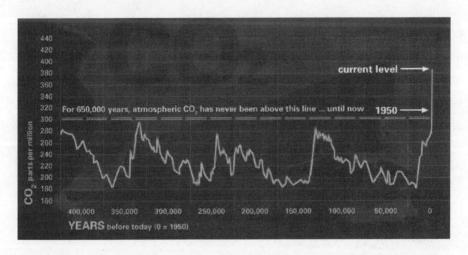

Figure 6.4: C02 Concentration with Reference to 1950 (Source: NASA)[42]

This graph synthesizing ice core proxy data for 650,000 years in the past capped by modern direct measurements. Source: http://climate.nasa.gov/evidence/

and direct measurement by NASA. Fossil fuel burning has produced about three-quarters of the increase in CO2 from human activity over the past 20 years.[41&42] Although since the early 20th century earth's mean surface temperature has increased by about 0.8 °C, about two-thirds of the increase occurring since

1980.[28] We can now relate that the sharp GDP growth since 1980 were the main drivers of increases in greenhouse gas emissions and corresponding sharp rise of the temperature level. Today's atmosphere contains 32 per cent more carbon dioxide than it did at the start of the industrial era.[36]

Global climate change has already had observable effects on the environment. NASA reports:

"The effects that scientists had predicted in the past would result from global climate change are now occurring: loss of sea ice, accelerated sea level rise and longer, more intense heat waves. Glaciers have shrunk, ice on rivers and lakes is breaking up earlier, plant and animal ranges have shifted and trees are flowering sooner."[43]

It has very drastic effects to humans include the threat to food security from decreasing crop yields and the loss of land and habitat from inundation, mass destruction by the catastrophes such as tsunamis and cyclones. Ironically similar to war, natural disasters actually adds to GDP during recovery and rebuild.[44] And in both the ways energy is spent to hold the economy on the same position.

Although 'Peak Oil' has not got enough attention from governments, industries or the big organizations like the United Nations, there is several organized bodies and movements for climate change. The most authoritative organization for climate change is Intergovernmental Panel on Climate Change (IPCC). Fossil fuel related CO2 emissions compared to five of the IPCC's Special Report Emissions Scenarios (SRES) emissions scenarios shown in Figure 6.5. The dips are related to global recessions. The IPCC has released several assessment reports over the years. About 3,000 scientific expert reviewers, more than 800 lead authors from over 130 countries contributed to the latest, the Fifth Assessment Report published recently in 2014.[46&47] The Fourth Assessment Report indicated that during the 21st century the global surface temperature is likely to rise a further 1.1 to 2.9 °C (2 to 5.2 °F) for their lowest emissions

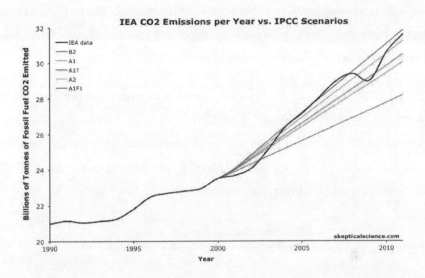

Figure 6.5: IEA C02 Emission per Year vs. IPCC Scenarios[45]

scenario and 2.4 to 6.4 °C (4.3 to 11.5 °F) for their highest.[48] The fifth assessment report assess that the global surface temperature increase by the end of the 21st century is likely to exceed 1.5° C relative to the 1850 to 1900 period for most scenarios, and is likely to exceed 2.0° C for many scenarios.[46&47]

In the fifth assessment report, IPCC admitted that carbon emission in the world is not reducing, it is increasing. This following figure (Figure 6.6) shows over the years China has been catching up to US's emission level and eventually crossed around 2005. And now China is the largest emitter of CO2 (10,540,750 kilo tons per year) produces one third of greenhouse gas about double than that of USA (5334,530 Kilo tons per year) because of growth of Chinese export market. According to a 2009 report by the Center for International Climate and Environmental Research:

"Half of the increase was due to export production, 60 per cent of which was exported to western countries."[50]

According to a recent study even if American emissions were to suddenly disappear tomorrow, world emissions would be back at the same level within four years as a result of China's growth alone.[52]

Recently United States and the People's Republic of China reached an historic agreement in the global effort to reduce greenhouse gas emissions. The U.S. President Obama announced plans to reduce greenhouse gas emissions 26–28 percent below 2005 levels by 2025. This will set the course for the U.S. to realize an 80 percent emissions reduction by 2050. Chinese President Xi also

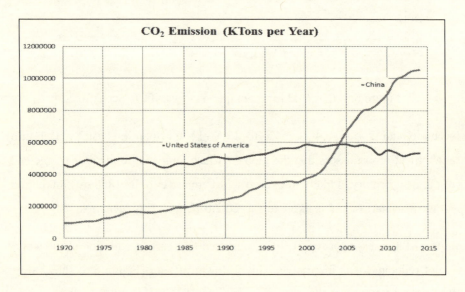

Figure 6.6: Carbon dioxide emissions by USA & China[49]

announced that zero-emissions, non-fossil energy sources would represent 20 percent of China's energy consumption by 2030. These two countries are jointly responsible for approximately 43 percent of global energy-related emissions.[53] As China is overusing its limited coal reserves–it has no choice but to replace declining coal with nuclear or renewable energy sources. On the other hand, to reduce greenhouse gas emission, USA will have to move the remaining manufacturing plants to China and impose high taxes on gasoline, car purchase etc., which will again bankrupt the industries. For China this agreement does not guarantee the total carbon emission will decrease since it was not meant to represent a ceiling on climate change policies but rather a floor.[54]

The global warming is also accompanied with rise of ocean temperature and increased rate of ocean acidification caused by increased atmospheric concentrations of carbon dioxide. Earth has been in radiative imbalance since at least the 1970s, where less energy leaves the atmosphere than enters it. As shown in Figure 6.7 that most of this extra energy has been absorbed by the oceans.[51] Increased ocean acidity decreases the amount of carbonate ions, which organisms at the base of the marine food chain, fishery products and food security.[55] According to research by Monash University Plankton, responsible for half of world's oxygen production, much of which may be killed by ocean

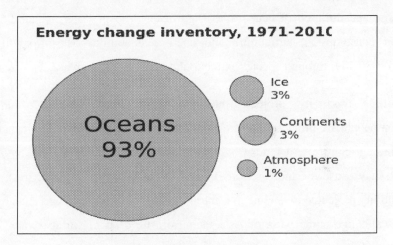

Figure 6.7 Energy Change Inventory 1971-2010[60]

acidification.[56] There is approximately 79 million tons of carbon dioxide (CO_2) released into the atmosphere every day, not only as a result of fossil fuel burning but also of deforestation and production of cement. Most the CO_2 released in the atmosphere since industrial revolution has been absorbed by the oceans, thus saving the earth for human beings and other species.[57]

Another large scale long-term impact of climate change is melting of ice sheets, which contributes to sea level rise. This could inundate low land countries, many of them are highly populated and drive away habitants from those areas, make people homeless, and salinate agricultural lands and eventually will cause severe food shortage and homelessness in many countries. As the world population is still increasing in developing countries, at the same time yields of crops will drop as a result of soil moisture and water supplies stressed by rising temperatures. In some regions of North America, the climate change will bring some benefits such as 5-20 percent increase in yields of rain-fed agriculture in some regions.[59] The top five countries generate 66% of CO_2 emission of the world. Unfortunately, the countries with less contribution to the greenhouse gases or global warming, will be affected more such as there will be increased frequency, intensity and duration of heat waves, significant drop in water availability for human consumption, agriculture and energy generation, risk of significant biodiversity loss through species extinction in many tropical areas.

In in IPCC report it is projected that in Africa by 2020, between 75 and 250 million people are projected to be exposed to increased water stress; yields from rain-fed agriculture will reduce by up to 50 percent in some regions by 2020, which may cause the more serious famine in the history.[59] In Asia, freshwater availability projected to decline in Central, South, East and Southeast Asia by the 2050s although some parts of Asia facing drastic drop of surface water level already. The report also says coastal areas in Asia will be at risk due to increased flooding; death rate from disease associated with floods and droughts expected to rise in some regions.[40&43] The reason is very little of Earth's trapped heat warms the atmosphere and land surface, over 90 percent of it is absorbed by the oceans. Figure 6.8 shows the global ocean heat content since 1955. This data shows global warming has accelerated since 1970 after the cheap oil has been available for burning and run the party of consumerism all over the world. It causes hurricanes, raise sea level, melt sea ice, destroy ocean food balance and

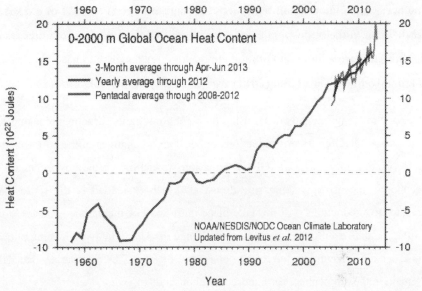

Figure 6.8 Ocean Heat Content (2012)[150]

eventually store potential heat for a more severe devastating calamity on earth. In 2013 the Earth's oceans accumulated energy at a rate of 12 Hiroshima atomic bombs per second, according to global ocean heat content records from the US National Oceanographic Data Center (NODC). This rapid heating in 2013 compares to an average of 4 Hiroshima bombs per second since 1998, and 2 bombs per second since records began in 1955. This means On July 26, 2015 at 7:35 PM our climate has accumulated 2, 252, 480, 973 Hiroshima atomic bombs of equivalent heat since 1998.[151] Although some scientists say global warming is slowed down or paused since the upper ocean, atmosphere and surface have warmed more slowly.[151] Heinberg argues "Global warming hasn't really "paused"; it's just gone to the depths."[147]

The IPCC defines mitigation as activities that reduce greenhouse gas emissions by energy conservation, increased energy efficiency, and using renewable energy and/or nuclear energy sources, or enhance the capacity of carbon sinks, such as reforestation to absorb Greenhouse Gases (GHG) from the atmosphere.

However, stabilizing CO2 emissions at current levels would not lead to stabilization in the atmospheric concentration of CO2 as human activities (fossil fuel burning) are adding CO2 to the atmosphere far faster than natural processes can remove it. Howard Latin (2012) argues:

"Most climate policymakers are using the wrong mitigation baseline, focusing on the annual GHG emissions reductions rather than on changes in the atmospheric GHG concentration.........GHG emissions-reduction programs, including economic incentive systems, are almost always back-loaded in the sense that most GHG reductions will not take place until 2050 or thereafter, which is "too little, too late" to prevent many climate change disaster. The back-loading policy is especially misguided due to the persistence of large CO2 discharges that will remain in the atmosphere for hundreds or thousands of years."[61]

In his book "Afterburn" Richard Heinberg also points out:

"That means curbing carbon emissions is even more urgent than almost anyone previously thought. The math has changed. At this point, the rate of reduction in fossil fuel consumption required in order to avert catastrophic climate change may be higher, possibly much higher, than the realistically possible rate of replacement with energy from alternative sources."[147]

Unfortunately, there is no sign that is happening in this world except few local discrete actions, which will not help much. At the end we will lose in two big ways. First, the earth will lose its carrying capacity because of the catastrophic climate change. And the second, ironically, as quoted from Heinberg

"[O]ur current infrastructure such as highways, skyscrapers, vehicles, factories that we have built using fossil fuel will be noting but casualties in future when all cheap oil will be gone".[147]

6.4 Fresh Water & Food Crisis

The similar to oil, water resource on earth's underground is also finite but impact of 'peak water' is more severe and deadlier than 'peak oil'. Only 3.5 percent of world's water reserve is fresh water but nearly 70 percent of that fresh water is frozen in the icecaps of Antarctica and Greenland. Most of the remainder is present as soil moisture or lies in deep underground aquifers as groundwater not accessible to human use. Less than 1% of the world's fresh water or 0.007 percent of all water on earth is accessible for direct human use.[62] This is the water found in lakes, rivers, reservoirs and those underground sources that are shallow enough to be tapped at an affordable cost. Only this minuscule amount is regularly renewed by rain and snowfall, and is therefore available on a sustainable basis.

The depletion of this water resource can be shown by a similar Hubbert curve as in Figure 6.1 since like "Peak oil", the usable fresh water is also harvested faster than it can be replaced. The impact of fresh water scarcity might be more severe on mankind since about 80 percent of the world's population (5.6 billion in 2011) lives in areas with threats to water scarcity.[63] Some parts are suffering from peak renewable water, where entire renewable flows are being consumed for human use. Also, some parts where groundwater aquifers are being over-pumped (or contaminated) faster than nature recharges them. The similar to peak oil, peak water is not about running out of fresh water, but about reaching physical, economic and environmental limits on meeting human demands for water and the subsequent decline of water availability.[64]

Water stress, which is difficulty of obtaining sources of fresh water for use, because of depletion.[65] According to the Falkenmark Water Stress indicator,[66] a region will experience 'water stress' when annual water supply drop below 1,700 cubic meters per person per year. A water crisis is a situation where the available potable, unpolluted water supplies within a region drop below 1,000 cubic meters per person per year.[67] In 1960 the world population was 3 billion during the time there was significant awareness about peak oil but common perception was that water was an infinite resource. On that time, we consumed fewer calories and ate less meat, so less water was needed to produce their food. As Figure 6.9 shows the world population has grown in pace with GDP and now there are over seven (7) billion people on earth, more than double of that time (1960).[67] However, the consumption of water-thirsty meat, crops and vegetables

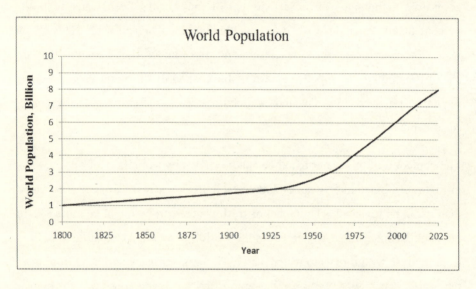

Figure 6.9 World Population Forecast 1800-2025[68]

is rising, and there is increasing competition for water from industry, urbanization biofuel crops, and now added huge water demand for non-conventional fossil fuel extraction. In future, even more water will be needed to produce food because the Earth's population is forecast to rise to 8 billion by 2025.[67&69] The united nations FAO states that by 2025, 1.9 billion people will be living in countries or regions with absolute water scarcity, and two-thirds of the population could be under stress condition.[70]

Water scarcity is also divided into 'physical' and 'economic' scarcity. Physical water scarcity is where there is not enough water to meet all demands, including that needed for ecosystems to function effectively. It also occurs where water seems abundant but where resources are over-committed, such as irrigation or hydraulic fracking using groundwater. Economic water scarcity is caused by insufficient investment in water supply or insufficient human capacity to satisfy the demand for water.[65] In many big crowded cities, water table has already dropped hundreds of feet because of extensive overdraft and causing big water crisis. As an example, a 2007 study by the Asian Development Bank showed that in 20 cities in India the average duration of supply was only 4.3 hours per day. None of the 35 Indian cities with a population of more than one million distribute water for more than a few hours per day, despite generally sufficient infrastructure.[71&72] How these cities will sustain with more population and depleted ground water at the same time where India is anticipated to overtake China as the world's most populous country by the mid-21st century?

The total amount of available freshwater supply is also decreasing because of climate change, which has caused receding glaciers, reduced stream and river flow, and shrinking lakes. Many aquifers have been over-pumped and are not recharging enough, become polluted, salted or unsuitable for drinking, industry and agriculture use. As an example, thousands of glaciers in the Himalayas are the source of water for Asia's biggest rivers - Ganges, Indus, Brahmaputra, Yangtze, Mekong, Salween and Yellow whose basins are home to 1.3 billion people. The Tibetan Plateau contains the world's third-largest store of ice and the glaciers are vital lifelines for Asian rivers, including the Indus and the Ganges.[73] "Temperatures are rising four times faster than elsewhere in China, and the Tibetan glaciers are retreating at a higher speed than in any other part of the world" said Qin Dahe, the former head of the China Meteorological Administration. These glaciers are at risk to disappear as temperatures rise.[73] "Once they vanish, water supplies in those regions will be in peril", Qin adds.[73] Over a billion people in India, China, Pakistan, Bangladesh, Nepal and Myanmar could experience floods followed by droughts in coming decades.

India has one fifth of the Earth's population, but only four per cent of its water. India withdraws 645.84 km^3/yr of fresh water, while only 8% is for domestic use, 5% in agriculture and 86% is used for agriculture.[74] Therefore, water tables are dropping fast in some of India's main agricultural areas. The mighty Indus and Ganges rivers are tapped so heavily that, except in rare wet years, they no longer reach the sea. The Ganges, the second largest river in India provides water for drinking and farming for more than 500 million people in India alone, 40% population in India in 11states, now one of the most polluted river basins in the world. An estimated 2.9 billion liters or more of human sewage is discharged into the Ganges daily and reported that its water is now deadly source of certain cancer.[75] Along with ever-increasing pollution, water shortages are getting worse. Some sections of the river are already completely dry. In the name of industrialization, countless tanneries, chemical plants, textile mills contribute to the pollution of the rivers that have damaged much of its fisheries and biodiversity. As an example, the leather industry in Kanpur, which employs only around 50,000 people in more than 400 tanneries use toxic chemicals compounds that can annihilate billions of fishes and cause deadly diseases of millions of people downstream. It has also been suggested that eighty percent of all illnesses in India and one-third of deaths can be attributed to water-borne diseases.[77] A rehabilitation project of the Ganges alone would cost about 25 to 30 years and about $20 billion, which is much worthier and sustainable than spending this money anywhere else.[78] Previously, the Ganga Action Plan or GAP was a program launched by Rajiv Gandhi in April 1986 in order to reduce the pollution load on the Ganges. However, the efforts to decrease the pollution level in the river became more after spending about $190 million since the sources of pollution-the sewage continues to flow into the river.[79] All water management projects in developing counties requires big money and are exposed to corruption and misuse.

Most of the fresh water is needed for growing food. As glaciers or snowpack disappears, the farmers make up for the loss of running surface water by pumping more from wells using significant amount of energy.[11] On one hand, glaciers are melting down in summer, on the other hand, the rivers are drying up in winter, and net result the streams are getting blocked because of sedimentation and which in turn increase salinity levels. Agriculture represents 70% of freshwater use worldwide. Industrial nations such as the United States (46%), Germany (68%), Russia (63%), Canada (69%) uses lots of water for industries. India consumes 86% of its fresh water for agriculture, Bangladesh and Pakistan used 96% for agriculture, the highest in the world, Thailand uses 95%.[80] The highest total annual consumption of water comes from the countries with large populations and extensive agricultural irrigation demand for food production. As an example, people in India consume a lot of rice that consumes a lot of water, but typically get less than half the yield per unit area by using 10 times more water than their counterparts in China do.

As the economy is developing, people's living standards are rising; they tend to eat more meat. A new report from the think tank Chatham House, Changing Climate, Changing Diets: Pathways to Lower Meat Consumption, states livestock farming and meat production is regarded as a driver of deforestation and habitat destruction around the world and accounts for 15 per cent of global greenhouse gas emissions equivalent to "tailpipe emissions from all the world's vehicles."[156] The report also argues that without concerted action to address over-consumption of meat, it will be near impossible to prevent global warming from passing the danger level of 2^0C.[157] The developed countries consumes highest amount of meat. As an example, an average American consumes about 250 g meats per day, whereas an average Indian consumes less than 10g of meat per day. BBC reports:

"While consumption levels have plateaued in industrialized countries, there is a general correlation between wealth and diet. As incomes rise in the emerging economies, meat consumption is booming. Left unchecked, shifting diets, coupled with a growing population, would see global consumption increase by more than 75% by 2050."[157]

It takes tremendous quantities of water to raise animals for food. Growing a ton of grain requires 1,000 tons of water, whereas to produce a ton of beef takes 15,000 tons of water. To make a single hamburger requires around 4940 liters (1,300 gallons) of water.[64&81] In summary, processed foods are much more water and energy intensive than unprocessed fresh foods.

China, the most populous country in the world, and second largest economy has the second largest water withdrawal out of all the countries in the world. Its 68% of that water goes to support agriculture and its growing industrial base is consuming 26%.[74] However, China is facing a water crisis where water resources are over-allocated, inefficiently used, and grossly polluted by human and industrial wastes. On the other hand, one third of China's population lacks access to safe drinking water. Rivers and lakes are dead and dying, groundwater aquifers are over-pumped, uncounted species of aquatic life have been driven to extinction, and direct adverse impacts on both human and ecosystem health are widespread and growing.[64]

The oil rich Middle East countries have a huge shortage of water. The highest is in Saudi Arabia short by 86% (14.9 km^3/yr), only 14% is fresh water need supplied by its declining 'fossil water' aquifers. Saudi Arabia reached peak water in the early 1990s, at more than 30 billion cubic meters per year, and declined afterward.[82] Saudi Arabian food production has been based on "fossil water", which is non-renewable, just as oil is, and it is unavoidable that it has to run out someday. Saudi Arabia has built desalination plants to provide about half the country's fresh water, which needs energy. The remainder comes from groundwater (40%), surface water (9%) and reclaimed wastewater (1%).[82] Today billions of dollars spent on desalination plant. Saudi Arabia has oil money and ceatoror stop.

cheap oil to produce water for its own need. Imagine the situation when all oil will be gone.

Another oil rich country Libya is working on a network of water pipelines to import water. It carries water from wells tapping fossil water in the Sahara desert to the cities of Tripoli, Benghazi, Sirte and others. Their water also comes from desalination plants.[83] Similarly, United Arab Emirates depends on have reached peak water and to solve this, UAE has a desalination plant near Ruwais that ships water to Abu Dhabi via pipeline.[84] In Yemen, the aquifer that supplies Sana'a, the capital of Yemen, depleted in 2009. In its search for water, the Yemeni government drilled test wells that are 2 kilometers (1.2 mi) deep, depths normally associated with the oil industry, but it has failed to find water. The pipeline option is complicated by Sana'a's altitude of 2,250 m (7,380 ft).[64] Yemen, which has no rivers and cannot afford desalination, is drawing water at around 400 times its replacement rate.[85] Christine Parthemore, a fellow at the Center for a New American Security says:

"Analysts are worried Yemen could be the first country in the world to effectively run out of water".[85]

The future oil and gas industry will be heavily dependent on water too. When the cheap oils in the Middle East will be gone, does not matter how much non-conventional heavy oil they have left in deep underground between the rocks, extraction possibility will depends on availability of water. Water is required at every stage of the mining, processing and production. About half the 410 billion gallons of water the U.S. withdraws daily goes to cooling thermoelectric power plants, and most of that to cooling coal-burning plants, according to the U.S. Geological Survey.[85] Since energy demand in the U.S. is expected to increase by 40 percent as the U.S. population rises above 440 million by 2050, the water supply will not be able to support that growth.[85] Even solar generating plants that use conventional cooling technology use two to three times more water as coal-fired power plants. Circle of Blue, a network of journalists and scientists dedicated to water sustainability calls the intersection of a rising demand for energy and diminishing supply water a "choke point" whether energy is generated using fossil fuel or renewable.[85] According to them it is just one aspect of the water scarcity crisis that is unfolding in various regions of the globe. Water scarcity may lead to water wars in many regions–which means burning more energy and faster reaching to the "choke point".

Water scarcity is already a serious problem in many countries in Asia, Africa and Latin America. Water demand already exceeds supply in many parts of the world, and as the world population continues to rise, many more areas are expected to experience this imbalance in the near future. To produce food for the 7 billion or so people today requires the water that would fill a canal ten meters deep, 100 meters wide and 7.1 million kilometers long – that's enough to circle the globe 180 times.[86] An additional 2.5 or 3 billion people, choosing to eat fewer cereals and more meat and vegetables could add an additional five million kilometers to the virtual canal mentioned above.[86&87] In other words, without this huge amount of water, millions or may be billions of people in the populated countries will starve and in the extreme case, will suffer from famine.

Apart from water, the challenge of food production is multifarious such as declination of fertility, topsoil erosion, declining seed diversity, mineral depletion.[88] In old days, farmers used to preserve their own seeds. Now the seeds of high yield energy and water intensive crops are produced and distributed by highly profitable centralized corporates who makes huge profits and more debts for farmers.[11] These high yield crops require pesticides and herbicides, higher doses every time as the pests are growing resistances.

Since fossil fuel is declining, many countries are increasing using biofuels by using food crops for making energy. Many governments now offer incentives or subsidies for turning biomass including food crops into fuel. As farmers are replacing wheat fields with more profitable biofuel crops, food prices are going up. In many developing countries, farmers are encouraged to grow tobacco instead to food crops by the corporates. On the other hand, genetically modified seed industry centralized production and distribution systems and use of more chemicals. Richard Heinberg describes:

"So far, gene splicing in food plants has succeeded mostly in generating enormous profits for an increasingly centralized corporate seed industry, and more debt for farmers.........Today's industrial farmer relies on an array of packaged products (seeds, fertilizers, pesticides, herbicides, feed, antibiotics), as well as fuels, powered machines and spare parts. The annual cash outlays for these can be daunting, requiring farmers to take out substantial loans."[11]

This situation is more severe in developing countries such as Bangladesh, India or Pakistan where the loans come from 'loan sharks' called 'mohajons' with an annual interest as high as 120% or more (10% in a month).

Another big issue regarding food production is depletion of minerals that is used to produce fertilizers, such as phosphate rock-based fertilizer. Canadian physicist and agricultural consultant Patrick Déry concluded that the peak of phosphate production has been passed for the world as a whole (1989).[89] The Soil Association report notes that, "When demand for phosphate fertilizer outstripped supply in 2007-08, the price of rock phosphate rose 800 percent."[90] On the other hand, without phosphate yields of food crops such as wheat could fall by half. Phosphate is essential and non-substitutable; therefore demand is inelastic.[11]

The contamination of rivers due to industrialization is extending to the seas and oceans and endangering sea species. On the other hand, the scarcity of fishes make the fishermen to go deep sea fishing which cost them more money such as higher costs for renting fishing boats, fuel, instruments, other incidental costs. The higher costs cause them borrowing more money and eventually over-fishing to pay off their loans. If steep declination of marine species continues to decline at current rate, the world will run out of seafood as early as mid of this century.[11] An international group of ecologists and economists warned that as of 2003, 29 percent of all fished species had collapsed and the rate of collapse continues to accelerate. Boris Worm, a leader of this group quoted as saying

> "We really see the end of the line now. It's within our lifetime. Our children will see a world without seafood if we don't change things."[91]

Infectious waterborne diseases such as diarrhea, typhoid, and cholera are responsible for 80 percent of illnesses and deaths in the developing world, many of them children. One child dies every eight seconds from a waterborne disease; 15 million children a year. About 25 million refugees were displaced by contaminated river in 2010 mostly in Africa. This number will continue to grow and spread in Asia, Latin America and eventually all over the world. Extensive research has shown the direct links between water resources, the hydrologic cycle, and climatic change. Evidence from the IPCC Working Group II, has shown climate change is already having a direct effect on not only human beings but also on animals, plants and water resources and systems. A 2007 report estimates that 75–250 million people across Africa could face water shortages by 2020. Agriculture fed by rainfall could drop by 50% in some African countries by 2020.[92] Already a severe drought, the worst in 60 years has been affecting the entire East Africa region. The drought has caused a severe food crisis across Somalia, Ethiopia and Kenya that threatens the livelihood of more than 9.5 million people.[93]

We need water everywhere from farming to mining, energy extraction, electricity production. Nuclear power plants also need substantial amounts of water to cool their reactors. Even manufacturing of photovoltaic solar panels requires water with very high purity. In summary, scarcity of water will affect at every stage of human activity. In the past, there were conflicts and wars over access and control over water resource. In West Africa today and in many other places in South East Asia, South America major changes in the rivers, generate a significant risk of violent conflict in coming years. The countries with dwindling water supplies compete for access for the remaining. Without rivers flow, many fertile regions in Asia and Africa would be desert.[94] Richard Heinberg summarizes the looming food crisis:

> "Demand for food is slowly outstripping supply. Food producers' ability to meet growing needs is increasingly being strained by rising human populations, falling freshwater supplies, the rise of biofuels industries, expanding markets within industrializing nations for more resource-intensive meat and fish-based diets; dwindling wild fisheries; and climate instability. The result will almost inevitably be a worldwide food crisis sometime in the next two or three decades."[94&11]

Nevertheless, the biggest of all crisis looming is fresh water scarcity that will severely impact all living beings in the world. In some parts of the world, access to water resources is causing conflicts or military tension among the countries. As an example, the Indus River is crucial to both India and Pakistan. Pakistan's 90 percent agriculture depends on this river. However, India on the upstream can control the flow of water of this river for its agriculture and hydroelectricity. As water demand is increasing and there are already massive shortages of water in both the countries, the risk of a big war between them is also increasing.[95] Since the economy of the Himalayan region such as China, India, Pakistan Bangladesh growing and producing more CO_2 emission and therefore, the glaciers are melting, extreme water shortage in this part of the world, home of 1.3 to 1.5 billion people is on the way. Many other parts of the world, in Asia, in the Middle East and in Africa are also at risk of war over water.

6.5 End of Growth

"Anyone who believes exponential growth can go on forever in a finite world is either a madman or an economist."[96]

- Kenneth Boulding (1966)

Why an economy should grow? Richard Heinberg answers this in his book "The end of Growth" as:

"We have relied on economic growth for the "development" of the world's poorest economies; without growth, we must seriously entertain the possibility that hundreds of millions—perhaps billions—of people will never achieve even a rudimentary version of the consumer lifestyle enjoyed by people in the world's industrialized nations."[18]

In every step of this consumer lifestyle such as production of raw materials, manufacturing, transportation, distribution and consumption we need oil. When our economies grow, it is all about consumption including rising consumption of fossil fuel. We focus on more consumption but we miss the point that the fossil fuel (oil, coal or natural gas) and all other natural resources on which the growth depends on are finite.

Now with globalization, the growth centers have moved from USA & Europe to Asia and South America but using up finite resources more quickly. As an example, after joining World Trade Organization in December 2001, China's energy consumption is increasing 15% each year to produce cheap products for the far away markets in USA and Europe. Although the developed countries such as USA and Europe are able to reduce per capita fuel consumption but their consumptions of manufactured products increased since they are now getting at lower price from China. Otherwise, as the people in developed countries spending more on commuting, they would cutback in discretionary non-food consumptions. In the US, increased consumption by printing money is showing positive growth figures despite debt of over \$17.9 trillion or about 105% of November 10, 2014 GDP.[97] On the other hand, China is using coal for 70% of its energy needs to reduce the impact of high oil price. As the coal is also finite resource, when its supply will decline if not already started to decline, China will no longer be able to produce products cheap or buy US treasuries. The two simultaneous crises, the massive debt and the high oil price or energy crisis will squeeze the biggest economy of the world faster than any other economies if its high dependency on debt and oil continues. Currently Greece's economy is contracting by roughly 5 percent a year.[98] Rubin comments "The EU can demand all the austerity measures it wants, but at that rate Greece's debt is only going to get bigger. That leaves the second option, default."[98] Without acceptance of USD as reserve currency, the economy of USA would bend backward in the same way as Greece.

As the EROEI (Energy Returned on Energy Invested) for oil extraction is getting lower, it will cause higher Energy Cost for Technology (ECT) for exploration. Economist Jeff Rubin argues:

"What geologists don't get is that peak oil isn't about supply: higher prices will always fetch more oil supply.....It doesn't matter if billions of barrels are waiting to be tapped in unconventional plays such as the tar sands or oil shale if the cost of extraction is beyond our capacity to pay."[98]

At some point, when the oil price will rebound, it may do it very sharply as the companies will try to recover their loss, pay the accumulated interests to the banks that the economy cannot afford–growth will stop. Rubin concludes:

"Some people might call that an oil peak. Others might just call it the end of growth."[98]

If an economy pays more money toward oil, it will have less money to grow. As an example, the more the oil price is, the more money a government spends on importing oil and therefore, more shortage of the money it requires to run itself and fund unbudgeted liabilities such as Medicare or social securities. The only sector will grow in a higher oil price is the oil industry and therefore, Optimal Capital for the Technological state (OCT) (see Chapter 4) will be lower. This means the money will recycle within a small part of the economy not the whole economy and the economy will shrink as shown in Figure 6.10. Therefore, higher oil price alone, at some point in future, is enough to bring down the

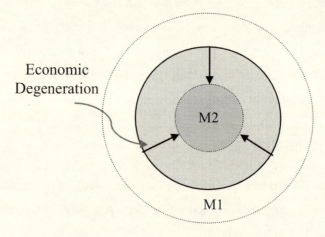

Figure 6.10: Economic Degeneration

growth of economic activity to zero and then negative. The corresponding technological state will change to negative direction and the economy will produce lesser amounts of products and food. Once the world economies will squeeze and begin to degenerate all that we will be achieving on that point of time the roads, highways, buildings, factories all will gradually become scraps.

On the other hand, when the oil price is low, it encourages more consumption. This means our earth is now warming faster, which is irreversibly depleting glaciers and fresh water. There could be two reasons for recent drop of oil price. First, Saudi Arabia and its OPEC allies do not want to lose their market share on the event the U.S. is posing to export shale oil & gas to overseas. The second reason could be, a Saudi and American joint effort to weaken Russia's recent move toward dumping US dollar.[99&100] The bottom line, both the high or the oil price is expediting the eventual end of growth.

Since the oil price is going down now, the possibility of very sharp rise is also looming. As oil backs almost all consumer products in the world, increase of oil price means lower the real income. If the cost of oil extraction increases faster than inflation, the oil price will increase and therefore, real wage will continue to fall in pace with the oil price. At the same time, many businesses will face difficulty to keep running because of higher oil price and therefore, they may lay off employees to reduce operational expenses. The governments will lose taxes and businesses will have hard times finding enough customers.

Nevertheless, globalization transfers part of this risk to developing countries who are adjusting their wages by depreciating own currencies. As Steve Baragona explains:

"Globalization transfers consumption of limited oil supply from developed countries to developing countries. If world oil supply isn't growing by very much, and demand is growing rapidly in developing countries, oil to meet this rising demand must come from somewhere. The way this transfer takes place is through the mechanism of high oil prices."[102]

One big effect after 'peak oil' may be inflation as prices of all products will increase by piggybacking the oil price. It will impact auto industry, the trucking industry, international shipping and the airlines and therefore, the economic globalization will collapse. Altogether, after 'peak oil' the whole world economy will turn to a negative growth as shown in Figure 6.11. Without oil, 'quantitative easing' or printing dollar no longer will work rather it will create inflations or in the worst case hyperinflation since there will be very limited products but some rich people will spend anything to grab them. According to the concept of "Biased Equilibrium" described in chapter 4, the collapse of globalization can be interpreted as breaking down global MMD, where no money and resource will come to the west or to the east through global channel. Heinberg describes

"If the oil stops flowing, global trade as we know it grinds to a standstill."[11]

The demand for USD will end and borrowing money by the US government will become more expensive, more difficult. Currently globalization allows Americans purchase more for every dollar of income. If the value of USD drops, People's Bank of China will receive less in return and therefore, US treasury will no more an attractive investment for China or other countries. As a result, the cost of borrowing will increase and Americans will have to pay more interest on their mortgages, car loans that will impact almost every Americans who hold debt or live on payrolls. On the other hand, as the unemployment will rise, the US federal tax will drastically decline. It will be very difficult for the companies

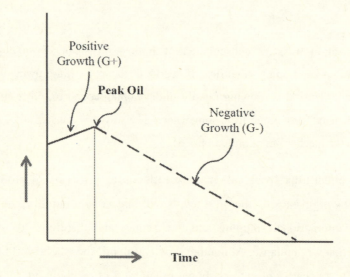

Figure 6.11 Economy before and after 'Peak oil'

to run, many will shut down, the businesses heavily dependent on oil like airline, transport will require subsidies to operate, whereas government will struggle to find money to run health care, welfare, food banks and even schools. Full day electricity or heating will become luxuries. Industries will begin to collapse, companies will file bankruptcies, and unemployment will begin to break records- the depression will be everlasting.

During Great Depression, unemployment rate in the U.S. had reached 23.6%, and it peaked in early 1933 at 25%.[103] The businesses and families defaulted on record numbers of loans, and thousands of banks had failed. Hundreds of thousands of people became homeless, and began congregating in shanty towns. Cars being pulled by horses called Bennett Buggies or Hoover Wagons became a common sight during the Depression (Figure 6.12).[104] This time everlasting depression following 'peak oil' will make many cars, buses, trains, aeroplanes and machineries scraps because they may never again be used. President Roosevelt's New Deal programs stimulated demand and provided work and relief for the impoverished through increased government spending and the institution of financial reforms. This time, there will be shortages of supply of goods and money. The U.S. government may fall in everlasting financial crisis

Figure 6.12: Bennett Buggies or "Hoover wagons"[104]

Bennett Buggy, 1935: Bennett buggies, or "Hoover wagons", cars pulled by horses, were used by farmers too impoverished to purchase gasoline.

as all sources of funds will squeeze. If the Chinese investors start selling their treasury bond, then the U.S. government will collapse. The people will begin to hoard what they can buy, which will make further shortage of supply of goods. The people who will be living cities or who will be working in non-farming, the technology and business people (majority of population of developed countries), and immigrants will be severely impacted by losing incomes and by the shortage of food and vital supplies. Heinberg describes this scenario as:

"With support services (in the U.S: Social Security, Medicare, public schools, the food stamp program) stretched beyond their limits, we could see more public resentment against immigrants, especially in border states. Of course, the economic pain gripping the United States will not actually be the fault of immigrants—or China, Muslims, environmentalists, or even terrorists."[105]

The concept of MMD (Chapter 4) in globalized world explains how developed countries holding most of the capitals generated around the world by means of contracts, rights or technologies they produce. In reality all these money is with the Global Pareto Coalition (GPC), whereas common people are more vulnerable to suffer the consequences of high oil price. Most severely, higher oil price affects food price. The high oil price increases food price because it adds cost in every stages from growing to distribution. Another reason is that diversion of arable lands to the production of biofuels. Even in the oil rich Arab world, although oil price increases, the high food price impacts the common Arabs. A recent study shows that 2011 food price spikes helped trigger the Arab Spring.[102] "In 2008, the last time global food prices spiked, Egypt was one of several countries hit by food riots and demonstrations".[102] Now although the Arab Spring already converted into political turmoil, whichever governments take the power will not be able to control the situation if oils run out. Will rest of the world be any different?

The example in Figure 6.13 below shows a DMM with an essential product (say, food) and two markets M1 and M2, where M2 represents the richer segment and

M1 represents the poorer segment. The two markets are in equilibrium at price level 'p'. The shortage of the product in the richer market M2 is shown by the shift of supply curve from S_2S_2' to S_2'S_2". As a result, the new equilibrium price will be '**p**''. After peak oil, many people in M2 who will not be able to afford

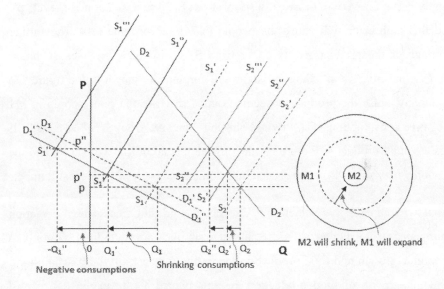

Figure 6.13 A basic demand & supply model after 'peak oil'

this price will fall to the lower market energy state M1 as their income will fall (reference: Figure 6.10). The Biased Equilibrium Barrier (BEB) between M2 and M1 will not be stable anymore and will continue to move upward by comprising fewer rich people in M2 but leaving more and more people in M1. Heinberg (2011) describes the similar situation as:

"[A] post-growth world characterized by heightened geopolitical and demographic competition, in which hundreds of millions who are currently enjoying or aspiring to a middle-class lifestyle may sink into poverty, and in which many millions more who are already poor may lose access to the barest elements of survival."[106]

449

The demand curve D_1D_1' in M1 will move down to $D_1'D_1''$ as the income of the people in M1 will severely reduce or become zero due to massive unemployment. The economy will shrink in both markets by the reduced supply of goods (opposed to supply driven economics after industrial revolution). The supply curve for M1will drastically shrink from S_1S_1' to $S_1'S_1''$ at price level '**p'**' and this high price will cause the people in M1 to consume less. The further shortage of the product supply curve from $S_2'S_2''$ to $S_2''S_2'''$ will cause father increase in price, say **p''**. This inflation will continue as shown in the figure and eventually cause the product to become out of reach to the poor people in M1 (negative consumption, $-Q1''$) by left shifting the curve from $S_1'S_1''$ to $S_1''S_1'''$. If this essential product is food, then most of the people in M1 will starve and the economy may suffer from severe malnutrition and consequently deepest famine.

What will happen if we factor in climate change and fresh water depletion culminated by oil bonanza? As fresh water supplies are dwindling, continuing economic growth and food production increasingly at risk. In the past failing to maintain growth of food production systems played a role in the collapse of previous civilizations, including the Roman Empire.[107] Mesopotamia, the green and lush center of the Sumerian and Babylonian civilizations, was largely turned to desert as a result of soil erosion. The Mayan civilization likewise succumbed to declining food production, according to recent archaeological research.[108] After fall of Roman Empire or after Mongol invasion (discussed in Chapter 2) that severe malnutrition and famine were followed by devastating plagues from China to Europe that killed millions of people. This time a plague of similar type might be more powerful, may count lives in hundreds of millions. Recent epidemic outbreak of Ebola spreading thousands of new cases a week with 70 percent mortality rate, World Health Organization (WHO) forecasts that there will be 10,000 new cases a week by the middle of November, 2014. According to Roger Kell, a York University professor, "Ebola is the scariest infectious disease that one can imagine. It really has Biblical plague connotations".[109] As

Green the Capitalists

long as economy is stable and we have resources, the possibility to control the outbreak of disease like Ebola is high. What if Ebola strikes back again in our weakest moment of global economic stability?

The two century old mainstream economic theories that we are obsessed with focuses on more production and more consumption have not factor the limited reserves of natural resources like fossil fuel or surface water in their models.

Richard C. Duncan defines a profile of Industrial Civilization as the ratio of world annual energy consumption and world population. He introduced a theory called Olduvai theory[110] shows the states that industrial civilization (as defined by per capita energy production) will have a lifetime around 100 years (1930-2030). Although civilization is not going to end so soon as he mentioned but couple of hid findings are incontrovertible.

As industrial civilization is dependent on energy that comes from finite resource of fossil fuel, it will be like a transient pulse in the perpetuity of human history as shown in Figure 6.14. According to Duncan's analysis, world total energy production outpaced world population growth from 1700 to 1979, but then from

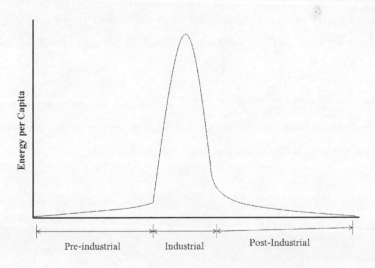

Figure 6.14: Olduvai theory: The short-lived industrial economy[110]

451

Monowar Zaman

1979 through 2003 total energy production and population growth went almost dead even at 1.5%/y each.[110] In Figure 6.14 the timeline estimated by Duncan is not shown since it is more of an academic concern. Although after publication of Duncan's paper, the trend of per capita energy consumption has increased but this trend will be difficult to sustain in the face of limits on finite resources such as oil, coal, and natural gas.[111] Once population is adjusted with earth's carrying capacity, society will approach the agrarian level of existence.

The declination of oil reserve and simultaneously, new demand for oil due to population growth would cause exponential rise of oil price and many of the technological advancements would be useless to most of people in the world. As an example, only super rich people would be able to drive cars and live in warm houses. As population will continue to grow but energy will decline, the Olduvai ratio will go steeply negative 'spreading epidemic of permanent blackouts', when population will decline to proximate the energy in an unpleasant and violent way. To avoid this extreme consequence on mankind, Chris Martenson (2011) suggests this:

"The best possible set of responses to Peak Oil will have been started two decades in advance of the actual peak, a much weaker set of responses one decade in advance, and the worst and the weakest set only after Peak Oil has already arrived."[5]

Then it will decline so rapidly that the world will not have enough time to develop alternate sources of energy, will lead to drastic social and economic impacts at the cost of the end of our civilization.[6]

6.6 The New Energy Outlook-Saudi America?

"The market is not laying the foundations for an era of unending oil-based prosperity. The market is pushing inexorably toward investment in expensive technologies to extract the last drop of profit through faster depletion of a resource that's guaranteed to run out"[117]

- Raymond Pierrehumbert (2013)

In 2010 World Energy Outlook, the International Energy Agency (IEA) announced that total annual global crude oil production will probably never surpass its 2006 level.[44&112] The usual forecast pattern of IEA and US Department of Energy's Energy Information Administration (EIA) is over-estimating future supplies and under-estimating future prices. Heinberg argues:

"During the past decade there has been one notable exception to the agencies' tendency toward over-optimism: in the years prior to 2009 the EIA and IEA failed to foresee the substantial increase in US natural gas and oil production resulting from the application of hydro-fracturing and horizontal drilling."[113]

In 2012 IEA has come up with some super-optimistic forecast because of a surge in unconventional supplies, mainly from light tight oil in the United States.[114] IEA (2012) also reports that there will be 'energy renaissance' in the United States which will allow USA become 'energy independent' and then a net oil exporter as light tight oil and shale gas resources will get competitive advantage and the oil price rises.[114] IEA Executive Director Maria van der Hoeven foresees this as "game changer" in oil based geopolitics. However, she admitted peak oil is always a concern which may just move to another decade.[115] In discussing the IEA report, a few analysts think that one of the objectives of IEA claims are essentially just efforts to avoid panicking the markets.[113]

Severely enough, using the IEA projections, an enthusiastic Wall Street journal article titled "Saudi America: The U.S. will be the world's leading energy producer, if we allow it."[116] This article boasts that America can be a fossil-fuel super power again by technological innovation "horizontal drilling and hydraulic fracking" and risk-taking funded by private capital but undermines investment needs for renewable energies. The article reads "Historians will one day marvel that so much political and financial capital was invested in a green-energy revolution at the very moment a fossil fuel revolution was aborning."[116]

According to Raymond Pierrehumbert, the Louis Block Professor in Geophysical Sciences at the University of Chicago, believes that the recent "abundance narrative" of American 'energy renaissance' or 'energy independence' comes primarily "on the heels of a report by Leonardo Maugeri", a former oil-industry top-executive and a fellow at Harvard's Belfer Center.[117] In his Wall Street journal article in 2009 Maugeri describes the U.S. oil reserve as 'huge' that is unexploited. According to him "Although the country's proven oil reserves are now only 29 billion barrels, the National Petroleum Council (NPC) estimates that 1.124 trillion barrels are still left underground, of which 374 billion would be recoverable with current technologies.[118] A Citigroup study forecasts U.S. shale oil production to rise by at least 2 million b/d by 2020.[119] The United States has almost a trillion recoverable barrels of shale oil.[120] After decades of decline, U.S. oil production is now on the rise, because of shale oil production, which could add around 3 million barrels a day to U.S. oil production by 2020.[121]

There were huge money invested in oil and gas exploration and production since 2003. Recently, between 2010 and 2012, around $1.5 trillion invested for oil and gas exploration and production.[122] In 2012, he forecasts additional production of oil and natural gas liquid (NGL) 29 million barrels per day (mpd) by 2020. However, by factoring depletion rate of currently producing oilfields and their "reserve growth" his net additional production forecast is 17.6 mbd by 2020, which will increase the world production to 110.6 mbd from 93 mbd in 2011. Figure 6.15 shows Maugeri's country wise forecast, where top 6 countries Saudi Arabia, United States, Russia, Iraq, Canada and Brazil will produce 83% of net

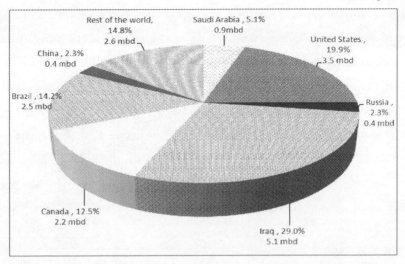

Figure 6.15 Forecast of net oil and NGL production, 2020 (17.6 mbd)[122]

additional capacity. Iraq will be the top most suppliers, one third of the net addition (29%), followed by USA, one fifth of the net addition, then Brazil (14.2%) and Canada (12.5%). The top four will contribute over three fourth (75.6%) of the world's net additional oil and NGL supply. The economic prerequisite for this new forecast is a long-term price of oil of $70 per barrel or higher in 2020.[122]

Robert Smith, an operations geologist explains "Shale play reserves are typically very thin in comparison to conventional wells, with layers of oil tightly sandwiched between layers of shale formation. Horizontal drilling of a shale play means the operator is going after the oil deposit from the side, which quickly draws the reserve away from the recovery point."[123] Pierrehumbert argues Maugeri's incorrectly compounded the decline rate of shale oil. In reality the decline rate of shale oil production from fracking and horizontal drilling is exponentially high.[117]

Geologist David Hughes examined proprietary data on 63,000 US shale gas and tight oil wells and calculated production decline rates in each active play, published in his book "Drill Baby Drill". He finds that individual shale gas well sharply declines from 80-95 percent after 36 months in the top five US plays.[124] Currently, more than 80 percent of tight oil production in the US comes from the Bakken and Eagle Ford, with the other 20 percent from 19 other formations. In Bakken, per-well production decline rates are between 81 and 90 percent in the first 24 months. The overall decline rate in Eagle Ford wells is 60 percent and at the end of the second year the decline rate is 89 percent.[113&124] Figure 6.16 is drawn depicting the declination rate of shale oil/gas from initial production rate based on the above information. Therefore, if someone such as Maugeri is overwhelmed with the future of shale gas or tight oil, he might be looking at the

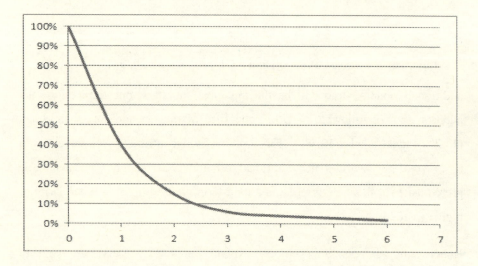

Figure 6.16 Shale oil/gas production decline rate pattern (For illustration only)

initial production rate in the sweet spots only and failing to see the sharp declination after a little beyond. Even OPEC's secretary general Abdalla Salem el-Badri, said at a conference in Kuwait that U.S. shale producers are "running out of sweet spots" and that output will peak in 2018.[164] Heinberg (2015) describes the reason why the decline of shale production may not be seen is because of "Red Queen" syndrome of Lewis Carroll's "Alice in Wonderland".[147] In the story, the fictional Red Queen runs at top speed but never gets anywhere; she explains to Alice, "It takes all the running you can do, to keep in the same place."[149] That is the drillers keep on drilling at higher rate to replace the high decline rates of the shale oil in order to keep the total production rate growing or even flat.[113]

In his field by field analysis, Hughes (2013) calculates that for the nation as a whole between 30 and 50 percent of shale gas production must be replaced annually with more drilling—amounting to roughly 7,200 new wells a year.[124&113] Undoubtedly, the net increase in global oil production will be driven entirely by unconventional oil, including a contribution from light tight oil that will exceed 4 million barrel per day for much of the 2020s, and by natural gas liquids.[114].The big oil companies and there are few reports funded by oil companies still says that there's trillions of barrels of oil underground and somehow technology will come to play a magical role to bring them out of the ground[122], which is exaggerated and misleading. In 2011, the world's proven (crude oil and natural gas liquids) reserves were about 1.3 trillion barrels, which is equivalent to 40 years of consumption.[125] However, the actual problems will begin far before oil fully runs out but as soon as market realizes that net declination has begun.

Let us check the real scenarios of shale oil in United States. According to Pierrehumbert (2013) although there are huge amounts of oil locked up in shale formations worldwide but a tiny fraction of this total is recoverable. As an example, Bakken (in Montana and North Dakota) and Eagle Ford (in Texas) tight oil contain up to 700 billion barrels and the Green River shale under Colorado, Wyoming, and Utah has a 2 trillion barrels, the estimated recoverable fraction ranges from 1 to 2 percent.[117] David Hughes estimates that the United States' total tight oil "technically recoverable unproved resources" is between 23 and 34.6 billion barrels, which presents 3-4 years of the domestic consumption. He adds "even if it all could be recovered—which would take decades."[124] In Eagle Ford, even with assumptions of 40 percent overall field decline rate and current rates of drilling (2011), Hughes estimates that a peak of 0.891 mbd production will reach in 2016 at and total oil recovery is estimated at about 2.23 billion barrels by 2025, which is a five-month contribution to US oil consumption.[124]

In the Green River, Pierrehumbert (2013) explains that the hydrocarbon in the Green River shale is not really oil at all but a waxy substance that must be cooked at around 500 degrees Celsius to turn it into flowing oil.[117] The technology for extracting oil from deposits like the Green River shale is never been profitably implemented at any significant scale. Therefore, there is no credible estimate of how much oil can be recovered from the Green River formation.[117] However, even if we consider the best case 2% recovery rate, among 2 trillion estimated reserve in Green River shale, only 40 billion barrel is recoverable, which is equivalent to 7-8 years US consumption at current rate. Altogether, in the best case scenario (2% recoverable rate) the equivalent recoverable reserve in America is less than a decade's "self-sufficiency" far from a sustainable self-sufficiency.

Deborah Rogers (2013), a former Wall Street financial consultant and member of the Advisory Council for the Federal Reserve Bank of Dallas from 2008 to 2011, Wall Street is orchestrating Shale gas and fracking mania in the same way as subprime lending crisis in connection with shale gas and tight oil companies.[163] In her article "Shale and Wall Street: Was the Decline in Natural Gas Prices Orchestrated?" She finds similarity with the shale boom and the boom of new financial products based on credit default swaps before 2008 mortgage crisis. As she describes:

"It was similar with shale. Due to the new technology of hydro-fracture stimulation, shale results could not be verified for a number of years. There simply was not enough historical production data available to make a reasonable assessment. It wasn't until Q3 of 2009 that enough production history on shale wells in the Barnett had been filed.....What emerged was significantly different from the operators' original rosy projections. Of further interest is the fact that once numbers could begin to be verified in a play, operators sold assets quickly. This has followed in each play in the U.S. as it matured. The dismal performance numbers were recognized as a potential drag on company share prices."[163]

According "World Market Report", IEA, the total U.S. crude oil production in November 2012 was about 6.8 mbd, and Saudi Arabia's production was 9.9 mbd, next to Russia (10.9 mbd). For the first time in 2013, the U.S. production becomes 7.3 mbd surpasses imports (7.27 mbd) for first time since 1997. Now to exceed Saudi production, new oil from tight-oil sources would have to more than offset declining production from existing wells.[117] Pierrehumbert (2013) refers the statistics presented by J. David Hughes at the American Geophysical Union (AGU) session, USA is now drilling 25,000 wells per year just to bring production back to the levels of the year 2000, when there were 5000 wells drilled per year. These new wells are as expensive as $10 million each in the Bakken but "give out rapidly".[117] Hughes concludes

"It is clear that even if we do manage somehow to temporarily exceed Saudi production rates, the party is not going to last very long."[117]

6.7 The Final Count Down

"What if our exponentially based economic and monetary systems, rather than being the sophisticated culmination of human evolution, are really just an artifact of oil? What if all of our rich societal complexity and all of our trillions of dollars of wealth and debt are simply the human expression of surplus energy pumped from the ground? If so, what happens to our wealth, economic complexity, and social order when they cannot be fed by steadily rising energy inputs? What happens then?"[5]

- Chris Martenson (2011)

Although global oil and gas production is expected to rise in some countries because of advancement of technologies such as hydraulic fracturing and horizontal drilling in tight shale reservoirs, some facts about oil (or fossil fuel) remains unchanged. First, there is a finite amount of fossil fuel reserve in our planet, where production follows the bell curve defined by Hubbert in 1956. This means the concept of 'peak oil' is an inevitable fact. It takes many millions of years to form oil and therefore, once it run out it goes for ever. Secondly, if the supply grows, the 'peak' will shift by few years but with increased uncertainty. Thirdly, the unconventional oil extracted using the new technologies has very sharp declination rate of the wells, which calls for continuous drilling of new wells. Fourthly, dropping of oil price will allow emerging nations to use more oil, the more quickly the conventional cheap oil will run out and open businesses for unconventional oil. Fifthly, the more we move toward conventional to unconventional oil, the less the EROEI, which calls for higher cost, more carbon emission and higher environmental risk of every unit barrel of oil produced.

Our world has limited amount of fossil fuels, the same is true for all minerals. Wall Street journal article, Leonardo Maugeri, also admits that "It is incontrovertible". However, he argues:

> "But even so, no one knows how finite they are. And since we don't know the total amount of oil resources existing underground, it's impossible to calculate the curve of future supply."[118]

Since 2003 when oil production approaching a saturation (Figure 6.2), there was huge investment in worldwide oil exploration & production, encouraged by increasing crude oil prices.[125] In last three years between in 2010 and 2011, the investment boomed, when the oil industry invested more than $1.5 trillion worldwide to explore and develop new resources.[125] According to IEA, in the New Policies Scenario, cumulative investment of $37 trillion will be needed in the world's energy supply system over 2012-2035. Oil and gas supply will require $19 trillion, of which 30% will be invested in North America.[114]

Again, IEA forecasts that after investment so huge money, the net increase in global oil production, driven entirely by unconventional oil such as light tight or shale oil that will contribute only 4 mbd for much of the 2020s during the peak supply.[114] This additional volume will only be economical if oil price is above a certain level. Therefore, the new unconventional oil and natural gas liquid extraction will not decrease the overall price. The total power sector will require investment over 2012-35 of $16.9 trillion. Two-fifths of this investment will be for distribution networks, while the rest will be for generation capacity.[114] Where will this money come from? IEA has this answer that by a more efficient allocation of resources, the world will be able to boost cumulative global economic output by $18 trillion through 2035. And an additional investment of $11.8 trillion in efficient end-use technologies will offset a $17.5 trillion reduction in fuel bills and a $5.9 trillion cut to supply-side investment.[114] Doesn't it resemble with George W. Bush's projection of $1.288 surplus from 2001 through 2004 before Iraq invasion[127] that ended up $851 billion deficit instead, a swing of $2.138 trillion.[128]

Interestingly, Iraq has big part in the IEA forecast. According to the forecast, Iraq's cumulative revenue will stand $5 trillion in revenues from oil export over the period to 2035. To achieve this, Iraq will need cumulative energy investment of over $530 billion, equivalent to just over 10% of the projected revenue from oil and gas exports.[114] As shown in Figure 6.15, Maugeri's (2012) positions Iraq as top most source of future oil supplier (29%) where he figured out the production will rise from 2.5 mbd to 7.6 mbd in 2020, net additional production increase 5.1 mbd. The United States has the second most growth, from 8.1 mbd to 11.6 mbd in 2020, net addition 3.5 mbd.[125] According to him the U.S. and Iraq together will hold about 50% of additional net supply of oil and NGL, although Saudi Arabia will top in production capacity with 13.2 mbd but net addition from 2011 to 2020 will be only 0.9 mbd. The total net addition from three countries,

USA, Canada and Iraq will be 10.8 mbd, 61.4% of total world additional forecast 17.6 mbd.[125]

An important note here is that Maugeri's growth forecast is based on unconventional oil, which has increasingly low Energy Return on Energy Invested (EROEI). This means to produce this much of additional oil, a big amount of conventional oil will have to be used, which USA can import by printing dollar. This means to meet demand for US unconventional oil sector, the world's conventional oil reserve will deplete faster and the oil price will enter into a vicious price cycle. Guess, what will be the implication to other countries? Nevertheless, the stocks of the U.S. based oil companies will soar but for time being. Heinberg (2013) explains the consequence:

"Often, financial speculation based on an extravagant (and sometimes deliberate) over-estimation of resource potential drives the peak of the boom higher than would otherwise be the case, thus making the bust all the more devastating."[113]

A study by the U.S. Energy Information Administration (EIA), published in April 2011, found technically recoverable resources, including U.S. is 6,620 trillion cubic feet (tcf) of shale gas deemed recoverable.[129] This report says a combined use of horizontal drilling and hydraulic fracturing brings an 'oil revolution' in the U.S. economy, which is the result of massive investment in exploration technologies by risk taking independent companies. This revolution will be very short lived as the shale gas and shale oil wells have proven to deplete quickly, the best fields have already been tapped.[114] In an interview in 2013, Bill Powers, author of the book "Cold, Hungry and in the Dark: Exploding the Natural Gas Supply Myth," explains this situation:

"The bigger North American companies are consolidating, because it is harder to acquire prospective land. Plus, the cost of drilling wells has gone up. But juniors that can find new reserves and that can increase production per share and cash-flow per share will have a wonderful rise over the next three to five years.

Companies are helped by the upward trend of ever-higher oil prices and we will soon see much higher gas prices. And remember, all of this is happening at a time of historically low interest rates. So companies that can get to critical size and borrow money at today's low rates have a chance to deploy that capital into some very high-return projects."[131]

At the same time in 2013, Heinberg (2013) also has very similar view:

"Their huge need of investment capital prompting them to ballyhoo fracking's significance....These companies need investors to believe that fracking is the Next Big Thing. As in every boomtown since the dawn of time, hyperbole has become a tool of survival."[126]

There is a big difference in the forecast made by the oil companies or funded by oil companies and the reality. As an example, Eady Ashley (2013) reports despite oil company predictions for some unconventional plays in Texas to last upwards of 15 years, after drilling they lasts no more than 18 months.[123] Robert Smith an operations geologist working there describes:

"An extremely dramatic decline curve....Operators ultimately end up chasing the deposit sideways constantly, and the cost of drilling horizontally in pursuit of the ever-retreating reserve quickly surpasses the recovered oil return... Eventually horizontal drilling is suspended because operators reach a point where they are just burning cash."[123]

According to Bill Powers "US Shale gas won't last ten years".[130] He comments about 'America's 100- year reserve of oil" as "This myth has been perpetuated by self-interested industry, media and politicians."[130] In another interview he points out the political game behind shale reserves as:

"Many of the people promoting the 100-year myth were doing it for either financial or political reasons. Let's look at why the U.S. government promoted the myth. The government has the idea that if the U.S. were to become an LNG exporter through the rapid development of shale, we would lessen the importance of Russia on the world's stage."[131]

According to history, dropping oil prices in the 1980s did help bring down the Soviet Union.[160] Since the dream of Saudi-America is no longer be true, the political game is being played using the old weapon again. This time, oil price is going down but Saudi Arabia and its OPEC allies do not want to cut production. There will two consequences of this political game. First, the oil reserve of Saudi Arabia is going to deplete quicker, that will impact on the supply and trigger oil price to rebound eventually, while demand is increasing in Asia. Second, the foreign currency reserve of Saudi Arabia is going to deplete that will make the country to seek fund from international financial industry.

Martenson emphasizes that the concern for everybody is that on that day real demand will outstrip available real supply. "In that moment", he continues "oil market will change forever, probably, quite suddenly".[5] According to him the food shortage seemingly erupted overnight in February 2008 were triggered by the perception of demand of oil exceeding supply, which led to an immediate export ban of food shipment in many countries. "This same dynamic of nation hoarding will certainly be a feature in global oil market when perception of shortage takes hold" he adds.[5]

For an analysis of the consequences, let us divide the world in two types of countries. Type A: a handful of countries such as United States, Russia, Iraq, Canada and Brazil that will experience a boom of unconventional oil production. Type B: the remaining countries in the world will who has no oil or will experience a declination of their oil production. The situation of Type B countries can be explained by the simple analysis based on the two-layer DMM and corresponding demand and supply curves in Figure 6.13. As the oil price will increase, it will cause cost-push inflation in the economy but the people in the lower MES (here M1) will be severely affected and their number will increase. Consumption in the economy will consistently fall, unemployment rate will rise. The only possibility to save a country from this consequence will be to borrow money to import oil.

As per IEA, the United States will be the strongest Type A country in 'New Policy Scenario'. It is currently the largest consumer, the second largest producer of coal and natural gas, and the largest importer and third largest producer of oil.[132] Citigroup estimated the impact of the 'oil revolution' in the US economy that the GDP will rise by 2% to 3.3%, or by $370 billion to $624 billion, by 2020 although budget deficit will still remain but may reduce from current 3% to anywhere between 1.2% of GDP to 2.4% of GDP.[133] This is not much compared to the huge unfunded liabilities the U.S. government have. As described in the new policy scenario, Type A countries either USA or Russia will drive the global economy. There will be a need huge investment for exploration and production of oil because of reduced Energy Return on Energy Invested (EROEI) of unconventional oil. If we assume factor of production is fixed for a country including investment capital, then because of the shift toward unconventional oil technology, there will be more investment growth for oil and NGL and related products. Let's define the products and services that are based on oil and NGL as Product Y and the products that are not related with oil as Product X. Figure 6.17 shows the production–possibility frontier (PPF) curve X'Y' after revolution of unconventional oil in a Type A country–a shift from existing PPF curve XY. Since the country will have to invest most of its income from oil export for oil exploration and production, the quantity of products and services that are non-oil based may fall as shown negative Q' in Figure 6.17. Again, as long as the country has oil (at economic level) the country may further increase oil & NGL export and therefore, allowing more quick depletion of the reserves. In this way, the government will earn more money and taxes to support Product X such as health care and social security as long as it can cover the cost from oil export. This is shown by the new PPF curve X"Y" in Figure 6.17. The economy will

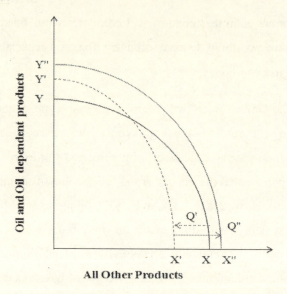

Figure 6.17 Production Possibility Frontier curves for Type A country

show good figures in consumption of non-oil based products and services as shown Q" in Figure 6.17. However, it will fall in a vicious cycle of export since more export will require more extraction of oil and gas and eventually it will cause sooner depletion from their finite reserves.

Although U.S. laws currently ban oil exports without specific federal approval, the above analysis shows that there is enough reason for U.S. government to allow bulk export of oil and NGL. In December, 2015, the U.S. government passed a bill for crude oil export. Bloomberg reports:

> "A 40-year ban on US crude oil exports was lifted just last week as part of a massive federal budget deal, and on first blush the new policy looks like a giant step backwards for global climate change."[161]

Earlier IEA forecasted that North America (means USA) will become a net oil exporter around 2030. In an interview with France 24, Maria Van Der Hoeven, IEA executive director admits that USA will be the initial winner of the unconventional fracking technology for producing shale oil around 2020 but for the time being as a first mover that technology. She also admitted that nevertheless it would follow the peak oil cycle, the oil production would flatten and then will go down.[134] In another interview with Reuter she also admits that the discussion around peak oil is only changed whether it will happen in this decade or another decade.[116] Following Maugeri if we accept the National Petroleum Council (NPC)'s super optimistic forecast that the U.S. has 374 billion barrels recoverable oil[125&132], at current rate of consumption, 20 mbd, it will serve the US economy about 51 years. However, if USA begins to export oil, all reserve will be gone much earlier. Eventually the situation of USA will be no better than a Type B country.

The Type A countries, which are depend on oil export but producing high cost oils or gas from Arctic or deep water (such as Russia) or sand oil (such as Canada) will have to produce more to run their budget and to pay the interest costs of their debts. Organization of Petroleum Exporting Countries (OPEC) has said in its latest World Oil Outlook report that oil demand to hit 111 million barrels per day by 2040 despite climate change as Asian demand grows.[269] It also sees that oil prices will average $177 per barrel by 2040.

Another fact, once a Type A country will become dependent on oil export, at some point, the country may suffer from inflation if it does not dispose some oil money outside the country. As an example, Type A countries may lend to Type B countries so that Type Bs can import oil and in return Type As get leverage of low cost labor in Type Bs. In this way, the global economic outlook will look healthy. The investors who will buy the bonds that allow governments to roll over the debt and they will be making larger and larger bets on future economic growth, which will lead to a bigger collapse when oil will begin to disappear.

China can be categorized as Type B country. However, China burns nearly twice as much coal as the United States. Currently coal accounts for three-quarters of the country's power which is also depleting in the same way as oil. Chinese economy it is booming for its growing international market as well as domestic market. In domestic market China has 1.3 billion potential consumers. Rubin (2012) gives an idea about Chinese appetite for oils by describing investment in infrastructure development:

"In the last five years, China has spent more than $700 billion on transportation infrastructure, more than twice as much as the United States. Construction of twelve national highways there was recently completed, roughly thirteen years ahead of schedule. China's expressways, most of them less than ten years old, now cover the same distance as the US Interstate system, which took three decades to build."[87]

Since with all these constructions, China is going to use up its vast coal reserve in a near future and therefore, it will increasingly become dependent on oil import. At some point of time, with declination of fossil fuel, oil price will go up and Chinese export market will not be able to cope up with increased oil price and then may decline. Ironically this may lead to de-globalization. Although China is in a better position than USA as it has massive sovereign wealth but once globalization will fail due to oil crisis, Chinese export industry will fall, unemployment will rise in urban industries and people begin to migrate back to rural areas. The dependency of increased population on limited agricultural land with reduced productivity will put pressure on food supply (Malthusian Catastrophe). Most likely China will back to de-privatization, and government will possibly take control of the lands again. China may roll back to pre-industrialized era leaving recently built cities, industrial plants, big highways, rail roads, high speed trains, millions of automobiles and aircrafts as scraps but with many times more population, more pollution, and much less energy.

Now let us take a look at the world's largest exporter of petroleum, Saudi Arabia. Its domestic oil consumption is increasing more than 5 percent a year.[87] Similarly, the domestic demand is also increasing elsewhere in the Middle East. The desert country's aquifers composed of rainfall from thousands of year ago, are already about 80% depleted. As the country running out of water, the Saudi government has built giant desalination plants to turn salty seawater into fresh water. These plants consumes huge amount of energy, currently burns more than a million barrels a day. The demand of fresh water is increasing at 7 percent a year.[87] Accordingly, the country's power generation capacity is increasing 10 percent a year. It is estimated that the domestic oil consumption in this country would hit 8.3 million barrels a day by 2028, nearly matching the current production.[2] This means at some point, Saudi Arabia will have to stop exporting. The petroleum sector accounts for roughly 45% of the country's budget revenues, 55% of GDP, and 90% of export earnings.[135&136] Now with depletion of the oil, not only the country's economy will collapse but also there will be severe consequence on all living beings in the desert country because of shortage of fresh water. The huge migrant workers (more than five million) working in Saudi Arabia will have to leave back home putting more pressure on the economy of their home country, which have been dependent on wage earners.

Now falling oil price, Saudi government is running under deficit.[154] To minimize this deficit, the countries currently holding conventional oil should produce more oil that will quickly deplete their existing reserve but will open business opportunities for unconventional oil, that is for Type A countries. Also the countries depend on oil import, will likely glut the oil and their investors will make high profit, a part of which will be out-flown out of the countries to off-shore or back to Type A countries and stay within Global Money Loop (GML).

Looking from financial perspective, increased income of the Type A country from oil export should cover the interest expense for increased investment in oil exploration and production and the induced price hike due to Inductive Market Energy (IKE and IPE), mathematically $\delta V \geq \delta M_{KME} + \delta M'_{IME} + \delta M'_{IME}$ (Ref: equation 4.31, Section 4.11, Chapter 4). As per EROEI of unconventional oils, is as low as 3:1 or lower, Energy Cost for the Technological state (ECT) will be high. If ECT increases rapidly, it will cross Optimal Energy for the Technological state (OET) and reinforce the pre-existing Market Loop (ML) that will potentially cause Bulling ML (BML). This will make cost of inductive price $\delta M'_{IPE\text{-}}$ asynchronously higher in every cycle of the ML, a very fertile ground for plotting Ponzi scheme ($\delta M_{KME}+\delta M'_{IME}+\delta M'_{IME} > \delta V$) (ref: equation 4.34, Section 4.11, Chapter 4). Richard Heinberg (2009) describes Ponzi scheme as:

"The collateral for that debt consists of a wager that next year's levels of production and consumption will be higher than this year's......Given that growth cannot continue on a finite planet, this wager, and its embodiment in the institutions of finance, can be said to constitute history's greatest Ponzi scheme. We have justified present borrowing with the irrational belief that perpetual growth is possible, necessary, and inevitable. In effect we have borrowed from future generations so that we could gamble away their capital today"[137]

As we discussed in the previous chapter that capitalism has now become debt driven and cannot be stopped. According to Martenson (2011) the underlying fact is that debt markets are making an enormous collective bet that the future economy will be exponentially larger than the present.[38] Unfortunately, the reality is opposite. The tax base of developed world has already set to decline, meaning more social security liabilities on government and in turn more dependency on debt. In other words, in the long run, the taxes to be collected by the governments will be spent for debt servicing. The worst to be the worst, with declination of the fossil fuel, unemployment rate might grow in a rate that might make impossible to exact more taxes from the people who cannot evade taxes similar to the Roman peasants.

The value of the Ponzi scheme may grow as high as hundreds of trillions dollars of IOUs, couple of time the world GDP. In both ways few capitalists of both the Type A and Type B countries will steer the Ponzi scheme as long as they get support from oil money. According to equation 4.28 ($\delta f(E,\ T) \geq \delta M'_{IPE}$), if cost of the inductive price due to Money Loop (ML) $\delta M'_{IPE}$ rises high due to Ponzi schemes, the economy will need to produce and export more oil and gas to keep pace with $\delta M'_{IPE}$ to protect the global financial system until it collapses as soon as oil become uneconomical and disappears from the market all of a sudden.

In his article David Stockman describes that Chinese economy is now a monumental Ponzi scheme. In last fourteen years since the beginning of 21st century, the credit market debt increased from \$1 trillion to \$25 trillion, a stupendous 25 times. The Chinese investors borrowed and built huge amount of infrastructures such as 70 million empty luxury apartments and vast stretches of over-built highways, fast rail, airports, shopping malls and new cities with these money.[152] Stockman goes into details about the Bulling Money Loop (BML) created by a Vertical Growth (VG) of the economy, which can collapse anytime:

"China has been on a wild tear heading straight for the economic edge of the planet–that is, monetary Terra Incognito–based on the circular principle of borrowing, building and borrowing. In essence, it is a giant re-hypothecation scheme where every man's "debt" become the next man's "asset"......Thus, local government's have meager incomes, but vastly bloated debts based on stupendously over-valued inventories of land. Coal mine entrepreneurs face collapsing prices and revenues, but soaring double digit interest rates on shadow banking loans collateralized by over-valued coal reserves. Shipyards have empty order books, but vast debts collateralized by soon to be idle construction bays. Speculators have collateralized massive stock piles of copper and iron ore at prices that are already becoming ancient history."[152]

The collapse of Chinese economy will not be limited to China. The whole world economy will be impacted by the severe blow from the world's second largest economy. In case, if China calls off the U.S. treasury bonds, enough to collapse the U.S. dollar and the rest of the world will get the hit at the same time.

On the other hand if Chinese economy and similarly all other emerging economies continue to grow for some time, and the world will need to find an additional 21 million barrels per day (bpd) of crude over the next 25 years to meet demand from rising global populations and rapid economic growth in Asia. The Telegraph reports:

"The findings of the report will come as a blow to climate change campaigners who are warning that unless serious action is taken to reduce greenhouse emissions the world will face a catastrophic global warming shock beyond 2025."[158]

In case of agriculture, the developing countries have now become dependent on centralized production and distribution of genetically modified seeds that has almost destroyed local storage system of the native breed seeds. Many agricultural scientists, and food system theorists including Wendell Berry, Wes Jackson, Vandana Shiva, Robert Rodale, and Michael Pollan, has argued against centralization, industrialization, and globalization of agriculture, and for an ecological agriculture with minimal fossil fuel inputs. Heinberg argues:

"Unfortunately, their recommendations have not become mainstream, because industrialized, globalized agriculture have proved capable of producing larger short-term profits for banks and agribusiness cartels. Even more unfortunately, the available time for a large-scale, proactive food system transition before the impacts of Peak Oil and economic contraction arrive is gone. We've run out the clock."[11]

At the time, globalization will stop working when production and transportation of seeds and other agricultural resources will become uneconomical, keeping up food production for huge population will be jeopardized, if preventive measures are not taken right now. As we have seen in the past that shortage of food production will cause food riots, malnutrition and may potentially be followed by epidemic diseases up to the scale of inter-continental plagues.

The long-term environmental impact of the energy revolution cannot be overlooked or discounted for the sake of our short lived comforts and luxuries. The Energy Return on Energy Investment (EROEI) of unconventional oils is as low as 3:1 or lower. This means the unconventional oil of higher amount will release more greenhouse gases. Pierrehumbert (2013) questions "Does all the new American oil give us yet another way to fry ourselves?"[127] He explains

"At 0.1159 metric tons of carbon per barrel of oil, the oil in Bakken and Eagle Ford amounts to a carbon pool of 81 Giga-tones (Gt), and the Green River shale adds up to 232 Gt. given that burning an additional 500 Gt of fossil fuel carbon is sufficient to commit the Earth to a practically irreversible warming of 2 degrees Celsius."[117]

"However", as he points out that if American Geophysical Union (AGU) are right, that is, almost all of this oil will remain inaccessible. The U.S. economy including the others will look for coal to cater their interest, which contains enough carbon to bring us to the danger level and beyond.[117]

According to IEA (2012),

"The climate goal of limiting warming to 2°C is becoming more difficult and costly with each year that passes."[138]

IEA also reports as global energy demand will increase by over one-third in the period to 2035, energy-related CO2 emissions will rise from an estimated 31.2 Gt in 2011 to 37.0 Gt in 2035, pointing to a long-term average temperature increase of 3.6 °C.[114] This will accelerate melting the glaciers and destructions of fresh water supplies. Melting the glaciers is one way journey. Once a glacier melts, the water reaches to the sea, it will never come back and dry up the rivers. At the same time every barrel of oil produced in an oil shale operation, between 1 and 3 barrels of water are required, which again will put pressure on the depleting fresh water reserves. There is about one million barrels of water are needed to frack one unconventional well, compared to 3 to 4,000 barrels of water needed for one conventional well drilling.[123] Heinberg warns

"The "shale revolution" will be short-lived, while the environmental, economic and societal costs of this drilling will last for generations."[3]

Unfortunately, the IEA reports and media do not highlight the inconvenient fact that according to the new forecast the 'peak oil' will just move few years only but overstates the prospects of shale gas and fracking technology. As a result, world oil reserves will deplete faster than would otherwise happen after spending trillions of dollars and consuming billions of liters fresh water, damaging environment that will leave an even further worse world for our next generations. Here is the fact what IEA chief economist Fatih Birol disclosed in an interview:

"We're not running out of oil today or tomorrow but we need to prepare ourselves for the day that we do. We have to leave oil before it leaves us."[139]

In other words, we have to plan now for a soft landing on a plain land rather than keep on high flying and then burst out on rocks.

Thomas Homer-Dixon[140] argues that a falling EROEI in the Later Roman Empire was one of the reasons for the collapse of the Western Empire in the fifth century CE. In his book "The Upside of Down" he suggests that EROEI analysis provides a basis for the analysis of the rise and fall of civilizations. At the maximum extent of the Roman Empire, there were 60 million people and its technological base the agrarian base of Rome was about 1:12 per hectare for wheat. One can then use this to calculate the population of the Roman Empire required at its height, on the basis of about 2,500–3,000 calories per day per person. It comes out roughly equal to the area of food production at its height. However later ecological damage such as deforestation, soil fertility loss saw a collapse in the system beginning in the second century, as EROEI began to fall. It bottomed in 1084 when Rome's population, which had peaked under Trajan at 1.5 million, was only 15,000.[140 & 141] Evidence also fits the cycle of Mayan and

Cambodian collapse too. Joseph Tainter suggests that diminishing returns of the EROEI is a chief cause of the collapse of complex societies.[141 & 142]

Falling EROEI due to depletion of high quality fossil fuel resources also poses a difficult challenge for industrial economies. Many researchers like Commoner (1971) accuse technology for intensifying "assaults on the environment, creating a debt to nature ultimately leading to ecosystem collapse".[143] He accuses "Modern technology extends man's effects on air, food and water, accumulating rubbish and junk."[143] After the end of fossil fuel, Commoner's comment about technology will become very visible. The technological advancements over hundreds of years, massive industrializations are now waiting for the final count down. Summing up all these, it can be said that the new unconventional oil will become uneconomical sooner than expected.

Suddenly, as Olduvai Theory[85] states we will discover a blackout as shown in Figure 6.18, an everlasting shortage of energy. As a result, growth will end, industries will be closed down, banking system and international trade would collapse and all the economies will fall in the deepest recession. The impact of blackout will not only involve power outage, closing down industries, collapse

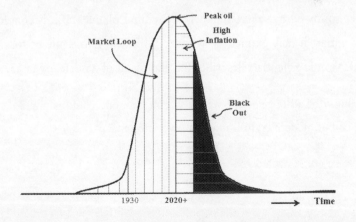

Figure 6.18 The consequence of economical depletion of unconventional oil

of financial system but also most severely, there will be civil war, starvation, And extreme famine. When 99% people will starve, the 1% rich people cannot live better. After all, the wealthy people can easily be accused for the crisis and a country may enter into an era of civil war. In the documentary "Collapse", Michael Ruppert portrays:

"There are homeless displaced people. The great may billionaires, who we call the elites. They great many very wealthy people are getting crashed, burned, eaten alive."[145]

The institutional structure may break down as no governments will have capacity to control the crisis or the riots. Paul Roberts (2008) of National Geographic warns:

"Ready or not, we will face a post-oil future–a future that could be marked by recession and even war."[146]

A war will make the situation worse. Even though there is no war, without oil or fossil fuel all the modern infrastructures built in many decades, the highways, vehicles, airport, aircrafts, skyscrapers, military establishments all will become environmentally dangerous scraps and casualty. As happened in the past, a big war may be followed by severe famine, devastating plagues. If it is coupled with nuclear weapons, it may extinct the whole civilization into a pile of fossils. The Bulletin of Atomic Scientists describes the end result of a nuclear war as:

"The possibility of all-out nuclear war--a war that no one could win and that could lead to the end of modern civilization--was ever present."[162]

CHAPTER 7

GREENING CAPITALISM

7.1 Introduction

Our earth producing oil can be compared with 'the Goose that laid the golden eggs' in Aesop's Fables, which was killed by her impatient greedy owner. In a similar manner, we are destroying our earth by quick extraction and burning the limited reserve of fossil fuels. On the other hand, the end of fossil fuel will be disastrous for mankind, if we do not switch to alternate energy sources. Green Economics could be a better choice for a sustainable well-being that positions economics within a very long-term, earth-wide, holistic context of reality as a part of nature.[1] The literatures in 'Green Economics' describes a nature bound utopia economy but ignore the question how is to transit from the existing growth based economics to there.

All or most of the fuel-dependent nations agree to cut carbon emission and reduce dependency on fossil-fuel including Paris Climate Change Agreement in 2015 but only if doing so does not threaten economic growth. All the recommendations for curbing carbon emission so far tried out such as Kyoto Protocols, 'cap and trade', 'carbon tax' produced no net positive result. After 2008 financial crisis, environmental concerns have taken a back seat. A new proposal called "Green New Deal (GND)" was put forth but in a way that is doing more to return to the path of growth than addressing the underlying causes of the financial or environmental crises. The information sharing strategies within a Pareto Coalition (PC) reveals that capitalists are in a dilemma, which is preventing them from co-operating toward a sustainable green economy and therefore, all of the exhortations about a green recovery is now overridden by growth compulsion.

7.2 Energy Return on Energy Invested (EROEI)

In the past the energy shift was toward efficiency gain. This time energy shift is different from what happened in the past. Prior to the development of coal in the mid-19th century, nearly all energy used was renewable. The oldest use of renewable energy was biomass to fuel fires. The second oldest usage of renewable energy was wind power in order to drive ships over water. This practice can be traced back some 7000 years, to ships on the Nile.[2] Moving into the time of recorded history, the primary sources of traditional renewable energy were human labor, animal power, water power, wind, in grain crushing windmills, and firewood, a traditional biomass.[3] In his article "A Farewell to Fossil Fuels: Answering the Energy Challenge", Amory B. Lovins describes the history of energy shift in nineteenth century as below:

"In 1850, most U.S. homes used whale-oil lamps, and whaling was the country's fifth-biggest industry. But as whale populations dwindled, the price of whale oil rose, so between 1850 and 1859, coal-derived synthetic fuels grabbed more than five-sixths of the lighting market. In 1859, Edwin Drake struck oil, and kerosene, thanks to generous tax breaks, soon took over. Whalers astounded that they had run out of customers before they ran out of whales, begged for federal subsidies on national security grounds, but Thomas Edison's 1879 invention of electric lighting snuffed out their industry. Whales had been accidentally saved by technological innovators and profit-maximizing capitalists."[4]

This time the energy shift is toward efficiency lose. The best way to define energy efficiency of a physical source of energy is Energy Return on Energy Invested (EROEI). It is the ratio of the amount of usable energy acquired from a particular energy resource to the amount of energy expended to obtain that energy resource.[5] At the time oil was originally discovered, it took on average one barrel of oil to find, extract, and process about 100 barrels of oil. That ratio has declined steadily over the last century to about three barrels gained for one barrel used up in the U.S. For Saudi Arabia this ration is about ten for one.[6&7]

When the EROEI of a resource is less than or equal to one, that energy source becomes an "energy sink", and can no longer be used as a primary source of energy.[5] EROEI sometimes is used in its short form EROI Figure 7.1 shows EROEI of different types of physical energy sources for USA. It shows EROEI of the U.S. physical energy sources are declining. As an example, EROEI for oil import has declined from 35 in 1990 to 12 in 2007. Although coal is in a better

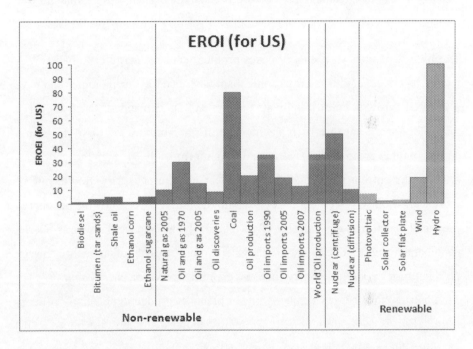

Figure 7.1: Energy Return on Energy Invested (for US) of various fuels[6]

position in terms of EROEI but environmental cost of coal is very high (due to high carbon emission). Again all these resources are finite and subject to decline. In the U.S. nearly half of electricity is made from coal, and almost none is made from oil but power plants and oil burning each account for over two-fifths of the carbon that is emitted by fossil-fuel use.[4] About three-fourths of electricity powers buildings, three-fourths of oil fuels transportation, and the remaining oil and electricity run factories.[4] If oil declines, the most affected sector of the U.S. economy will be transportation-the backbone of the U.S. economy. The biased equilibrium theory in this book (Chapter 4) describes that economic activities of a country or of the whole world are integrated as Money Market Dynamics (MMD) on high-EROEI fuels. As Heinberg explains in his book "Snake Oil"

"We built industrial societies on high-EROEI fuels that enabled a small amount of investment, and relatively few workers, to supply enough cheap, concentrated energy so that the great majority of citizens could use ever-increasing amounts of energy and thereby become more productive."[8]

The high dependency on energy poses problem cause "energy cannibalism". A related recent concern is energy cannibalism where energy technologies can have a limited growth rate if climate neutrality is demanded. Many energy technologies are capable of replacing significant volumes of fossil fuels and corresponding greenhouse gas emissions. Unfortunately, neither the enormous scale of the current fossil fuel energy system nor the necessary growth rate of these technologies is well understood within the limits imposed by the net energy produced for a growing industry. This technical limitation is known as energy cannibalism and refers to an effect where rapid growth of an entire energy producing or energy efficiency industry creates a need for energy that uses (or cannibalizes) the energy of existing power plants or production plants.[6&9] Energy cannibalism is using up high EROEI energy sources. If supply of high-EROEI energy reduces, MMD will slow down and may eventually stop. As a result the backbone of the capitalist economy will disintegrate and fail. We may not be able to prevent this disintegration but we can save local economies.

Figure 7.1 shows nuclear energy has better EROEI compared to any renewable energy sources except hydro. However, according to Scientific American, when the construction and decommissioning of power plants, and the mining and processing of uranium are all taken into account it also offers a relatively low EROEI.[137] Uranium, the predominant fuel for nuclear power, are limited anyway and even with no major expansion of power plants, there will be shortages by mid-century.[138] Nuclear plants have high up-front investment costs. There is still no good solution for storing the radioactive waste produced even when reactors are operating as planned.[139] In her article "Nuclear vs. renewables: Divided they fall", Dawn Stover argues that nuclear proponents have failed to come to terms with issues of safety, security, and waste disposal. Accidents and security breaches will never be entirely preventable, and there is no safe plan on the horizon for dealing with waste.[12] Expansion of nuclear energy may potentially put all of the earth's inhabitants including human beings vulnerable to extinction since atomic power plants are tied to nuclear weapons proliferation.[136]

Nevertheless Nuclear energy was in the front line as an alternative to fossil fuel, before recent incidence in Fukushima nuclear disaster on March 11, 2011. According to The Japan Times, the disaster changed Japan's national debate over energy policy almost overnight "By shattering the government's long-pitched safety myth about nuclear power, the crisis dramatically raised public awareness about energy use and sparked strong anti-nuclear sentiment."[10] Most of the nuclear power plants were established during 1970s and 80s and following another increase in new constructions from 2007 to 2010, there was a decline after the Fukushima nuclear disaster. However, because of the debate between nuclear versus renewables, use of coal and other fossil fuel rises.[38] As an example, in Germany, the renewables-only approach that will phase out nuclear power by 2022 drove coal consumption to a new high in 2013.[12] In Japan, today only 2 out of 54 of the nation's atomic power plants are operating. In 2012, The Economist magazine devoted a special issue to a report on nuclear energy titled, "Nuclear Power: The Dream that Failed."[140] It concluded: the nuclear industry may be on the verge of expansion in just a few nations, principally China; elsewhere, it's on life support.[140]

A newer version of nuclear reactor technology is called Integral Fast Reactor (IFR). Unlike existing light water reactors, IFRs would use sodium as a coolant. The IFR nuclear reaction features fast neutrons, and it more thoroughly consumes radioactive fuel, leaving less waste. That is, IFR theoretically "transmutes," rather than eliminates, radioactive waste and alleged to offer greater operational safety and less risk of weapons proliferation.[136] However, earlier versions of the fast breeder reactor were commercial failures and safety disasters.[136] Unfortunately, the technology IFR is decades away from widespread implementation, and its use of liquid sodium as a coolant can lead to fires and explosions.[141] In his book "Afterburn", Richard Heinberg warns:

> "The challenges of climate change and fossil fuel depletion require action now, not decades hence....we don't have the luxury of limitless investment capital, and we don't have decades in which to work out the bugs and build out this complex, unproven technology."[136]

David Biello (2010) in Scientific American found "To date, fast neutron reactors have consumed six decades and $100 billion of global effort but remain 'wishful thinking."[142] After all these, as The Economist concludes "Nuclear power will not go away, but its role may never be more than marginal."[140]

Low EROEI means reduced net supply the energies from the physical sources, which triggers energy price. Higher energy price is an incentive for extraction of more oil and gas from underground, which has further lower EROEI and thus rapid declination of the earth's energy budget.

The left hand side of the graph in Figure 7.1 shows alternate non-renewable sources of energy such as Shale oil, biodiesel, tar sand, ethanol, all of them have very low EROEI that require ever more extreme up-front investment and environmentally risky extraction methods.[143] Tight oil wells show such steep production decline rates that a peak and sharp drop in output.[143] Canada's tar sands have an EROEI ratio that ranges from 3.2:1 to 5:1. The petroleum industry promotes using natural gas more widely as a transport fuel, since shale gas is currently plentiful and cheap. However, in reality, shale gas resources suffer from the same problems as rapid per-well decline rates.[143]

According to experts, we need EROEI 10:1 for a sustainable industrial civilization.[145] Figure 7.2 shows most of the future energy sources such as shale

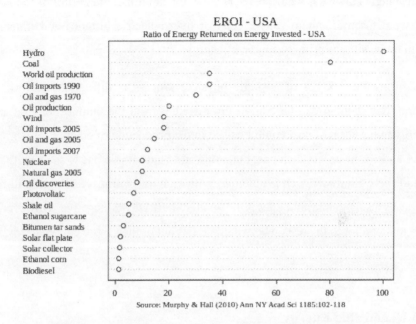

Figure 7.2: Ratio of Energy Returned on Energy Invested[11]

oil, solar, biofuel has less than this ratio. The amount of energy required growing the corn crop, harvest and collect and process into nearly pure alcohol to be used as biofuel require close to the amount of energy that the fuel itself would yield when burned in an engine. This means the EROEI of corn ethanol is close to 1:1 or in some cases lower. Therefore, biofuel does not have the ability to become substitute for fossil fuel but may be used for emergency transport only or low scale use only. As we are moving toward lower EROEI for fossil fuel and no better economic substitution is available, a larger proportion of our energy need to be diverted toward production of energy itself.

As a result of earth's declining energy budget, billions of people and species will be out of its capacity. To avoid this, we have to gradually switch over to renewable energy on time before it becomes too late. As Figure 7.1 and 7.2

shows EROEI for most renewables is currently lower than that for fossil fuels. But the EROEI of oil and gas is declining, while the EROEI of renewables is improving.[8] However, we need fossil fuels for rapid manufacturing of the parts for wind turbines, photo-voltaic cells or hydro-electric turbines and transport them to the sites as primary source of energy.

Measuring the EROEI of a single physical process is difficult. The form of energy of the input can be completely different from the output. For example, energy in the form of coal could be used in the production of ethanol. This might have an EROEI of less than one, but could still be desirable due to the benefits of liquid fuels. Similarly, rich people may still want to fly or drive using liquid fuel made by using renewable energy no matter if EROEI is negative. However, it will matter a lot to the rests who would be left out of their basic energy needs.

7.3 Renewable Energy

Since we are reaching to the economic point of diminishing returns for non-renewable energy sources, we have to move toward renewable energy sources. The right hand side of Figure 7.1 shows EROEI of renewable energy sources. For renewables, while the required initial investment is high, renewable generating systems are cheap to run because there is no fuel cost.[143] Based on REN21's 2014 report, renewables contributed 19 percent to global energy consumption and 22 percent to our electricity generation in 2012 and 2013, respectively. Worldwide investments in renewable technologies amounted to more than US$ 214 billion in 2013, with countries like China, the United States and European Union are heavily investing in renewable energy.[130] Figure 7.3 shows share of renewables in power generation is growing in USA, particularly accelerated after 2007 high oil price although not enough to replace fossil fuel any time soon.[14] President Barack Obama called for the expanded use of renewable energy to meet the twin challenges of energy security and climate

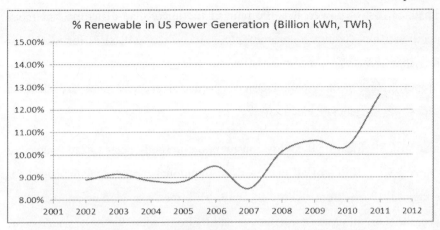

Figure 7.3: Share of Renewable Fuel in US Power Generation[15]

change. He envisioned the United States will "harness the sun and the winds and the soil to fuel our cars and run our factories."[16]

Some countries are seeing relatively quick adoption: At least 25 countries in the world are already produce 80%, 17 countries produce over 90%, 10 countries produce over 99% and at least three (3) countries, Albania, Iceland, Paraguay produce 100% of electricity demand from renewable energy.[131] However, none of them are big enough can be compared with the volume of U.S. electricity demand. Yet the IEA notes that "worldwide renewable electricity generation since 1990 grew an average of 2.8 percent per year, which is less than the 3 percent growth seen for total electricity generation."[17]

According to International Renewable Energy Agency (IRENA), in 2011 additions included 41 GW of new wind power capacity, 30 GW of solar photovoltaic (PV), 25 GW of hydropower, 6 GW of biomass, 0.5 GW of concentrated solar power (CSP) and 0.1 GW of geothermal power.[18] The rapid deployment of renewable technologies in a larger market may significantly reduce cost because of high learning rate.[4] For instance, for every doubling of the installed capacity of solar PV, module costs will decrease by as much as 22%.[4] IRENA uses the term Levelised Cost of Electricity (LCOE) to measure normalized cost of power. It is the ratio of lifetime costs to lifetime electricity generation using a common discount rate.[18] According to IRNEA, the LCOE for wind, solar PV, CSP and some biomass technologies are declining, while hydropower and geothermal electricity produced at good sites are still the cheapest way to generate electricity.[18]

About 16% of global final energy consumption presently comes from renewable resources, with 10%[16] of all energy from traditional biomass, mainly used for heating, and 3.4% from hydroelectricity. This means excluding biomass and hydro, the share of other renewables (small hydro, modern biomass, wind, solar, geothermal, and biofuels) account for another 3%. At the national level, at least 30 nations around the world already have renewable energy contributing more than 20% of energy supply.[19] And some 120 countries have various policy targets for longer-term shares of renewable energy, including a 20% target of all electricity generated for the European Union by 2020.[17]

According to Renewable Energy Policy Network for 21st Century (REN21), renewable energy replaces conventional fuels in four distinct areas: electricity generation, heating, transport fuels, and rural off-grid energy services.[19]

Power generation: Renewable energy provides 19% of electricity generation worldwide. Renewable power generators are spread across many countries, and wind power alone already provides a significant share of electricity in some areas: for example, For the record, there is already so much wind power in Denmark that one day earlier this year it produced 140 per cent of its energy needs from the technology, sending the excess power out to its European neighbours.[176] Some countries get most of their power from renewables, including Iceland (100%), Norway (98%), Brazil (86%), Austria (62%), New Zealand (65%), and Sweden (54%).[17]

Heating: Solar hot water makes an important contribution to renewable heat in many countries, most notably in China, which now has 70% of the global total

(180 GWth). Most of these systems are installed on multi-family apartment buildings and meet a portion of the hot water needs of an estimated 50–60 million households in China. Worldwide, total installed solar water heating systems meet a portion of the water heating needs of over 70 million households. The use of biomass for heating continues to grow as well. In Sweden, national use of biomass energy has surpassed that of oil. Direct geothermal for heating is also growing rapidly.[17] In India, Bangalore has the largest deployment of roof top solar water heaters growing with government incentives. In 2009, these heaters generate an energy equivalent of 200 MW. These systems are now mandatory for all new structures.[190]

Transport fuels: Renewable biofuels have contributed to a significant decline in oil consumption in the United States since 2006. The 93 billion liters of biofuels produced worldwide in 2009 displaced the equivalent of an estimated 68 billion liters of gasoline, equal to about 5% of world gasoline production.[17] However, the use of ethanol for fuel has had very negative impact on food market by increasing corn price making unaffordable to many poor people. Nevertheless demand for transport fuel is ever increasing, especially exponential demand of automobiles in emerging economies such as China and India. The disappearance of oil cannot to be meet by ethanol since the crop fields will have to be used for food as the most priority not for transport fuel.

Electric Vehicles: Electric Vehicles s include road and rail vehicles, surface and underwater vessels, electric aircraft and electrically-powered space vehicles.[20] Among them electric trains are commonplace since the fixed nature of a rail line makes it relatively easy to power through permanent overhead lines or electrified third rails, eliminating the need for heavy onboard batteries. Electric trains can have very good power-to-weight ratios. This allows high speed trains such as France's double-deck TGVs to operate at speeds of 320 km/h or higher.[20]

Electric vehicle were among the earliest automobiles, and before the preeminence internal combustion engines in 1900s. Robert Anderson of Scotland invented the first crude electric carriage; powered by non-rechargeable primary cells in 1840s.[21] Edison also favored earliest rechargeable batteries, the nickel-iron battery for use in electric cars. At one point in history electric vehicles out-sold gasoline-powered vehicles. In fact, in 1900, 28 percent of the cars on the road in the USA were electric. They were so popular that even President Woodrow Wilson and his secret service agents toured Washington DC in their Milburn Electrics, which covered 60–70 miles per charge.[21] Finally, the initiation of mass production of gasoline-powered vehicles by Henry Ford in 1913 reduced significantly the cost of gasoline cars as compared to electric cars and kicked off electric cars from the market.[21]

During the last few decades, environmental impact of the fossil fuel based transportation infrastructure, along with the peak oil, has led to renewed interest for electric vehicles.[23] Electric vehicles differ from fossil fuel-powered vehicles in that the electricity they consume can be generated from a wide range of sources, including fossil fuels, nuclear power, and renewable sources such as tidal power, solar power, and wind power or any combination of those. The electricity may then be stored on board the vehicle using a battery, flywheel, or super capacitors. A key advantage of hybrid or plug-in electric vehicles is regenerative braking due to their capability to recover energy normally lost during braking as electricity is stored in the on-board battery.[20]

Beside electric cars, electric buses were also introduced in many places. Chattanooga, Tennessee operates nine zero-fare electric buses, which have been in operation since 1992 and have carried 11.3 million passengers and covered a distance of 3,100,000 kilometers, They were made locally by Advanced Vehicle Systems.[24] The 2008 Beijing Olympics used a fleet of 50 electric buses, which have a range of 130 km with the air conditioning on.[25] The batteries are replaced with fully charged ones at the recharging station to allow round the clock operation of the buses.[26]

A movie made on electric vehicle in 2005-2006 titled "Who Killed the Electric Car?" was released in 2006. The film explores the roles of automobile manufacturers, oil industry, the U.S. government, and consumers, and each of their roles in limiting the deployment and adoption of this technology.[27] The electric cars produced during that time were offered in market only for a short term closed-end lease. After the lease General Motors (GMs) crushed its EV1. The lucky few who leased EV1s never wanted to give them up since the cars had great range, cost of fuel was much lower since it required no gas or oil.[27] The crushing has variously been attributed to 1) the auto industry's successful federal court challenge to California's zero-emissions vehicle mandate, 2) a federal regulation requiring GM to produce and maintain spare 3) the success of the oil and auto industries' media campaign to reduce public acceptance of electric vehicles. Following GM, others big automakers, Ford, Honda, Nissan also reprocessed and crushed most of their electric vehicles. In March 2009, however, the outgoing CEO of GM, Rick Wagoner, said the biggest mistake he ever made as chief executive was killing the EV1 car, and failing to direct more resources to electrics and hybrids after such an early lead in this technology.[29]

Tesla Motors, named after Nikola Tesla is an American company that designs, manufactures, and sells electric cars and electric vehicle and powertrain components. The Tesla Roadster introduced in July 2006, the company's first vehicle, is the first production automobile to use lithium-ion battery cells and the first production electric vehicles with a range greater than 200 miles (320 km) per charge.[30] Tesla CEO Elon Musk announced in a press release and conference call on June 12, 2014, that the company will allow its technology patents be used by anyone in good faith.[31] The reasons for this generosity attracting and motivating talented employees, as well as to accelerate the mass market advancement of electric cars for sustainable transport. In 2012, Tesla Motors began building a network of 480-volt Supercharger stations to facilitate longer distance journeys in the Model S. As of 26 September 2014, there are 200 stations operating on three continents. Eventually, all Supercharger stations are to be supplied by solar power. [32] Electric vehicles either from Tesla, or Nissan or Ford are still long way to go to pass the threshold to outpace the gasoline-power vehicle. Like iPhone, as explained in chapter 4, if Tesla were able to bypass the inflated costs arises because of Money Loop (ML) such as warranty, commission, media & marketing, its price would reach the threshold much earlier. Government policy support may help this area. As an example, in the U.S. federal tax credits of up to $7,500 and state incentives that might effectively knock another $2,500 off the amount buyers pay for the electric vehicles.[29] Now the sale of electric cars are going up eventhough oil price is low.

The engine capacities of battery operated electric vehicle are limited by the ability of batteries to store energy, as compared to conventional liquid fuels. A gallon of gasoline carries 46 Mega-joules of energy per kilogram (MJ/kg), while lithium-ion batteries can store only 0.5 MJ/kg. Improvements are possible, but the ultimate practical limit of chemical energy storage is still only about 6–9 MJ/kg.[33] According to Heinberg

"This is why we'll never see battery-powered airliners: the batteries would be way too heavy to allow planes to get off the ground."[34]

Many of the components of batteries, engines and body of the vehicles are made from byproducts of petroleum or cannot be economically produced without fossil fuel. However, widespread use of electric vehicle may slow down the pace of declination of fossil fuel and reduce carbon emission.

We are dependent on fossil fuel for almost everything is our modern life, whether staying at home or going outside. Here are some details about mainstream alternate technologies including their recent performance.

Hydroelectric: Hydroelectric power has perfect EROEI (100). Therefore, it is the largest producer of renewable power in the U.S. According to Renewable Energy Agency (IRENA), global installed capacity of hydroelectric power was around 970 GW at the end of 2011. However, it has already become saturated since it requires building dams blocking fresh water supply, which often creates huge environmental impact and therefore, it can't grow by very much in most part of the world.[8] Hydroelectric plants exist in at least 34 US states. Table 7.1 shows hydroelectric plants produces around 8% of the total electricity in 2010 which was 60.2% of the total renewable power in the U.S.[14] Hydropower is unique among other renewable power generation technologies in that it also provides other services, such as water storage, irrigation opportunities and flood control. Hydropower is a mature technology, with limited cost reduction potentials in most settings. Hydropower is produced in 150 countries, with the

Year	Hydro	Geothermal	Waste	Wood	PV	Wind	Renewable Total	US Total	% Renewable
2002	264.33	14.49	15.04	38.66	0.555	10.34	343.44	3858.45	8.90%
2003	275.81	14.24	15.81	37.53	0.534	11.19	355.29	3883.18	9.15%
2004	268.42	14.81	15.42	38.12	0.575	14.14	351.48	3970.56	8.85%
2005	270.32	14.69	15.42	38.86	0.55	17.81	357.65	4055.42	8.82%
2006	289.25	14.57	16.1	38.76	0.508	26.59	385.77	4064.7	9.49%
2007	247.51	14.64	16.52	39.01	0.612	34.45	352.75	4156.74	8.49%
2008	254.83	14.84	17.73	37.3	0.864	55.36	417.72	4119.39	10.14%
2009	273.44	15.01	18.16	36.05	1.83	74.12	419.59	3950.31	10.62%
2010	257.08	15.67	18.59	37.61	4.49	94.95	428.38	4125.06	10.38%
2011	325.07	16.7	19.79	36.95	1.81	119.75	520.07	4105.73	12.67%

Table 7.1: Distribution of Renewable Fuels used in Power Generation in USA (Billion kWh, TWh)[14]

Asia-Pacific region generating 32 percent of global hydropower in 2010. China is the largest hydroelectricity producer, with 721 Terawatt-hours (TWh) of production in 2010, representing around 17 percent of domestic electricity use. There are now three hydroelectricity plants larger than 10 GW in the world: the Three Gorges Dam in China, Itaipu Dam across the Brazil/Paraguay border and Guri Dam in Venezuela.[35]

Solar Photovoltaic: Unlike hydroelectric power, solar Photovoltaics (PV), is one of the most "democratic" renewable technologies, in that their modular size means that they are within the reach of individuals, co-operatives, small-scale businesses. A solar photovoltaic plant can be installed in large spaces, buildings and even in vehicles. A PV is an electronic device that converts sunlight directly into electricity. The initial credit of PV should go to Albert Einstein, who invented the concept of photoelectric effect in 1905, for which he received the Nobel Prize in Physics in 1921. The modern form of the solar cell was invented in 1954 at Bell Laboratories.

At the end of 2012 the photovoltaic (PV) capacity worldwide was 100,000 MW, and PV power stations are popular in Germany and Italy. Solar thermal power stations operate in the USA and Spain, and the two largest of these in the world are in California, the biggest one, 392 MW Ivanpah Solar Power Facility in San Bernardino and the second largest 354 MW SEGS power plant in the Mojave Desert.[36] India has planned to install the world's largest solar power station of capacity 750 MW on 305 hectares of land in Madhya Pradesh, expected to operate by March 2017.

The cumulative installed capacity of solar PV grew by around 70% in 2011 and it has resulted in significant price declines over recent years. As an example, the highly growing German residential systems have fallen from around USD 7/W (USD 7 000/kW) in the second quarter of 2008 to just USD 2.2/W in the second quarter of 2012. In contrast, average prices for residential systems in the United States, in the second quarter of 2012 had only fallen to USD 5.5/W.[18]

The first-generation PV systems (fully commercial) use the wafer-based crystalline silicon (c-Si) technology. Second-generation PV systems (early market deployment) are based on thin-film PV technologies. Third-generation PV systems include technologies, such as concentrating PV (CPV) and organic PV cells, which are still under demonstration or have not yet been widely commercialized.[18] It is one of the fastest-growing renewable energy technologies. As a consequence, according to IRENA crystalline silicon (c-Si) PV module prices have fallen by more than 65% over the last two years.[18] Therefore, advanced technology to more efficient use of solar power with lower cost can be achieved by concentrating solar power and limited use of photovoltaic materials such as polysilicon.[41]

Physicists claim that recent technological developments bring the cost of solar energy more in parity with that of fossil fuels. Figure 7.4 shows per watt cost for PV cells reduced from $76 in 1977 to $0.30 in 2015 and now can compete with any other energy source such as oil or natural gas and even hydro. This happened primarily due to the reduction in processing costs, the fall in polysilicon costs

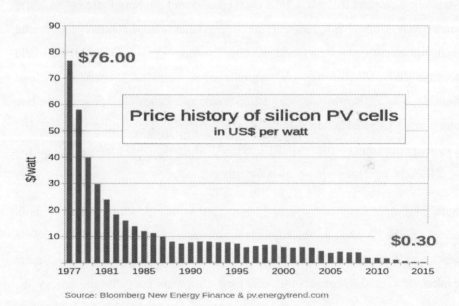

Figure 7.4: Price history of silicon PV cells since 1977[40]

and improvement in conversion efficiencies. That represents a fall of around 60 per cent in just three years.[171] Technologies such as reflector dish along with mirror and lenses to focus and intensify the sun's light can produce far more electricity at lower cost.[41] Jon Wellinghoff, chairman of Federal Energy Regulatory Commission (FERC) predicted in 2013 that solar will overtake wind in about ten years.[172] According to Deutsche Bank's analyst Vishal Shah, the cost may further down by 40% in next two years.[171] Many countries or states have introduced feed-in tariff as incentive to encourage residents install PV panels in their roof-top. As an example, in 2005, Washington state introduced a feed-in tariff of 15 ¢/kWh which increases to 54 ¢/kWh if components are manufactured in the state.[37]

The company that led the world in low cost solar energy is SunEdison, Inc., which is now the largest renewable energy company in the world. Originally this was a silicon-wafer manufacturer established in 1959 as the Monsanto Electronic Materials Company (MEMC). In 2006 it entered into the burgeoning solar wafer market, via long-term agreements to supply China-based Suntech Power and many other companies in Germany and Taiwan.[7&179] By 2007, MEMC held approximately 14% of the solar wafer market.[178] In 2009, when it acquired SunEdison LLC, North America's largest solar energy services provider, it had more than 600 worldwide patents on silicon products and processes and 300 patent applications on file.[7] In 2013, MEMC adopted its the name to SunEdison to reflect the company's focus on solar energy.[179]

SunEdision was founded by Jigar Shah in 2003 with 113,000 from line of credit on his home.[181] He introduced a new business model focusing "solar as a service" by using available technology on that time that brought mainstream capital flow in this industry but charging customers only for the energy the consumed, a very similar approach as utility companies. In his book "creating Climate Wealth" Jigar Shah describes his model as:

"I'll pay for the power plant; you just pay me every month for electricity you use"[181]

This model helped SunEdision to grow 1,000 percent per year in 2005.[181] After acquired by Monsanto Electronic Materials Company (MEMC), SunEdision became world's largest renewable energy company for developing, building, owning, and operating solar power plants and wind energy plants, in addition to manufacturing high purity silicon wafers, solar modules and solar energy systems. By October 2014, the plant began producing the world's first high-pressure fluidized bed reactor (HP-FBR) polysilicon, enabling sizeable reductions in the cost of solar energy ($0.40/W). HP-FBR is a high-purity polysilicon up to 10 times more efficiently and with 90% less energy used than non-FBR technologies.[182] In June 2015, it sold off its semiconductor business SunEdison Semiconductor to become a fully dedicated renewable-energy company.[183] Now most of the successful solar companies in the world are now following Jigar Shah's model.[181] In 2015, MIT Technology Review named SunEdison #6, and the top energy company, in its annual "50 Smartest Companies" list. The review characterized SunEdison as "Aggressively expanding its renewable energy products and building a business to provide electricity to the developing world."[180]

Concentrating Solar Power (CSP) or Concentrated Photovoltaics (CPV) is a power generation technology that uses mirrors or lenses to concentrate the sun's rays to heat a fluid and produce steam. The steam drives a turbine and generates power in the same way as conventional power plants. However, according to International Renewable Energy Agency (IRNEA), other concepts are being explored and not all future CSP plants will necessarily use a steam cycle.[42] Solar concentrators such as luminescent solar concentrators (when combined with a PV-solar cell) may be used. These are often mounted on a solar tracker in order to keep the focal point upon the cell as the sun moves across the sky that can improve efficiency of PV-solar panels drastically.[43]

A fully fossil fuel independent sustainable energy supply can be possible by using a recent advancement, called solar breeder. A solar breeder is a photovoltaic panel manufacturing plant which can be made energy-independent by using energy derived from its own roof using its own panels. Such a plant becomes not only energy self-sufficient but a major supplier of new energy, hence the name solar breeder. The reported investigation establishes certain mathematical relationships for the solar breeder which clearly indicate that a vast amount of net energy is available from such a plant for the indefinite future.[44] In 2009 the Sahara Solar Breeder Project was proposed by the Science Council of Japan as a cooperation between Japan and Algeria with the highly ambitious goal of creating hundreds of GW of capacity within 30 years.[45] This is now possible because of technological advancements in solar photovoltaic capacity along with recent progress in high-Tc superconducting cable technology. Although this project declared goal is to provide 50% of the world's electricity by 2050, using superconductors to deliver the power to distant locations.[46] However, this project could not draw interests of media and big investors. There is not enough information available about any progress of this project in the project website (http://www.ssb-foundation.com/).

A 4,000MW Ultra Mega Green Solar Power Project (UMPP) is being built near in Rajasthan, India. Upon Completion, it would be world's largest Solar Power Plant. The total cost of each phase of the project is estimated to be US$1.0 billion and the entire project is expected to be completed in 7 years.[191]

Solar Power Windows: A recent technological development enables transparent solar cells could turn windows into generators.[192] Electricity from the sunlights that hits solar cell glasses in modern buildings and even cards is a new magnificent technology and it is now ready for production.[193] The first challenge for researchers was to make the solar power windows transparent at the same time increase efficiency.[193] Oxford University researchers invented a neutral-colored, semi-transparent solar cells, called perovskite could be used in building and car windows to generate electricity with high efficiency.[192] According to an article in Computerworld, there are at least two companies who are ready to bring solar window in market.[193] One company is targeting its technology for windows that will be installed in newly constructed buildings and its technology is now 8% efficient.[194] This means 8% of all the sunlight that strikes the glass is converted into electricity. According to Suvi Sharma, CEO of Solaria:

"If you look at the glass that's manufactured worldwide today, 2% of it is used for solar panels; 80% of it is used in buildings. That's the opportunity"[194]

A second company uses a different form of transparent organic photovoltaic cell technology that is suitable for new construction, replacement windows and retrofits to existing windows. Its organic photovoltaics can vary in color and transparency, depending on the needs of the customer. The company has not released data on the efficiency of its technology.[194&193]

Wind Power: Another big renewable source of energy is wind power. Wind power is growing at the rate of 30% annually, with a worldwide installed capacity of 282,482 megawatts (MW) at the end of 2012, and is widely used in Europe, Asia, and the United States. It is the fastest growing renewable energy sectors in the world. Large wind farms consist of hundreds of individual wind turbines which are connected to the electric power transmission network. It is the conversion of wind energy into a useful form of energy, such as using wind turbines to make electrical power, windmills for mechanical power, wind pumps for water pumping or drainage, or sails to propel ships.[17] Airflows can be used to run wind turbines. Modern utility-scale wind turbines range from around 600 kW to 5 MW of rated power, although turbines with rated output of 1.5–3 MW have become the most common for commercial use.[47] The power available from the wind is a function of the cube of the wind speed, so as wind speed increases, power output increases dramatically up to the maximum output for the particular turbine.[17] Areas where winds are stronger and more constant, such as offshore and high altitude sites, are preferred locations for wind farms.

The principal determinants of the Levelised Costs of Electricity (LCOE) of wind power systems include total capital costs, wind resource quality, technical characteristics of the wind turbines, operations and maintenance costs and the discount rate. According to IRNEA, wind turbine costs in 2011 ranged from around USD 600/kW in China up to around USD 1,350/kW in developed countries. Operations and maintenance costs vary from a best practice case of around USD 0.01/kWh in the United States to a more typical USD 0.025/kWh in Europe.[18] The global long-term technical potential of wind energy is believed to be five times total current global energy production, or 40 times current electricity demand, assuming all practical barriers needed were overcome.[17]

Biomass & Biofuel: The oldest known use of renewable energy was from biomass. It is still the largest source of renewable energy in the world, especially in the developing countries. In 2010 renewable energy accounted for 17% of total energy consumption. Biomass heat accounted for 11% and hydropower 3%. Figure 7.1 shows that EROEI for biomass is very low. Biomass is biological material derived from living, or recently living organisms. It most often refers to plants or plant-derived materials which are specifically called lignocellulosic biomass. Wood remains the largest biomass energy source today. Biomass includes plant or animal matter that can be converted into fibers or other industrial chemicals, including biofuels. Industrial biomass can be grown from numerous types of plants, hemp, corn, poplar, willow, sorghum, sugarcane, bamboo, and a variety of tree species, ranging from eucalyptus to palm oil. The grain can be used for liquid transportation fuels while the straw can be burned to produce heat or electricity. Plant biomass can also be degraded from cellulose to glucose through a series of chemical treatments, and the resulting sugar can then be used as a first generation biofuel. Crops, such as corn and sugar cane, can be fermented to produce the transportation fuel, ethanol. Brazil has one of the largest renewable energy programs in the world, involving production of ethanol fuel from sugar cane, and ethanol now provides 18% of the country's automotive fuel. Ethanol fuel is also widely available in the USA.[17] Ethanol can be used as a fuel for vehicles in its pure form, but it is usually used as a gasoline additive to increase octane and improve vehicle emissions. Another form of biofuel is called biodiesel, which is made from vegetable oils, animal fats or recycled greases. It can be used as a fuel for vehicles in its pure form.

There is a great deal of research involving algal, or algae-derived, biomass due to the fact that it's a non-food resource and can be produced at rates 5 to 10 times those of other types of land-based agriculture, such as corn and soy. Once harvested, it can be fermented to produce biofuels such as ethanol, butanol and methane, as well as biodiesel and hydrogen. The biomass used for electricity generation varies by region. Feedstock costs for biomass can represent 40% to 50% of the total cost of electricity produced by biomass technologies. The lowest cost feedstock is typically agricultural residues such as straw and bagasse from sugar cane, as these can be collected at harvest. The LCOE of biomass-fired electricity generation ranges from a low of USD 0.06/kWh to a high of USD 0.29/kWh in the OECD. Where capital costs are low and low-cost feedstocks are available, bioenergy can provide competitively priced, dispatchable electricity generation with an LCOE as low as around USD 0.06/kWh. In developing countries biomass is the most available and cheapest source of energy since feedstock costs can be zero for wastes and residues, which are locally available.[18]

Geothermal: Geothermal energy is from thermal energy generated and stored in the Earth. It is cost effective, reliable, sustainable, and environmentally friendly but has historically been limited to areas near tectonic plate boundaries. Recent technological advances have dramatically expanded the range and size of viable resources, especially for applications such as home heating, opening a potential for widespread exploitation. Thermal energy is the energy that determines the temperature of matter. Earth's geothermal energy originates from the original formation of the planet (20%) and from radioactive decay of minerals (80%).[48]

The geothermal gradient, which is the difference in temperature between the core of the planet and its surface, drives a continuous conduction of thermal energy in the form of heat from the core to the surface.

The heat that is used for geothermal energy can be from deep within the Earth, all the way down to Earth's core 4,000 miles (6,400 km) down. At the core, temperatures may reach over 9,000 °F (5,000 °C). Heat conducts from the core to surrounding rock. Extremely high temperature and pressure cause some rock to melt, which is commonly known as magma. Magma convects upward since it is lighter than the solid rock. This magma then heats rock and water in the crust,

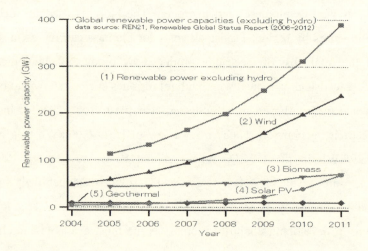

Figure 7.5: Global renewable power capacity excluding hydro[38]

sometimes up to 700 °F (371 °C).[6] The International Geothermal Association (IGA) has reported that 10,715 MW of geothermal power in 24 countries is online, which will grow to 18,500 MW by 2015. The world's largest geothermal power installation is The Geysers in California, with a rated capacity of 750 MW.[6] The Philippines follows the US as the second highest producer of geothermal power in the world, with 1,904 MW of capacity online; geothermal power makes up approximately 18% of the country's electricity generation.[49] In 2011, geothermal energy provided about 65 percent of primary energy in Iceland

and about 85% of all houses in Iceland are heated with geothermal energy.[50] Renewable energy provides almost 100 percent of electricity production in Iceland with about 75 percent coming from hydropower and 25 percent from geothermal power.[51]

Enhanced Geothermal Systems (EGS) are a new type of geothermal power technologies that do not require natural convective hydrothermal resources. The vast majority of geothermal energy within drilling reach is in dry and non-porous rock.[52] EGS technologies "enhance" and/or create geothermal resources in this "hot dry rock (HDR)" through hydraulic stimulation. EGS / HDR technologies, like hydrothermal geothermal, are expected to be baseload resources which produce power 24 hours a day like a fossil plant. Distinct from hydrothermal, HDR / EGS may be feasible anywhere in the world, depending on the economic limits of drill depth. There are HDR and EGS systems currently being developed and tested in France, Australia, Japan, Germany, the U.S. and Switzerland.[17&52] According to IRENA,

> "The role of geothermal and marine power on the 2030 horizon will be limited on a global scale and confined to regions and countries where these options can play a vital role."[39]

Hydrogen Fuel: Hydrogen fuel is could be a miracle fuel if the cost of producing hydrogen and storage become cheaper. It can be produced from water using a technology called electrolysis and contains almost three times as much energy as natural gas. It is a zero-emission fuel which uses electrochemical cells, or combustion in internal engines, to power vehicles and electric devices.[132] Hydrogen gas must be produced, and that production always requires more energy than can be Retrieved on from the gas as a fuel later on.[133] It has the problem of storage, and a new "hydrogen battery" can be used to power vehicles. Toyota is about to release its first commercial hydrogen-powered car. The car name is Mirai–a Japanese word that means future.[134] It uses a hydrogen fuel cell generate electricity instead of batteries recharges in three minutes. The engine is powered by an electric engine and has a maximum speed of 180 km/h.[134] However, producing hydrogen (H_2) from water by electrolysis from water using solar or wind-based electricity is very expensive. Currently most commercially produced hydrogen is currently made from natural gas, because the gas-reforming process is inherently more efficient and therefore almost always cheaper than electrolysis.[129] To bring hydrogen car in market, enough support infrastructure is to be built from the current very handful of filling stations.[143]

The European Commission developed a set of possible principles of Energy Policy for Europe was elaborated at the Commission's green paper A European Strategy for Sustainable, Competitive and Secure Energy on 8 March 2006. It is claimed that Europe will lead to a 'post-industrial revolution', or a low-carbon economy, in the European Union, as well as increased competition in the energy markets, improved security of supply, and improved employment prospects.[54] The Commission's proposals was approved at a meeting of the European Council in March 2007.[55] The proposal mainly set targets for reduction of greenhouse gas but also it included minimum target of using biofuel and development of a European Strategic Energy Technology Plan to develop technologies in areas including 60% share of renewable energy by 2050 and energy efficiency by 50% by 2050, energy conservation, low-energy buildings, fourth generation nuclear reactor, clean coal and carbon capture.[55]

The German energy policy was framed following the European Union proposal that required a 20% reduction of carbon dioxide emissions before the year 2020 and the consumption of renewable energies to be 20% of total EU consumption (compared to 7% in 2006).[56] Germany's renewable energy sector is among the most innovative and successful worldwide. Germany reached the EU 20 percent mark during the first half of 2011 from 6.3 percent of 2000.[57] In 2010, investments totaling 26 billion euros were made in Germany's renewable energies sector to boost up the capacity and reach the 20% EU target. It reached about 25 percent in the first half of 2012. Figure 7.6 shows share of renewable sources for electricity generation in Germany. The German renewable energy sector benefited when the Green party joined the Federal Government between 1998 and 2005. Hans-Josef Fell and Hermann Scheer the two members of the

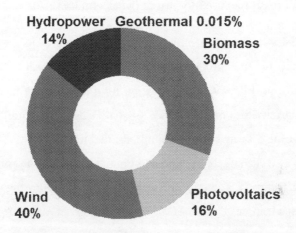

Figure 7.6: Share of Renewable Electricity Generation in Germany[58]

Green Party framed the German Renewable Energy legislation.[59] The renewable energy sector was aided especially by the Renewable Energy Sources Act that renewable energy mainly by stipulating feed-in tariffs that grid operators must pay for renewable energy fed into the power grid. People who produce renewable energy can sell their 'product' at fixed prices for a period of 20 or 15 years. This has created a surge in the production of renewable energy.[59] Energy co-operatives have been created, and efforts were made to decentralize control and profits. The large energy companies have a disproportionately small share of the renewables market. In 2012, Siemens estimated the total cost of renewable energy would come to at least €1.4 trillion (US$1.8 trillion) by 2030.[60] For the 2005–2010 period the Federal Government set aside nearly 800 million euros for scientific research in the country. The key policy document outlining the Energiewende was published by the German government in September 2010, some six months before the Fukushima nuclear accident. After the Fukushima incident, Germany decided to end of nuclear energy was set to 2022 abrogating the 2001 law to close all nuclear power plants within a period of 32 years.[59] Already most of the nuclear power plants were closed, and the existing 9 plants will close earlier than planned for, in 2022.[59] Energiewende targets a 60 percent reduction in all fossil fuel use (not just in the electricity sector) by 2050.[177]

Denmark has set a target to meet more than 50 percent of its electricity supply with renewables by 2020, 100 percent of electricity and heat by 2035, and 100 percent in transport by 2050.[53] Today wind turbines generate nearly 30 percent of Danish electricity. But of course that's not all. The Danes didn't stop with just wind. They've also been building hundreds of biogas digesters and waste-to-energy plants as well. Together, wind and biomass provide 44% of the electricity consumed by Denmark's nearly six million inhabitants. Portugal's 10 million people produced more than half their electricity in 2010 from their own indigenous renewable resources. Spain's 40 million people meet one-third of their electrical consumption from renewables. The similar other European Union members who have already achieved good progress toward renewable energy are now suggesting that Europe could move toward 100% renewable energy by 2050. Some of them such as Austria, Scotland already have set up ambitious target to reach 100 percent renewables by 2030. [53]

In her article "The Myth of Renewable Energy", Dawn Stover identifies "one big problem" regarding renewable energy.[13] The materials such photovoltaic panels, rare earth materials and ground water are not renewable. Therefore, Richard Heinberg called them as fossil fuel extenders:

> "Wind and sunlight are abundant and free, but the technology used to capture energy from these ambient sources is made from nonrenewable minerals and metals. The mining, manufacturing, and transport activities necessary for the production and installation of wind turbines and solar panels currently require oil. It may theoretically be possible to replace oil with electricity from renewables in at least some of these processes, but for the foreseeable future wind and solar technologies can best be thought of as fossil fuel extenders."[143]

Other than high purify silica wafer and rare earth metal, solar panel requires huge amount of flat glass. To manufacture one MW one MW capacity solar PV modules, 100 to 150 tons of flat glass is used in manufacturing. Low iron flat glass or float glass is manufactured from soda ash and iron free silica, all of which are highly energy intensive process.[189]

Dawn Stover estimates the American Wind Energy Association that the 5,700 turbines installed in the United States in 2009 required approximately 36,000 miles of steel rebar and 1.7 million cubic yards of concrete (enough to pave a four-foot-wide, 7,630-mile-long sidewalk).[13] She further estimates that to meet the world's total energy demands in 2030 with renewable energy alone would take an estimated 3.8 million wind turbines, 720,000 wave devices, 5,350 geothermal plants, 900 hydroelectric plants, 490,000 tidal turbines, 1.7 billion rooftop photovoltaic systems, 40,000 solar photovoltaic plants, and 49,000 concentrated solar power systems. In summary, she concludes

"[U]ntil we find a way to reduce our energy consumption and to share Earth's finite resources more equitably among nations and generations, "renewable" energy might as well be called "miscellaneous".[13]

Richard Heinberg also argues about maintaining consumption or growth and pursuing renewable energy at the same time as:

"Thus there seems to be no realistic way to bootstrap the energy transition (for example, by using the power from solar panels to build more solar panels) while continuing to provide enough energy to keep the rest of the economy expanding. In effect, to maintain growth, the energy transition would have to be subsidized by fossil fuels—which would largely defeat the purpose of the exercise."[143]

On the other hand, at the same time of reducing overall energy consumptions, we will have to build renewable energy infrastructure at a "ferocious pace"[8] during the economic lifetime of fossil fuel.

7.4 The Grid Goliath

The U.S. national electrical grid system is the largest centralized electrical distribution system in the world distributed over 2.7 million miles of power lines that carries electricity from 3,200 utility companies.[148] It connects three big interconnect-grids the Texas, Eastern and Western interconnects. There are regional nodes, which interlock the nation's grid.[169] The U.S. electric demand today is 10 percent higher than 2001, which represents an increase equal to Italy's entire annual electric use. The Energy Information Administration forecasts at least another 10 percent rise over the next fifteen years (2030).[146]

According to Forbes, this grid system is too big at the same time too vulnerable to any terrorists' attack.[169] If any of the regional nodes are knocked out by either a physical or a cyber attack, it could have a major destabilizing effect on the entire grid system. If there are multiple node outages it could be many weeks or months to bring the system back to normal because of their complexity and highly and customized designs.[169] By referring to an interview with former Federal Energy Regulatory Commission (FERC) chief Jon Wellinghoff, Forbes magazine describes the severity of such an instance of attack or outage as:

> "America would literally go dark. No phones. No money. No heat. No running water. No medicine. No police.... Congressional studies quoted by Woolsey estimate that two-thirds of the population would die of starvation, disease, exposure or violence related to social breakdown in the first twelve months alone....And to make matters worse, we would never even know what hit us, because we would have no means to investigate, to say nothing of respond. Just darkness."[169]

To protect this grid system from attack, billions of dollar investment is required that Wellinghoff describes as building a wall, which will only lead to potential attacks designing higher ladders and eventually keep on spending billions of dollars for this purpose only.[169]

Now President Obama's "Clean Power Plan" will increase the share of renewable energy from existing 13 percent to 23 percent in 2030, majority of which will come from solar and wind power plants.[147] However wind power and solar power are intermittent energy sources – they have very low average availability compared to conventional power plants and very low capacity factors that matters for a large scale grid level deployment. That is the reason, replacing natural gas will be harder, because gas-fired plants are often used to buffer the intermittency of industrial-scale wind and solar inputs to the grid.[177] To keep operational dynamics, over 99 percent of all electricity carried over the grid has to be generated at the same instant that it is consumed.[146]

According to IRNEA, Solar and Wind technologies are mature, proven technologies that have achieved grid parity in a number of markets. [18] However, Mark Mills in his Forbes article argues:

"[Y]ou need to build three wind or solar megawatts of capacity to equal the energy produced by one megawatt of turbine capacity. (Obviously the exact ratio depends on how windy or sunny the locale.) That means it is just nonsensical to claim a solar or wind plant with a capital cost per "nameplate" megawatt equal to a conventional power plant has achieved the Holy Grail of "grid parity." And even if you build extra wind and solar capacity, the extra capacity is worthless if it's not available when needed."[146]

Despite all these technologies the laws of physics matters to store electricity from of solar and wind power plans by using batteries to overcome intermittency or low availability at volumes that matter. Mark Mills explains this as:

"Elon Musk has given us a way to illustrate the challenge to store power at grid levels. The astoundingly big $5 billion Tesla battery factory under construction in Nevada, the so-called "gigafactory," is slated to produce more than all of the world's existing lithium battery factories combined. For battery cognoscenti, that represents a quantity of batteries each year that can store 30 billion watt-hours of electricity. A big number. But the United States consumes about 4,000,000 billion watt-hours a year. Thus the entire annual output of the gigafactory can store about five minutes worth of U.S. electric demand."[146]

Moreover, the lifespan of batteries is very short that is counted in years not the decades needed for grid-scale power systems.[146] That is, to keep one hour worth battery backup for the U.S. national grid system, it would require 12 years production of the gigafactory and in every few years the batteries are to be replaced–a guaranteed long term business opportunity for the battery companies such as gigafactory. Mills further adds:

"Storing electricity in expensive short-lived batteries is not a little more expensive but tens of thousands of times more expensive than storing gas in tanks or coal in piles adjacent to idle but readily available long-lived power plants."[146]

Therefore, implementing "Clean Power Plan (CPP)" in national grid system will require huge private and public investment that eventually be translated into higher utility bills to normal consumers. As happened previously, if private investors are reluctant investing in grid system, the U.S. government alone will have to bear the cost by further borrowing from the banks. As a result, electricity cost will increase and therefore, increasingly more numbers of consumers may choose to go off grid and install solar panels in their roof tops or buy electricity from shared community solar gardens or small utility-scale systems with utility off-takers or from local or regional wind farms. If this happens, economic viability of CPP will be a big challenge just because of the huge appetite of the centralized grid for investment to achieve its parity with renewable energy.

However, off-grid PV systems have traditionally used rechargeable batteries to store excess electricity. In a grid system, excess electricity can be sent to the transmission grid. The Institute for Solar Energy Supply Technology of the University of Kassel pilot-tested a combined power plant linking solar, wind, biogas and hydro storage to provide load-following power around the clock, entirely from renewable sources.[53] According to REN21, many experts disputed this view, saying that the wide range of other options to manage variability mean that high shares are possible without storage. As the report explains the views of the experts on storage that storage will indeed be needed before 2030, but for now, the immediate need can be managed with pumped hydro and gas, even up to high levels.[19] As discussed, currently adding storage system with solar and wind power, the cost will increase may seem uneconomical.[129] The cost of storage has to come down to one-tenth the cost of generation for us to use it in a big way. Referring to another expert REN21 report quotes,

> "We don't need any storage breakthroughs over the next 15–20 years, so we have something of a '15-year reprieve' from needing storage because we can accomplish grid stability with other options, foremost among them demand-response."[19]

It will take time and enormous capital to accommodate intermittent renewable energy to existing electricity grid system, where the grids are already overdue for a massive upgrade but neglected by investors. Richard Heinberg emphasizes:

> "The world may have a fairly brief window of time in which major investments in renewable energy are feasible. Beyond that point, the volatility of fossil fuel prices and declining overall societal EROEI may drain the vitality of economies to the point that financing major new projects will become ever more difficult."[8]

7.5 Green Economics Utopia

The only way to reduce energy consumption is stopping economic growth. After brining the ecological and 'peak oil' concern in the 1972 Club of Rome report "Limits to Growth", there have been two approaches tried by economists to deal with the problem of growth within capitalist framework. In one approach, ecological economist like Herman Daly and his school propose a "Steady-State

Economy", where they imagine that capitalism could be reconstructed such that it would develop qualitatively instead of growing quantitatively.[54] He suggests growth should be optional rather than built-into capitalism but market forces prevail for qualitative development.[61] He defines a steady state system as "a system that permits qualitative development but not aggregate quantitative growth."[61] Smith (2010) strongly opposes Daly's opinion and argues "capitalism cannot exist without constant revolutionizing of productive forces, without constantly expanding markets, without ever-growing consumption of resources."[62] Daly distinguishes growth and development as "growth is more of the same stuff; development is the same amount of better stuff (or at least different stuff)."[61]

Herman Daly suggests a "Steady State Economics (SSE)" where no growth but environmentally rational economy that conserves nature and resources for the benefit of future generations. SSE suggests reducing growth and consumption to save the humans by limiting the scale of "resource throughput". He defines "throughput" as "the flow beginning with raw materials inputs, followed by their conversion into commodities, and finally into waste outputs".[61] Then he explains "Once the level of resource throughput is reduced to a sustainable level, the pattern of consumption will automatically adapt."[61] For poverty alleviation he criticizes World Bank for promoting rich to grow to provide markets for the poor and to accumulate capital to invest in poor countries. Then he comments "The steady state answer is that the rich should reduce their throughput growth to free up resources and ecological space for use by the poor, while focusing their domestic efforts on development, technical and social improvements that can be freely shared with poor countries."[61] All of these are good words as our holy books teach for thousands of years but in reality, wealthy people never gave up neither their resources nor their hunger for getting more.

In another approach called "sustainable development", Paul Hawken, Lester Brown and other proponents imagined that capitalism could keep on growing in a benign way for the environment by fostering an eco-entrepreneurial-led "green industrial revolution".[62&63] Previously, in his book 'Ecological Commerce" Paul Hawken wrote "restoring the environment and making money become one and the same process."[64] In "Natural Capitalism" he extends his thoughts as argues that "Industrial capitalism...neglects to assign any value to the largest stocks of capital it employs—the natural resources and living systems, as well as the social and cultural systems that are the basis of human capital."[63] The authors say this devaluing allows for the externalization of costs onto the environment, into the future, and onto less politically powerful populations. [63&65] These costs may affect the welfare of people living in the future, as well as affecting the natural environment.[66&67] According to them "sustainable development" might work in two ways. First, as resources such as energy become scarcer and therefore more expensive, businesses will have to figure out how to be more efficient that is how to do more with less. Second, businesses will have to come up with new ideas for capital accumulation using alternate energy.[63]

The definition of 'sustainable development' has been given in the year 1987 by the World Commission of Environment and Development of the United Nations: "A development that meets the needs of the present without compromising the

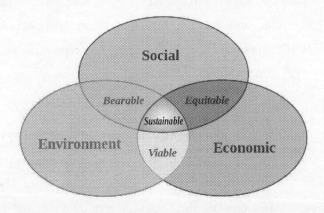

Figure 7.7: Three Pillars of Sustainable Economy[71]

ability of future generations to meet their own needs."[68] At the 2005 World Summit it was noted that this requires the reconciliation of environmental, social and economic demands - the "three pillars" of sustainability.[69] This view has been expressed as an illustration using three overlapping ellipses indicating that the three pillars of sustainability are not mutually exclusive and can be mutually reinforcing as shown in Figure 7.7.[71] The UN Report of the World Commission on Environment and Development emphasizes "The goals of economic and social development must be defined in terms of sustainability in all countries - developed or developing, market-oriented or centrally planned."[69] This approach argues for a more enlightened globalization to reach sustainability and to resolve environmental degradation.[1]

According to World Wide Fund for Nature (WWF) "Living Planet Report 2012", "it is taking 1.5 years for the Earth to fully regenerate the renewable resources that people are using in a single year. Instead of living off the interest, we are eating into our natural capital."[72] WWF further calculates that if current trends continue, and no ecological 'tipping points' are reached in the meantime, this overshoot will reach 100 percent in the 2030s, meaning we would need two planet Earths to sustain our population and consumption levels.[72] The report concludes "We can reduce our footprint by producing more with less, and consuming better, wiser and less."[72] This view is completely opposite to neo-classical values of economics either capitalists or non-capitalists, which are the foundations for the commodification of nature.[1]

Frank Rotering (2009) develops an economic model called Economics of Needs & Limits (ENL) not ignoring the existence of our capitalist economy but gradually shifting from there to a sustainable well-being through a conscious era. He shows that a sustainable trajectory of our economy cannot be achieved through policy initiatives within the present economic order, but will instead require its revolutionary transformation. As he describes

"Our economies are inherently unsustainable that moderate reforms cannot resolve our predicament. Instead, we must radically transform our economic systems so that they operate on an entirely different set of principles."[73]

Although there is no guideline from economists on how the revolution will happen but most of the economists agree that to save our earth from the potential disasters and crises poised by traditional economic theories, we have to limit our economic activities within the carrying capacity of nature.

Outside mainstream economic model there are heterogeneous approaches in economic theories describing 'sustainable economics'. The International Chamber of Commerce (ICC) representing global business defines green economy as "an economy in which economic growth and environmental responsibility work together in a mutually reinforcing fashion while supporting progress on social development".[74] In 2012, the ICC published the Green Economy Roadmap that highlights the essential role of business in bringing solutions to common global challenges. It addresses the four categories of significant and increasing problems: eco, intellectual, political and moral.[74]

Green economy is a sustainable development approach that includes green energy generation based on renewable energy to substitute for fossil fuels and energy conservation for efficient energy use. Although much of the renewable energy can be produced locally but many of the components used for renewable energy cannot be produced locally. Because the market failure related to environmental and climate protection as a result of external costs, high future commercial rates and associated high initial costs for research, development, and marketing of green energy sources and green products prevents firms from being voluntarily interested in reducing environment-unfriendly activities.[74] Therefore, the green economy may need government subsidies as market incentives to motivate firms to invest and produce green products and services. The German Renewable Energy Act, legislations of many other member states of the

European Union and the American Recovery and Reinvestment Act of 2009, all provide such market incentives.[70]

On the other hand, Kennet and Heinemann (2006) argue against "sustainable development" approach as "Acknowledging that many nation states are weaker than global corporations, sustainable development argues in favor of benevolent corporations being the agents of global problem solving."[1] They regard corporations as agents of hegemony[75], being undemocratic, unelected, uniform, lacking in transparency and being the fundamental causes of the problem. They argue against dogma and externally imposed systems, believing that local economic control, access, survivability and diversity are key. Instead they advocates "Green Economics" that tells about promoting local production for local needs, and reusing, reducing, repairing and possibly recycling, rather than global expansion of corporations.[1]

The concept of 'Green Economics' was first captured by Carson (1962) as in his book Silent Spring he criticized the chemical industry.[76] Some economists view Green Economics as a branch or subfield of more established schools. According to Kennet & Heinemann (2006) classical economic approach originally developed by Smith (1976) was broad, diverse and philosophical in nature. Basic fundamental principles have been developed out of it to form the narrower and more conservative foundation of economics as a new science, which tends to misrepresent the original classical texts.[1] In classical economics traditional land is generalized to natural capital and has some attributes in common with labor and physical capital.[70]

Green Economics is completely different approach from Green Economy since it seeks to reconnect the values and costs of transactions with the natural world and with social structures by enhancing local economy supporting bio-regional developments, democracy and access for all.[1] Kennet and Heinemann (2006) define 'Green Economics' as:

"Green Economics positions economics within a very long-term, earth-wide, holistic context of reality as a part of nature. It also incorporates and celebrates 'difference', diversity, equity and inclusiveness within its concepts of society and community. Its philosophy is to manage economics for nature as usual, rather than to manage the environment for business as usual."[1]

The above definition is taking a holistic approach blended with any number of other theories such as welfare economics, feminist economics, eco-feminism, eco-socialism, environmental economics and ecological economics.[1] Therefore, Green Economics is loosely defined as any theory of economics by which an economy is considered to be component of the ecosystem in which it resides.[70] 'Green Economics' school of thought that brings to economics the core drivers of ecology, equity, social and environmental justice.[70] It claims "to replace the axis of the dualism of the worker versus the owner of production with concern for people, society, non-human species, nature and the biosphere as a holistic whole, life-world."[1] They describe "Green Economics strongly advocates the need for each generation to leave behind an adequate bundle of resources and a habitable planet."[1] It can be inferred that there will be full employment within the ecosocialist system of 'Green Economics'. The effect of poverty is increase in food and commodity prices that are addressed by defending local food sovereignty and creating sustainable agro-ecosystems.[1]

The solutions of the economic problems we are facing now have been largely caused by the industrial transformation require a switch from fossil fuel to alternate energy sources. Gerhard Schick, a Green Party representative in German parliament criticizes 'Green Economics' for its 'highly ecological basis' for our 'highly problematic economic system'.[77] Green Economics is an absolute detachment from existing growth centric capitalist economy.[77] However, he supports the main idea is to change our economy to live within the earth's environmental budget.[77]

There are lots of similarities between Herman Daly's 'steady-state economics (SSE)' and green economics such as no growth but environmentally rational economy that conserves nature and resources for the benefit of future generations except SSE depends on some market magic to achieve its goal. Smith (2010) argues that however market-driven economic development has big consequences especially overconsumption and environmental destruction.[62] In his another article he argues "We can't shop our way to sustainability because the problems we face cannot be solved by individual choices in the marketplace."[78] The question arises, who will control the throughput of the raw materials supply? Daly's answer is that the government or "some democratically elected body" should set "controls" or "quotas" on consumption of particular resources.[61&62] Smith argues "under capitalism that just means recession, unemployment, falling revenues, or worse."[62] No government will do that since there is no public support out there for a capitalist steady-state economy. As described in chapter 4, capitalists control supply side economics, not the government. If government dictates the throughput, capitalism will fall down from "free market" ride. Smith (2010) concludes

> "[E]cological economists should abandon the fantasy of a steady-state capitalism and get on with the project figuring out what a post–capitalist economic democracy could look like."[62]

Nevertheless, according to the definitions, 'Green and mainstream neoclassical economics are playing their theoretical games in two different fields. As an example, 'Green Economics' appears to be completely ignorant about the forthcoming crisis of 'peak oil' or fossil fuel depletion. Neoclassical economics kicks the 'peak oil' ball but 'Green Economics' does not see that within its boundary. Although Green Economics does not address the issues of 'peak oil' directly but emphasis on replacement of nonrenewable energy sources with renewable energy sources is sought in this model. The renewable energy can replace a very small part of the world's energy requirement now and after 'peak oil' the global economy will continue to shrink and there will be devastating long-term consequences. Similar to ecosocialist system, 'Green Economics' addresses the climate and global warming issues by development of clean energy sources and drastic and enforceable reduction in the emission of greenhouse gas through gradually replacing production and consumption patterns by sustainable goods and green architecture. Again, this is a hypothetical model. A realistic model will require more conceptual groundwork as discussed in the next chapter. The literatures in 'Green Economics' describes a nature bound utopia economy and emphasis on how a green world can be kept green but ignore the question how is to take the existing economy to 'green' economy.

Frank Rotering (2009) critically analyzes the few other alternatives of his model aside from Green Economics and 'Steady State Economics' and groups them into three categories: green reformism, spontaneous change, and political revolution.[73] According to him, 'green reformism' is sometime misinterpreted as a version of 'Green Economics' although they are completely different concepts. He further argues this:

"If green reformism has a bible, it is Natural Capitalism. This book's core message is that the power of capitalist markets can dramatically increase resource productivity, thus allowing growth to continue indefinitely without causing excessive ecological damage. This mean, that the system can re-orient capital, its defining component, to embrace natural sources and sinks. This is impossible because it would require capitalism to alter its essential nature; in effect rendering itself obsolete....The goal isn't progressive policy within the prevailing order, but a sharp break with this order."[73]

The proposers of 'spontaneous change' like Bill McKibben (2011) believe that a change will emerge through the leadership of millions of people creating new cultural and institutional reality from the bottom up."[79] Rotering argues

"They lack an independent logic to guide the massive economic change they know is required....They laud this bottom-up approach as a virtue of democracy and community, but it is instead an alarming dereliction of intellectual leadership."[73]

Instead, Rotering proposes strategy for economic change consists of three steps: First, acknowledge the realities of humankind and capitalism, thus placing our actions on a sound empirical foundation. Second, emancipate ourselves conceptually from capitalism's grasp through a new guiding logic. Third, vigorously apply this logic in order to revolutionize the economy.[73] He concludes his arguments as

"If localization is an essential aspect of humankind's future, this formation will arise organically from the change process suggested above. As a general statement, we must remain agnostic about the structure of future economies. Our task is not to find or envision a solution, but to organically create one."[73]

7.6 Carbon Capitalisation

Samuelson proposed that atmosphere is an international public good since it has two properties: non-rivalry and non-excludability.[66] Paul Hawken's concept of "Ecological Commerce" or "Natural Capitalism" says there must be a cost for natural resource that industries externalize onto the environment.[46&49] These external costs can be estimated and converted in a common (monetary) unit and then be added to the private costs that the emitter faces.[63&82] This has been discussed in "Climate Change 1995: Economic and Social Dimensions of Climate Change" report of Intergovernmental Panel on Climate Change (IPCC), published in 1997.[81] According to this report

"Because the costs of taking action today are borne by the current generation, whereas the benefits that accrue will be felt possibly hundreds of years in the future, the world community is now faced with issues of intergenerational equity on an unprecedented scale."[81]

Here Figure 7.8 gives an idea about how stabilizing the atmospheric concentration of carbon dioxide at a constant level would require carbon dioxide

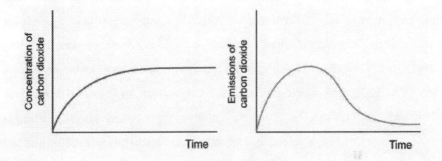

Figure 7.8a Concentration of CO_2, 7.8b Elimination of CO_2 emission required[83]

emissions to be effectively eliminated (Figure 7.8b). According to Helm (2005)

"These changes will be costly, and a natural way to make the transition to a more sustainable economy is to use the price mechanism and markets. Economic instruments, correcting for the market failures, are an obvious route forward for environmental policy, harnessing the market to deliver the economic transformation required."[84]

Heinberg argues about this market approach as:

"One of the fundamental problems with markets, acknowledged by nearly all economists, is the tendency for businesses to externalize costs."[85]

All the debates around will need to transform current modes of capitalism into a new form or something beyond capitalism.

Looking back to history the climate change issues were pointed out in Arrhenius (1896) or earlier scientific studies. According to Oppenheimer (2004)

"But it was not until the mid-1970s that a broader expert community, including policy-makers, began to focus on the questions of whether, when and how to limit warming."[86]

IPCC was formed by the United Nations Environment Programme (UNEP) and the World Meteorological Organization (WMO) in 1988. In the same year, conference held in Toronto recommended that by 2005, industrialized countries should reduce their carbon dioxide emissions by 20 percent, compared to 1988 levels.[86] In 1992 The UN Conference on the Environment and Development was held in Rio de Janeiro, where a Framework Convention on Climate Change was established. In 1995, specific targets on emissions were outlined in Berlin, which led formulation of the Kyoto Protocol in Kyoto Japan in 1997, in which the parties agreed to the broad outlines of emissions targets.[87] The Kyoto Protocol urged the industrialized countries to cut carbon emissions by an average of 5.2 percent below 1990 levels by 2008-2012. There were 192 countries present at the conference, only 30 nations produced 90% of the world's emission.[88]

Smith (2011) points out that the voluntary approach embodied in the 1997 Kyoto Protocols, was a failure.[78] He explains

"Virtually no country honestly lived up to its promises. For example, Japan, the strongest promoter of the Kyoto Protocol, promised to reduce emissions 6 percent below 1990 levels by 2008. Instead, by 2009 Japan's emissions exceeded its 1990 levels by 9 percent. Most of the rest of the world did much worse than that. Emissions skyrocketed."[78&88]

The U.S. was accounted for 36% of global emissions in 1990. The U.S. signed the Protocol, but did not ratify it. Therefore, even though the Clinton administration signed the treaty,[89] it remained only a symbolic act and was never submitted to the Senate for ratification. After being elected as president in 2000, George W. Bush opposed the Kyoto treaty, because according to him "it exempts 80% of the world, including major population centers such as China and India, from compliance, and would cause serious harm to the US economy".[90] In 2002 Russia and Canada ratify the Kyoto Protocol bringing the treaty into effect on 16 February 2005.

In 2006 China's 2006 CO2 emissions surpassed those of the USA by 8%. On that time, global CO2 emissions from fossil fuel use increased by about 2.6%, mainly due to a 4.5% increase in global coal consumption, of which China contributed more than two-third.[91] Smith (2011) points out

"By 2006, scientists reported that global emissions were then rising four times faster than they were a decade earlier. Thirteen of the 15 original EU signers of the accords increased their emissions, many sharply. Germany did better, almost meeting its target, but only because it incorporated East Germany and thus bettered its average by closing down dirty, inefficient communist-era plants. The U.K. also did better but only because North Sea gas discoveries enabled it to close coal mines and replace coal-fired power with gas – a situation that is unlikely to last because North Sea gas peaked in 1999 and will be two-thirds gone by 2015."[78&92]

In the wake of Kyoto's failures, on 16 February 2007, 'Washington Declaration', heads of governments from Canada, France, Germany, Italy, Japan, Russia, the United Kingdom, the United States, Brazil, China, India, Mexico and South Africa agreed in principle on the outline of a successor to the Kyoto Protocol called "cap and trade" system.[78] The key energy proposal of European Union in 2007 includes a cut of at least 20% in greenhouse gas emissions from all primary energy sources by 2020 (compared to 1990 levels), while pushing for an international agreement to succeed the Kyoto Protocol aimed at achieving a 30% cut by all developed nations by 2020.[54] A cut of up to 95% in carbon emissions from primary energy sources by 2050, compared to 1990 levels.[92] The idea is under this scheme, governments or intergovernmental bodies set an overall legal limit on CO2 emissions in a certain time period and then grant industries a certain number of permits to pollute. Smith (2011) explains

"Permits could be bought, sold, traded, or banked for the future…..Thus efficient plants would profit from clean technology by trading their permits to the polluters."[78]

It sets legal limits for emissions reductions, letting the market price of tradable carbon allowances vary. The proponents of 'cap and trade' envision that permit price will rise because of scarcity, then fossil fuel costs will exceed renewable energy prices and thus fossil fuels use will be phased out.[78] A declining cap gives allowance and flexibility for reduction emission targets. However, a sudden lowering of the cap may prove detrimental to economies and a gradual lowering of the cap may risk future environmental damage.[67]

Canada was committed to cutting its greenhouse emissions to 6% below 1990 levels by 2012, but in 2009 emissions were 17% higher than in 1990.[94&95] The Canadian government announced its withdrawal from the Kyoto Protocol, which was allowed at any time three years after ratification otherwise Canadian government would have to pay "enormous financial penalties".[95] In 2011, Canada, Japan and Russia stated that they would not take on further Kyoto targets.[94] Canada's then environment minister Peter Kent said that signing Kyoto was one of the previous government's biggest blunders. He explains this

"To meet the targets under Kyoto for 2012 would be the equivalent of either removing every car, truck, ATV, tractor, ambulance, police car and vehicle of every kind from Canadian roads or closing down the entire farming and agriculture sector and cutting heat to every home, office, hospital, factory and building in Canada."[94]

According to the World Resources Institute, by 2007 some 65% of the companies participating in the European trading system were making investment decisions based on having a carbon price.[88] In anticipation of the United States joining Europe and other countries around the world to create a market that would reduce the emission of greenhouse gases Chicago Climate Exchange

(CCX) was set up in 2000. It operated North America's largest comprehensive cap and trade program from 2003 to 2010. According Fox News "which was envisioned to be the key player in the trillion-dollar "cap and trade" market"[97] After win, Obama administration proposed a bill that would give emission targets to factories, utilities and other businesses. Those that emitted less fewer regulated gases than their target could sell the "excess" to someone who was above target.[97] Each year, the target would be reset lower. Although the U.S. House of Representatives passed the bill but unfortunately, it was not passed in the senate. Following this, in 2010 CCX ceased trading.[97] On August 3, 2015 President Obama declared "Clean Power Plan" to reduce national electricity sector emissions by an estimated 32 percent below 2005 levels by 2030, while the power plants account for nearly 40 percent of U.S. carbon dioxide emissions.[147]

Carbon Trade Watch describes a major drawback of 'cap and trade' as "The "cap" has too many holes and sometimes caps nothing. The cap is only as tight as the least stringent part of the system. This is because permits are sold by those with a surplus, and the cheapest way to produce a surplus is to be given too many permits in the first place."[96] This system allowed the surplus holders make wind-fall money. In December 2010, New York Times reports "it is becoming clear that system has so far produced little noticeable benefit to the climate-but generated a multibillion-dollar windfall for some of the Continent's biggest polluters."[98] Smith (2011) describes "As governments caved, emissions soared, and the profits went to the polluters and the traders."[78] Lohmann (2009) points out that emissions trading schemes create new uncertainties and risks, which can be commoditized by means of derivatives, thereby creating a new speculative market.[99] Steffen Bohm and others argue

"Carbon market serve as creative new modes of accumulation, but are unlikely to transform capitalist dynamics in ways that might foster a more sustainable global economy."[100]

Another criticism of carbon trading is that carbon trading may become a form of colonialism, where rich countries maintain their levels of consumption while getting credit for carbon savings in inefficient industrial projects since they can afford it.[94] The big oil companies such as British Petroleum, Shell Oil, Chevron sold off their solar power ventures and ramped up fossil-fuel exploration, including tar sands and hydraulic fracking.[101] The poor nations may find that they cannot afford the permits necessary for developing an industrial infrastructure, thus inhibiting these countries economic development. On the other hand, in the developing countries where monitoring of carbon trading is difficult, this approach may promote fraudulent practices. As an example, in China some companies started artificial production of greenhouse gases with sole purpose of their recycling and gaining carbon credits.[102] Similar practices happened in India. The earned credits were then sold to companies in US and Europe.[103] The Critics of carbon trading, such as Carbon Trade Watch argues

"It distracts attention from the wider, systemic changes and collective political action that needs to be taken to tackle climate change."[104]

There is another initiative called 'carbon offsets' taken by the UN. This is created to supposedly compensate for continued pollution in industrialized countries in the North. It generates "credits" which permit pollution over and above this limit. The UN's Clean Development Mechanism (CDM) is the largest offsetting scheme with almost 1,800 registered projects in developing countries in September 2009, and over 2,600 further projects awaiting approval. Based on current prices, the credits generated by approved schemes will be worth around $35 billion by 2012.[105] Carbon Trade Watch (CTW) points out that offsetting does not reduce emissions at source, but allows companies and governments in the North that have the historical responsibility to clean up the atmosphere to buy credits from projects in the South by making dubious "equivalences" between very different economic and industrial practices.[105] They also describe

"Offsetting rests on "additionally" claims about what "would otherwise have happened," offering polluting companies and financial consultancies the opportunity to turn stories of an unknowable future into bankable carbon credits. The net result for the climate is that offsetting tends to increase rather than reduce greenhouse gas emissions."[105]

As of September 2009, three-quarters of the offset credits issued were manufactured by large firms making minor technical adjustments at a few industrial installations to eliminate HFCs (refrigerant gases) and N_2O. It is estimated that a straightforward subsidy to regulate HFC emissions would have cost less than 100 million – yet, by 2012, up to 4.7 billion in carbon credits will have been generated by such projects. In a memorandum to the Government of India in November 2009, Joint statement of Indian Climate Justice and Social Movements says "Carbon offsets perpetuate elite consumption in the misplaced hope that it can be compensated for. CDM in India is dominated by polluting industries that continue to harm communities and ecosystems, emit toxic fly ash and carbon, pollute rivers and underground aquifers. Corporations with bad environmental track records earn huge money through flimsy, non-verifiable and mostly false claims of emissions reductions."[105] Now putting 'cap and trade' and offsetting together, CTW argues "Offsets burst the cap" as

"While cap and trade in theory limits the availability of pollution permits, offset projects are a license to print new ones. When the two systems are brought together, they tend to undermine each other – since one applies a cap and the other lifts it."[105]

After failure of cap and trade and carbon offsets, James Hansen, the prominent climate scientist who headed the NASA Goddard Institute for Space Studies argued for a simpler, more transparent direct approach a flat carbon tax, which require no more lobbying. In James Hansen's words:

"All sweet deals will be wiped off the books by a uniform carbon fee at the sources, which will affect all fossil fuel uses."[106]

His proposal entitled "fee and dividend" tells that a gradually rising tax on carbon would be imposed and collected at the "port of entry" for fossil fuels (including oil, gas and coal). The fees, expressed in a uniform cost per ton of CO_2, would be returned to the public in the form of dividends.[88]

The carbon tax was first introduced in Finland in 1990 and many other developed countries.[78] Both the approaches, carbon taxes and cap and trade, adopt classical economists' assumption that if the market is transparent and consumers have full information for making rational choices and in turn, those marketplace decisions will encourage ecologically favorable production. In reality, the market-driven growth is taking us toward collapse. A carbon tax is an indirect tax that sets a price for carbon dioxide emissions. According to Arthur Pigou, pollution can be considered a negative externality, a negative effect on a party not directly involved in a transaction, which results in a market failure.[107] To confront parties with the issue, Pigou proposed taxing the goods (in this case hydrocarbon fuels), which was the source of the negative externality (carbon dioxide) thereby internalizing the costs associated with the goods' production to society.[107&108] Heinberg explains

"One strategy is to collect "Pigovian" taxes from businesses equal in amount to their negative, externalized costs to society. Another solution is to define property rights more carefully (e.g., the right of residents in a community to clean air and water) so that efforts to remedy violations of those rights carry legal weight."[34]

According to Krugman, both the approaches, carbon trade and "cap and trade" ultimately produce the same result. "The only difference is the nature of uncertainty over the aggregate outcome," as he explains

"If you use a tax, you know what the price of emissions will be but you don't know the quantity of emissions; if you use a cap, you know the quantity but not the price."[89]

Ultimately, Krugman favors cap and trade because it is

"[T]he only form of action against greenhouse gas emissions we have any chance of taking before catastrophe becomes inevitable."[88&109]

Likewise financial innovations, a carbon cap may open the system wide to gaming by industry and traders, where the "trade" component does not require any emissions reductions. A technological transition would require scrapping the technology and using a different one. Therefore, the immediate impact of emission cap would be production reduction, unemployment and eventually foreclosure of industries.[96] This is acceptable neither to investors nor to the workers. Eventually, businesses outside core economics, such as bureaucracy, lobbying, lawsuits become lucrative out of carbon trading than pursuing for energy efficiency or emission control.

Finally, on December 12, 2015, representatives of 195 countries reached to an "historic" "break-through" agreement, that commits "to hold the increase in the global average temperature to well below 2^0C above pre-industrial levels and to pursue efforts to limit the temperature increase to 1.5^0C."[174] Will this new deal solve global warming problem? New York Times explains:

"At best, scientists who have analyzed it say, it will cut global greenhouse gas emissions by about half enough as is necessary to stave off an increase in atmospheric temperatures of 2 degrees Celsius. That is the point at which, scientific studies have concluded, the world will be locked into a future of devastating consequences, including rising sea levels, severe droughts and flooding, widespread food and water shortages and more destructive storms."[175]

The implicit assumption of any climate protection proposal is that technology will keep on advancing toward energy efficiency or emission efficiency. If this were possible, the best place in the world would be the developed countries such as Germany, Japan or USA where all top energy research centers are located. In reality, it cannot happen in this way. Environmental groups such as the Corner House have argued that the market will choose the easiest means to save a given quantity of carbon in the short term, which may be different to the pathway required to obtain sustained and sizable reductions over a longer period, and so a market-led approach is likely to reinforce technological lock-in.[75]

7.7 Green New Deal was Flipped

The industrial capitalism was developed two hundred years back during industrial revolution. It prompted supply side classical economics that remained unchallenged for a long time until Keynes (1936) introduced demand-side revolution following the Great Depression. In the early to mid-1930s President Franklin D. Roosevelt, seeking to pull the US economy out of The Great Depression, introduced a series of economic programs which are collectively referred to as The New Deal.[110] It focused heavily on fiscal stimulus in order to help the economy escape what John Maynard Keynes called the 'paradox of thrift'.[111] Keynesian economics lost ground when demand-side management resulted in high public debt, inflationary problems, and poor growth rates.

In her article "A Tale of Two Crises: What the Global Financial Crisis Means for the Global Environmental Crisis" Tienhara argues

"While Keynes was preoccupied with the 'paradox of thrift', some commentators have suggested that in light of recent events perhaps there should be more attention given to the "paradox of gluttony" put forth by Hyman Minsky."[111]

Cooper (2008) explains "The paradox of gluttony" as it occurs when "higher borrowing produces higher profits, thereby ratifying the decision to borrow and spend more".[112] Tienhara explains the root of financial crisis and environmental crisis is the same as:

"It leads to a self-reinforcing cycle of economic expansion through debt creation. This cycle has serious consequences, not only for the global economy, but also for the global environment."[111]

Following the green capitalism concepts, environmental movement geared up in many countries. As an example, Smith (2011) further describes

"The "sustainable" "green" "natural" capitalism movement took off in the 1980s and 90s: Organic farming came into the mainstream and whole foods became the fastest growing sector of the grocery industry. Green businesses sprouted up in every sector from renewable energy to organic cottons to eco-travel. Stores added green products in every aisle…mutual funds looked to fund renewable energy……Even big corporations like 3M and Wal-Mart eventually embraced green 'business practices' such as cutting waste, recycling, producing and adopting less toxic products."[78]

Unfortunately, in his "The green capitalist god that failed"[78] Smith (2011) describes that the enthusiasm for 'sustainable economy' could not sustain as profit making got precedence over 'saving the world'. We see now that instead of producing products in environment friendly way, capitalists rather prefer 'Greenwashing', in which green marketing is deceptively used to promote the perception that their products, aims and policies are environmentally friendly.[80]

The United Nation's Intergovernmental Panel on Climate Change (IPCC) defines social cost of carbon (SCC) as the marginal cost of emitting one extra ton of carbon (as carbon dioxide) at any point in time. If SCC estimates were complete and markets were perfect, a carbon tax should be set equal to the SCC. Emission permits would also have a value equal to the SCC. In reality, however, markets are not perfect, and SCC estimates are not complete.[81] Although we cannot measure SCC of carbon in an imperfect market but we may measure the impact of carbon tax on consumption. According to a Cambridge University research paper, in most instances, firms pass the costs of a carbon price onto consumers. However, as poor consumers spend a greater proportion of their income on energy-intensive goods and fuel, cost increases in energy tend to impact the poor worse than the rich.[113]

Let an imperfect market is modeled as two layer DMM for a carbon product (say, gasoline) as shown in Figure 7.9, where M2 represents the upper layer Market Energy State (MES) (rich people) and M1 represents the lower layer MES (poor people). The corresponding demand and supply curves are shown as D_2D_2' and S_2S_2' for M2 and D_1D_1' and S_1S_1' for M1 that are in equilibrium at price level p. There is a new equilibrium price p', when carbon tax is imposed. However, this new price does not decrease in consumption in M2 as they spend a

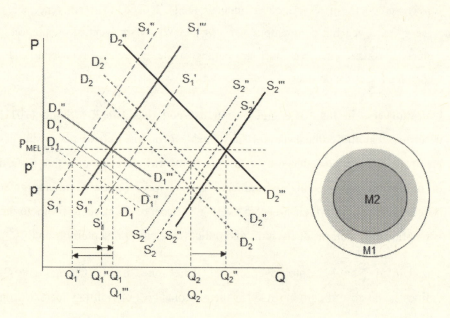

Figure 7.9: Impact of carbon tax in a two layer DMM

very insignificant portion of their income on carbon products or they have enough bargaining power to get a wage raise. The adjusted demand and supply curves in M2 after the price rise are shown as $D_2'D2''$ and $S_2'S_2''$. On the other hand, to comply with the new equilibrium price, the supply curve in M1 moves leftward from S_1S_1' to $S_1'S_1''$ and consumption of carbon products in M1 will decrease from Q_1 to Q_1'. Therefore, if carbon tax reduced emission, poor people would have to bear the cost, which is not good for economy and politically not acceptable. Therefore, in reality, to relieve this situation, central bank lowers interest rates so that the poor people in M1 can hold their consumption close totheir current level, economy is saved and politicians can save their back. This is shown in Figure 7.9 by moving the demand curve rightward from D_1D_1' to $D_1'D_1''$ where corresponding net reduction of consumption from original Q_1 to Q_1''. This also can be seen as increases in quantity consumption from Q_1' to Q_1'' based on debt.

On the other hand, lowering interest rate is an incentive for existing Money Loop (ML), which reinforces existing Market Energy Loop (MEL) as shown in Figure 4.15. The effect of MEL is reflected as rightward shift of demand curve from $D_2'D_2''$ to $D''D_2'''$, which increases price level from p' to P_{MEL} and consumption from Q_2' to Q_2''. It is also increases Border Propensity of Consumption (BPC) based on debt following Minsky's cycle of debts, hedge, speculation and Ponzi until reaches Minsky Moment (Chapter 4). This situation is called as Minsky's "paradox of gluttony".[112] In this way, the economy creates money through more production and more consumption but at the same time run the risk of being collapsed. As the cycle progresses, interest rate of lending continues to be low and flexible. The BPC in M1 may also increase from Q_1'' to Q_1''' riding over debt, particularly in the border area as shown as the shaded area within M1. And to be worse, every debt servicing is energy intensive.[66] The part where quantity consumption does not increase since the people cannot afford debt or Price

Pressure as shown as the non-shaded area of M1 is Residual Market Energy State (RMS), where the consumption reduces because of carbon tax.

The above analysis shows that on one hand, if a government imposes carbon tax, in response central bank has to cut interest rate to keep up the level of consumption (or production). Smith (2011) argues

"This means the carbon tax strategy to stop global warming is a non-starter. And without green taxes, the entire green capitalist project collapses."[78]

A more realistic and comprehensive solution is proposed by 'The Green New Deal Group (GND group)' in 2007 of NEF (the New Economics Foundation) and United Nations Environment Program (UNEP) in 2009[114] called "Green New Deal (GND)" following the New Deal (ND) program proposed by President Roosevelt in 1930s to revive the U.S. economy from 'The Great Depression'. Likewise ND, GND is a package of policy proposals that not only addresses looming ecological crisis but also address financial crisis, namely 'triple crunch' economic problem, which is a combination of a credit-fuelled financial crisis, accelerating climate change and soaring energy prices underpinned by an encroaching peak in oil production.[115] In the context of ecological crisis, the GND mainly focuses on policies and financing of carbon reduction solutions including rising carbon taxes, increasing prices on traded carbon for reducing carbon emissions, and increasing investments in energy infrastructure.[116]

UNEP (2009) has argued that the global financial crisis provides an opportunity for broad, neutral and equitable tax reform, such that the tax burden is shifted away from economic 'good' such as jobs, income, fuel efficient vehicles and other activities providing environmental and social benefits, to economic 'bad' such as carbon, pollution and dirty and inefficient vehicles.[115] By following Keynesian school of thought, the ND programs include several sets of stimulus during the crisis when the economy suffers from lack of demand. Following the 2007-2008 financial crisis that began in 2006, the U.S. government bailed out trillions of dollars to banks and auto-industries to stimulate the economy. In this context, the US secretary-general Ban Ki-moon and former US vice-president Al Gore warns as:

"continuing to pour trillions of dollars into carbon-based infrastructure and fossil-fuel subsidies would be like investing in subprime real estate all over again".[117]

Even if there is stimulus package to improve energy efficiency as happened during 2008 financial crisis, the Big Three automakers received funding for a $25 billion government loan to help them re-tool their factories to meet new fuel-efficiency standards of at least 35 mpg-US (6.7 L/100 km; 42 mpg-imp) by 2020,[184] the new volume of vehicles will generate more carbon emission. As Tienhaara (2009) argues:

"If 30 percent of a stimulus package goes to improving energy efficiency in buildings but 70 percent goes to large infrastructure projects such as coal-fired power stations, is it really possible to call it 'green' stimulus? Or is this instead another example of 'greenwash'?"[111]

Chinese green programs, which has been lauded for its high proportion of green programs; here stimulus money has been used to boost car sales, which has helped China overtake the US as the world's biggest automobile market.[118] There has also been a surge of spending on energy-intensive cement and steel infrastructure projects.[119] The only reason is that politicians and economists cannot give up the idea of economic growth. Australian Prime Minister Kevin Rudd has acknowledged that the global recession has made it harder to get his emission trading scheme passed through parliament.[120] At a Senate Hearing Meeting on the scheme, National Party Senator Ron Boswell accused the country's leading climate scientists of living in "a Pollyanna world", arguing that deep cuts in greenhouse gas emissions was simply not practical given the financial crisis.[121] The Green New Group describes that questioning the primacy of the growth imperative

"[R]emains an economic heresy, punishable by excommunication from the company of the professional commentariat".[111&122]

Likewise the ND, the GND group proposes two main public investment strands of GND. "First, it outlines a structural transformation of the regulation of national and international financial systems, and major changes to taxation systems. And, second, it calls for a sustained program to invest in and deploy energy conservation and renewable energies, coupled with effective demand management."[115] Gerhard Schick (2010), financial policy spokesman of the Green Party and a member of the German Parliament identifies that there are three pillars of 'The Green New Deal':[77]

1. financial market regulation,

2. ecological modernization of the economy, and

3. new social balance

The Green New deal (GND) is a set of proposals but do not follow any specific economic model or theory. The initial proposals were to encourage use of renewable energy. As an example, in making 'every building a power station' involving tens of millions of properties, building human resources for a vast environmental reconstruction program, safety net fossil fuel price to support vulnerable people and re-regulating financial market for financial stability, social justice and environmental stability. One of the core elements of GND is to build a green public infrastructure via smart grid technologies, green transportation through investing in rail, public transportation and electric cars, and also by establishing recycling markets. Our children will not drive electric cars or live in a warm house if we do not create a path for them to be there. The second one is leapfrogging opportunities. These opportunities can be provided from implementing green technology, improving efficiency, and restructuring management practices. The third element states that for green revolution, high quality digital infrastructures reduce environmental impact. A fourth, additional element is the restructuring of prices and markets to promote a green economy.[116]

The Green Job Report by the Green Job Initiatives describe green jobs as "work in agricultural, manufacturing, research and development (R&D), administrative, and service activities that contribute substantially to preserving or restoring environmental quality. Specifically, but not exclusively, this includes jobs that help to protect ecosystems and biodiversity; reduce energy, materials, and water consumption through high efficiency strategies; de-carbonize the economy; and minimize or altogether avoid the generation of all forms of waste and pollution.[116] Some developing countries and organizations based in developing countries have expressed some concerns over the proposals of the Green New Deal, sending the message that environmental "global challenges are as much about transformation of the political system as about the need for economic system reforms". Some countries also imply that the proposal may undermine national sovereignty when it comes to control over own natural resources.[110] Opponents have argued that the emphasis should be on a continued search for sustainable development rather than a "Green New Deal". As far as states are concerned, China and Indonesia have voiced basic support for the Green New Deal, but particularly China worried that one may face "trade protectionism under the pretext of environmental protection". Brazil, Mexico and India have emphasized national sovereignty when discussing the Green New Deal, with India also expressing fears of a green "economic straightjacket". Bolivia, on their part, have worried that the Green New Deal signals a "privatization and commodification of nature"[123] Despite the above constructive criticism, the proposals of GND were highly hailed by many 'green minded' intellectuals, politicians and parliamentarians but they could not attract enough attentions of investors or capitalists. Unfortunately, the Green New Deal is not moving since practically, under capitalist biasing the objective of financial stimulus to boost up economy and saving environment or dealing with peak oil crisis are mutually

exclusive. In her article "Nuclear vs. Renewables: Divided They Fall", Dawn
Stover argues as:

"People who agree that climate change is a dire problem often disagree about how to
solve it."[12]

According to the US Energy Information Administration, in 2012 nuclear and
renewables each provided between 8 and 9 percent of all energy used in the
United States. Petroleum, natural gas, and coal together provided 81 percent.[124]
Although nuclear and renewable energy are making compatible contributions in
U.S. economy, policy makers and politicians are now polarized on nuclear vs.
renewable to address the climate issue. By considering the magnitude of climate
crisis, Dawn Stover (2014) urges

"If climate activists are to have any hope of real progress in the policy arena, they
must present a united front. There are plenty of policies they can jointly support:
the elimination of tax privileges for fossil fuels, stricter rules for mining and
fracking, a massive ramp-up in requirements and support for energy efficiency
and conservation, and a carbon tax that would force polluters to pay for the
damage they do to the environment and human health."[12]

A new policy paper by researchers at the University of California, Berkeley
suggests that instead of emphasizing cap-and-trade schemes and penalties on
greenhouse gas emissions policymakers need to build political support by
investing or providing incentives such as subsidies and tax rebates in clean-
energy industries to speed up progress in tackling climate change.[170&173]

The corporate law dictates that the corporate managements are obligated to
maximize profits, the very interests of their companies' shareholders. They bias
information instead of sharing in the market place. Smith (2011) argues

"But saving the world requires that the pursuit of profits be systematically
subordinated to ecological concerns."[78]

As shown in Figure 7.1 that in context of declining conventional reserves and a low EROEI of unconventional hydrocarbons, the oil and gas industry launched a public relations campaign in media exaggerating the actual performance of the wells or "forecast supported only by cherry-picked statistics".[28] Instead of supporting GND, according to Deborah Rogers (2013), Wall Street is orchestrating Shale gas and fracking mania in the same way as subprime lending crisis in connection with shale gas and tight oil companies.[126] In her article "Shale and Wall Street: Was the Decline in Natural Gas Prices Orchestrated?" she points out this:

> "Banks no longer held on to mortgages. Instead it became lucrative to make loans, package the mortgages, have a ratings agency pronounce it a safe investment and then flip them to investors, thereby collecting large fees. This is not unlike the land grab which shale operators engaged in by leasing millions of acres of land, drilling a handful of wells and pronouncing the field "proved up" and thereby a "safe" investment, and then flipping such parcels to the highest bidder."[126]

The aftermath of the Wall Street game is the Green New Deal (GND) is lost from focus. Tienhaara (2009) points out this:

> "What they are likely to accomplish (at least in the short term) is what they were intended to accomplish; a return to the path of economic growth."[111]

There have been very few articles were written, few research was done or data was published on GND after the shale or fracking hype in the media. Figure 7.10 shows renewable power generation and capacity as a proportion of change in global power increased dramatically from 2007 to 2009 but between 2009 and 2010 it became flat. The renewable energy sector grew during 2011-2014 due to higher amount of investment and loan available in this sector during higher oil price. However, the stocks of renewable energy companies plummeted because of falling oil price since third quarter to 2014. Although there are several

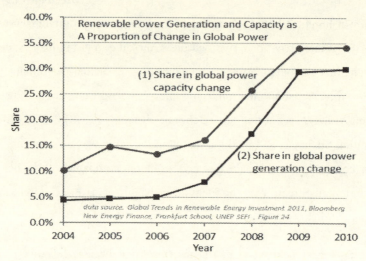

Figure 7.10: Renewable Power as a Proportion in Global Power Supply[128]

opinions on why the oil price is falling but this time OPEC did not cut production since Saudi Arabia and their Gulf allies did not want to lose their market share to the surging American shale oil producers.[185] Whatever is the reason for falling oil price, either threat of shale boom, over-glut or geopolitics it killed the "Green New Deal" immaturely.

As an example, SunEdision's stock price fell down by 96% in six months from $32.13 to $1.37 in February, 2016.[186] Many analysts blames SunEdision's business model accompanied with its management's inept financial decisions for this big down fall.[187] However, it was bad timing too for expanding business through creating yieldcos. In mid-2014, SunEdison created its first yieldco subsidiary, called Terraforms Power, Inc. so that it can sell its installed solar power plants to the yieldco and in turn guarantees streams of cash flow to itself (SunEdison) for long-run.[188] In 2015, to manage renewable-energy projects in emerging markets like Brazil, China, and India, it formed another yieldco TerraForm Global. However, due to falling share price and lack of funding SunEdision is hanging with whopping 2.9 GW of renewable energy projects under construction on one hand and shortage of cash on the other.[187] Riding on debt, SunEdision's financial condition might be very close to Minsky Moment (Section 4.11, Chapter 4) when its cash on hand would dry up servicing outstanding debt and income or cash flow would become insufficient for paying off the interests. To overcome this crisis moment, it needs a big boost that could be possible if GND were in place.

Tragically, if we fail transitioning from non-renewable to renewable, the whole humanity will inevitably fail. Our policy makers and capitalists cannot escape from their responsibilities. Nevertheless, capitalist system is structurally dependent on growth, which has conflict of interest with 'green recovery'. The GND has lost its ground in the battle with the financial Frankenstein. Now the growing renewable energy industry is caged by the Frankenstein and ironically, now the industries survival depends on the its blessing.

7.8 Capitalists Dilemma

"Maximizing profit and saving the planet are inherently in conflict and cannot be systematically aligned even if, here and there, they might coincide for a moment."[78]

- Richard Smith (2011), "Green Capitalism: the god that failed"

Green New Deal (GND) calls for government policies and spending for renewable energy, low carbon emission and environment friendly products to address credit crunch, global poverty and environmental issues. Scientists gathered at the Nature conference, held at the International Institute of Social Studies in The Hague in 2011 hold a different view. According to them, these are inherently political and social problems embedded in globally dominant ideas of human development and progress. They suggests that a more positive and realistic way forward necessarily has to start by addressing 'economic power structures' (of the capitalists) and 'social inequalities'.[150]

We have seen that government policies are not sufficient for motivating the capitalists co-operate toward green economy. If government has to spend money building renewable energy infrastructures and upgrade national grid system, where will the government get the money from since most of the governments are already overly indebt? The New Deal (ND) introduced by Roosevelt in 1930s to revive the U.S. economy from 'The Great Depression' by increasing government stimulus spending and for public demand creation, in other words, promoting consumption. Kovel (2002) sees this as the major reason behind rapid industrialization during the 1960s, with the help of the import-substitution policies in developing as well as developed countries, led to increasing pressure on nature that now leads us to an ecological crisis.[151]

On the other hand, Pollin et al. (2008) calculated that the short term $100 billion green recovery package of U.S. would create almost four times more total jobs than the oil industry can create with the same amount.[152] However the policy makers are more interested to bail out banks and auto industry to promote growth and consumption. Have the bailouts worked? The bailouts have worked at least for strengthening the preexisting Money Loop (ML) but by making the governments and common people dependent on debts. The intention of government spending or policies is that eventually market will take over and generate money for the economy. A perfect takeover is when there is no MEL or ML. As discussed in Chapter 4 that Money Loops (MLs) are the reasons for over-consumption or Market Energy Loop (MEL) and driving force of capitalism. In the previous chapters we have seen that the bail outs are not much successful in creating jobs rather it makes rich people richer and in turn, creates context for another looming financial crisis. While the governments in USA and most of European countries such as Greece, Spain, and Italy are drowning in debt, many of the Green New Deal (GND) proposals seeking government spending are not realistic.

Many economists like Asici et al. (2011) comments that "New Deal type policies, which helped to revive the economies in the 1930s, cannot solve but can only aggravate the problems in today's world." [153] Finally, it was not only government spending in New Deal (ND) which overcomes the Great Depression but also it was the expansion of military spending for World War II. After the War, the use of oil exponentially increased in the U.S. economy so as the public debt. During that time of the 'Great Depression', the 'peak oil' fact was not known. However, now a new war will 'burn' much of the remaining oil, perhaps much more devastating way than the two World Wars leaving noting for rebuilding and making profit except few arms industry.

Although the New Deal program was derived from Keynes's book "The General Theory of Employment, Interest and Money" published in 1936, economists on that time failed to integrate this earlier work in his "Treatise on Money" published in 1930.[154&155] There his proposal was for economic stability at the limits of growth, what we would now call a "sustainable design" for capitalism. It was not at all well received.[156] He explained that it was for some future time when increasing capital investment would reach to a climax when continuing increases in investment by the wealthy would then cause over-investment and result in "conditions sufficiently miserable" to bring the net savings rate of the economy to zero. As a response to the natural over-investment crisis it would have relied on the good will (co-operation) of the wealthy (capitalists) in spending enough of their own earnings to restore profitability to the rest of the economy.[26] Unfortunately, the original misinterpretation was that it was intended to restore growth rather than to allow growth to end without conflict.[154]

In the big picture, capitalists are myopic captured with their Pareto Coalition (PC). More than 200 years back during peak of colonial era and after invention of steam engine, the capitalism might look promising. At this point of time, it is blasphemous to blame capitalism as a whole and thus we will be nowhere. Frank Rotering argues:

"Anyone who seriously contemplates humankind's future will quickly encounter the dilemma posed by capitalism. On one hand, the system's growth compulsion is environmentally suicidal, which implies that capitalism must be abolished. On the other hand, the system is deeply entrenched and no clear alternatives exist, which implies it must be retained."[157]

Asici et al. (2011) argues that Green New Deal (GND) represents yet another exit strategy of the mainstream capitalist system to overcome the crisis situation.[153] The "Biased Equilibrium" model described in Chapter 4 tells that to better address capitalism we need to focus on the core capitalists–the people who run capitalism.

Haque (2011) defines 'capitalists' dilemma' as the more same old prosperity required more and more harm to economy, society and nature.[158] That is capitalists choose to 'defects' the societal and natures good for achieving their own good. No government in the world is run by "green" agenda rather run by the "growth" agenda. If the U.S and EU governments had enough money to spend, it might not go for 'greening' rather for continuity of "growth" of productions and consumptions as the top most priority. According to HSBC research, renewable energy is more labor intensive than traditional fossil fuel industries.[29] Solar panels, wind turbine, weatherizing buildings, planting trees, green roofs all these activities require human labor.[159] Tienhaara argues

"Recognizing this simple fact helps to undermine the myth that ecological restoration must always be at odds with economic performance."[111]

However, capitalists are not likely interested since green energy contributes less money to their control in form of Money Loop (ML) but more benefits to Residual Market Energy States (RMS) and local economy.

In 2009 report, World Economic Forum (WEF) estimated that $500 billion per year would be required by 2020 to limit global warming to 2°C.[160] However, only a half of the financing target has been achieved so far.[160] Nevertheless we

542

do not see the market has responded to the amount of money already spent on 'Greenwashing'.

A market cannot be explained based on how much money is spent, rather on how money fundamentally holds the capitalists in their Pareto Coalition (PC). As long as this money grows, the bonding of the PC is reinforced. Therefore, financial market is based on making larger and larger bets on future economic growth. Since they are part of a coalition, the dilemma is that any individual capitalist cannot unilaterally come out of it to co-operate with "no-growth" such as "green economy", while the others are defecting and competing for "growth". This can be named as **"Capitalists Dilemma (CD)"**. Unfortunately, this dilemma is driving our civilization toward a systemic collapse. Arms race is just another form of CD. In his "A Strategy of Peace" speech in American University, Washington, Kennedy mentioned the following about nuclear arms race:

"Today the expenditure of billions of dollars every year on weapons acquired for the purpose of making sure we never need to use them is essential to keeping the peace. But surely the acquisition of such idle stockpiles--which can only destroy and never create–is not the only, much less the most efficient, means of assuring peace."[189]

Let us assume that there are only two capitalists 'A' & 'B' in an economic world who constitute a Pareto Coalition (PC) and maintains a biased equilibrium with the rest of the people of the economy. It tells that if the economy has a strong Money Loop (ML), it will put a growth pressure on their businesses. As per above discussion, to reach to the ultimate goal of holding 1.5^0C to 2.0^0C temperature from pre-industrial level set in Paris Agreement of Climate Conference, 2015, they need to 'cooperate' to "green" actions by retrenching the use of fossil fuel and strengthening local economies.

Carbon Trade Watch describes this:

"The cap is supposed to reduce emissions over time. However, setting a limit on pollution can be highly susceptible to corporate lobbying and favoritism, to such an extent that companies can frequently continue to increase pollution while remaining within the cap."[96]

As shown in Figure 7.11, when oil price is lower than renewable energy, if 'A' cooperates and sets a 'cap' on fossil fuel use and gradually switch to renewable energies, the company's expenditure on energy will increase in turn, there will be cut in other expenditures such as raw materials, payroll, benefits etc. that will

B A	Co-operates	Defects
Co-operates	Sustain	A:Sink B:Soar
Defects	A:Soar B:Sink	Smash (Economic & environmental Crisis)

Figure 7.11: Capitalists' Dilemma (Capitalists' Square)[161]

negatively impact A's growth and its market capitalization. As a result corresponding dividends or bonuses of 'A' will reduce and the overall company's businesses may 'sink'. On the other hand if 'B' continues to use more fossil fuel (defects), its business will '**surge**' since over-consumption or Market Energy Loop (MEL) and Money Loop (ML) paradigm will prevail, which will be reflected in its increased market capitalization. Economist Paul Krugman (1999) explains this as:

"There is a strong element of rat race in America's consumer-led boom, but those rats racing in their cages are what keeps the wheels of commerce turning."[162]

It can be argued if there were no ML or MEL, the rats would not race in a cage but in an open space in a healthy environment. Smith (2011) argues this:

"We can't stop consuming more and more because if we stop racing, the system collapses into crisis."[149]

He perhaps indicates collapse of the financial paradigm (ML) of the capitalists who dominate the economic game. As long as the racing game continues, consumptions and use of fossil fuel will also grow. Under globalization, if A and B are in different countries then this situation will be more complex to manage. In reality, we see while China and India are rising, the slowing down economic growth of the U.S. or the European countries are making their debt and unemployment situations worse. In a recent report, International Energy Agency (IEA) forecasts that by 2040, China's oil imports to be five times those of the U.S., while India's will "easily exceed" the European Union's.[167]

In European countries 20 to 40 percent or more youths are already unemployed. According to National Geographic we need to keep emissions below 350 ppm, then not only cannot we keep on growing but we would have to make radically deeper cuts in GDP than even the -7 percent per year.[163] Under capitalism, this level of economic contraction would mean economic collapse and depression.[163] Figure 7.11 shows that if both the 'A' and 'B' cooperate to cap fossil fuel usage, their businesses will 'squeeze' and so will their 'profits'. Smith (2011) further explains this as:

"For example, the science says that to save the humans, we have to drastically cut fossil fuel consumption, even close down industries like coal. But no corporate board can sacrifice earnings to save the humans because to do so would be to risk shareholder flight or worse."[78]

Now we are in "Capitalists' Dilemma (CD)" whether to choose collapse of capitalism (squeeze) or to choose collapse of the civilization (smash). This model tells that their rational decisions guide them toward the latter option. In that respect, the probability of achieving 2015 Paris Agreement among 195 countries for holding the increase in the global average temperature to well below $1.5^{0}C$–$2^{0}C$ above pre-industrial levels is very low under Capitalists' Dilemma (CD). The ideal expectation here is that the participating countries will be stick to it even though their economies "squeeze". However, in reality, each individual country will still pursue growth ("soar"), while they are competing with each other and therefore, may end up at the same level of risk as if there were no agreement.

The capitalists will invest to produce green products and follow environment friendly processes, if they get higher return on their investment. The EROEI chart in Figure 7.1 shows EROEI of renewable energy is too low compared to non-renewable energy sources to attract the capitalists follow this approach. Whichever approach or instruments we choose dealing with fossil fuel depletion or global warming, James Hansen (2010) points out

> "The problem is that our governments, under the heavy thumb of special interests, are not pursuing policies that would restrict our fossil fuel use. Quite the contrary, they are pursuing policies to get every last drop of fossil fuel, including coal, by whatever means necessary, regardless of environmental damage."[93]

We also see the reflection of CD in derivative contracts of the top capitalists. As discussed in Chapter 3 and 5 that there are couple of hundred trillion dollar Over the Counter (OTC) derivative contracts (over USD $700 trillion in 2007)[164] in nominal value. Since OTC derivatives are not traded on an exchange, there is no central counter-party. Therefore, they are subject to counterparty risk, like an ordinary contract, since each counter-party relies on the other to perform.[165]

An individual capitalist without "Capitalists Dilemma (CD)" may agree that we need to open up new opportunities of 'green businesses' to save our only livable place in the universe, 'the earth'. Unfortunately, similar to Prisoner's Dilemma

(PD), under CD the rational decision always drives an individual capitalist toward his own myopic benefit. This turns into as "defection" from the sides of the both the capitalists 'A' and 'B. In this way, our industrial civilization is going to hit the limits of the earth with high velocity that it will eventually be 'smashed'. This dilemma can be applied universally to all capitalists' and their organizations. Therefore, Smith explains this:

"Corporations aren't necessarily evil. They just can't help themselves. They're doing what they're supposed to do for the benefit of their owners. But this means that, so long as the global economy is based on capitalist private/corporate property and competitive production for market, we're doomed to collective social suicide and no amount of tinkering with the market can brake the drive to global ecological collapse."[149]

In the extended form the PD game, it is verified that if the game is played over and over, the two prisoners will betray each other repeatedly. The same is true for Capitalists' Dilemma (CD). This dilemma prevents the capitalists from co-operating for sustainability and peace. A recent study by UC Berkeley recommends "not to fight on climate change but to co-operate to any best solution". An analysis by Ben Knight based on this research explains:

"The thing about opposing something, if you think about it, is that whatever you're opposing will inevitably oppose you back. That eats up a lot of valuable time, energy and resources."[168]

Edenhoffer and Stern suggest that if action is not taken to reduce reliance on fossil fuels "the next economic crisis is pre-programmed".[166]

Perhaps, to be more specific, it is Capitalists Dilemma (CD) that prevents capitalism changing from its status quo that is leading us toward eco-suicidal collapse. Ironically, end of civilization is also end of capitalization but end of capitalization might be beginning on new era of civilization.

CHAPTER 8

CAPITALISTS BIASING

8.1 Introduction

This chapter narrows down our information biasing structure that simplifies modeling of human values and institutions to formulate appropriate strategies and actions for the sustainability. A social or economic problem can be subjectively modeled as an information biasing chain where individuals are positioned in different abstract coalitions. The topmost layer coalition may be called as "The Core Capitalists" virtually control the institutions and they have greater influences on our economy.

8.2 Poverty Trap

In previous chapters we have discussed about financial and environmental crises. The reality is that whatever is the crisis, the poor people in the Residual Market Energy State (RMS) of a 'biased equilibrium' model become the ultimate sufferers although they are not responsible. These crises leave us the challenge to let the poor people access to the economic development concentrated in a Market Energy Loop (MEL) at the same time keep fossil fuel and fresh water reserves for our future generations as much as possible. If there exists a strong MEL, the poor people in the RMS can be assumed are in a 'poverty trap' since MEL will create a 'Price Pressure (PP)" on them.

According to World Bank Poverty Measurement and Analysis report there are three ingredients required in computing a poverty measure. First, one has to choose the relevant dimension and indicator of well-being. Second, one has to select a threshold or a poverty line below which a given household or individual will be classified as poor. Finally, one has to select a poverty measure to be used for reporting for the population as a whole.[2] The World Bank's international poverty line definition is based on Purchasing Power Parity (PPP) basis, at $1.25 per day. Figure 8.1 shows World Bank 2014 poverty benchmarks based on 2011

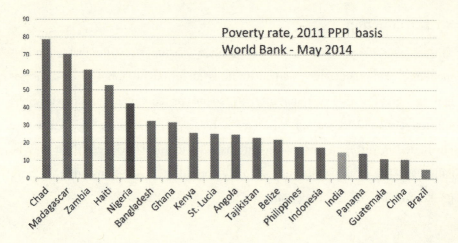

Figure 8.1: Poverty rate chart 2014 based on World Bank new 2011 PPP[3]

purchasing power parity basis.[4] This measure provides a partial snapshot of poverty but it does not tell that many of the poor people under poverty line are in a 'poverty trap' who may never be able to make escape due to overhanging Market Energy Loop (MEL) (Chapter 4). However, those who are at the border of poverty line live a fragile economic life.[5] Lack of basic essentials of life such as safe drinking water, sanitation, housing, health infrastructure as well as malnutrition impact the lives of hundreds of millions. A recent proposal from Oxford Poverty and Human Development Initiative (OPHI) introduces some semi-economic and non-economic indices for poverty measurement. As an example, a poverty rate measure so-called Multi-dimensional Poverty Index (MPI), which put only 6.25% weight to assets owned by a person and placed 33% weight on education and number of years spent in school.[6] These non-economic measures remain controversial and contested as a measure of poverty rate of any nation.[7]

Let us go back to the example of the rickshaw puller Ayat Ali in Chapter 1. During his lifetime he has pedaled equivalent to seven times around the world or three quarters the way to the moon but he owns virtually nothing.[8] According to a recent research, rickshaw pulling provides them with relatively easy access to the urban labor market, higher income but it does not provide any better well-being such as better accommodation, better access to amenities, kids' education or healthcare.[9] It is found, not unusually, that many of them are working with severe illness just because hunger is unendurable. Perhaps slavery is better than this because slaves get food without working when they are sick. The research paper concludes that

"But the initial trend of modest upward mobility from rickshaw pulling is not sustained in the long run. For the sample in this study, almost all economic and social indicators – including income poverty – deteriorated with the length of involvement in rickshaw pulling. The unsustainability of the livelihood is related to the extreme physical demands of the activity, which are unrealistic in the context of poverty and malnutrition, and which result in high vulnerability to health shocks."[9]

Study shows most of the rickshaw pullers in Bangladesh were marginal farmers by origin but had to migrate from rural village farmlands after losing their land to pay off their debt from private money-lenders called "mohajons" (the local loan sharks). The mohajons charge a pernicious 20% per month or 240% per year interest for a small amount of loan given for example paying, agricultural accessories, medical bill, outstanding rent or dowry for daughter's wedding. Then borrowers (typically marginal farmers) scramble for paying the interest months after months as long as they can and eventually lose their land to the mohajons. As an example, let's take a look at the recent harvest season of a southern district village in Bangladesh that is known as crop house of the country. Habibur, a marginal farmer in Bangladesh took 20,000 taka ($285) agriculture loan for production of rice in a piece of land. According to last year's higher rice price, the cost of production due to higher price of fertilizer and other components like irrigation, seed were higher in this year and eventually his outstanding loan became 35,000 taka ($500) in few months. Now during harvest season, the paddy price is dropped by 30% to 40% than last year, which will not cover his production cost and cause him in huge net loss. These lower prices of agricultural products are deliberately fixed by the middlemen, whereas all other products are suffering from inflation. It leaves no other choice for the marginal farmers but to sell out their produce during the harvest season since they need to pay their loan installments so that they can further borrow and also they need to feed their families. As a result they will fall in the vicious cycle of debt-trap and eventually will be bound to sell their remaining pieces of land.

Obviously after few days when the entire paddy will be sold out from the farmers to the stockers, the price will go up so that stockers and the other middlemen can make exorbitant profits without doing anything and taking any risk. If there is any risk like drought or any other natural calamity, the farmers have no choice but to bear it. The middlemen like the mohajons, stockers, bankers, lawyers, bureaucrats, businessmen and politicians explicitly or implicitly, consciously or unconsciously collaborate to grab the money generated by the farmers. There is also a process in place to grab the money of the farmers by engaging them in lawsuits. Majority of the civil and criminal lawsuits in Bangladesh are directly and indirectly related to land. The mohajons are backed by local political parties and informal institutions and therefore, their presence in rural, suburb and slum areas in Bangladesh are so deep rooted that they are enough reasons for creating and raising poverty. This match with Quigley's observation about inefficient middle layer of Chinese society that allows a large portion of the wealth which was being drained from the farmers to be diverted and diffused among the middlemen.[10]

Another reason for the farmers and poor villagers falling into debt-trap is high cost of medical bills. Normally they do not have enough cash-flow to afford medical bills of sudden sickness of any of their family members. Medical expenses are always increases due to over-hanging Money Loop (ML) or Market Energy Loop (MEL). It is common that the farmers have to sell or mortgage their crop lands to pay the medical bills to the rich villagers or mohajons and eventually they become landless.

In India, the debt burden on the marginal farmers is so severe that in 2012, 13,754 farmers suicide because of debt.[11] According to the National Crime Records Bureau (NCRB) total 216,500 farmers committed suicide since 1997 including 17,368 in 2009. According to P. Sainath, a journalist and the Rural Affairs Editor of The Hindu who covered the Covering farmers' suicides in India, later won the 2007 Ramon Magsaysay Award , the farmers' suicides have occurred with cash crops, because with food crops such as rice, even if the price falls, there is food left to survive on.[12] The indebted farmers has taken loans from money lenders is highest (29%), followed by banks (27%), co-operative society (26%) and government (3%). The co-operative institutions were established help farmers in their monetary needs but as Assadi analyzed the reason of farmers' suicide in India that the failure of the co-operatives has further made the large number of farmers to fall back on money lenders (mohajons) who charge exorbitant interest. This is not only debt alone caused so many suicides as Assadi analyzed, the farmers were made responsible for any ecological, economic and social crises, and each inter-linked with the other.[13]

The micro-credit programs introduced by Muhammad Yunus thirty years back in the early 1980s appeared as comfortable substitute of the private money lenders (mohajons) and targeted to rescue the landless people. Mohajons are still doing their business targeting the marginal farmers in the villages and urban poor people. Sometimes mohajons are the only quick source of money to them since micro-credit organizations are not lending money for paying medical bills or to the urban poor people due to their unsettled life. Grameen Bank the iconic institution for micro-credit founded in Bangladesh by Muhammad Yunus gives loan to rural poor people for cow rearing, paddy husking, rural trading that are organizing production there even in small scale. If one of a family member takes loan, due to "high" concern within the family in a rural area, the other members will virtually share the liability of the loan. That is why normally a loan is given to a woman (97% of 7.0 million borrowers are woman), particularly to a mother whose concern for the family is the highest so that the combined efforts of the family make her able to pay the monthly installments. Thus the micro-credit organizations are working under capitalist framework and become sustainable. The fact is that only the family members knows how difficult now in these days to cope with high inflation and then to pay the installments over the time. Many of them are just surviving on waves of borrowings shifting from one lender to another (Bateman, 2010).[14] One may ask why there is so much relish about micro-credit. Why we are not emphasizing industrial development to create employments, co-operatives and implement pro-poor policies like land reform? Thus the poor people would get higher incomes and stronger supports for their real immediate needs and eventually they would become less dependent on borrowings. After thirty five years of operations, micro-credit programs are blamed for facilitating infantilisation of the local economy.[14]

Despite many micro-credit programs, huge numbers of landless people are migrating from rural areas to urban areas but to live unsettled and uncertain life, without having savings, health security, education facility etc. According to World Bank, the number of poor people in Bangladesh has declined by 26 percent between 2000 and 2010 because of growth of labor income, which does not consider high inflation during the time. The growth of income is particularly because of high growth in readymade garments industry, which is now $20 billion industry and employs about 4 million people, mostly women. The women workers work 12 to 14 hours a day for only $50 per month without any long-term benefits but generates huge money for the overhanging MEL. Many of them have to work all of the holidays just to get a little bonus on top of their small salaries. As discussed earlier that the poverty measurement based on income growth will not reflect the true picture of poverty if Price Pressure (PP) due to overhanging ML or MEL and inflation are more than income growth. Instead a better approach could be to measure and benchmark how much they get in real value with respect to their contributions.

8.3 Real Income to Contribution Ratio (RICR)

In previous chapters we have discussed about financial and environmental crises. The reality is that whatever is the crisis, the poor people in the Residual Market Energy State (RMS) of a 'biased equilibrium' model become the ultimate victims. In neoclassical world there are two types of income. One type of income goes to the contributor of "labor" and the remaining or majority goes to the owner of "capital". In neoclassical 'utopia', income due to "labor" and contribution of "laborers" are not distinguished since it inherently considers them as the same things. The price taking behavior of income from a perfectly competitive market, essentially tells that a worker is always paid as per his or her marginal contribution. Therefore, the income to marginal contribution ratio in neoclassical economics can be considered as 1 at any time as shown in Figure 8.2 below.[17] In case we deal with poverty, the relationship between income and contribution may play a significant role in defining economic performance. A capitalist economy works in combination of people having income to marginal contribution ratio less than 1 (I/C < 1) and greater than 1 (I/C >1), in real terms. It does not mean all the people who are paid less than their contribution are poor, at least from Pareto improvement perspective. However in a country having poverty, a subset of this population (I/C < 1) is poor. Increase in per capita income or GDP reduce may reduce poverty. As in China poverty rate declined from 85% in 1981 to 16% in 2005 (poverty being defined as the number of people living on < \$1.25/day). However, in this way poverty reduction based on export market and urbanization may not sustain if growth rate slows down or the economy fall in recession. In many countries, the benefits of GDP growth based

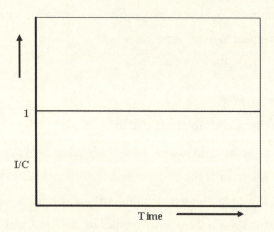

Figure 8.2: Real Income to Marginal Contribution Ratio in Neoclassical Economics[17]

on export market reduce income of its poor people in real values since most of the money is trapped in the overhanging Market Energy Loop (MEL). As Tienhaara explains:

"It is not difficult to imagine that declining incomes in developed countries (e.g. through reduced working weeks) could put pressure on producers in developing countries to export even cheaper goods, resulting in poorer conditions for workers as well as no or minimal decline in overall consumption."[1]

Every economy has certain degree of Market Energy Loop (MEL). However, in case of high MEL, where almost all benefits of economic development are trapped within certain upper layer market energy states, poverty is a likely phenomenon. In a 'biased equilibrium' economy if contributions of poor people increase for whatever reasons even without their direct effort like new technologies, new investments or new business opportunities etc., most of the money will go to non-poor people in MEL and it will be trapped there. As a result, the market prices of all basic goods and services like food, accommodation, education, health care etc. increase and consequently, real income of the poor people decrease. To capture this situation in this model, let us

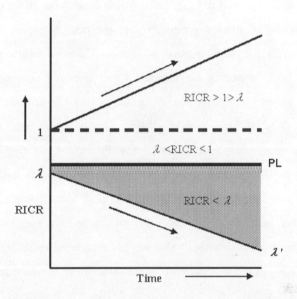

Figure 8.3: Real income to contribution ratio (RICO) in poverty situation[17]

consider the term 'income' as real income based on absolute purchasing power of the poor people. Now if we consider only existing employed people, the term "marginal" can be dropped and the ratio discussed here can be called as 'Real Income to Contribution Ratio (RICR)'. In this paper, we are concerned about RICR < 1 part of the economy as shown in Figure 8.3. Let us define a poverty line by using the concept of RICR. The people who have RICR below a certain level may be considered as poor people. As an example, we may draw an Indian Poverty Line (IPL) at \$2 per day income level, which accounts for about a billion people (2010 reference). If we keep aside the 9.4% unemployed people in

India, then the Poverty Line (PL) can be better represented in terms of a constant RICR line in time dimension as shown in Figure 8.3.

Economy of a poor country is likely to be labor intensive and they are the core workforce of the country. The farmers, factory workers, day laborers, peddlers, porters, housekeepers, rickshaw pullers all are making the right contributions for the economy. They do not deserve the miserable lives that they are living in the poor countries in Africa, Latin America or South East Asia. In those countries, most of the additional money produced gets trapped in pre-existing Market Energy Loop (MEL). In this situation, a subset of people below poverty line (RICR<λ<PL), become poorer as their RICR fall over the time shown by the downward line λλ' in Figure 8.3. Therefore, they can be positioned on Residual Market Energy State (RMS) outside a MEL. On the other hand, a subset of population (including corporates) above the Poverty Line (RICR>1>PL>λ) become richer as their RICR go up shown by the upward RICR line and therefore, they can be positioned inside the MEL.[17] As a simple example, if contribution (not necessarily productivity) of an average individual worker increase by 10% in current market value but his income is increased by 2%, the remaining 8% goes to the others in MEL. Accumulating the sum from millions of workers is huge money gets trapped in the MEL, which certainly impacts the prices of all basic goods and services that the workers need and in turn the real income of the workers drops over the time. If the money in Switch banks were in India as idle money, the inflation would be much more and we would see a sharper downward line λλ' in Figure 8.3.

Measurement of contribution is a politically sensitive term. How can we measure contributions of the poor workers in an industry if they are not equal to their salaries or incomes? Let us simplify our math here. According to the pattern of RICR curve (line) λλ', we may assume that in some –T time in the past, average RICR of our workers were 1 and in some +T time in future it will be so small that close to zero (when the our workers will be considered as mere "means" of production not a human being at all). In this way if we assume we are now just in the middle between -T and +T, then RICR will be 0.5. This value can be used as a reference or bench mark.[17] The existing market price of some selected basic goods and services can be taken as reference for calculating the real income. Therefore, reference contribution can be assumed as just two (2) times of average salary of the workers. Alternatively a benchmark may also be set based on the information available in the market. As an example, a recent pay scheme in Bangladesh increased minimum salary of the garments workers from $25 per month to $45 per month after four years whereas demand from the workers was to set at $75 since the living costs increased at least three times. Using these figures, RICR can be benchmarked as 0.6 instead. In summary, whatever the method of calculating the value, to alleviate poverty, RICR of the poor people will have to increase in a consistent manner. See Chapter 9 for more discussion.

8.4 Economics of Information Biasing (EIB)

"But if the engine of capitalist growth and consumption can't be stopped, or even throttled back, and if the logic of capitalist efficiency and capitalist rationality is killing us, what choice to we have but to rethink the theory?"[18]

-Smith, Richard (2010)

Capitalism became dominant in the world following the demise of feudalism.[19] Feudal society was hierarchical in the sense that virtually no upward mobility was possible.[20] The feudal system was maintained by static institutional hierarchy marked with traditions and ceremonies in a land based economy for more than thousand years ranged from fall of Rome (476) to the European Renaissance (about 1500). As Pluta (2011) summarizes feudalism in Europe, "[T]echnology stagnated. Innovation was minimal. Human knowledge regressed, largely because of a repressive Church, the only institution whose power grew during this period. The manor, the guilds, and the Church were institutions committed to maintaining the status quo among general population. For most of this period, they succeeded in doing precisely that."[20]

Pluta further elaborates the status quo

"[A]t the very bottom of the feudal structure were peasants or serfs. Generation after generation was born into serfdom and remained in that state of life until death. Hard-working, productive serfs did not become lords, and ineffective lords did not one day find themselves demoted to serfs…the rich and powerful overate and overdrank, while many peasants suffered from hunger"[20]

He explains a series of forces that eroded the European feudal institutions and eventually led to collapse of the system. First, The Crusades sent people of different social classes to the Middle East, where they observed more advanced cultures and sought change when they returned to their drab manors and villages. The second, markets started to develop locally as serfs started to sell surplus products in local markets. Third, cities were reborn and encouraged international trade, industries developed and a new middle class emerged. Fourth and perhaps the most important was use of currency (money) replacing barter economy. Finally, the enclosure movement enabled lords to convert their fiefs into privately owned land, increased agricultural productivity and forced redundant serfs to seek employment. However, one thing in common as a cause of transformation from feudalism to capitalism that is overlooked by most of the economists is that information flow gradually increased among the people along the way of capitalist synthesis by economic means. After invention of printing, the information spread among the population that aligned their actions by integrating their common economic interests. As an example, Pluta (2011) explains the big change in information flow after invention of printing as:

"[T]he rapid spread of the written word in an inexpensive form caused an equally rapid growth in literacy which, in turn, enabled instructions for the operation of the new machinery to be communicated effectively to a required newly trained labor force.....curiosity among the population at large expanded, enabling further advances in knowledge at a later date."[20]

Pluta also concludes that as a result of increased information sharing "Technology finally overcame ceremonialism"[20] and the major economic goal changed from survival to accumulation of capital.[20] As explained in Chapter 4 that accumulation of money has direct relationship with biasing of information. In simple terms, capitalists are those who accumulate capitals (or money) from the non-capitalists who produce them by their labors and skills. Thus a new type of dynamic hierarchy began replacing the static feudal hierarchy. Capital accumulation and biasing was also present during feudalism but on that time it was discrete and static. Although there were rivalry among the feudal lords but in terms of biasing no feudal lord was interested to spend money for their serfs – the productive forces but for their military forces or building palaces and mansions. Mercantilism and colonization created dynamics in the capital accumulation process. 'Capitalist synthesis' has streamlined the dynamic capital accumulation process following industrial and fossil fuel revolution.

In neoclassical paradigm of economics, natural resources are scarce but adjustable to the market as long as we are ready to pay the economic cost of extraction, which we now know is absolutely wrong in time dimension. The mainstream economic theories that policymakers rely on are environment agnostic. Now we know that the growth focused economic activities will turn out 'bad' from apparent 'good' as more we approach to the 'peak oil' and realize the environmental disasters like global warming. The 'biased equilibrium' model in Chapter 4 explains that information biasing is essentially the building blocks of capitalism that help the capitalists hold control of the capitalists system and align others work for them. In a two layer Differential Market Model (DMM) described in Chapter 4, capitalists can be positioned in the central layer and non-capitalists are positioned in the outer layer. The dependency of non-capitalists on the capitalists is artificially created by means of information biasing that we now know is not sustainable when the growth will stop. In fact, once the age of oil will over, almost all of the so called capital may turn useless and the two layers may potentially merge into one layer again or a new type of civilization and economic system will be born.

The 'methodological individualism' foundation of neoclassical economics (NCE) does not allow any differentiation among the individuals although many classical economists like Karl Marx, distinguished capitalists from non-capitalists (e.g., workers). Therefore, NCE essentially assumes that each individual of an economy have equal access to the information. Stiglitz describes "for more than a hundred years, formal modeling in economics has focused on models in which information was perfect."[21] If this were the case, then slowing down economic growth in the advent of an environmental or economic crisis would be a natural outcome, whereas we see the opposite in the real world. The concept of 'Biased Equilibrium' brings modification in the core NCE assumption that information is much more a strategic tool to the interacting individuals rather than a given parameter of economic system (Chapter 4).

The concept 'Information Economics' is a branch of microeconomic theory that studies how information affects an economy and economic decisions. Much of its relevant literatures considers information as given parameter of economic systems and describes impacts of imperfect and asymmetric information on the capital based micro economic structure, for example, on price systems or on contracts. The consolidated economic model described in Chapter 4 defines that information has a fundamental role in economic systems by its cause and effect relationship on utility maximization goals of individual economic agents. The causal aspect of information tells that the decision an individual takes is made based on the information available to him at the point of decision. On the other hand, every individual is a source of information that he or she may strategically share with others to achieve his or her personal objective functions.

An individual has multi-valued or multi-dimensional utility vectors. A group of individuals have common or similar set of objective functions (objective palette). Otherwise economic problems would be specific to individuals and would never be a collective issue. Let us go back to the example of information sharing in Figure 4.2 of chapter four and replace Z with remaining population outside the coalition A1. It does not make sense that a small coalition establishes a biased

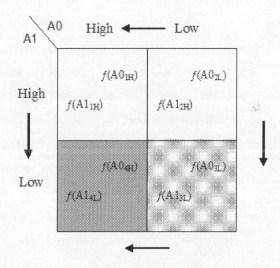

Figure 8.5: Biasing of information by coalition A1[17]

equilibrium with the remaining population. Here individual Z can be replaced with another coalition A0. The combinations of the possible outcomes are listed below and shown in Figure 8.5.

1.   High (A1) - High (A0): the two coalitions will share the same level of information that will result in a win-win outcome. This situation complies with the concept of neoclassical economics.

2.   High (A1) - Low (A0): A0 will establish biased equilibrium with A1.

3.   Low (A1) - Low (A0): interaction between two coalitions will be unproductive and therefore can be ignored.

4.   Low (A1) - High (A0): This situation describes exactly the same thing as of 2 above but A1 will establish biased equilibrium with A0.

The concept of coalition tells that a coalition implies a win-win situation among the players. On the other hand, two coalitions have win-lose relationship where one dominates over the other. In this example eventually one will dominate over the other. If the dominance is sustainable, we may say that the winner will bias the loser. Similar to the example described in Figure 4.2, let us assume that, A1 tries to dominate over A0 in a way that A1 is tuned up to share always "Low" information with A0 so that whatever strategy A0 takes, an individual of A1 will receive higher payoff than that of an individual of A0. That is, f (A1$_{4L}$) > f (A0$_{4H}$) and f (A1$_{3L}$) > f (A0$_{3L}$). This game remains at equilibrium at (Low, High) quadrant as shown in the figure below if f(A0$_{4H}$) is always greater than f(A0$_{3L}$). This game of two coalitions is indeed a biased game where A1 biases information by overriding natural information to increase probability of its winning over A0. This situation can be denoted as A0←A1. Let's call A1 as the "biasing source" and A0 as the "biased load".[17]

The size of the biased load depends on biasing conditions of its biasing source. An individual's objective functions and their priorities are dependent on information available to him. Therefore, a biasing source influences the individuals of its biased load to set their objective functions and their priorities in compliance with the common objective functions of the individuals of biasing source. These objective functions can be named as biased objectives. Theoretically an individual in a biased load may qualify to move to the biasing source if he or she can acquire the same level of information or knowledge as of the biasing source. New institutional economics define the need of acquiring information is the source of transaction cost (Coase, 1937).[22] Thus biasing imposes transaction cost on the biased load. The concept of information biasing implies that improvement of socioeconomic conditions of the individuals of a biased load requires that the biasing on them must change in favour of that.

The concept of information biasing is apparently similar to 'principal-agent problem'[23] (Ross, 1973) at micro-level. A real life example of principal agent problem can be mentioned as a job market of a worker, where a worker is like lots of others looking for a job and there are very limited employers who are offering jobs. The employers expect that they will get required numbers of workers from huge number of candidates. Therefore, they may communicate with the prospective workers so conservatively that a worker has two options; to accept a job at low salary or to be unemployed, although depending on unemployment rate in the economy. Whatever is the choice of a worker, in a viable production system, the employer must always be the winner. Although the employers do not communicate with each other to form a coalition but the whole community of the employers can be abstracted as virtual coalition because of their uniform nature of interaction with workers. On the worker's part, if a worker is employed, then cooperation and dedication will allow him or her get high salaries than that of non-cooperation with his or her employer although in either case he or she will be always paid less than his contribution in real terms considering there an overhanging Money Loop (ML) exists. This example indeed tells how an employer ensures profit by creating employment opportunities for others.

As discussed earlier in Chapter 4 that in case of principal-agent, the principal and agent are complementary to each other. On the other hand, in case of information biasing, the individuals in a biasing source are substitutes of the individuals in a biased load. For example, if the individuals who have good jobs or good business are abstracted as biasing source, then the identical individuals who are unemployed because of the reasons beyond their control can be abstracted as biased load. That is, have-nots of an economy are separated from the people who have a lot by a biasing spell from the later. However, this is not enough to explain how few rich people control the fate of many poor people throughout the human history.

Another example, farmers in developing countries are getting poor net incomes even though food production capacity per unit of land has increased with technological advancement. If there is bumper crop in a year, the farmers will get low price. On the other hand, non-farmers in the village like lenders, middlemen, lawyers, traders get benefit of the bumper crop. An initial biased equilibrium model can be made by putting the farmers as biased load and the all other individuals as biasing source. Farmers exchange their yields with high interest on their debt and high costs for all other goods and services they need. The initial model will give us start up clues toward a solution of a particular economic problem. On next step we may further peel off the biasing source to build a robust model.

Let us go back to our previous example described in Figure 8.5. There are chances that some individuals of one or both coalitions will gain enough potential to constitute another coalition A2. If a new coalition A2 comes to play

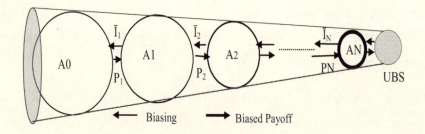

Figure 8.6: Information biasing chain[24]

this game with the other coalitions, there will be only two possible outcomes. It will either win or lose in the game. And whatever is the outcome, the three coalitions A0, A1 and A2 will construct a biasing chain where they will be positioned one after another as shown in Figure 8.6. If our analysis involves all people of an economy, this biasing chain will continue until the last set of individuals of the economy is included. In a biasing chain, a biased load in turn acts as biasing source except the last biased load. Therefore, the last biased load (e.g., A0) can be called as the Absolute Biased Load (ABL) or the 'Absolute 'Pareto Space (APS)'. The reason for biasing is keeping the biased loads in compliance with the objectives of biasing sources. In our capitalist world, this compliance is for streamlining flow of payoffs or capital toward the biasing sources. The coalitions are linked based on interdependencies of their payoff functions. The bigger the size of a biased load at the bottom, the more capital goes up to its biasing source and on the contrary, the less the size of the biasing source, the more per capita it has for its constituents. This is why we see the biasing chain is cone shaped as shown in the above Figure 8.6. There $\bar{I}_0$, $\bar{I}_1$ or $\bar{I}_2$ indicates biasing of information and P_0, P_1 or P_2 indicates the corresponding "biased payoffs". The topmost coalition, AN can be called as primary biasing source (PBS). The coalitions positioned above the primary biasing source may be abstracted as 'Universal Biasing Source (UBS)'.

The constituents of UBS can be imagined as inter-biased and therefore UBS cannot be broken into further coalitions. A PBS is a biased load of UBS. A biasing chain always starts from UBS and ends up at the last set of individuals of concern. Individuals of concern are those who fulfill the criteria of economic problems that we are analyzing. The economics that uses the concept of information biasing to analyze and interpret economic problems can be named as Economics of Information Biasing (EIB). This concept explains James Kunen's statement "A highly intelligent mind can be programmed by the Establishments" in his book "The Strawberry Statement", a first-person documentary of the Columbia University protests of 1968.[25] In his documentary "The Capitalists Conspiracy" Edward Griffin describes

"The human mind is like a computer. No matter how efficient it may be, its reliability is only as great as the information fed into it. If it is possible to control the input of human mind, then no matter how intelligent a person may be, it is entirely possible to program what he will think."[26]

This means the concept of EIB tells us how information is spreading in an economy. In other words, biasing of information is the building blocks of the information available in an economy by overriding the natural information.

As described earlier that information biasing in turn imposes transaction cost and thus keeps the biased load in equilibrium with the biasing source. That is, it describes how transaction costs are staged in an economy. According to Stigler (1961) this is how equilibrium in the whole economy.[27] In capitalist economy, the transaction cost increases and size of the coalition is restricted toward the upward direction that restricts the size of the coalitions on that direction. From this model it can be said that neoclassical economics assumes all individuals of an economy are in the same state and there is no biasing, transactions are costless and markets are efficient.

The concept of EIB substantiates that the major determinant of one's environment is the behavior of others, and their behavior may in turn depend on their beliefs about others' behavior. The extension of biasing chain is political interplay may be driven by incentives come from diverse opportunities found in the nature or in the market. For example, 'fossil fuel' is a big incentive for integrating our existing globalized information biasing chain structure. This is the reason that few 'oil investors' can control the political lifeline of many countries. They could play a big positive role building alternatives for our societies during transitioning to peak oil. Instead they are funding for politicians' election campaigns in order to gain perks for their industry and to put off higher efficiency standards and environmental protections and distorting climate science and discouraging a transition to renewable energy.[83] The most they are doing toward climate change is no more than greenwashing their huge profit from high oil price. As an example, Heinberg points out that ExxonMobil's 10 million dollar for a year investment in the Global Climate and Energy Project is equivalent to three hours' worth of earnings for the company in 2010.[83] On the other hand, aggregate production and return on investment on fossil fuel is declining. All new production are coming from expensive unconventional sources such as tar sands, tight oil, and deep-water oil, which requires very high investment but has very high decline rate. However, the fossil fuel industry does not want to admit the facts "as the industry needs investors to pony up ever-larger bets to pay for ever-more-extreme production projects"[83]. This means their position on top of the biasing chain is negatively impacting transition to the 'peak oil' until oil fully depletes.

The concept of biasing chain describes that capitalists try to keep their position up of the biasing chain. The upper the position of a biasing source, the more power it holds to control of the overall economy. This model can be used for analysis of many socio-economic and political issues like causes of war, leadership and motivation, corporate governance or high payout for CEO and top executives etc. As an example, only few people who are top on the information biasing chain may motivate common people into a war to establish their narrow political or religious views. The people positioned at the top of an information biasing chain bear great responsibilities for the people positioned below them. Unfortunately, their actions always concentrate for the benefits of the coalition where they belong. A small mistake from the part of the leaders at the top may cause big sufferings of the others at the bottom. On the other hand, a visionary leader can see outside the coalition and may lead a nation through crisis toward greater benefits. The concept of EIB also tells that the individuals positioned at the topmost coalition of global economic biasing chain can take independent decisions for their own absolute benefits although they are not beyond their Capitalists' Dilemma (CD) (reference: Section 7.8 in Chapter 7).

8.5 Institutions Redefined

The concept of "Economics of Information Biasing (EIB)" tells that institutions are fundamentally born in information sharing strategies of individual economic agents. It is based on information asymmetry however, focuses on impact of information sharing strategies of individuals on institutions and human values. This model provides an analytical framework to model our broad perspective social and economic problems in terms of information biasing so that we can extract underlying institutional structure specific to the problem. In our real world, natural information is overridden or biased by means of preaching, publicizing, advertising, motivation, legislation, norms or whatsoever. The biasing of information integrates diversified payoff maximization interests, one dependent on another but segregates the individuals in different coalitions. The coalitions are abstracted as long as neoclassical aggregation or methodological individualisms are presumably valid. This abstraction is absolutely subjective that varies from few individuals to the whole population of a country. EIB fully complies with new institutional economics for the whole economy but it ignores the role of the institutions within a coalition.

The economic history of last two centuries has been centered around the impact of government intervention on the efficiency of the market economy. As Stiglitz refers Adam Smith "that free markets led to efficient outcomes "as if by an invisible hand" has played a central role in these debates: it suggested that we could, by and large, rely on markets without government intervention."[44] He argues "they have suggested that the reason that the hand may be invisible is that it is simply not there – or at least that if is there, it is palsied."[28] Neoclassical Economics (NCE) describes a perfect market as the most efficient engine for distribution of resources. Such a 'perfect' market is only a theoretical idea and is not possible in real world. On the other hand, in absence of invisible hand, EIB more closely represents real world economies with imperfect information. If we can enhance information sharing among the coalitions, an EIB will gain distributional efficiency. This is where the concept of government comes in this model. Here a government can be defined as an absolutely independent body outside the information biasing chain that can enhance information sharing among the coalitions defined in the model. As mentioned in Chapter 4 that enhancement of information has to be reflected in all institutional matters like policies, regulations, practices, systems, norms, motivation, laws and orders and so on. Now the challenge is to form an independent government out of the individuals who already belong to those upper layer coalitions. This is the reason for why a government power is always preferred to be centralized.

Joseph Tainter (1990) describes the growth of civilization as a process of investing societal resources in the development of ever-greater complexity in order to solve problems.[84] The biasing chain is the best example of a complex system that organized flow of resources from villages to more centralized urban areas and then to the hand of the riches in the world. The institutions have become more complex as the biasing become bigger. Much of the economic problems that our rural people had been facing could be solved in a much simpler way locally without forming complex institutions. As an example, the solution of rural poverty in India could be to address the root causes of poverty such as protecting them from loan sharks and lawsuits, provide access to good health care and education. Instead the rural poverty created an influx of migration to urban areas overcrowded and polluted the urban areas and created more complex problem – now nearly impossible to solve. As Tainter puts describes "More complex societies are costlier to maintain than simpler ones and require higher support levels per capita."[84] Now the policy makers have no choice but to maintain these costs, which so far have been manageable because of cheap energy from fossil fuel. As Heinberg describes:

"The dramatic increase in societal complexity seen during the past two centuries (measured, for example, in a relentless trend toward urbanization and soaring volumes of trade) resulted primarily from increasing rates of energy flow for manufacturing and transport. Fossil fuels provided by far the biggest energy subsidy in human history, and were responsible for industrialization, urbanization, and massive population growth."[83]

As an example, the scarcity and fall of water level in the city of Mumbai or Chennai could be solved by using high capacity pumps and more electricity that use fossil fuel as primary source of energy. What will happen if the water crisis in those cities becomes severe as the oil price becomes unaffordable and water level falls further down? Won't it create the situation more complex?

According to Stiglitz, much the economic problems cannot be fully resolved, but there are laws and institutions which can decidedly improve matters.[28] He contends for laws and institutions like Right-to-know laws, demanding transparency that have been part of governance in Sweden for two hundred years which can decidedly improve the matters created from information imperfection.[29] The concept of Economics of Information Biasing goes one step deeper to address the unsolved or aggravated economic and social problems since in this model, existing institutions are seen as effects not as a tool for solving specific problems.

The new institutional economics generalizes the involvement of human beings in evolution of institutions ignoring differential influence of some individuals on the institutions. The institutions are defines as "humanly devised constraints that structure human interaction."[30] In fact, the same institutions are constraints for a group of individuals however, opportunities for another group of individuals. This model is intended to provide analytical framework to distinguish these different groups based on a particular subject of analysis. To overcome the constraints created by existing institutions we usually talk about institutional reform. If the individuals empowered for institutional reform are not affected or they are the beneficiaries of existing institutional structure, why they will go for any reform or changes? Institutions are not about constraints also "such a constraint can open up possibilities."[31] We may use the definition of institutions from Hodgson as "systems of established and prevalent social rules that structure social interactions. Language, money, law, systems of weights and measures, table manners, and firms (and other organizations) are thus all institutions."[30]

The neoclassical economics applies methodological individualism that starts from the ultimate constituents of the world, "the individual people and relations between them."[31] It ignores "the incentive structure embodied in institutions".[30] The concept of coalition is a meeting point of methodological individualism and institutions since institutions do not matter within a coalition but they do matter when the coalitions interact. The concept of methodological individualism is valid only for a coalition. A coalition acts as a single actor in economic games and when two coalitions interact, the institutions become visible. The concept of information biasing supports "downward causation" concept of institution originated by Sperry (1991)[32] and Hodgson (2003)[33]. Hodgson and many others indicated that institutions have "significant downward effects" and equilibrium-like qualities.[47] Our real world optimization games are not evenly played. Some agents are in advantageous positions but they leave limited options for their counterparts to secure their chances to win. Many of the constraints we face in our real life are created by information biasing strategies of some other people. At aggregate level, the sustainability of information biasing is achieved by means of rules of laws, formal or informal norms, beliefs, prejudice, practices and so on otherwise the biasing would be continually or dynamically redefined. Therefore, in our information biasing chain model, institutions can be simply defined as means to stabilize information biasing between two coalitions. The concept of information biasing does not provide any general definition of institutions but help us model our economic and social problems in terms of most relevant institutions.

The term 'institution' is very comprehensive that sometimes makes difficult finding a realistic or workable solution of a social or economic problem. The concept of coalition hides all complexities of institutions within a coalition and the concept of information biasing highlights the impacting institutions between two coalitions. The following figure (Figure 8.7) shows a simple cone shaped information biasing model as described in section 8.3 but comprising of only one Biasing Source (BS), one Biased Load (BL) between the Universal Biasing Source (UBS) and the Absolute Biased Load (ABL). An economic system is an interdependent process by involving many individuals and coalitions. We may imagine that the information biasing system is a **Biased Learning Process (BLP)** occurs in vertical direction from biasing source to biased load. There is also a feedback process flows opposite direction from a biased load to a biasing source and all the way up to UBS. The feedbacks are captured by the biasing sources to make necessary corrections and adjustments to have better control over others all the way down the chain. Therefore, the feedback process is in fact a learning process for all the biasing sources. In a biasing chain model, since this learning occurs in the vertical direction, it can be named as **Vertical Feedback Process (VFP)** as shown in Figure 8.7. BLP and VFP together can be called as **Biased Vertical Learning Process (BVLP)**. There are also incentives for learning within a coalition that leads to consistent development of mental models of the individuals and changes in the institutional structure of an economy within

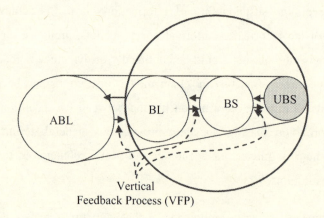

Vertical
Feedback Process (VFP)

Figure 8.7: Biased Vertical Learning Process (BVLP)

it. This learning can be named as **Horizontal Learning Process (HLP)** or endogenous learning. The horizontal learning describes natural human learning processes within a coalition. Although every individual within a coalition share the same level of information but learning is different because each individual has different knack and ability for learning. North (1993) defined the learning process as "the informational feedback process and arbitraging actors will correct initially incorrect models, punish deviant behavior and lead surviving players to correct models."[34] North defines a general learning process. If we try to fit this definition into our model, it will be much of a horizontal learning as the arbitraging actors are peers positioned in the same coalition. On the other hand, it will be more of a BVLP if they are positioned in two different coalitions. If knowledge development is a HLP, then BVLP will tell about how is to use that knowledge. For example, gun powder is result of horizontal learning but to use gun powder for colonization is result of BVLP. The ways we have ordered our modern world like technological advancement, specialization, division of labor, competition are the results of combination of both the learning processes. However, we need to distinguish between them to evaluate quality and efficiency of the ordering in terms of the benefits of human being. For example, competition is good but we need to evaluate whether the competition will be for transforming all of our milks into candy or for keeping the milk as much as possible for our kids. Since policy making is a top down process, vertical learning should worth outmost importance to economists and social scientists. It also explains evolution of our institutions with time.

The market fundamentalists say institutions do not matter—an efficient market takes care of our economic problems, they ignore the functional presence of information biasing on vertical direction. If both context of information (horizontal and vertical) are not taken into account, the capacity of a market may be misunderstood. In his proposal 'Steady-State Economy' Herman Daly proposes non-growth but a market driven economy. Daly says that "the market is the most efficient institution we have come up with". "Markets single-mindedly aim to serve allocative efficiency."[35] He believes that the role of the state should just be to "impose . . . quantitative limits on aggregate throughput . . . within which the market can safely function, and then the market is left alone."[35] How will the market solve 'Capitalists Dilemma (CD)'? Most importantly, CD is fully supported by corporate laws. Canadian law professor Joel Bakan (2004)[36] summed up after interview with Milton Friedman "the corporation, as created by law, most closely resembles Milton Friedman's ideal model of the institution: it compels executives to prioritize the interests of their companies and shareholders above all others and forbids them from being socially responsible – at least genuinely so."[36] Smith (2010) argues Daly's comments as "and by leaving the corporations "alone" to maximize capitalist efficiency and optimality according to their interests, doesn't this just open the way to further social and environmental destruction, and thus to undermine Daly's social and environmental goals?"[18] Arnott-Stiglitz analyze that it was only under very special circumstances that markets could be shown to be efficient.[37] Although Stiglitz further argues "the so-called Washington consensus policies, which have predominated in the policy advice of the international financial institutions over the past quarter century, have been based on market fundamentalist policies which ignored the information-theoretic concerns, and this explains at least in part their widespread failures."[28] According to the concept of EIB, the long persistent gap between these policies and the fact of functional level of the institutions in turn fill out the market with corruption and exploitation.

The learning environments are not the same for every individual since information availability or the cost of acquiring information differs among them. In a biasing chain model, since vertical learning occurs on the upward direction, it increases transaction costs on the downward direction. There are chances that learning may concentrate within upper layer coalitions and that may cause them to merge by defining common interests and create a big "Pareto Coalition (PC)" shown as a big circle in Figure 8.7. However, the coalitions at the bottom of the biasing chain may worse off because of the learning loop on upper layer. If VLP gets confined then in the long run, ideological or behavioral stereotyping may take over any initiatives to change our existing social and political system.

8.6 The Concept of Values Framework

Although we have assumed that everyone in a coalition shares the same level of information but each individual has different history since they have not been always in the same coalition. There are differences in beliefs, choices and characteristics among individuals within a coalition. The concept of information biasing complies with Herbert Simon's concept of bounded rationality that every individual is limited in terms of rational choices and decision making.[38]

The ability of an individual to rationally optimize his objective functions under a biased environment can be defined as his **Rationality Index (RI)**. To comply with the definition of coalition in Chapter 4, we may assume that in a sustainable biasing environment, every individual in a coalition has the same rationality index. In a biasing chain model, the lower the position of a coalition on the biasing chain is, the more the individuals are limited to optimize their rational decisions. Therefore, the coalitions can be ranked in terms of RI along the biasing chain. The "**Universal Biasing Source (UBS)**" that is positioned above a primary source can have the highest RI=1 and the absolute biased load placed at the bottom most level of a biasing chain may have the lowest RI=0. All other coalitions are to be ranked between 1 and 0. As an example, the colonists in America had superior information about warfare than that of natives. However, when they provoked the natives for fighting against them leaving no option of denying, it was the situation of information biasing. In that case, colonists could have RI close to 1 just below the UBS on that time and the natives had RI close or equal to zero (0). Since a biasing chain model is a subjective model, this ranking of middle order coalitions will also vary based on the problem we are trying to solve. The concept of bounded rationality tells us the reason for making sub-optimal decisions, whereas the definition of rationality index tells about level of the sub-optimality of any decision.

The definition of rationality index does not distinguish among individuals within a coalition. The uniqueness in terms of rationality of an individual toward a particular objective function can be defined by introducing a new term called Elasticity of Rationality (EoR). It can be defined as responsiveness of an individual's rationality index toward a common objective function with respect to corresponding information biasing. Everyone in a coalition will not respond in the same way when the biasing toward them changes. The Rationality Index (RI) of an individual provides indication of his existing position on a biasing chain whereas EoR provides a forecast about his future position. The rational behavior of an individual toward a certain objective function will change if his or her rationality index is elastic for that objective with respect to corresponding information biasing. In our world, most of the individuals are more elastic to those objectives which can be measured in monetary value than those are not. This is why capital based market interest overrides our natural human interest so strongly that we have no other choice but to accept its blessings and sufferings.

In this model, the concept of bounded rationality is described in terms of RI and EoR. The both are seen from a biased load perspective. On the other hand, a biasing source is responsible for limiting rational choices of the individuals it biases. Therefore, it is important to know how much the individuals of a biasing source are concerned about the benefits of the other individuals positioned below them along the biasing chain. Doing well of others is not an individual's objective, it is a strategy. This strategy of an individual largely depends on his learning or the information he has received and how that has shaped his logical mindsets and values. We may assume that the individuals of a biasing source use their values to prioritize their objective functions. And there is an implicit agreement among the individuals of a biasing source to create resonance effect toward their biased load. This agreement can be translated in terms of values and may be called as coalition values.

In reality, we see our values have been changing consistently in long-run and also they vary demographically even within the same country in different time-frame. There is a big difference between Japanese values before and after the World War II. Our personal values are inherited from coalition values and modified according to our personal characteristics and learning processes we have come through. This is how our values are preserved and transformed inter-generationally from one individual to another individual. The concept of coalition values differ from collective value. The collective values define some normative values of our cultural, society or religion, whereas our coalition values are always subjective and define implicit common values of an abstract coalition. This model also tells that coalition values of individuals in the upper layer biasing source are sometimes more powerful than collective values.

A Pareto efficient economy describes a utopia where the whole biasing chain would become a single coalition and everybody would become concerned about everybody. Our real economy is not at all comprised of philanthropists but every individual has a combination of good and bad values. In normal circumstances we observe a very slow and consistent change of our coalition values. Any big change in any part of a biasing chain like military intervention, civil war, revolution or motivation does not come suddenly rather it come as a consequence of a series of biasing adjustments along the biasing chain. For example, a country where there are lots of corrupted people, we need to investigate the biasing that caused their coalition values to deteriorate in course of time. Since biasing works in the form of biasing chain, it is nearly impossible to deal with corruption by charging corrupted individuals only rather than counteracting its biasing root. In summary, we may conclude that every coalition has certain values that are the building blocks of a country's qualitative economic structure. The whole biasing chain represents a **Values Framework (VF)** where each coalition holds certain values.[24]

Each country has unique value framework that translates the economic cost and output produced in the country into human cost and human value respectively at each level of the biasing chain. The "values framework" of the entire world evaluates our economic efforts in terms of benefits of whole mankind. An economy always works within a "values framework" on which the characteristics of the institutions depend. Institutional framework is just an outfit of the values framework. Our institutions are greatly influenced by the values of those coalitions that are positioned on the uppermost levels of the biasing chain. The concept of value framework will help us to deal with the issues like environmental damages, spreading of corruption or cultural detachment for which quantitative economics alone is not enough.

Smith (2010) argues "So it follows that we need a completely different kind of economic system, a non-capitalist economic system based on human needs, environmental needs, and a completely different value system, not on profit."[18] His 'green proposals' describes "They call for a redistribution of wealth to those who are in need and for the construction of a society based not on possessive individualism but on a decent material sufficiency for everyone on the planet. And they call for a moral and spiritual transformation of our values away from materialism."[18] Why not we shall also refer our spiritual books which guide us toward restrained use of resources and lifestyle long before the ecological crisis began due to excessive use of natural resources?

In the short-run, the values framework may be invariable, however, in the long-run, the path of economic history takes many turnings, rises and falls so does the composition of our values. Our values preserve our history, evaluate our present economic activities and provide guidelines for the future. There is a gap remains between existing institutional framework and the institutions that will be required in future. The whole effort of this model is to show that we can deliberately improve our human values to create a better economy, a better society and a better environment.

8.7 The Core Capitalists

The mainstream economists are not concerned about values framework or any institutional influence, since they assume institutions does not matter in a well-functioning (competitive) economic system. As discussed in Chapter 4 that institutions matter when a Pareto Coalition interacts with A Pareto Space but may not matter within a Pareto Coalition. However, in a biasing chain model, institutions matters in varying degree but less toward center of a Differential Market Model (DMM) since the probability of achieving Pareto Efficiency is the highest at the center of a DMM. In other words, the center of a DMM can be defined as the Market Energy State (MES) which is perfectly Pareto Efficient. This means the individuals positioned at center of a global DMM has the highest level of co-operation or bonding for achieving their common objective functions such as accumulation of capitals. Alternatively, they can be positioned at the top most coalition of a global biasing chain model described in section 8.3. However and whatever an economy performs, they are the ultimate destination for capital accumulation of all the economies in the world. Accordingly, they are the Core Capitalists or the Absolute Biased Source (ABS) who hold highest level of control of the world economy to achieve their objectives. The question is whether The Core Capitalists are the result of market dynamics or it has been a long-term planned effort to be on the top?

The literatures that projects power relations in social group chiefly psychological or socio-political origins regarded as conspiracy theory.[39] In an article in Time Magazine, Justin Fox describes that Wall Streeters like conspiracy theories "because (1) some financial market conspiracies are real and (2) without theories of some sort to grasp on to, you're going to get completely lost in the chaos of the market's day-to-day movements."[40] Griffin argues "Yet there is hardly a single page of history that does not partially reveal the deadly eye of conspiracy at work."[26] Therefore, exploring The Core Capitalists is nothing but exploring the books and research papers on the richest people in the world, which are regarded as "conspiracy theory". The single most important such book named "Tragedy and Hope"[41] is written by Carroll Quigley, eminent American historian and theorist, professor at Georgetown University.

Quigley identifies The Core Capitalists as "secret society" or "secret group". Quigley himself was permitted to examine its papers and secret records for two years and spent twenty years writing this book. In his book, "Tragedy and Hope" published in 1966, Carroll Quigley, In the preface of his book Quigley describes:

"The powers of financial capitalism had another far-reaching aim, nothing less than to create a world system of financial control in private hands able to dominate the political system of each country and the economy of the world as a whole. This system was to be controlled in a feudalistic fashion by the central banks of the world acting in concert, by secret agreements arrived at in frequent meetings and conferences. The apex of the systems was to be the Bank for International Settlements in Basel, Switzerland, a private bank owned and controlled by the world's central banks which were themselves private corporations. Each central bank...sought to dominate its government by its ability to control Treasury loans, to manipulate foreign exchanges, to influence the level of economic activity in the country, and to influence co-operative politicians by subsequent economic rewards in the business world."[42]

According to Quigley, the third stage of capitalism in European civilization is financial capitalism (1850-1931) followed by commercial capitalism, industrial capitalism (1770-1850). As a quick recap from Chapter 2 that industrial capitalism embarked in England with the wealth brought by East India Company from Asia through opium trade to China from their occupied Bengal followed by

Battle of Plassey in 1757. Through 1790-East India Company established a monopoly on Opium trade and poppy growers in Indian could sell only to the East India Company. William Digby and British historians agree that without the "Venture Capital" which was brought from Bengal, the Industrial Revolution might not have happened.[43] A small group of merchant bankers of London had acquired all gems and wealth of East India Company 'which lay ready for use when the need of financial capitalist innovation became urgent'[44]. They owned London Stock Exchange, the Bank of England, and the London money market, which are indirectly is the basis for the establishment of almost all of the banking institutions of India and also many around the world. Sequentially, Britain conquered the whole of India and colonies all over the world, thus giving it more capital, more raw materials and a larger market, which help accelerate its Industrial Revolution.[43]

London based merchant bankers brought their financial networks into a single financial system on an international scale which manipulated the quantity and flow of money "so that they were able to influence, if not control, government on one side and industries on the other"[22]. They aspired to establish dynasties of international bankers and were at least as successful at this as were many of the dynastic political rulers.[60] Quigley (1966) describes establishment of Rothschild dynasty as:

> "The greatest of these dynasties, of course, were the descendants of Meyer Amschel Rothschild (1743-1812) of Frankfort, whose male descendants, for at least two generations, generally married first cousins or even nieces. Rothschild's five sons, established at branches in Vienna, London, Naples, and Paris, as well as Frankfort, cooperated together in ways which other international banking dynasties copied but rarely excelled."[44]

The strategically located Rothschild five sons began their lucrative operations in government finance. In his book "The World Order: A Study in the Hegemony of Parasitism" Eustace Mullins writes "The first precept of success in making government loans lies in "creating a demand", that is, by taking part in the creation of financial panics, depressions, famines, wars and revolutions. The overwhelming success of the Rothschilds lay in their willingness to do what had to be done."[45] As Frederic Morton writes in the preface to "The Rothschilds":

"For the last one hundred and fifty years, the history of the House of Rothschild has been to an amazing degree the backstage history of Western Europe... Because of their success in making loans not to individuals but to nations, they reaped huge profits... Someone once said that the wealth of Rothschild consists of the bankruptcy of nations."[46]

In the wake of free trade, according to Quigley, the English have not always been unanimous in regarding the empire as a source of pride and benefit. He describes:

"In fact, the middle generation of the nineteenth century was filled with persons, such as Gladstone, who regarded the empire with profound suspicion. They felt that it was a source of great expense; they were convinced that it involved England had no need to fight; they could see no economic advantage in having an empire, since the existence of free trade would allow commerce to flow no matter who held colonial areas; they were convinced that any colonial areas, no matter at what cost they might be acquired, would eventually separate from the mother country, voluntarily if they were given the rights of Englishman, or by rebellion, as the American colonies had done, if they were deprived of such rights. In general, the "Little Englanders", as they were called, were averse to colonial expansion on the grounds of cost."[47]

However, the new imperialism after 1870 changed on grounds of moral duty and of social reform and not, as earlier, on grounds of missionary activity and material advantage. According to Quigley the man most responsible for this change was John Ruskin.[48] In 1870, John Ruskin, a wealthy British socialist was appointed as professor of fine arts at Oxford University in London. He urged the Oxford undergraduates as members of the privileged to extend their magnificent tradition of education, beauty, rule of law, freedom, decency, and self-discipline to the lower classes in England itself and to the non-English masses throughout the world.[48]

According Quigley, Ruskin's inaugural lecture was copied out in longhand by one undergraduate, Cecil Rhodes (1853-1902), who kept it with him for thirty years. During the second half of Britain's "imperial century" between 1815 and 1914, Cecil Rhodes advocated the British Empire re-annexing the United States of America and reforming itself into an "Imperial Federation" to bring about a hyper-power and lasting world peace. At his death he was considered one of the wealthiest men in the world. In his first will, written in 1877 before he had accumulated his wealth, Rhodes wanted to create a secret society (known as the Society of the Elect) that would bring the whole world under British rule.[49] The exact wording from this will is:

"To and for the establishment, promotion and development of a Secret Society, the true aim and object whereof shall be for the extension of British rule throughout the world, the perfecting of a system of emigration from the United Kingdom, and of colonization by British subjects of all lands where the means of livelihood are attainable by energy, labor and enterprise, and especially the occupation by British settlers of the entire Continent of Africa, the Holy Land, the Valley of the Euphrates, the Islands of Cyprus and Candia, the whole of South America, the Islands of the Pacific not heretofore possessed by Great Britain, the whole of the Malay Archipelago, the seaboard of China and Japan, the ultimate recovery of the United States of America as an integral part of the British Empire, the inauguration of a system of Colonial representation in the Imperial Parliament which may tend to weld together the disjointed members of the Empire and, finally, the foundation of so great a Power as to render wars impossible, and promote the best interests of humanity." [50&51]

Rhodes, with financial support from Rothschild and Alfred Beit, made one of the world's greatest fortunes from businesses by monopolizing diamond and controlling most of the gold mines of South Africa. He organized a secret society and spent his wealth to federate the ruling class of English-speaking peoples and to bring all the habitable portions of the world under their control. The central part of the society was established by March 1891, where Rhodes was the leader, surrounded by an executive committee comprised of powerful journalist William T. Stead and Lord Alfred Milner and then a "Circle of Initiates" where Lord Rothschild was a member and an outer circle "Association of Helpers".[48] At the center, usually depicted as the all-seeing eye, there is a tiny group in complete control.[42] Next comes a circle of secondary leadership that, for the most part, is completely unaware of an inner core. This all-seeing eye also appears on the reverse side of the Great Seal of the United States (1776) and on the back of the U.S. one-dollar bill since 1935 as shown in Figure 8.8.[53] The phrase "Annuit Coeptis" translates to "He approves (or has approved) [our] undertakings".[54] This reflects the founding fathers belief that God favors the creation the United States and will bless its future prosperity. In reality has the word "God" changed to "Financial God"? The Latin phrase "novus ordo seclorum", meaning "New Order of the Ages"[55] appears on the reverse side of the Great Seal since 1782.

Figure 8.8: The Eye of Providence, seen here on the US $1 bill[52]

The conspiracy theorists claim this was an allusion to the "New World Order".[56] The unprecedented transformation of the world economies, societies, businesses and polities was not a coincidence. Would these happen that fast without big financial investments in science and technologies such as in rail roads, electricity, petroleum, automobiles, telecommunications and manufacturing by The Core Capitalists?

After death of Rhodes in 1902, the group was able to access Rhodes's money to extend and execute his ideas. Milner who became Governor General and High Commissioner of South Africa led this group a dominant force in British imperial and foreign affairs.[48] Milner recruited a group of young men mostly from Oxford and Toynbee Hall and according to Quigley:

"Through his influence these men were able to win influential posts in government and international finance in British imperial and foreign affairs up to 1939. Under Milner in South Africa, they were known as Milner's Kindergarten until 1910. In 1909-1913 they organized semi-secret groups, known as The Round Table Groups in the chief British dependencies and the United States."[48]

Milner became one of the greatest political and financial powers in the world. Later it formed an outer circle organization in many other countries such as Royal Institute of International Affairs (RIIA) in British dominions, Council on Foreign Relations (CFR) in the United States.[48] Figure 8.9 below zooms in the center of a Differential Market Model (DMM) showing the position of CFR/RIIA and The Round Table. According to Quigley, the innermost position was the circle of initiates was led by Milner or Rhodes. However, according to the concept of Economics of Information Biasing (EIB), their biasing still exists in form of an information biasing chain built historically since then. Therefore, we may assume the existence of the Absolute Capitalists or the Core Capitalists is in fact institutional not physical. As an example, although Milner or Rhodes does not exist anymore but the biasing chain they have initiated has now been fully established. Importantly, Milner and Rhodes were initially funded by international bankers. Therefore, they were the front end of the international bankers and ultimately they have established objectives of the banking houses

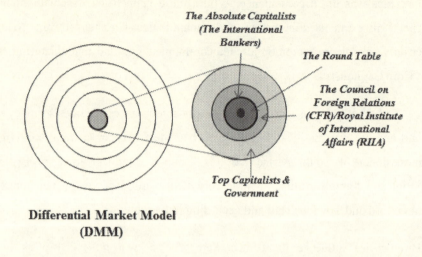

Differential Market Model (DMM)

Figure 8.9: An exemplary model of The Core Capitalists

(Elaborated using the concept of Carroll Quigley's book "Tragedy & Hope"[48])

not even Ruskin's. In Figure 8.9, the outer circle of the center of the DMM represents government and all other top capitalists. In his documentary "The Capitalists Conspiracy", Edward Griffin describes "The outer circle, for the most part, is completely unaware of an inner core. "They are led to believe that they are inner-most ring."[57] Quigley argues that although the Round Table still exists today, its position in influencing the policies of world leaders has been much reduced from its heyday during World War I and slowly waned after the end of World War II and the Suez Crisis. However, according to the concept of "Economics of Information Biasing (EIB)" the institutional existence of core capitalists at the top most position of a biasing chain model or the center most position of a DMM is stronger than ever.

According to Mullins, J.P. Morgan's principal role at the beginning was "to secretly carry out commissions for the House of Rothschild".[45] According to

Quigley, CFR was a was a front for J. P. Morgan and Company in association with the very small American Round Table Group.[58] Mullins describes another revelation of the hidden power of the Rothschild interests in America through Rockefeller, the oil tycoon and the richest man in the world. As Mullins writes "Not only has it directed the Rockefeller enterprises from the time that National City Bank of Cleveland, a Rothschild bank, financed the early expansion of Rockefeller, South Improvement Co., which enabled him to crush his competitors through illegal railway rebates."[45] Does it mean that the house of Rothschild is the inner most core of the International Bankers?

Rockefeller was also considered a supporter of capitalism based in a perspective of social Darwinism, and is often quoted saying "The growth of a large business is merely a survival of the fittest".[59] He was well positioned to take advantage of postwar oil-fueled economy and the great westward expansion fostered of railroads financed by J. P. Morgan's partnered National City Bank. As of 1906, two-thirds of the rail mileage in the U.S. was controlled by seven entities, with the New York Central, Pennsylvania Railroad (PRR), and Morgan having the largest portions.[50] In 1911, with the dissolution of the Standard Oil trust into 33 smaller companies, Rockefeller became the richest man in the world.[51] Quigley describes the reason for the co-operation among The Core Capitalists such as J.P. Morgan and Rockefeller as:

"The structure of financial controls created by the tycoons of "Big Banking" and "Big Business" in the period 1880-1933 was of extraordinary complexity, one business fief being built on another, both being allied with semi-independent associates, the whole rearing upward into two pinnacles of economic and financial power, of which one, centered in New York, was headed by J.P. Morgan and Company, and the other, in Ohio, was headed by Rockefeller family. When these two co-operated, as they generally did, they could influence the economic life of the country to a large degree and could almost control its political life, at least on the Federal level. The former point can be illustrated by a few facts. In the United States the number of billion-dollar corporations rose from 32 percent in 1909 to 49 percent in 1930 and reached 57 percent in 1939...In fact, in 1930, one corporation (American Telephone and Telegraph, controlled by Morgan) had greater assets than the total wealth in twenty-one states of the Union."[62]

President Roosevelt, on one hand had to deal with big conglomerate businesses such as Standard Oil and on the other hand big banking houses and politicians who supported them. Their combined effort created Panic of 1907 and consolidated the preeminence of the banks controlled by J.P. Morgan. In 1890–1913, 42 major corporations such as Federal Steel Company, AT&T, General Electric and 24 railroad companies were organized or their securities were underwritten, in whole or part, by J.P. Morgan and Company.[63] The partners of J.P. Morgan & Co. and directors of First National and National City Bank controlled aggregate resources of over $22 billion, which Louis Brandeis, which was equivalent to all the properties in the twenty-two states west of the Mississippi River.[64] The he Rockefeller Chase Bank was merged with the Warburg's Manhattan to form the Chase-Manhattan, one of the most powerful financial combines in the world today. Acting in concert with Morgan banking dynasty, they spent untold millions of dollars to promote the Federal Reserve Act.[57] As discussed in section 4.2, the concept of 'Biased Equilibrium' explains why the institutions built by initial big capitalists 'Big Bankers' and 'Big Oil' companies still dominate the financial world. It also explains why most of the European central banks or the U.S. Federal Reserve is owned by a private coalition of "Big Bankers".

Why the richest people are interested in banking? Quigley explains from the quotation of William Paterson, on obtaining the charter of the Bank of England in 1694, to use the moneys he had won in privateering, said, "The Bank hath benefit of interest on all moneys which it creates out of nothing".[48] The Panic of 1907 in the United States was a financial crisis that began with a stock manipulation scheme to corner the market in F. Augustus Heinze's United Copper Company.[65] During the Panic of 1907, when major New York banks were on the verge of bankruptcy, a private conglomerate led by J. P. Morgan stepped in and set themselves up as "lenders of last resort".[66] Europe's most famous banker, Lord Rothschild, sent word of his "admiration and respect" for Morgan.[65] The event led to the passage of Aldrich–Vreeland Act in 1908, which established the National Monetary Commission, sponsored and headed by Nelson Aldrich, a prominent American businessman and a leader of the Republican Party. He worked with several key bankers and economists to design a plan for an American central bank following the models of privately owned European central banks. One of them was Paul Warburg, a German immigrant banker from Warburg banking family in Hamburg, Germany who masterminded the plan for Federal Reserve System.

Aldrich's bill met much opposition from politicians. Critics charged Aldrich of being biased due to his close ties to wealthy bankers such as J. P. Morgan and John D. Rockefeller, Jr., Aldrich's son-in-law.[67] After winning in 1912 presidential election, Democrat Woodrow Wilson had tried to find a middle ground between conservative Republicans, led by Senator Nelson W. Aldrich, and the powerful left wing of the Democratic Party, led by William Bryan, who wanted a government-owned central bank that could print paper money as Congress required. Wilson convinced Bryan's supporters that because Federal Reserve notes were obligations of the government, the plan met their demands for an elastic currency. Having 12 regional banks was meant to weaken the influence of the powerful New York banks.[68] Meanwhile, a key meeting that shaped the Federal Reserve Act was held in secret including Aldrich, J.P. Morgan, Paul Warburg at the Jekyll Island Club, where both were members of the club.[69] In 1913 President signed the Federal Reserve Act into law. This act established a privately owned Federal Reserve System. In reality, while power was supposed to be decentralized, the New York branch has been dominating the

Federal Reserve as the "first among equals".[70] When the federal government goes into debt, it borrows the money from the Federal Reserve System that it creates out of nothing on which huge interests to be paid by the U.S. taxpayers. In the 2013 Federal Budget, the interest expense was $221 billion.[57]

If the Federal Reserve System established before they had formed their coalition, would it be publically owned? Or would the rail roads and all other big investments be financed from competitive capital market? Quigley explains:

"In the various actions which increase or decrease the supply of money, governments, bankers, and industries have not always seen eye to eye. On the whole, in the period up to 1931, bankers especially the Money Power controlled by the international investment bankers, were able to dominate both business and government. They could dominate business, especially in activities and in areas where industry could dominate business, especially in activities and in areas where industry could not finance its own needs for capital, because investment bankers and the ability to supply or refuse to supply such capital. Thus, Rothschild interests came to dominate many of the railroads of Europe, while Morgan dominated at least 26,000 miles of American railroads. Such bankers went further than this. In return for floatation of securities of industry, they took seats on the boards of directors of industrial firms, as they had already done on commercial banks, insurance firms, and finance companies. From these lesser institutions they funneled capital to enterprises which yielded control and away from those who resisted. These firms were controlled through interlocking directorships, holding companies, and lesser banks. They engineered amalgamations and generally reduced competition, until by the early twentieth century many activities were so monopolized that they could raise noncompetitive prices above costs to obtain sufficient profits to become self-financing and were thus able to eliminate the control of bankers. But before that stage was reached a relatively small number of bankers were in positions of immense influence in European and American economic life."[71]

After building 6,365 miles Trans-Siberian railroad in the fourteen years 1891-1905, according to Quigley "Russia was able to increase her political pressure in the Far East, brought Britain into an alliance with Japan (1902) and brought Russia into war with Japan (1904-1905). The railroads had a most profound effect on Russia from every point of view, binding one-sixth of the earth's surface into a single political unit and transforming that country's economic, political, and social life."[44] Russia grew in export of her Petroleum from Baku and Grozny oil field, minerals such as iron and coal agricultural products such as grains, sugar and cotton allowed siphoning wealth into urban areas and to export market. According to Quigley, this caused a "quick turnover middlemen who swarmed like ants".[72] At the same time Russia's balance of trade grew, providing gold and foreign exchange which allowed her building up its gold reserve and capital for industrial development.[72] The Czar personally owned 150 million acres of lands.[73] Between 1905 and 1910 the Czar had sent hundreds of millions of dollars in six leading New York banks: Chase, National City Bank, Guaranty Trust, J.P. Morgan, Hanover, and Manufacturers Trust and also similar amount in four European banks.[73] During communist revolution in 1917, Czar Nicholas II, and his family were killed. None of the Czar's money deposited in European and American banks ever been disbursed.[73]

Griffin analyzes "the Communist movement, not only in the United States, but around the world always has been financed by the International banking Establishment."[26&74] Quigley explains why the Establishment has never greatly worried about the Communist movement in America. He writes

"It must be recognized that the power that these energetic left-wingers exercised was never their own power or Communist power but was ultimately the power of the International financial coterie."[75]

He also writes this:

"There does exist, and has existed for a generation, an international Anglophile network which operates, to some extent, in the way the Radical right believes the Communists act. In fact, this network, which we may identify as the Round Table Groups, has no aversion to cooperating with the Communists, or any other group, and frequently does so."[75]

Almost all economies before integration with The Core Capitalists were comprised of some sorts of biasing chain where productive class at the bottom such as peasants or 'proletariat', a middle men class called gentry or 'bourgeois' and a imperial class or government on the top. The middle layer is the dominant element who protects the vested interests by creating a strong Biased Equilibrium (BE). The effect of integration of the core capitalist superstructure reinforces the Biased Equilibrium Barrier (BEB) by creating or reinforcing a Money Loop (ML) and Market Energy Loop (MEL) described in Chapter 4. Conspiracy theorists describes that to obtain its share of the wealth flowing upward from the bottom, The Core Capitalists apply a strategy called "Hegelian dialectic" (see Chapter 3). This philosophy of calls for setting up two opposing forces, thesis and anti-thesis, which would be thrown against each other in conflict to produce an outcome, synthesis.[76] In his documentary "The Capitalist Conspiracy", Griffin called "Pressure from above and below" is the revolutionary strategy of deliberately creating problems and then offering only those solutions that result in the expansion of government in control by them from behind the scenes.[57] This spreads corruptions and inefficiency among bureaucracy or excessive wealth in private hands ultimately flows out of the country to tax heavens or to other favorable countries of The Core Capitalists.

According to Tax Justice Network, global super-rich has at least $21 trillion hidden in secret tax heavens and there may be as much as $32 trillion of hidden assets held offshore by high net worth individuals (HNWIs) at the end of 2010.[79] In his book, "Treasure Islands (2011)" Nicholas Shaxson, a political analyst and associate Fellow of the Royal Institute of International Affairs (RIIA), describes every FTSE 100 company has subsidiaries or partners in tax havens to avoid tax. He believes that the United States and the United Kingdom are the biggest tax havens in the world, claiming that the US is responsible for approximately 21 percent of offshore business, while the UK is responsible for about 20 percent. Switzerland is responsible for around 6 percent of the offshore trade. London is described as the center of a spider web that links to the Channel Islands, the Isle of Man and the Caribbean, serving the needs of global capital.[80]

The term "neocolonialism" is now used to describe the role of international bankers in changing the world order. Edward Griffin describes "It is a sobering fact that the hidden power structure of international finance has exerted tremendous influence over public opinion in this country through its virtual control of higher education and major segments of mass communications."[26] Dean Henderson argues that the international bankers have a different way of using Hegel's 'synthesis' theory. The states that subscribes to the geopolitical interests of the international bankers are in fact markets of the colonial powers ('thesis'). This causes anarchies, political unrests and civil war that accuse the colonial power sponsoring anti-democratic governments, whose regimes do not represent the interests of the majority of the populace ('antithesis').[77] At the end he describes the 'synthesis' as "The ensuing conflict, which manifest in the Cold War produced a huge market for arms and oil which their trusts manufactured."[77]

Heinberg explains Wall Streets another approach of synthesis "Wall Street always benefits from manias—at least in the short term. Investment banks make money on sales of shares in companies whose activities spur speculative bubbles. The Street also profits from mergers and acquisitions when bubbles burst and companies go bust. For the most part, it's not their money being invested—it's more likely yours if you have any kind of retirement account."[78] The Core Capitalists control not only present wealth of the world but also contracts for future wealth or derivatives of the world. The Economist magazine has reported that as of June 2011, the over-the-counter (OTC) derivatives market amounted to approximately $700 trillion, and the size of the market traded on exchanges totaled an additional $83 trillion.[81] However, these are "notional" values, and some economists say that this value greatly exaggerates the market value and the true credit risk faced by the parties involved. Nevertheless, the multiplicity of wealth or derivatives whether it is physical or "notional" is the result of 'capitalist dilemma' of The Core Capitalists with an assumption of unlimited supply of fossil fuel. Imagine if oil is gone, all these wealth will also be gone, the superstructure of the 'financial gods' will fall apart and all the wealth will turn into dusts. With disappearance of oil, the capitalists will no more be the fittest to survive. Its consequence will affect all of us, so badly.

CHAPTER 9

A SWITCH OVER STRATEGY (SOS)

9.1 Introduction

Our industrial civilization now riding on financial capitalism has taken off the ground after financial deregulation for reaching to its tragic end just like a moth to a flame. On its way, it is irreversibly and progressively damaging the environment and exhausting the fossil fuel reserves at exponential rate. If we continue this path then at some point of time, after 'peak oil', the existence of our civilization will be challenged. On the other hand, the clear path for survival is renewable energy, distributed resources and steady state economy. According to a recent study by University of California, Berkeley, confrontation of the policy makers on these two opposite positions will bring the worst result; eat up a lot of valuable time, energy and resources.[41]

This chapter describes a strategy for a smooth switch-over from existing growth based economics to a steady state economics, while solving current economic problems in real time. A steady-state economics is much of a Horizontal Learning Process (HLP). Therefore, to reach there we will have to counteract the existing biasing forces through an Unbiased Vertical Learning Process (UVLP). This can be achieved by systematically bringing the existing and future sufferers–eventually everyone under a common economic framework, primarily forming two coalitions, Green Coalition Zero (GC0) and Green Coalition "Z" (GCZ). The efforts for formation of these two coalitions will spur many other coalitions and liberate HLP until our economies are auto adjusted with the earth's carrying capacity.

9.2 The Road Taken

"Burning fossil fuels is changing the climate to such a degree, and at such a pace, that economic as well as ecological ruin may ensue within the lifetimes of today's schoolchildren. The science is in: either we go cold turkey on our coal, oil, and gas addictions, or we risk raising the planet's temperature to a level incompatible with the continued existence of civilization."[50]

– Richard Heinberg (2015), "Our Renewable Future"

A child born in 2014, if he is lucky born in a developed society, he will grow up in an isolated and sophisticated environment always occupied with little devices either chatting in Facebook and a fantasy world of video games. Isn't there is a big similarity between this and opium addiction in China in early nineteen century followed by "century of humiliation"? What if before his teen age the world reaches 'peak oil'?

At the end of uphill path of fossil fuel now we are observing a bumpy plateau of oil price. All those politics around the oil are also accelerating the decline at the point when the oil price will spike again for the final time, no will be able to afford to buy the oil. A collapse must happen – we will see major bankruptcy, starvation dislocation happening very fast, while infrastructures standing unrepaired as witnesses of a past wasting civilization. In a documentary called "Collapse", the author of "Confronting Collapse: The Crisis of Energy and Money in a Post Peak Oil World" Michael Ruppert describes:

"We live in an infinite growth paradigm, which requires growth for ever...The hole economy is a pyramid scheme. The whole global economy cannot be sustained-requires infinite growth. But infinite growth collides with finite energy.....you have finite energy and you have a financial paradigm that demands infinite growth. We are at the point of human history where infinite growth paradigm collides with something that is more powerful than money is."[1]

Once the oil supply will begin to decline, further growth will be over. After then it will sharply fall on a basin by basin basis.[2] As of 2010 there were more than one billion motor vehicles in use in the world excluding off-road vehicles and heavy construction equipment. Now there are more than 1.2 billion and it is estimated that it will reach to 2 billion by 2035.[3] If we imagine 5 liters of oil per vehicle per day, it will be equivalent to 6.0 billion liters of oil right now every day just to run them. Not to mention how much oil was burnt to produce them and how much will require to build new roads and highways for doubling them. In 2014, USA alone had 240 million vehicles. Now China is chasing USA, which had 154 million vehicles, next to the U.S.[35] However, in 1993 China had 730.000 cars on the road and by the start of 2004 they had 6 million cars. By the end of 2004 they had 8 million cars. The demand is increasing. In an interview in the video documentary "The Power of Community: How Cuba Survived Peak Oil", Megan Quinn from the Community Solution describes the reason:

"The whole vision for these developing countries is that they're going to be like America someday and that the people are going to be able to consume the way that the Americans have consumed. But that's not going to be able to happen and that's not even possible for America. Americans won't be able to consume like Americans today."[26]

Unfortunately we are now obsessed with the lifestyle based on high consumption that is taking us toward a tragic end of our civilization, leaving the ashes and toxic scraps of our burnings of fossil fuels for our future generations. We are already at or passed "peak oil", which means we have already extracted cheap and easily accessible oil and gas leaving more expensive and harder to extract inside the ground. The "peak oil" situation may not be recognized at the beginning but according to the prediction of "peak oil" researchers bumpy plateau of oil price and inflation may be considered as early symptoms.[1] At the point extraction of this oil or gas will no more be economically viable, it will disappear from the market.

Will the nuclear power nations survive? The biggest sustainable alternative of fossil fuel is nuclear power, which is inherently contains radiation threats, a lethal long-term danger to mankind and environment in case of a disaster. Nuclear power does not contribute to air pollution and greenhouse gas emissions, but a good solution to safely storing tons and tons of radioactive waste, a nuclear byproduct that remains dangerous to all life-forms for thousands of years, remains elusive. Except few developed countries, most of the poor countries will not be able to build nuclear plants not only because of high installation costs but also because of political and safety issues. Again, like the other non-renewable energies, the planet's supply of uranium is limited and hazardous to human health. There is a big preoccupation among policymakers, economists with potential technological solutions for "peak oil". Martenson argues,

"Nobody has advanced any candidate for our next source of energy. Technology is not a source of energy. It may be used for more efficient use energy but not as energy source."[4] Tienhaara argues "technologies developed to resolve one problem often end up creating myriad new, often unanticipated, problems."[5]

When we talk about technology such as nuclear power, horizontal fracking, non-conventional oil, there are huge cost implications. Distributing the cost to the economy, oil price is going up and causing governments, most common businesses and individuals run by debts. In his book 'The End of Growth" Richard Heinberg explains this as:

"We have accumulated too many financial- monetary claims on real assets—consisting of energy, food, labor, manufactured products, built infrastructure, and natural resources. Those claims, essentially IOUs, exist in the forms of debt and derivatives."[6]

While most of the governments are drowning into debts, the core capitalists are making billions of dollars in their financial casinos. According to The Economist', the over-the-counter (OTC) derivatives market amounted to approximately $700 trillion in June 2011, about 10 times of the world's GDP.[7] This means that the world economy is sold ten times already. No wonder why the core capitalists can control lifeline of many governments including USA.

The child born in U.S.A in 2014, will incumbent $53,000 per-capita debt during his birth.[8] This will certainly go up before he begins his life at his own. There will be no more dreams for him about his future. Apparently, only super rich people would be able to drive cars (electric cars) and live in warm houses. Beside this, all others will have to learn how is to survive without heating and without enough warm cloths as all those will become expensive. Our children will face the harsh reality and will have to be prepared for the worse. In developing countries, the most severe impact would be on food supply. Beside fossil fuel, another grave scarcity is looming in the world is fresh water scarcity. Together they will cause hike in food price and in the worst case, increased food price may cause social instability at the beginning and eventually lead to mass starvation and famine. As Heinberg describes in the initial impact of food crisis:

"Climate change, water scarcity, high oil prices, vanishing credit, and the leveling off of per-hectare productivity and the amount of arable land are all combining to create the conditions for a historic food crisis, which will impact the poor first and most forcibly. High food prices breed social instability— whether in 18th century France or 21st century Egypt. As today's high prices rise further, social instability could spread, leading to demonstrations, riots, insurgencies, and revolutions."[11]

Capitalism has been constructed with rampant supply of fossil fuel (e.g., oil or coal) on its uphill direction. Financial capitalism is based on assumptions that future economy will be larger than the present.[6] Following this assumption the path of capitalism has been marked by war, creation and destruction of wealth burning fossil fuels in both ways. This time, after realization of fossil fuel declination the growth rate will sharply fall and the future economy will become smaller ever. The shrinking economy means lower tax revenues for government and therefore, will make it harder for governments to repay debt. In order to avoid a credit downgrade, governments must cut social spending for Residual Market Energy State (RMS). As the economy will continue to shrink, RMS will become bigger and bigger – the need for social spending will increase as unemployment, homelessness, and malnutrition increase, while the availability of social services declines. Initially, these symptoms can be relieved by increasing flow of debts but to chase huge debts with declining oil, the governments, businesses and individuals will face financial trouble together and eventually will become bankrupts.

More debt means more burning and quicker depletion of fossil fuel and further rise of global temperature, worst enough to melt the glaciers and dry out the rivers. Aren't we experiencing this already? IEA reports as global energy demand will increase by over one-third in the period to 2035, energy-related CO_2 emissions will increase a long-term average temperature of 3.6 °C.[9] This will accelerate melting the glaciers and destructions of fresh water supplies. The melting of ice sheets will contribute sea level rise and depletion of the water source in all rivers which will have severe consequences on food chain for all living beings, human beings will not be exceptions. This will inundate low land countries, many of them are highly populated and drive away habitants from those areas, make people homeless, and salinate agricultural lands and eventually will cause severe food shortage and homelessness in many coastal areas and countries where the population densities are high. On the other hand, most of the rivers will eventually dry out when their sources, the glaciers will melt down. The yields of crops will drop as a result of low soil moisture and a severe food and water crisis will begin. This means the carrying capacity of our earth will drastically reduce. If this continues, all of a sudden there will be a big collapse – a blackout of the whole system. There is a little chance that the societies will be able to preserve the achievements in science and technologies, books, research papers, history and culture without enough preparation before-hand. As happened in the past, during the process of decline and collapse they were able to give insufficient thought to preserving the best of their achievements. Indeed, the reverse happened such as libraries and museums were burned, scholars were killed, and tombs were looted.[11]

The impact of fresh water scarcity might be more severe on mankind since about 80 percent of the world's population (5.6 billion in 2011) lives in areas with threats to water scarcity.[10] Unfortunately, the countries with less contribution to the greenhouse gases or global warming, will be more affected because of already infested poverty. In 1960 the world population was 3 billion and we consumed fewer calories and ate less meat, so less water was needed to produce their food. Now there are over seven (7) billion people on earth, more than double of that time (1960). However, the consumption of water-thirsty meat, crops and vegetables is rising, and there is increasing competition for water from industry, urbanization biofuel crops, and now added huge water demand for non-conventional fossil fuel extraction. In future, even more water will be needed to produce food because the Earth's population is forecasted to rise to 8 billion by 2025.[10] However, if there is a drastic reduction of this capacity, what will represent the overcapacity? The child who has born now, he deserves to live more than us. Are we leaving enough resources and time for them?

Figure 9.1 shows the downhill part of Figure 6.19 showing the blackout point of economic collapse as we are going to hit the wall of the earth's limit with high velocity of fossil fuel consumption. At the point of collapse, oil will be scarce and unaffordable. Foods, groceries will run out of market. Electricity and water supply will shut down since there will be no energy to generate or pump them. All the service sectors, manufacturing will be closed, no more jobs—no more pay checks, inflation will go out of control. The urban poor people, beginning with immigrants will suffer the most by losing their jobs, shelters leaving no choices but to starve. This will increase risk of robbery, plundering civil war and severely enough, may be followed by plague and famine in many places in the

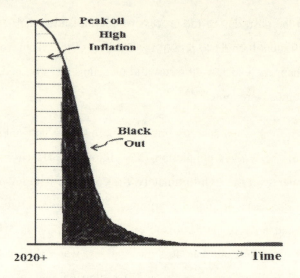

Figure 9.1: The Downhill Destruction

world. Eventually the blackout will touch all the urban people of industrial civilization who be virtually trapped in concretes, pollution from falling structures without food, water, heating or electricity. The rural areas will be little better at the beginning as long as they can protect themselves from urban invasion. In the documentary "Collapse", Michael Ruppert describes:

"If you are not on the land, don't even try to go, you gonna fail miserably and you might be shot by the people who got there ahead of you."[1]

Unfortunately, Capitalism or the capitalists will no more the fittest to survive on the downhill of economic growth. Once oil is gone, it will no more be possible any airstrike or deploy heavy weapons. We should keep in mind that any sorts of war at this point of time will quickly burn the remaining oil reserve and eventually will close all doors toward a new civilization. Will the countries be borderless? What will happen if those who were abused or deprived by capitalism including our children rise against the capitalists? As described in Chapter 2 that all of the massive invasions such as the barbarian invasion in the

Roman Empire or the Mongol massacre in Europe or in Asia or British invasion in India were followed by famine or plagues.

Capitalism, on its uphill has increased the carrying capacity of the earth through exploration of new resources and technological innovations. And the path of financial capitalism has speeded up consumption but now turns out as an uncontrolled Frankenstein, which will bring our industrial civilization to the end. The time left from today we should consider as transition period toward the very harsh reality awaiting after disappearance (economically) of fossil fuel. We and our children are going to experience a dire crisis marked as "blackout" in Figure 9.1 if we just let it come. Are we prepared for this big confrontation?

9.3 The Road to be Taken

"Together let us explore the stars, conquer the deserts, eradicate disease, tap the ocean depths and encourage the arts and commerce."[51]

–John F. Kennedy

The 2015 universal Paris Agreement among 195 participating countries for holding the increase in the global average temperature to well below 2^0C or to pursue efforts to limit the temperature increase to 1.5^0C above pre-industrial levels has created tremendous hope among common people. Previously, in all other climate agreements under United Nations Framework Convention on Climate Change (UNFCCC) framework since Kyoto imposed obligations for developed countries to reduce their greenhouse gas emissions. According to the concept of Capitalists Dilemma (CD), there was less possibility for this to be successful since the emerging countries such as China & India were able to "soar" by emitting more. On the other hand, the 2015 agreement is universal, that each participating or signing country will have to reduce their emission at the same time. The ideal expectation here is that the participating countries will be stick to it even though their economies "squeeze". However, in reality, each individual country will oppose squeezing their economies and still pursue growth, while they are competing with each other and therefore, may end up at the same level of risk as if there were no agreement. To minimize this risk, information sharing and collaboration among the participating nations are extremely important.

We are now passing the transition period before the blackout and therefore, every moment is very important. On the other hand if we are well prepared now with what we have at hand, a new civilization may begin bypassing the blackout where our future economy will have to be operated within the non-negotiable natural limits that is, within our earth's budget of energy and resources.[4]

One year back, in November 2014, U.S. Present Obama announced commitment to reduce greenhouse gas emissions 26–28 percent below 2005 levels by 2025.[12] Chinese President Xi also announced China will increase the share of zero-emissions, non-fossil energy sources (i.e., nuclear and renewables) up to 20 percent of total energy consumption.[12] We may assume two things will continue:

1. This target is to be achieved while globalization will continue.

2. To achieve the target economic growth will not be compromised.

This means China will still be supplying its cheap manufacturing products to the U.S. market carried all the way through pacific. The U.S. super giant business houses such as General Motors, McDonald and Walmart will keep on trying to penetrate Chinese market. On the other hand China will continue to support the U.S. government's unfunded liabilities. The agreement allows China to peak carbon emissions by 2030 although at the same time, China will need to deploy between 800 and 1,000 Gigawatts of nuclear, hydro, solar or wind power.[12] To build such huge infrastructure, China will need a huge amount of fossil fuel any way. On the other hand, supporting growth and globalization of auto-industry and manufacturing will move China out of track. The previous track record shows that China could not meet target to reduce the energy intensity of GDP by 20 percent by 2010.[13] It has almost used up its high grade coal, now if China has to keep up its growth, it will have no choice other than to use low grade coal, which will cause more emission. How much is the chance that China will be able to push its energy transition to renewable?

If a country is to maintain current growth trajectory it will need more energy. However it is hard to use renewable energy for this, while at the same time being economically viable. Here for any country, the ideal target for future incremental energy should be something like 80% zero-emission energy, preferably renewable and 20% from fossil fuel to reach to a sustainable economy for which the economy should use less energy. After Fukushima crisis, Japanese are using substantially less electricity than normal, where businesses and households have slashed energy use, driven by a collective ethical imperative. Nevertheless it is suicidal for the policy makers of a country to call for national policies to shrink economic throughput. In this situation Heinberg (2015) puts this forward:

"Localism offers a third approach that does not directly conflict with either of these. Simply: Let's do what we can locally to reduce consumption, thereby lessening the global carbon burden while building personal and community resilience so we can better respond to the now-unavoidable climatic and economic impacts. Typically, it's easier to change personal behavior or local ordinances than to enact national or international policies – so why not start small?"[11]

To change local economy toward sustainability in a massive scale we need a different strategy–a systems approach. In fact, there is no time wasting by holding the obsession about growth and 'globalization' here.

Herman Daly, in his book "A Steady-State Economy" defines a steady state economy that aims for stable consumption of energy and materials.[14] The economy of China and USA are trapped in a 'Capitalist Dilemma (CD)'[15] and therefore, steady state economy is a mission impossible for them. They cannot target to gradually replace fossil fuel with the zero-carbon emission energy sources. It is certain that globalization cannot continue when oil will disappear. We have seen that all efforts of "carbon capitalism" have failed and the carbon emission has increased. In his article "Beyond Growth or Beyond Capitalism", Richard Smith argues:

> "Daly and the anti-growth school are right that we need to break out of the "iron cage of consumerism," "downshift" to a simpler life, find meaning and self-realization in promoting the common good instead of accumulating stuff. They call for an environmentally rational economy that conserves nature and resources for the benefit of our children and theirs instead of consuming the whole planet right now."[16]

Here is the dilemma, in either way, continuing or stopping growth, the system will collapse. However, the concept of Capitalist Dilemma (CD) indicates that the only workable solution calls for a concerted co-operation from all of the core capitalists of the world for a transition from growth economy to non-growth green economy.[15] Now the big question is who will bell the big capitalist cat?

The problem is that capitalism neither can be overlooked nor can be withdrawn to solve the collapse of civilization until that actually happens. To continue with capitalism, we have to figure out what has gone wrong in capitalism beyond the thoughts of the economists irrespective of who supported capitalism or not. As an example, Marx thought capitalism would be adjusted through communism. However, he never thought about reduction of the earth's carrying capacity from which communism has no immune. In his lecture "The End of Laissez-Faire" at University of Berlin in 1924, Keynes talked about socialization of investment:

> "A point arrives in the growth of a big institution . . . at which the owners of the capital, i.e. the shareholders, are almost entirely dissociated from the

management, with the result that the direct personal interest of the latter in the making of great profit becomes quite secondary. When this stage is reached, the general stability and reputation of the institution are more considered by the management than the maximum of profit for the shareholders. The shareholders must be satisfied by conventionally adequate dividends; but once this is secured, the direct interest of the management often consists in avoiding criticism from the public and from the customers of the concern."[17]

Keynes presumed the big corporates will be required to spend money for the benefits of the societies and to the environment to avoid public criticism. Later on big corporations started to promote their little contribution to the societies under the new term Corporate Social Responsibility (CSR). Literally it means that a company's business model should be socially responsible and environmentally sustainable. Now we see, corporate profit has grown exponentially but their 'responsibilities' were not materialized more than the level of 'window-dressing'.[5] Many argue that CSR is an attempt to preempt the role of governments as a watchdog over corporations.

While the best we can achieve within our corporate dominated capitalist framework is CSR, another group of economists call for 180 degree phase shift, called ecological economics. A recent book "The General Theory of Eco-Social Science" by Jianfang Jin he defines five paradigms eco-entity, eco-resources, ecological society, eco-economics and eco-currency.[42] As an example, he defines "the doctrine of an "ecological society" where the rule of law is replaced by the "rule of organicism,". He claims that his concept "Theory of Ecological Economics," has been adopted into the major policies of Chinese government. In reality, China is not making any deliberate effort to subdue its growth trajectory, rather struggling to prop up the economy with falling growth rate. A recent research by University of California, Berkeley confirms that calamity of climate change is still solvable but not by sitting on two opposing poles like fossil fuel fans and ecological economists. Ben Knight of Geekquinox highlights:

"The thing about opposing something, if you think about it, is that whatever you're opposing will inevitably oppose you back. That eats up a lot of valuable time, energy and resources."[43]

According to Sagar Dhara, two countries Germany and Cuba can be used as model who experienced the most success in moving away from fossil fuels. As

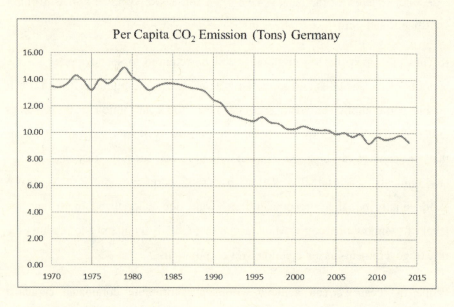

Figure 9.2: Per Capita CO_2 emission, Germany 1970-2014[47]

discussed in Chapter 7, Germany developed a transition plan to renewable energy called "Energiewende". This plan targets a 60 percent reduction in all fossil fuel use by 2050, achieving a 50 percent cut in overall energy use through efficiency in power generation, buildings, and transport.[46] Figure 9.2 shows that per capita emission reduced by about 38% from its "peak" 14.9 tons per year in 1979 to 9.30 tons per year. Energiewende targets a 60 percent reduction in all fossil fuel use (not just in the electricity sector) by 2050.[46] Germany guarantees fixed tariffs to producers of renewable energy. A large percentage of its renewable-generator owners are individuals, cooperatives, or communities.[46]

Dhara recommends that the German model might be replicated in developed countries, but not in developing ones.[46]

Many other European countries as shown in Figure 9.3, such as Georgia, Ukraine, Romania, Slovakia, Czech Republic, Estonia, United Kingdom, Hungary, Denmark, Sweden, Switzerland and Italy were able to reduce per capita emission by more than 25% between 1980 and 2014 by taking different measures similar to German model by switching to renewable energy, increasing

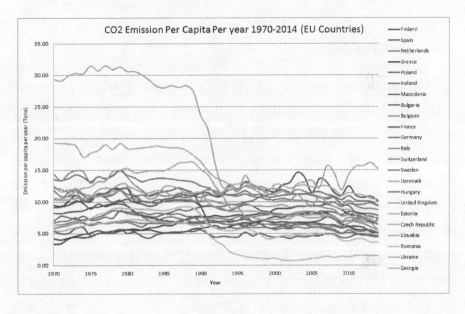

Figure 9.3: Per Capita CO_2 emission per year, European Union 1970-2014[47]

efficiency and behavioral changes. After breaking down Soviet Union, many of the east European countries reduced their energy consumptions. Formation of European Union might have played significant role in sharing information among that nations. From this perspective, this was a unique situation, which cannot be easily replicated in other parts of the world such as in Asia, Africa or South America considering their given level of financial and technological capacities, demographic and social varieties, and political complexities.

For North America, that is for United States & Canada the European model can be replicated. However, USA has its own model already. As Heinberg describers the success of California as a state for reducing carbon emission:

> "Look to California: its economy has grown for the past several decades while its per capita electricity demand has not. The state encouraged cooperation between research institutions, manufacturers, utilities, and regulators to figure out how to keep demand from growing by changing the way electricity is used. This is not a complete solution, but it may be one of the top success stories in the energy transition so far, rivaling that of Germany's Energiewende. It should be copied in every state and country."[50]

According to Heinberg even Germany's Energiewende plan is not a perfect one as he thinks it should aim emission reduction higher than 60 percent. Germany has made a good start to address its own energy future, which was revised as they learned from practical experience during deployment. Nevertheless Germany, California or the European Union will still have to go long way to reach to a sustainable economy. No country or state will be able to reach stainability standalone during crisis time; it is to be achieved with neighbors. Similarly, it is to be achieved for each community in urban or in rural areas of a country that includes each and every person in that community and it cannot be achieved overnight, it is a long term process, especially for a country with immigrants. During crisis time, rural areas will be in a better position as they are closer to land or food production. If rural areas isolate them from urban areas, much of their time will be spent for their protection instead of engaging them in food production. Therefore, we have to formulate a switch over strategy in a more fundamental way.

9.4 Unbiased Pareto Improvement (UPI)

The University of California, Berkeley researchers emphasize that to address the gap between science and policy, we should hugely step up investment in clean alternatives. The industrial policy should provide direct incentives for growth of green industries, which builds political support for carbon regulation.[41&44]

Here the challenges are, first, the fossil fuel or growth supporters are still far more powerful than the climate change activists or supporters of renewable energy. Therefore, building a coalition of the two opposing policy makers, still raise the question, who will bell the big powerful **ca**pitalists? Second, in a biasing chain model, the status quo supporters are positioned on upper layer, that is they are the biasing source. And third, they themselves are caught in a strong Capitalists Dilemma (CD) and therefore, they cannot change their position.

As discussed in Chapter 8 that a capitalist economy follows much of the concept of Economics of Information Biasing (EIB) to streamline flow of capital toward a Universal Biasing Source (UBS).[18] In this model, the definition of coalition has two aspects. In one aspect, it is defined as "Pareto Coalition (PC)" and in another aspect it is defined as "biasing source" or "biased load". One may argue that a biasing source or a biased load may have one to many relationships. However, it is not difficult to extend our imagination to merge a number of coalitions into one if not otherwise required for analysis. When there is a merging, the corresponding information can be called as information palette. The learning environments are not the same for every individual since information availability or the cost of acquiring information differs among them. According to definition of "Biased Equilibrium" the probability of finding common interests among upper layer coalitions is very high that they can be imagined to be merged into a single coalition to achieve that interest. In a linear biasing chain model, if one or more number of biasing sources merge with the "Universal Biasing Source (UBS)" as shown as big dotted circle in Figure 9.4, then it can be abstracted as a big Pareto Coalition (PC). Similarly if a number of biased loads at the bottom, the remaining population of the country merge with the ABL, there will be a big Pareto Space (PS) separated by a biased equilibrium barrier (BEB) as defined in chapter four. The merging will depend on the problem that we are analyzing.

Keynes did not tell how the investors' priority would change from making profit to socializing where in reality investors are never satiate with profit. However, the concept of 'Values Framework' describes that these challenges will require our values framework to improve. How can we make sure that the 'capitalists' values will change toward society and environment? The difference between Keynesian model and 'Biased Equilibrium" is that Keynes did not consider the differential positions of the major investors or capitalists and the people who suffer are separated by a Biased Equilibrium Barrier (BEB).

The scope of Pareto improvement in a Pareto Space (PS) can be defined in two ways. If Pareto improvement is made in compliant with existing biasing, it may be called as Biased Pareto Improvement (BPI). On the other hand, the absolute Pareto improvement that can be applied to a PS, independent of any biasing may be called as **Unbiased Pareto Improvement (UPI)**.[15] The approach Germany or

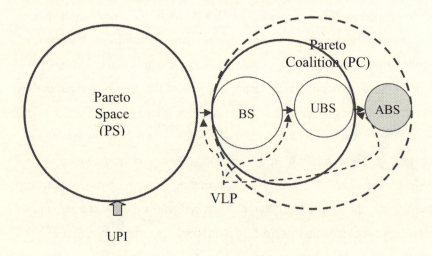

Figure 9.4: Unbiased Pareto Improvement (UPI) for PS

Denmark has taken to reduce its carbon emission is much of a UPI. The approach Berkeley researchers propose, simply move ahead with green industrial investment is a UPI. As Nina Kelsey says:

> "It's probably politically easier to start with direct measures that build industries directly rather than trying to filter it through a very broad, shallow policy like carbon pricing,"[44]

How can we build green industries and infrastructures in large scale? Solar panels are not yet commonly seen on the rooftops. On the other hand, an important criterion of BPI is that it is driven by market and therefore, it can be measured in price dimension. However, in presence of Money Loop (ML), price only convey inflated information not the actual value. In some other cases, price undermines the real worth of the things that have very high importance for humanity. Martenson (2011) explains:

> "Currently, fossil energy sources are 'valued' by an abstraction called money, which does an incredibly good job of masking their true worth by concealing the fact that they are limited and depleting."[4]

In his recent article "Our Renewable Future", Richard Heinberg mentions about of the Google's 2007 project to solve the world's climate and energy problems through steady improvements to today's renewable energy technologies but the researchers finally concluded "to be a false hope."[19] Heinberg argues that they may have been posing the wrong question.

> "They were, in effect, asking whether renewables can support our current growth-based industrial economy while saving the environment. They might more profitably have inquired what kind of economy renewable energy can support."[19]

Here what the Google engineers were trying to achieve was a Biased Pareto Improvement (BPI). But what Heinberg recommends is an Unbiased Pareto Improvement (UPI).

President Obama's Clean Power Plan (CPP) to reduce carbon dioxide emissions from electrical power generation by 32 percent within fifteen years relative to 2005 levels is a BPI but it was triggered by many UPI efforts and campaigns. According to White House, following this plan, 81 companies will have signed the American Business Act on Climate Pledge to demonstrate their support for action on climate change and the conclusion of a climate change agreement in Paris that takes a strong step forward toward a low-carbon, sustainable future. These 81 companies have operations in all 50 states, employ over 9 million people, represent more than \$3 trillion in annual revenue, and have a combined market capitalization of over \$5 trillion.[45] Nevertheless the corporates are in Capitalists Dilemma (CD) to maintain their growth. Therefore, their BPI efforts do not obviate the need of massive UPI each and every corner of the world.

Every Pareto improvement has price dependent (BPI) and price independent (UPI) components but in different combinations. As an example, using fossil fuel to heat water or household electricity is much of a BPI. On the other hand, using solar panel to do the same job is much of a UPI. The first one focuses on better off in monetary values whereas the other focuses on better off in real human value and sustainability. For the same reason, using lower quality solar panels as for "green-washing" may be a BPI not a UPI. From income perspective, BPI will be achieved if dollar income increases, that is, the ultimate outcome is 'growth'. However, in case of UPI, human value has to be increased in a sustainable way. For simplicity, if a target group is bettered off at lower than market price, then it can be treated as UPI. Those who do not fit within MEL, that is who are positioned on Residual Market Energy State (RMS) (see Chapter 4), UPI may care and protect them. As an example, as shown in Figure 9.5, if the people in Market Energy State 1 (Pareto Space) are able to buy the product in less than market price (P_{UPI}) the consumption will increase Q'_1 to Q_1'', while it will remain the same in Market Energy State 2 (MES2). This will increase the real income of the people in MES1. If planned properly, the additional consumption may be produced by using green technologies such as organic

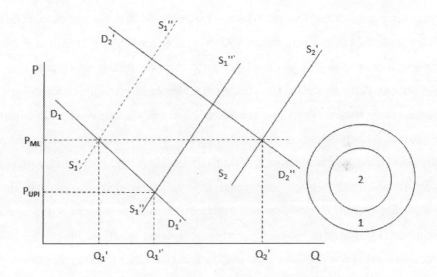

Figure 9.5: Price equilibrium for Unbiased Pareto Improvement

fertilizers, renewable energies etc., changing food habits—eating more plant food and less meat, and adopting green policies.

In cases of rural poverty in many developing countries, if the poor farmers begin to keep much of their produce (say, milk) for themselves, it will increase P_{UPI} in MES1 and may cut 'fat' consumption (say, candy) in MES2, while it will add essential nutrient in MES1. In a multilayer DMM, the price pressure will shift from MES1 to the middle market energy states, which are closer to MES1. This problem may be solved by merging the affected middle Market Energy State (MES) with MES1 or creating another layer of differential price model (P_{UPI}) for them. If this process continues, it will become a growing concern of the policy makers as at some point they will be triggered for a big policy reform like land reform or green reform. This example also shows where innovations are to be applied. As an example, for achieving better health care in MES1 in lower cost, more health care professionals have to be trained from MES1.

The concept of UPI tells that it is possible to achieve better economy, better human values or better environment even without monetary input but by increasing information sharing between Dominant Market Energy State (DMS) and Residual Market Energy State (RMS). As an example, a transition from a growth economy to a steady-state economy requires reform of corporate law. Republican Party candidate for Senate from Maine, Robert Monks remarks in a documentary movie "The Corporation" as "The corporation is an externalizing machine."[20] Corporations in this model, on one hand are biasing sources and on the other hand, suffering from Capitalist Dilemma (CD). Therefore, no single corporation in this world can take any unilateral decision outside their externalizing goal. In many cases, Unbiased Pareto Improvement (UPI) can be achieved by actively bypassing corporate biasing such as liberating local economy, using more organic fertilizers or less pesticide for food production and becoming less reliant on medicine but on exercise for better health, may counteract the corporate biasing forces.

If we recognize the crisis or economic problems we are facing such as climate change, financial crisis, poverty, inequalities all are result of Economics of Information Biasing (EIB), the solution is Unbiased Pareto Improvement (UPI) with a greater force. This strategy may be called as **"UPI Fast" Strategy (UFS)**. UFS is distributive not accumulative and therefore, it will liberate local economies for solution of their economic problems depending on local strengths. Rapid localization using renewable energy will counteract the biasing chain. The model of biasing chain says that easiest way is to counteract the biasing chain is from the very bottom of the chain that is from ABL (Absolute Biased Load) who are the ultimate victims now or will be victim in future. In fact, each and every individual in this world will be future victim of climate change and fossil fuel disappearance–just a matter of rational intuition.

On the other hand, good thing about Biased Pareto Improvement (BPI) is that it is market driven and therefore, it has inherent mechanism to scale-up and spread itself. Therefore, the best approach to address the challenges caused by 'Capitalists Dilemma' like debt crisis, poverty, inequality is rapid and comprehensive UPI for the Effective Pareto Space (EPS) and then complemented by BPI. As an example, to move to renewable energy, one of the hardest parts is to transform the transport sector to adapt renewable energy. It will require longer-term over-haul and capital intensive substitutions. However, we could reduce our need for cars by UPI efforts such as decentralizing our cities and suburbs, changing behaviors toward bicycling, and walking. It will reduce transport requirement significantly and help us plan how much we need to electrify all motorized human transport by building more electrified public transit and intercity passenger rail links, use fuel cells for trucking etc as BPI. If we can follow UFS, it will tells us how much we can produce locally and how much we should import from outside, which will lead to de-globalization of manufacturing. Therefore UFS will not only save time, which is the essence but also save money and vulnerability of financial market.

Another example, meeting local food demand by local food production using organic fertilizers and then scaling up the production by integrating with external market potential to complement any gap. This means UFS will help identify the areas where external involvements will be required. As an example, involvements of corporates to speed up this process such as establishment of green infrastructures, hospitals etc. may increase information sharing between corporates and public that may prevent corporations to externalize costs but benefits to public. This would not be otherwise possible through paying taxes or contributing in mere CSR. Without information sharing, the corporates and politicians may play political blame games to divert the public attention from the onset of the most disastrous but preventable crisis of human history to something else, which will make the transition worse.

In real life, Cuba survived in an absolute oil crisis when the Soviet Union collapsed in 1990s. Cuban economy was absolutely and totally dependent on Soviet oil. The breakup of the Soviet Union, Cuba almost lost its oil supply that created a major economic crisis in Cuba known as the Special Period. Jorge Mario, a Cuban economist describes this as "free fall" of the economic tool. As he explains "When I tell you, free fall of the economy try to imagine an airplane suddenly lose its engines.it was really a crash."[26] During the special period, Cuba lost 80% of its export and import markets and oil imports dropped by more than half. As a result, buses stopped running factories closed, electricity blackouts were common, and food was scarce. People almost starved.[26]

In a documentary called "Collapse", the author of "Confronting Collapse: The Crisis of Energy and Money in a Post Peak Oil World" Michael Ruppert describes the two opposing strategies taken when oil disappeared after breakdown of Soviet Union by North Korea and Cuba, who were totally dependent on Soviet oil.[1] North Korean government was very rigid to respond the situation. Its hierarchical, top down, bureaucratic regime. All of a sudden, there was no oil, no fertilizer, no electricity and North Korea starved. On the other hand, Michael Ruppert describes Cuba's response as:

> "Cuban government reverted one of the purest forms of capitalism. It said everybody start restoring the soil and grow food. You will grow food where you live. If you find any piece of arable land that is not being used, you occupy it and you start farming and you start growing food right now. The Cuban government did everything it could till liberate local food growing. And what happened was after a very tough period, the Cuban people were eating better that it had ever..... every square inch in Havana that had soil, on roof top, flower boxes was growing food.....And Cuba survived."[1]

As a centrally managed economy under biasing of communist government, Cuba had committed to the "Green Revolution". Its agriculture was more industrialized than any other Latin America country and exceeded the US in its use of fertilizer.[26] This required the massive use of fossil fuels in the form of natural gas based fertilizers oil based pesticides, and diesel fuel for tractors and other farm machinery. However, as Robert Perez, Cuba's Sustainable Urban Development Program describes:

"Cuban agricultural "green revolution" system never was able to feed the people. We had high yields but was a lot oriented to the plantation agriculture of an economy, we export citrus, tobacco, sugar cane, and we import the basics 55% of the rice, more than about 50% of the vegetable oil and lard that we consumed. So the system, even in the good times how people here remember never fulfilled the basic needs."[40]

Aggravatingly, in 1992 the U.S. tightened its embargo on Cuba. Any ship that docked in the Cuban port was denied access to the U.S. for 6 months afterwards. As an effect, almost over nights 750 million dollar worth of food and medical supplies to Cuba were halted.[26] Cuba's access to foreign capital was also crippled. In this situation, when outside options are closed, Robert Perez, describes Cuba's only option left "everything had to happen from the inside".[26]

Now Cubans have learned how to live with less energy. Figure 9.6 shows Cuba's per capita energy consumption from 1970-2014. It went up about 4.0 tons per capita and now reduced by about its half. Now Cuba produces all foods they need organically and locally. As an example, urban agriculture provides 50% to 100% of the urban vegetable needs. It has changed food consumptions from fat to vegetables. Increased physical activities reduced diabetes and the number of heart attacks and strokes. Universities are decentralized and multiplied. Cuba now produces more doctors and scientists for home and overseas. Farmers are among the highest earners. Now Cuba has achieved true "Green Revolution".[26] North Korea & Cuba are both communist countries but the fundamental difference on the event of disappearance of oil was that North Korea government was inflexible to respond on this emergency. In North Korea, the whole economic system remained biased to the government. On the other hand, Cuba

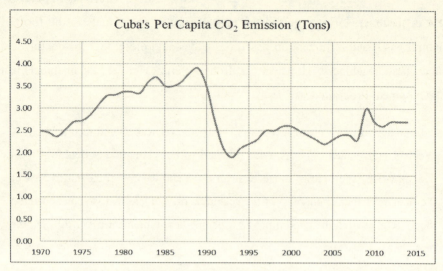

Figure 9.6: Per Capita CO_2 emission, Cuba 1970-2014[47]

not only responded promptly but also took an Unbiased Pareto Improvement strategy (UFS) to motivate local food production and a degree of sustainability. In this case, both the responses were reactive not proactive. North Korea suffered temporarily as China filled the gap left by the Soviet Union's collapse and propped up food supply with significant aid. By 1993, China was supplying North Korea with 77 percent of its fuel imports and 68 percent of its food imports.[21] In case, if China cuts aid or fuel supply, North Korea will fall in another disaster and may be worse than before if no preparation has been taken. On the other hand, Cuban UPI Fast (UFS) strategy has given Cuba an opportunity to reach to sustainability.

9.5 Auto-Adjust Switch-Over (A2S)

"I am talking about genuine peace, the kind of peace that makes life on earth worth living, the kind that enables men and nations to grow and to hope and to build a better life for their children–not merely peace for Americans but peace for all men and women--not merely peace in our time but peace for all time."[53]

-John F. Kennedy, speech, at American University

This is how the then U.S. President in 1963 John F. Kennedy was defining peace in the commencement address at American University. Peace and sustainability goes hand on hand but both are contrary to Capitalists Dilemma (CD) and less exciting to the core capitalists and our policy makers than war and growth. As Kennedy continues his speech:

"I realize that the pursuit of peace is not as dramatic as the pursuit of war–and frequently the words of the pursuer fall on deaf ears."[53]

As discussed in earlier chapters that when fossil fuel will be gone, there will be no growth anyway but transiting period will not be peaceful but bloodily painful if we don't take actions now toward peace and sustainability. As Kennedy further defines peace:

"It must be dynamic, not static, changing to meet the challenge of each new generation. For peace is a process--a way of solving problems."[53]

Like Kennedy's definition of peace, the sustainability we should achieve must be a dynamic process through solving real life problems such as poverty, inequality, diseases and climate change.

Cuba and North Korea were the first countries to face the crisis equivalent to Peak Oil Crisis that all the countries in the world will eventually face. Pat Murphy, Executive Director of The Community Solution and author of "Plan C: Community Survival Strategies for Peak Oil and Climate Change" describes:

"And what we've discovered is that Cuba, because their own artificial Peak Oil was imposed on them when the Soviet Union collapsed, is actually a model for what's going to take place in the rest of the world."[26]

We may follow the Cuban model but the problem is none of the country in the world is match to Cuba. Since 1965 Cuba has been governed as a single-party state by the Communist Party. It already has highly motivated and peaceful people under the leadership of Fidel Castro. This is not the case for rest of the world. In many or most places of the world, transition may be violent as discussed in section 9.2 if we continue existing path– that is, if a proper strategy is not taken and implemented on time. The rest of the world, including communist China is under capitalists biasing. If we follow UPI Fast Strategy (UFS) at a very high speed that can beat the biasing signal, after a transition period, we will reach to a steady state economy. As Bulletin of Atomic Scientists emphasis that:

"If the world is to avoid "severe, widespread, and irreversible [climate] impacts," carbon emissions must decrease quickly—and achieving such cuts, according to the Intergovernmental Panel on Climate Change, depends in part on the availability of "key technologies"."[46]

In fact, UFS does not suggest to wait for any "key technology" but to choose from what is available on that point of time and can be achieved relatively quickly, cheaply and sustainably. Nevertheless, what we will have to do is, we have to learn how is to survive with less. As Heinberg writes:

"We are at one of history's great turning points. During your lifetime you will see world changes more significant in scope than human beings have ever witnessed before. You will have the opportunity to participate in the redesign of the basic systems that support our society—our energy system, food system, transport system, and financial system."[11]

Unfortunately, we are moving to opposite direction. As Jeff Rubin argues:

"[T]he world's governments are getting it wrong. Instead of moving us toward economic recovery, measures being taken around the globe right now are digging us into a deeper hole. Both politicians and economists are missing the fact that the real engine of economic growth has always been cheap, abundant fuel and resources. But that era is over."[22]

"The end of cheap oil", Rubin argues, "signals the end of growth--and the end of easy answers to renewing prosperity."[22] Now oil price are showing a bumpy plateau, rise and drop of oil price. According to Michael Ruppert the bumpy plateau has been described by peak oil researchers many years ago.[1] The bumpy oil price coupled with financial boom riding on debt masking the real situation. The concept of Money Loop (ML) in chapter 4 can be considered a reason for financial boom, which runs the progression of irreversible environmental damage. As an example, increase of car loan, increase number of cars on the road. In other words, by controlling or unwinding ML of an economy, the progression of environmental damage might be slowed down (reference equation 4.28). However, unwinding ML is not possible because of Capitalists Dilemma (CD). The biggest challenge in front of us is to counteract the CD or help capitalists including the core capitalists to come out of their CD.

The documentary movie "Collapse" ended with a story of hundredth monkey. Michael Ruppert describes the story that in a pacific island after testing an atom bomb, scientists wanted to answer questions like, how soon after this testing any kind of life can start. So they went back to re-populate with monkeys. Monkeys ate coconuts but husks of the coconuts were slightly radio-active. The scientists took 10 Monkeys and taught them to wash coconuts in fresh water stream. Pretty soon may be 12 monkeys out of 10,000 were washing the coconuts, then 20, as soon as the 100th monkey started to wash coconut husks, all 10,000 started washing simultaneously.[1] The theory behind this phenomenon called "Hundredth monkey effect." originated with Lawrence Blair and Lyall Watson in the mid-to-late 1970s, who claimed that it was the observation of Japanese scientists on the

Japanese island of Koshima in 1952.[23&24] They observed that some of these monkeys learned to wash sweet potatoes because they found the dirt on them unpleasant, and gradually this new behavior spread across the water to monkeys on nearby islands and even through their generations.[25] Although apparently the two forms of the story are similar but there is an important difference. In the first case the monkeys were trained to do something that solved a problem (the radiation) unknown to them. And in the second case, the monkeys were solving a real life problem by washing the dirt on the potatoes. If the monkeys in the first case have had learned washing potatoes at the first place and we replace the story coconuts with potatoes, they would have washed potatoes by themselves–thus saved them from radiation. Similarly, if we can solve real life problems such as poverty, health care for a small group of people in certain locality by empowering them through UFI First Strategy (UFS) now, it will spread across the country and beyond rapidly that will eventually auto-adjust with the changing circumstances of fossil fuel disappearance.

The challenges like fossil fuel declination, climate change, poverty or cultural deterioration that are created within existing institutional and market structure have not been properly addressed by mainstream economic theories but they are now challenges to our policy makers. This model explains that the concept of green economics is much of a Horizontal Learning Process (HLP), which is deviated and distorted in course of time by information biasing chain works on it from vertical direction. A biasing chain constitutes a "values framework".[18] The solution of many economic, social and ecological problems that are yet challenges to our policy makers may require our existing values framework to improve. The concept of values framework in previous chapter describes that the composition of values of the top order coalitions limits or controls opportunities in down order layers in a biasing chain model. Therefore, this model defines that leadership plays very important role in changing economic structure of a country. However, a country cannot wait for a revolutionary leader to come out of its poverty or crisis. We have to set a realistic strategy and establish a system accordingly so that existing biasing is counteracted, while it solves current economic challenges in real time.

According to the concept of "Economics of Information Biasing (EIB)"[18], individuals of an economy are positioned in different coalitions. And due to their relative positions and binding in a biasing chain it is impossible to reform the economy in the middle of the biasing chain. The concept of Differential Market Model (DMM) also tells that every individual of an economy has a relative position in the market that resists any radical or sudden change in the existing economic and social structure. The poorest people having lowest level of economic freedom are vulnerable part of the economy and ultimate suffers of any economic or environmental crisis. In an Economics of Information Biasing (EIB)[18] chain model described in Chapter 8, they can be positioned at the end of an information biasing chain and can be called as "Absolute Biased Load (ABL)". It is a "Pareto space (PS)" and therefore does not represent a coalition.

There is a communication gap between the people in need positioned in a Pareto Space (PS) or in ABL and the people who control their fate–the Pareto Coalitions (PC) above them. We need to establish PS as a source of information to counteract the existing biasing to solve the problems caused by information biasing. In a highly biased economy, it is very difficult to better off poor and vulnerable people since its underlying values framework is supportive to poverty and inequality. The Pareto improvement of the PS is reflection of the Biased Vertical Learning Process (BVLP) of the biasing sources (PC) positioned above it, where the PS is an Absolute Biased Load (ABL) in an EIB chain model. Now the challenge to us is how can we achieve comprehensive **"UPI Fast (UFS)"** in a massive scale within an absolutely biased economy?

According to a forecast by Energy Watch Group of Germany in 2007 a peak of production of Chinese coal will be in 2015 with a rapid production decline commencing in 2020.[27] China has no choice but to replace declining coal with some other alternate energy. The recent (November, 2014) joint agreement with USA says that non-fossil energy sources would represent 20 percent of China's supply mix by 2030, while the U.S. agreed to reduce carbon emissions by 26-28 percent of 2005 levels by 2025. Although this agreement is a landmark in climate change agreement but a Biased Pareto Improvement (BPI) implementation of this agreement will pose a sufficient challenge to China to reach to a sustainable economy. Moreover, Sara Hsu of "The Diplomat" writes "It is also worth keeping in mind that this agreement was not meant to represent a ceiling on climate change policies but rather a floor."[13] Following this, on August 3, 2015, the U.S. President Obama announced the 'Clean Power Plan' to reduce carbon emission from the power sector by an ambitious 32% by 2030 compared to 2005 levels.[40] However, as discussed in section in Section 7.4 (Chapter 07) that a BPI implementation of this will require a huge investment to accommodate intermittent wind or solar energy in national grid system.

On the other hand, a UPI implementation would require China and USA to reduce total energy consumption. In that case, it might target its future energy growth, 80% from renewable energy and 20% from fossil fuel instead. To achieve this China would need to focus on local economic and community development – a complete turnaround from its existing export based economy. China's most coal reserves are located in the north and north-west of the country, which requires a larger amount of coal burning for supplying electricity to the more heavily populated coastal industrial areas. However, much of the local energy needs may be produced locally if China focuses on renewable energy and build the required infrastructures using the money earned from export market and prudently managing whatever coal they have now. This means, China needs to follow a comprehensive UFS to formulate its overall future economic strategy.

How can we implement comprehensive UFS for our economic policies? Let us go back to the example described in Figure 4.2 in section 4.2. If another individual joins with Z and they make another coalition A1 and gain more bargaining power to deal with coalition A0, theoretically, the outcome will be equivalent to the result of win-win 'payoff sharing in case of perfect information'. As a result the causes of biased equilibrium will be counteracted and the Biased Equilibrium Barrier (BEB) will be weakened. The two coalitions will not merge into one coalition as long as the causes of biased equilibrium will be in effect but counter-forced. Applying the same concept, we may say that if we can establish a system so that the individuals in the PS constitute a virtual coalition, then the biasing on them will be weakened by systematically counteracting the existing biasing forces. As an example, we may imagine that before Newton discovered gravitation in 1687, there might be some others also got this idea but that could not breakthrough science of physical universe since they were not able overcome the biasing forces on their times against any scientific knowledge to spread. However, on Newton's time, his book "Principia Mathematica" induced other like-minded scientists to be aligned by forming some kind of virtual coalition strong enough to beat the anti-science biasing forces that unlocked the Horizontal Learning Process (HLP) of science.

As per discussion in previous chapter, liberating local economy is much of a HLP. A Pareto Space (PS) is not a coalition however, if we can establish an aggressive and comprehensive UFS movement so that the individuals in Pareto Space (PS) will form a virtual coalition through HLP, then the upstream reciprocal Vertical Learning Process (VLP) will act against the biasing forces. This learning process can be called as **Unbiased Vertical Learning Process (UVLP) or Reciprocal Vertical Learning Process (RVLP)**. As a result of UVLP, the Capitalist Dilemma (CD) will be counteracted and the HLP will unleash. However, there is no apparent incentive for the individuals in PS to be linked together. They need external induction or motivation to form a virtual coalition through a comprehensive UFS. If they are exposed to market as virtual coalition and tracked by some measurements, they can trap more economic benefits for them by means of better values, welfare and job opportunities.

In Cuba, the economic crisis helped constitute the coalitions and improve the values framework through UVLP for organic "green revolution" without fossil fuel. Contrarily, the previous Soviet biased values framework induced a fossil fuel based "green revolution". The new 'values framework' has fostered the power of community to run the Cuban economy without any revolt against government or a civil war. According to Heinberg (2015)

> "[E]ven in the absence of effective action to avert economic and environmental crises, we still have the capacity to set ourselves up to be either more competitive or more cooperative in times of scarcity and crisis. With the right social structures and the right conditioning, whole societies can become either more cutthroat or more amiable. By building community organizations now, we are improving our survival prospects later."[11]

As a community we can reduce consumption of energy locally, grow foods locally and help each other's needs as UPI. It will also better prepare ourselves to respond to the climatic and economic impacts when the time will come. If substantial number localities begin to respond on this and they will motivate other as HLP, in turn, it will lessen the global carbon burden as UVLP.

The topmost coalition of an EIB chain placed above UBS may be called as "Absolute Biasing Source (ABS)" or "Absolute Capitalists (AC)" who independently holds control of the EIB but they are also not immune from Capitalist Dilemma (CD). An aggressive and comprehensive green UPI movement focusing local economy will make the PS a green source of information. The information will go up all the way to the ABS through vertical learning feedback channel. This will eventually influence the ABS to comply with the objectives of steady-state economy such as Green Economy (GE) that will act against the CD. Once the ABS complies, the whole EIB will tend to comply with Green Economy (GE). This is how an economy will be able to switch over from growth to 'no-growth' green economy over the time. At the highest level of imagination, if UVLP works perfectly, the economy will run by itself but by true human values. For now, let us call it as **"Auto-Adjust' Switch-Over (A^2S)** to a steady-state economy. This strategy is very important because of the following reasons:

1. The end of oil will also be end of globalization. Much of the local needs are to be locally produced and locally consumed. Local economy, local food production is to be strengthened and liberated right now.

2. Continuity of energy supply for sustainability. Build sufficient renewable energy infrastructure for future use. If there is a disconnect, it will be much difficult to produce solar panels or batteries after economic depletion of the fossil fuel. Economic depletion of fossil fuel will happen long before the actual depletion of fossil fuel may be followed by a long-term financial crisis.

3. Keep baseline reserve of fossil energy until we are prepared to live without. We will have to set priority, where we will continue fossil fuel and where fossil fuel must be replaced by renewable energy sources.

4. Buy time so that our kids are prepared to embrace the new challenges. If there is disconnect from the continuity of energy supply for sustainability, there will be no way to produce 'green' renewable energy like solar panels or batteries after depletion of the fossil fuel. For that we will have to set priority, where we will continue fossil fuel and where fossil fuel must be replaced by renewable energy sources.

5. Preserve our knowledge and continue research for new technology (e.g., new powerful batteries, less irrigation high yield crops).

6. Protect the world from 'blackout', the potential disaster like civil war, famine etc. (the blackout) during the transition. If there is a war it will burn the remaining reserve of fossil fuel and leave us in an irrevocable eternal disaster.

7. Smooth institutional reform for Green Economy.

8. Develop and empower communities based on human relationships for meeting most of the local economic and social needs such as food, healthcare, education, entertainment and even renewable energy locally as much as possible.

There are two kinds of challenges that are big global concern now. The first is ecological crisis, the global warming and fossil fuel depletion that call for slowing down economic growth to a sustainable 'steady-state' economy such as 'Green Economy' shown in Figure 9.7. The second challenge is poverty, inequality and unemployment that call for more growth. All the countries in the world are now dependent on growth to keep their economic engines running and

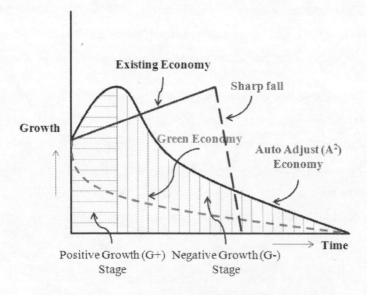

Figure 9.7: The Strategy-Auto Adjust (A^2) Economy

632

to solve their own poverty and unemployment. If the existing growth continues, a M.I.T. research in 2000 using computer simulation shows that within as little as 70 years, our social and economic system will collapse as shown as a 'sharp fall' in Figure 9.7 unless drastic changes are made very soon.[28] As discussed earlier that without growth, the economic engines (MMD) will stop. Although we have seen in previous chapters that growth does not solve the inequality problems rather widen the gap between rich and poor. Following the existing trend of growth, the economies are going to crash by burning most of the fossil fuel reserves (up to its economic limit) and heating up the planet. We are now in such a dilemma that none of the paths, growth or no-growth we can choose from.

Many European nations such as Sweden, Denmark, Japan, and Germany have reached situation in which they do not depend on high rates of growth to provide for their people. Heinberg recommends:

"We must discover how life in a non-growing economy can actually be fulfilling, interesting, and secure. The absence of growth does not necessarily imply a lack of change or improvement. Within a non-growing or equilibrium economy there can still be continuous development of practical skills, artistic expression, and certain kinds of technology."[29]

The 'UPI Fast strategy (UFS)' looks at this problem little differently. At the beginning the objective of UFS should be to make the PS or ABL as a green source of information for an end to end communication through Vertical Learning Process up to the UBS (Universal Biasing Source). During this time the economies will grow due to better information flow within an economy. Therefore, this will be the time for addressing the problems like poverty and inequalities. This will also be the time to set up priorities to reduce per capita energy usage and roadmap toward a sustainable economy such as building renewable energy infrastructure, promoting local agriculture and food sustainability, empowering community relationship and so on. Once the end to end communication is established from ABL (or PS) to UBS through Unbiased

Vertical Learning Process (UVLP), the Biased Vertical Learning Process (BVLP) will be weakened and the Horizontal Learning Process (HLP) will be strengthen. This means local economy and community relationship will be liberated or empowered to run the economy during this process. This cannot happen overnight. In this way, the economy should respond based on the reality of climate change and resource depletion or in other words, economic growth will be auto adjusted with carrying capacity of the earth.

This strategy for 'Auto-Adjust Switch-Over (A2S)' is very important to protect the world from potential disaster like civil war and famine (the blackout) during the transition from 'peak oil' to 'oil depletion'. This strategy is aimed to connect all the people of the world for smooth institutional reform toward Green Economy. As shown in Figure 9.7, the 'A^2 Economy' has two stages. The first stage may be called 'positive growth stage' or 'G+ Stage' and the second stage may be called as 'negative growth stage' or 'G- Stage'. The 'G+ Stage' can be green focused, for example, setting up renewable energy and its spare parts plants, electric vehicles, using bicycles, creating water reservoirs, growing fruits and vegetables using organic fertilizers, encouraging tree plantations and creating green jobs. The countries with high export earnings, can build these infrastructures during this phase. The first stage (G+) will be the most challenging part and it will require comprehensive UPI efforts to address poverty and unemployment but by reducing per capita energy usages. If the end to end communication from the ABL to UBS is established considering the ABL as a green source of unbiased information, the 'auto-adjust' transition process will begin to work.

As discussed in Chapter 4 that a Market Energy Loop (MEL) externalizes costs to Residual Market Energy States (RMS), which means to poor people and to future generation. Before entering into the transition we need to solve cost externalization problems. As an example, the local poor people of a community can be brought under virtual coalition so that they can counteract externalization of the costs to them. Similarly, another virtual coalition can be formed comprised of Generation Z people of an economy who are supposed to bear the future costs of externalization. These types of coalitions can be called as "Green Coalitions Zero" and "Green Coalitions Z" respectively. The coalitions can be formed to solve their specific problems following various comprehensive "UPI Fast" strategies. The efforts for formation of these two coalitions will spur many other coalitions of green activists, scientists, politicians and so on through HLP and all will send signals to the upper layer capitalists until our economies are auto adjusted with the earth's carrying capacity through UVLP.

Finally when the transition will be completed, the economy will land to a full-fledged steady-state economy or 'Green Economy' guided by natural information of Horizontal Learning Process (HLP) alone as opposed to existing Biased Vertical Learning Process (BVLP). Therefore, if we follow UPI Fast strategy (UFS), we will find light at the end of the tunnel and a smooth transition to a sustainable economy. Undoubtedly, the challenge for each individual will be to save himself during the transition period. This strategy will create opportunities for every individual for their own survival but staying together.

9.6 Green Coalition Zero (GC0)

Sharan Burrow of International Trade Union Confederation has called for the goal to be "zero carbon, zero poverty".[48] This worth deep analysis why zero carbon should be accompanied with zero poverty? Is it really achievable?

In his book "Afterburn: Society Beyond Fossil Fuel" Heinberg describes that the conflicts during the transition time following "peak-oil" will likely center on the four factors of money, energy, land, and food. In his recent article "Renewable Energy after COP21: Nine issues for climate leaders to think about the journey home", he describes, As he describes the impact of shrinking economy on the poor people as:

"Pursuing the renewable energy transition without equity in mind would likely doom the entire project. Unless the interests of people at lower economic levels are taken into account and existing inequalities are reduced, the inevitable stresses accompanying this all-encompassing societal transformation could result in ever-deeper divisions both between and within nations, and lead to open conflict. On the other hand, if everyone is drawn into a visionary project that entails shared effort as well as shared gains, the result could be overwhelmingly beneficial for all of humanity. This is true, of course, not only for the renewable energy transition but also for our response to impacts of climate change that are by now unavoidable."[11]

In case of poverty, economic efforts of poor people are continuously undervalued because of Biased Vertical Learning Process (BVLP). Therefore, true welfare across an economy cannot be achieved without protecting the poor people for their immediate economic needs and simultaneously counteracting the biasing forces. Their immediate need includes food, shelter, medical care etc. Charity and donations discretely serves immediate needs in small scale. As Heinberg puts forward this:

"The cost of covering the basics for everyone is within the means of most nations. Providing human necessities would not remove all fundamental problems now converging (climate change, resource depletion, and the need for fundamental economic reforms), but it would provide a platform of social stability and equity to give the world time to grapple with deeper, existential challenges."[11]

In Section 8.2, whatever the method of calculating the value of Real Income to Contribution Ratio (RICR)[15], to alleviate poverty, RICR of the poor people or RMS will have to increase in a consistent and concerted manner. This will be possible in a massive scale by applying a comprehensive "UPI Fast" strategy to help them form a virtual coalition. It is useless to advice the government of a poor country to increase welfare contributions not only because it puts huge burden on state funding but also there is very high probability that the money will again be spent in the same old way and therefore, will be trapped in the pre-existing Market Energy Loop (MEL). At this given level of complexity, a better option is to create incentives for our entrepreneurs to extend their existing domain toward poor people apart from BPI. The good thing about BPI is that it is market driven and therefore, it has inherent mechanism to scale-up and spread itself. The trick here is using a comprehensive 'UPI Fast' strategy to provide the incentives for BPI in favor of poor people in a more energy-saving green manner. The local food production is one single biggest sector can be changed in fully environmental sustainable way, for example, storing seeds, using bio or organic fertilizer to restore or revitalize soil, digging water reservoirs, tree plantation and so on. Poor people of a developing country are directly involved in food production and they are the most vulnerable people to the ecological crisis. They can be supported and organized in all stages of food production, processing and marketing by choosing 'green' options bypassing the loan sharks, merchandizers, and middlemen. Motivation is a powerful UPI tool to bring big comprehensive changes to an economy. Since there is no apparent incentive for the poor people to be united, they need external induction or motivation to come under a common virtual framework. Under such a framework, they may be named as **"Green Coalition Zero or GC0"**. If they are exposed to market as virtual coalition and tracked by some measurements, they can hold more economic benefits within themselves by means of better values, welfare and job opportunities.

We are assuming there is market failure or an uncontrolled Market Energy Loop (MEL) in an the economy since the government of the country has failed to take proper measures such as imposing progressive taxes on the riches or reducing corruptions or reducing per capita energy usage by the rich people. The central bank of the country has also failed to control inflation through its management of interest rates and the money market. In this circumstance, the proposed poverty alleviation strategy should focus precisely on the triangular area above line $\lambda\lambda'$ where RICR $< \lambda$ as shown in Figure 9.8. We will have to increase the productivity as well as the real income of our labour force from a benchmark position. This is shown as an anti-clockwise rotation of RICR line $\lambda\lambda'$ in Figure 9.8. In an ideal economy, if no money goes out of the economy or comes in from outside, the RICR for an average individual will be equal to 1. Therefore, an anti-clockwise rotation of RICR line $\lambda\lambda'$ will cause a clock-wise rotation of the upward RICR line through an Unbiased Vertical Learning Process (UVLP) as shown in Figure 9.7. If this happens in an economy, we may say that the communication from the poor people to the rich people is established through a bottom up economic channel. Quadir (2003) proposed an idea called "bottom-up

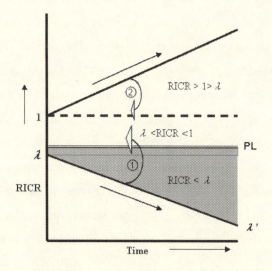

Figure 9.8: Poverty Alleviation Strategy using RICR

economics" to nurture and promote innovations and entrepreneurship at the level of the poor people in developing countries like village phone program in Bangladesh or Stirling engine in Africa.[31] The concept of UVLP theoretically substantiates his idea and therefore, tells of how those discrete efforts can be integrated with mainstream market and extensively used in an economy.

As the poor people of a country are the most vulnerable to any economic and ecological crisis and they bear the most risks and uncertainties, they can be more easily motivated than the rich people to bring any positive changes in an economy. If they are encouraged and supported to use and promote 'green' technologies in a progressive manner, the bottom up flow of information will counteract Capitalist Dilemma (CD) and therefore, MEL will squeeze, inflation and corruptions will reduce and eventually the economy will generate more value in real term for both the rich and the poor people. Trying to solve poverty by reducing corruptions or improving bureaucracy at the very first place will end up to the same failure as before and we cannot afford it anymore. However, there is a synergy if a country tries in both directions simultaneously.

The anti-clock wise rotation of RICR line $\lambda\lambda'$ calls for two kinds of objectives. The first objective is to improve of RICR of the poor people who are directly or indirectly employed or who have regular earnings. As an example, if Indian farmers were tracked by RICR, they would be far better by now by means of real values and quality of lives staying in the same profession as farmer. The second objective is to create new jobs for the poor people and improve their operational holdings, which will increase their productivity and contribution over time. To create new jobs emphasis should be given to liberate local economy in a sustainable way such as producing and using renewable energy, building water reservoirs, using organic and bio-technologies, 'green' health care etc.

At the beginning, the existing conditions of the poor people particularly their average real incomes, average productivities, per capita energy usage as well as several industry parameters have to be benchmarked. If the sectors grow or the people they serve improve their lives, then they should get numerical scores in their contributions. In a labor intensive growing economy, there is no way the contribution of the labor force will decrease if calculated properly even there is no additional direct effort from the workers. As an example, if Bangladesh gets a new quota for exporting garments products to Europe and the therefore, export volume doubles but by employing 25% additional workers only, then the contribution of laborers will have to be considered increased by 60% although the laborers are not involved in the negotiation.

To improve the RICR, the real incomes of the poor people should rise at a higher rate than their contributions from the existing reference value. It does not necessarily mean that this can be achieved by higher wage or monetary increase of their income but it will enable them to buy more value regardless of their incomes, such as better health care and education using their unit incomes than they were previously able to do. This means $1 of a poor person has to be more powerful than $1 of a rich person when buying specific goods and services. This new characteristics of money can be called as 'Dual Value of Money (DVM)'. The concept DVM can be justified as it may compensate the Price Pressure or cost externalization caused by Market Energy Loop (MEL) and Money Loop (ML) as a market failure of the economy. Now DVM can be a tool for fixing this failure and to extend the market toward the poor people, not necessarily reflected in monetary terms. The next chapter (Chapter 10) elaborates more on how the concept of DVM can be implemented in real economy.

9.7 Green Coalition "Z" (GCZ)

"We cannot walk alone. And as we walk we must make the pledge that we shall always march ahead."[52]

– Martin Luther King, Jr

As the economic and ecological crises are converging along with the decline of resources including fossil fuel and fresh water, the existing economic and governmental power structures will break up. When the crisis will begin, the young people will be in the front line either in conflict or in co-operation. They will after all, are the ones who will most forcibly face the consequences of climate change, and their attitude toward older generations may not be forgiving.[30] As the impacts of shrinking economy and climate change will become intense, the history tells the impoverished masses and deprived new generation may revolt against the power elites who control the biasing chain. Heiberg refers to the French Revolution as:

"History teaches us at least as much as scenario exercises can. The convergence of debt bubbles, economic contraction, and extreme inequality is hardly unique to our historical moment. A particularly instructive and fateful previous instance occurred in France in the late 18th century. The result then was the French Revolution, which rid the common people of the burden of supporting an arrogant, entrenched aristocracy, while giving birth to ideals of liberty, equality and universal brotherhood. However the revolution also brought with it war, despotism, mass executions—and an utter failure to address underlying economic problems."[16]

The elderly generations who are still on control of the biasing chain may redirect the conflicts toward different directions – religions, immigrants, leftists or rightists that will make the situation worse. On the other hand, if the younger generations are educated, trained and prepared for facing the crisis pro-actively such as building community relationship, grow gardens, permaculture, reuse, repair, help, share and care, they can lead us toward comfortable transition to sustainable economy.

The older generation who has their mindset attached with abundant fossil fuel still seeks to maintain the complexity of centralized government. However, with declination of fossil fuel or cheap energy a centralized government will become weaker, revenue will fall and debt burden will increase. Therefore, it may find no way other than to withdraw support for poor and elderly people. On the other hand, local communities may find no value supporting to centralized government anymore. As a result, the whole system may breakup and we will have to begin from scratch. Then why not to plan now for gradual shift from central to local provision of basic needs?

We have seen in Chapter 7 that "Carbon Capitalism" has failed to control emission after decades of buzzes among old bureaucrats, policy makers and activists. As an example, one of the proposals is to collect "Pigovian" taxes from businesses equal in amount to their negative externalized costs to society.[6] Herman Daly and Josh Farley have argued that the interests of future generations are still not taken into account.[32] One remedy that they suggest is making the rights of future generations to certain resources, such as to the ecosystems responsible for generating life-support functions, explicit and inalienable.[32] In reality, we have seen none of these laws concerning future generations are getting any attention to the policy makers other than putting forward another line item in the tax bills.

Generation Z is the last in line of all living human beings to take us to the next generations. Accordingly, we will have to take all-out efforts to save our earth now for Generation Z and so on. On the other hand, if we do nothing or do very little for them, we will be accused for endangering their future survival.

A Canadian magazine Maclean's cover article "Are you Ready for Generation Z" writes "They're smarter than boomers and way more ambitious than millennials".[33] According to the magazine, Generation Z who are born after 1995 when the World Wide Web and personal computers was already commonly used. Now it is a big group, two billion worldwide, and one-quarter of the North American population.[33] Social researcher Mark McCrindle who has been looking at Gen Z for seven years points out "They are the most years "connected, educated and sophisticated generation in history."[33] Now in fact Generation Z has the potential to be global in thinking, while acting locally for the community where they live if we allow them the freedom. As an example, when fossil fuel will disappear (this means fossil fuel will be no more economical), they will less likely travel beyond their country but still they will like to be connected over internet and concern over others living in the other parts of the world. Over the internet, they should be able to exchange knowledge, views and their feelings for a better world. This means they will like to have internet alive although it will have no commercial backup. If this is the case, we have to plan now–put internet as priority, make sure the switches, the routers, transports are powered and maintained for all the time. These equipment do not need so much power that cannot be generated by renewable energy with sufficient backups. We have to find a way to preserve our documents, technologies and cultures for them using our all-out efforts. On this regard, Heinberg expresses his worries as:

"In some respects our culture is arguably more ephemeral than most others, and a surprisingly large proportion of our cultural materials is in danger of being swept away with astonishing speed, leaving virtually no trace—like a candle flame vanishing in a puff of wind. The Egyptians carved their thoughts in enduring stone; we post ours on websites that change with lightning speed and sometimes vanish altogether. If we want future generations to have the benefit of our achievements, we should start thinking more seriously about what to preserve, and how to preserve it."[11]

A New York based advertising agency Sparks & Honey performed a study on Generation Z and found 60 percent of Generation Zers want jobs that had a social impact, compared with 31 percent of Generation Ys.[33] Although both Generation Z and Y are generally marked by an increased use and familiarity with communications, media, and digital technologies, Generation Z are more interested to be community oriented and more prudent (56 percent said they were savers, not spenders).[33] Although 72 percent of those surveyed want to start their own business, in the U.S., the unemployment for young has reached a record level (19.1%, July 2010). This problem is particularly acute in Europe, 40% in

Spain, 35% in the Baltic states, 19.1% in Britain and more than 20% in many more that has led to speculation about possible long term economic and social damage to this generation (Travis, 2009).[34] On the other hand, in the U.S. alone, they have a trillion dollar outstanding amount of student loan on their shoulder. In April 2012 it was reported that 1 in 2 new college graduates in the US were still either unemployed or underemployed.[34] One of the reason of unemployment is that as discussed the economies in the developed countries are already shrinking. Job markets of many previously attractive subjects are squeezing too. As Generation Z already have changed their mindsets from becoming an employee to become self-dependent, they can be taught and made aware about relationship between human beings and nature for their survival in their new world without fossil-fuel. As Heinberg highlights:

"our sustenance and survival will increasingly depend on relationships with the people and natural systems around us; as we nourish and protect them, they will have greater capacity to do the same for us".[11]

The next earlier inline of Generation Z is Generation Y. In developed countries, during 2007-2012 global financial crises, Generation Y were major impacted. It has been argued that this unemployment rate and poor economic situation has given Generation Z and Y a rallying call with the 2011 Occupy Wall Street movement although the movement included participants that vary from the very young to very old. If we want to analyze the reason for massive unemployment of Generation Y, then they are not to be blamed as they and are just a biased load of those who are before them as shown in Figure 9.9. The generations before them are Generation X who born after baby boomers generally includes people born from the mid-1960s.[36] They and the baby boomers are now leading corporate world, and the governments. They have witnessed several wars, oil & energy crisis, nuclear disasters and several financial crises. However the most important thing about them is often overlooked is most of them are 'spell bound' by the neoclassical 'growth' concept of economics. This is what they implanted

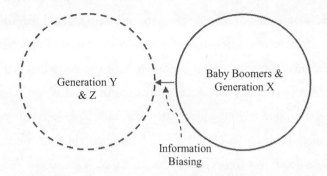

Figure 9.9: Existing intergenerational information biasing

into their next generation's brain by all means like showing, practicing, grooming, educating, preaching etc. Although the information that the world will run out of oil was predicted in 1960s but the Generation X who were responsible did not prepare any plan B for the next generation. Hubert (1956) accurately predicted in 1956 that United States oil production would peak between 1965 and 1970.[37] However, there has been absolutely no action taken so far to address the dire consequences ahead and we have been still continuing the 'growth path'. There are some buzzes around the climate change initiative but the politicians, policy makers are trying to make it "cry wolf". As Latin explains

"[T]he great majority of climate change programs, from American congressional bills to cap-and-trade economic incentive schemes to the Kyoto Protocol and other international treaties, rely on greenhouse gas emissions-reduction targets that will prove "too little, too late" by deferring strict pollution controls too far into the future."[38]

It is true that the growth in the developed countries slowed down already due to their overwhelming debts. Matter of fact the growth center has changed and moved from North America and Europe to China, India, South America and also some countries in Africa. The biggest economies in the world are running on debt over or close to their GDP from the growing countries. Who will stop China

Russia & India from growing further? In context of global economy, the situation is such worse that if China stops or oil disappears, the financial paradigm of U.S. economy will collapse as it is to some extent is dependent on borrowing from Chinese investors or petro dollar. Chinese or Indian cannot be stopped burning energy from outside influences. And inside the countries Generation X has not done anything since they are fully obsessed with growth. Generation Y is already struggling in a brutal job market.[33] In his book "Grown up Digital" Don Tapscott says Generation Z does not have a choice:

> "My generation is leaving them with a mess. These kids are going to have to save the world literally."[39]

Considering the so far progress we made in last decades and the direction we are heading on, we are going to hit the point of 'free fall' in any time soon. We are preparing our kids (Generation Z) for the best fit in the capitalist economy but tragically, they are going to be the worst fit for their future. Instead, if we can

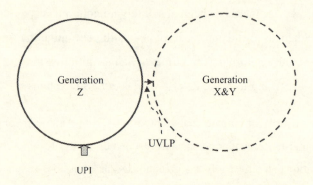

Figure 9.10: UPI Strategy for Green Coalition Z (GCZ)

organized and united under a common platform, may be called as 'Green Coalition Z (GCZ)", their collective consciousness will act as a counterforce against the capitalist dilemma of their senior generations, Generation X and Y through an Unbiased Vertical Learning Process (UVLP)' as shown in Figure 9.10. They need to be well informed about depleting resources and global warming, whereas they are already globally connected by social media. If GCZ takes strong position on the side of renewable energy and strengthening their local communities, the influence of powerful financial and fossil fuel industries and centralized powers will recede. They already have shown their potentials. Tapscott writes

"This is the first time in history kids know more than adults about something really important to society-may be the most important thing."[39]

Monowar Zaman

CHAPTER 10

GREENHOUSE CARE ECONOMICS

10.1 Introduction

After the end of fossil fuel (this means when fossil fuel will become economical), everything or most of the things that will be used by mankind will be local in the new paradigm as opposed to existing paradigm of globalization. Why is not then to strengthen the local economy and start building the new paradigm right now?

This chapter proposes "Greenhouse Care Economics (GhCE)" for building the new paradigm of sustainable economics by applying the UPI Fast Strategy (UFS). Until the policymakers or the capitalists are sufficiently motivated for concerted action, let the people who are suffering now or who may potentially suffer the most from the existing paradigm constitute Green Coalition 0 (GC0) and Green Coalition Z (GCZ) respectively under a common economic framework called Greenhouse Care Economics Framework (GhCEF). This framework will enrich local economy and solve many of their economic problems in real time. Moreover, the formations of GC0 and GCZ under GhCEF will spur many new green coalitions through Horizontal Learning Process (HLP) and eventually they will together counteract the existing paradigm of growth and globalization through Unbiased Vertical Learning Process (UVLP) toward a new metric of well-being –the age of sustainability.

10.2 Greenhouse Care Economics (GhCE)

The recent report of Intergovernmental Panel on Climate Change (IPCC), for the first time since 2007, states that tackling carbon emission is economically affordable.[1] Sam Smith, from World Wide Fund for Nature (WWF) says "What is needed now is concerted political action."[2] By referring the rapid response of politicians to the recent global financial crisis, Smith argues that "they could act quickly and at scale if they are sufficiently motivated".[2]

The existing global financial system has big impact on both ecological and economic systems. In case of global financial crisis and global environmental crises both mostly affect the poor the most even though they are largely caused by the rich. Although we cannot motivate the policymakers for an action to prevent the biggest disaster of human history but we may try to motivate poor people to solve poverty problem through "**UPI Fast Strategy (UFS)**". There are historical and institutional reasons behind poverty but if poverty problem is not solved before peak oil, the post peak period will be disastrous for both the riches and the poor. Interestingly, solving poverty problems, the mainstream theories say to increase competition for more growth and consumption for better distribution of wealth. In reality, due to "Biased Equilibrium" between rich and poor, increased consumption generates more wealth for the rich but may trickle down some to the poor. According to discussion in the previous chapter, if the poor people are exposed to the market as a collective body "Green Coalition Zero (GC0)", their collective presence not only will counteract the causes of poverty but will also create immunity against poverty.

Similar to poor people, Generation Z is going to be the most vulnerable population for the future when the economy will undergo into crisis. Their senior generations, Generation X and Y are so obsessed with the mainstream economic theories based on over production and over production can do nothing but to submit themselves to the capitalist Frankenstein they have inherited and nourished. However, as discussed earlier that the collective presence of

Generation Z as "Green Coalition Z (GCZ)" will act as a counterforce against the Capitalist Frankenstein through Unbiased Vertical Learning Process (UVLP) to a new metric of well-being during downhill economic growth path. As an example, making them conscious about the 'limits to growth' not only will help them prepare themselves for their future but also motivate their parents and eventually policy makers build green infrastructure to support the minimum energy requirement for their future well-being.

Although our growth compulsive and capitalist economy could not solve the problems of poverty and inequality, we have already used up the major part of our scare reserve of fossil fuel and surface water and caused an ecological crisis like global warming or greenhouse effect. We have two major challenges: The first is to reduce dependency on fossil fuel and to maintain a reserve for Generation Z and beyond. The second one is to let the poor people get access to the prosperity we have already achieved. There is a synergy if we address both of them by formation of Green Coalitions 0 (GC0) and Green Coalition Z (GCZ) for the poor people and Generation Z respectively, the primary sufferers of existing and potential economic or environmental crisis under a common framework. The traditional biased approach does the opposite; it has left the poor people and our kids on the bottommost position of a capitalists biasing chain. They are a huge population close to three fourth population of the world. However, we can focus on a tiny fraction of them to begin with.

This chapter aims to discuss or provide recommendations for creation and nurturing GC0 and GCZ in a way that will eventually spurs similar or many other green coalitions of scientists, politicians, green activists and so on through Horizontal Learning Process (HLP) around the world. These coalitions will counteract the biasing chain of the core capitalists and therefore, any biasing will be auto-negotiated to a win-win outcome through Unbiased Vertical Learning Process (UVLP). These learning processes will create an immune system within a local economy against external biasing. The economics of establishing these learning processes can be called as **'Greenhouse Care Economics' (GhCE)**.[3] It will call for a coherent co-operation from the core capitalists in the pursuit of sustainable economy, energy access, energy security and low-carbon economic growth and prosperity. Although focus of GhCE is poor people and Generation Z, however, there will be no breakthrough for sustainable economics until the core capitalists change their values framework. In primitive time, women might have started plantation however, the breakthrough for transition from hunter-gatherer to agricultural societies might not happen until men involved in plantation (Figure 10.1). Similarly, the ultimate objective of GhCE is to 'green

Figure 10.1: "First Plantation" Painting by S.M. Sultan (1975)[4]

the core capitalists' to reach to a new sustainable human paradigm bypassing the 'downhill collapse'. Although we say a sustainable economy is a no-growth economy, but green economy should grow in every locality. This will be a new human paradigm based on local economy. To achieve this, during the transition period, UVLP should counteract BVLP in a way that the net effect should auto adjust our existing growth based globalized economy with the earth's carrying capacity focusing local economy. After transition, green economics 'managing economics for nature as usual' will be much of a HLP. GhCE is analogous to the care and protections for tender plants grow in a greenhouse in a protective environment from cold weather by sharing each other's warmth.

The poorest people of a country and our kids (Generation Z) have the lowest level of economic freedom and they are the most vulnerable part of our economies and the ultimate sufferers of any economic or environmental crisis. Therefore, they need more attention within a protected economic system for their immediate economic needs. The idea of GhCE is to create an institutional framework that will provide care and economic protections for who will come under this framework from adverse effects of Economics of Information Biasing (EIB). In course of time, every success of GhCE can counteract and prevent the causes of existing economic problems such as poverty and ecological crisis on the uphill path of economic growth and provide incentives for markets, societies and institutions to change to the right direction to avoid potential blackout or collapse on the downhill path of economic growth.

Here some high level objectives of GhCE can be summarized as:

1. To organize Green Coalition 0 (GC0) in an economic system that will improve their Real Income to Contribution Ratio (RICR) while meeting their immediate economic and social needs.

2. To organize Green Coalition Z (GCZ) in a social environment that will prepare them for their future survival with declination of fossil energy availability and resources while keeping them healthy and involved.

3. To support Horizontal Learning Process (HLP) for spurring similar or many other green coalitions around the world who will act as green sources of information for the core capitalists for a breakthrough transition from a unsustainable growth economy to sustainable green economy through Unbiased Vertical Learning Process (UVLP).

To achieve the first objective, some small projects can be initiated for improving RICR of some small segments of poor people in a local economy, may be in a big city or in a small town. A successful implementation of such a project will breed a bigger project and so on. The second objective can be achieved if our kids are educated and motivated in healthy lifestyle with in conservation of energy and at the same time they are involved in campaigning building sustainable economy for their future survival. As Heinberg emphasizes:

"We need public messages that emphasize the personal and community benefits of energy conservation, and visions of an attractive future where human needs are met with a fraction of the operational and embodied energy that industrial nations currently use. We need detailed transition plans for each major sector of the economy."[5]

Many organizations already are working on formulating transition strategies and these campaigns. In North America, the Post Carbon Institute, the Transition Network, the Arthur Morgan Institute for Community Solutions, the Simplicity Institute and many other organizations have already begun pioneering this work, and deserve support and attention. The concept of GhCE recommends involving Generation Z as Green Coalition Z (GCZ) to make these campaigns more effective, more laud so that the policymakers cannot continue to be deaf. The campaigns can be as simple as participating small 'green' campaigns such as independence in local food production, building fresh water reservoirs, "go organic", "go green" or "go local" etc. Their participation will spread consciousness to every corner of the country for achieving self-sufficiency in sustainable renewable energy. The third objective tells that together the first two objectives have a synergistic effect if pursued under an institutional framework.

The urban population of a country uses much higher amount of energy from fossil fuel than rural population. Therefore, with declination of fossil fuel availability, they will suffer the most. At the beginning of this event, the urban people will begin to lose their jobs. As a result, they default in mortgage, pay utility bills (as also utility bills will be high) or buy food. The cities will lose taxes; the financial industry will be bankrupts because of increased number of foreclosures. Many U.S. cities are already showing these early symptoms. Many of the residents of those cities have moved to other cities or their home towns from where they migrated during economic boom. However, ironically with fossil fuel declination, this situation will cause urban people to migrate to rural areas but a fraction of them may be lucky enough to enter and find jobs or businesses there. The most of us may be trapped in urban concretes leaving no choice but to starve. If this information is communicated properly, a coalition of urban people (say, Green Coalition Urban or GCU) may be formed through Horizontal Learning Process (HLP).

It is much safer to be aggressive in helping poor people or building green infrastructures for our future generation than creating panic. The concept of GhCE aims at shifting generalized focus of economic theories to specific target groups among GC0 and GCZ. Once a positive change starts for a target group, it will spur more and more types of Green Coalitions through Horizontal Learning Process (HLP) extended to all other population of a country primarily who are at most risk such as urban population of a country (say, Green Coalition Urban (GCU)) or to the whole world to counteract the existing biasing chain (Chapter 8) through UVLP. We do not have much time left. If we do not plan now, we will let our economies to collapse.

10.3 Greenhouse Care Economics Framework (GhCEF)[3]

The objectives of Greenhouse Care Economics (GhCE) can be achieved if a number of institutions either dedicated or undedicated to the target people collaborate under some defined guidelines. The institutional framework to support GhCE can be named a Greenhouse Care Economics Framework (GhCEF).[3] A realistic model of GhCEF should displace complex solutions to the environmental, financial and economic problems with that are simple and yet effective. As an example, empowering community relationship, living healthy lives, building green homes, installing energy efficient light bulbs, installing solar panels on roofs or buying smaller homes are simpler and sustainable. Martenson (2011) explains this:

> "By simply reorienting our priorities we can simultaneously buy ourselves time and assure that we choose prosperity over growth....we already know how to build houses that face the sun and use almost no energy; we know how to build smaller and more fuel-efficient vehicles."[6]

There is a lot to learn and follow from Cuba model after its 'artificial' 'peak oil' crisis called special period following breakdown of Soviet Union (see Chapter 09) was without any money or help from outside. Immediately after the crisis and for next five first five years of the special period government introduced food rationing that kept the crisis at bay.[51] These food distributions guaranteed a minimum level of food to each of Cuban citizens and prevent the people who had more money couldn't just swipe and go away with everything on the counters, and others would go hungry.[50] Similarly not only food rationing but also rationing of many other essential items such as clothes, toys, health care can be introduced for the have-nots using the concept Dual Value of Money (DVM), where poor people will pay much less than those who can afford under GhCEF.

During the special period, Cuban government imported 1.2 million bicycles from China, and manufactured another half a million.[50] Since bicycle will be most important short distance transport, why don't we establish bicycle manufacturing plants using green energy right now under GhCEF so that people become get used to with bicycles. Many developed countries in Europe already came forward doing that, whereas many developing countries such as China and India are doing the opposite, opening the door for fossil fuel based automobiles. Encouraging use of bicycles instead under GhCEF will create awareness among the people and then will spread from one community to the other and then to small towns to all over the country.

Back in the 1970s, during the first energy shocks, Australians David Holmgren and Bill Mollison, came up with a system they called "permaculture". The term permaculture (as a systematic method) was first coined by Australians Bill Mollison and David Holmgren in 1978. The word permaculture originally referred to "permanent agriculture"[51&52] Bill Mollison defines "permaculture" as:

> "Permaculture is a philosophy of working with, rather than against nature; of protracted and thoughtful observation rather than protracted and thoughtless labor; and of looking at plants and animals in all their functions, rather than treating any area as a single product system."[53]

More specifically, Permaculture is a branch of ecological design, ecological engineering, environmental design, construction and integrated water resources management that develops sustainable architecture, regenerative and self-maintained habitat and agricultural systems modeled from natural ecosystems.[52&54] As an example, Agroforestry is an integrated approach that combines agricultural and forestry technologies to create more diverse, productive, profitable, healthy and sustainable land-use systems.[55] There are many other techniques and technologies practiced in permaculture such as rainwater harvesting to accumulate and store rainwater for reuse before it reaches the aquifer, sheet mulching to reducing evaporation of water, providing nutrients, increasing organic matter in soil, feeding and creating habitat for soil organisms, suppressing weed growth, Keyline design for maximizing beneficial use of water resources and so on.[52] Greenhouse Care Economics (GhCE) may adopt this concept as its ultimate goal. To reach there we need to build a GhCEF to promote permaculture throughout a country.

Urban Agricultural Movement and growing organic food using the concept "Permaculture" was another big movement during the special period in Cuba. Cuba made a drastic move to convert every piece of arable land to organic agriculture. Organic agriculture includes rebuilding the top soil using organic seeds, bio-fertilizers, bio-pesticides, organic composts and worm humus. Today 80% of Cuba's agricultural production is organic.[50] Heinberg argues:

> "The Cuban example is encouraging, but it is often called into question on the grounds that what worked on an island with an authoritarian government might not work so well in a large, pluralistic democracy such as the United States."[11]

If planned properly under GhCEF, agricultural sectors of a country can be transformed into permaculture before the "peak oil" crisis hits the economy. Like Cuba, it would take couple of years to make the lands fertile without expensive and fossil fuel based chemical fertilizers and pesticides. Popularizing organic agriculture will reduce dependency on borrowings from loan sharks, good for the farmers (the Pareto Space (PS)) and bad for the businessmen and the lenders who are in fact form a virtual Pareto Coalition (PC).

As happened in Cuba, when the "peak oil" crisis will begin to appear, hundreds of thousands of families will move to rural areas putting pressure on the food supply. This may turn into a miserable situation or conflict if the rural areas are not ready to accept that huge migration. Therefore, a land reform is very important to increase food production and strengthen the community relationship and liberate local economies. The urban people may buy lands but it will be very difficult to take possession on the event of the crisis if they are not on the lands already. The price of agricultural lands may suddenly go up and many people will not be able to buy any and that will be a big source of conflict when the crisis will knock the door. A land reform should be inclusive of all the people, rich or poor, farmers or non-farmers, local or migrants. Shared ownership and co-operatives may be a good solution for land distribution. As an example, the urban people who are not on any rural lands may wish to buy lands in rural areas but the GhCEF may make sure that they still share the ownership with the previous small owners and build a long term relationship by sharing the efforts of food production. There could be many arguments and debates but it will not be difficult to figure out a fair solution that can be implemented uniformly in the whole country.

Cuba already had free healthcare and high quality system for its citizens. Still Cuba produces more doctors and health care professionals than it needs and many of them are serving in many other countries in Latin America. In rest of the world under "capitalists biasing", the conventional medical system is designed to generate more money for big pharmaceutical companies and hospital corporates, create more employments and generate more tax revenues for government. Actually for government, the net revenue from health sector might be negative considering government pays billions of dollars of hospital bills for treatment of diseases like cancer, heart disease at least for elderly and poor people. According to Dr. Charles B. Simone, founder of Simons Protective Cancer Center, we made little no progress in conventional treatment of adult cancer since 1920 although there are hundreds of millions dollars spent on it.[7] American Cancer Society reports that surgary, radiation, therapy and chemotherapy seldom produce a cure of cancer.[8] Chemotherapy destroys natural immune system whereas a plant based diet is a foundation for good immune system and even can reverse cancer and many other deadly diseases.[7] Nevertheless diseases that is produced by over consumptions, unhealthy lifestyle make the big pharmaceutical companies wealthy. Figure 10.2 shows the biased Generation Z in developed countries and also among rich families in developing countries are well suited for unhealthy lifestyle such as sitting in front of computers or spending most of the time with electronic devices, avoiding plant food and complete dependency on animal protein, more severely on junk foods.

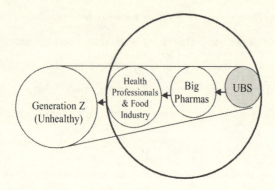

Figure 10.2: Unhealthy Gen Z due to Information Biasing

They are actually helping the medical industry and processed food industry and eventually the pharmaceutical companies and their investors but not helping themselves nor helping their countries. No doubt they need to make a U-turn and counteract this biasing not only for their healthy lives but also for saving their countries from the post-peak oil crisis.

In a developed country, implementation of GhCEF can be as simple as motivating Generation Z in healthy lifestyle such as involving them in lots of physical activities, eating lots of plant foods and avoiding animal fat whereas the opposites are the widespread practices. Every school in a community can be brought under GhCEF. Healthy Generation Z means more active work-force, less disease, less health care expenses and less borrowing for government. At the beginning a small percentage of Generation Z will come under GhCEF. We may call them a starter Green Coalition Z (GCZ). If hundred percent of a starter GCZ can change their lifestyle, it will motivate many others from Generation Z, X and Y including many patients suffering from cancer or heart diseases to do so. Figures 10.3 shows healthy lifestyle of GCZ will weaken the biasing chain comprised of healthcare professionals-doctors, pharmacists, technicians, food industries, pharmaceutical industries, bio-medical equipment companies and against capitalist dilemma of their investors through Unbiased Vertical Learning Process (UVLP). On the other hand, it will promote local food production, organic foods, sports, cultural activities and medical treatments based on less on expensive medicines but more on nutrition, changing lifestyle, herbs, yoga, meditation etc., wherever suits best and appropriate. As an example, vitamin is a multi-billion dollar industry but according to a series of recent studies in North America where people get enough nutrition is not making people healthier, and

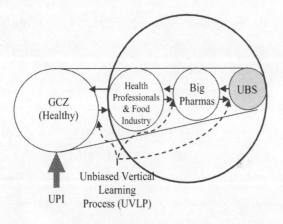

Figure 10.3: Healthy GCZ under GhCEF

they might even be doing the opposite.[9] As more and more people will be aware of this and practice healthy lifestyle, they will virtually be joining in Green Coalitions. As a result the corresponding Money Loop (ML) or the Market Energy Loop (MEL) caused by conventional medical system will degenerate but focus now will change to right medical cares and treatments at much reduced cost extended to Residual Market Energy States (RMS). The key here is education, sharing and motivation which do not infer any cost.

Renewable energy infrastructure development can be the next big target of Greenhouse Care Economics Framework (GhCEF) in a developed country. In 2011, the United Nations Secretary-General launched the Sustainable Energy for All (SE4ALL) initiative with three interlinked objectives to be achieved by 2030: ensure universal access to modern energy services; double the global rate of improvement in energy efficiency; and double the share of renewable energy in the global energy mix.[10] Accordingly, this global share of renewable energy to be made as high as 36% by 2030 with technologies that are already available today as well as with improved energy efficiency and energy access. International Renewable Energy Agency (IREA) assures

"The good news is that the technology already exists to achieve that aspirational goal by 2030, and even to surpass it. Strikingly, taking external costs into account, the transition to renewables can be cost-neutral."[11]

Technology costs for renewable energy will continue to decline through technology innovation, competition and growing markets. A GhCEF may be designed in a way to stimulate market growth and enable short-term and long-term investments for renewable energy infrastructure. Therefore, it should promote widespread adoption and sustainable use of all forms of renewable energy, including bioenergy, geothermal, hydropower, solar and wind energy, in the pursuit of sustainable economy, climate control and prosperity.

Energy transition has huge implications for finance not only from investment perspective but also from debt perspective[5]. As an example, recovery of high investment for grid upgrade will heighten government debt since private investors are not likely to invest in grids. This will require high growth and consumption so that the government can collect taxes to pay off the debts, whereas we need to reduce consumption.[5] Therefore, Heinberg recommends:

"Transition strategies should therefore include goals such as the cancelation of much existing debt and reduction of the size and role of the financial system.

Increasingly, we must direct investment capital toward projects that will tangibly benefit communities, rather than leaving capital investment primarily in the hands of profit-seeking individuals and corporations."[5]

A government may introduce 'green bonds' or 'green infrastructure bond' that will allow individuals to invest in building and operating low-carbon infrastructure, such as offshore wind turbines and grid connections, which will also create green jobs. This means green bonds will be asset backed and sustainable and survive even when fossil fuel will become expensive and unavailable. A government may also introduce registered green bonds, which may be tax deductible similar to registered retirement savings plan in Canada. It is very important to note that the renewable energy sector is not fully independent since still we need carbon products and fossil fuel for manufacturing parts for solar panels, wind turbine, blades, storage system such as batteries, grid upgrade etc. A country may build these industries locally under GhCEF as well and save fossil fuel instead of burning much of it for transportation by the name of globalization. After deregulation in utility sectors there are competition created for power generation and distribution or reseller companies but there was no interest for investing in grids. Grid upgrade for making compatible with renewable energy for both solar and wind will be a huge investment cannot be achieved with profit making goal. There are trillions of dollars long-term assets are held by capitalists, a part of which can be allocated for buying green bonds or green infrastructure development otherwise their values will sharply decline when 'peak oil' will be visible. It is also important to highlight here that 'peak oil' may not be visible when physical reserve reaches at 'peak' since economic 'peak' can be masked by debt market.

According to Ben Caldecott, the head of UK & EU policy at Climate Change Capital low-carbon infrastructure projects are generally unable to access capital held by institutional investors because most of the projects are individual projects that institutional investors are highly unlikely to invest.[11] On the other hand, green bond market hasn't taken off. Ben explains the reason as:

"There is also a chicken-and-egg problem, where little or no liquidity in this bond market means that few investors want to buy them, and without buyers, few want to issue them, which in-turn, results in little liquidity."[12]

The green infrastructural bonds under GhCEF may solve this problem if it targets a massive scale green infrastructure development by bringing initial investors in a Green Coalition of Investors (GCI). Once few projects are successful, CGI will grow bigger and it may become similar massive infrastructure building activities as building railroads during Victorian era.

One interesting and may be a breakthrough idea for reducing dependency on fossil fuel is "solar highway" put forward by a U.S. couple Scott Brusaw and Julie Brusaw in 2006. The plan is to replace asphalt surfaces of roads and highways with structurally-engineered strong solar panels with necessary traction and impact-resistance properties. In an interview Scott Brusaw describes its potential as:

"We learned that the U.S. had over 72,000 square kilometers of asphalt and concrete surfaces exposed to the sun. If we could cover them with our solar road panels, then we could produce over three times the amount of energy that we use as a nation—that's using clean, renewable energy instead of coal."[13]

This vision will be equivalent to covering a small country with solar road panels, which will require huge amount of money and energy to begin with. Scott Brusaw estimates a cost of $10,000 for a 12-foot-by-12-foot segment of Solar Roadway, or around $70 per square foot, whereas asphalt, costs somewhere around $3 to $15, depending on the quality and strength of the road.[14] The total cost to redo America's roadways with Solar Roadways would be $56 trillion, which looks to be a crazy amount.[14] This may be too late for this massive idea. It would be good to adopt this kind of idea when King Hubbert alerted the U.S.

"peak oil" or the U.S. really reached peak oil during 1970 or Club of Rome warned us about "The Limits to Growth" in 1972 since many of the roads and highways were being constructed. Now it is too late for the debt ridden U.S. government for such a big investment. It will be hard to motivate profit driven private investors because of the same reason as they are uninterested in investing for grids. Solar panel in every roof top is more important than building solar highways. We need to set priorities. Once every community or local economy is motivated for solar power under GhCEF, solar highways may come next provided that the energy requirement will become a fraction of existing and cost effective economics of scale benefit can be achieved.

Apart from this big vision, building green homes or using solar electricity in a massive scale will also bring economics of scale benefits, reducing prices of solar panel. Rocky Mountain Institute (RMI) forecasts a massive growth prospect of community-scale solar electricity.[58] According to its recent report community-scale solar can become cost-competitive with utility-scale solar and wholesale electricity rates. As it describes the reason:

"Community-scale solar is at a sweet spot between utility-scale and behind-the-meter solar. It is neither too big nor too small; it is just the right size to capture community and distributed energy benefits on one hand and utility-scale solar's economies of scale on the other."[58]

A massive deployment of community-scale solar is possible under GhCEF bypassing the vulnerability of financial market. Green Coalition Z (GCZ) may take frontline position to promote community solar and to pursue with government and municipalities for incentives and appropriate legislations. They may convince school boards to allow building solar panels on roof tops of every school. In this way, students of the school will develop affinity for renewable energy and their sustainable future. And thus it will create appeals to the other parts of societies for supporting them. In big cities such as New York, London or Tokyo, the majority of the population does not own houses or live in high rise buildings or apartments that are not suitable for solar panels. Therefore, cities would be the biggest potential market for community scale solar. Rocky Mountain Institute (RMI) calculates that USA has more than 750 GW potential markets for this.[58]

GhCEF should comply with the market based economy but based on the fact of differential markets in pricing for these products for poor and rich people. This means when a poor people will buy a house, he should get incentives for buying a green home but not the rich people. Instead rich people who buy big houses should pay more taxes for not having green homes. In reality it is very hard to differentiate the actual rich and poor people where tax evasion is a norm for huge amount of self-employed and rich people. Developed countries such as USA and Canada are not very exception to this norm. Therefore, a proper database of the poor people is very important for a success of the GhCEF, which can be newly built by launching some creative programs under this framework. As an example, a certain percentage of Green Coalition Z (GCZ) in a community are poor families and the rest are rich families. If a family house of a member of GCZ is bigger than a certain size, the family can be considered as rich family. The poor families may get government subsidies and the rich families may have to pay green taxes otherwise they may have to convert their houses into green homes. In this way, hundred percent of the families can be targeted to have green homes. GCZ may motivate their parents to convert their homes to green homes. Eventually when hundred percent of the children of a community will be under GCZ, all houses in that community may potentially become green homes. Similarly, if hundred percent houses of a community have green homes, the same for the rest of the communities under a municipality is just matter of time. The local school database can be used for this purpose and each member of GCZ can be tracked by a number instead of true profile of a student's family house to conceal the real identity for information security. Highly motivated students from high schools may volunteer for collecting information from neighborhood and bring a participatory success.

Once there is a market for green home, investors and builders will be interested in investing more money in this industry. And the market will get benefits of economics of scale that will drive the costs down with increasing use of renewable energy or gaining efficiencies of these technologies. After global financial crisis, governments worldwide slashed solar power subsidies that left China sitting on idle capacity and mounting losses. To help prop up the solar industry, Beijing plans to more than quadruple solar power generating capacity to 35 Gigawatts (GW) by 2015 to use up some of the huge domestic panel glut.[15] Under GhCEF, economic policies and strategies are to be set by the government of a country to produce renewable energy parts as much as possible in own country to become energy independent in future. At least 25 countries in the world are already produce 80% of electricity demand from renewable energy.[16] The countries where per capita energy consumptions are very low, it is not difficult to generate 100% of electricity from renewable energy. As an example, in Bangladesh installed electric generation capacity was 10289 MW in January 2014 for 150 million people, with a per capita availability of 321 kWh per annum. However, contribution of renewable energy is as low as 4.43%, among which solar energy contributes 15 MW in rural households and wind energy contributes 1.9 MW.[17] More than 60% this electricity caters export industries and commercial sectors, much of which will not be required when globalization will fall down after disappearance of cheap oil. It will be not difficult to increase from 4.43% to 40-60% of the share from renewable energy, which might be equivalent to 100% of considering domestic demand in an un-globalized world.

On the other hand, the countries with high per capita energy consumption should reduce it, while increase the use of renewable energy as much as possible. At the national level, at least 30 nations around the world already have renewable energy contributing more than 20% of energy supply.[18] This percentage is lower compared to renewable energy for electricity since transportation is a major stakeholder of non-renewable energy. The per capita energy usage in the U.S. is 7 times higher than that of China, 15 times of India and twice more than of the U.K. and the most of the European countries.[19] If the U.S. reduces half their per capita energy usage, it will be equal to the usage of the U.K., not too bad.

An independent National Research Council in the U.S. has noted that "Renewable energy is an attractive option because renewable resources available in the United States, taken collectively, can supply significantly greater amounts of electricity than the total current or projected domestic demand."[20] Mark Z. Jacobson, professor of civil and environmental engineering at Stanford University and director of its Atmosphere and Energy Program says producing all new energy with wind power, solar power, and hydropower by 2030 is feasible and existing energy supply arrangements could be replaced by 2050. Barriers to implementing the renewable energy plan are seen to be "primarily social and political, not technological or economic". Jacobson says that energy costs with a wind, solar, water system should be similar to today's energy costs.[17&21] There are also technologies emerging for desalination of water that can produce fresh water from salty sea water. A recent study shows that graphene oxide filters may unlock our most abundant water source since it can desalinate using 100 times less energy than conventional filters.[22] The technology is there but we need to redesign our whole infrastructure based on energy efficient technologies. According to the 2013 Post Carbon Pathways report, which reviewed many international studies, the key roadblocks are: climate change denial, the fossil fuels lobby, political inaction, unsustainable energy consumption, outdated energy infrastructure, and financial constraints.[23] Here GhCE will provide a unique pathway to bypass the roadblocks for an initial success for solving existing problems such as poverty, health and safety, scarcity of fresh water everything using less energy and strengthening local economy which may potentially eliminate all the roadblocks.

Although GhCE advocates for creating an economic system without growth compulsion, green products and services are exceptions, which should grow dynamically. A government may take a radical step by imposing tax on accumulated wealth that is sitting idle or not invested for a green cause such as buying green bonds or investing directly in renewable energy, growing organic foods, building green homes or buying electric cars. Currently governments impose tax on the current years earning only that requires continuous growth and profit. A government may take a further more radical step by introducing workers share in green sectors to achieve dynamic growth in green sectors, which are sustainable. If workers of an industry share little ownership of the company, a concern to the other workers and a family attitude in a wage employment sector will develop. Therefore, in this way the workers will form a Green Coalition Zero (GC0) under a GhCEF, which will change the focus of the other investors from merchandizing to establishing local industries for producing of green products such as electric cars, solar panels, polysilicon, wind turbines blades & other parts, batteries, graphene filter etc.

Figure 10.4 below shows GhCEF for GC0, which will counteract the Money Loop (ML) and Market Energy Loop (MEL) in the economy. In case of worker's share, one's 'ownership entitlement (Sen, 1981)[24], becomes a part of his operational holding that increases with the rise of his marginal productivity and creates an internal and external dynamics. Therefore, it will not only be beneficial for them but also for all other investors in the company. By course of time a unit green industry will have a growth and each of the workers will have more capital to work with. Their wage rate will rise along with the rise of their marginal productivities. There will be more income for the workers and ideally, they will not intend to withdraw their capital as long as it will provide higher wages and other benefits. The workers' share must be protected by a legal and policy framework, which must accommodate and extend existing legal and

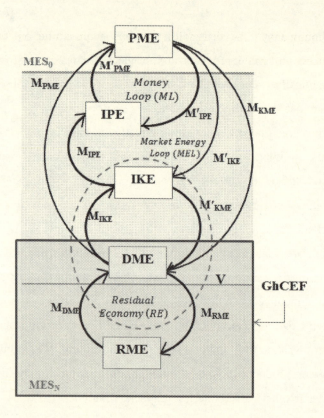

Figure 10.4: Greenhouse Care Economics Framework (GhCEF) for GC0

policy framework, as well as the workers' right to realize commercial value of their share any time on demand by keeping total investment intact.

Are we transforming the poor workers into capitalists under this framework? As an example, let us consider a solar panel manufacturing company in which workers receive low wages, but yet are holding a portion of the company's stocks, purchased with their little savings. If the company's profit is poor, it will not be an attractive investment for them. In this situation, let us assume that the government decides to give incentives, such as tax refunds equivalent to their proportionate share. Eventually, the workers collective share will be accumulated more rapidly than that of their employer. Someday in the period of perpetuity the workers collectively will intend to dominate over their employer as shown in Figure 10.5. We may call this tendency of **Internal Green Dynamics (IGD)** of the company.[25] As shareholders, to get more value out of their shares, the workers will prefer modernization to support the future growth of the industry. The portfolio nature of investment suggests that entrepreneurs do not put all their

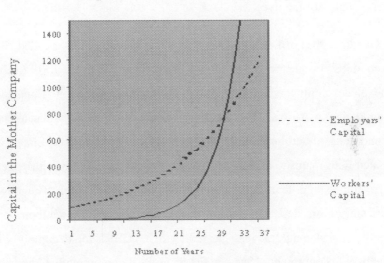

Figure 10.5: workers' dominance in a green industry[25]

eggs in one basket. The investors of the company must withdraw a part of their profit (say, in terms of dividends) from the mother industry for other investments. Their investment portfolios will be triggered by the IGD for diversified investments in new green sectors. Thus it will expand the green industry with economics of scale and create new jobs and opportunities. This tendency may be called as **External Green Dynamics (EGD)**.[25]

The workers share option will give them the opportunity to participate in decision making for better healthcare, education and other welfare support from their companies. By contributing more on welfare, their employer can delay the pressure of workers dominance in the mother industry. The EGD will act as a potential source of local industrial development in green sectors and welfare of an economy. In the long run, it will be realized that a workers share is not a tool to provide higher income for the workers, but to provide them with better access to healthcare, education and housing services etc. under GhCEF, thus will create a green dynamics in health and education sectors. Eventually industrial dynamics of the green sectors will create more services and opportunities to enhance the workers' quality of the lives.

Iqbal Quadir (2003) of Legatum Center at MIT proposed an idea called "bottom-up economics" to nurture and promote entrepreneurship at the level of the poor people in developing countries like village phone program in Bangladesh or Stirling engine in Africa.[26] The concept of GhCE theoretically substantiates this idea and tells about how those discrete efforts in local economies can be integrated with mainstream market. The countries are infested with poverty are less developed and therefore, less dependent on fossil fuel. The developed countries are more dependent on fossil fuel and responsible for their depletion and ecological damage. A realistic model of GhCEF should comply with the market based economy but based on the fact of differential market in pricing and services. A higher level of economic freedom calls for the need to develop human capital, which requires good education and health care. In a developing country, one way or another, poor people are the major work force of a country's major industrial and agricultural sector but they are deprived of accessing the two basic needs, good healthcare for their family and good education for their children. GhCEF should translate the real income of the poor people in terms of access to affordable but good quality education and healthcare so that their Real Income to Contribution Ratio (RICR) improves (Chapter 9). Although these two sectors require massive restructuring and reform for good services, much of the improvements can be achieved directly through GhCEF.

A radical step from GhCEF would be 'land reform' in developing countries. Unfortunately, the politics in those countries are too complicated to make any revolutionary decisions like pro-poor land reform or welfare reform. In rural areas poverty caused by information biasing is directly enforced by local loan sharks (mohajons), middlemen so that they can maximize rents and interests on

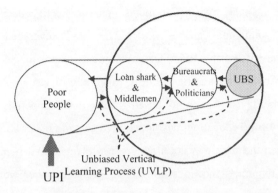

Figure 10.6: Unbiased Poverty Alleviation

which they live and indirectly by deliberately inefficient bureaucracy, politics and businesses. If a huge number of poor people are steadily and aggressively taken under GhCEF as Green Coalition Zero (GC0), the biasing forces against them will begin to change through an 'Unbiased Vertical Learning Process (UVLP)' as shown in Figure 10.6. That means this framework will work in two ways. Firstly, it will provide comfort level for the poor people and secondly, it will align them together and give signals about their bargaining power to government and other institutions for making and implementing pro-poor economic policies and strategies. This may lead to human development, build community relationship, improve of healthcare services, housing and amenities for the poor people and eventually revolutionary outcomes like land-reform. Greg Downey, a Journalism professor shares his experience regarding a revolutionary example of land reform in Brazil as:

"I saw something very similar in camps of the Movimento Sem Terra (the MST or 'Landless Movement') in Brazil. Roadside shanty camps attracted former sharecroppers, poor farmers whose small plots were drowned out by hydroelectric projects, and other refugees from severe restructuring in agriculture toward large-scale corporate farming." These farmers were victims, but they were by no means helpless. "Activists and religious leaders were helping these communities to set up their own governments, make collective decisions, and eventually occupy sprawling ranches. . . . The MST leveraged the land occupations to demand that the Brazilian government adhere to the country's constitution, which called for agrarian reform, especially of large holdings that were the fruits of fraud. . . . community-based groups, even cooperatives formed by people with very little education, developed greater and greater ability to run their own lives when the state was not around. They elected their own officials, held marathon community meetings in which every member voted (even children), and, when they eventually gained land, often became thriving, tight-knit communities."[56]

The concept of Unbiased Pareto Improvement (UPI) tells that many of the problems the poor people face locally can be dealt with locally rather than waiting for policy level change. Let us imagine that an economy is composed of many quanta of economics. A geographical region may be considered as a quantum economy. As an example, a rural or a suburban area of underdeveloped Indian states such as Bihar or Urissa or a slum of Mumbai can be considered as a quantum economy. The key of GhCEF will be proper modeling of an economic challenge based on the concept of a 'DMM'. To implement GhCE massively throughout a country, we will need to translate the high-level model to a further low-level based on the real needs and opportunities of each quantum economy. At first, it will be required to conduct a very comprehensive study to define the criteria of the target people and to narrow down the local needs and opportunities for a particular area.

A good example is Ralegan Siddhi, a rural village in western India, in 1975 which was afflicted by drought, poverty prevailed, and trade in illicit liquor was widespread. Anna Hazare, a social activist and reformist changed the village to a model village of environmental conservation demonstrates that it is possible to rebuild natural capital in partnership with the local economy. Now it uses non-conventional energy solar power, biogas and a windmill.[27] All the village street lights each have separate solar panels. Also, the village has carried out programs like tree planting, terracing to reduce soil erosion and digging canals to retain rainwater.[27] The World Bank Group has concluded that the village of was transformed from a highly degraded village ecosystem in a semi-arid region of extreme poverty to one of the richest in the country.[28]

A GhCEF may facilitate movement such as The Green Belt Movement (GBM) in Kenya organized by Professor Wangari Maathai in 1977 under the auspices of the National Council of Women of Kenya. It organizes women in rural Kenya to plant trees, combat deforestation, restore their main source of fuel for cooking, generate income, and stop soil erosion. Since 1977 then over 51 million trees have been planted. Over 30,000 women trained in forestry, food processing, bee-keeping, and other trades that help them earn income while preserving their lands and resources.[29] Maathai received Nobel Peace Prize in 2004 for her work with the Green Belt Movement. Her movement has been motivating both men and women to prevent further environmental destruction and restore that which has been damaged.

At the beginning GhCEF may establish some research and development centers of GhCE in some areas where the primary target people mostly live or where to begin a movement. The focus of the research and development centers will be to identify local common needs for the people and for the environment and formulate a framework to integrate them through environmental friendly locally significant programs. For example, by applying a self-selection (Rothschild and Stiglitz, 1976)[30] method the target people may be motivated to voluntarily enroll in a database through participation in some prudently designed programs. The database will represent them as an organized segment of an economy so that they can be cared for, educated and entertained in an organized way. The next step will be to design the best suitable plan for that quantum economy based on the study result. Once the small sized local projects are locally successful, this framework can be extended to more primary target people through prudently designed local and national level programs. Small scale implementation of GhCEF will be a learning experience for large scale implementation.

No other institution can be a better alternative to a government because of not only its policy making capacity but also workforce and infrastructural capacity to improve the RICR. The most weakness of a government of a poor country is that it is very inefficient in service delivery, which means it needs help in this part. The poorest people have lowest level of economic freedom are vulnerable part of the economy and the most sufferers of any economic or environmental crisis. If economic growth gives birth of opportunist people, then it will reinforce the preexisting MEL and boost up costs of all products and services increasingly unreachable by the poor people. The core idea of GhCEF is to create a protected economic system for their economic and human needs so that they can share and hold the reflection of their own efforts. At the same time, if they are exposed to market as a collective body, their collective presence will not only provide an incentive for the existing market to be stretched toward them with differential prices but also insist government to provide pro-poor policy supports.[31]

An ideal government must ensure education and healthcare for the poor people. In an under developed country, these two sectors are full of inefficiency and corruption. On the other hand, they are also two flourishing private sectors. In this reality, let us assume that poor people deserve healthcare and education at a cost they can afford. Thus, we can make the health and education sectors more accountable to poor people. This is where we may introduce an insurance service for the poor people. A certain percentage of one participant's monthly tiny deposit may be assumed as a premium of his insurance policy.[32] The question may arise which hospital or school will provide the welfare services to the poor people at a lower cost? Their employers must provide some welfare to their workers. There is no reason for not choosing existing government subsidized hospitals or schools to provide healthcare and education services, respectively, in GhCEF in the first place. The subsidized welfare services should be continued under GhCEF by introducing lower prices for poor people and higher prices for rich people since they are already classified by the framework. The service delivery of the government hospitals and schools can also be improved under the same framework. This is how a poor man's unit money can buy more value in terms of welfare and improve their RICR. To offset the costs and distribute risks, the insurance service shall also be extended to non-poor people with differentiated premiums and services by setting up another interface.

A huge number of poor people in a country may be considered as opportunity for local market for green products such a locally produced green electricity and green foods. On the other hand, when the poor people decide to sell their products and services, the GhCE will virtually empower them with collective bargaining power. Therefore, they will get better price for the products and services they produce. Eventually, the poor people like share crop workers, small farmers, craftsmen or day workers will be benefited. This framework should accommodate business opportunities involving poor people such as the social businesses promoted by Nobel peace laureate professor Yunus.[33] It should promote innovation for creating new business opportunities involving poor people particularly in supply chain and service delivery of agricultural products.

In case of poverty alleviation, a two layer DMM model, the inner layer may represent market of rich people and the outer layer may represent market of poor people. In the outer market, the businesses may be benefited from "economics of scale" to reach huge number of new customers (poor people). Therefore, the prices of the same or similar services or products of the outer market will fall and it will always be lower than that of the inner market. In other words, an individual on the outer layer will be able to buy more values such as health care with his unit money than that of an individual of the inner layer.[25&31] The lower price in the outer market will be offset by the higher price and enhancement of quality of services or products on the inner market. Thus GhCEI may create a competitive business environment for both quantity and quality, which may result in stronger local market before entering into a sustainable green economy.

There the welfare expenses and foreign aid programs by the government and non-government organizations are not efficiently managed, because of their weak service delivery systems. The dedicated institutions under GhCEF may keep track of the individuals who truly need welfare support, thus acting like a watchdog to support the low cost insurance service and to improve services and efficiencies of the existing welfare services like healthcare or education. They can also act as a platform to influence and motivate the existing businesses, corporate or employers to build and support welfare infrastructures for poor people beside the government. Once the welfare infrastructure will be built along with brining the poor people under GhCEF as GC0, they will not be left off during and after the transition to sustainable economy. Similarly, when renewable energy infrastructure will be built along with brining Generation Z under GhCEF as GCZ, they will be well prepared to survive with less energy and less consumptions with depletion of resources availability such as fossil fuels, vital minerals and surface water. Pursuing GC0 and GCZ together have a synergic effect since that may spur similar or many other green coalitions through Horizontal Learning Process (HLP), who will act as green sources of information for the core capitalists. Therefore, extending GhCEF from a quantum economy to the whole country and then to the whole world for a breakthrough transition from growth economy to sustainable green economy.

10.4 Greenhouse Care Economics Institutes (GhCEI)

Greenhouse Care Economics can counteract and prevent the causes of poverty and ecological damage and provide incentives for the markets, societies and the institutions to change to the right direction. A well designed GhCEF may not only unlock market potential of an economy but also make the market more meaningful to mankind. An aggressive implementation of GhCE requires standardization of GhCEF. The institution for setting up, standardization and accreditation of the methods, procedures and policies for large scale implementation of GhCEF can be called "Greenhouse Care Economics Institute (GhCEI)". The standards can be set for community power, organic agriculture, low carbon businesses, green bonds, renewable energy infrastructure, worker's share, as well as healthcare reform, education, rural business support, quality of life, and so on. It may standardize the implementation of GhCEF in massive scale worldwide The GhCEI may also be responsible for research & development on GhCE and also for setting up and monitoring standards for businesses and organizations that will follow the concept of GhCE. They may also define specifications for governments to support this.

A GhCEI should focus on overall system design rather than pursuing many discrete efforts to reach the objectives of GhCE. However, at the beginning some small projects can be initiated for research and development of the overall system design for a larger scale. As an example, it may define Unbiased Pareto Improvement (UPI) strategies for formation of Green Coalitions, particularly for GC0 and GCZ based on local situation and specify how to use and maintain their database. If target people are correctly classified, then it will be much easier to organize them and achieve the objectives.

The first and foremost of objective of GhCEF will be independence in local food production, particularly in urban areas. Following the Cuban Urban Agricultural Movement model in 1990s, we will need to motivate and train the urban people to grow foods on rooftops, any empty or squatting places by themselves using permaculture. Following the Cuban model, a training institute may be set up for "train the trainer course" for training a number of highly motivated individuals from every community or locations about permaculture. Now in Havana 50% of the demand of fruits and vegetables comes from urban agriculture in the city. In an interview in the video documentary "The Power of Community: How Cuba Survived Peak Oil" Robert Perez, Cuba's Sustainable Urban Development Program describes the benefits of such training courses:

Not only has through these workshops and courses, has the community learned about permaculture, but they here in the center have learned a lot about the community. For example if someone comes here and they have a health problem, they do whatever they can to help with that, but also they service kind of a reference point. They will go and look for the specialists and bring them here, so it's a mutual relationship. The people cooperating with, and caring about each other are the main factors that we need to encourage. We can all plant fruit trees, we can all have water catchment devices on our roofs. It's not the technology, it's the human relationships.[50]

Following the Cuba model, training institutes can be set up for "train the trainer courses" on permaculture in a way that enhance human and community relationship. The profession training courses needs to be redesigned that will best suit for the new post fossil-fuel economy. The educational institutes, the total health care system will need to be decentralized and therefore, more healthcare professionals, more doctors, teachers will be needed. The existing highly paid doctors of private hospitals or teachers of private universities will not be willing to go rural areas but they may be motivated and engaged for training others from different locations of a country under GhCEF. Again Cuba is the best example, the number of universities in Cuba increased from three (3) to fifty (50) after the special period. Only seven (7) of them are in Havana. After the crisis, now many more medical clinics and schools have been set upacross the country.[50]

A large scale deployment of GhCEF will require co-operation from people involved–rich and poor, urban and rural, governments, non-government organizations, investment companies, local authorities and even international organizations such as United Nations and International Renewable Energy Agency (IRENA). As an example, governments must ensure renovating and building welfare infrastructure in compliance with GhCEF. As part of supporting renewable infrastructure a government should support the development of enabling infrastructure, including power grids and storage, to support the integration of high shares of variable renewables. Since with depletion of fossil fuel availability, economic growth will also deplete but renewable energy will become demanding, GhCEF compliances may become a necessity of time.

According to IRENA, 9% of Total Final Energy Consumption (TFEC) TFEC was from traditional use of biomass and 9% of TFEC is modern renewable energy resulting in a total renewable energy share of 18% of TFEC in 2010, which is targeted to reach 36% by 2030.[34] In light of this target, UK government founded Green Investment Bank (GIB) in October 2012 as public limited company to attract private funds for the financing of the private sector's investments for environmentally sustainable projects such as renewable energy, carbon capture and storage and energy efficiency both in the UK and overseas with an initial capital £3 billion.[35] Among the £3billion, £2billion is coming from the sale of nationally owned assets hoping that private sector will match the huge investment ranging from £200 billion and £1 trillion required over the next two decades. GIB's biggest project is £100 million project to convert a Drax coal power station to three of its six MW coal units to operate biomass with equivalent capacity to powering 2 million homes. The problem with this project is although the GIB and Drax have said the biomass will be sourced sustainably, they haven't explained how exactly this will be done.[35] International Energy Agency (IEA, 2012) defines traditional use of biomass as: "the use of wood, charcoal, agricultural residues and animal dung for cooking and heating in the residential sector. It tends to have very low conversion efficiency (10% to 20%) and often relies on unsustainable biomass supply".[36] Biomass is one of the biggest portfolio of GIB that includes new plants and upgrade capacity of existing plants.[37] The bank's initial engagement with many biomass projects means it has failed to think further than "outside the box".

On the other hand, under GhCEF, biomass will be a less preferred option in large scale because it is an incredibly heavy fuel and will cause air pollution during transport and may require forest harvesting or use of crop lands and huge amount of surface water which will harm the environment. If there were a GhCEF, the 2 million homes can be powered by solar panels by involving Generation Z in GCZ of the neighborhoods for promotion. If the solar panels were produced locally in U.K., it would create new employments and at the same time workers share would create a 'dynamic green growth' as explained in previous section. Once this project would gain momentum, it would attract private investors to buy green bonds that would multiply the funds for green sectors with every successful project under GhCEF. Accordingly, a type of GhCE institute can be called Green Investment Support (GIS), which might look after policy framework for issuing green bonds, investment portfolio guidelines and workers green share. A new green investment bank or a green investment company in a country of in a location can be formed by inheriting the policy framework of GIS under GhCEF.

According to Lovins, Amory B., Chief Scientist of Rocky Mountain Institute, the net benefit from sources of energy in order from greatest to lowest is, first hydro (on his purely economic assumptions) and gas (only if we omit its price volatility), then wind, solar, and last of all nuclear. If the volatility of gas price were counted, as any prudent investor would do, the priority sequence would probably be first hydro (on his purely economic assumptions), then wind, solar, gas, and last of all nuclear.[38] Hydro power plants depend on geographic positions and its opportunity is almost saturated in the world. Recently the Green

Investment Bank, UK has become interested in offshore wind farms. It recently invested £461m into two "next generation" wind farms in March, 2014. And in June, 2014 it unveiled new plans to raise a £1 billion private fund to support Britain's offshore wind farms.[39] Its recently published 2013-14 results showed that in the financial year from March 31 2013, the bank committed £668 million to 18 new projects, making it the most active investor in the UK's green economy. Private investors followed, pledging a further £1.9 billion to the projects, adding up to a total of £2.5 billion of new investment. Most of the projects in the GIB's portfolio remain under construction, but when completed, they are expected to reduce the UK's carbon emissions by 3.5 million tons per year.[39] Even if all these projects are successful, Laura Cloutman writes:

> "The [UK] government has kept one promise, but it has been breaking other promises to reduce emissions. The recent dash for gas, continued extraction of oil and gas in the North Sea and £3 billion of tax breaks for such companies in the 2012 budget alone has left little hope. Emissions were up 4.5% in 2012 due to cheap coal, meaning the UK Climate Change Act is no longer being followed as a legally binding document and more as an advisory report."[35]

The North Sea extraction or cheap coal projects will cater only unsustainable Money Loop (ML) or Market Energy Loop (MEL) under capitalist biasing over the UK economy. In presence of a GhCEF, this would be prevented by collective conscientious of green coalitions such as GCZ and GCI.

Many environmentalists argue that the GIB is still not fulfilling its potential and therefore called for the government to give the bank freedom to borrow.[39] The leader of the UK Green Party Caroline Lucas, criticized GIB "it would be a fund –that is, a pot of money that, once used up, is gone forever."[40] Under GhCEF, this would not be the case since one of the main objectives of GIB would be channeling funds from existing growth sector (Money Loop) to green sector as the existing growth sector will become unsustainable and green sectors are sustainable. Additionally under GhCEF workers share in these projects would create dynamicity since workers share in an existing project (say, an offshore wind energy project) would increase but the other investors share would decrease (internal dynamics) but the other investors would keep on investing for more and more new projects (external dynamics).[32]

We have to keep alive our financial-monetary system but in a new dimension. Heinberg argues "if the financial-monetary system seizes up, this will imperil society's ability to respond to any and all other crises."[41] A new dimensional financial system can be introduced, called Greenhouse Care Bank that may operate to support workers share and financial services such as savings and loans to its members. Members will not be the green workers but also anyone who want to support green causes. This bank can be an interest free bank similar to Swedish or Danish JAK bank, which is an interest free, members owned bank. JAK bank does not charge any interest but those members who borrow money also to save money. As of 2011 members had accumulated 131 million euros in savings, of which 98 million have been allocated as loans to the members.[42] If JAK grants more loans with a similar amount of expenses then cost of loan-cost percentage can go down, but if JAK grants fewer loans, then this percentage can go up. This means under GhCEF, the members of Green Coalitions can be readily available members to join in a Greenhouse Bank. As their numbers will increase the cost of borrowing will decrease. As an example, the loan-cost for Swedish JAK bank is currently 3% considering its 38,000 members.[42] If the members increase by two or three times, then the loan-cost will definitely will be more competitive than conventional banks, who charge around 2.5%. In the long run when Greenhouse Care Bank will approach green economy, the loan-cost may reach to a nominal value, less than one percent. The Greenhouse Care Bank will provide opportunities for everyone for channeling moneys from an unsustainable financial-monetary system to green banking system. In other words, the Greenhouse Care Bank may gradually eliminate any Market Loop.

Greenhouse Care Economics Institution (GhCEI) may adopt the models of eco-municipalities and extend the model as eco-village and eco-cities as inspired by economist Torbjörn Lahti and by Karl Henrik Robèrt, founder of the Natural Step Movement.[43&44] The concept "eco-municipality" originated in there in 1983 in Sweden with the founding of the first eco-municipality, Övertorneå. It saw a 20 percent unemployment rate during the recession of the early 1980s and lost 25 percent of its population, but now boasts a thriving ecotourism economy based on organic farming, sheepherding, fish farming, and the performing arts. The town has reached its 2010 goal of being a free of fossil fuels. These municipalities once became depressed industrial towns, which now have made official and deliberate commitments to "dematerialize" their economies and to foster social equity.[43&45] Hällefors, a former steel town that also suffered from high unemployment 20 years ago, now has a successful economy based on renewable energy, organic farming, and culinary arts. Other eco-communities exist in some small parts of USA, Norway, Finland, and Denmark[43&45]

The American Planning Association's four objectives of sustainability are:[45]

1. Reduce dependence upon fossil fuels, underground metals and minerals

2. Reduce dependence upon synthetic chemicals and other unnatural substances.

3. Reduce encroachment upon nature

4. Meet human needs fairly and efficiently.

The difference between the existing U.S. approach about sustainability model and Swedish approach is that many U.S. communities are carrying out sustainable development projects such as emission control initiatives, green building programs, smart growth are largely occurring on a project-by-project basis and called "silo approach".[45] In contrast, the eco-municipality model uses a systems approach as also proposed by GhCEF that involves widespread community awareness-raising and integrated municipal involvement, and using a common language to identify what sustainability means.

The most important part of a GhCEF will be creating awareness among people about green options, particularly among Generation Z. Research shows Generation Z is a stellar generation: educated, industrious, collaborative and eager to build a better planet.[46] A recent issue (July 21, 2014) of Canadian magazine Maclean's writes about some exemplary achievements by this generation at their teen. Sixteen year old Ann Makosinski invented a flashlight powered by the heat of a human hand. 15-year old Jack Andraka made headlines with his inexpensive, accurate sensor, able to detect pancreas cancer. Angela Zhang, a 17-year old revealed a protocol that allowed doctors to better detect cancerous tumors on MRI scans. There are many others who demonstrate they are ahead of their age in many areas such as social activists, or a successful chef or successful fashion writer. [46] No doubt, if they are collectively organized, they will become a huge force for a big change. The best way to achieve that is to encourage them to write for themselves in a new platform-in a magazine may be circulated in every school with all over sharing their constructive thoughts under close guidance from qualified moderators about our history, people, peak oil, renewable energy, innovations, lifestyle, science, literature, culture, music and so on. Imagine who will be other audiences, their parents who are from their earlier generation (Generation Y) from every corner of the society, teachers, bankers, businessmen, doctors, lawyers or even politicians can be "reverse mentored" by them. There may be different newsletters and magazines for different age groups primarily focusing on their local economy and community and local peers as audiences. Selected articles may be re-published for bigger audiences, for example, for the whole region or the whole province and then for the whole country and may be for the whole world. They are already demonstrating their potentials that they can do it. Adora Svitak, 16-year old in-demand speaker talks about "What adults can learn from kids". Her speeches have 3.4 million views and been translated into over 40 languages.[46] On the other side, there are consequences of the digital lives centered over a small piece of device. The proposed newsletter or magazines will bring them in open space of minds for thinking about their present and future beyond their small horizon of handheld devices for sure.[46]

A type of green institute may promote use of green technologies such as organic seeds, fertilizers, green methodologies and technologies, high efficiency filters for water desalination or renewable energies locally. For each type of local institute, there may be a global interface for acquiring knowledge and supports connected globally. In summary, in the above discussions we have discussed several instances of Greenhouse Care Economics Institute (GhCEI) in the context of a developed country:

1.   Green Research and Development

2.   Green training centers for permaculture

3.   Green Technology Adoption

4.   Greenhouse Care Bank and Investment Support

5.   Green Publishing & Archiving.

The above institutes of GhCEF are related to some specific areas of GhCEF. To avoid bureaucratic tendency, these institutes might not have any functional power such as issuing licenses or permissions but compliances of GhCEF may become a market requirement. The idea is that to ensure that the best GhCEF standards will be replicated in all markets.

A GhCEI may also accredit organizations that carry out services for poor people in accordance with requirements defined by GhCEF standards. The above mentioned five institutes can be adjusted to support poor people. As an example, Greenhouse Care Bank may take care of workers share, banking and insurance services for poor people. According to the discussions in section 10.3, the following two additional institutes of GhCEF can also be proposed:

6.   Health, Education and Entertainment.

7.   Social Business and Small Business Support.

Nevertheless, there may be a central GhCEI that will communicate with different organizations such as for education and healthcare, businesses, institutes, other accreditation bodies and organizations at national and international level. It may also lobby with policy making organizations like respective government and international organizations such as United Nations, IEA, IRENA etc.

10.5 Age of Sustainability

Is there any possibility to reach to some sorts of sustainability if we do nothing—just follow the path we have already taken? Even though there is—but after passing a long misery and devastating transition period may be accompanied with huge die off due to starvation, conflict, civil war and eventually famine and plague. On the other hand, the path Greenhouse Care Economics (GhCE) proposes will prepare the whole economy for a smooth transition to an age of sustainability by auto-adjusting with the carrying capacity of the earth.

We know the existing path is failing but we are just part of an information biasing chain dominated by financial capitalism and we can do nothing from the middle. The recent report of Intergovernmental Panel on Climate Change (IPCC) makes clear that carbon emissions from burning fossil fuel are currently rising to record levels, not falling although the deadline for international action on global climate change is just over a year away.[47] As Kevin Anderson analyzes the short time-frame that we have to switch over to renewable energy:

"According to the IPCC's Synthesis Report, no more than 1,000 billion tonnes (1,000 Gt) of CO_2 can be emitted between 2011 and 2100 for a 66% chance (or better) of remaining below 2 °C of warming (over preindustrial times)... However, between 2011 and 2014 CO_2 emissions from energy production alone amounted to about 140 Gt of CO_2... the remaining budget for energy-only emissions over the period 2015–2100, for a 'likely' chance of staying below 2 °C, is about 650 Gt of CO2."[59]

According to Heinberg it will take only 19 years to produce 650 gigatons of carbon from fossil fuel.[60] This is the window we have left to make a complete transition to renewable energy to limit the global temperature below 2^0C above pre-industrial level. IPCC does not take into account the fundamental problems with our monetary and financial systems but only with climate matters. Although financial crisis prompts policymakers act quickly but with bailouts and policies that eventually contributes to Money Loop (ML). The onset of catastrophic climate change and depleting fossil fuel–the far more severe crises for mankind cannot urge them on taking quick decisive action. However, as discussed in Chapter 4 that excessive use of fossil fuel and consumption is driven by financial capitalism. Therefore, a fix of the issue of climate change may reside in fixing our financial and monetary systems in a controlled economic environment as possible under a Greenhouse Care Economics Framework (GhCEF). On the other hand, if these systems break up by themselves because of inherent vulnerabilities of these systems, we will be doomed to the consequences of the first path.

A Money Loop (ML) is sustainable as long as it is backed by an increased flow of money generated using cheap energy. However, since our resources and energy reserves are declining, at some point the ML will stop as shown in Figure 10.7. The Figure shows sudden stopping the ML will reduce the circulation of money from banks (PME) to the industries. The stock market will collapse. Industries will be closed down. The whole financial and monetary system will fail. Governments will become bankrupt. At individual level, savings will be evaporated as banks will run out. No employment, no income. There will be huge shortage of food, which will have severe consequences in urban areas. People will revolt. It may turn into an everlasting civil war. Governments will collapse. As a result our industrial civilization will collapse.

As Heinberg describes the financial collapse:

> "Our financial-monetary system is not just vulnerable to periodic internal disruptions like credit crises, it is inherently unsustainable in the emerging context of energy and resource constraints. And if the financial-monetary system seizes up, this will imperil society's ability to respond to any and all other crises. This means that, whatever our other priorities may be, we must also immediately devote effort to reforming the financial-monetary system."[43]

Therefore, financial reform needs to be addressed along with climate matters under a common framework as proposed in GhCEF. Without a reform, on the other hand, continuing existing business as usual our economics will eventually explode into pieces that will be very hard to put together. Although resource

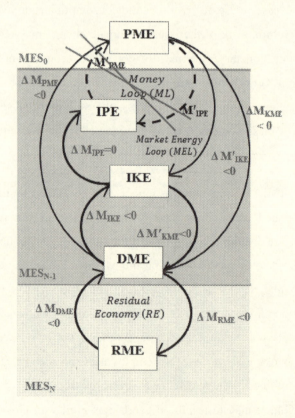

Figure 10.7: Financial Collapse

depletion or climate change is a slowly progression process but a financial-monetary explosion may destroy all options for survival. Risks loom around all over the global economy for a full force explosion unless they are not mitigated by taking actions such as building renewable infrastructures or green banking through GhCEF or any other means.

According to Heinberg, a mitigation plan must also include a 'universal haircut' strategy that will create "time and space" to avert immediate collision of any financial crisis. He proposes strategy for gaining time as "re-set" in the relationship between claims and real assets to restructure our economic and financial systems to be more sustainable and resilient. He describes this example:

"Government by edict would reduce all debt by a certain percentage — let's say, somewhere between 75 and 90 percent. At the same time, all investments and savings accounts above a certain figure (allowance would have to be made for pensioners and low income individuals) would get the same treatment...... Let's say, as a starting point, that we wanted to protect all assets below a certain level. In the US, perhaps all assets below $25,000 could remain untouched. Then, one simple way to administer the "haircut" would be to slice a decimal place off everyone's debts, savings, and other accounts. If you had a $250,000 mortgage, it would be knocked down to $25,000 — but your $20,000 savings account would survive unscathed, as it fell below the $25,000 limit designed to protect pensioners and other low-income individuals. Your debt overhang would have shrunk from $230,000 to $5,000. A wealthy person who had gained $5 billion through investing in hedge funds would now have only $500 million. A business that owed $750,000 in loans would now owe $75,000. And so on."[43]

According to the concept of 'biased equilibrium' Heinberg's "re-set" proposal will work on Money Loop (ML) and as a result, the corresponding Market Energy Loop (MEL) will also be "re-set". However, it will require curbing "capitalist biasing" first, which would take us to square one again. Greenhouse Care Economics (GhCE) at the very first place will allow channeling money from the ML to GhCEF as green investment. A full-fledged implementation of GhCEF will provide opportunities for protection for everyone not limited to poor people or Generation Z from the looming disaster if pursued aggressively and on time. Figure 10.8 shows that once a strong GhCEF will be established, a 'reset' will just cut off the ML and MEL without making any impact on those who are already under protection of GhCEF. The Figure shows that under GhCEF a sustainable Money Market Dynamics (MMD) still may present, where Dominant Market Energy (DME) will be replaced by Green Potential Market Energy (GPE). And Residual Market Energy (RME) will be replaced by Green Kinetic Market Energy (GKE). At some point we can expect a government will be run by Generation Z. If hangover debts still be a problem, government would buy up

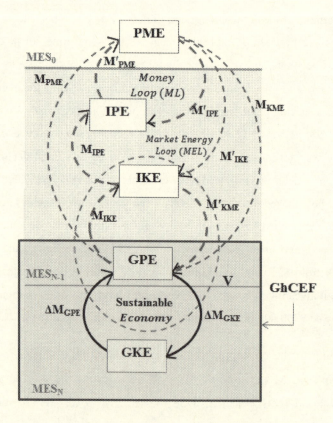

Figure 10.8: Sustainable Green Economy under GhCEF

all the debts with condition of switching to GhCEF. What will happen to the core capitalists? When oil will be gone, they will lose their dominance anyway. If we can counteract the Capitalists Dilemma (CD) of the core capitalists, at some point of time, the concept of "core capitalists" will no more and the transition will end up in a soft landing to a new matric of wellbeing.

In a sustainable economy, energy usage will be a fraction of existing usage because of less consumption, more dependency on agriculture not on industries, localized production and consumption limited by the availability of local resources. As an example, Bangladesh economy with 160 million people largely depends on its big export market of ready-made garments industry. Bangladesh is the second largest exporter of ready-made garments in the world. The existing electricity generation capacity in Bangladesh is about 10,000 MW. Much of the high demand of electricity is to support increased demand in this sector and urbanization. In a sustainable economy, when "cheap" oil will be gone, Bangladesh economy will require a fraction of this electrical energy, which can be produced from renewable energy in few years. The existing solar energy capacity of Bangladesh is 150 MW increased 10 times from 15 MW in 5 years and serving about 3.5 million households or about 20 million people.[48] If Bangladesh can keep the same growth rate, in next 5 years Bangladesh can produce at least 1500 MW of electricity and in next 7 years more than 3,700 MW of electricity, which might be enough for meeting the need of the whole population excluding the export industry. Moreover, much of the renewable energy infrastructure in rural areas will not require any big footprint since solar can use existing rooftops and canal banks, and wind turbines can share space with food crops.

However, there is a big difference in government perception. Bangladesh government is forecasting that the country will produce 24,000MW electricity by 2021, with 10 percent from solar power. How much fossil fuel to be burnt to generate this amount of electricity? By adopting renewable energy for 100%

electricity, much of this fossil fuel could be reserved for future generations to produce solar panels, batteries, wind turbines, health-care, live saving medicines, aviation, that otherwise will be impossible to produce. The way Bangladesh government is planning and the path of sustainable economics are very different. The switch over will require a Greenhouse Care Economics Framework (GhCEF) in Bangladesh economy. As an example, the solar panels will need to be produced locally including spare parts with minimum supply of input or raw materials from overseas. Other sources of renewable energy also need to be explored and applied wherever fits the best. At the same time, the country should figure out how is to become less dependent on energy such as eating less meat, creating water reservoirs, organic farming, producing organic foods and products using technologies that require less energy such as graphene filters for desalination and after all saving all energy sources such as forests.

There are few important movements are trying to take ground in Bangladesh by organizations such as Bangladesh Organic Products Manufacturers Association (BOPMA) established in 2002.[49] Since then it is pushing Bangladesh government for enabling and implementing the National Organic Policy. BOPMA's main goal is to save the nation from poverty, hunger, malnutrition and from diseases as well as to save public health, soil health, fisheries and environment through the following objectives. The proposed policy includes establishment of an organic fertilizer factory at every sub-division to meet total demands of fertilizer throughout the country. According to them, organic fertilizer reduces the usage of pesticides up to eighty percent. They also propose plantation and production of herbal pesticides industries throughout such as Neem, Mehagani etc. This initiative will stop importation of chemical and toxic pesticides and fertilizers. Currently, chemical fertilizer, pesticide and poultry or livestock feed meal are powerful trading businesses having strong lobby with government and politicians. According to BOPMA statistics some national and multinational companies pour 50,000 metric tons of harmful and hazardous pesticides every year in Bangladesh, which is not only damaging environment but also destroying fisheries, increasing health bills through slow poisoning.[49] To reach to sustainability Bangladesh just needs to switch from traditional agriculture to permaculture.

Robert Perez, Cuba's Sustainable Urban Development Program describes the age of sustainability by creating food forests of permaculture as this:

"Nobody fertilizes a forest, nobody irrigates the forest, the forests do by itself. So if you are able to create something like a food forest, your main effort is to pick the fruits and pick the produce and so in that way the effort is less. You work hard in the very beginning, but once the system is established you work a lot less. It's what we call lazy people agriculture, but it's because you are working with nature not against nature."[50]

Let's take a look of a real life story of a man in a remote area in Assam, India, who single-handedly turned once barren river island of the river Brahmaputra into 1,400 acres of forest reserve over the span of 36 years. His name is Jadav Payen, honored with title "Forest Man", a 52 year old dairy farmer lives in a small hut in the forest. He planted trees such as bamboo, teak to protect the river island from accelerated erosion caused by global warming. He nourished, watered the plants and also relocated red ants, earthworms and other insects to the area to help the soil until the plants grew by themselves. Today it is a lush sanctuary for hundreds of elephants, deer and thousands of migratory birds. And even endangered animals such as the one-horned rhino and Royal Bengal tiger started appearing.[57] He expresses his deep concern to protect this forest as:

"I will continue to plant till my last breath. I tell those people cutting those trees will not get you nothing. Cut me before you cut my trees."[57]

On the other side of the world, the so called developed world, the path we have already taken is complex, unhealthy, individualistic based on more production and consumption of futile goods such as fats, drugs, plastics, mileage, radiation, carbon monoxides and crimes but generates huge money for riches by means of profits, medical bills, lawsuits, bribes or usury and at the end leads to collapse. The other path is greener, simpler, healthy, inclusive based on natural rate of production and consumption, knowledge, co-operation and sharing and eventually will lead to sustainability, happiness and peace. Which path will a rational mind of an unbiased individual choose? Jadav Payeng, the Forest Man is an example. His rational mind has established deep bonding with the nature he developed by his own. The whole idea of Greenhouse Care Economics Framework (GhCEF) is to create bonding among people as well as bonding with nature. It will not happen overnight. If a poor man can create a big forest from scratch, then why cannot we the seven billion people together create a sustainable earth?

REFERENCES

Chapter 1: The Crises

1. "A Green New Deal", by Larry Elliott et el., New Economics Foundation, July 21, 2008, http://www.neweconomics.org/publications/entry/a-green-new-deal

2. Heinberg, Richard (2015), "Afterburn: Society Beyond Fossil Fuels", New Society Publishers, Canada, January 2015.

3. Gallagher, Robert (1992), "Rickshaws of Bangladesh", May 1, 1992, University Press Limited, Dhaka, Bangladesh.

4. "Rickshaw pullers in Dhaka city, Bangladesh", photograph by K.M. Mokbul Hossain, March 3, 2015 on behalf of the Author.

5. Tienhaara, Kyla. (2009), "A Tale of Two Crises: What the Global Financial Crisis Means for the Global Environmental Crisis", Global Governance Working Paper No 37. Amsterdam et al.: The Global Governance Project. Available at http://www.glogov.org/images/doc/WP37.pdf

6. Stephen Broadberry et al., "British Economic Growth, 1270–1870," University of Warwick, UK, December 6, 2010, http://www2.warwick.ac.uk/fac/soc/economics/staff/academic/broadberry/wp/british gdplongrun8a.pdf

7. Heinberg, Richard (2011), "The End of Growth: Adapting to our New Economic Reality", New Society Publishers, Canada. pp. 1-25.

8. Martenson, Chris (2011). The Crash Course: "The Unsustainable Future of Our Economy, Energy, and Environment". John Wily & Sons, Inc., Hoboken, New Jersey, pp.125-157.

9. Heinberg, Richard (2015) "Afterburn: Society Beyond Fossil Fuels", New Society Publishers, Canada, page-57-64.

10. Ravallion, M. (2007) Inequality is bad for the poor in S. Jenkins and J. Micklewright, (eds.) Inequality and Poverty Re-examined, Oxford University Press, Oxford.

11. Donella H. Meadows, Jorgen Randers, Dennis L. Meadows. Limits to Growth: The 30-Year Update. White River Junction, Vermont : Chelsea Green, 2004.

12. Schnaiberg, Allan. The Environment: From Surplus to Scarcity. New York: Oxford University Press.

13. "Bangladesh collapse search over; death toll 1,127" by Julhas Alam and Farid Hossain, Yahoo News. http://news.yahoo.com/bangladesh-collapse-search-over-death-toll-1-127-122554495.html, Retrieved on 30 November 2014.

14. "Dhaka Savar Building Collapse", This image, which was originally posted to Flickr.com, was uploaded to Commons using Flickr upload bot on 19:05, 12 May 2013 (UTC) by Rijans007 (talk). On that date it was licensed under the Creative Commons Attribution-Share Alike 2.0 Generic license at Wikipedia. http://commons.wikimedia.org/wiki/File:Dhaka_Savar_Building_Collapse.jpg

15. "How to Put a Stop to Sweatshop Abuse?", by John Miller, Tripple Crisis, http://triplecrisis.com/how-to-put-a-stop-to-sweatshop-abuse/#more-8625

16. Collier, Paul (2008), "The Bottom Billion: Why the Poorest Countries are Failing and What Can Be Done About It", August 22, 2008, http://www.amazon.com/The-Bottom-Billion-Poorest-Countries/dp/0195373383

17. "Poverty in Africa", Wikipedia, http://en.wikipedia.org/wiki/Poverty_in_Africa

18. Quammen, David (2005), "Views of the Continents", National Geographic, Vol.208, No.3, September 2005, pp. 2-35.

19. "Occupy Wall Street", http://occupywallst.org/

20. "Creative destruction: A cost crisis, changing labout markets and new technology will turn an old institution on its head", Higher education, June 28, 2014, The

Economist, http://www.economist.com/news/leaders/21605906-cost-crisis-changing-labour-markets-and-new-technology-will-turn-old-institution-its

21. Slaughter, Anne-Marie, "Occupied Wall Street, Seen From Abroad", Sunday Book Review, The New York Times, October 6, 2011, http://www.nytimes.com/2013/03/10/books/review/sheryl-sandbergs-lean-in.html?pagewanted=all&_r=0

22. "Charts: Here's what the Wall Street protestors are so angry about...", by Henry Blodget, October 11, 2011, http://www.businessinsider.com/what-wall-street-protesters-are-so-angry-about-2011-10?op=1

23. "Who is Occupy Wall Street? After six weeks, a profile finally emerges.". Archived from the original on December 14, 2013. The Christian Science Monitor By Gloria Goodale, November 1, 2011, http://web.archive.org/web/20131214210751/http://www.csmonitor.com/USA/Politics/2011/1101/Who-is-Occupy-Wall-Street-After-six-weeks-a-profile-finally-emerges/(page)/2

24. Giove, Candice (January 8, 2012). "OWS has money to burn". New York Post. Archived from the original on April 18, 2012, http://web.archive.org/web/20120418103631/http://www.nypost.com:80/p/news/local/manhattan/ows_has_money_to_burn_zbjQcSF86gzz8vvVDSNZgM

25. "The Single Largest Benefactor of Occupy Wall Street is a Mitt Romney Donor", by Max Read, October 17, 2011, http://gawker.com/5850730/the-single-largest-benefactor-of-occupy-wall-street-is-a-mitt-romney-donor

26. Kunen, James Simon "The Strawberry Statement: Notes of a College Revolutionary", Wiley-Blackwell, Aug. 3 1995, pp.130

27. "Stagflation", Wikipedia, http://en.wikipedia.org/wiki/Stagflation Retrieved on January 8, 2015.

28. World Bank, Gross Domestic Product for World [MKTGDP1WA646NWDB], retrieved from FRED, Federal Reserve Bank of St. Louis https://research.stlouisfed.org/fred2/series/MKTGDP1WA646NWDB/, April 3, 2015.

29. "A Short History of Financial Deregulation in the United States", by Matthew Sherman, Center for Economic and Policy Research, Washington, July, 2009, http://www.cepr.net/documents/publications/dereg-timeline-2009-07.pdf Retrieved on January 10, 2015.

30. Pluta (2011) Joseph E., "Human Progress Amid Resistance to Change", FriesenPress, Victoria, BC, Canada, April, 2011.pp-149-183.

31. Strange, Susan (1986), "Casino Capitalism", ISBN 0-7190-5235-1, Manchester University Press.

32. "Clear and Present Danger: Clearing-houses may add danger as well as efficiency", The Economist, April 7, 2012, Retrieved on January 1, 2014. http://www.economist.com/node/21552217

33. Heinberg, Richard (2011), "The End of Growth: Adapting to our New Economic Reality", New Society Publishers, Canada.

34. "Buffett warns on investment 'time bomb'", BBC News, March 4, 2003, http://news.bbc.co.uk/2/hi/2817995.stm

35. Friedman, Thomas L. (2009), "The Inflection Is Near?", The New York Times, 7 March, 2009, http://www.nytimes.com/2009/03/08/opinion/08friedman.html?_r=0 Retrieved on August 10, 2014

36. Schick, Gerhard, "Greening Capitalism is not Enough", Tripple Crisis, http://triplecrisis.com/author/gerhard-schick/

37. "US Crude Oil Production 1900 to 2010 matched against a typical Hubbert Curve", Retrieved on from Wikipedia http://commons.wikimedia.org/wiki/File:US_Crude_Oil_Production_versus_Hubbert_Curve.png on 30 November, 2014. Wikipedia produced this graph using data from the US Energy Information Administration". This file is licensed under the Creative Commons (http://en.wikipedia.org/wiki/Creative_Commons) Free to Share Attribution-Share Alike 3.0 Unported license.

38. "Saudi America, The U.S. will be the world's leading energy producer, if we allow it," The Wall Street Journal, November 14, 2012,

http://online.wsj.com/article/SB100014241278873238947045781145911744453074.html

39. Hughes, David (2013), " Drill Baby Drill: Can Unconventional Fuels Usher in a New Era of Energy Abundance?", Post Carbon Institute, http://www.postcarbon.org/reports/DBD-report-FINAL.pdf

40. http://en.wikipedia.org/wiki/Club_of_Rome

41. Donella H. Meadows, Jørgen Randers, Jorgan Randers, Dennis Meadows"The Limits to Growth: The 30-year Update", Taylor & Francis, 2005.

42. http://en.wikipedia.org/wiki/The_Limits_to_Growth

43. Malthus, Thomas "An Essay on the Principle of Population", Oxford University Press, UK, 1993, ISBN0191605948, 9780191605949.

44. Campbell, Colin (2003), "When will the world's oil and gas production peak?", http://www.feasta.org/documents/wells/contents.html?one/campbell.html oroginally published in Before the Wells Run Dry: Ireland's Transition to Renewable Energy, edited by Richard Douthwaite, Green Books, UK.

45. IPCC Synthesis Report (2007), Fourth Assessment Report, Chapter 1 Observed changes in climate and their effects, in IPCC AR4 SYR. http://www.ipcc.ch/publications_and_data/ar4/syr/en/mains1.html

46. "Global Annual Mean Surface Air Temperature Change", http://data.giss.nasa.gov/gistemp/graphs_v3/, National Aeronautics and Space Administration, Goddard Institute for Space Studies. This file is in the public domain because it was solely created by NASA. NASA copyright policy states that "NASA material is not protected by copyright unless noted". (See Template: PD-USGov, NASA copyright policy page or JPL Image Use Policy.)

47. "Sustained warming could lead to severe impacts, p.5, in Synopsis, in National Research Council 2011, http://en.wikipedia.org/wiki/Global_warming

48. "Global Warming: Challenges, Opportunities and a Message of 'Be Prepared'", Green Evolution: Managing the Risks, Reaping the Benefits, March 2010, Initiative for Global Environmental Leadership (IGEL), Whatron, University of Pennsylvania,

http://knowledge.wharton.upenn.edu/papers/download/030310_green_evolution_ss. pdf

49. Smith Richard (2011), "Green capitalism: the god that failed", real-world economics review, issue no. 56, 11 March 2011, pp. 112-144, http://www.paecon.net/PAEReview/issue56/Smith57.pdf

50. "Jim Hansen's arguments for a carbon tax in Storms, p. 215ff. For Al Gore's arguments see his Our Choice (Emanus, PA: Rodale, 2009), pp. 342-45 & p. 210.

51. Quigley, Carroll (1966), "Tragedy and Hope: A History of The World in Our Time", The Macmillan Company, New York, pp.39.

52. Charles A. S. Hall, "Provisional Results from EROI Assessments," The Oil Drum, posted April 8, 2008, http://www.theoildrum.com/node/3810.

53. David Murphy and Charles A. S. Hall, "EROI, Insidious Feedbacks, and the End of Economic Growth," pre-publication, 2010.

54. "China's housing market is on the brink of collapse. Should Australia be worried?", by Greg Jericho, 8 September 2014, http://www.theguardian.com/business/grogonomics/2014/sep/08/why-a-collapse-in-chinas-housing-market-will-hurt-australia Retrieved on 01 December, 2014

55. "China real estate: A bubble bursting?", by Dhara Ranasinghe, 31 Aug 2014, CNBC, http://www.cnbc.com/id/101945949# Retrieved on 01 December, 2014.

56. "Is China's Property Market Heading Toward Collapse?", by Li-Gang Liu, Peterson Institute for international economics, Policy Brief, Number PB14-21, August 2014, http://www.iie.com/publications/pb/pb14-21.pdf Retrieved on 01 December, 2014.

57. "Brent Spot monthly 1987-2013", Retrieved on from Wikipedia http://en.wikipedia.org/wiki/File:Brent_Spot_monthly.svg on 30 November, 2014. Wikipedia produced this graph using data from the US Energy Information Administration". This file is licensed under the Creative Commons (http://en.wikipedia.org/wiki/Creative_Commons) Free to Share Attribution-Share Alike 3.0 Unported license.

58. "Vladimir Putin: oil price decline has been engineered by political forces", by Peter Spence, 06 November 2014, The Telegraph, http://www.telegraph.co.uk/finance/newsbysector/energy/oilandgas/11215063/Vladimir-Putin-oil-price-decline-has-been-engineered-by-political-forces.html

59. "Russia Dumps 20% Of Its Treasury Holdings As Mystery "Belgium" Buyer Adds Another Whopping $40 Billion", by by Tyler Durden, 05 May, 2014, Zero Hedge, http://www.zerohedge.com/news/2014-05-15/russia-dumps-20-its-treasury-holdings-mystery-belgium-buyer-adds-another-whopping-40?page=2

60. "Oil price drop may drive Europe back to Russian gas next year", by Nina Chestney and Oleg Vukmanovic, 28 November 2014, Reuters, http://uk.reuters.com/article/2014/11/28/europe-energy-prices-idUKL6N0TI2YF20141128

61. "Opec: Oil demand to hit 111m barrels by 2040 despite climate change", By Andrew Critchlow, 06 November 2014, The Telegraph, http://www.telegraph.co.uk/finance/newsbysector/energy/oilandgas/11213302/Opec-Oil-demand-to-hit-111m-barrels-by-2040-despite-climate-change.html

62. "World population to reach 9.1 billion in 2050, UN projects". United Nations. 24 February, 2005, http://www.un.org/apps/news/story.asp?NewsID=13451&Cr=population&Cr1, Retrieved on August 23, 2014

63. Asian Development Bank:2007 Benchmarking and Data Book of Water Utilities in India, 2007, p. 3, http://www.adb.org/publications/2007-benchmarking-and-data-book-water-utilities-india

64. By 2050 Warming to Doom Million Species, Study Says", by John Roach, National Geographic News, July 12, 2014, http://news.nationalgeographic.com/news/2004/01/0107_040107_extinction.html Retrieved on 23 August, 2014

65. "How Safe are we from Ebola", by Jonathon Gatehouse, 16 October 2014, Macleans, http://www.macleans.ca/news/world/how-safe-are-we-from-ebola/

66. "20 Deadliest Effects of Global Warming", Simmons, 11 September, 2007, http://scribol.com/science/20-deadliest-effects-of-global-warming Retrieved on 23 August 2014.

67. Heinberg, Richard (2013), "Snake Oil: How Big Energy's Misleading Promise of Plenty Imperils Our Future", Chapter 1.

68. "List of countries by percentage of population living in poverty - Wikipedia", https://www.google.com/fusiontables/DataSource?docid=1thvK57pjXG73-Fb-5z4dUZoRQVuF4QdK_bWI7C4#rows:id=1

69. "The global contribution to world's GDP by major economies from 1 AD to 2003 AD according to Angus Maddison's estimates", Retrieved on from Wikipedia. http://commons.wikimedia.org/wiki/File:1_AD_to_2003_AD_Historical_Trends_in_global_distribution_of_GDP_China_India_Western_Europe_USA_Middle_East.png. M Tracy Hunter from Wikipedia produced this graph using data from Data table in Maddison A (2007), Contours of the World Economy I-2030AD, Oxford University Press, ISBN 978-0199227204" This file is licensed under the Creative Commons Attribution-Share Alike 4.0 International license.

70. Maddison, Angus (2006). The World Economy - Volume 1: A Millennial Perspective and Volume 2: Historical Statistics. OECD Publishing by Organisation for Economic Co-operation and Development. p. 656. ISBN 9789264022621.

71. "The World Economy (GDP): Historical Statistics by Angus Maddison". http://www.theworldeconomy.org/MaddisonTables/MaddisontableB-18.pdf Retrieved on 25 August, 2014.

72. Quigley, Carroll (1966), "Tragedy and Hope: A History of The World in Our Time", The Macmillan Company, New York, pp.176-179.

73. Heinberg, Richard (2011), "The End of Growth: Adapting to our New Economic Reality", New Society Publishers, Canada. pp. 1-25.

74. Heinberg, Richard (2015), "Our Renewable Future", Post Carbon Institute, January 21, 2015, http://www.postcarbon.org/our-renewable-future-essay/ Retrieved on January 31, 2015.

75. Lebow, Victor (1955), "Journal of Retailing", http://www.gcafh.org/edlab/Lebow.pdf Retrieved on July 8, 2015.

76. "Furia Ashe Gas", 7 August, 2015, Daily Ittefaq, http://www.now-bd.com/ittefaq/2015/08/07/67489.htm Retrieved on August 7, 2015

77. "Greece's Debt Crisis Explained", The New York Times, July 8, 2015, http://www.nytimes.com/interactive/2015/business/international/greece-debt-crisis-euro.html?_r=0 Retrieved on July 10, 2015

78. "Greece debt crisis: Finance Minister Varoufakis resigns", July 6, 2015, http://www.bbc.com/news/world-europe-33406001 Retrieved on July 11, 2015.

79. Graph prepared by the author by using data from (http://www.imf.org/external/pubs/ft/weo/2013/01/weodata/index.aspx), Retrieved on from http://en.wikipedia.org/wiki/List_of_countries_by_public_debt, March 07, 2014.

80. Dhara , Sagar (2015) "The challenge is deeper than technology", Technology's role in a climate solution, Bulletin of the Atomic Scientists, 20 November, 2015 http://thebulletin.org/technologys-role-climate-solution Retrieved on December 9, 2015

81. "Club of Rome", Wikipedia, https://en.wikipedia.org/wiki/Club_of_Rome

82. "United Nations Framework Convention on Climate Change", United Nations, FCCC/Informal/84/GE 05-62220 (E) 200705, https://unfccc.int/resource/docs/convkp/conveng.pdf

83. 'Historic' Paris climate deal adopted, CBC News, December 12, 2015, http://www.cbc.ca/m/touch/canada/montreal/story/1.3362354 Retrieved on December 12, 2015

84. Vásquez, Ian (2015) "Ending Mass Poverty", Cato Institute, http://www.cato.org/publications/commentary/ending-mass-poverty Retrieved on December 4, 2015

85. "24.6% rate is based on 2005 PPP at $1.25 per day" The World Bank (2015), https://openknowledge.worldbank.org/bitstream/handle/10986/20384/978146480361 1.pdf

86. "8% GDP growth helped reduce poverty: UN report", Puja Mehra, February 6, 2015, The Hindu, http://m.thehindu.com/news/national/8-gdp-growth-helped-reduce-poverty-un-report/article6862101.ece/

87. "India's economic growth slows to 7%", BBC News, 31 August, 2015, http://www.bbc.com/news/business-34107648 Retrieved on December 4, 2015

88. "List of countries by carbon dioxide emissions", Wikipedia, https://en.wikipedia.org/wiki/List_of_countries_by_carbon_dioxide_emissions Retrieved on December 4, 2015.

89. "The paradox of Paris", Jennie C. StephensElizabeth J. Wilson, Roundtable: Technology's Role in a Climate Solution, Bulletin of the Atomic Scientists, 9 December, 2015, http://thebulletin.org/technologys-role-climate-solution/paradox-paris Retrieved on December 9, 2015

90. "CO2 time series 1990-2014 per capita for world countries". Netherlands Environmental Assessment Agency. http://edgar.jrc.ec.europa.eu/overview.php?v=CO2ts_pc1990-2014 Retrieved on December 4, 2015

91. "World's richest 10% produce half of global carbon emissions, says Oxfam", The Guardian, December 2, 2015, http://www.theguardian.com/environment/2015/dec/02/worlds-richest-10-produce-half-of-global-carbon-emissions-says-oxfam Retrieved on Dec. 5, 2015

92. Burrow, Sharan, "Back to the Future: Our Journey to Zero Carbon, Zero Poverty World", Huff Post, 24, September, 2015, http://www.huffingtonpost.com/sharan-burrow/back-to-the-future---our_b_8187960.html Retrieved on December 5, 2015.

93. "Paris UN Climate Conference 2015: 5 things we learnt on day 3", by Tom Arup & Peter Hannam, December 3, 2015, http://www.smh.com.au/environment/un-climate-conference/paris-un-climate-conference-2015-5-things-we-learnt-on-day-3-20151203-gle039.html?skin=text-only Retrieved on December 5, 2015

94. "World Economic Outlook Database, April 2015". http://www.imf.org/external/pubs/ft/weo/2015/02/weodata/index.aspx Retrieved on December 5, 2015.

95. Graph prepared by the author by using data from " CO2 time series 1990-2014 per capita for world countries". Netherlands Environmental Assessment Agency, http://edgar.jrc.ec.europa.eu/overview.php?v=CO2ts_pc1990-2014 Retrieved on December 7, 2015

96. Graph prepared by the author by using data from "CO2 time series 1990-2014 per region/country". Netherlands Environmental Assessment Agency, http://edgar.jrc.ec.europa.eu/overview.php?v=CO2ts1990-2014&sort=des9 Retrieved on December 7, 2015

97. "It is 3 Minutes to Midnight", Doomsday Clock, Bulletin of the Atomic Scientists, http://thebulletin.org/timeline Retrieved on December 7, 2015

98. "India's Need for Coal-Fueled Growth Complicates Paris Climate Summit", Nikhil Kumar, Time, December 1, 2015, http://time.com/4131236/india-coal-climate-change-paris-summit/ Retrieved on December 8, 2015.

99. "Explained in 90 Seconds: Why 1.5 Degrees Matters", by Time McDonnell, 10 December, 2015, http://www.motherjones.com/environment/2015/12/paris-climate-agreement-could-be-more-ambitious-anyone-expected Retrieved on: December 12, 2015

100. Heinberg, Richard (2014), "Renewable Energy after COP21: Nine issues for climate leaders to think about the journey home", Post Carbon Institute, December 14, 2015, http://www.postcarbon.org/renewable-energy-after-cop21/ Retrieved on December 15, 2015

101. David Braun (October 20, 2010). "Bangladesh, India Most Threatened by Climate Change, Risk Study Finds". National Geographic, http://voices.nationalgeographic.com/2010/10/20/bangladesh_india_at_risk_from_cl imate_change/ Retrieved on: December 14, 2015

102. Heinberg, Richard (2015), "Afterburn: Society Beyond Fossil Fuels", New Society Publishers, Canada, January 2015.

103. Kevin Anderson, "Duality in climate science," Nature Geoscience 8 (2015), pp. 898–900, http://www.nature.com/ngeo/journal/v8/n12/full/ngeo2559.html Retrieved on: December 14, 2015

104. Shah, Jigar (2013), "Creating Climate Wealth: Unlocking the Impact Economy", ICOSA, ISBN-10: 0989353109

105. "Hedge Fund Managers Cash Out of SunEdison: Should You Too?" by Zacks Equity Research, November 18, 2015, http://www.zacks.com/stock/news/198443/hedge-fund-managers-cash-out-of-sunedison-should-you-too#sthash.4QshrfDE.dpuf Retrieved on January 23, 2016

106. "SunEdison Inc. (SUNE) Interactive Stock Chart", http://www.nasdaq.com/symbol/sune/interactive-chart Retrieved on February 12, 2016.

107. Kennedy, John F. (1963), "A Strategy of Peace", Commencement Address at American University, June 10, 1963, John F. Kennedy Presidential Library and Museum, http://www.jfklibrary.org/Asset-Viewer/BWC7I4C9QUmLG9J6I8oy8w.aspx Retrieved on February 10, 2016.

108. "Rigging The Oil Market: 'Perhaps 60% of Today's Oil Price is Pure Speculation'" by By F. William Engdahl, Global Research, May 2, 2008, http://www.globalresearch.ca/perhaps-60-of-today-s-oil-price-is-pure-speculation/8878 Retrieved on February 10, 2016

109. "New Balance of Power" by Clifford Krauss, , New York Times, April 22, 2015, http://www.nytimes.com/2015/04/23/business/energy-environment/new-balance-of-power.html Retrieved on February 10, 2016

110. US. Energy Information Administration, Crude Oil Prices: Brent - Europe [DCOILBRENTEU], retrieved from FRED, Federal Reserve Bank of St. Louis https://research.stlouisfed.org/fred2/series/DCOILBRENTEU, February 11, 2016.

111. "Oil Prices: What's Behind the Drop? Simple Economics" by Clifford Krauss, , New York Times, February 9, 2016, http://www.nytimes.com/interactive/2016/business/energy-environment/oil-prices.html?_r=0 Retrieved on February 10, 2016

112. "Deferred upstream projects tally reaches 68", WoodMackenzie, 14 January, 2016, http://www.woodmac.com/media-centre/12530462 Retrieved on February 10, 2016

113. "Shale Drillers' Safety Net Is Vanishing", by Asjylyn Loder and Bradley Olson, Bloomberg Business, July 1, 2015, http://www.bloomberg.com/news/articles/2015-07-01/shale-driller-losing-their-insurance-against-price-drops Retrieved on February 10, 2016

114. "Changing contract expiration dates will affect crude oil futures comparisons", U.S. Energy Information Administration (EIA), January 26, 2016, http://www.eia.gov/todayinenergy/detail.cfm?id=24692 Retrieved on February 10, 2016

115. "The clean energy giant has seen its stock plunge and faced a string of lawsuits over the past year" by Katie Fehrenbacher, Fortune, February 11, 2016, http://fortune.com/2016/02/11/sunedison-latin-america-power/ Retrieved on February 11, 2016.

116. "U.S. Shale-Oil Boom May Not Last as Fracking Wells Lack Staying Power" by Asjylyn Loder, BloombergBusiness, October 10, 2013, http://www.bloomberg.com/news/articles/2013-10-10/u-dot-s-dot-shale-oil-boom-may-not-last-as-fracking-wells-lack-staying-power Retrieved on March 16, 2016.

117. "5 Reasons Community-Scale Solar is a Multi GW Market Opportunity" by Kevin Brehm and Joseph Goodman, Rocky Mountain Institute, March 17th, 2016, http://cleantechnica.com/2016/03/17/5-reasons-why-community-scale-solar-is-a-multi-gw-market-opportunity/ Retrieved on March 20, 2016.

118. Krugman, Paul (1999), "Money Can't Buy Happiness. Er, Can It?", The New York Times, June 1, 1999 http://www.nytimes.com/1999/06/01/opinion/money-can-t-buy-happiness-er-can-it.html Retrieved on May 31, 2014.

Chapter 2: A Brief History of Capitalist Synthesis

1. Quigley, Carroll (1966), "Tragedy and Hope: A History of The World in Our Time", The Macmillan Company, New York, pp.3

2. "History of Economic Thought", Wikipedia, http://en.wikipedia.org/wiki/History_of_economic_thought

3. "Usury", Wikipedia, http://en.wikipedia.org/wiki/Usury

4. Balbir S. Sihag (2007), "Kautilya on Administration of Justice During the Fourth Century B.C.", Journal of the History of Economic Thought, Vol.29, No.3 (September 2007), pp.359-377.

5. Pluta (2011) Joseph E., "Human Progress Amid Resistance to Change", FriesenPress, Victoria, BC, Canada, April, 2011.pp-53, 62, 73

6. "Really Old School" Garten, Jeffrey E. New York Times, 9 December 2006.

7. Foltz, Richard C. (1999). Religions of the Silk Road: Overland Trade and Cultural Exchange from Antiquity to the Fifteenth Century. New York: St Martin's Press. p. 38.

8. "Economic History of China before 1912", Wikipedia, http://en.wikipedia.org/wiki/Economic_history_of_China_before_1912

9. Bentley, Jerry H. (1993), "Old World Encounters: Cross-Cultural Contacts and Exchanges in Pre-Modern Times" , Oxford University Press, NY, pp. 43-44

10. "Silk Road", Wikipedia, http://en.wikipedia.org/wiki/Silk_Road

11. Parker,W N. Europe, America and the Wider World: Essays on the Economic History of Western Capitalism. Cambridge University Press, 26 Apr 1991. ISBN ISBN 0521274796. Retrieved on 2012-06-08.

12. Zgur, Andrej (2007), "The economy of the Roman Empire in the first two centuries A.D., An examination of market capitalism in the Roman economy", Aarhus School of Business, December 2007, pp. 252–261.

13. Slavery," The Encyclopedia Americana, 1981, page 19

14. Arnold J. Toynbee (1947). A Study of History: Abridgement of Volumes I to VI. Oxford University Press. p. 273.

15. "Decline of Roman Empire", Wikipedia, http://en.wikipedia.org/wiki/Decline_of_the_Roman_Empire

16. Young, Frances: Christian Attitudes to Finance in the First Four Centuries, Epworth Review 4.3, Peterborough, September 1977, pp. 81–82.

17. "History of Europe", Wikipedia, http://en.wikipedia.org/wiki/History_of_Europe

18. "Physiocracy", Wikipedia, http://en.wikipedia.org/wiki/Physiocracy

19. "History of Europe", 2008/9 Schools Wikipedia Section, McGill University, http://www.cs.mcgill.ca/~rwest/link-suggestion/wpcd_2008-09_augmented/wp/h/History_of_Europe.htm

20. "History of Slavery", Wikipedia, http://en.wikipedia.org/wiki/History_of_slavery

21. Junius P Rodriguez, Ph.D. (1997). The Historical Encyclopedia of World Slavery. vol 1. A – K. ABC-CLIO. p. 674.

22. "History of Economic Thought", Wikipedia, http://en.wikipedia.org/wiki/History_of_economic_thought

23. Pluta (2011) Joseph E., "Human Progress Amid Resistance to Change", FriesenPress, Victoria, BC, Canada, April, 2011.pp-100-101.

24. "History of Capitalism", Wikipedia, http://en.wikipedia.org/wiki/History_of_capitalism

25. Brenner, Robert, 1977, "The Origins of Capitalist Development: a Critique of Neo-Smithian Marxism," in New Left Review 104: 36-37, 46.

26. Nicolle, Davis (1994). Yarmuk AD 636. Osprey Publishing. ISBN 1-85532-414-8. pp.45.

27. Esposito, John (1998). Islam: The Straight Path. Oxford University Press. ISBN 0-19-511233-4.

28. Hourani, Albert, A History of the Arab Peoples, Faber and Faber, 1991. P.23.

29. Dubnow, Simon (1968). History of the Jews: From the Roman Empire to the Early Medieval Period 2. Cornwall Books. p. 326. ISBN 9780845366592.

30. "Umar ibn Khattab", Wikipedia, http://en.wikipedia.org/wiki/Umar_ibn_Khattab

31. The Cambridge economic history of Europe, p. 437. Cambridge University Press, ISBN 0-521-08709-0.

32. Blankinship, Khalid Yahya (1994), The End of the Jihad State, the Reign of Hisham Ibn 'Abd-al Malik and the collapse of the Umayyads, State University of New York Press, p. 37, ISBN 0-7914-1827-8.

33. Robert Sabatino Lopez, Irving Woodworth Raymond, Olivia Remie Constable (2001), Medieval Trade in the Mediterranean World: Illustrative Documents, Columbia University Press, ISBN 0-231-12357-4.

34. Timur Kuran (2005), "The Absence of the Corporation in Islamic Law: Origins and Persistence", American Journal of Comparative Law 53, p.785-834.

35. Subhi Y. Labib (1969), "Capitalism in Medieval Islam", The Journal of Economic History 29 (1), p. 79-96.

36. "Islamic Economics in the World", Wikipedia, http://en.wikipedia.org/wiki/Islamic_economics_in_the_world

37. Jairus Banaji (2007), "Islam, the Mediterranean and the rise of capitalism", Historical Materialism 15 (1), p. 47-74, Brill Publishers.

38. Richard W. Bulliet (2010). The Earth and Its Peoples: A Global History. Cengage Learning. p. 226.

39. Davis, Robert (2004), "Christian Slaves, Muslim Masters: White Slavery in the Mediterranean, the Barbary Coast and Italy", 1500–1800. p.45. ISBN 1-4039-4551-9.

40. Europe: A History, p 257. Oxford: Oxford University Press 1996. ISBN 0-19-820171-0.

41. "Khazars", Wikipedia, http://en.wikipedia.org/wiki/Khazars

42. Noonan, Thomas S. (2007). "The Economy of the Khazar Khaganate". In Golden, Peter B.; Ben-Shammai,, Haggai; Róna-Tas, András. The World of the Khazars:New Perspectives. Handbuch der Orientalistik: Handbook of Uralic studies 17. BRILL. pp. 207–244. ISBN 978-9-004-16042-2. pp.493

43. "Umayyad Caliphate", Wikipedia, http://en.wikipedia.org/wiki/Umayyad_Caliphate

44. "Abbasid Dynasty", The New Encyclopædia Britannica (2005).

45. Vartan Gregorian, "Islam: A Mosaic, Not a Monolith", Brookings Institution Press, 2003, pg 26–38 ISBN 0-8157-3283-X.

46. "Islamic Golden Age", Wikipedia, http://en.wikipedia.org/wiki/Islamic_Golden_Age

47. Mark Edward Lewis (2009). China's Cosmopolitan Empire: The Tang Dynasty. Harvard University Press. ISBN 978-0-674-05419-6, p. 158.

48. Bloom, Jonathan (2001). Paper Before Print: The History and Impact of Paper in the Islamic World. New Haven: Yale University Press. ISBN 0-300-08955-4.

49. Ji, Jianghong; et al (2005), Encyclopedia of China History (in Chinese) 3, Beijing publishing house, ISBN 7900321543.

50. "Economic history of China before 1912", Wikipedia, http://en.wikipedia.org/wiki/Economic_history_of_China_before_1912

51. "Abbasid Caliphate", Wikipedia, http://en.wikipedia.org/wiki/Abbasid_Caliphate

52. Rubenstein, R. E. (2003). Aristotle's children: how Christians, Muslims, and Jews rediscovered ancient wisdom and illuminated the dark ages (1st ed.). Orlando, Fla: Harcourt, pp. 16-17.

53. "Al-Andalus", Wikipedia, http://en.wikipedia.org/wiki/Al-Andalus

54. "Lombardy", Wikipedia, http://en.wikipedia.org/wiki/Lombardy

55. "Emergence of Merchant Banks", World Heritage Encyclopedia, http://worldheritage.org/articles/History_of_banking Retrieved on: Jan 28, 2014

56. "Crusades", Wikipedia, http://en.wikipedia.org/wiki/Crusades

57. Tyerman, Christopher (2006), "God's War: A New History of the Crusades", Cambridge, MA: Belknap Press. ISBN 978-0-674-02387-1. pp. 156–158.

58. "History of Banking", Wikipedia, http://en.wikipedia.org/wiki/History_of_banking

59. Martin, Sean (2005), "The Knights Templar: The History & Myths of the Legendary Military Order", ISBN 1-56025-645-1.

60. "Saladin", Wikipedia, http://en.wikipedia.org/wiki/Saladin

61. Asbridge, Thomas (2011). The Crusades: The Authoritative History of the War for the Holy Land. Ecco. ISBN 978-0-06-078729-5.

62. Norman, Housley (2006). Contesting the Crusades. Malden, MA: Blackwell Publishing. ISBN 1-4051-1189-5, pp. 152–154.

63. Strayer, Joseph R. (1969). "The Crusades of Louis IX" (http://digicoll.library.wisc.edu/cgi-bin/History/History-idx?type=article&did=HISTORY.CRUSTWO.I0023&isize=M). In Wolff, R. L. and Hazard, H. W. The Later Crusades, 1189–1311. pp. 487–521.

64. "Anti-Semitism", The New World Encyclopedia, http://www.newworldencyclopedia.org/entry/Anti-Semitism

65. "Usury", Wikipedia, http://en.wikipedia.org/wiki/Usury

66. "Lombard Banking", Wikipedia, http://en.wikipedia.org/wiki/Lombard_banking

67. "Genghis Khan", Wikipedia, http://en.wikipedia.org/wiki/Genghis_Khan

68. "Khwarazmian Dynasty", Wikipedia, http://en.wikipedia.org/wiki/Khwarezmid_Empire#Khwarezmian_Dynasty

69. Mongol Empire, New World Encyclopedia, http://www.newworldencyclopedia.org/entry/Mongol_Empire

70. The Cambridge History of China: Alien regimes and border states, 907–1368, 1994, p.622, cited by White.

71. "Mongol Empire", Wikipedia, http://en.wikipedia.org/wiki/Mongol_Empire

72. Ji, Jianghong; et al (2005), Encyclopedia of China History (in Chinese) 2, Beijing publishing house, ISBN 7900321543, p. 72.

73. Hsiao, Ch'i-Ch'ing (1994), "Mid-Yuan politics", in Franke, Herbert and Twitchett, Denis (eds.), Alien Regimes and Border States, 710–1368, The Cambridge History of China 6, Cambridge: Cambridge University Press, pp. 492, ISBN 9780521243315.

74. Dreyer, Edward H. (1988), "Military origins of Ming China", in Twitchett, Denis and Mote, Frederick W. (eds.), The Ming Dynasty, part 1, The Cambridge History of China 7, Cambridge: Cambridge University Press, pp. 58–107, ISBN 9780521243322.

75. Li, Bo; Zheng, Yin (2001), 5000 years of Chinese history (in Chinese), Inner Mongolian People's publishing corp, ISBN 7-204-04420-7. p. 950.

76. Maddison, Angus (2007): "Contours of the World Economy, 1–2030 AD. Essays in Macro-Economic History", Oxford University Press, ISBN 978-0-19-922721-1, p. 382, table A.7.

77. "Marco Polo", Wikipedia, http://en.wikipedia.org/wiki/Marco_Polo

78. Landström, Björn (1967), Columbus: the story of Don Cristóbal Colón, Admiral of the Ocean, New York City: Macmillan, p. 27.

79. "Franco-Mongol Alliance", Wikipedia, http://en.wikipedia.org/wiki/Franco-Mongol_alliance

80. "Silk Road", Wikipedia, http://en.wikipedia.org/wiki/Silk_Road

81. Robert L. Canfield, Robert L. (1991). Turko-Persia in historical perspective, Cambridge University Press, p.20. "The Mughals-Persianized Turks who invaded from Central Asia and claimed descent from both Timur and Genghis – strengthened the Persianate culture of Muslim India".

82. "Crisis of the Late Middle Ages", Wikipedia, http://en.wikipedia.org/wiki/Crisis_of_the_Late_Middle_Ages

83. J. M. Bennett and C. W. Hollister, Medieval Europe: A Short History (New York: McGraw-Hill, 2006), p. 326.

84. "Black Death", Wikipedia, http://en.wikipedia.org/wiki/Black_Death

85. Austin Alchon, Suzanne (2003). A pest in the land: new world epidemics in a global perspective. University of New Mexico Press. p. 21. ISBN 0-8263-2871-7.

86. Daileader, Philip, "The Late Middle Ages", audio/video course produced by The Teaching Company, (2007) ISBN 978-1-59803-345-8.

87. "Hundred Years' War", Wikipedia, http://en.wikipedia.org/wiki/Hundred_Years%27_War

88. Neillands, Robin (1990). The Hundred Years War, Revised ed. London: Routledge. ISBN 0-415-26131-7, p. 110-111.

89. "Joan of Arc", Wikipedia, http://en.wikipedia.org/wiki/Joan_of_Arc

90. Holmes, Jr, Urban T; Schutz, Alexander H (1948). A History of the French Language, Revised ed. Columbus, OH: Harold L. Hedrick., p. 61.

91. Stone, Norman (2005). "Turkey in the Russian Mirror". In Mark Erickson, Ljubica Erickson. Russia War, Peace And Diplomacy: Essays in Honour of John Erickson. Weidenfeld & Nicolson. p. 94. ISBN 978-0-297-84913-1. Retrieved on 11 February 2013.

92. Parker,W N. Europe, America and the Wider World: Essays on the Economic History of Western Capitalism. Cambridge University Press, 26 Apr 1991. ISBN ISBN 0521274796. Retrieved on 2012-06-08.

93. İnalcik, Halil (1997). An economic and social history of the Ottoman Empire. Cambridge University Press. p. 213.

94. "Ottoman Empire", Wikipedia, http://en.wikipedia.org/wiki/Ottoman_Empire

95. "Jan Hus", Wikipedia, http://en.wikipedia.org/wiki/Jan_Hus

96. "Renaissance" Wikipedia, http://en.wikipedia.org/wiki/Renaissance

97. "Leonardo da Vinci", Wikipedia, http://en.wikipedia.org/wiki/Leonardo_da_Vinci

98. Eisenstein, Elizabeth L. (1980), The Printing Press as an Agent of Change, Cambridge University Press, ISBN 0-521-29955-1

99. "Martin Luther", Wikipedia, http://en.wikipedia.org/wiki/Martin_Luther

100. Andrew Cunningham, The Four Horsemen of the Apocalypse: Religion, War, Famine and Death in Reformation Europe, Cambridge: Cambridge University Press, 2000, ISBN 0-521-46701-2, 141; Mullett, 239–40; Marty, 164.

101. "Thirty Year's War", Wikipedia, http://en.wikipedia.org/wiki/Thirty_Years'_War

102. "History of Germany", Wikipedia, http://en.wikipedia.org/wiki/History_of_Germany

103. Herbert, Klein (1999), "The Atlantic Slave Trade", Cambridge University Press, 0521465885, 9780521465885

104. "Dutch East India Company", Wikipedia, http://en.wikipedia.org/wiki/Dutch_East_India_Company

105. "Spanish Armada", Wikipedia, http://en.wikipedia.org/wiki/Spanish_Armada

106. Milan N. Vego (2003). Naval Strategy and Operations in Narrow Seas. Frank Cass. p. 148.

107. "East India Company", Wikipedia, http://en.wikipedia.org/wiki/East_India_Company

108. Heinberg, Richard (2015), "Afterburn: Society Beyond Fossil Fuels", New Society Publishers, Canada, January 2015, page-115.

109. "Economic History of Japan", Wikipedia, http://en.wikipedia.org/wiki/Economic_history_of_Japan

110. "Jacques Specx", Wikipédia, http://en.wikipedia.org/wiki/Jacques_Specx

111. "Fur Trade", Wikipedia, http://en.wikipedia.org/wiki/Fur_trade

112. "North American Fur Trade", Wikipedia, http://en.wikipedia.org/wiki/North_American_fur_trade

113. "New England", Wikipedia, http://en.wikipedia.org/wiki/New_England

114. "Bank of England", Wikipedia, http://en.wikipedia.org/wiki/Bank_of_England

115. Bagehot, Walter (1873). Lombard Street : a description of the money market. London: Henry S. King and Co.

116. Burnham, Peter (2003). Capitalism: The Concise Oxford Dictionary of Politics. Oxford University Press.

117. Painting. Court. Jahangir investing a courtier with a robe of honour watched by Sir Thomas Roe, English ambassador to the court of Jahangir at Agra from 1615-18, and others. Calligrapher: As`af `Ibadallah al-Rahim and date 23 Ramadan 985/4 December 1577. Source: http://www.britishmuseum.org/research/search_the_collection_database/search_object_details.aspx?objectid=231669&partid=1&searchText=mughal&fromADBC=ad&toADBC=ad&numpages=10&images=on&orig=%2fresearch%2fsearch_the_collection_database.aspx&currentPage=43 This work is in the public domain in its country of origin and other countries and areas where the copyright term is the author's life plus 100 years or less, Retrieved on 10 June, 2015.

118. "Indian History Sourcebook: England, India, and The East Indies, 1617 A.D", Fordham University, http://legacy.fordham.edu/halsall/india/1617englandindies.asp

119. James Harvey Robinson, ed., Readings in European History, 2 Vols. (Boston: Ginn and Co., 1904-1906), Vol. II: From the opening of the Protestant Revolt to the Present Day, pp. 333-335.

120. Rommelse, "Prizes and Profits: Dutch Maritime Trade during the Second Anglo-Dutch War," International Journal of Maritime History (2007) pp 139-159.

121. "East India Company" (1911). Encyclopedia Britannica Eleventh Edition, Volume 8, p.835.

122. Burgess, Douglas R. (2009). "The Pirates' Pact: The Secret Alliances Between History's Most Notorious Buccaneers and Colonial America". New York, NY: McGraw-Hill. ISBN 978-0-07-147476-4.

123. Hunter, Sir William Wilson (2005) [1886 (London:)]. The Indian Empire: Its People, History, and Products (Reprinted ed.). New Delhi: Asian Educational Services. p. 311. ISBN 9788120615816.

124. A Guide Book.Calcutta, Agra, Delhi, Karachi and Bomabay. The American Redcross of the China-Burma-India Command.

125. Newton took the post of warden of the Royal Mint in 1696, a position that he had obtained through the patronage of Charles Montagu, 1st Earl of Halifax, then Chancellor of the Exchequer and founder of Bank of England. Later Newton became perhaps the best-known Master of the Mint upon the death of Thomas Neale in 1699, a position Newton held for the last 30 years of his life. the famous physicist and mathematician. http://en.wikipedia.org/wiki/Sir_Isaac_Newton Retrieved on 5 December, 2014.

126. Mays, Andrew and Shea, Gary S.(2011),"East India Company and Bank of England Shareholders during the South Sea Bubble: Partitions, Components and Connectivity in a Dynamic Trading Network", School of Economics and Finance, University of St. Andrews, http://www.st-andrews.ac.uk/economics/CDMA/papers/wp1109.pdf Retrieved on 5 December, 2014

127. "South Sea Company", Wikipedia, http://en.wikipedia.org/wiki/South_Sea_Company Retrieved on 5 December, 2014

128. "Economic History of France", Wikipedia, http://en.wikipedia.org/wiki/Economic_history_of_France Retrieved on 5 December, 2014

129. DeJean, Joan (2005). "The Essence of Style: How the French Invented Fashion, Fine Food, Chic Cafés, Style, Sophistication, and Glamour", Free Press, New York.

130. "Seven Years' War", Wikipedia, http://en.wikipedia.org/wiki/Seven_Years%27_War Retrieved on 5 December, 2014

131. Harrington, Peter (1994). "Plassey 1757, Clive of India's Finest Hour", Osprey Publishing, London, ISBN 1-85532-352-4. pp.9.

132. "Battle of Plassey", Wikipedia, http://en.wikipedia.org/wiki/Battle_of_Plassey Retrieved on 5 December, 2014.

133. "Robert Clive and Mir Jafar after the Battle of Plassey, 1757", Author: Francis Hayman oil on canvas, circa 1760, http://www.npg.org.uk/collections/search/portrait/mw01347/Robert-Clive-and-Mir-Jafar-after-the-Battle-of-Plassey-1757 This work is in the public domain in the United States, in the European Union and non-EU countries because its copyright has expired, Retrieved on 10 June, 2015.

134. Sengupta, Shombit (2010), "Bengal's plunder gifted the British Industrial Revolution",The Financial Express,Feb 07 2010, http://www.financialexpress.com/news/bengal-s-plunder-gifted-the-british-industrial-revolution/576476 Retrieved on: 5 December, 2014

135. "Indian Rebellion of 1857", Wikipedia, http://en.wikipedia.org/wiki/Indian_Rebellion_of_1857 Retrieved on: 5 December, 2014

136. Dutt, Romesh Chunder (1908). The economic history of India under early British rule. Kegan Paul, Trench, Trübner & Co.

137. "Bengal Famine of 1770", Wikipedia, http://en.wikipedia.org/wiki/Bengal_famine_of_1770 Retrieved on: 5 December, 2014

138. Gray, Jack (2002). "Rebellions and Revolutions: China from the 1800s to 2000", New York: Oxford University Press. pp. 22–23. ISBN 978-0-19-870069-2.

139. Chaudhury, Sushil (1999). From Prosperity to Decline: Eighteenth Century Bengal. Manohar Publishers and Distributors.

140. Ebrey, Patricia Buckley, ed. (2010). "9. Manchus and Imperialism: The Qing Dynasty 1644–1900". The Cambridge Illustrated History of China (second ed.). Cambridge University Press. p. 236. ISBN 978-0-521-19620-8.

141. Hanes III, W. Travis; Sanello, Frank (2002). The Opium Wars. Naperville, Illinois: Sourcebooks, Inc. p. 20.

142. Chisholm, Hugh (1911). The Encyclopædia Britannica: A Dictionary of Arts, Sciences, Literature and General Information. p. 130.

143. Salucci, Lapo (2007). Depths of Debt: Debt, Trade and Choices. University of Colorado.

144. Bertelsen, Cynthia (2008). "A novel of the British opium trade in China." 19 October , 2008, Roanoke Times & World News.

145. "Economic History of United Kingdom", Wikipedia, http://en.wikipedia.org/wiki/Economic_history_of_the_United_Kingdom Retrieved on: 5 December, 2014

146. Foster, Charles (2004). Capital and Innovation: How Britain Became the First Industrial Nation. Northwich: Arley Hall Press.

147. "Industrial Revolution", Wikipedia, http://en.wikipedia.org/wiki/Industrial_Revolution Retrieved on: 5 December, 2014.

148. Gerald M. Meier, James E. Rauch (2000), "Business and Economics. Leading Issues in Economic Development", Oxford University Press.

149. Kiely, Ray (Nov 2011). "Industrialization and Development: A Comparative Analysis". UGL Press Limited: 25-26.

150. Robb, Peter (2004), A History of India (Palgrave Essential Histories), Houndmills, Hampshire: Palgrave Macmillan. pp. 131–134.

151. "Muslin", Wikipedia, http://en.wikipedia.org/wiki/Muslin

152. Peers, Douglas M. (2006), India under Colonial Rule 1700–1885, Harlow and London: Pearson Longmans. pp. 48–49, ISBN 058231738.

153. Farnie, D. A. (1979), The English Cotton Industry and the World Market, 1815-1896, Oxford, UK: Oxford University Press. Pp. 33, ISBN 0-19-822478-8.

154. "Economic History of India", Wikipedia, http://en.wikipedia.org/wiki/Economic_history_of_India

155. "GDP of United Kingdom and India during the Colonial Era", 1700 AD through 1950 AD per capita GDP of United Kingdom and India during the Colonial Era .All GDP numbers are inflation adjusted to 1990 International Geary-Khamis dollars. Data Source: Tables of Prof. Angus Maddison (2010), http://www.ggdc.net/maddison/oriindex.htm, Date 19 July 2014, Author: M Tracy Hunter at Wikimedia. This file is licensed under the Creative Commons Attribution-Share Alike 4.0 International license, http://commons.wikimedia.org/wiki/File:1700_AD_through_1950_AD_per_capita_GDP_of_United_Kingdom_and_India_during_the_Colonial_Era.png

156. Mabel C. Buer (1926), Health, Wealth and Population in the Early Days of the Industrial Revolution, London: George Routledge & Sons, 1926, page 30 ISBN 0-415-38218-1

157. Galbi, Douglas A. Child Labor and the Division of Labor in the Early English Cotton Mills. Journal of Population Economics, Vol. 10, No. 4.

158. Venning, Annabel (2010). "Britain's child slaves: They started at 4am, lived off acorns and had nails put through their ears for shoddy work. Yet, says a new book, their misery helped forge Britain". dailymail.co.uk (London), 17 September 2010, http://www.dailymail.co.uk/news/article-1312764/Britains-child-slaves-New-book-says-misery-helped-forge-Britain.html

159. "A young "drawer" pulling a coal tub along a mine gallery. Image is a copy of one from an official report of a parliamentary commission done in the mid-18th century, In Britain laws passed in 1842 and 1844 that improved working conditions in mines. http://en.wikipedia.org/wiki/File:Coaltub.png 21 February 2007 This artistic work created by the United Kingdom Government is in the public domain, This image (or other media file) is in the public domain in United States because its copyright has expired.

160. Laura Del Col (1988), The Life of the Industrial Worker in Nineteenth-Century England, West Virginia University.

161. Broadberry, Stephen & Bishnupriya Gupta (2005). Cotton Textiles and the Great Divergence: Lancashire, India and Shifting Competitive Advantage, 1600-1850. The Rise, Organization, and Institutional Framework of Factor Markets, 23-25 June 2005.

162. Wayne Smith, Joe Tom Cothren , "Cotton: Origin, History, Technology, and Production" Page viii. Published 1999. John Wiley and Sons. Technology & Industrial Arts. 864 pages. ISBN 0-471-18045-9.

163. Ray, Indrajit (2009), Identifying the woes of the cotton textile industry in Bengal: Tales of the nineteenth century, Economic History Review, Nov 5896, Vol. 62 Issue 4, pp 857-892.

164. "Life in Great Britain during the Industrial Revolution" Wikipedia, http://en.wikipedia.org/wiki/Life_in_Great_Britain_during_the_Industrial_Revolutio n

165. Ray, Rajat Kanta (1998), Indian Society and the Establishment of British Supremacy, 1765-1818, The Oxford History of the British Empire: vol. 2, The Eighteenth Century" ed. by P. J. Marshall, (1998), pp 508-529.

166. Madison, Angus (2006). The world economy, Volumes 1–2. OECD Publishing. p. 638. doi:10.1787/456125276116. ISBN 92-64-02261-9.

167. "The Age of Enlightenment" Wikipedia, http://en.wikipedia.org/wiki/The_Age_of_Enlightenment

168. Morgan, Edmund S. and Morgan, Helen M. (1963), The Stamp Act Crisis: Prologue to Revolution.

169. Thies, Clifford F.,"Wanton Inflation", The Mises Institute monthly, , http://mises.org/freemarket_detail.aspx?control=336

170. Greene, Jack P. and Richard M. Jellison. "The Currency Act of 1764 in Imperial-Colonial Relations, 1764–1776". The William and Mary Quarterly, Third Series, Vol. 18, No. 4 (October 1961), 485–518.

171. Labaree, Benjamin Woods. The Boston Tea Party. Originally published 1964. Boston: Northeastern University Press, 1979. ISBN 0-930350-05-7.

172. "Boston Tea Party", http://www.general-books.net/sw2.cfm?q=Boston_Tea_Party

173. "The Destruction of Tea at Boston Harbor", lithograph depicting the 1773 Boston Tea Party Some colonist disguised themselves as Native Americans., Author: Nathaniel Currier, http://www.loc.gov/pictures/item/91795889/ Repository: Library of Congress Prints and Photographs Division Washington, D.C. 20540 USA . Rights Advisory confirms "No known restrictions on publication", Retrieved on June 10, 2015.

174. "Boston Tea Party", Wikipedia, http://en.wikipedia.org/wiki/Boston_Tea_Party

175. Brinkley, Douglas (2010). The Sparck of Rebellion. American Heritage Magazine 59 (4).

176. Greene and Pole (2004), "A Companion to the American Revolution", chapters 42, 48.

177. Tombs, Robert and Isabelle (2007). "That Sweet Enemy: The French and the British from the Sun King to the Present", Random House.

178. Jensen, Merrill (2004), "The Founding of a Nation: A History of the American Revolution 1763–1776." Hackett Publishing.

179. Labaree, Benjamin Woods. The Boston Tea Party. Originally published 1964. Boston: Northeastern University Press, 1979. ISBN 0-930350-05-7.

180. Cooke, Jacob Earnest. Alexander Hamilton. Charles Scribner's Sons, 1982. ISBN 0-684-17344-1.pp.89, pp.100.

181. "Alexander   Hamilton",   Wikipedia, http://en.wikipedia.org/wiki/Alexander_Hamilton

182. "You should hope that this game will be over soon." The Third Estate carrying the Clergy and the Nobility on its back, Source, http://www.loc.gov/pictures/item/2004676889/, Author M. P., Repository: Library of Congress Prints and Photographs Division Washington, D.C. 20540 USA. Rights Advisory confirms "No known restrictions on publication", Retrieved on June 10, 2015.

183. "French Revolution" Wikipedia, http://en.wikipedia.org/wiki/French_Revolution

184. "Rothschild Family", Wikipedia, http://en.wikipedia.org/wiki/Rothschild_family

185. "Napoleonic Wars", Wikipedia, http://en.wikipedia.org/wiki/Napoleonic_Wars

186. "The History of Money Part 1", XAT3, http://www.xat.org/xat/moneyhistory.html

187. Quigley, Carroll (1966). Tragedy And Hope. New York: Macmillan. p. 515. ISBN 0-945001-10-X.

188. "Louisiana Purchase" Wikipedia, http://en.wikipedia.org/wiki/Louisiana_Purchase

189. Gray, Victor; Aspey, Melanie (May 2006) [2004]. "Rothschild, Nathan Mayer (1777–1836)". Oxford Dictionary of National Biography (Online ed.). Oxford University Press.

190. "Nathan   Mayer   Rothschild",   Wikipedia, http://en.wikipedia.org/wiki/Nathan_Mayer_Rothschild

191. "Arthur   Wellesley,   1st   Duke   of   Wellington",   Wikipedia, http://en.wikipedia.org/wiki/Arthur_Wellesley,_1st_Duke_of_Wellington

192. "United   Kingdom   National   Debt",   Wikipedia, http://en.wikipedia.org/wiki/United_Kingdom_national_debt

193. "Rothschild", 1906 Jewish Encyclopedia, http://www.jewishencyclopedia.com/articles/12909-rothschild

194. Rommelse (2007), "Prizes and Profits: Dutch Maritime Trade during the Second Anglo-Dutch War," International Journal of Maritime History pp 159.

195. Todd Estes, "Shaping the Politics of Public Opinion: Federalists and the Jay Treaty Debate." Journal of the Early Republic (2000) 20(3): 393–422. in JSTOR.

196. White, Richard (2010). The Middle Ground: Indians, Empires, and Republics in the Great Lakes Region, 1650-1815. Cambridge U.P. p. 416. ISBN 9781107005624.

197. "War of 1812", Wikipedia, http://en.wikipedia.org/wiki/War_of_1812

198. Dangerfield, George. 1965. The Awakening of American Nationalism: 1815-1828. Harper & Row. New York, p12-13, p. 32-33, p. 73-74, p. 90-91, p. 88-89.

199. Wilentz, Sean. 2008. The Rise of American Democracy: Jefferson to Lincoln. W.W. Horton and Company. New York. p. 206.

200. "Second Bank of the United States", Wikipedia, http://en.wikipedia.org/wiki/Second_Bank_of_the_United_States

201. "President Jackson's Veto Message Regarding the Bank of the United States",Lillian Goldman Law Library, Yale Law School, July 10, 1832, http://avalon.law.yale.edu/19th_century/ajveto01.asp

202. Wilentz, Sean. 2005. Andrew Jackson (American Presidents Series). Times Books, New York, p. 396-397, p. 399-400, p. 401.

203. "General Jackson Slaying the Many Headed Monster", Source: Brown University Library Center for Digital Initiatives, Print, Drawings & Watercolors from the Anne S. K. Brown Military Collection,ID 119817787962500., Author: N.Y. : Printed & publd. by H.R. Robinson, 1836 http://en.wikipedia.org/wiki/File:General_Jackson_Slaying_the_Many_Headed_Mo nster.jpg This work is in the public domain in the United States because it was published before January 1, 1923.

204. Schlesinger, Arthur M. 1945. The Age of Jackson. Little, Brown and Company (1953). Boston, Massachusetts, p. 106.

205. Hammond, Bray. 1956. Jackson's Fight with the Money Power. American Heritage, June 1956, Volume VII, Number 4. American Heritage Publishing Company, p. 102-103.

206. "Early American Trade", April, 16, 2007, http://h2g2.com/approved_entry/A21388322

207. John Gallagher and Ronald Robinson. "The Imperialism of Free Trade," Economic History Review (August 1953) 6#1 pp 1–15 in JSTOR.

208. Smith, Simon (1998). British Imperialism 1750–1970. Cambridge University Press. ISBN 978-3-12-580640-5, p.20 Retrieved on 22 August 2013.

209. "British Empire", Wikipedia, http://en.wikipedia.org/wiki/British_Empire

210. Fairbank, John K. (1978), "The Canton trade and the Opium War", in Fairbank, John K. (ed.), Late Ch'ing 1800–1911, Part 1, The Cambridge History of China 10, Cambridge: Cambridge University Press, pp. 163–213, ISBN 9780521214476.

211. "Economic History of China Before 1912", Wikipedia, http://en.wikipedia.org/wiki/Economic_history_of_China_before_1912

212. Patricia Buckley Ebrey, Anne Walthill James B. Palais., East Asia (Boston, MA: Houghton Mifflin, 2006), pp.378–82.

213. Sun, Jian (2000), Economic history of China, (1840–1949) (in Chinese) 2, China People's University Press, ISBN 7300029531, p. 712.

214. Ludden, David (2002), India And South Asia: A Short History, Oxford: Oneworld, xii, 306, ISBN 1-85168-237-6.

215. "Company Rule in India", Wikipedia, http://en.wikipedia.org/wiki/Company_rule_in_India

216. "Indian Rebellion of 1857", Wikipedia, http://en.wikipedia.org/wiki/Indian_Rebellion_of_1857

217. Spear, Percival (1990), A History of India, Volume 2, New Delhi and London: Penguin Books, ISBN 978-0-14-013836-8, pp. 147-148.

218. "Royal African Company", Wikipedia, http://en.wikipedia.org/wiki/Royal_African_Company

219. "Early American Trade", April, 16, 2007, http://h2g2.com/approved_entry/A21388322

220. Paul E. Lovejoy (1982) 'The Volume of the Atlantic Slave Trade: A Synthesis.' The Journal of African History, Vol. 23, No. 4.

221. David P. Forsythe (2009). "Encyclopedia of Human Rights, Volume 1". Oxford University Press. p. 399. ISBN 0195334027.

222. Hoyos, Carola (2009), Rothschild and Freshfields founders linked to slavery,Global Research, June 28, 2009 http://www.globalresearch.ca/rothschild-and-freshfields-founders-linked-to-slavery/14147

223. Hochschild, Adam (2005) "Bury the Chains: Prophets and Rebels in the Fight to Free an Empire's Slaves" Houghton Mifflin, New York, p.347.

224. "Mexican–American War", Wikipedia, http://en.wikipedia.org/wiki/Mexican%E2%80%93American_War

225. "American imperialism", Wikipedia, http://en.wikipedia.org/wiki/American_imperialism

226. Jaffa, Harry V. (2000). A New Birth of Freedom: Abraham Lincoln and the Coming of the Civil War. Rowman & Littlefield. ISBN 0-8476-9952-8, p.299-300.

227. White, Jr., Ronald C. (2009). A. Lincoln: A Biography. Random House, Inc. ISBN 978-1-4000-6499-1, p.251.

228. "American Civil War", Wikipedia, http://en.wikipedia.org/wiki/American_Civil_War

229. Brown, Ellen (April 8, 2009). "Revive Lincoln's Monetary Policy". webofdebt.com, http://www.webofdebt.com/articles/lincoln_obama.php

230. Brown, Ellen Hodgson; Simpson, Reed (2012). Web of Debt: The Shocking Truth About Our Money System and How We Can Break Free, Third Millennium Press. ISBN 0983330859, p.85.

231. Donald, David Herbert (1996) "Lincoln", Simon and Schuster. ISBN 978-0-684-82535-9.p. 453-466.

232. "Second Industrial Revolution", Wikipedia, http://en.wikipedia.org/wiki/Second_Industrial_Revolution

233. Marx, Karl (1859) A Contribution to the Critique of Political Economy, Das Kapital.

234. Wells, David A. (1890). Recent Economic Changes and Their Effect on Production and Distribution of Wealth and Well-Being of Society. New York: D. Appleton and Co. ISBN 0-543-72474-3.

235. "Life in Great Britain during the Industrial Revolution", Wikipedia, http://en.wikipedia.org/wiki/Life_in_Great_Britain_during_the_Industrial_Revolutio n

236. "A capitalism's social pyramid", Industrial Workers of the World, 1911, http://commons.wikimedia.org/wiki/File:Anti-capitalism_color.jpg This work is in the public domain in the United States, and those countries with a copyright term of life of the author plus 100 years or less.

237. Engels, Friedrich (1892). The Condition of the Working-Class in England in 1844. London: Swan Sonnenschein & Co. pp. 45, 48–53.

238. "History of rail transport in Great Britain 1830–1922", Wikipedia, http://en.wikipedia.org/wiki/History_of_rail_transport_in_Great_Britain_1830%E2 %80%931922

239. Royle, Trevor Crimea: The Great Crimean War, 1854–1856 (2000) Palgrave Macmillan ISBN 1-4039-6416-5.

240. "Crimean War", Wikipedia, http://en.wikipedia.org/wiki/Crimean_War

241. "Alaska Purchase", Wikipedia, http://en.wikipedia.org/wiki/Alaska_Purchase

242. Hunt, Lynn, Thomas R. Martin, Barbara H. Rosenwein, R. Po-chia Hsia et al.. The Making of the West, Peoples and Cultures. Vol. C. 3rd ed. Boston: Bedford/ St. Martin's, 2009. 712-13.

243. "Economic history of Japan", Wikipedia, http://en.wikipedia.org/wiki/Economic_history_of_Japan

244. "Japan Answers the Challenge of the Western World". The Meiji Restoration and Modernization. Columbia University. Retrieved on 3 September 2012.

245. "Meiji Restoration", Wikipedia, http://en.wikipedia.org/wiki/Meiji_Restoration

246. "First Sino Japanese War", Wikipedia, http://en.wikipedia.org/wiki/First_Sino-Japanese_War

247. "Austro-Prussian War", Wikipedia, http://en.wikipedia.org/wiki/Austro-Prussian_War

248. "History of Germany", Wikipedia, http://en.wikipedia.org/wiki/History_of_Germany

249. Taylor, AJP (1969), Bismarck: the Man and the Statesman, New York: Alfred A Knopf, p. 203.

250. Hennock, E. P. (2007), The Origin of the Welfare State in England and Germany, 1850–1914: Social Policies Compared.

251. Hermann, Beck (1995), Origins of the Authoritarian Welfare State in Prussia, 1815-1870.

252. "Long Depression", Wikipedia, http://en.wikipedia.org/wiki/Long_Depression

253. Huberman, Michael (Dec. 2004). "Working Hours of the World Unite? New International Evidence of Worktime, 1870-1913". The Journal of Economic History 64 (4): 971.

254. Moberg, David. "Antiunionism". Encyclopedia of Chicago. Chicago History Museum, Newberry Library, Northwestern University. Retrieved on April 2, 2012.

255. Reiff, Janice L. "The Press and Labor in the 1880s". Encyclopedia of Chicago. Chicago History Museum, Newberry Library, Northwestern University. Retrieved on 2 March, 2013.

256. Avrich, Paul (1984),"The Haymarket Tragedy", Princeton, NJ: Princeton University Press. ISBN 0-691-00600-8, p. 393.

257. Smil, Vaclav (2005). Creating the Twentieth Century: Technical Innovations of 1867–1914 and Their Lasting Impact. Oxford; New York: Oxford University Press. ISBN 0-19-516874-7.

258. Arthur J Taylor, "The Economy," in Simon Nowell-Smith, ed., Edwardian England: 1901-1914 (1964) pp105-138.

259. Charles Feinstein, "Britain's Overseas Investments in 1913," Economic History Review (1990) 43#2 pp. 288-295 in JSTOR.

260. "History of rail transport in the United States", Wikipedia, http://en.wikipedia.org/wiki/History_of_rail_transport_in_the_United_States

261. "Statue: George Peabody statue" , London Remembers, http://www.londonremembers.com/memorials/george-peabody-statue

262. Linda Hall Library, Kansas City, Missouri. The Search for the Ancient Suez Canal, accessed 20 August 2008.

263. "Suez Canal", Wikipedia, http://en.wikipedia.org/wiki/Suez_Canal

264. Stephen J. Lee (2005), "Gladstone and Disraeli", Routledge, pp. 107.

265. Panama Canal, Wikipedia, http://en.wikipedia.org/wiki/Panama_Canal

266. Sherman Antitrust Act, Wikipedia, http://en.wikipedia.org/wiki/Sherman_Antitrust_Act

267. "Panic of 1893", Wikipedia, http://en.wikipedia.org/wiki/Panic_of_1893

268. "J.P. Morgan", Wikipedia, http://en.wikipedia.org/wiki/J._P._Morgan

269. Baldwin, Neil (2001). Edison: Inventing the Century. University of Chicago Press. ISBN 978-0-226-03571-0. p. 37.

270. "Thomas Edison", Wikipedia, http://en.wikipedia.org/wiki/Thomas_Edison

271. "Nikola Tesla", Wikipedia, http://en.wikipedia.org/wiki/Nikola_Tesla

272. Thomas Parke Hughes, Networks of power: electrification in Western society, 1880–1930 (1983), page 119.

273. Emerson, D. T. (1997). "The work of Jagadis Chandra Bose: 100 years of MM-wave research". IEEE Transactions on Microwave Theory and Research 45 (12): 2267–2273. doi:10.1109/MWSYM.1997.602853. ISBN 9780986488511.

274. Sen, A. K. (1997). "Sir J.C. Bose and radio science". Microwave Symposium Digest 2 (8–13): 557–560. doi:10.1109/MWSYM.1997.602854.

275. Mahanti, Subodh. "Acharya Jagadis Chandra Bose". Biographies of Scientists. Vigyan Prasar, Department of Science and Technology, Government of India.

276. "Henry Ford", Wikipedia, http://en.wikipedia.org/wiki/Henry_Ford

277. Nevins, Allan; Frank Ernest Hill (1957). Ford: Expansion and Challenge, 1915–1933. New York: Charles Scribners' Sons.

278. "Wright Brothers", Wikipedia, http://en.wikipedia.org/wiki/Wright_brothers

279. "First flight of the Wright Flyer I, December 17, 1903, Orville piloting, Wilbur running at wingtip", Author: Author John T, Daniels. Source: The United States Library of Congress's, digital ID ppprs.00626, Retrieved on from http://www.loc.gov/pictures/resource/ppprs.00626/ Repository: Library of Congress Prints and Photographs Division Washington, D.C. 20540 USA. Rights Advisory confirms "No known restrictions on publication", Retrieved on June 10, 2015.

280. "AEA June Bug", Wikipedia, http://en.wikipedia.org/wiki/AEA_June_Bug

281. Alexander Graham Bell, Wikipedia, http://en.wikipedia.org/wiki/Alexander_Graham_Bell

282. "Helen Keller", Wikipedia, http://en.wikipedia.org/wiki/Helen_Keller

283. Petrie, A. Roy. Alexander Graham Bell. Don Mills, Ontario: Fitzhenry & Whiteside Limited, 1975. ISBN 0-88902-209-7, p. 17.

284. "Standard Oil", Wikipedia, http://en.wikipedia.org/wiki/Standard_Oil

285. Chernow, Ron (1998). Titan: The Life of John D. Rockefeller, Sr. Random House. ISBN 978-0-679-43808-3.

286. "The Gospel According to Andrew: Carnegie's Hymn to Wealth", North American Review (June 1889). Reprinted in The Annals of America, vol. 11, 1884–1894 (Chicago: Encyclopaedia Britannica, 1968), 222–226.

287. Dostrovsky, I. (1988). Energy and the Missing Resource: A View from the Laboratory. Cambridge University Press. p. 18. ISBN 978-0-521-31965-2.

288. Moody, Richard (2007-04-20). Oil & Gas Shales, Definitions & Distribution In Time & Space. In The History of On-Shore Hydrocarbon Use in the UK (PDF). Geological Society of London.

289. Francu, Juraj; Harvie, Barbra; Laenen, Ben; Siirde, Andres; Veiderma, Mihkel (May 2007). A study on the EU oil shale industry viewed in the light of the Estonian experience. A report by EASAC to the Committee on Industry, Research and Energy of the European Parliament (PDF). European Academies Science Advisory Council. pp. 1; 5; 12.

290. History of the petroleum industry, Wikipedia, http://en.wikipedia.org/wiki/History_of_the_petroleum_industry

291. Gordon, John Steele (2007), "10 Moments That Made American Business", American Heritage, February/March 2007.

292. "Royal Dutch Shell", Wikipedia, http://en.wikipedia.org/wiki/Royal_Dutch_Shell

293. "British Petroleum", Wikipedia, http://en.wikipedia.org/wiki/BP

294. Bamberg, James H (1994). The History of the British Petroleum Company: The Anglo-Iranian Years, 1928–1954. vol. II. Cambridge: Cambridge University Press. ISBN 9780521259507, pp. 3-7, pp. 177.

295. Nelson W. Aldrich, Wikipedia, http://en.wikipedia.org/wiki/Nelson_W._Aldrich

296. "Federal Reserve Act", Wikipedia, http://en.wikipedia.org/wiki/Federal_Reserve_Act

297. Vladimir Ilyich Lenin. Imperialism, the Highest Stage of Capitalism. transcribed from Lenin's Selected Works, Progress Publishers, 1963, Moscow, Volume 1, pp. 667–766.

298. "Imperialism and Capitalism" in the Communist International, No. 18, October 1921. p. 3. http://www.fordham.edu/halsall/mod/1916lenin-imperialism.html#bm3.

299. "Russian Revolution", Wikipedia, http://en.wikipedia.org/wiki/Russian_Revolution

300. Mullins, Eustace (1984) "The World Order: A Study in the Hegemony of Parasitism", Chapter 1.1: Mayer Rothschild and the Five Arrows", Ezra Pound Institute of Civilization. http://modernhistoryproject.org/mhp?Article=WorldOrder&C=1.1

301. "World War I", Wikipedia, http://en.wikipedia.org/wiki/World_War_I

302. Willmott, H.P. (2003), "World War I, New York: Dorling Kindersley", ISBN 0-7894-9627-5, OCLC 52541937, p. 21, p. 307.

303. Prior, Robin (1999), The First World War, London: Cassell, pp. 18.

304. Fromkin, David (2004), Europe's Last Summer: Who Started the Great War in 1914?, New York: Alfred A. Knopf, ISBN 0-375-41156-9, OCLC 53937943, p. 94.

305. Sachar, Howard Morley (1970), The emergence of the Middle East, 1914–1924, Allen Lane, ISBN 0-7139-0158-6, OCLC 153103197.

306. Evans, Leslie (27 May 2005), Future of Iraq, Israel-Palestine Conflict, and Central Asia Weighed at International Conference, UCLA International Institute.

307. "History of Iran", Wikipedia, http://en.wikipedia.org/wiki/History_of_Iran

308. Metz, Helen Chapin, ed. (1988). "The Turkish Petroleum Company". Iraq: A Country Study, http://countrystudies.us/iraq/53.htm. Retrieved on 29 December 2013.

309. Myers, Kevin (3 September 2009). "The greatest 20th century beneficiary of popular mythology has been the cad Churchill". Irish Independent, http://www.independent.ie/opinion/columnists/kevin-myers/the-greatest-20th-century-beneficiary-of-popular-mythology-has-been-the-cad-churchill-26563434.html

310. "Red Line Agreement", Wikipedia, http://en.wikipedia.org/wiki/Red_Line_Agreement

311. Longrigg, Stephen Hemsley (1961). Oil in the Middle East. New York: Oxford University Press. OCLC 237163.

312. Carment, David (1981) D'Arcy, William Knox (1849–1917), http://adb.anu.edu.au/biography/darcy-william-knox-5882

313. Bamberg, James H (2000). The History of the British Petroleum Company: British Petroleum and Global Oil, 1950–1975: The Challenge of Nationalism. vol. III. Cambridge: Cambridge University Press. ISBN 9780521785150, pp. 109–110.

314. "Russian Revolution", Wikipedia, http://en.wikipedia.org/wiki/Russian_Revolution

315. Carmichael, Joel (1966), A short history of the Russian Revolution, Nelson, pp 23-4

316. Olivia Fleming (2012). "Meet the 14th Century African king who was richest man in the world of all time (adjusted for inflation!)", 15 October, 2012,Daily Mail, http://www.dailymail.co.uk/news/article-2218025/Meet-14th-Century-African-king-richest-man-world-time-adjusted-inflation.html

317. Marrs, Jim "Rule by Secrecy: The Hidden History that Connects the Trilateral Commission, the Freemasons and the Great Pyramids.", HarperCollins Publishers, New York, 2000. P.195.

318. "Woodrow Wilson", Wikipedia, http://en.wikipedia.org/wiki/Woodrow_Wilson

319. Wells, David A. (1890). Recent Economic Changes and Their Effect on Production and Distribution of Wealth and Well-Being of Society. New York: D. Appleton and Co. ISBN 0-543-72474-3.

320. George F. Kennan, Russia Leaves the War, p. 472, et passim. 1956, repr. 1989, ISBN 0-691-00841-8.

321. Robert J. Maddox, The Unknown War with Russia (San Rafael, CA: Presidio Press, 1977), pp.137.

322. Kitchen, Martin (2000) [1980], Europe Between the Wars, New York: Longman, ISBN 0-582-41869-0, OCLC 247285240, pp. 22.

323. Ewald, Paul (1994), Evolution of infectious disease, New York, Oxford University Press, 1994, pp. 110.

324. Stacey L, ed. (2005), The Threat of Pandemic Influenza: Are We Ready? Workshop Summary, Washington DC: National Academies Press, ISBN 0-309-09504-2, OCLC 57422232.

325. "Fourteen Points Speech", Wikipedia, http://en.wikisource.org/wiki/Fourteen_Points_Speech

326. President Woodrow Wilson speaking on the League of Nations to a luncheon audience in Portland OR. 66th Cong., 1st sess. Senate Documents: Addresses of President Wilson (May–November 1919), vol.11, no. 120, p.206.

327. "Treaty of Versailles", Wikipedia, http://en.wikipedia.org/wiki/Treaty_of_Versailles

328. World War Reparations, Wikipedia, http://en.wikipedia.org/wiki/World_War_I_reparations

329. Keynes, John Maynard (1919). The Economic Consequences of the Peace, London : Macmillan, 1919.

330. "Aftermath of World War I", Wikipedia, http://en.wikipedia.org/wiki/Aftermath_of_World_War_I.

331. Eichengreen, Barry J. (1995). Golden Fetters: The Gold Standard and the Great Depression, 1919–1939. New York City: Oxford University Press. ISBN 0-19-510113-8. OCLC 34383450.

332. "What's a little debt between friends?" by Finlo Rohrer, BBC News. 10 May 2006.

333. "Gold Standard", Wikipedia, http://en.wikipedia.org/wiki/Gold_standard

334. Elwell, Craig K. (2011). Brief History of the Gold Standard in the United States. Congressional Research Service.

335. "World War II", Wikipedia, http://en.wikipedia.org/wiki/World_War_II

336. Fergusson, Adam (2010). When money dies : the nightmare of deficit spending, devaluation, and hyperinflation in Weimar Germany (1st [U.S.] ed. ed.). New York: PublicAffairs. ISBN 1-58648-994-1, pp.10, p.254.

337. Hyperinflation in the Weimar Republic, Wikipedia, http://en.wikipedia.org/wiki/Hyperinflation_in_the_Weimar_Republic

338. Parsson, Jens O. (1974). Dying of Money : Lessons of the Great German and American Inflations. Boston: Wellspring Press, p. 116-117.

339. Balderston, prepared for the Economic History Society by Theo (2002). Economics and politics in the Weimar Republic (1. publ. ed.). Cambridge [u.a.]: Cambridge Univ. Press. ISBN 0-521-77760-7, p.21.

340. "Weimar Republic hyperinflation from one to one trillion paper Marks per gold Mark; on a logarithmic scale", Logarithmic chart of German Hyperinflation. Based on the values in Table IV (page 441) of The Economics of Inflation by Costantino Bresciani-Turroni, published 1937 http://commons.wikimedia.org/wiki/File:Germany_Hyperinflation.svg This file is made available under the Creative Commons CC0 1.0 Universal Public Domain Dedication, created on 12 December 2014 at Wikipedia, Retrieved on 5 February, 2015.

341. Civilization in the West, Seventh Edition, Kishlansky, Geary, and O'Brien, New York, page 807.

342. Mussolini, Benito. 1935. Fascism: Doctrine and Institutions. Rome: Ardita Publishers. p 14.

343. Cyprian Blamires. World Fascism: A Historical Encyclopedia, Volume 1. Santa Barbara, California, USA: ABC-CLIO, 2006. p. 189.

344. Joseph, Frank (2010). Mussolini's War: Fascist Italy's Military Struggles from Africa and Western Europe to the Mediterranean and Soviet Union 1935–45. West Midlands, England, UK: Helion & Company. p. 50.

345. Kitchen, Martin, A History of Modern Germany, 1800–2000 (Malden, Massaschussetts, USA; Oxford, England, UK; Carlton, Victoria, Australia: Blackwell Publishing, Inc., 2006),p. 205.

346. "Great Depression", Wikipedia, http://en.wikipedia.org/wiki/Great_Depression

347. Frank, Robert H.; Bernanke, Ben S. (2007). Principles of Macroeconomics (3rd ed.). Boston: McGraw-Hill/Irwin. p. 98. ISBN 0-07-319397-6.

348. Romer, Christina D. (1992), "What Ended the Great Depression?". Journal of Economic History 52 (4).

349. Bank for International Settlements, Wikipedia, http://www.wikipedia.or.ke/index.php/Bank_for_International_Settlements

350. Quigley, Carroll (1966). Tragedy And Hope. New York: Macmillan. p. 515. ISBN 0-945001-10-X, p.324.

351. Eichengreen, Barry J. (2008). Globalizing Capital: A History of the International Monetary System. Princeton University Press. ISBN 978-0-691-13937-1, pp. 61.

352. Willoughby, Douglas; Susan Willoughby (2000). The USA 1917-45 (2000 ed.). Heinemann. ISBN 978-0-435-32723-1, p. 72.

353. "Young Plan", Wikipedia, http://en.wikipedia.org/wiki/Young_Plan

354. Temin, Peter & Toniolo, Gianni (2008). The World Economy between the Wars. Oxford University Press, USA. ISBN 978-0-195-30755-9, p. 137-8.

355. Ian Kershaw. Hitler, 1889–1936: hubris. New York, New York, US; London, England, UK: W. W. Norton & Company, 2000. p. 182.

356. Republic of China (1912–49), Wikipedia, http://en.wikipedia.org/wiki/Republic_of_China_%281912%E2%80%9349%29

357. "Economy of the People's Republic of China", Wikipedia, http://en.wikipedia.org/wiki/Economy_of_the_People's_Republic_of_China

358. Cyprian Blamires. World Fascism: A Historical Encyclopedia, Volume 1. Santa Barbara, California, USA: ABC-CLIO, Inc., 2006. p. 542.

359. Keith H. Pickus. Constructing Modern Identities: Jewish University Students in Germany, 1815-1914. Detroit, Michigan, USA: Wayne State University Press, 1999. p. 86.

360. Jonathan Olsen. Nature and Nationalism: Right-wing Ecology and the Politics of Identity in Contemporary Germany. New York, New York, USA: Palgrave Macmillan, 1999. p. 62.

361. Overy, R.J., The Dictators: Hitler's Germany and Stalin's Russia, W. W. Norton & Company, Inc., 2004. p. 399.

362. Bendersky, Joseph W. A History of Nazi Germany: 1919-1945. 2nd ed. Burnham Publishers, 2000. p. 72.

363. Blamires, Cyprian; Jackson, Paul. World Fascism: A Historical Encyclopedia: Volume 1. Santa Barbara, California, USA: ABC-CLIO, Inc, 2006. p. 62.

364. Eastman, Lloyd E. (1986). "Nationalist China during the Sino-Japanese War 1937–1945". In John K. Fairbank and Denis Twitchett, eds., The Cambridge History of China, Volume 13: Republican China 1912–1949, Part 2. Cambridge: Cambridge University Press. ISBN 978-0-521-24338-4.

365. Niewyk, Donald L., Nicosia, Francis (2000). The Columbia Guide to the Holocaust. New York, NY: Columbia University Press. ISBN 978-0-231-11200-0., pp. 45–52.

366. Blamires, Cyprian; Jackson, Paul. World Fascism: A Historical Encyclopedia: Volume 1. Santa Barbara, California, USA: ABC-CLIO, Inc, 2006. p. 62.

367. Peukert, Detlev (1994). "The Genesis of the 'Final Solution' from the Spirit of Science". In David F. Crew. Nazism and German Society, 1933–1945. London: Routledge. pp. 274–299.

368. Burleigh, Michael (2000). "Psychiatry, Society and Nazi 'Euthanasia'". In Omer Bartov. The Holocaust: Origins, Implementation, Aftermath. London: Routledge. pp. 43–62.

369. Bauer, Yehuda (2002). Rethinking the Holocaust. New Haven, CT: Yale University Press, p. 48.

370. Friedländer, Saul (2007). The Years of Extermination: Nazi Germany and the Jews 1939–1945. London: Weidenfeld & Nicolson, p. xxi.

371. Rummell, R. J. "Statistics". Freedom, Democide, War. The University of Hawaii System. Retrieved on 25 January 2010.

372. Johnson, Chalmers, "The Looting of Asia", London Review of Books, http://www.lrb.co.uk/v25/n22/chalmers-johnson/the-looting-of-asia.

373. Hosking, Geoffrey A. (2006). Rulers and Victims: The Russians in the Soviet Union. Cambridge, MA: Harvard University Press. ISBN 978-0-674-02178-5., p. 242.

374. Kolko, Gabriel (1990) "The Politics of War: The World and United States Foreign Policy", 1943–1945. New York, NY: Random House. ISBN 978-0-679-72757-6, pp. 211, 235, 267–268.

375. Neale, Jonathan (2001). The American War: Vietnam, 1960–1975. London: Bookmarks. ISBN 978-1-898-87667-0, p. 17. p. 20, p. 24, p.25.

376. Kolko, Gabriel (1985). Anatomy of a War: Vietnam, the United States, and the Modern Historical Experience. New York: Pantheon Books. ISBN 978-0-394-74761-3., p. 36, p 457.

377. Peter Dennis (1987). Troubled days of peace: Mountbatten and South East Asia command, 1945–46. Manchester University Press ND. p. 179. ISBN 978-0-7190-2205-0.

378. Amartya Sen (1981). Poverty and Famines: An Essay on Entitlement and Deprivation. London: Oxford University Press. p. 203. ISBN 9780195649543.

379. "Bengal famine of 1943", Wikipedia, http://en.wikipedia.org/wiki/Bengal_famine_of_1943

380. Mishra, Pankaj "Exit Wounds", The New Yorker, 13 August 2007, http://www.newyorker.com/arts/critics/books/2007/08/13/070813crbo_books_mishr a?currentPage=3 Retrieved on January 31, 2014.

381. Richard Symonds, 1950, The Making of Pakistan, London, OCLC 245793264, p 74.

382. Judd, Dennis, The Lion and the Tiger: The rise and Fall of the British Raj,1600– 1947. Oxford University Press: New York. (2010) p. 138.

383. United Nations Monetary and Financial Conference, Final Act (London et al., 1944), Article IV.

384. "Bank for International Settlements", Wikipedia, http://en.wikipedia.org/wiki/Bank_for_International_Settlements.

385. Eichengreen, Barry J. (1995). Golden Fetters: The Gold Standard and the Great Depression, 1919–1939. New York City: Oxford University Press. ISBN 0-19- 510113-8. OCLC 34383450.

386. John Fforde, The Role of the Bank of England, 1941–1958 (1992).

387. "Bretton Woods Conference", Wikipedia, http://en.wikipedia.org/wiki/Bretton_Woods_Conference

388. "World Bank", Wikipedia, http://en.wikipedia.org/wiki/World_Bank.

389. "Flight and expulsion of Germans (1944–50)", Wikipedia, http://en.wikipedia.org/wiki/Flight_and_expulsion_of_Germans_%281944%E2%80 %9350%29

390. Swain, Geoffrey (1992). "The Cominform: Tito's International?". The Historical Journal 35 (3): pp.641–663.

391. Stueck, William (2010). "The Korean War". In Melvyn P. Leffler and Odd Arne Westad, eds., The Cambridge History of the Cold War, Volume I: Origins (pp. 266– 287). Cambridge: Cambridge University Press. ISBN 978-0-521-83719-4.

392. Lynch, Michael (2010). "The Chinese Civil War 1945–49. Oxford: Osprey Publishing". ISBN 978-1-84176-671-3., pp. 12–3.

393. "Marshall Plan", Wikipedia, http://en.wikipedia.org/wiki/Marshall_Plan

394. Volkogonov, Dmitri. Stalin: Triumph and Tragedy. Forum, 1996, p.531.

395. Hogan (1987) p. 427-45; Barry Eichengreen, The European Economy since 1945: Coordinated Capitalism and Beyond, (2008) pp 64-73.

396. Barry Eichengreen, The European Economy since 1945: Coordinated Capitalism and Beyond, (2008) p. 57.

397. Milward, Alan S. The Reconstruction of Western Europe 1945-51 (Berkeley: University of California Press, 2006), p. 466.

398. Wolf, Holger C. (1993). "The Lucky Miracle: Germany 1945–1951". In Rudiger Dornbusch, Wilhelm Nölling and Richard Layard, eds., Postwar Economic Reconstruction and Lessons for the East Today (pp. 29–56). Cambridge, MA: MIT Press. ISBN 978-0-262-04136-2, pp. 29, 30, 32.

399. "Germany makes final payment for WWI reparations", The Jerusalem Post, September 29, 2010, http://www.jpost.com/International/Germany-makes-final-payment-for-WWI-reparations.

400. Minford, Patrick (1993). "Reconstruction and the U.K. Postwar Welfare State: False Start and New Beginning". In Rudiger Dornbusch, Wilhelm Nölling and Richard Layard, eds., Postwar Economic Reconstruction and Lessons for the East Today (pp. 115–138). Cambridge, MA: MIT Press. ISBN 978-0-262-04136-2., p. 117.

401. Schain, Martin A., ed. (2001). The Marshall Plan Fifty Years Later. London: Palgrave Macmillan. ISBN 978-0-333-92983-4.

402. Smith, Alan (1993). Russia and the World Economy: Problems of Integration. London: Routledge. ISBN 978-0-415-08924-1., p. 32.

403. Genzberger, Christine (1994). China Business: The Portable Encyclopedia for Doing Business with China. Petaluma, California: World Trade Press. p. 4. ISBN 0-9631864-3-4.

404. "Economy   of   Germany",   Wikipedia,
http://en.wikipedia.org/wiki/Economy_of_Germany

405. Beschloss, Michael R (2003). The Conquerors: Roosevelt, Truman and the Destruction of Hitler's Germany, 1941-1945. Simon and Schuster. ISBN 0-7432-6085-6, p.277.

406. "Wirtschaftswunder", Wikipedia, http://en.wikipedia.org/wiki/Wirtschaftswunder

407. Bayne Fisher, W. William; Avery, P.; Hambly, G. R. G.; Melville, C. (1991). The Cambridge History of Iran, Volume 7. Cambridge University Press. p. 665.

408. Sztucki, Jerzy (1984). Interim measures in the Hague Court. Brill Archive. ISBN 9789065440938., p. 43.

409. "Oil Company Histories". Virginia University. Retrieved on 30 December 2013, http://www.virginia.edu/igpr/APAG/apagoilhistory.html

410. Citino, Nathan J. (2012) "From Arab Nationalism to OPEC: Eisenhower, King Sa'ūd, and the making of U.S-Saudi relations", Indian University Press, 2002.

411. Riley, Kevin M. (2011), "Oil and the U.S. Dollar", Columbia University, https://www.academia.edu/1253274/Oil_and_the_U.S._Dollar, June 27, 2011, Retrieved on: January 5, 2014.

412. OPEC, Wikipedia, http://en.wikipedia.org/wiki/OPEC

413. Maugeri, Leonardo, "The Age of Oil: The Mythology, History, and Future of the World's Most Controversial Resource", Greenwood Publishing Group,http://books.google.fr/books?id=mzHt5hYeXllC&printsec=frontcover&dq=The+Age+of+Oil:+The+Mythology,+History,+and+Future+of+the+World's+Most+... amazon&hl=fr&sa=X&ei=LbLBUuPnHeyuyAG25YHACw&ved=0CElQ6AEwAA #v=onepage&q&f=false, page 113.

414. Horton,Sarah,"The 1973 Oil Crisis", http://www.envirothonpa.org/documents/The1973OilCrisis.pdf

415. Spiro, David E. The Hidden Hand of American Hegemony: Petrodollar Recycling and International Markets. Ithaca, NY: Cornell UP, 1999.

416. "Saudi Aramco", Wikipedia, http://en.wikipedia.org/wiki/Saudi_Aramco

417. Financial Times Non-public Top 150". The Financial Times. http://www.ft.com/intl/cms/s/2/5de6ef96-8b95-11db-a61f-0000779e2340.html#axzz2oyzgkKq1, Retrieved on 5 January 2014

418. Riley, Kevin M. (2011), "Oil and the U.S. Dollar", Columbia University, https://www.academia.edu/1253274/Oil_and_the_U.S._Dollar, June 27, 2011, Retrieved on: 5 January 5, 2014.

419. Albert, David (1980), "Tell the American People: Perspectives on the Iranian Revolution", Movement for a Free Society, Philadelphia, p.24.

420. Henderson. Dean (2010), "Big Oil & Their Bankers in the Persian Gulf", Bridger House Publishing, Lexington, KY, USA.

421. "Iranian Revolution", Wikipedia, http://en.wikipedia.org/wiki/Iranian_Revolution

422. "History of Iraq", Wikipedia, http://en.wikipedia.org/wiki/History_of_Iraq

423. "Hundred Flowers Campaign", Wikipedia, http://en.wikipedia.org/wiki/Hundred_Flowers_Campaign

424. Harry Wu; Hongda Harry Wu; George Vecsey (30 December 2002). Troublemaker: One Man's Crusade Against China's Cruelty. NewsMax Media, Inc. pp. 49–55. ISBN 978-0-9704029-9-8.

425. Philip Short (2001). Mao: A Life. Macmillan, 1 February, 2001. pp. 470. ISBN 978-0-8050-6638-8.

426. McNamara, Robert S., with James Blight, Robert Brigham, Thomas Biersteker, Herbert Schandler (1999). Argument Without End: In Search of Answers to the Vietnam Tragedy. New York: PublicAffairs. ISBN 978-1-891-62087-4., pp. 377–9, p.19.

427. Pentagon Papers, Gravel, ed, Chapter 2, 'U.S. Involvement in the Franco-Viet Minh War', p. 54.

428. Zinn, A People's History of the United States, p. 471.

429. "Geneva Conference (1954)", Wikipedia, http://en.wikipedia.org/wiki/Geneva_Conference_(1954)

430. "Cold War", Wikipedia, http://en.wikipedia.org/wiki/Cold_War

431. Leffler, Melvyn P.; Westad, Odd Arne, eds. (2010). The Cambridge History of the Cold War (3 volumes). Cambridge: Cambridge University Press. ISBN 978-0-521-83938-9.

432. Bourne, Peter G. (1986). Fidel: A Biography of Fidel Castro. New York City: Dodd, Mead & Company. ISBN 978-0-396-08518-8.. pp. 64–65.

433. "Bay of Pigs Invasion", Wikipedia, http://en.wikipedia.org/wiki/Bay_of_Pigs_Invasion

434. "Apollo Program", Wikipedia, http://en.wikipedia.org/wiki/Apollo_program

435. Allen, Bob (ed.). "NASA Langley Research Center's Contributions to the Apollo Program". Langley Research Center. NASA, http://www.nasa.gov/centers/langley/news/factsheets/Apollo.html Retrieved on March 13, 2014.

436. Lexington, ed. (May 21, 2011). "Apollo plus 50". The Economist (London: The Economist Newspaper Limited). p. 36, http://www.economist.com/node/18712369 Retrieved on: March 13, 2014.

437. The History of the Vietnamese Economy (2005), Vol. 2, edited by Dang Phong of the Institute of Economy, Vietnamese Institute of Social Sciences.

438. Gerdes (ed.) Examining Issues Through Political Cartoons: The Vietnam War p. 19. Charles Hirschman et al., "Vietnamese Casualties During the American War: A New Estimate," Population and Development Review, December 1995.

439. Kolko, Gabriel (1985). Anatomy of a War: Vietnam, the United States, and the Modern Historical Experience. New York: Pantheon Books. ISBN 978-0-394-74761-3., p. 36, p 457.

440. Charles Hirschman et al., "Vietnamese Casualties During the American War: A New Estimate," Population and Development Review, December 1995.

441. Shenon, Philip (23 April 1995). "20 Years After Victory, Vietnamese Communists Ponder How to Celebrate". The New York Times.

442. Weiner, Tim (July 6, 2009). "Robert S. McNamara, Architect of a Futile War, Dies at 93 - Obituary". New York Times, http://www.nytimes.com/2009/07/07/us/07mcnamara.html?pagewanted=5&_r=2&hp& Retrieved on 18 January, 2014.

443. Khrushchev, Nikita (1970), "Khrushchev's Memoirs", Little Brown & company. pp. 250-257. ISBN 0316831409.

444. Lardy, R. Nicholas; Fairbank, K. John (1987). "The Chinese economy under stress, 1958–1965", P.368.

445. "Great Leap Forward", Wikipedia, http://en.wikipedia.org/wiki/Great_Leap_Forward

446. Dikötter, Frank (2010), "Mao's Great Famine: The History of China's Most Devastating Catastrophe, 1958-62". Walker & Company.

447. Datt, Ruddar; Sundharam, K.P.M. (2009). Indian Economy. New Delhi: S. Chand Group. p. 976. ISBN 978-81-219-0298-4. p.179.

448. Panagariya, Arvind (2004). India in the 1980s and 1990s: A Triumph of Reforms. http://ideas.repec.org/p/wpa/wuwpit/0403005.html. p.24

449. Gurcharan Das (2002). India Unbound. Anchor Books. pp. 167–174. ISBN 978-0385720748.

450. Fitzgerald, Stephanie (2011), "Children of the Holocaust", Compass Point Books, Mankato, MN, pp.6

451. "Bangladesh Liberation War", Wikipedia, http://en.wikipedia.org/wiki/Bangladesh_Liberation_War

452. "Genocide in Bangladesh, 1971", Gendercide Watch, Gendercide.org. Archived from the original on 26 July 2011. http://www.gendercide.org/case_bangladesh.html Retrieved on 23 June 2011.

453. Sharlach, Lisa (2000). "Rape as Genocide: Bangladesh, the Former Yugoslavia, and Rwanda". New Political Science 1 (22): 89. doi:10.1080/713687893", pp. 92–93.

454. Scott, Paul (21 December 1971). "Naval 'Show of Force' By Nixon Meant as Blunt Warning to India". Bangor Daily News (Google News), http://news.google.com/newspapers?id=HUU0AAAAIBAJ&sjid=IeEIAAAAIBAJ &pg=5099,2016461&dq=nixon+pakistan+military&hl=en Retrieved on: January 4, 2014.

455. Orton, Anna (2010), "India's Borderland Disputes: China, Pakistan, Bangladesh, and Nepal", Epitome Books, New Delhi.pp.116.

456. "Library of Alexandria", Wikipedia, https://en.wikipedia.org/wiki/Library_of_Alexandria

457. Iqbal, Muhammed Zafar "Aro Aktukhani Bigyan", Kakali Prokashoni, Dhaka.

458. "South Africa", Wikipedia, https://en.wikipedia.org/wiki/South_Africa Retrieved on February 5, 2016

459. "History of slavery and early colonisation in South Africa", South African History Online, http://www.sahistory.org.za/south-africa-1652-1806/history-slavery-and-early-colonisation-sa Retrieved on February 5, 2016.

460. Eric Williams, Capitalism & Slavery, University of North Carolina Press, 1944, pp. 98–107, 169–177.

461. Inikori, Joseph E.; Engerman, Stanley L. The Atlantic Slave Trade: Effects on Economies, Societies and Peoples in Africa, the Americas, and Europe, http://www.livescience.com/6986-skeletons-discovered-african-slaves-world.html Retrieved on February 6, 2016

462. Marx, Karl. "Chapter Thirty-One: Genesis of the Industrial Capitalist". https://www.marxists.org/archive/marx/works/1867-c1/ch31.htm Retrieved on February 6, 2016

463. David Richardson, "The British Empire and the Atlantic Slave Trade, 1660-1807," in P. J. Marshall, ed. The Oxford History of the British Empire: Volume II: The Eighteenth Century (1998), pp. 440-64

464. Stanley L. Engerman. "The Slave Trade and British Capital Formation in the Eighteenth Century" 46: 430–443. JSTOR 3113341

465. Martin E. Hellman, Resist Not Evil in World Without Violence (Arun Gandhi ed.), M.K. Gandhi Institute, October 2, 1994, http://www-ee.stanford.edu/~hellman/opinion/Resist_Not.html Retrieved on February 6, 2016

466. Parel, Anthony J. (2002), "Gandhi and Tolstoy", in M. P. Mathai, M. S. John, Siby K. Joseph, Meditations on Gandhi : a Ravindra Varma festschrift, New Delhi: Concept, pp. 96–112

467. "Mahatma Gandhi", Wikipedia, https://en.wikipedia.org/wiki/Mahatma_Gandhi Retrieved on February 6, 2016.

468. Johnson, Richard L. (2006). Gandhi's Experiments With Truth: Essential Writings By And About Mahatma Gandhi. Lexington Books. p. 11. ISBN 978-0-7391-1143-7. Retrieved on 9 May 2012.

469. "John F Kennedy", Wikipedia, https://en.wikipedia.org/wiki/John_F._Kennedy Retrieved on February 7, 2016.

470. Ellis, Joseph J. (2000). "Making Vietnam History". Reviews in American History 28 (4): 625–629.

471. Talbot, David (June 21, 2007). "Warrior For Peace". Time Magazine. http://content.time.com/time/specials/2007/article/0,28804,1635958_1635999_1634954-5,00.html Retrieved on February 7, 2016.

472. Wang, Joy Y. "Obama to follow in John F. Kennedy's historic footsteps", MSNBC, August 4, 2015, http://www.msnbc.com/msnbc/obama-follow-john-f-kennedy-historic-footsteps, Retrieved on 6 August 2015.

473. Dallek, Robert (2003). An Unfinished Life: John F. Kennedy, 1917–1963. Boston, MA: Little, Brown and Co. ISBN 978-0-316-17238-7. P. 624.

474. Rhodes, Nick (2003). William Cowper: Selected Poems. Routledge, 2003, p.84.

475. Muir, Hugh (2014), "Livingstone weeps as he apologises for slavery", The Guardian, 24 August 2007,

http://www.theguardian.com/politics/2007/aug/24/london.humanrights Retrieved on February 6, 2016

476. Reeves, Richard (1993). President Kennedy: Profile of Power. New York: Simon & Schuster. ISBN 978-0-671-64879-4, p. 345-426.

477. Kennedy, John F. (1963), "A Strategy of Peace", Commencement Address at American University, June 10, 1963, John F. Kennedy Presidential Library and Museum, http://www.jfklibrary.org/Asset-Viewer/BWC7I4C9QUmLG9J6I8oy8w.aspx Retrieved on February 10, 2016.

478. Anstey, Roger (1975), "The Atlantic Slave Trade and British Abolition", 1760–1810. London: Macmillan, 1975.

479. Patrick Manning, "The Slave Trade: The Formal Dermographics of a Global System" in Joseph E. Inikori and Stanley L. Engerman (eds), The Atlantic Slave Trade: Effects on Economies, Societies and Peoples in Africa, the Americas, and Europe (Duke University Press, 1992), pp. 117-44, online at pp. 119-20.

Chapter 3: Economic Theories and Practices

1. Tucker, Irvin B. (1997). Macroeconomics for Today. pp. 553.

2. Case, Karl E. (2004). Principles of Macroeconomics. Prentice Hall.

3. Heinberg, Richard (2011), "The End of Growth: Adapting to our New Economic Reality", New Society Publishers, Canada. pp. 27-51.

4. William Greider, "The Education of David Stockman," Atlantic Magazine, December, 1981.

5. "History of Capitalism", Wikipedia, http://en.wikipedia.org/wiki/History_of_capitalism

6. "History of Economic Thought", Wikipedia, http://en.wikipedia.org/wiki/History_of_economic_thought

7. Marx, Karl (1859) A Contribution to the Critique of Political Economy, Das Kapital.

8. Marx, Karl (1867) 1976 Capital: A Critique of Political Economy Volume One trans. Ben Fowkes. Harmondsworth and London: Penguin Books and New Left Review. pp.875.

9. Pluta (2011) Joseph E., "Human Progress Amid Resistance to Change", FriesenPress, Victoria, BC, Canada, April, 2011.pp-149-183.

10. Pluta (2011) Joseph E., "Human Progress Amid Resistance to Change", FriesenPress, Victoria, BC, Canada, April, 2011.pp-100-114.

11. Smith, A. (1776), The Wealth of Nations edited by R.H. Campbell and A.S. Skinner, The Glasgow edition of the Works and Correspondence of Adam Smith, vol. 2b.

12. "History of Economic Thought", Wikipedia, http://en.wikipedia.org/wiki/History_of_economic_thought

13. "Physiocracy", Wikipedia, http://en.wikipedia.org/wiki/Physiocracy

14. Marroquin, Andres (2002), Invisible Hand: The Wealth of Adam Smith, The Minerva Group, Inc., 2002, ISBN 1-4102-0288-7, page 123.

15. Smith, Roy C. (2004), "Adam Smith and the Origins of American Enterprise: How the Founding Fathers Turned to a Great Economist's Writings and Created the American Economy", Macmillan, ISBN 0-312-32576-2, pp. 13–14.

16. Kennet, M. and Heinemann, V. (2006), Green Economics: setting the scene. Aims, context, and philosophical underpinning of the distinctive new solutions offered by Green Economics, Int. J. Green Economics, Vol. 1, Nos. 1/2, pp.68–102.

17. Ekelund, Robert B. and Hebert, Robert F. (1997), A History of Economic Theory and Method, 4th ed., McGraw Hill, New York, pp-118.

18. http://en.wikipedia.org/wiki/Capitalism_and_Islam

19. Said Amir Arjomand (1999), "The Law, Agency, and Policy in Medieval Islamic Society: Development of the Institutions of Learning from the Tenth to the Fifteenth

Century", Comparative Studies in Society and History 41, pp. 263–93. Cambridge University Press.

20. Jairus Banaji (2007), "Islam, the Mediterranean and the rise of capitalism", Journal Historical Materialism 15 (1), Brill Publishers. Pp. p. 47-74.

21. Ibn Khaldun, The Muqaddimah, An Introduction to History (Princeton:Princeton University Press, 1967) (translated by Franz Rosenthal). In this book (pp273-338), Khaldun also presented a forerunner of the multiplier principle, which John Maynard Keynes would advance in the 1930s. Khaldun stated the concept that income equals expenditures, argued that capital accumulation lead to economic growth, encouraged low rates of taxation, presented a modern theory of the role of money, and even developed versions of cost-push and demand-pull inflation.

22. Hamid Hosseini, "Seeking the Roots of Adam Smith's Division of Labor in Medieval Persia," History of Political Economy, 30 (4) (Winter 1998), p.655.

23. Bentham, Jeremy (1789) "An Introduction to the Principles of Morals and Legislation".

24. Malthus, Thomas R (1798), An Essay on the Principle of Population, London.

25. Who is Thomas Malthus?, All About Science, http://www.allaboutscience.org/malthus-faq.htm

26. BBC, Historical figures–Thomas Malthus (1766–1834), http://www.bbc.co.uk/history/historic_figures/malthus_thomas.shtml.

27. "Thesis, Antithesis & Synthesis", Wikipedia, http://en.wikipedia.org/wiki/Thesis,_antithesis,_synthesis

28. "The Accessible Hegel", Michael Allen Fox. Prometheus Books. 2005. p.43. Also see Hegel's preface to the Phenomenology of Spirit, trans. A.V. Miller (Oxford: Clarendon Press, 1977), secs. 50, 51, p.29. 30.

29. Immanuel Kant (Stanford Encyclopedia of Philosophy)". Plato.stanford.edu. 20 May 2010, http://plato.stanford.edu/entries/kant/ Retrieved on: January 4, 2013.

30. "Dialectical Materialism", Wikipedia, http://en.wikipedia.org/wiki/Dialectical_materialism

31. "Capitalism", Wikipedia, http://en.wikipedia.org/wiki/Capitalism

32. "Antoine   Augustin   Cournot",   Wikipedia,
    http://en.wikipedia.org/wiki/Antoine_Augustin_Cournot

33. "Nash Equilibrium", Wikipedia, http://en.wikipedia.org/wiki/Nash_equilibrium

34. Pluta (2011) Joseph E., "Human Progress Amid Resistance to Change",
    FriesenPress, Victoria, BC, Canada, April, 2011.pp-185-212.

35. Quigley, Carroll (1966), "Tragedy and Hope: A History of The World in Our Time",
    The Macmillan Company, New York, pp.41

36. Marx, Capital, ch. 32, 837.

37. Spencer, Herbert (1864), "Principles of Biology", vol. 1, p. 444.

38. Steve J. Shone, "Cultural Relativism and the Savage: The Alleged Inconsistency of
    William Graham Sumner," American Journal of Economics and Sociology 63, no.3,
    July 2004, pp.697-716 and Rick Tilman, "Herbert Spencer and Political Economy of
    Mean-Spiritedness Revived," Journal of the History of Economic Thought, 21, no 2,
    June 1999, pp.137-144.

39. Claeys, Gregory (2000). "The "Survival of the Fittest" and the Origins of Social
    Darwinism", Journal of the History of Ideas 61 (2):223-240.

40. Peukert, Detlev (1994), "The Genesis of the 'Final Solution' from the Spirit of
    Science" pages 274–299 from Nazism and German Society, 1933–1945 edited by
    David F. Crew, London: Routledge, 1994 page 288.

41. Burleigh, Michael (2000), "Psychiatry, Society and Nazi "Euthanasia" pages 43–62
    from The Holocaust: Origins, Implementation, Aftermath edited by Omer Bartov,
    London: Routledge, 2000, pages 47–48.

42. Sonja M. Hedgepeth; Rochelle G. Saidel (2010). Sexual violence against Jewish
    women during the Holocaust. UPNE. p. 16. ISBN 978-1-58465-905-1.

43. Weintraub, E. Roy (2007). Neoclassical Economics. The Concise Encyclopedia Of Economics. Retrieved on September 26, 2010, from http://www.econlib.org/library/Enc1/NeoclassicalEconomics.html

44. Jevons, William S. (1871), "Theory of Political Economy", Macmillan and Co., London.

45. Walras, Leon (1954), "Elements of Pure Economics", Augustus M Kelley Pubs.

46. Alan Kirman (2008). "Pareto, Vilfredo (1848–1923)", Efficiency or 'Pareto optimality', The New Palgrave Dictionary of Economics. Abstract. Pareto (1897). "Cours d'économie politique", v. 2. Pareto (1906). "Manual of Political Economy", ch. 6, Mathematical Appendix, sect. 145-52. Translation of French edition from 1927.

47. Marshall, Alfred (1920). Principles of Economics (Revised Edition ed.). London: Macmillan; reprinted by Prometheus Books.

48. "Partial Equilibrium", Wikipedia, http://en.wikipedia.org/wiki/Partial_equilibrium

49. Dieterle, David A. (2013), "Economic Thinkers: A Biographical Encyclopedia: A Biographical Encyclopedia", ABC-CLIO, 2013, ISBN 0313397473, 9780313397479

50. Pigou, A.C. (1934), "The Theory of Unemployment", Routledge; New issue of 1933 ed edition (March 9, 1968)

51. "Neoclassical Economics", Wikipedia, http://en.wikipedia.org/wiki/Neoclassical_economics

52. Arrow, Kenneth J. (1994), "Methodological Individualism and Social Knowledge," American Economic Review, 84(2), p p. 1-9

53. Schumpeter, Joseph (1908). "Methodological Individualism" (PDF). Das Wesen und Hauptinhalt der theoretischen Nationalokonomie (The Nature and Essence of Theoretical Economics).

54. Schumpeter, Joseph (2013). "Capitalism, Socialism and Democracy" Routledge,2013 ISBN 1134841507, 9781134841509.

55. "General Equilibrium Theory", Wikipedia, http://en.wikipedia.org/wiki/General_equilibrium_theory

56. Roncaglia, Alessandro (2005). The wealth of ideas: a history of economic thought. Cambridge University Press. 2005.

57. "Capitalism", Wikipedia, http://en.wikipedia.org/wiki/Capitalism

58. Wittman, Donald (2004), The Encyclopedia of Public Choice, edited by Charles Rowley, Friedrich Schneider, "Efficiency of Democracy", pp.186

59. Stiglitz, J.E. & Greenwald B. "Keynesian, New Keynesian and New Classical Economics", Oxford Economic Papers, New Series, Vol. 39, No. 1 (Mar., 1987), pp. 119-133, http://www.jstor.org/stable/2663132

60. Keynes, John Maynard (1936), "The General Theory of Employment, Interest, and Money", Chapter 19, Palgrave Macmillan, UK.

61. "Keynesian Economics", Wikipedia, http://en.wikipedia.org/wiki/Keynesian_economics

62. "Great Depression", Wikipedia, http://en.wikipedia.org/wiki/Great_Depression

63. Fisher, Irving (1933), "Debt- Deflation Theory of Great Depressions", https://fraser.stlouisfed.org/docs/meltzer/fisdeb33.pdf

64. "The Classic view of Saving & Investment.", This graph is created at the English language Wikipedia on 23 July 2004 and licensed under the Creative Commons Attribution-Share Alike 3.0 http://en.wikipedia.org/wiki/File:CLASSIX.png Retrieved on January 16, 2014.

65. "The Keynesian view of Saving & Investment". This graph is created at the English language Wikipedia and licensed under the Creative Commons Attribution-Share Alike 3.0 Unported license. Wikipedia. Permission was granted to copy, distribute and/or modify this document under the terms of the GNU Free Documentation

License, Version 1.2 or any later version published by the Free Software Foundation http://en.wikipedia.org/wiki/File:KEYNES.png Retrieved on January 16, 2014.

66. Keynes, John Maynard (1924). "The Theory of Money and the Foreign Exchanges". A Tract on Monetary Reform.

67. Klein, Lawrence R. (1947), "The Keynesian Revolution", Macmillan, New York: . pp. 56–58, 169, 177–79. Rosenof, Theodore (1997). Economics in the Long Run: New Deal Theorists and Their Legacies, 1933–1993. Chapel Hill: University of North Carolina Press. ISBN 0-8078-2315-5.

68. Romer, Christina D. (1992), "What Ended the Great Depression?". Journal of Economic History 52 (4).

69. "Patience Is a Virtue When Normalizing Monetary Policy", Speech by Charles Evans, Federal Reserve Bank of Chicago, 24 September, 2014 http://www.chicagofed.org/webpages/publications/speeches/2014/09-24-14-charles-evans-patience-monetary-policy-peterson-institute.cfm

70. "Economic Policy - Intervention Strategy Matrix", This table is created at Wikipedia and licensed under the Creative Commons Attribution-Share Alike 3.0 Unported license. Permission was granted to copy, distribute and/or modify this document under the terms of the GNU Free Documentation License, Version 1.2 or any later version published by the Free Software Foundation http://en.wikipedia.org/wiki/File:Economic_Policy_-_Intervention_Strategy_Matrix.png

71. David M. Kennedy (1999), "Freedom From Fear, The American People in Depression and War 1929 – 1945", Oxford University Press, 1999, ISBN 0-19-503834-7, p. 122, 123

72. Eichengreen, Barry (1992). Golden Fetters: The Gold Standard and the Great Depression, 1919–1939. New York: Oxford University Press. ISBN 0-19-506431-3

73. Phillips, A. W. (1958). "The Relationship between Unemployment and the Rate of Change of Money Wages in the United Kingdom 1861-1957". Economica 25 (100): 283–299.

74. "Phillips Curve", Wikipedia, http://en.wikipedia.org/wiki/Phillips_curve

75. Samuelson, Paul (2008), Foreword to "Understanding Inflation and the Implications for Monetary Policy: A Phillips Curve Retrospective", FRBB Conference Series 53, Chatham, Massachusetts.

76. Friedman, Milton (1968). "The role of monetary policy". American Economic Review 68 (1): 1–17. JSTOR 1831652

77. Phelps, Edmund S. (1968). "Money-Wage Dynamics and Labor Market Equilibrium". Journal of Political Economy 76 (S4): 678–711. doi:10.1086/259438.

78. Short-Run Phillips Curve before and after Expansionary Policy, with Long-Run Phillips Curve (NAIRU)", This file is licensed under the Creative Commons Attribution-Share Alike 3.0 Unported license. Permission was granted to copy, distribute and/or modify this document under the terms of the GNU Free Documentation License, Version 1.2 or any later version published by the Free Software Foundation. http://en.wikipedia.org/wiki/File:NAIRU-SR-and-LR.svg

79. Domitrovic, Brain (10 October 2011). "The Economics Nobel Goes to Sargent & Sims: Attackers of the Phillips Curve". Forbes.com. http://www.forbes.com/sites/briandomitrovic/2011/10/10/the-economics-nobel-goes-to-sargent-sims-attackers-of-the-phillips-curve.

80. "Larry Summers: 'I think Keynes mistitled his book'", by Ezra Klein, The Washington Post, July 26, 2011, http://www.washingtonpost.com/blogs/wonkblog/post/larry-summers-i-think-keynes-mistitled-his-book/2011/07/11/gIQAzZd4aI_blog.html

81. Lucas, Robert E. Jr. Models of Business Cycles. Oxford: Basil Blackwell, 1987.

82. Kennet, Miriam. and Heinemann, V. (2006), Green Economics: setting the scene. Aims, context, and philosophical underpinning of the distinctive new solutions offered by Green Economics, Int. J. Green Economics, Vol. 1, Nos. 1/2, pp.68–102.

83. Snowdon and Vane (2005), "Modern Macroeconomics: Its Origins, Development And Current State", Edward Elgar Pub, p. 388.

84. Shapiro, C. and Stiglitz, J. (1984), "Equilibrium unemployment as a worker discipline device," American Economic Review, June 1984.

85. "Efficiency wage Shapiro Stiglitz", This graph is created at Wikipedia and licensed under the This file is licensed under the This file is licensed under the Creative Commons Attribution-Share Alike 3.0 Unported license. Permission was granted to copy, distribute and/or modify this document under the terms of the GNU Free Documentation License, Version 1.2 or any later version published by the Free Software   Foundation http://en.wikipedia.org/wiki/File:Efficiency_wage_Shapiro_Stiglitz.svg

86. Araujo, Ricardo and Sachsida, Adolfo (2010), "Adverse Selection in an Efficiency Wage Model with Heterogeneous Agents", Revista Economia, September/December 2010.

87. Mankiw, Gregory N. & Taylor, Mark P. (2008), Macroeconomics (European edition), pp. 181–182.

88. "Dynamic   Stochastic   General   Equilibrium",   Wikipedia, http://en.wikipedia.org/wiki/Dynamic_stochastic_general_equilibrium

89. Bartlett, Bruce. "Supply-Side Economics: "Voodoo Economics" or Lasting Contribution?". Laffer Associates: Supply-Side Investment Research (November 11, 2003). http://web.uconn.edu/cunningham/econ309/lafferpdf.pdf Retrieved on 2014-02-22.

90. "Supply   Side   Economics",   Wikipedia,   http://en.wikipedia.org/wiki/Supply-side_economics

91. Malabre, Jr., Alfred L. (1994). Lost Prophets: An Insider's History of the Modern Economists, p. 182. Harvard Business School Press. ISBN 0-87584-441-3

92. Harper, David (2013) "Understanding Supply-Side Economics", Investopedia, November 04, 2013, http://www.investopedia.com/articles/05/011805.asp

93. "Monetary Policy", Wikipedia, http://en.wikipedia.org/wiki/Monetary_policy

94. Friedman, Milton (1948). "A Monetary and Fiscal Framework for Economic Stability". American Economic Review 38 (3): 245–264, http://www.hilbertcorporation.com.ar/amonetaryandfiscaleconomicstability.pdf

95. Friedman, Milton (1960). A Program for Monetary Stability. Fordham University Press.

96. Bernanke, Ben (2006). "Monetary Aggregates and Monetary Policy at the Federal Reserve: A Historical Perspective". Federal Reserve.

97. Laffer, Arthur (2004) "The Laffer Curve, Past, Present and Future." Heritage Foundation, http://www.heritage.org/research/reports/2004/06/the-laffer-curve-past-present-and-future Retrieved on: February 27, 2014

98. "How Far Are We From The Slippery Slope? The Laffer Curve Revisited" by Mathias Trabandt and Harald Uhlig, NBER Working Paper No. 15343, September 2009, http://www.nber.org/papers/w15343 Retrieved on: February 25, 2014.

99. "The standard Laffer Curve", Permission is granted to copy, distribute and/or modify this document under the terms of the GNU Free Documentation License, Version 1.2. This file is licensed under the Creative Commons Attribution 3.0 Unported license. Permission:CC-BY-3.0; Attribution: Vanessaezekowitz at en.wikipedia, http://en.wikipedia.org/wiki/File:Laffer-Curve.svg Retrieved on February 25, 2014.

100. Stuart, C. E. (1981). "Swedish Tax Rates, Labor Supply, and Tax Revenues". The Journal of Political Economy 89 (5): 1020–1038. doi:10.1086/261018. JSTOR 1830818.

101. Ali, Imam (1978). "Nahjul Balagha". Imam Ali. http://www.imamalinet.net/old/en/nahj/nahj.htm Retrieved on: March 1, 2014.

102. The White House, Economic Report of the President, January 1963.

103. This image displays U.S. federal government tax receipts as a percentage of GDP from 1945 to 2015 according to data from the Office of Management and Budget's Historical Tables, Table 1.2. This work has been released into the public domain by its author at the Wikipedia. The author grants anyone the right to use this work for

any purpose, without any conditions, unless such conditions are required by law. http://en.wikipedia.org/wiki/File:U.S._Federal_Tax_Receipts_as_a_Percentage_of_GDP_1945%E2%80%932015.jpg Retrieved on February 21, 2014.

104. Blinder, A. S. (2006). "Can fiscal policy improve macro-stabilization". In Kopcke, E.; Tootell, G. M. B.; Triest, R. K. The macroeconomics of fiscal policy. Cambridge, MA: MIT Press. pp. 23–62. ISBN 0-262-11295-7.

105. Quote from Mankiw with source in Bartels, L. M. (2008). Unequal democracy: The political-economy of the new gilded age. Princeton, NJ: Princeton University Press. ISBN 978-0-691-13663-9.

106. Tobin, J. (1992). "Voodoo curse". Harvard International Review 14 (4): 10.

107. Case, K. E.; Fair, R. C. (2007). Principles of Economics (8th ed.). Upper Saddle Rive, NJ: Prentice Hall. ISBN 0-13-228914-8, p.695.

108. Mundell, Robert A (1999), "A Reconsideration of the Twentieth Century", December 8, 1999, Aula Magna, Stockholm University, http://www.nobelprize.org/nobel_prizes/economic-sciences/laureates/1999/mundell-lecture.pdf

109. Heinberg, Richard (2015), "Afterburn: Society Beyond Fossil Fuels", New Society Publishers, Canada, January 2015.

110. Federal Government Finances and Employment 1990, US Census Bureau, http://www2.census.gov/prod2/statcomp/documents/1990-04.pdf

111. "Analyzing the Economic and Budgetary Effects of a 10 Percent Cut in Income Tax Rates", Congressional Budget Office, December 1, 2005 http://www.cbo.gov/sites/default/files/cbofiles/ftpdocs/69xx/doc6908/12-01-10percenttaxcut.pdf Retrieved on: February 27, 2014.

112. Krugman, Paul (2005-12-23). "The Tax Cut Zombies". New York Times.

113. Galbraith, John Kenneth (1982-02-04). "Recession Economics". New York Review of Books.

114. "Welfare Capitalism", Wikipedia, http://en.wikipedia.org/wiki/Welfare_capitalism

115. Crone, Patricia (2005), Medieval Islamic Political Thought, Edinburgh University Press, pp. 308–9, ISBN 0-7486-2194-6.

116. "The Contradiction of Capitalism in the Search for Democracy", Latin American Perspectives, Vol. 24, No. 3, Ecuador, Part 1: Politics and Rural Issues (May, 1997), pp. 116-122

117. R.R. Palmer, "How Five Centuries of Educational Philanthropy Disappeared in the French Revolution," History of Education Quarterly (1986) 26#2 pp. 181–197 in JSTOR.

118. "French Revolution", Wikipedia, http://en.wikipedia.org/wiki/French_Revolution

119. A. L. Morton. The Life and Ideas of Robert Owen (London, Lawrence & Wishart, 1962).

120. Esping-Andersen, Gosta (1990) "The Three Worlds of Welfare Capitalism", Princeton University Press, ISBN-10: 0691028575.

121. R. Jagannathan, Socio-Capitalism Set to Become the New Economic Doctrine, May 10, 2009, available at http://www.dnaindia.com/report.asp?newsid=1254764

122. Emanuele Ferragina and Martin Seeleib-Kaiser (2011). Welfare regime debate: past, present, futures. Policy & Politics. p. 584.

123. John McManners, The French Revolution and the Church, p 5.

124. R. Jagannathan, Socio-Capitalism Set to Become the New Economic Doctrine, May 10, 2009, available at http://www.dnaindia.com/report.asp?newsid=1254764 Retrieved on: 12 March, 2013.

125. Steven A. Ramirez, Fear and Social Capitalism: The Law and Macroeconomics of Investor Confidence, available at http://papers.ssrn.com/sol3/papers.cfm?abstract_id=1088436

126. Kevin Rudd, The Global Financial Crisis, The Monthly, Feb. 2009 available at http://www.themonthly.com.au/node/1421

127. Kees van Kersbergen, Social Capitalism: A Study of Christian Democracy and the Welfare State (Routledge 1995) available at http://search.barnesandnoble.com/Social-Capitalism/Kees-Van-Kersbergen/e/9780415116701

128. Corfe, Robert (2008), "The People's Capitalism-- Volume 2 of Social Capitalism in Theory and Practice: People's Capitalism v. II", Arena Books Ltd, ISBN-10: 0955605547.

129. "Social Market economy", Wikipedia, http://en.wikipedia.org/wiki/Social_market_economy

130. Müller-Armack, A., Wirtschaftslenkung und Marktwirtschaft, Hamburg, 1946, p. 88. However, the question of the origins of the term Soziale Marktwirtschaft is still controversial. In his autobiography Wahrheit und Wirklichkeit. Der Weg aus den Weltkriegen in die Soziale Marktwirtschaft und eine künftige Weltordnung, Homburg-Saarplatz, 1996, pp. 571 ff., Karl Günther Weiss, academic assistant to the former permanent representative of the State Secretary in the Reich Ministry of Economics, Otto Ohlendorf, argues, the term 'Social Market Economy' was the outcome of a discussion with Ludwig Erhard on 12 Jan 1945. There is also some evidence that Harold Rasch, who in 1946/47 was deputy head of the inter-zonal economic administration in Minden, used the term in late 1947 and early 1948 independently of Müller-Armack (1901–1978); cf. Rasch, H., Grundlagen der Wirtschaftsverfassung, Bad Godesberg, 1948.

131. Koppstein, Jeffrey; Lichbach, Mark Irving (2005), Comparative Politics: Interests, Identities, And Institutions In A Changing Global Order, Cambridge University Press, ISBN 0-521-60359-1 , p. 156

132. Müller-Armack, A., Auf dem Weg nach Europa. Erinnerungen und Ausblicke, Tübingen/ Stuttgart, 1971, pp. 50.

133. Oppenheimer, F., System der Soziologie (III/1). Band 3: Theorie der reinen und politischen Ökonomie, Teil 1: Grundlagen, Jena, 1910, p. 9. The economist Franz Oppenheimer (1864-1943) also published his economic conception in Sprung über ein Jahrhundert, Bern/ Leipzig, 1935 under the pseudonym F. D. Pelton.

134. Oppenheimer supervised Erhard's doctoral thesis titled 'Wesen und Inhalt der Werteinheit', namely a study on various historical schools' perception of character and content of value, in the years 1922 to 1925.

135. Crouch, Colin; Streeck, Wolfgang (2000), Political Economy of Modern Capitalism: Mapping Convergence and Diversity, SAGE Publications Ltd., ISBN 0-7619-5653, p. 56

136. "Japanese Post war Economic Miracle", Wikipedia, http://en.wikipedia.org/wiki/Japanese_post-war_economic_miracle

137. "Japan GDP Growth Rate 1980-2014", Trading Economics, http://www.tradingeconomics.com/japan/gdp-growth

138. Albert, Michel: Capitalism Against Capitalism. London: Whurr, 1993. -ISBN 1-870332-54-7.

139. Veblen, Thorstein. 1898. "Why is Economics Not an Evolutionary Science." The Quarterly Journal of Economics. vol. 12, 1898.

140. Pluta (2011) Joseph E., "Human Progress Amid Resistance to Change", FriesenPress, Victoria, BC, Canada, April, 2011.pp-251-324.

141. "Institutional Economics", Wikipedia, http://en.wikipedia.org/wiki/Institutional_economics

142. Brown, Christopher (2005), "Is There an Institutional Theory of Distribution", Journal of Economic Issues, 39, no.4, p.926.

143. Berle, Adolf and Gardiner C. Means (1967) The Modern Corporation and Private Property, 2nd edn Harcourt, Brace and World, New York, 1967, ISBN 0-88738-887-6.

144. Galbraith, John Kenneth, (1973). "Power & the Useful Economist," American Economic Review 63:1-11.

145. Coase, Ronald (1937). "The Nature of the Firm". Economica (Blackwell Publishing) 4 (16): 386–405.

146. Coase, Ronald (1960). "The Problem of Social Cost". Journal of Law and Economics 3: 1-44.

147. North, Douglass C., (1994). Economic Performance through Time, American Economic Review, Vol.84, No.3, pp-359-368.

148. Wallis, John J., and Douglass C. North, (1986) "Measuring the Transaction Sector in the American Economy, " in S.L. Engerman and R.E. Gallman, (eds.), Long Term Factors in American Economic Growth, Chicago: University of Chicago Press.

149. From the Introduction. Kwame Nkrumah. Neo-Colonialism, The Last Stage of Imperialism. First Published: Thomas Nelson & Sons, Ltd., London (1965). Published in the USA by International Publishers Co., Inc., (1966);

150. Vladimir Ilyich Lenin. Imperialism, the Highest Stage of Capitalism. transcribed from Lenin's Selected Works, Progress Publishers, 1963, Moscow, Volume 1, pp. 667–766.

151. Ernest Mandel, "Semicolonial Countries and Semi-Industrialised Dependent Countries", New International (New York), No.5, pp.149-175.

152. "Neocolonialism", Wikipedia, http://en.wikipedia.org/wiki/Neocolonialism

153. Anuradha M. Chenoy. "Soviet New Thinking on National Liberation Movements: Continuity and Change", Soviet Foreign Policy in Transition pp. 145–162. Roger E. Kanet, Deborah Nutter Miner, Tamara J. Resler, International Committee for Soviet and East European Studies. Cambridge University Press, (1992) ISBN 0-521-41365-6; See pp. 149–150 for the Soviet Bloc academic definitions of "Neo-colonialism".

154. Henderson, Dean (2010), "Big Oil & Their Bankers in the Persian Gulf: Four Horsemen, Eight Families & Their Global Intelligence, Narcotics & Terror Network", Createspace, ISBN-10: 1453757732, pp.345-348.

155. Richard Nixon, "25 - Address on the State of the Union Delivered Before a Joint Session of the Congress", January 30, 1974, http://www.presidency.ucsb.edu/ws/?pid=4327 Retrieved on: January 6, 2013.

156. Riley, Kevin M. (2011), "Oil and the U.S. Dollar", Columbia University, June 27, 2011, https://www.academia.edu/1253274/Oil_and_the_U.S._Dollar Retrieved on: January 5, 2014.

157. Spiro, David E (1999), "The Hidden Hand of American Hegemony: Petrodollar Recycling and International Markets", Ithaca, NY: Cornell UP, 1999. pp.31.

158. "Economy of Saudi Arabia", Wikipedia, http://en.wikipedia.org/wiki/Economy_of_Saudi_Arabia

159. Mosley, Paul; Harrigan, Jane; Toye, John (1995). Aid and Power: The World Bank and Policy Based Lending, 2nd Edition 1. Abington, UK: Routledge. ISBN 978-0-415-13209-1.

160. Cornia, Giovanni Andrea; Jolly, Richard; Stewart, Frances, eds. (1987). Adjustment with a Human Face: Protecting the Vulnerable and Promoting Growth. New York, NY: Oxford University Press USA. ISBN 978-0-19-828609-0.

161. Committee on Foreign Relations, United States Senate, 111th Congress (2010). The International Financial Institutions: A Call For Change (Report). U.S. Government Printing Office. http://www.foreign.senate.gov/imo/media/doc/55285.pdf.

162. Tan, Celine (2007). "The poverty of amnesia: PRSPs in the legacy of structural adjustment". In Stone, Diane; Wright, Christopher. The World Bank and Governance: A Decade of Reform and Reaction. New York, NY: Routledge. ISBN 978-0-41-541282-7.

163. Chossudovsky, Michel (1997). The Globalisation of Poverty: Impacts of IMF and World Bank Reforms. London, UK: Zed Books. ISBN 978-1-85-659401-4.

164. Perkins, John (2005), "Confessions of an Economic Hit Man", Plume, ISBN-10: 0452287081, ISBN-13: 978-0452287082

165. Heinberg, Richard (2011), "The End of Growth: Adapting to our New Economic Reality", New Society Publishers, Canada. pp. 189-230.

166. Quammen, David (2005), "Views of the Continents", National Geographic, Vol.208, No.3, September 2005, pp. 2-35.

167. "Petroleum Industry in Nigeria", Wikipedia, http://en.wikipedia.org/wiki/Petroleum_industry_in_Nigeria

168. Okonta, Ike & Douglas, Oronto (2003) ,"Where Vultures Feast: Shell, Human Rights, and Oil in the Niger Delta", Verso,ISBN-10: 1859844731.

169. "Health Care in Nigeria", Wikipedia, http://en.wikipedia.org/wiki/Health_care_in_Nigeria

170. "AIDS in Nigeria", Wikipedia, http://en.wikipedia.org/wiki/HIV/AIDS_in_Nigeria

171. "World Bank, IMF Threw Colombia Into Tailspin" The Baltimore Sun, April 4, 2002, http://articles.baltimoresun.com/2002-04-04/news/0204040117_1_colombia-bank-and-imf-industrial-sector Retrieved on: January 10, 2014.

172. "Bangladesh Takes Step to Increase Lowest Pay", by Jim Yardley, November 4, 2013, The New York Times, http://www.nytimes.com/2013/11/05/world/asia/bangladesh-takes-step-toward-raising-38-a-month-minimum-wage.html Retrieved on: January 10, 2014.

173. "Will the Bangladesh factory collapse change global apparel supply chains? By: Marty Lariviere May 10, 2013, Chicago Business, http://www.chicagobusiness.com/article/20130510/OPINION/130509707/will-the-bangladesh-factory-collapse-change-global-apparel-supply-chains# Retrieved on: January 10, 2014.

174. "The Contradiction of Capitalism in the Search for Democracy", Latin American Perspectives, Vol. 24, No. 3, Ecuador, Part 1: Politics and Rural Issues (May, 1997), pp. 116-122

175. "Financial Capitalism", Wikipedia, http://en.wikipedia.org/wiki/Finance_capitalism

176. Frederic Jameson, 'Culture and Finance Capital', in The Jameson Reader (2005) p. 257

177. Quoted in E. H. Carr, The Bolshevik Revolution 2 (1971) p. 137

178. Sherman, Matthew (2009), "A Short History of Financial Deregulation in the United States", Center for Economic and Policy Research, July 2009, http://www.cepr.net/documents/publications/dereg-timeline-2009-07.pdf

179. "Big Bang", Wikipedia, http://en.wikipedia.org/wiki/Big_Bang_(financial_markets)

180. Strange, Susan (1986), "Casino Capitalism", ISBN 0-7190-5235-1, Manchester University Press.

181. Thomas Palley, From Financial Crisis to Stagnation (2012) p. 218

182. PBS Frontline, "The Long Demise of Glass-Steagall," The Wall Street Fix, May 8, 2003. http://www.pbs.org/wgbh/pages/frontline/shows/wallstreet/weill/demise.html

183. Broome, Lissa Lamkin; & Markham, Jerry W. (2001). The Gramm–Leach–Bliley Act: An Overview. Retrieved on from http://www.symtrex.com/pdfdocs/glb_paper.pdf. .

184. Barth, James R., R. Dan Brumbaugh Jr. and James A. Wilcox, "The Repeal of Glass Steagall and the Advent of Broad Banking," Journal of Economic Perspectives, vol. 14, no. 2, Spring 2000. http://www.business.auburn.edu/~barthjr/papers/The%20Repeal%20of%20Glass-Steagall.pdf

185. "Derivatives: Innovation in the Era of Financial Deregulation", by Wallace C. Turbeville, Demos, 13 June 2013, http://www.demos.org/publication/derivatives-innovation-era-financial-deregulation

186. Faiola, Anthony, Ellen Nakashima and Jill Drew, "What Went Wrong," Washington Post, October 15, 2008, http://www.washingtonpost.com/wp-dyn/content/story/2008/10/14/ST2008101403344.html

187. Blumenthal, Paul, "Read the Bill: The Commodity Futures Modernization Act," Sunlight Foundation, April 1, 2009, http://blog.sunlightfoundation.com/2009/04/01/read-the-bill-the-commodity-futures-modernization-act/

188. "A price worth paying?". Analysis. 1 February 2010. 0-13 minutes in. BBC Radio 4, http://www.bbc.co.uk/radio/player/b00qbxwj Retrieved on 23 November, 2014.

189. "Gordon Brown admits 'big mistake' over banking crisis". The BBC. 11 April 2011, http://www.bbc.co.uk/news/business-13032013 Retrieved on 23 November 2014.

190. Goodman, Peter S., "Taking Hard New Look at a Greenspan Legacy," New York Times, October 8, 2008. http://www.nytimes.com/2008/10/09/business/economy/09greenspan.html

191. "Total world wealth versus total notional value in derivatives contracts, 1998-2007", This graph is created at Wikipedia self-made using world derivatives data from the Bank for International Settlements at: http://www.bis.org/statistics/derstats.htm The file with the data from 1998-2007 is: http://www.bis.org/statistics/otcder/dt1920a.csv The world wealth is in the United Nations report on household wealth in the year 2000 at: http://www.wider.unu.edu/research/2006-2007/2006-2007-1/wider-wdhw-launch-5-12-2006/wider-wdhw-report-5-12-2006.pdf. The author of this work, hereby release it into the public domain. http://en.wikipedia.org/wiki/File:Total_world_wealth_vs_total_world_derivatives_1998-2007.gif

192. "Clear and Present Danger: Clearing-houses may add danger as well as efficiency", The Economist, April 7, 2012, Retrieved on January 1, 2014. http://www.economist.com/node/21552217

193. "Derivative (finance)", Wikipedia, http://en.wikipedia.org/wiki/Derivative_%28finance%29

194. Stever, Ryan; Upper, Christian; Peter, Goetz von (2007). BIS Quarterly Review (PDF) (Report). Bank for International Settlements, December 2007, http://www.bis.org/publ/qtrpdf/r_qt0712.pdf

195. Liu, Qiao; Lejot, Paul (2013). "Debt, Derivatives and complex interactions". Finance in Asia: Institutions, Regulation and Policy. Douglas W. Arne. New York: Routledge. p. 343. ISBN 978-0-415-42319-9.

196. "Gross Domestic Product 2013" (PDF). The World Bank DataBank. 2014., http://databank.worldbank.org/data/download/GDP.pdf

197. Gabriel O'Hara, "The $531 Trillion Dollar Derivatives Time Bomb", Wise Up Journal, September 1, 2009, http://www.infowars.com/the-531-trillion-dollar-derivatives-time-bomb/

198. "Buffett warns on investment 'time bomb'", BBC News, March 4, 2003, http://news.bbc.co.uk/2/hi/2817995.stm

199. "Greenspan Discusses Risks of Derivatives", May 09, 2003, The New York Times, May 09, 2003, http://www.nytimes.com/2003/05/09/business/greenspan-discusses-risks-of-derivatives.html?fta=y

200. "Taking Hard New Look at a Greenspan Legacy", by Goodman, Peter, The New York Times, October 8, 2008, http://www.nytimes.com/2008/10/09/business/economy/09greenspan.html?pagewanted=all

201. "Greenspan Concedes Error on Regulation", by Andrews, Edmund, The New York Times, October 23, 2008, http://www.nytimes.com/2008/10/24/business/economy/24panel.html?_r=0

202. Edlin, A. and J. E. Stiglitz (1995), "Discouraging Rivals: Managerial Rent–Seeking and Economic Inefficiencies", American Economic Review 85(5): pp. 1301–12.

203. Greenwald, Bruce and Joseph E. Stiglitz (1986), "Externalities in economies with imperfect information and incomplete markets". Quarterly Journal of Economics 101: 229-264.

Chapter 4: New Concept "Biased Equilibrium"

1. Stiglitz, Joseph E. (2002) Information and the Change in the Paradigm in Economics, The American Economic Review, Vol. 92, No. 3 (Jun., 2002), pp. 460-501.

2. "The Fundamental Difference Between Mainstream and Heterodox Economics", Unlearning Economics, http://unlearningeconomics.wordpress.com/2012/07/09/the-

fundamental-difference-between-mainstream-and-heterodox-economics/ Retrieved on September 4, 2014.

3. Zaman, M. (2012), "A Consolidated Economic Model Based on a New Concept of Biased Equilibrium", International Journal of Green Economics 2012 - Vol. 6, No.1 pp. 55 - 72.

4. "Information Economics", Wikipedia, http://en.wikipedia.org/wiki/Information_economics

5. Zaman, M. (2009), "Welfare Dynamics Based on a New Concept of Biased Equilibrium", Oxford Business and Economics Conference, Oxford University.

6. Nash, John (1951) "Non-Cooperative Games" The Annals of Mathematics 54(2):286-295.

7. Stiglitz, J. E. and A. Weiss (1983), "Incentive Effects of Termination: Applications to the Credit and Labor Markets," American Economic Review, 73(5), pp. 912–927.

8. "The Accessible Hegel", Michael Allen Fox. Prometheus Books. 2005. p.43. Also see Hegel's preface to the Phenomenology of Spirit, trans. A.V. Miller (Oxford: Clarendon Press, 1977), secs. 50, 51, p.29. 30.

9. Scott, John (2005). Industrialism: A Dictionary of Sociology. Oxford University Press.

10. Marx, Karl (1859) A Contribution to the Critique of Political Economy, Das Kapital.

11. Stiglitz, J.E. and Greenwald, B.C. (1986), "Externalities in Economies with Imperfect Information and Incomplete markets", Quarterly Journal of Economics, Vol. 101, No. 2, pp.229–264.

12. Sen, A.K. (1985), "Commodities and Capabilities," Oxford University Press, Oxford.

13. "Pareto Efficiency", Wikipedia, http://en.wikipedia.org/wiki/Pareto_efficiency

14. Debreu, G. (1959), "Theory of Value", Wiley, New York.

15. Arrow, K.J. and Debreu, G. (1954) "The existence of an equilibrium for a competitive economy", Econometrica, Vol. XXII, pp.265–290.

16. Wittman, Donald (2004), The Encyclopedia of Public Choice, edited by Charles Rowley, Friedrich Schneider, "Efficiency of Democracy", pp.186.

17. "Fundamental Theorems of Welfare Economics", Wikipedia, http://en.wikipedia.org/wiki/Fundamental_theorems_of_welfare_economics

18. Smith, A., 1976, The Wealth of Nations edited by R.H. Campbell and A.S. Skinner, The Glasgow edition of the Works and Correspondence of Adam Smith, vol. 2b.

19. Feldman, A.M. (1987), "Welfare Economics", The New Palgrave: A Dictionary of Economics, Vol. 4, pp.889–895.

20. "General Equilibrium Theory", Wikipedia, http://en.wikipedia.org/wiki/General_equilibrium_theory

21. Stiglitz, Joseph E. (1991). The Invisible Hand and Modern Welfare Economics, National Bureau of Economic Research, Massachusetts, Cambridge, Working Paper No-3641.

22. Ng, Yew-Kwang (1984), "Quasi-Pareto Social Improvements", American Economic Review, Vol. 74, No. 5, pp.1033–1050.

23. Quigley, Carroll (1966), "Tragedy and Hope: A History of The World in Our Time", The Macmillan Company, New York, pp.184-187.

24. Blodget, Henry (2011) CHARTS: "Here's What The Wall Street Protesters Are So Angry About". Available online at: http://www.businessinsider.com/what-wall-street-protesters-are-so-angry-about-2011-10# Retrieved on January 11, 2014.

25. Kopczuk, Wojciech; Saez, Emmanuel and Song, Jae, "Uncovering the American Dream: Inequality and Mobility in Social Security Earnings Data since 1937", The National Bureau of economic Research, NBER Working Paper No. 13345, Issued in August 2007, http://www.nber.org/papers/w13345 Retrieved on: April 14, 2015. Published with permission.

26. Kenworthy, L. (2010), "The best inequality graph, updated. Consider the Evidence". The above illustration24 3.4 shows changes in real incomes in top 1%, middle 60%, and bottom 20% after inflation adjustment. The data are averages within each group. Incomes in 1970 and 2007:$15,500-$17,500 for the bottom 20%; $44,000-$57,000 for the middle 60%; $350,000-$1.3 million for the top1%. The years listed on the horizontal axis are business-cycle peaks. Using data from the Congressional Budget Office. Available online at: http://www.cbo.gov/publications/collections/collections.cfm?collect=13, Retrieved on from Wikipedia, http://en.wikipedia.org/wiki/File:Inequality-by-Kenworthy.png Retrieved on 16 June 2014, Published with permission.

27. Deborah, J.L. (2011), "Occupy Wall Street and the Rhetoric of Equality", Forbes, 1 November.

28. Coase, R.H. (1960), "The Problem of Social Cost", Journal of Law and Economics, Vol. 3, No. 1, pp.1–44.

29. Stiglitz, J. E. (1989)," The Economic Role of the State", A. Heertje (ed.), Basil Blackwell and Bank Insinger de Beaufort NV, 1989a, pp. 9–85.

30. Stiglitz, Joseph E. (1991). The Invisible Hand and Modern Welfare Economics, National Bureau of Economic Research, Massachusetts, Cambridge, Working Paper No-3641.

31. North, D.C. (1994), "Economic Performance Through Time", American Economic Review, Vol. 84, No. 3, pp.359–368.

32. Sen, Amartya (1999), "Poverty as Capability Deprivation". Development as Freedom. New York: Anchor Books.

33. Fukuda-Parr, Sakiko (2003), "The Human Development Paradigm: Operationalizing Sen's Ideas on Capabilities", Feminist Economics 9(2/3): 301–17.

34. UNDP (1990) Human Deuelopment Report, Oxford University Press, New York

35. Pluta, J.E. (2011), "Human Progress Amid Resistance to Change", FriesenPress, Victoria, BC, Canada, pp.149–159.

36. Alkire, S and Deneulin, S. (2009). "The Human Development and Capability Approach." An Introduction to the Human Development and Capability Approach (accessed Oct. 28, 2010). Sterling, VA: Earthscan, http://www.idrc.ca/EN/Resources/Publications/Pages/IDRCBookDetails.aspx?PublicationID=62, Retrieved on 16 June 2014

37. Krugman, P. (1992), "A Dynamic Spatial Model, Working Paper No.4219", National Bureau of Economic Research, Cambridge, MA.

38. "Production–Possibility Frontier", Wikipedia, http://en.wikipedia.org/wiki/Production%E2%80%93possibility_frontier

39. Smith, Richard (2010) "Beyond Growth or Beyond Capitalism?", real-world economics review, issue no. 53, 26 June 2010, pp. 28-42, http://www.paecon.net/PAEReview/issue53/Smith53.pdf

40. Farrell, C. (2011), "Can the Jobs-and-Income Crisis End Well?", Bloomberg Businessweek, 25 November. Available online at: http://www.businessweek.com/finance/can-thejobsandincome-   crisis-end-well-11252011.html, Retrieved on 16 June 2014

41. Hutt, W. H. (1974), "A Rehabilitation of Say's Law", Ohio University Press, Athens, 1974

42. Martenson, Chris (2011). The Crash Course: "The Unsustainable Future of Our Economy, Energy, and Environment". John Wily & Sons, Inc., Hoboken, New Jersey, pp.35-39.

43. "Keynesian Economics", Wikipedia, http://en.wikipedia.org/wiki/Keynesian_economics, Retrieved on 16 June 2014

44. Minsky, H.P. (1992), "The Financial Instability Hypothesis", Working Paper No. 74, Handbook of Radical Political Economy.

45. Robert Nozick. Anarchy, State, and Utopia. New York: Basic Books, 1974, pp151-152.

46. Sen, Amartya, Poverty and Famines : An Essay on Entitlements and Deprivation, Oxford, Clarendon Press, 1982 via Questia via Oxford Press.

47. Heinberg, Richard (2011), "The End of Growth: Adapting to our New Economic Reality", New Society Publishers, Canada.

48. Mahmud, W. (2001). "Bangladesh: Structural Adjustment and Beyond." The Reform Experience in South Asia. Basingstoke, U.K: Palgrave-Macmillan in association with International Economic Association.

49. Samuelson, Robert J. (2005), "The Global Savings Glut", *The Washington Post*, published on April 27, 2005. http://www.washingtonpost.com/wp-dyn/content/article/2005/04/26/AR2005042601394.html, Retrieved on 16 June 2014

50. "Inflation", Wikipedia, http://en.wikipedia.org/wiki/Inflation, Retrieved on 16 June 2014

51. Sachs, Jeffrey (26 October 1998). "The real causes of famine: a Nobel laureate blames authoritarian rulers". Time Magazine, http://content.time.com/time/magazine/article/0,9171,989405,00.html Retrieved on 16 June 2014.

52. Pigou, A.C. (1932) "Chapter IX: Divergences Between Marginal Social Net Product and Marginal Private Net Product" The Economics of Welfare.

53. Goldin, Claudia, and Robert Margo (1992), "The Great Compression: The Wage Structure in the United States at Mid-Century," Quarterly Journal of Economics, CVII, 1–34.

54. "M2 Growth and Inflation (10 year average)", Chart of M2 money supply growth and inflation as measured by the GNP price deflator. Data from 1875 to 1959 are taken from Appendix B of The American Business Cycle: Continuity and Change (edited by Robert Gordon). Data available here: http://www.nber.org/data/abc/ . Data from 1959 onward are taken from the Fred database. Series IDs GNPDEF and MSNS. See for similar charts: http://research.stlouisfed.org/publications/review/98/11/9811wd.pdf and https://www.clevelandfed.org/Research/Commentary/1999/0801.pdf. This is a file from This file is licensed under the Creative Commons Attribution-Share Alike 3.0 Unported license created on 21 January 2012 at the English language Wikipedia. http://en.wikipedia.org/wiki/File:M2andInflation.png

55. "Margaret Thatcher", Wikipedia, http://en.wikipedia.org/wiki/Margaret_Thatcher

56. Heinberg, Richard (2011), "Fight of Our Lives: Moore's Law vs. Murphy's Law", Post Carbon Institute, http://www.postcarbon.org/article/299173-fight-of-our-lives-moore-s-law

57. Simon, Julian L. (1993), "When Will We Run Out of Oil? Never!" The Ultimate Resource II: People, Materials, Environment", www.juliansimon.com/writings/Ultimate_Resource/TCHAR11.txt.

58. Data is provided by Freddie Mac®, 30-Year Fixed Rate Mortgage Average in the United States© [MORTGAGE30US], Retrieved on from FRED, Federal Reserve Bank of St. Louis https://research.stlouisfed.org/fred2/series/MORTGAGE30US/, April 15, 2015. Published with permission. Also please see the note in https://research.stlouisfed.org/fred2/series/MORTGAGE30US/. And US. Bureau of the Census, Median Sales Price for New Houses Sold in the United States [MSPNHSUS], Retrieved on from FRED, Federal Reserve Bank of St. Louis https://research.stlouisfed.org/fred2/series/MSPNHSUS/, April 15, 2015.

59. Molly Oswaks (2012), "The iPhone 5 Costs $8 More to Build Than it Does to Buy (UPDATED)", Sep.19, 2012 http://gizmodo.com/5944446/the-iphone-5-costs-8-more-to-build-than-it-does-to-buy

60. "Supply-Side Economics and Austrian Economics", APRIL 01, 1987 by Bruce Barlett, http://www.fee.org/the_freeman/detail/supply-side-economics-and-austrian-economics#axzz2tGp2qZbk

61. Krugman, Paul (1995), "Peddling Prosperity: Economic Sense and Nonsense in the Age of Diminished Expectations", W.W. Norton, 1995.

62. "Demand Side Economics", Wikipedia, http://rationalwiki.org/wiki/Demand_side_economics

63. Friedman, Milton (1968). "The role of monetary policy". American Economic Review 68 (1): 1–17. JSTOR 1831652

64. Harper, David (2013) "Understanding Supply-Side Economics", Investopedia, November 04, 2013, http://www.investopedia.com/articles/05/011805.asp

65. "Time Series Chart of Federal Income Taxes", http://www.usgovernmentrevenue.com/revenue_chart_1910_2010USp_XXs1li011m cn_11f12f_Federal_Income_Taxes#copypaste

66. "Supply Side Economics", Wikipedia, http://en.wikipedia.org/wiki/Supply-side_economics

67. Laffer, Arthur (2004) "The Laffer Curve, Past, Present and Future." Heritage Foundation, http://www.heritage.org/research/reports/2004/06/the-laffer-curve-past-present-and-future Retrieved on: February 27, 2014

68. Stiglitz, Joseph E. (2000). The Contributions of the Economics of Information to Twentieth Century Economics, The Quarterly Journal of Economics, November, p-1441-1478.

69. "Phillips Curve", Wikipedia, http://en.wikipedia.org/wiki/Phillips_curve

70. "Wages as a percent of the economy", Source: St. Louis Fed (http://research.stlouisfed.org/) [A576RC1/GDP], Retrieved on from "Here's one way to help the economy: Walmart Could Give Every U.S. Employee A $5,000 Raise" by Henry Blodget, http://www.businessinsider.com/walmart-raises-2011-12, Retrieved on January 15, 2012.

71. Snowdon and Vane (2005), "Modern Macroeconomics: Its Origins, Development And Current State", Edward Elgar Pub, p. 388.

72. Shapiro, C. and Stiglitz, J. (1984), "Equilibrium unemployment as a worker discipline device," American Economic Review, June 1984.

73. Araujo, Ricardo and Sachsida, Adolfo (2010), "Adverse Selection in an Efficiency Wage Model with Heterogeneous Agents", Revista Economia, September/December 2010.

74. Mankiw, Gregory N. & Taylor, Mark P. (2008), Macroeconomics (European edition), pp. 181–182.

75. Smith, Richard (2011), "Green capitalism: the god that failed", real-world economics review, issue no. 56, 11 March 2011, pp. 112-144,

http://www.paecon.net/PAEReview/issue56/Smith56.pdf "Finance Capitalism", Wikipedia, http://en.wikipedia.org/wiki/Finance_capitalism

76. "The Contradiction of Capitalism in the Search for Democracy", Latin American Perspectives, Vol. 24, No. 3, Ecuador, Part 1: Politics and Rural Issues (May, 1997), pp. 116-122.

77. "Financial Crisis", Wikipedia, http://en.wikipedia.org/wiki/Financial_crisis

78. Heinberg, Richard (2011), "The End of Growth: Adapting to our New Economic Reality", New Society Publishers, Canada.

79. "Stagflation", Wikipedia, http://en.wikipedia.org/wiki/Stagflation

80. "Phillips Curve", Wikipedia, http://en.wikipedia.org/wiki/Phillips_curve

81. Bradford DeLong (3 October 1998). "Supply Shocks: The Dilemma of Stagflation". University of California at Berkeley. Retrieved on 2008-01-24.

82. Burda, Michael; Wyplosz, Charles (1997). Macroeconomics: A European Text, 2nd ed. Oxford University Press. pp. 338–339.

83. Barsky, Robert; Kilian, Lutz (2000). A Monetary Explanation of the Great Stagflation of the 1970s. University of Michigan, http://fordschool.umich.edu/rsie/workingpapers/Papers451-475/r452.pdf

84. Heinberg, Richard (2015), "Afterburn: Society Beyond Fossil Fuels", New Society Publishers, Canada, January 2015.

85. Azzopardi, Paul V. (2010), Behavioural Technical Analysis, Harriman House Limited, ISBN 9780857190680, p. 116.

86. Cooper, George (2008), "The Origin of Financial Crises: Central Banks, Credit Bubbles, and the Efficient Market Fallacy", Vintage.

87. "Minsky Moment", Wikipedia, http://en.wikipedia.org/wiki/Minsky_moment

88. Lahart, Justin (2007), "In Time of Tumult, Obscure Economist Gains Currency— Mr. Minsky Long Argued Markets Were Crisis Prone; His 'Moment' Has Arrived",

18   August,   2007,   The   Wall   Street   Journal, http://online.wsj.com/news/articles/SB118736585456901047

89. "Economic Bubble", Wikipedia, http://en.wikipedia.org/wiki/Economic_bubble

90. King, Ronald R.; Smith, Vernon L.; Williams, Arlington W. and van Boening, Mark V. (1993). "The Robustness of Bubbles and Crashes in Experimental Stock Markets". In R. H. Day and P. Chen. Nonlinear Dynamics and Evolutionary Economics. New York: Oxford University Press. ISBN 0-19-507859-4.

91. Tienhaara, Kyla, A Tale of Two Crises: What the Global Financial Crisis Means for the Global Environmental Crisis (2010). Environmental Policy and Governance, Vol. 20, pp. 197-208, 2010. Available at SSRN: http://ssrn.com/abstract=1740086 Retrieved on: March 10, 2014.

Chapter 5: The Take Off

1. Krugman, Paul (2007). "The Conscience of a Liberal", New York:

2. Noah, Timothy (2011), "The United States of Inequality". Slate, September 7, 2010,http://www.slate.com/articles/news_and_politics/the_great_divergence/feature s/2010/the_united_states_of_inequality/did_immigration_create_the_great_divergen ce.html Retrieved on: January 17, 2014.

3. Piketty, Thomas and Saez, Emmanuel (2003), "Income Inequality in the United States, 1913–1998, The Quarterly Journal OF Economics, Vol. CXVIII, Issue 1.

4. This graph demonstrating increases in the annual income of the top 1% of wealthy persons in the U.S. before economic crises. It is created by Wikipedia, http://en.wikipedia.org/wiki/File:2008_Top1percentUSA.png, using data initially published as Thomas Piketty and Emmanuel Saez (2003), Quarterly Journal of Economics, 118(1), 2003, 1-39. Data (and updates) available here and shown here: http://inequality.org/income-inequality

5. "Income Inequality in the United States", Wikipedia, http://en.wikipedia.org/wiki/Income_inequality_in_the_United_States Retrieved on July 20,

6. Goldin, Claudia, and Robert Margo (1992), "The Great Compression: The Wage Structure in the United States at Mid-Century," Quarterly Journal of Economics, CVII, 1–34.

7. Samuelson, Paul (1948), "Economics: An Introductory Analysis",ISBN 0-07-074741-5; with William D. Nordhaus (since 1985), 2009, 19th ed., McGraw–Hill. ISBN 978-0-07-126383-2.

8. Zaman, M. (2012), "A Consolidated Economic Model Based on a New Concept of Biased Equilibrium", International Journal of Green Economics 2012 - Vol. 6, No.1 pp. 55 - 72.

9. Shapiro, C. and Stiglitz, J. (1984), "Equilibrium unemployment as a worker discipline device," American Economic Review, June 1984.

10. Frydman, Carola and Saks, Raven E., Executive Compensation: A New View from a Long-Term Perspective, 1936-2005 (June 2008). NBER Working Paper No. w14145. Available at SSRN: http://ssrn.com/abstract=1152686

11. Brown, Christopher (2005). "Is There an Institutional Theory of Distribution?" Journal of Economic Issues, 39, no 4, p.926

12. http://en.wikipedia.org/wiki/File:Nominalrealoilprices1968-2006.png Oil prices 1968–2006; peak is 1980, with steep decline over 1980. Data from http://www.eia.doe.gov/emeu/aer/pdf/pages/sec5_50.pdf

13. Mankiw, Gregory; Scarth William (2003). Macroeconomics: Canadian Edition Updated. New York: Worth Publishers. p. 270. ISBN 978-0-7167-5928-7.

14. Pluta, J.E. (2011) Human Progress Amid Resistance to Change, FriesenPress, Victoria, BC, Canada, pp.241–250.

15. Spiro, David E. The Hidden Hand of American Hegemony: Petrodollar Recycling and International Markets. Ithaca, NY: Cornell UP, 1999.

16. "Employment status of the civilian noninstitutional population 16 years and over, 1940 to date". United States Bureau of Labor Statistics, http://www.bls.gov/cps/prev_yrs.htm Retrieved on 16 September, 2014.

17. "The Coming Stock Market Crash and The Death of Money with Jim Rickards",https://www.youtube.com/watch?v=tQBia1Mw9Vw&gclid=CJbLtZjLgs ECFcRAMgodHmAAvw, Money Morning, Retrieved on September 28, 2014.

18. Heinberg, Richard (2015), "Afterburn: Society Beyond Fossil Fuels", New Society Publishers, Canada, January 2015.

19. Bernanke, Ben (2006). "Monetary Aggregates and Monetary Policy at the Federal Reserve: A Historical Perspective". Federal Reserve, http://www.federalreserve.gov/newsevents/speech/bernanke20061110a.htm Retrieved on: March 1, 2014.

20. Nelson, Edward (2007). "Milton Friedman and U.S. Monetary History: 1961–2006". Federal Reserve Bank of St. Louis Review (89 (3)): 171, http://research.stlouisfed.org/publications/review/07/05/Nelson.pdf Retrieved on: March 1, 2014.

21. Silber, William L. (2012), "Volcker: The Triumph of Persistence", Bloomsbury Press, p.8

22. Mitchell, Daniel J. (1996). "The Historical Lessons of Lower Tax Rates". The Heritage Foundation, July 19, 1996. http://www.heritage.org/Research/Taxes/BG1086.cfm.

23. "Average Tax Rates for the Highest-Income Taxpayers, 1945-2009", This work is in the public domain in the United States. Author: Thomas L. Hungerford, U.S. Congressional Research Service, Source: http://online.wsj.com/public/resources/documents/r42729_0917.pdf, CRS Report for Congress no.7-5700/R42729, p.3. This work is in the public domain in the United States because it is a work prepared by an officer or employee of the United States Government as part of that person's official duties under the terms of Title 17, Chapter 1, Section 105 of the US Code. See Copyright. Retrieved on from http://commons.wikimedia.org/wiki/File:US_high-income_effective_tax_rates.png on 16 September, 2014.

24. Mandel, Michael J. (2004), "Reagan's Economic Legacy", Bloomberg BusinessWeek, June 20, 2004. http://www.businessweek.com/stories/2004-06-20/reagans-economic-legacy

25. Bartlett, Bruce (June 5, 2012). "Rich Nontaxpayers". NY Times. http://economix.blogs.nytimes.com/2012/06/05/rich-nontaxpayers/?gwh=01897A4E09CA7986B86648979A5CD26F, Retrieved on 16 September, 2014

26. Kocieniewski, David (2012). "Since 1980s, the Kindest of Tax Cuts for the Rich". The New York, January 18, 2012. Times. http://www.nytimes.com/2012/01/18/us/politics/for-wealthy-tax-cuts-since-1980s-have-been-gain-gain.html.

27. Karaagac, John (2000). Ronald Reagan and Conservative Reformism. Lexington Books. p. 113. ISBN 0-7391-0296-6. http://books.google.com/books?id=ZFhGnjKqjgAC&pg=PA113.

28. Krugman, Paul (1995) "Peddling Prosperity: Economic Sense and Nonsense in the Age of Diminished Expectations", W.W. Norton, p.95.

29. "Ronald Reagan", Wikipedia, http://en.wikipedia.org/wiki/Ronald_Reagan

30. "Historical Budget Data". Congressional Budget Office. March 20, 2009. Archived from the original on July 30, 2008. http://web.archive.org/web/20080730192808/http://www.cbo.gov/budget/historical.shtml.

31. "Federal receipts by Source Historical 1950-2010", This file is licensed under the Creative Commons Attribution-Share Alike 3.0 Unported license created on 6 June 2012 by English language Wikipedia. http://en.wikipedia.org/wiki/File:Federal_receipts_by_Source_Historical_1950-2010.jpg Retrieved on 16 September, 2014

32. "Historical Budget Data". Congressional Budget Office. March 20, 2009. Archived from the original on July 30, 2008. http://web.archive.org/web/20080730192808/http://www.cbo.gov/budget/historical.shtml.

33. Dreier, Peter (2011), "Don't add Reagan's Face to Mount Rushmore", The Nation, April 3, 2011.

34. US. Bureau of Economic Analysis, Gross Domestic Product [GDP], Retrieved on from FRED, Federal Reserve Bank of St. Louis https://research.stlouisfed.org/fred2/series/GDP/, February 11, 2016.

35. US. Bureau of Economic Analysis, Corporate profits after tax [A055RC0A144NBEA], Retrieved on from FRED, Federal Reserve Bank of St. Louis, https://research.stlouisfed.org/fred2/series/A055RC0A144NBEA/, February 16, 2016.

36. Rosenbaum, David E (1986). "Reagan insists Budget Cuts are way to Reduce Deficit". The New York Times, January 8, 1986. http://www.nytimes.com/1986/01/08/us/reagan-insists-budget-cuts-are-way-to-reduce-deficit.html. Retrieved on 17 September, 2014

37. "Views from the FoKMEr Administrators". EPA Journal. Environmental Protection Agency. November 1985. http://web.archive.org/web/20080715143637/http://www.epa.gov/history/topics/epa/15e.htm. Retrieved on 17 September, 2014

38. Martenson, Chris (2011). The Crash Course: "The Unsustainable Future of Our Economy, Energy, and Environment". John Wily & Sons, Inc., Hoboken, New Jersey, pp.65-122.

39. Jones, Brent (2010-02-04). "Medical expenses have 'very steep rate of growth'". USA Today. http://www.usatoday.com/news/health/2010-02-04-health-care-costs_N.htm Retrieved on 17 September, 2014.

40. US. Bureau of Economic Analysis, Personal consumption expenditures: Services: Health care (chain-type price index) [DHLCRG3A086NBEA], Retrieved on from FRED, Federal Reserve Bank of St. Louis https://research.stlouisfed.org/fred2/series/DHLCRG3A086NBEA/, Retrieved on February 11, 2016.

41. US. Bureau of Economic Analysis, Personal Consumption Expenditures: Nondurable Goods [PCND] & Personal Consumption Expenditures: Durable Goods

[PCEDG], Retrieved on from FRED, Federal Reserve Bank of St. Louis https://research.stlouisfed.org/fred2/series/PCND/, December 27, 2014.

42. Bacon, Edwin; Sandle, Mark (2002) "Brezhnev Reconsidered", Palgrave Macmillan. ISBN 978-0333794630, p. 1.

43. Service, Robert (2009). History of Modern Russia: From Tsarism to the Twenty-first Century (3 ed.). Penguin Books Ltd. ISBN 978-0674034938, p.416.

44. "Trouble in Ukraine – part 2", Renegade Tribune, 13 March, 2014, http://renegadetribune.com/trouble-in-ukraine-part-2/

45. Bacon, Edwin; Sandle, Mark (2002). Brezhnev Reconsidered. Palgrave Macmillan. ISBN 978-0333794630, p.28.

46. "Cold War", Wikipedia, http://en.wikipedia.org/wiki/Cold_War

47. "Prestroika", Wikipedia, http://en.wikipedia.org/wiki/Perestroika

48. Ulfelder, Jay (2004), "Baltic Protest in the Gorbachev Era: Movement Content and Dynamics", The Global Review of Ethnopolitics, Vol. 3, no. 3-4, 2004, p. 23-43, http://www.ethnopolitics.org/ethnopolitics/archive/volume_III/issue_3-4/ulfelder.pdf Retrieved on 18 September, 2014

49. Gaddis, John Lewis (2005). The Cold War: A New History. Penguin Press. ISBN 1-59420-062-9, p.247.

50. "The K.G.B.'s Bathhouse Plot" by Victor Sebestyen, The New York Times, 20 August, 2011, http://www.nytimes.com/2011/08/21/opinion/sunday/the-soviet-coup-that-failed.html?pagewanted=all&_r=0, Retrieved on 27 December, 2014.

51. Aslund, Anders (2007) "Russia's Capitalist Revolution: Why Market Reform Succeeded and Democracy Failed", Peterson Institute for International Economics, p.109.

52. Erlanger, Steven (1993), "For Sale, Cheap: Russia's Once-Mighty Industrial Base", The New York Times, 23 May, 1993, http://www.nytimes.com/1993/05/23/weekinreview/for-sale-cheap-russia-s-once-mighty-industrial-base.html

53. "Economic History of the Russian Federation", Wikipedia, http://en.wikipedia.org/wiki/Economic_history_of_the_Russian_Federation

54. World Bank, Inflation, consumer prices for the Russian Federation [FPCPITOTLZGRUS], Retrieved on from FRED, Federal Reserve Bank of St. Louis, https://research.stlouisfed.org/fred2/series/FPCPITOTLZGRUS/, December 27, 2014.

55. "Voucher Privatization", http://www.allrussias.com/rf/privatiz_2.asp

56. Orlov,Dmitry (2011), "Reinventing Collapse: The Soviet Experience and American Prospects",New Society Publishers; Revised edition, May 31, 2011.

57. "How Harvard lost Russia" by David McClintick, Institutional Investor. 27 February 2006, http://www.institutionalinvestor.com/Article/1020662/How-Harvard-lost-Russia.html#.VJ9BfF4DJB Retrieved on 24 July 2014.

58. "Russia's Defense Industry: Breakthrough or Breakdown?", By Richard Weitz, The International Relations and Security Network (ISN), 6 March 2015, http://www.isn.ethz.ch/Digital-Library/Articles/Detail/?id=188933 Retrieved on 15 March, 2015.

59. Nicholson, Alex. "Metal is the latest natural resource bonanza for Russia", http://www.iht.com/articles/2007/08/14/business/metal.php International Herald Tribune.

60. "Russia: Clawing Its Way Back to Life (int'l edition)". BusinessWeek, http://www.businessweek.com/1999/99_48/b3657252.htm Retrieved on 27 December, 2014.

61. "Dissolution of the Soviet Union", Wikipedia, http://en.wikipedia.org/wiki/Dissolution_of_the_Soviet_Union Retrieved on: 25 December, 2014

62. Page, Jeremy (16 May 2005). "Analysis: punished for his political ambitions". The Times (UK). Retrieved on 27 December 2007.

63. "Economy of Russia", Wikipedia, http://en.wikipedia.org/wiki/Economy_of_Russia Retrieved on: 25 December, 2014

64. Graph prepared by the author by using data from " CO_2 time series 1990-2014 per capita for world countries". Netherlands Environmental Assessment Agency, http://edgar.jrc.ec.europa.eu/overview.php?v=CO2ts_pc1990-2014 Retrieved on December 7, 2015 Retrieved on: 7 December, 2015

65. "Russia's economy under Vladimir Putin: achievements and failures", RIA Novosti,01 March, 2008, http://sputniknews.com/analysis/20080301/100381963.html Retrieved on 27 December, 2014.

66. "Russians weigh an enigma with Putin's protégé", MNBC News, 5 March, 2008 http://www.nbcnews.com/id/24443419/ Retrieved on May 3, 2008.

67. "Russia Today Atlas: Strategic Information for Business and Political Decision Makers Strategic Information and Developments", International Business Publications, USA, p-85

68. "World Development Indicators: Contribution of natural resources to gross domestic product", World Bank, http://wdi.worldbank.org/table/3.15 Retrieved on 27 December 2014.

69. "Russian economy since fall of the Soviet Union (2008 international dollars)", Source: http://www.imf.org/external/pubs/ft/weo/2009/02/weodata/index.aspx, This graph is created by Wikipedia and licensed under the Creative Commons Attribution-Share Alike 3.0 Unported, 2.5 Generic, 2.0 license, http://commons.wikimedia.org/wiki/File:Russian_economy_since_fall_of_Soviet_Union.PNG Retrieved on 27 December, 2014.

70. International Monetary Fund, General government gross debt for Russia© [GGGDTARUA188N], Retrieved on from FRED, Federal Reserve Bank of St. Louis General government gross debt for Russia© - FRED - St. Louis Fed https://research.stlouisfed.org/fred2/series/GGGDTARUA188N/, Retrieved on February 11, 2016. Published with permission from IMF.

71. Elliott, Larry (2014). "Fears for Russian rouble as plunging oil price dents markets". The Guardian, 15 December 2014, http://www.theguardian.com/business/2014/dec/15/fears-russian-rouble-oil-price-markets, Retrieved on 27 December 2014.

72. "Emerging Markets 2014: How Russian Ruble Crisis, Tumbling Oil Prices Will Affect Bond Markets" by Jessica Menton, International Business Times, 22 December, 2014, http://www.ibtimes.com/emerging-markets-2014-how-russian-ruble-crisis-tumbling-oil-prices-will-affect-bond-1764834 Retrieved on 25 December, 2014

73. "U.S. Won't Ease Sanctions to Stem Russia's Economic Crisis". by Mike Dorning and Ian Katz, Bloomberg, 16 December 2014, http://www.bloomberg.com/news/2014-12-16/u-s-won-t-ease-sanctions-to-prevent-economic-meltdown-in-russia.html Retrieved on 16 December 2014.

74. "Russia to Dip Into Wealth Fund as Ruble Crisis Pressures Economy", by Olga Tanas, Anna Andrianova and Ksenia Galouchko, 14 January, 2015 http://www.bloomberg.com/news/articles/2015-01-14/russia-to-convert-currency-from-wealth-fund-to-arrest-ruble-drop

75. "West behaving like an 'empire': Russian president." Special Broadcasting Service, 19 December 2014, http://www.sbs.com.au/news/article/2014/12/18/west-behaving-empire-russian-president Retrieved on 25 December 2014.

76. US. Bureau of Labor Statistics, Import (End Use): Fuel oil [IR10010], Retrieved on from FRED, Federal Reserve Bank of St. Louis https://research.stlouisfed.org/fred2/series/IR10010/ and US. Department of the Treasury. Fiscal Service, Federal Debt: Total Public Debt [GFDEBTN], Retrieved on from FRED, Federal Reserve Bank of St. Louis https://research.stlouisfed.org/fred2/series/GFDEBTN/, January 18, 2015.

77. Blodget, Henry (2011) CHARTS: "Here's What The Wall Street Protesters Are So Angry About". Available online at: http://www.businessinsider.com/what-wall-street-protesters-are-so-angry-about-2011-10#

78. Federal Reserve Bank of St. Louis and US. Office of Management and Budget, Federal Debt Held by the Public as Percent of Gross Domestic Product [FYGFGDQ188S], Retrieved on from FRED, Federal Reserve Bank of St. Louis https://research.stlouisfed.org/fred2/series/FYGFGDQ188S/, Retrieved on February 11, 2016.

79. Lorin, Janet (2012), "U.S. student loan debt reaches record US$1-trillion", Bloomberg March 22, 2012, http://www.bloomberg.com/news/2012-03-22/student-loan-debt-reaches-record-1-trillion-u-s-report-says.html

80. US. Bureau of Economic Analysis, Personal Saving Rate [PSAVERT], Retrieved on from FRED, Federal Reserve Bank of St. Louis https://research.stlouisfed.org/fred2/series/PSAVERT/, Retrieved on February 11, 2016.

81. Simkovic, Michael (2011), "Bankruptcy Immunities, Transparency, and Capital Structure", Presentation at the World Bank.

82. Samuelson, Robert J. (2005), "The Global Savings Glut", The Washington Post, published on April 27, 2005. http://www.washingtonpost.com/wp-dyn/content/article/2005/04/26/AR2005042601394.html Retrieved on 20 September, 2014

83. "Social Security Trust Fund 2010 Report Summary". Status of the Social Security and Medicare Programs, http://www.ssa.gov/oact/trsum/index.html Retrieved on 20 September, 2012.

84. "Financial crisis of 2007–08", Wikipedia, http://en.wikipedia.org/wiki/Financial_crisis_of_2007%E2%80%9308

85. Bernanke, Ben S (2007). "Global Imbalances: Recent Developments and Prospects", At the Bundesbank Lecture, Berlin, Germany September 11, 2007. http://www.federalreserve.gov/newsevents/speech/bernanke20070911a.htm.

86. Austvik, Ole Gunnar. "Oil Prices and the Dollar Dilemma." OPEC Review 11.4 (1987): 399-412.

87. Riley, Kevin M. (2011), "Oil and the U.S. Dollar", Columbia University, June 27, 2011, https://www.academia.edu/1253274/Oil_and_the_U.S._Dollar Retrieved on: January 5, 2014.

88. Spiro, David E (1999), "The Hidden Hand of American Hegemony: Petrodollar Recycling and International Markets", Ithaca, NY: Cornell UP, 1999.pp. 121-122.

89. Krugman, Paul "Nobody Understands Debt". New York Times, January 1, 2012, http://www.nytimes.com/2012/01/02/opinion/krugman-nobody-understands-debt.html?_r=2&ref=paulkrugman& Retrieved on 2012-02-04.

90. "National Debt of the United States", Wikipedia, http://en.wikipedia.org/wiki/National_debt_of_the_United_States

91. US. Department of the Treasury. Fiscal Service, Federal Debt Held by Foreign & International Investors [FDHBFIN], Retrieved on from FRED, Federal Reserve Bank of St. Louis https://research.stlouisfed.org/fred2/series/FDHBFIN/, February 11, 2016.

92. Graph prepared by the author, Data source: "Major Foreign Holders of Treasury Securities". treasury.gov. 17 July 2012. http://www.treas.gov/tic/mfh.txt.

93. Wilkinson, Will (2009), "Thinking Clearly About Economic Inequality", Cato Institute.

94. "Quantitative Easing", Wikipedia, http://en.wikipedia.org/wiki/Quantitative_easing December 28, 2014.

95. Plumer, Brad (2012), "QE3: What is quantitative easing? And will it help the economy?", The Washington Post, September 13, 2012. http://www.washingtonpost.com/blogs/ezra-klein/wp/2012/09/13/qe3-what-is-quantitative-easing-and-will-it-help-the-economy/ December 28, 2014.

96. US. Department of the Treasury. Fiscal Service, Federal Debt Held by Federal Reserve Banks [FDHBFRBN], Retrieved on from FRED, Federal Reserve Bank of St. Louis https://research.stlouisfed.org/fred2/series/FDHBFRBN/, February 11, 2016.

97. "Dependency Theory", Wikipedia, http://en.wikipedia.org/wiki/Dependency_theory

98. "President Bush's Address to Nation". The New York Times. 24 September, 2008, http://www.nytimes.com/2008/09/24/business/economy/24text-bush.html?_r=3&pagewanted=1&oref=slogin& Retrieved on 24 September, 2010.

99. Krugman, Paul (2010), "Creative Destruction", New York Times, January 2010.

100. King, Ronald R.; Smith, Vernon L.; Williams, Arlington W. and van Boening, Mark V. (1993). "The Robustness of Bubbles and Crashes in Experimental Stock Markets". In R. H. Day and P. Chen. Nonlinear Dynamics and Evolutionary Economics. New York: Oxford University Press. ISBN 0-19-507859-4.

101. "Economic Bubble", Wikipedia, http://en.wikipedia.org/wiki/Economic_bubble

102. Minsky, Hyman P.(1992) "The Financial Instability Hypothesis", Working Paper No. 74, Levy Economics Institute of Brad College, http://www.levyinstitute.org/pubs/wp74.pdf Retrieved on 28 December, 2014.

103. Lei, Vivian; Noussair, Charles N.; Plott, Charles R. (2001). "Non-speculative Bubbles in Experimental Asset Markets: Lack of Common Knowledge of Rationality Vs. Actual Irrationality". Econometrica 69 (4): 831. doi:10.1111/1468-0262.00222.

104. Saez, Emmanuel (2012), "Striking it Richer: The Evolution of Top Incomes in the United States", http://elsa.berkeley.edu/~saez/saez-UStopincomes-2010.pdf

105. Board of Governors of the Federal Reserve System (US), Excess Reserves of Depository Institutions (DISCONTINUED SERIES) [EXCRESNS], Retrieved on from FRED, Federal Reserve Bank of St. Louis https://research.stlouisfed.org/fred2/series/EXCRESNS/, December 28, 2014.

106. "Federal Reserve slashes interest rates to nearly zero", by Larry Elliott & Ashley Seager, 17 December, 2008, The Guardian, http://www.theguardian.com/business/2008/dec/16/federal-reserve-interest-rates-cut 25 September, 2014.

107. "Top 6 U.S. Government Finanmcial Bailouts", by Marc Davis, Investopedia, http://www.investopedia.com/articles/economics/08/government-financial-bailout.asp Retrieved on 28 December, 2014.

108. Simkovic, Michael (2009), "Secret Liens and the Financial Crisis of 2008", American Bankruptcy Law Journal, Vol. 83, p. 253.

109. Simkovic, Michael (2010), "Paving the Way for the Next Financial Crisis", Banking & Financial Services Policy Report, Vol. 29, No. 3.

110. BIS survey: The Bank for International Settlements (BIS) semi-annual OTC, derivatives market report, for end of June 2008, shows US$683.7 trillion total notional amounts outstanding of OTC derivatives with a gross market value of US$20 trillion. See also Prior Period Regular OTC Derivatives Market Statistics.

111. Office of Management and Budget, Executive Office of the President (April 9, 2001) *Fiscal year 2002: Budget of the United States Government*, p. 224.

112. Office of Management and Budget, Executive Office of the President (July 30, 2004). Fiscal year 2005: Midsession review: Budget of the U.S. Government, p. 28. GPO Access.

113. CBO Long-Term Budget Outlook-Historical Budget Data-January 2012, http://www.cbo.gov/publication/21999

114. "United States Federal Budget", Wikipedia, http://en.wikipedia.org/wiki/United_States_federal_budget

115. US. Office of Management and Budget, Federal Surplus or Deficit [-] [FYFSD], Retrieved on from FRED, Federal Reserve Bank of St. Louis https://research.stlouisfed.org/fred2/series/FYFSD/, February 11, 2016.

116. "Budget Control Act of 2011", Wikipedia, http://en.wikipedia.org/wiki/Budget_Control_Act_of_2011 December 21, 2014.

117. Bumiller, Elisabeth (2011). "Despite Threat of Cuts, Pentagon Officials Made No Contingency Plans". The New York Times, 22 November, 2011, http://www.nytimes.com/2011/11/23/us/despite-threat-of-cuts-pentagon-made-no-contingency-plans.html?_r=0 Retrieved on 21 December, 2014.

118. Hand, Eric. (2011). "Debt deal sets day of reckoning". Nature 476 (7359): 133–134. doi:10.1038/476133a. PMID 21833060, http://www.nature.com/news/2011/110809/full/476133a.html

119. Ham, Becky (2011). "Science, Engineering Groups Urge Lawmakers to Protect R&D". Science 334 (6059): 1079. doi:10.1126/science.334.6059.1079, 25 November, 2011, http://www.sciencemag.org/content/334/6059/1079 Retrieved on 21 December, 2014.

120. "Census: U.S. Poverty Rate Spikes, Nearly 50 Million Americans Affected" CBS. 15 November, 2012, http://washington.cbslocal.com/2012/11/15/census-u-s-poverty-rate-spikes-nearly-50-million-americans-affected/ Retrieved on 26 September, 2014.

121. Smith, Donna (2010) "Poverty rate hits 15-year high" Reuters. 17 September, 2010, http://www.reuters.com/article/2010/09/17/us-usa-economy-poverty-idUSTRE68F4K520100917 Retrieved on 26 September, 2014

122. "The Fall of the American Empire...and What We Can do About It", By Joachim Hagopian, Global Research, June 04, 2014, http://www.globalresearch.ca/the-fall-of-the-american-empire-and-what-we-can-do-about-it/5385506 Retrieved on August 9, 2015

123. Berlinger, Joshua (2012). "A New Poverty Calculation Yields Some Surprising Results". Business Insider, 12 November, 2012, http://www.businessinsider.com/new-census-data-on-poverty-rates-yields-some-pretty-shocking-results-2012-11 Retrieved on 26 September, 2014.

124. Walker, Duncan (2013). "The children going hungry in America", BBC News, 6 March 2013, http://www.bbc.com/news/magazine-21636723 Retrieved on 26 September, 2014.

125. Fisher, Max (15 April 2013). Map: How 35 countries compare on child poverty (the U.S. is ranked 34th). The Washington Post. Retrieved on 16 February 2014. See also: Child well-being in rich countries: A comparative overview. UNICEF office of Research. p. 7.

126. Drum, Kevin (2013). New Study Says Poverty Rate Hasn't Budged For 40 Years. Mother Jones, 9 December 2013, http://www.motherjones.com/kevin-drum/2013/12/new-study-says-poverty-rate-hasnt-budged-40-years Retrieved on 26 September, 2014.

127. Kenworthy, L. (1999). "Do Social-Welfare Policies Reduce Poverty? A Cross-National Assessment" Social Forces 77(3), 1119–1139. Bradley, D., E. Huber, S. Moller, F. Nielsen, and J. D. Stephens (2003). "Determinants of Relative Poverty in Advanced Capitalist Democracies". American Sociological Review 68 (1): 22–51.

128. US. Bureau of Economic Analysis, Personal current taxes [W055RC1], Retrieved on from FRED, Federal Reserve Bank of St. Louis https://research.stlouisfed.org/fred2/series/W055RC1/, December 21, 2014.

129. "The federal government's financial health: a citizen's guide to the 2008 financial report of the United States government", pp. 7–8. United States Government Accountability Office (GAO). http://www.gao.gov/financial/citizensguide2008.pdf Retrieved on February 1, 2011.

130. David Friedman, New America Foundation (2002),"No Light at the End of the Tunnel", Los Angeles Times, June 15, 2002. http://www.newamerica.net/publications/articles/2002/no_light_at_the_end_of_the_tunnel

131. Hira, Ron and Anil Hira with forward by Lou Dobbs, (May 2005). Outsourcing America: What's Behind Our National Crisis and How We Can Reclaim American Jobs. (AMACOM) American Management Association. Citing Paul Craig Roberts, Paul Samuelson, and Lou Dobbs, pp. 36–38.

132. Elliott, Larry & Rushe, Dominic (2011), "US Credit Rating Downgrade Prompts Warning From China", The Guardian, London, http://www.guardian.co.uk/business/2011/aug/06/us-credit-rating-downgrade-china

133. BRICS Bank to be headquartered in Shanghai, India to hold presidency". Indiasnaps.com. 16 July 2014, http://indiasnaps.com/brics-bank-to-be-headquartered-in-shanghai-india-to-hold-presidency/ Retrieved on 23 December, 2014.

134. Powell, Anita (2013) "BRICS Leaders Optimistic About New Development Bank". Voice of America, 27 March, 2013 http://www.voanews.com/content/brics-summit-leaders-optimistic-about-new-development-bank/1629583.html Retrieved on 23 December 2014.

135. "BRIC wants more influence". Euronews. Archived from the original on 21 June 2009, http://www.euronews.com/2009/06/16/bric-wants-more-influence/ Retrieved on 23 December 2014.

136. "BRICS morphing into anti-dollar alliance", The Voice of Russia, voiceofrussia.com, 3 Jul 2014, http://sputniknews.com/voiceofrussia/2014_07_03/BRICS-is-morphing-into-an-anti-dollar-alliance-6229/ Retrieved on 23 December, 2014.

137. Brown, Carrie Budoff (2011), "Obama's 'Buffett Rule' to call for higher tax rate for millionaires". Politico, September 17, 2011

138. O'Connor Clare (2012), "The Buffett Rule's Billionaire Backers: Meet The Super-Rich Who Want To Pay More Taxes", Forbes, April 10, 2012. http://www.forbes.com/sites/clareoconnor/2012/04/10/the-buffett-rules-billionaire-backers-meet-the-super-rich-who-want-to-pay-more-taxes/ Retrieved on 23 December, 2014.

139. NYT Editorial Board, "The Need to Agree to Agree", 10 July, 2012, http://www.nytimes.com/2012/07/10/opinion/a-challenge-on-middle-class-tax-cuts.html?src=rec&recp=15&_r=0 Retrieved on 23 December, 2014.

140. "Senate fails to advance Buffett rule" by Susan Davis, USA Today, April 16, 2012, http://usatoday30.usatoday.com/news/washington/story/2012-04-16/senate-fails-to-pass-buffett-rule/54324786/1 Retrieved on: 23 December, 2014.

141. "Decline of the Roman Empire", Wikipedia, http://en.wikipedia.org/wiki/Decline_of_the_Roman_Empire

142. Arnold J. Toynbee (1947). A Study of History: Abridgement of Volumes I to VI. Oxford University Press. p. 273.

143. Rubin, Jeff (2012), "The End of Growth", Random House Canada, pp. 46-75.

144. Whitehouse, Steve (June 30, 2008). "BIS says global downturn could be 'deeper and more protracted' than expected". Forbes. Archived from the original on June 1, 2010. Thomson Financial News https://web.archive.org/web/20100601020319/http://www.forbes.com/feeds/afx/2008/06/30/afx5166493.html Retrieved on 23 December, 2014

145. Benedict Brogan (2009), "The debt crisis of 1976 offers a vision of the blood, sweat and tears facing David Cameron", The Telegraph.

http://www.telegraph.co.uk/comment/columnists/benedict-brogan/6410123/The-debt-crisis-of-1976-offers-a-vision-of-the-blood-sweat-and-tears-facing-David-Cameron.html Retrieved on: March 07, 2014.

146. Burk, Kathleen (1992) "Good-bye Great Britain: 1976 IMF Crisis", Yale University Press UK SR, ISBN 0-300-05728-8

147. "Britain may need IMF bail-out, warns David Cameron", reported by Andrew Porter and Matthew Moore, The Telegraph, 23 January, 2009, http://www.telegraph.co.uk/news/politics/conservative/4319385/Britain-may-need-IMF-bail-out-warns-David-Cameron.html, Retrieved on: March 07, 2014.

148. Childs, David (2006). Britain since 1945: a political history (6th ed.). Taylor & Francis. ISBN 978-0-415-39326-3, p. 185

149. Margaret Thatcher", Wikipedia, http://en.wikipedia.org/wiki/Margaret_Thatcher

150. Middleton, Roger (1996) "Government versus the market: the growth of the public sector, economic management, and British economic performance c. 1890-1979", E. Elgar, ISBN:1852780312, 9781852780319, p. 630.

151. "Annual U.K. GDP Growth, 1948 to 2012", his graph shows the annual U.K. GDP Growth from 1948 to 2012, expressed in percentage terms, with data taken from the Office of National Statistics. The years under Prime Minister Margaret Thatcher, who administered the government from 1979 to1990, are highlighted. This file is made available under the Creative Commons CC0 1.0 Universal Public Domain Dedication created on 19 April 2013, Retrieved on from http://commons.wikimedia.org/wiki/File:Annual_U.K._GDP_Growth,_1948_to_201 2_(Thatcher)_(alt).png

152. "Inflation-CPI", Wikipedia, http://www.tradingeconomics.com/united-kingdom/inflation-cpi

153. Childs, David (2006). Britain since 1945: a political history (6th ed.). Taylor & Francis. ISBN 978-0-415-39326-3

154. Seldon, Anthony; Collings, Daniel (2000). Britain Under Thatcher. Longman. ISBN 978-0-582-31714-7, p-27.

155. Feigenbaum, Harvey; Henig, Jeffrey; Hamnett, Chris (1998). Shrinking the State: The Political Underpinnings of Privatization. Cambridge University Press. ISBN 978-0-521-63918-7., p. 71

156. Marr, Andrew (2007). A History of Modern Britain. Pan. ISBN 978-0-330-43983-1., p. 428

157. Rogers, Simon (2013-05-22). "Deficit, national debt and government borrowing - how has it changed since 1946?". http://www.theguardian.com/news/datablog/2010/oct/18/deficit-debt-government-borrowing-data#zoomed-picture Retrieved on: March 07, 2014.

158. World Bank, Central government debt, total (% of GDP) for the United Kingdom [DEBTTLGBA188A], Retrieved on from FRED, Federal Reserve Bank of St. Louis https://research.stlouisfed.org/fred2/series/DEBTTLGBA188A/, December 31, 2014.

159. "Government Spending under Labour", by Tejvan Pettinger, July 11, 2012 in Economics, http://www.economicshelp.org/blog/5509/economics/government-spending-under-labour/

160. "ECB ratings: Pound sterling in Euros". European Central Bank, http://www.ecb.europa.eu/stats/exchange/eurofxref/html/eurofxref-graph-gbp.en.html Retrieved on: March 07, 2014.

161. "Pound Sterling", Wikipedia, http://en.wikipedia.org/wiki/Pound_sterling

162. "78 Theses About The U.S. Economy", The Acamedic Activist, 15 August, 2014, http://theacademicactivist.org/78%20Theses%20About%20The%20US%20Economy Retrieved on: 31 December, 2014.

163. "It's All Connected: A Spectator's Guid to the Euro Crisis", The New York Times, October 22, 2012 http://www.nytimes.com/imagepages/2011/10/22/opinion/20111023_DATAPOINTS.html?ref=sunday-review Retrieved on: February 3, 2014.

164. "Euro", Wikipedia, http://en.wikipedia.org/wiki/Euro

165. Brown,Mark and Chambers,Alex "How Europe's governments have enronized their debts", Euromoney, September 2005, http://www.euromoney.com/Article/1000384/How-Europes-governments-have-enronized-their-debts.html Retrieved on: February, 3, 2014.

166. "What Greece Needs", by Aristos Doxiadis, The New York Times, http://www.nytimes.com/2015/02/26/opinion/what-greece-needs.html?_r=0 Retrieved on July 21, 2015.

167. Rubin, Jeff (2012), "The End of Growth", Random House Canada, pp. 46-75.

168. "OPEC", Wikipedia, http://en.wikipedia.org/wiki/OPEC

169. "Greece debt crisis: Has Grexit been avoided?", by Paul Kirby, 20 July, 2015, BBC News, http://www.bbc.com/news/world-europe-32332221 Retrieved on July 21, 2015 Retrieved on: July 21, 2014.

170. "China's Monumental Ponzi: Here's How It Unravels", by David Stockman, Contra Corner, March 31, 2014, http://davidstockmanscontracorner.com/chinas-monumental-ponzi-heres-how-it-unravels/ Retrieved on: July 23, 2015

171. "G-20: The new global economy – CNNMoney.com". CNN. http://money.cnn.com/news/economy/g20/interactive/index.html?cnn=yes.

172. Adam, Shamim (2010). "China to Exceed U.S. by 2020, Standard Chartered Says". Bloomberg Businessweek. http://www.businessweek.com/news/2010-11-14/china-to-exceed-u-s-by-2020-standard-chartered-says.html.

173. "Economy of the People's Republic of China", Wikipedia, http://en.wikipedia.org/wiki/Economy_of_the_People's_Republic_of_China

174. World Bank, Gross Domestic Product for China [MKTGDPCNA646NWDB], Retrieved on from FRED, Federal Reserve Bank of St.Louis,https://research.stlouisfed.org/fred2/series/MKTGDPCNA646NWDB/, February 11, 2016.

175. "U.S. Trade Deficit With China Sets New Record In 2013", by Alliance for American Manufacturing, 02 June, 2014, http://www.inddist.com/news/2014/02/us-trade-deficit-china-sets-new-record-2013

176. "Manufacturing and Trade". Greyhill Advisors, October 6, 2011. http://greyhill.com/blog/2011/10/6/manufacturing-and-trade.html.

177. "The China Bubble Is Going to Burst", BloombergBusiness, June 16, 2015, http://www.bloomberg.com/news/articles/2015-06-16/china-bubble-debate-turns-to-when-not-if-stocks-will-tumble   Retrieved on: July 23, 2015

178. "Chinese Economic Reform", Wikipedia, http://en.wikipedia.org/wiki/Chinese_economic_reform

179. "Online Extra: "China Is a Private-Sector Economy", August 21, 2005, http://www.businessweek.com/stories/2005-08-21/online-extra-china-is-a-private-sector-economy Retrieved on 31 December, 2014.

180. Allen, Franklin et al. (2008), "China's Financial system: Past, present and future", China's Great Transformation, Cambridge university press. P.556.

181. Naughton, Barry et al. (2008), "A Political Economy of China's Economic Transition in China's Great Transformation", China's Great Transformation, Cambridge: Cambridge university press.

182. "Shanghai Stock Exchange", Wikipedia, http://en.wikipedia.org/wiki/Shanghai_Stock_Exchange

183. Svejnar, Jan et al. (2008), "China in light of other transition economies", in Brandt, Loren and Rawski, G. Thomas, China's Great Transformation, Cambridge: Cambridge university press. P68-76.

184. Huang, Jikun et al. (2008), "Agriculture in China's Development: Past Disappointments, Recent Successes, and Future Challenges", China's Great Transformation, Cambridge: Cambridge university press. P. 478-482.

185. Dollar, David (2007), "Poverty, Inequality, and Social Disparities During China's Economic Reform", World Bank, Washington, DC. https://openknowledge.worldbank.org/handle/10986/7404. Retrieved on 24 March, 2014.

186. Cai, Fang et al. (2008), "The Chinese labor market in the reform era", China's Great Transformation, Cambridge: Cambridge university press, p.184.

Green the Capitalists

187. Chovanec, Patrick (2009). "China's Real Estate Riddle". Far East Economic Review. http://www.feer.com/economics/2009/june53/Chinas-Real-Estate-Riddle Retrieved on 24 March, 2014.

188. Yao, Yang (2010), "No, the Lewisian turning point has not yet arrived", The Economist, July 16, 2010.

189. Eastman, R. and M. Lipton (2004), "Rural and Urban Income Inequality and Poverty: Does Convergence between Sectors Offset Divergence within Them?" in G. A. Cornea, ed., Inequality, Growth and Poverty in an Era of Liberalization and Globalization, Oxford U. Press, 112-141.

190. Bernanke, Ben S.(2005), "The Global Saving Glut and the U.S. Current Account Deficit", The Federal Reserve Board, http://www.federalreserve.gov/boarddocs/speeches/2005/200503102/default.htm

191. Ma, Guonan & Yi Wang (2010), "China's High Saving Rate: Myth and Reality", Bank for International Settlement Working Papers No 312, Switzerland. http://www.bis.org/publ/work312.pdf

192. "China's economic boom leaves a trail of ghost cities" by Rob Schmitz, Marketplace, June 2, 2014, http://www.marketplace.org/topics/world/marketplace-25/chinas-economic-boom-leaves-trail-ghost-cities Retrieved on 23 December, 2014

193. "Double Bubble Trouble :China's property prices appear to be falling again", 22 March, 2014, Hong Kong, The Economists, http://www.economist.com/news/china/21599395-chinas-property-prices-appear-be-falling-again-double-bubble-trouble, Retrieved on 23 December, 2014

194. "Coal in China", Wikipedia, http://en.wikipedia.org/wiki/Coal_in_China

195. NationMaster.com. Energy Statistics > Coal consumption (most recent) by country, http://www.nationmaster.com/country-info/stats/Energy/Coal/Consumption. Retrieved on from http://en.wikipedia.org/wiki/Coal_in_China

196. Graph prepared by the author by using data from "CO2 time series 1990-2014 per capita for world countries". Netherlands Environmental Assessment Agency,

http://edgar.jrc.ec.europa.eu/overview.php?v=CO2ts_pc1990-2014   Retrieved on December 7, 2015 Retrieved on: 7 December, 2015

197. Peter   Fairley,   Technology   Review.   Part   I: China's   Coal   Future, http://www.technologyreview.com/article/407110/part-ii-chinas-coal-future/?p=1 Retrieved on from http://en.wikipedia.org/wiki/Coal_in_China

198. "China is now the world's largest net importer of petroleum and other iquid fuels", Energy   Information   Administration   (EIA),   24   March,   2014, http://www.eia.gov/todayinenergy/detail.cfm?id=15531 Retrieved on 1 January, 2015.

199. Yao, Yang (2010), "No, the Lewisian turning point has not yet arrived", The Economist,   July   16,   2010,   http://www.economist.com/economics/by-invitation/guest-contributions/no_lewisian_turning_point_has_not_yet_arrived   22 March, 2014.

200. "Moving on up: The government unveils a new "people-centred" plan for urbanisation",   The   Economists,   22   March,   2014, http://www.economist.com/news/china/21599397-government-unveils-new-people-centred-plan-urbanisation-moving-up Retrieved on 23 December, 2014

201. "China's housing market is on the brink of collapse. Should Australia be worried?" Posted   by   Greg   Jericho,   The   Guardian,   8   September   2014, http://www.theguardian.com/business/grogonomics/2014/sep/08/why-a-collapse-in-chinas-housing-market-will-hurt-australia Retrieved on 22 December 2014. Retrieved on 23 December, 2014

202. "America's   disappearing   middle   class",   by   Tami   Luhby,   CNN   Money, http://economy.money.cnn.com/2014/01/28/middle-class/ Retrieved on July 24, 2015

203. The   times,   China's   New   Healthcare   could   cover   millions   more, http://www.time.com/time/world/article/0,8599,1890306,00.html

204. Scissors,   Derek   (2009),   Liberalization   in   reverse, http://www.heritage.org/Research/Commentary/2009/05/Liberalization-in-Reverse

205. Lewis, W. Arthur (1954). "Economic Development with Unlimited Supplies of Labor". Manchester School of Economic and Social Studies, Vol. 22, pp. 139-91.

206. "China Reaches Turning Point as Inflation Overtakes Labor". Bloomberg. June 11, 2010. http://www.bloomberg.com/apps/news?pid=20601068&sid=aZGJ0mc_Dm5o

207. "Shortage of Migrant Workers Suggests Arrival of Lewisian Turning Point-Industrial Upgrading Likely to Accelerate as a Result", Reaserch Institute of Economy, Trade & Industry, China in Transition, April 28, 2010. http://www.rieti.go.jp/en/china/10042801.html#figure5.

208. Ma, Guonan & Yi Wang (2010), "China's High Saving Rate: Myth and Reality", Bank for International Settlement Working Papers No 312, Switzerland. http://www.bis.org/publ/work312.pdf

209. "Russia signs second China gas deal, but falling prices raise doubts", by Vladimir Soldatkin and Chen Aizhu, Reuters, 10 November, 2014, http://www.reuters.com/article/2014/11/10/us-russia-china-gas-idUSKCN0IU17K20141110 Retrieved on 24 December, 2014

210. Barth, Chris (2012), "Why India Won't Be The Next China...And That's Bullish", June 6, 2012. http://www.forbes.com/sites/chrisbarth/2012/06/06/why-india-wont-be-the-next-china-and-thats-bullish/ Retrieved on 25 March, 2014.

211. Roy, Satyaki (2007): Structural change in employment in India since 1980s: How Lewisian is it? Social Scientist , Vol. 36, No. 11-12 (2008): pp. 47-68. Online at http://mpra.ub.uni-muenchen.de/18009/ Retrieved on 25 March, 2014.

212. "Combating Poverty and Inequality: Structural Change, Social Policy and Politics", United Nations Research Institute for Social Development (UNRISD), 2010. http://www.unrisd.org/, 3 September, 2010, ISBN: 978-92-9085-076-2.

213. "Number and Percentage of Population Below Poverty Line". Reserve Bank of India. 2012, http://www.rbi.org.in/scripts/PublicationsView.aspx?id=15283 Retrieved on 24 December, 2014.

214. "India – New Global Poverty Estimates". World Bank. http://povertydata.worldbank.org/poverty/country/IND. Retrieved on 24 December, 2014.

215. "India Factsheet UNDP India: Economic and Human Development Indicators", http://www.in.undp.org/content/dam/india/docs/india_factsheet_economic_n_hdi.pdf Retrieved on 24 December, 2014.

216. "Five Myths About India's Poverty", by Richard Dobbs & Anu Madgavkar, The World Post, 6 February, 2014, http://www.huffingtonpost.com/richard-dobbs-/india-poverty-myths_b_5429858.html Retrieved on: 24 December, 2014

217. "Economy of India", Wikipedia, http://en.wikipedia.org/wiki/Economy_of_India

218. "RBI governor Raghuram Rajan meets Narendra Modi", LiveMint, 1 June 2014, http://www.livemint.com/Politics/Jh1N8RUWG7J5BKZfTSyYZO/RBI-governor-Raghuram-Rajan-meets-Narendra-Modi.html Retrieved on: 23 December, 2014

219. Madison, Angus (2007). Contours of the world economy, 1-2030 AD: essays in macro-economic history. Oxford University Press. p. 379. ISBN 0-19-922720-9.

220. Madison, Angus (2006). The world economy, Volumes 1–2. OECD Publishing. p. 638. ISBN 92-64-02261-9.

221. "Of Oxford, economics, empire, and freedom". The Hindu, 10 July, 2005 http://www.hindu.com/2005/07/10/stories/2005071002301000.htm. Retrieved on 28 March, 2014.

222. "Indira Gandhi", Wikipedia, http://en.wikipedia.org/wiki/Indira_Gandhi

223. Graph based on information: "Historic inflation India - CPI inflation", http://www.inflation.eu/inflation-rates/india/historic-inflation/cpi-inflation-india.aspx

224. Brass, Paul R. (1994), "The Politics of India Since Independence", Cambridge University Press. pp. 40–50. ISBN 978-0-521-45970-9.

225. "Moraji Desai", Wikipedia, http://en.wikipedia.org/wiki/Morarji_Desai

226. "Rajiv Gandhi", Wikipedia, http://en.wikipedia.org/wiki/Rajiv_Gandhi

227. Unequal effects of Liberalization – Dismantling the license raj in India. http://www.princeton.edu/~reddings/pubpapers/ABRZ_AER_Sept2008.pdf.

228. Ghosh, Arunabha (2006) "Pathways Through Financial Crisis", Understanding Pathways Through Financial Crises and the Impact of the IMF, Global Governance volume 12, No 4, Lynne Rienner Publishers, p413-429, http://www.jstor.org/discover/10.2307/27800629?sid=21105548990773&uid=2&uid=4

229. "Economic reforms in India: Task force report" (http://harrisschool.uchicago.edu/News/press-releases/ IPP Economic Reform in India. pdf) (PDF). University of Chicago. p.7-20.

230. Arackal, Peter (2010), "HNI contribution to society is low", The Times of India, Mar 23, 2010, http://articles.timesofindia.indiatimes.com/2010-03-23/india-business/28121860_1_fund-manager-bain-social-sector 23 December, 2014

231. World Bank, Gross Domestic Product for India [MKTGDPINA646NWDB], Retrieved on from FRED, Federal Reserve Bank of St. Louis https://research.stlouisfed.org/fred2/series/MKTGDPINA646NWDB/, February 11, 2013.

232. Nayar, Kuldip (2011), "Laundering black money", Deccan Herald, India. 03 February 2011, http://www.deccanherald.com/content/134580/laundering-black-money.html Retrieved on 23 December, 2014

233. "External debt up at $440 bn pumped by NRI deposits", Ians, Business Standard, 29 August 2014, http://www.business-standard.com/article/news-ians/external-debt-up-at-440-bn-pumped-by-nri-deposits-114082900547_1.html Retrieved on 02 January, 2014

234. "List of Countries by Income Euality", Wikipedia, http://en.wikipedia.org/wiki/List_of_countries_by_income_equality

235. CIA-"The World Factbook-India", https://www.cia.gov/library/publications/the-world-factbook/geos/in.html Retrieved on 30 March 2014

236. "A flourishing slum The residents of Dharavi, allegedly Asia's biggest slum, are thriving in hardship", Urban poverty in India, The Economists, Dec 19th 2007, http://www.economist.com/node/10311293 Retrieved on 30 March 2014

237. "Indian landless march into Delhi ", BBC News, 28 October 2007, http://news.bbc.co.uk/2/hi/south_asia/7065888.stm Retrieved on 30 March 2014

238. "Rajiv Gandhi aimed at value based education in rural India through JNVs". Press brief. http://www.basearticles.com/Art/65874/216/Rajiv-Gandhi-aimed-at-value-based-education-in-rural-India-through-JNVs.html. 30 March 2014

239. Kalam, A. P. J Abdul, Rajan, Y. S. (1998), "India 2020: A Vision for the New Millennium", ISBN 0-670-88271-2.

240. "Fact Sheet on Foreign Direct Investment", March 2012, http://dipp.nic.in/English/Publications/FDI_Statistics/2012/india_FDI_March2012.pdf

241. "India Nutrition", UNICEF, http://www.unicef.org/india/nutrition.html, Retrieved on 30 March 2014

242. Country Strategy for India (CAS) 2009–2012" (PDF). World Bank. http://www.ukibc.com/ukindia2/files/India60.pdf.

243. Wright, Tom and Gupta, Harsh (2011). "India's Boom Bypasses Rural Poor". The Wall Street Journal, 29 April 2011. http://online.wsj.com/article/SB10001424052748704081604576143671902043578.html.

244. "Indian rural welfare – Digging holes". The Economist. 5 November 2011. http://www.economist.com/node/21536642.

245. "Highlights of Union Budget 2011-2012", The Times of India, February 28, 2012, http://timesofindia.indiatimes.com/home/union-budget-2011/Highlights-of-Union-Budget-2011-2012/articleshow/7592642.cms?

246. "Illicit Financial Flows from Developing Countries:2003-2012", Global Financial Integrity, http://www.gfintegrity.org/wp-content/uploads/2014/12/Illicit-Financial-Flows-from-Developing-Countries-2003-2012.pdf Retrieved on 24 December, 2014.

247. Rubin, Jeff (2012), "The End of Growth", Random House Canada, pp. 37-70.

248. Shangquan, Gao (2000), "Economic Globalization: Trends, Risks and Risk Prevention", Economic & Social Affairs, United Union, p.3-10, http://www.un.org/en/development/desa/policy/cdp/cdp_background_papers/bp2000_1.pdf

249. "World Economy", Wikipedia, Retrieved on from http://www.scribd.com/doc/234796197/World-Economy#scribd

250. "U.S. FDI and site selection". Greyhill Advisors. http://www.esa.doc.gov/Reports/foreign-direct-investment-united-states.

251. "U.S. trade gap with China cost 2.7 million jobs: study" Yahoo! News. August 23, 2012.

252. "Manufacturing and Trade". Greyhill Advisors. http://greyhill.com/blog/2011/10/6/manufacturing-and-trade.html.

253. US. Bureau of Economic Analysis, Balance on Merchandise Trade [BOPBMA], Retrieved on from FRED, Federal Reserve Bank of St. Louis https://research.stlouisfed.org/fred2/series/BOPBMA/, January 2, 2015.

254. Bastiat, Frederic (1848), "The Balance of Trade", Selected Essays on Political Economy. http://www.econlib.org/library/Bastiat/basEss13.html

255. Krugman, P. and A. Venables (1995), Globalization and the Inequality of Nations, Quarterly Journal of Economics, 110, 857-880.

256. Economic Focus:". The Economist (London: The Economist Group): p. 81. 2008-04-19.

257. "Chinese Auto Sales Set New World Record of 18 Million Units in 2010". ChinaAutoWeb.com. http://chinaautoweb.com/2011/01/chinese-auto-sales-set-new-world-record-of-18-million-units-in-2010/.

258. Rawski, G. Thomas et al. (2008), "China's Industrial Development", China's Great Transformation, Cambridge university press. P.588-593

259. "Chinese Auto Sales Set New World Record of 18 Million Units in 2010". ChinaAutoWeb.com. http://chinaautoweb.com/2011/01/chinese-auto-sales-set-new-world-record-of-18-million-units-in-2010/.

260. "The Debt to the Penny and Who Holds It", Treasury Direct, http://www.treasurydirect.gov/NP/debt/current

261. "China must keep buying US Treasuries for now-paper". Reuters. August 19, 2009, http://www.reuters.com/article/2009/08/20/china-usa-treasuries-iduspek16627420090820

262. "Comparative Advantage", Wikipedia, http://en.wikipedia.org/wiki/Comparative_advantage

263. Roberts, Paul Craig (August 7, 2003). Jobless in the USA Newsmax, http://archive.newsmax.com/archives/articles/2003/8/6/132901.shtml.

264. Mack, Eric (2012), "iPhone manufacturing costs revealed?", CNET, February 22, 2012. http://news.cnet.com/8301-17938_105-57382995-1/iphone-manufacturing-costs-revealed/

265. Jackson, James K. (2013) "U.S. Direct Investment Abroad: Trends and Current Issues", Congressional Research Service, http://fas.org/sgp/crs/misc/RS21118.pdf

266. "Shale Oil: In a bind: Will falling oil prices curb America's shale boom?", by Lindsay, Oklahoma, 6 December 2014, The Economists, http://www.economist.com/news/finance-and-economics/21635505-will-falling-oil-prices-curb-americas-shale-boom-bind Retrieved on 29 December 2014

267. Henry, James (2012), "The Price of Offshore Revisited: New Estimates for Missing Global Private Wealth, Income, Inequality and Lost Taxes"", Tax Justice Network.

268. "Super rich hold $32 trillion in offshore havens", Reuters, 22 July, 2012, http://uk.reuters.com/article/2012/07/22/uk-offshore-wealth-idUKBRE86L03W20120722?feedType=RSS&feedName=topNews Retrieved on: 25 December, 2014

269. "Opec: Oil demand to hit 111m barrels by 2040 despite climate change" By Andrew Critchlow, 06 November 2014, The Telegraph,

http://www.telegraph.co.uk/finance/newsbysector/energy/oilandgas/11213302/Opec-Oil-demand-to-hit-111m-barrels-by-2040-despite-climate-change.html

270. "Oil Prices: What's Behind the Drop? Simple Economics", by Clifford Krauss, October 5, 2015, http://www.nytimes.com/interactive/2015/business/energy-environment/oil-prices.html?_r=0 Retrieved on November 23, 2015.

271. "Oil Prices Will Take 5 Years To Recover - IEA", by Geoffrey Smith, Fortune, November 10, 2015, http://fortune.com/2015/11/10/iea-low-oil-prices-outlook-2015/ Retrieved on November 23, 2015.

272. United States Congress, Government Accountability Office, FY 2007 Financial Report, p. 47, http://www.gao.gov/financial_pdfs/fy2007/07frusg.pdf Retrieved on August 3, 2015.

273. "EU growth gets boost from oil but risks 'intensify'" By Bruno Waterfield, 05 Feb 2015, The Telegraph, http://www.telegraph.co.uk/news/worldnews/europe/eu/11392039/EU-growth-gets-boost-from-oil-but-risks-intensify.html Retrieved on November 22, 2015.

274. "The World's Most Powerful People", Forbes, http://www.forbes.com/profile/vladimir-putin/

275. "Tech Billionaires Team Up to Take On Climate Change", Wired, November 30, 2015, http://www.wired.com/2015/11/zuckerberg-gates-climate-change-breakthrough-energy-coalition/ Retrieved on December 8, 2015.

276. "India's Need for Coal-Fueled Growth Complicates Paris Climate Summit", Nikhil Kumar, Time, December 1, 2015, http://time.com/4131236/india-coal-climate-change-paris-summit/ Retrieved on December 8, 2015.

277. "Technology's role in a climate solution", Bulletin of Atomic Scientists, http://thebulletin.org/technologys-role-climate-solution Retrieved on December 9, 2015

278. Graph prepared by the author by using data from "CO2 time series 1990-2014 per region/country". Netherlands Environmental Assessment Agency,

http://edgar.jrc.ec.europa.eu/overview.php?v=CO2ts1990-2014&sort=des9
Retrieved on December 7, 2015 Retrieved on: 7 December, 2015

279. "China's strategies to combat climate change", Climate Group's July report, by Changhua Wu, 7 OCTOBER 2008, extracted from http://thebulletin.org/chinas-strategies-combat-climate-change

280. "Most glaciers in Mount Everest area will disappear with climate change – study", John Vidal, The Guardian, 27 May 2015, http://www.theguardian.com/environment/2015/may/27/most-glaciers-in-mount-everest-area-will-disappear-with-climate-change-study Retrieved on December 8, 2015

281. Joseph R. Curray and David G. Moore, "Growth of the Bengal Deep-Sea Fan and Denudation in the Himalayas," Geological Society of America Bulletin 82, no. 3 (1971): 563-72.

282. India government reveals progress to 100GW solar; Modi focuses on solar parks, by By Tom Kenning, PVTech, October 01, 2016, http://www.pv-tech.org/news/india_government_reveals_progress_to_100gw_solar_modi_focuses_on_solar_park Retrieved on 22 March, 2016.

283. Saudi Arabia's Post-Oil Plan Starts April 25, Prince Says by Riad Hamade & Alaa Shahine, Bloomberg, April 16, 2016, http://www.bloomberg.com/news/articles/2016-04-16/saudi-arabia-to-launch-plan-for-the-future-april-25-prince-says Retrieved on April 17, 2016

284. Carroll, Lewis (1865), "Alice's Adventures in Wonderland", Templar, Slp edition (Sept. 22 2009), Slp edition (Sept. 22 2009).

Chapter 6: Toward Fossil Civilization

1. Quigley, Carroll (1966), "Tragedy and Hope: A History of The World in Our Time", The Macmillan Company, New York, pp.3

2. "Revealing Statements from a Bush Insider about Peak Oil and Natural Gas Depletion", June 12, 2003, The Wilderness Publications, http://www.fromthewilderness.com/free/ww3/061203_simmons.html Retrieved on 29 September, 2013.

3. Heinberg, Richard (2013), "Snake Oil: How Big Energy's Misleading Promise of Plenty Imperils Our Future", Chapter 1, pp.19-36.

4. Yunus, Mohammad (2006). 'The Nobel Peace Prize Laureate 2006', Oslo. The fipbel Foundation. Stockholm, Sweden.

5. Martenson, Chris (2011). The Crash Course: "The Unsustainable Future of Our Economy, Energy, and Environment". John Wily & Sons, Inc., Hoboken, New Jersey, pp.125-157.

6. "US Crude Oil Production and Imports by year in millions of barrels per day", US Energy Information Administration. This is a file from the Wikimedia Commons. This file is licensed under the Creative Commons Attribution-Share Alike 3.0 Unported, 2.5 Generic, 2.0 Generic and 1.0 Generic license. http://en.wikipedia.org/wiki/File:US_Crude_Oil_Production_and_Imports.svg September 29, 2013.

7. Meadows, Donella H; Randers, Jorgen; Meadows, Dennis L.; Behrens, William W. "The Limits to growth: A report for the Club of Rome's Project on the Predicament of Mankind", Universe Books, 2nd edition February 18, 1974.

8. "The Limits to Growth", wikipedia, http://en.wikipedia.org/wiki/The_Limits_to_Growth September 29, 2013.

9. "Club of Rome", Wikipedia, http://en.wikipedia.org/wiki/Club_of_Rome September 29, 2013.

10. Campbell, Colin (2003), "When will the world's oil and gas production peak?", http://www.feasta.org/documents/wells/contents.html?one/campbell.html originally published in Before the Wells Run Dry: Ireland's Transition to Renewable Energy, edited by Richard Douthwaite, Green Books, UK.

11. Heinberg, Richard (2011), "The End of Growth: Adapting to our New Economic Reality", New Society Publishers, Canada. pp. 105-145.

12. Appenzeller, Tim (June 2004). "The End of Cheap Oil". National Geographic. http://ngm.nationalgeographic.com/ngm/0406/feature5/fulltext.html September 29, 2013.

13. "World Oil Depletion Per Major Producer" A time chart of oil depletion at each oil producing country, created by Wikipedia. The author has released this work into the public domain., http://commons.wikimedia.org/wiki/File:Oil_depletion_per_country.jpg Retrieved on September 29, 2013.

14. "World Oil Crisis: Driving forces, Impact and Effects", http://www.world-crisis.net/oil-crisis.html September 29, 2013.

15. Downs, Erica (2014), "A Grand Bargain", GavekalDragonomics Global Research, Ideas, Thursday, May 22, 2014, http://www.brookings.edu/~/media/research/files/articles/2014/05/28%20russia%20china%20gas%20grand%20bargain%20downs/28%20grand%20bargain%20downs.pdf Retrieved on September 30, 2013.

16. Heinberg, Richard (2013), "Snake Oil: How Big Energy's Misleading Promise of Plenty Imperils Our Future", Campaign Webpage, http://www.indiegogo.com/projects/snake-oil-how-big-energy-s-misleading-promise-of-plenty-imperils-our-future September 29, 2013.

17. Graph drawn based on data from "International Petroleum Monthly, December 2010", Energy Information Administration, http://www.eia.gov/petroleum/supply/monthly/ Retrieved on 19 October, 2013.

18. Heinberg, Richard (2011), "The End of Growth: Adapting to our New Economic Reality", New Society Publishers, Canada. pp. 63

19. Heinberg, Richard (2011), "The End of Growth: Adapting to our New Economic Reality", New Society Publishers, Canada. pp. 1-26.

20. "A Green New Deal: Joined-up policies to solve the triple crunch of the credit crisis, climate change and high oil prices", Green New Deal Group, http://s.bsd.net/nefoundation/default/page/file/8f737ea195fe56db2f_xbm6ihwb1.pdf Retrieved on: March 19, 2014.

21. Hagens, Nate (2008). "Unconventional Oil: Tar Sands and Shale Oil-EROI on the Web, Part 3 of 6." Oil Drum, April 15, 2008. www.theoildrum.com/node/3839 Retrieved on: March 19, 2014.

22. Cutler J. Cleveland and Peter O'Connor (2010), "An Assessment of the Energy Return on Investment (EROI) of Oil Shale," Western Resource Advocates. www.westernresourceadvocates.org/land/pdf/oseroireport.pdf Retrieved on: March 19, 2014.

23. Rubin, Jeff (2012), "The End of Growth", Random House Canada, pp.99-121.

24. "Graph of types of coal produced in China", created by Wikipedia, http://en.wikipedia.org/wiki/File:China_coal_prod.PNG. The author has released this work into the public domain, Data Source: http://www.iea.org/w/bookshop/add.aspx?id=355, Retrieved on September 29, 2014.

25. "Capacity of China's straw-fueled power plants reaches 1.2 mln kw". Xinhua. 16 January, 2007, http://english.people.com.cn/200701/16/eng20070116_341780.html Retrieved on: March 19, 2014.

26. Peter Fairley, Technology Review. Part I: China's Coal Future, January 5, 2007.

27. Cohen, Armond (2014). "Learning from China: A Blueprint for the Future of Coal in Asia?". The National Bureau of Asian Research, April 21, 2014, http://www.nbr.org/research/activity.aspx?id=418 Retrieved on November 14, 2014.

28. "Warm February", by Andy Soos, Environmental News Network, March 15, 2013, http://www.enn.com/top_stories/article/45725

29. Heinberg, Richard (2011), "The End of Growth: Adapting to our New Economic Reality", New Society Publishers, Canada. pp. 189-229.

30. Zittel, Werner & Schindler, Jorg (2007), "Coal:Resources and Future Production", EWG-Paper 1/07, Ottobrunn, Germany:Energy Watch Group.

31. Patzek, Tadeusz & Croft, Gregory D. (2010), "A Global Coal Production Forecast with Multi-Hubbert Cycle Analysis, " Energy 35, Source: Energy Information Administration

32. Brown, Lester R. (2007). "Biofuels Blunder:Massive Diversion of U.S. Grain to Fuel Cars is Raising World Food Prices, Risking Political Instability". Testimony before U.S. Senate Committee on Environment and Public Works.

33. Mitchell, Donald (2008). "A note on Rising Food Crisis". The World Bank. http://wwwwds.worldbank.org/external/default/WDSContentServer/IW3P/IB/2008/07/28/000020439_20080728103002/Rendered/PDF/WP4682.pdf Retrieved on November 14, 2014.

34. Environment Protection Agency, "Biofuels and the Environment: The First Triennial Report to Congress", Draft Report EPA/600/R-10/183A, January 28, 2011.

35. Pimentel, David & Patzek, Tad W. (2005), "Ethanol Production Using Corn, Switchgrass and Wood; Biodiesel Production Using Soybean and Sunflower", National Resources Research 14, no 1.

36. David Suzuki Foundation, http://www.davidsuzuki.org/issues/climate-change/ Retrieved on November 14, 2014.

37. "Greenhouse Effect", Wikipedia, http://en.wikipedia.org/wiki/Greenhouse_effect Retrieved on November 14, 2014.

38. IPCC Synthesis Report (2007), Fourth Assessment Report, Chapter 1 Observed changes in climate and their effects, in IPCC AR4 SYR. http://www.ipcc.ch/publications_and_data/ar4/syr/en/mains1.html Retrieved on November 14, 2014.

39. E. Claussen, V. A. Cochran, and D. P. Davis, Climate Change: Science, Strategies, & Solutions, University of Michigan, 2001. p. 373.

40. IPCC Synthesis Report (2007), Fourth Assessment Report, in Solomon, S.; Qin, D.; Manning, M.; Chen, Z.; Marquis, M.; Averyt, K.B.; Tignor, M.; and Miller, H.L., Climate Change 2007: The Physical Science Basis, Contribution of Working Group I, Cambridge University Press, ISBN 978-0-521-88009-1 (pb: 978-0-521-70596-7), http://www.ipcc.ch/publications_and_data/ar4/wg1/en/faq-1-3.html Retrieved on November 14, 2014.

41. Petit, J. R.; et al. (1999). "Climate and atmospheric history of the past 420,000 years from the Vostok ice core, Antarctica" (PDF). Nature 399 (6735): 429–436. http://www.daycreek.com/dc/images/1999.pdf Retrieved on November 14, 2014.

42. "Global Climate Change, Evidence: How do we know?", NASA, Author: Global Climate Change -- Earth Science Communications Team at NASA's Jet Propulsion Laboratory/California Institute of Technology http://climate.nasa.gov/evidence/, This file is in the public domain because it was solely created by NASA. NASA copyright policy states that "NASA material is not protected by copyright unless noted". (See Template:PD-USGov, NASA copyright policy page or JPL Image Use Policy.) http://commons.wikimedia.org/wiki/File:Evidence_CO2.jpg Retrieved on November 14, 2014.

43. "The current and future consequences of global change", Global Climate Change-Effects, NASA, http://climate.nasa.gov/effects Retrieved on November 14, 2014.

44. Heinberg, Richard (2011), "Earth's Limits: Why Growth Won't Return", http://www.postcarbon.org/article/254838-earth-s-limits-why-growth-won-t-return Retrieved on November 14, 2014.

45. The graph shows the projected increase in carbon dioxide (CO2) emissions from fossil fuels in five of the emissions scenarios used by the IPCC, compared to the International Energy Agency's (IEA's) actual observational CO2 emissions data from fossil fuel consumption. Between the years 2000-2009, growth in CO2 emissions from fossil fuel burning was, on average, 3% per year, which exceeds the growth estimated. (Source: http://en.wikipedia.org/wiki/File:Global_Warming_Observed_CO2_Emissions_from_fossil_fuel_burning_vs_IPCC_scenarios.jpg (Authored by Dana Nuccitelli, data from IPCC emissions scenarios; Data spreadsheet included with International Energy Agency's "CO2 Emissions from Fuel Combustion 2011 - Highlights"; and

Supplemental 2010 IEA data; and Supplemental 2011 IEA data, Copied under the Creative Commons Attribution-Share Alike 3.0 Unported license from Wikimedia Commons. Retrieved on November 14, 2014.

46. "Fifth Assessment Report (AR5)", Intergovernmental Panel on Climate Change (IPCC), , http://www.ipcc.ch/report/ar5/ Retrieved on November 14, 2014.

47. "IPCC Fifth Assessment Report", Wikipedia, http://en.wikipedia.org/wiki/IPCC_Fifth_Assessment_Report Retrieved on November 14, 2014.

48. Meehl et al. (2007), "Chap. 10: Global Climate Projections, Sec. 10.ES: Mean Temperature", IPCC AR4 WG1 2007 http://www.ipcc.ch/publications_and_data/ar4/wg1/en/ch10s10-es-1-mean-temperature.html Retrieved on November 14, 2014.

49. Graph prepared by the author by using data from "CO2 time series 1990-2014 per region/country". Netherlands Environmental Assessment Agency, http://edgar.jrc.ec.europa.eu/overview.php?v=CO2ts1990-2014&sort=des9 Retrieved on December 10, 2015.

50. Rees, Eifion (2011). "UK's greenhouse gas emissions reductions an 'illusion'". Ecologist, February 2, 2011 http://www.theecologist.org/News/news_analysis/753571/uks_greenhouse_gas_emissions_reductions_an_illusion.html, Retrieved on 11 November, 2014.

51. Rhein, M., et al. (7 June 2013): Box 3.1, in: Chapter 3: Observations: Ocean (final draft accepted by IPCC Working Group I), pp.11-12 (pp.14-15 of PDF chapter), in: IPCC AR5 WG1 2013

52. Muller, Elizabeth "China Must Exploit Its Shale Gas" The New York Times, 12 April 2013, http://www.nytimes.com/2013/04/13/opinion/china-must-exploit-its-shale-gas.html?_r=1& 11 November, 2014

53. "Notwithstanding Significant Uncertainties, the U.S.-China Joint Announcement on Climate Change Is a Big Deal", by Tim Boersma, Brookings, November 13, 2014, http://www.brookings.edu/blogs/planetpolicy/posts/2014/11/13-us-china-joint-announcement-on-climate-change-boersma 11 November, 2014

54. "China's Reality in the US-China Climate Change Deal", by Sara Hsu, The Diplomat, November 14, 2014, http://thediplomat.com/2014/11/chinas-reality-in-the-us-china-climate-change-deal/ Retrieved on November 14, 2014.

55. Wang, M; J.E. Overland (2009). "A sea ice free summer Arctic within 30 years?". Geophys. Res. Lett 36 (7), Pacific Marine Environmental Laboratory, http://www.pmel.noaa.gov/publications/search_abstract.php?fmContributionNum=3261 Retrieved on November 14, 2014.

56. Ocean acidification may weaken or kill plankton, responsible for half of world's oxygen production", Monash University, May 4, 2012, http://dgrnewsservice.org/2012/05/04/ocean-acidification-may-weaken-or-kill-plankton-responsible-for-half-of-worlds-oxygen-production/ Retrieved on September 29, 2014.

57. Sabine C. L. et al., 2004. The oceanic sink for anthropogenic CO2. Science 305:367-371.

58. "European Project on OCean Acidification (EPOCA)", http://www.epoca-project.eu/index.php/what-is-ocean-acidification.html Retrieved on September 29, 2014.

59. Schneider et al. (2007), "Chapter 19: Assessing Key Vulnerabilities and the Risk from Climate Change, Section 19.3.3: Regional vulnerabilities", IPCC AR4, WG2. http://www.ipcc.ch/publications_and_data/ar4/wg2/en/ch19.html Retrieved on September 29, 2014.

60. "Energy change inventory, 1971-2010", Data reference from Rhein, M., et al. (2013-06-07), "Box 3.1, in: Chapter 3: Observations: Ocean (final draft)", in Qin, D. and T. Stocker, Climate Change 2013: The Physical Science Basis. Working Group I Contribution to the Intergovernmental Panel on Climate Change (IPCC) 5th Assessment Report, IPCC, http://www.climatechange2013.org/images/uploads/WGIAR5_WGI-12Doc2b_FinalDraft_Chapter03.pdf, pp.11-12 (pp.14-15 of PDF chapter), Wikipedia dedicated this graph to the public domain, https://commons.wikimedia.org/wiki/File:Energy_change_inventory,_1971-2010.svg Retrieved on December 9, 2015

61. Latin, Howard A. (2012), "Climate Change Policy Failures: Why Conventional Mitigation Approaches Cannot Succeed", World Scientific, Singapore.

62. "Human Appropriation of the World's Fresh Water Supply", January 04, 2006 http://www.globalchange.umich.edu/globalchange2/current/lectures/freshwater_supply/freshwater.html Retrieved on September 29, 2014

63. Gilbert, Natasha (2010), "Balancing water supply and wildlife", Nature, Published online 29 September 2010, http://www.nature.com/news/2010/100929/full/news.2010.505.html Retrieved on September 29, 2014

64. "Peak Water", Wikipedia, http://en.wikipedia.org/wiki/Peak_water Retrieved on September 29, 2014

65. "Water Scarcity", Wikipedia, http://en.wikipedia.org/wiki/Water_scarcity Retrieved on September 29, 2014

66. Falkenmark and Lindh (1976), quoted in UNEP/WMO. "Climate Change 2001: Working Group II: Impacts, Adaptation and Vulnerability". UNEP. http://www.grida.no/publications/other/ipcc_tar/?src=/climate/ipcc_tar/wg2/180.htm Retrieved on September 29, 2014

67. "World Population", Wikipedia, http://en.wikipedia.org/wiki/World_population Retrieved on September 29, 2014

68. Author's own graph from information from http://en.wikipedia.org/wiki/World_population Retrieved on September 29, 2014

69. United Nations Press Release POP/952, 13 March 2007. World population will increase by 2.5 billion by 2050, http://www.un.org/News/Press/docs/2007/pop952.doc.htm Retrieved on September 29, 2014.

70. Samuel T. L. Larsen. "Lack of Freshwater Throughout the World". Evergreen State College. http://academic.evergreen.edu/g/grossmaz/LARSENST/ Retrieved on September 29, 2014.

71. "Water Supply and Sanitation in India", Wikipedia, http://en.wikipedia.org/wiki/Water_supply_and_sanitation_in_India Retrieved on September 29, 2014.

72. "2007 Benchmarking and Data Book of Water Utilities in India", Asian Development Bank.

73. "Vanishing Himalayan Glaciers Threaten a Billion", Planetark.com, 2007-06-05. http://www.planetark.com/dailynewsstory.cfm/newsid/42387/story.htm Retrieved on October 10, 2014.

74. Gleick, Peter H. (2008). "The World's Water 2008-2009". Island Press, Washington, D.C. pp. Table 2, http://www.worldwater.org/data.html Retrieved on October 10, 2014.

75. "Ganga is now a deadly source of cancer", http://timesofindia.indiatimes.com/india/Ganga-is-now-a-deadly-source-of-cancer-study-says/articleshow/16842966.cms Retrieved on October 10, 2014.

76. Heinberg, Richard (2015), "Our Renewable Future", Post Carbon Institute, January 21, 2015, http://www.postcarbon.org/our-renewable-future-essay/ Retrieved on January 31, 2015.

77. Puttick, Elizabeth (2008), "Mother Ganges, India's Sacred River", in Emoto, Masaru, The Healing Power of Water, Hay House Inc. Pp. 275, pp. 241–252, ISBN 1-4019-0877-2

78. Udasin, Sharon (2012), "Preserving a highly polluted holy river", The Jerusalem Post, May 03, 2012, http://www.jpost.com/Enviro-Tech/Preserving-a-highly-polluted-holy-river Retrieved on October 10, 2014.

79. "Ganga Action Plan bears no fruit". The Hindu (Chennai, India). 28 August 2004. http://www.hindu.com/2004/08/28/stories/2004082807430400.htm Retrieved on October 10, 2014.

80. Water Resources, Wikipedia, http://en.wikipedia.org/wiki/Water_resources Retrieved on October 10, 2014.

81. Lewis, Leo (2009). "Ecologists warn the planet is running short of water". London: Times Online, http://www.thetimes.co.uk/tto/environment// Retrieved on October 10, 2014.

82. Bardi, Ugo (2008) Peak water in Saudi Arabia, The Oil Drum:Europe, January 29, 2008, http://www.theoildrum.com/node/3520

83. Omar Salem (2007-04). "Water Resources Management in Libya" (PDF). Global Water Partnership Mediterranean. http://www.gwp.org/en/GWP-Mediterranean/

84. "Shuweihat Water Transmission Scheme, United Arab Emirates". water-technology.net., http://www.water-technology.net/projects/shuweihat/ Retrieved on October 10, 2014.

85. Boaz, Peter and O. Berger, Matthew (2010), "Rising Energy Demand Hits Water Scarcity 'Choke Point'". Inter Press Serivce News Agency, September 22, 2010, http://www.ipsnews.net/2010/09/rising-energy-demand-hits-water-scarcity-choke-point/ Retrieved on October 10, 2014.

86. Water, Wikipedia, http://en.wikipedia.org/wiki/Water Retrieved on October 10, 2014.

87. "Highlights of GCM Predictions: Surface Water", College of Earth and Mineral Science, Pennsylvania State University, John A Dutton, e-Education Institute, https://www.e-education.psu.edu/earth103/node/684 Retrieved on October 10, 2014.

88. Horrigan Leo, Lawrence Robert S., and Walker Polly (2002), "How Sustainable Agriculture Can Address the Environmental and Human Health Harms of Industrial Agriculture," Environmental Health Perspectives 110, no.5, May, 2002.

89. Déry, Patrick (2007), "Pérenniser l'agriculture, Mémoire pour la Commission Sur l'Avenir de l'Agriculture du Québec", GREB,April 2007.

90. "New Threat to Global Food Security as Phosphate Supplies Become Increasingly Scarce," Soil Association, November 29, 2010.

91. "World's Fish Supply Running Out, Researchers Warn", by Juliet Eilperin, The Washington Post, November 3, 2006, http://www.washingtonpost.com/wp-

dyn/content/article/2006/11/02/AR2006110200913.html Retrieved on: November 12, 2014

92. "Africa", Intergovernmental Panel on Climate Change (IPCC), http://unfccc.int/essential_background/the_science/climate_change_impacts_map/items/6224txt.php Retrieved on: November 12, 2014

93. "UN: Somali famine is over, but action still needed". Thejournal.ie. http://www.thejournal.ie/un-somalian-famine-is-over-but-action-still-needed-347449-Feb2012/ Retrieved on: November 12, 2014

94. Julian Cribb, The Coming Famine: The Global Food Crisis and What We Can Do to Avoid It (Berkeley and Los Angeles: University of California Press, 2010).

95. "Pakistan and India to go to War over Water?", by John Daly, Oilprice, 04 April, 2012, http://oilprice.com/Geopolitics/Asia/Pakistan-and-India-to-go-to-War-over-Water.html Retrieved on 7 March, 2015.

96. Boulding, Kenneth E . (1996) [1966] "The Economics of the Coming Spaceship Earth", in Victor D. Lippit, ed., Radical Political Economy, Armonk, NY: M.E. Sharpe. p 362.

97. "The Debt to the Penny and Who Holds It", Treasury Direct http://www.treasurydirect.gov/NP/debt/current Retrieved on January 11, 2015.

98. Rubin, Jeff (2012), "The End of Growth", Random House Canada.

99. "The Coming Stock Market Crash and The Death of Money with Jim Rickards", Money Morning, https://www.youtube.com/watch?v=tQBia1Mw9Vw&gclid=CJbLtZjLgsECFcRAMgodHmAAvw Retrieved on October 10, 2014.

100. "As Oil Prices Plummet, Saudi Arabia Faces a Test of Strategy" by By Ben Hubbard and Clifford Krauss, http://www.nytimes.com/2014/10/16/world/middleeast/as-oil-prices-plummet-saudi-arabia-faces-a-test-of-strategy.html?_r=0 Retrieved on October 19, 2014.

101. Tverberg, Gail (2013), "Twelve Reasons Why Globalization is a Huge Problem", http://ourfiniteworld.com/2013/02/22/twelve-reasons-why-globalization-is-a-huge-problem/ Retrieved on October 19, 2014

102. Baragona, Steve (2011), "2011 Food Price Spikes Helped Trigger Arab Spring, Researchers Say", Voice of America, December 13, 2011, http://www.voanews.com/content/article-2011-food-price-spikes-helped-trigger-arab-spring-135576278/149523.html Retrieved on October 19, 2014

103. Swanson, Joseph; Williamson, Samuel (1972). "Estimates of national product and income for the United States economy, 1919–1941". Explorations in Economic History 10: 53–73. doi:10.1016/0014-4983(72)90003-4.

104. "A Bennett Buggy, 1935", University of Saskatchewan, University Archives and Special Collections photograph collection : A-3412 http://en.wikipedia.org/wiki/File:35bennettbuggy.jpg Retrieved on 8 March, 2015.

105. Heinberg, Richard (2011), "The End of Growth: Adapting to our New Economic Reality", New Society Publishers, Canada. pp. 231-266.

106. Heinberg, Richard (2011), "The End of Growth: Adapting to our New Economic Reality", New Society Publishers, Canada. pp. 189-230.

107. David Montgomery (2007), "Dirt: The Erosion of Civilizations", Berkeley and Los Angeles: University of California Press.

108. Beach, T. et al. (2006), "Impacts of the Ancient Maya on Soils and Soil Erosion in the Central Maya Lowlands," Catena 65, no.2, February 28, 2006, pp. 166–178.

109. Gatehouse, Jonathon (2014), "How safe are you?", Maclean's, October 27, 2014, Canada.

110. Duncan, Richard C. (1996), "The Olduvai Theory: Sliding Towards a Post-Industrial Stone Age", Institute on Energy and Man, June 27, 196, http://www.jayhanson.us/page125.htm Retrieved on: November 14, 2014.

111. "Revisiting the Olduvai Theory", The Oil Drum, March 6, 2006, http://www.theoildrum.com/story/2006/3/6/135437/7111 Retrieved on: November 14, 2014.

112. World Energy Outlook 2010". International Energy Agency. 2010, http://www.worldenergyoutlook.org/ Retrieved on: November 14, 2014.

113. Heinberg, Richard (2013), "Snake Oil: How Big Energy's Misleading Promise of Plenty Imperils Our Future", Chapter 3.

114. World Energy Outlook 2012 Factsheet, "How will global energy markets evolve to 2035?", International Energy Agency. http://www.worldenergyoutlook.org/media/weowebsite/2012/factsheets.pdf. Retrieved on December 10, 2014.

115. "U.S. to overtake Saudi as top oil producer: IEA", Interview with Maria Van Der Hoeven, Executive Director of the IEA, Reuters TV, November 12, 2012, http://www.reuters.com/article/video/idUSBRE8AB0IQ20121112?videoId=239070 930 Retrieved on December 10, 2014.

116. "Saudi America, The U.S. will be the world's leading energy producer, if we allow it," The Wall Street Journal, November 14, 2012, http://online.wsj.com/article/SB10001424127887323894704578114591174453074. html Retrieved on December 10, 2014.

117. Pierrehumbert, Raymond T. (2013), "The Myth of "Saudi America": Straight talk from geologists about our new era of oil abundance", Slate, http://www.slate.com/articles/health_and_science/science/2013/02/u_s_shale_oil_ar e_we_headed_to_a_new_era_of_oil_abundance.single.html Retrieved on December 10, 2014.

118. Maugeri, Leonardo (2009). "Leonardo Maugeri: The Crude Truth About Oil Reserves ", 04 November, 2009, The Wall Street Journal, http://online.wsj.com/article/SB10001424052748704107204574470700973579402. html#articleTabs%3Darticle Retrieved on December 10, 2014.

119. Citigroup Inc, "Resurging North American Oil Production and the Death of the Peak Oil Hypothesis", https://www.citigroupgeo.com/pdf/SEUNHGJJ.pdf, pp. 9-10, Retrieved on December 10, 2014.

120. Institute for Energy Research, "New Oil Finds Around the Globe: Will the U.S. Capitalize on Its Oil Resources?"

http://www.instituteforenergyresearch.org/2011/09/13/new-oil-finds-around-the-globe-will-the-u-s-capitalize-on-its-oil-resources/ Retrieved on December 10, 2014.

121. McCracken, Ross (2012), "Tight Gas to Tight Oil: Squashing Hubbert's Bell Curve", International Association for Energy Economics, http://www.iaee.org/en/ Retrieved on December 10, 2014.

122. Maugeri, Leonardo (2012), "Oil: The Next Revolution: The Unprecedented Upsurge of Oil Production Capacity and What It Means for the World ", John F. Kennedy School of Government, Harvard University, http://belfercenter.ksg.harvard.edu/files/Presentation%20on%20Oil-%20The%20Next%20Revolution.pdf Retrieved on December 10, 2014.

123. Eady, Ashley (2013) "Oil industry insiders divided over longevity, feasability of shale play: Key players expand 2013 drilling budgets as play timeframe is extended", Lubbock Avalanche-Journal, February 3, 2013 , http://lubbockonline.com/business/2013-02-02/oil-industry-insiders-divided-over-longevity-feasability-shale-play?v=1359873091 Retrieved on December 10, 2014.

124. Hughes, David (2013), " Drill Baby Drill: Can Unconventional Fuels Usher in a New Era of Energy Abundance?", Post Carbon Institute, http://www.postcarbon.org/reports/DBD-report-FINAL.pdf Retrieved on December 10, 2014.

125. Maugeri, Leonardo (2012) "Oil: The Next Revolution", The Geopolitics of Energy Project,Harvard Kennedy School, Belfer Center for Science and International Affairs, June 1012, http://belfercenter.ksg.harvard.edu/files/Oil-%20The%20Next%20Revolution.pdf Retrieved on December 10, 2014.

126. Heinberg, Richard (2013), "Snake Oil: How Big Energy's Misleading Promise of Plenty Imperils Our Future", Chapter 2.

127. Office of Management and Budget, Executive Office of the President (April 9, 2001) Fiscal year 2002: Budget of the United States Government, p. 224. http://www.gpoaccess.gov/usbudget/fy02/pdf/budget.pdf Retrieved on December 15, 2014.

128. Office of Management and Budget, Executive Office of the President (July 30, 2004). Fiscal year 2005: Midsession review: Budget of the U.S. Government, p. 28. GPO Access.

129. U.S. Energy Information Administration (EIA), "Technically Recoverable Shale Oil and Shale Gas Resources: An Assessment of 137 Shale Formations in 41 Countries Outside the United States", http://www.eia.gov/analysis/studies/worldshalegas/ Retrieved on December 15, 2014.

130. Byrne, Peter (2012) "US Shale Gas Won't Last Ten Years: Bill Powers", The Energy Report, November 8, 2013, http://www.theenergyreport.com/pub/na/14705 Retrieved on December 15, 2014.

131. "Bill Powers: Give Up the Shale Gas Fantasy and Profit When the Bubble Bursts", The Energy Report, Source: Zig Lambo of The Energy Report, 17 September, 2013 http://www.theenergyreport.com/pub/na/bill-powers-give-up-the-shale-gas-fantasy-and-profit-when-the-bubble-bursts Retrieved on December 15, 2014.

132. "Hard Truths: Facing the Hard Truths about Energy", National Petroleum Council, July 2007, http://www.npchardtruthsreport.org/ Retrieved on December 15, 2014.

133. Morse, Ed. "Move Over, OPEC—Here We Come", The Wall Street Journal, 19 March, 2012, http://online.wsj.com/articles/SB10001424052702304459804577285972222946812 Retrieved on December 15, 2014.

134. "The Interview: Maria Van Der Hoeven, Executive Director of the International Energy Agency", France 24, 09 April, 2013, http://www.france24.com/en/20130404-interview-maria-van-der-hoeven-executive-director-of-the-international-energy-agency-oil-summit Retrieved on December 15, 2014.

135. "Economy of Saudi Arabia", Wikipedia, http://en.wikipedia.org/wiki/Economy_of_Saudi_Arabia Retrieved on December 15, 2014.

136. "New plan to nab illegals revealed". Arab News. 16 April 2013, http://www.arabnews.com/news/448234 Retrieved on 30 April 2013

137. Heinberg, Richard (2009), "Temporary Recession or the End of Growth?" http://richardheinberg.com/208-the-end-of-growth Retrieved on December 15, 2014.

138. "World Energy Outlook 2012" International Energy Agency. http://www.iea.org/publications/freepublications/publication/English.pdf Retrieved on December 15, 2014.

139. "IEA economist: 'We have to leave oil before it leaves us", EurActiv, 07 November, 2011, http://www.euractiv.com/climate-environment/iea-economist-leave-oil-leaves-u-interview-508763 Retrieved on December 15, 2014.

140. Homer-Dixon, Thomas (2007). The Upside of Down; Catastrophe, Creativity and the Renewal of Civilisation. Island Press. ISBN 978-1-59726-630-7.

141. "Energy Returned on Energy Invested", Wikipedia, http://en.wikipedia.org/wiki/Energy_returned_on_energy_invested Retrieved on December 15, 2014.

142. Tainter, Joseph (1990). The Collapse of Complex Societies. Cambridge University Press. ISBN 052138673X.

143. Commoner, B. (1971) The Closing Circle, Nature, Man and Technology, Kopf, NY, pp.267–276.

144. Heinberg, Richard (2013), "Snake Oil: How Big Energy's Misleading Promise of Plenty Imperils Our Future", Chapter 6.

145. "Collapse", an American documentary film directed by Chris Smith, interview of author Michael Ruppert on his book "Confronting Collapse: The Crisis of Energy and Money in a Post Peak Oil World", https://www.youtube.com/watch?v=IVd-zAXACrU Retrieved on 22 February, 2015.

146. Roberts, Paul (2008), "Tapped Out", National Geographic, http://ngm.nationalgeographic.com/2008/06/world-oil/roberts-text Retrieved on 22 February, 2015.

147. Heinberg, Richard (2015), "Afterburn: Society Beyond Fossil Fuels", New Society Publishers, Canada, January 2015.

148. "Global Oil Market Forecasting: Main Approaches & Key Drivers", Steven Kopits, Columbia University, February 11, 2014, http://energypolicy.columbia.edu/events-calendar/global-oil-market-forecasting-main-approaches-key-drivers Retrieved on: July 26, 2015

149. Carroll, Lewis (1865), "Alice's Adventures in Wonderland", Templar, Slp edition (Sept. 22 2009), Slp edition (Sept. 22 2009).

150. "Ocean Heat Content (2012)", Author: National Oceanic and Atmospheric Administration, Source: http://www.nodc.noaa.gov/OC5/3M_HEAT_CONTENT/, This image is in the public domain, Available in https://commons.wikimedia.org/wiki/File:Ocean_Heat_Content_(2012).png Retrieved on July 26, 2015.

151. "Global Warming not slowing-It's Speeding Up", by James Wight, 12 March, 2014, Skeptical Science, http://www.skepticalscience.com/global-warming-not-slowing-its-speeding-up.html Retrieved on July 26, 2015.

152. "China's Monumental Ponzi: Here's How It Unravels", by David Stockman, Contra Corner, March 31, 2014, http://davidstockmanscontracorner.com/chinas-monumental-ponzi-heres-how-it-unravels/ Retrieved on: July 23, 2015

153. "Oil Prices: What's Behind the Drop? Simple Economics", by Clifford Krauss, October 5, 2015, http://www.nytimes.com/interactive/2015/business/energy-environment/oil-prices.html?_r=0 Retrieved on November 24, 2015.

154. "Saudi Arabia Credit Rating Cut by S&P After Oil Prices Sink", by Richard Richtmyer & Elena Popina, BloombergBusiness, http://www.bloomberg.com/news/articles/2015-10-30/saudi-arabia-cut-to-a-from-aa-by-s-p-after-oil-prices-plunge Retrieved on November 24, 2015.

155. "Oil Prices Will Take 5 Years To Recover - IEA", by Geoffrey Smith, Fortune, November 10, 2015, http://fortune.com/2015/11/10/iea-low-oil-prices-outlook-2015/ Retrieved on November 24, 2015.

156. "Changing Climate, Changing Diets: Pathways to Lower Meat consumption", by Laura Wellesley, Catherine Happer and Antony Froggatt, Chatham House, November 2015,

https://www.chathamhouse.org/sites/files/chathamhouse/publications/research/2015 1124DietClimateChangeWellesleyHapperFroggatt.pdf Retrieved on December 11, 2015

157. Can eating less meat help reduce climate change?, by Laura Wellesley, Science & Environment, BBC, 24 November 2015, http://www.bbc.com/news/science-environment-34899066 Retrieved on: December 9, 2015

158. "Opec: Oil demand to hit 111m barrels by 2040 despite climate change" By Andrew Critchlow, 06 November 2014, The Telegraph, http://www.telegraph.co.uk/finance/newsbysector/energy/oilandgas/11213302/Opec-Oil-demand-to-hit-111m-barrels-by-2040-despite-climate-change.html

159. "Bulletin of the Atomic Scientists", Doomsday Clock, Overview, http://thebulletin.org/overview#sthash.a3WMcsKi.dpuf Retrieved on: December 11, 2015.

160. "Oil Prices: What's Behind the Drop? Simple Economics" by Clifford Krauss, , New York Times, February 9, 2016, http://www.nytimes.com/interactive/2016/business/energy-environment/oil-prices.html?_r=0 Retrieved on February 12, 2016

161. "U.S. Crude Oil Export Ban: A 40-Year Restriction Comes to an End", by Brian Wingfield and Isaac Arnsdorf, Bloomberg, December 18, 2015, http://www.bloombergview.com/quicktake/u-s-crude-oil-export-ban Retrieved on February 12, 2016

162. "It is 3 Minutes to Midnight", Doomsday Clock, Bulletin of the Atomic Scientists, http://thebulletin.org/timeline Retrieved on February 12, 2015

163. Rogers, Deborah (2013) "Shale and Wall Street: Was the Decline in Natural Gas Prices Orchestrated?" Energy Policy Forum, February 2013, http://shalebubble.org/wall-street/ Retrieved on February 12, 2015

164. "U.S. Shale-Oil Boom May Not Last as Fracking Wells Lack Staying Power" by Asjylyn Loder, BloombergBusiness, October 10, 2013, http://www.bloomberg.com/news/articles/2013-10-10/u-dot-s-dot-shale-oil-boom-may-not-last-as-fracking-wells-lack-staying-power Retrieved on March 16, 2016.

Chapter 7: Greening Capitalism

1.   Kennet, Miriam and Heinemann, Volker (2006), "Green Economics: setting the scene. Aims, context, and philosophical underpinning of the distinctive new solutions offered by Green Economics", Int. J. Green Economics, Vol. 1, Nos. 1/2, pp.68–102.

2.   "The Encyclopedia of Alternative Energy and Sustainable Living", http://www.daviddarling.info/encyclopedia/W/AE_wind_energy.html   Retrieved on: May 4, 2014.

3.   "Renewable Energy", Wikipedia, http://en.wikipedia.org/wiki/Renewable_energy

4.   Lovins, Amory B. (2012), "A Farewell to Fossil Fuels: Answering the Energy Challenge", http://www.rmi.org/

5.   Murphy, D.J.; Hall, C.A.S.. (2010), "Year in review EROI or energy return on (energy) invested", Annals of the New York Academy of Sciences 1185: 102–118. doi:10.1111/j.1749-6632.2009.05282.x

6.   This graph is made by the author based on information from http://en.wikipedia.org/wiki/Energy_returned_on_energy_invested

7.   Swinger, Patricia (2009), "Building on the Past, Ready for the Future: A Fiftieth Anniversary Celebration of MEMC Electronic Materials, Inc", Donning Company Publishers, http://www.memc.com/assets/file/company/MEMC_book-optimized.pdf Retrieved on 2 February, 2015.

8.   Heinberg, Richard (2013), "Snake Oil: How Big Energy's Misleading Promise of Plenty Imperils Our Future", Post Carbon Institute, Santa Rosa.

9.   Pearce, J.M. (2008). "Limitations of Greenhouse Gas Mitigation Technologies Set by Rapid Growth and Energy Cannibalism". Klima, http://www.climate2008.net/?a1=pap&cat=1&e=61 Retrieved on 14 November, 2014

10. Nagata, Kazuaki, "Fukushima meltdowns set nuclear energy debate on its ear", The Japan Times, January 03, 2012, http://www.japantimes.co.jp/news/2012/01/03/national/fukushima-meltdowns-set-nuclear-energy-debate-on-its-ear/ Retrieved on: May 9, 2014.

11. "EROI - Ratio of Energy Returned on Energy Invested - USA", Murphy, D. J. and Hall, C. A. S. (2010), Year in review—EROI or energy return on (energy) invested. Annals of the New York Academy of Sciences, 1185: 102–118. http://onlinelibrary.wiley.com/doi/10.1111/j.1749-6632.2009.05282.x/pdf This file is licensed under the Creative Commons Attribution-Share Alike 3.0 Unported at the Wikipedia, Retrieved on from http://commons.wikimedia.org/wiki/File:Nuclear_power_plant_construction.jpg on February 14, 2014

12. Stover, Dawn "Nuclear vs. renewables: Divided they fall", Bulletin of the Atomic Scientists". Thebulletin.org. January 30, 2014, http://thebulletin.org/nuclear-vs-renewables-divided-they-fall Retrieved on May 5, 2014

13. Stover, Dawn "The myth of renewable energy", Bulletin of the Atomic Scientists". Thebulletin.org. 2011-11-22. http://thebulletin.org/myth-renewable-energy Retrieved on May 5, 2014

14. "Renewable Energy in United States", Wikipedia, http://en.wikipedia.org/wiki/Renewable_energy_in_the_United_States

15. This graph is made by the author based on information from http://en.wikipedia.org/wiki/Renewable_energy_in_the_United_States

16. US Department of Energy (2009), "President Obama Calls for Greater Use of Renewable Energy", Energy Efficiency Renewable Energy, January 21, 2009, http://apps1.eere.energy.gov/news/news_detail.cfm/news_id=12194

17. Renewables, International Energy Agency, http://www.iea.org/topics/renewables/

18. "Renewable Power Generation Costs in 2012: An Overview", IRNEA, http://irena.org/menu/index.aspx?mnu=Subcat&PriMenuID=36&CatID=141&SubcatID=277

19. REN21 (2013). "Renewables global futures report 2013", http://www.ren21.net/Portals/0/REN21_GFR_2013_print.pdf

20. "Electric Vehicle", Wikipedia, http://en.wikipedia.org/wiki/Electric_vehicle

21. Bellis, Mary (2010). "Inventors - Electric Cars (1890 - 1930)". Inventors.about.com, June 16, 2010, http://inventors.about.com/od/estartinventions/a/History-Of-Electric-Vehicles.htm Retrieved on 2010-12-26.

22. AAA World Magazine. Jan-Feb 2011, p. 53

23. Eberle, Ulrich; von Helmolt, Rittmar (2010-05-14). "Sustainable transportation based on EV concepts: a brief overview". http://www.researchgate.net/publication/224880220_Sustainable_transportation_based_on_electric_vehicle_concepts_a_brief_overview Royal Society of Chemistry. Retrieved on 2010-06-08.

24. "Success Stories", Smart Communities Network, http://www.smartcommunities.ncat.org/success/chattano.shtml , Retrieved on October 24, 2014

25. "UNDP donates electric buses to Beijing Olympic Games", Xinhua, July 31, 2008, http://news.xinhuanet.com/english/2008-07/31/content_8880067.htm Retrieved on October 24, 2014

26. "Battery Electric Vehicle", Wikipedia, http://en.wikipedia.org/wiki/Battery_electric_vehicle

27. "Who Killed the Electric Car", Documentary, Directed by Chris Paine, Sony Pictures. Also at Wikipedia, http://en.wikipedia.org/wiki/Who_Killed_the_Electric_Car Retrieved on 28 February, 2015.

28. Heinberg, Richard (2015), "Afterburn: Society Beyond Fossil Fuels", New Society Publishers, Canada, January 2015, page-1-36.

29. Neil, Dan. "The Rick Wagoner vehicles: Hits and misses", LA Times, March 31, 2009, http://articles.latimes.com/2009/mar/31/business/fi-gm-cars31 Retrieved on 7 March 2015.

30. "Tesla Motors Moving Quickly to Commercialization of an Electric Car". GreenCar Magazine, http://www.greencarmagazine.net/2009/07/tesla-motors-moving-quickly-to-commercialization-of-an-electric-car/2009-07-09 Retrieved on 24 October, 2014.

31. Musk, Elon (2014), "All Our Patent Are Belong To You", Tesla Motors,June 12, 2014, http://www.teslamotors.com/blog/all-our-patent-are-belong-you Retrieved on October 24, 2014

32. Eric Loveday (2014-09-26). "Tesla Opens Supercharger #200". InsideEVs.com, http://insideevs.com/tesla-opens-supercharger-200/ Retrieved on October 24, 2014.

33. Kurt Zenz House, "The Limits of Energy Storage Technology," Bulletin of the Atomic Scientists, January 20, 2009.

34. Heinberg, Richard (2011), "The End of Growth: Adapting to our New Economic Reality", New Society Publishers, Canada. Chapter 4.

35. Worldwatch Institute (January 2012). "Use and Capacity of Global Hydropower Increases", http://www.worldwatch.org/node/9527 Retrieved on: May 4, 2014.

36. "List of Thermal Power Stations", Wikipedia, http://en.wikipedia.org/wiki/List_of_solar_thermal_power_stations

37. Broehl, Jesse (2005), "Washington State Passes Progressive Renewable Energy Legislation", Renewable Energy World, May 10, 2005, http://www.renewableenergyworld.com/rea/news/article/2005/05/washington-state-passes-progressive-renewable-energy-legislation-28478

38. "Global Renewable Power Capacities (excluding hydro)", This graph is prepared by Wikipedia, dedicated to the public domain and made available under the Creative Commons CC0 1.0 Universal Public Domain Dedication. http://commons.wikimedia.org/wiki/File:GlobalREPowerCapacity-exHydro-Eng.png Data Source: Data compilation of annual reports since 2006, the latest being: REN21, Renewables Global Status Report 2012, http://ren21.net/Portals/0/documents/activities/gsr/GSR2012_low%20res_FINAL.pdf Retrieved on, Retrieved on May 9, 2014

39. "Doubling the Global Share of Renewable Energy A Roadmap to 2030", IRNEA, https://www.irena.org/DocumentDownloads/Publications/IRENA%20REMAP%202030%20working%20paper.pdf

40. "Price history chart of crystalline silicon solar cells in US$ per watt since 1977", Wikipedia's own work released into the public domain. Original source data 1977–2013: Bloomberg, New Energy Finance, 2014: based on average sales price of $0.36/watt on 26 June 2014 from EnergyTrend.com, 2015: based on average sales price of $0.30/W on 29 April 2015 from EnergyTrend.com, https://commons.wikimedia.org/wiki/File:Price_history_of_silicon_PV_cells_since_1977.svg Retrieved on July 4, 2015.

41. At the Zenith of Solar Energy, Neal Sandler, BusinessWeek, 26 March 2008, http://www.businessweek.com/stories/2008-03-26/at-the-zenith-of-solar-energybusinessweek-business-news-stock-market-and-financial-advice

42. "Sweet sorghum for food, feed and fuel", New Agriculturist http://resourcespace.icrisat.ac.in/filestore/8/4/0_6c06c9b61b19c20/840_be710da94740b90.pdf

43. Layton, Julia (5 November 2008). "What is a luminescent solar concentrator?" http://science.howstuffworks.com/environmental/green-science/luminescent-solar-concentrator1.htm Retrieved on May 8, 2014

44. Lindmayer, Joseph (1977). The Solar Breeder. NASA, http://www.researchgate.net/publication/23885550_Solar_breeder_Energy_payback_time_for_silicon_photovoltaic_systems

45. Koinuma, H.; Kanazawa, I.; Karaki, H.; Kitazawa, K. (Mar 26, 2009), Sahara solar breeder plan directed toward global clean energy superhighway, G8+5 Academies' meeting in Rome, Science Council of Japan

46. Darren Quick, "Sahara Solar Breeder Project aims to provide 50 percent of the world's electricity by 2050" Gizmag, 24 November 2010, http://www.gizmag.com/sahara-solar-breeder-project/17054 Retrieved on: 25 November 2014.

47. "Wind Energy The Facts An Analysis of Wind Energy in the EU-25", European Wind Energy Association, http://www.ewea.org/fileadmin/ewea_documents/documents/publications/WETF/Facts_Summary.pdf , Retrieved on May 5, 2014

48. Turcotte, D. L.; Schubert, G. (2002), "4", Geodynamics (2 ed.), Cambridge, England, UK: Cambridge University Press, pp. 136–137, ISBN 978-0-521-66624-4

49. Geothermal Energy Association. "Geothermal Energy: International Market Update May 2010", page. 4-7. http://www.geo-energy.org/pdf/reports/GEA_International_Market_Report_Final_May_2010.pdf Retrieved on May 8, 2014.

50. "Renewable Energy in Iceland", http://en.wikipedia.org/wiki/Renewable_energy_in_Iceland

51. "The Energy Sector", Askaja Energy, The http://askjaenergy.org/iceland-introduction/iceland-energy-sector/

52. Duchane, Dave; Brown, Don (December 2002). "Hot Dry Rock (HDR) Geothermal Energy Research and Development at Fenton Hill, New Mexico". Geo-Heat Centre Quarterly Bulletin 23 (4) (Klamath Falls, Oregon: Oregon Institute of Technology). pp. 13–19. ISSN 0276-1084.

53. Paul Gipe, "100 Percent Renewable Vision Building", Renewable Energy World, http://www.renewableenergyworld.com/rea/news/article/2013/04/100-percent-renewable-vision-building?amp;buffer_share=fdc06

54. http://en.wikipedia.org/wiki/Energy_policy_of_the_European_Union

55. Rettman, Andrew, "EU sticks out neck in global climate change battle", March 09, 2007, Eurobserver, http://euobserver.com/economic/23665

56. "Historical agreement on climate protection", http://www.eu2007.de/en/News/Press_Releases/March/0309BKBruessel.html

57. "Crossing the 20 Percent Mark: Green Energy Use Jumps in Germany", Spiegel Online International, August 30, 2011, http://www.spiegel.de/international/crossing-the-20-percent-mark-green-energy-use-jumps-in-germany-a-783314.html

58. Germany percentage of renewable electricity by source in 2011. In all, 20.5% of electricity consumed in 2011 came from these renewable sources. Biomass includes the following: solid biomass 11.9 TWh, liquid biomass, vegetable oil included, 1.5 TWh, biogas, 17.5 TWh, sewage gas, 1.3 TWh, landfill gas, 0.6 TWh, and biogenic fraction of waste, 4.8 TWh. In all, 123.5 TWh was generated from renewable sources in 2011., Source: http://www.erneuerbare-energien.de/fileadmin/Daten_EE/Bilder_Startseite/Bilder_Datenservice/PDFs__XL S/20130110_EEiZIU_E_PPT_2011_FIN.pdf This file is made available under the Creative Commons CC0 1.0 Universal Public Domain Dedication created on 26 September 2011 by S-kei at the English language Wikipedia. http://commons.wikimedia.org/wiki/File:Germany_renewable_electricity_generatio n_percentage-2011.png

59. "Renewable Energy in Germany", Wikipedia, http://en.wikipedia.org/wiki/Renewable_energy_in_Germany

60. "Eye-watering cost of renewable revolution", World Nuclear News, January 23, 2012, http://www.world-nuclear-news.org/NP_Eye_watering_cost_of_renewable_revolution_2301121.html

61. Daly, Herman E. (2008) "A Steady-State Economy", Sustainable Development Commission, UK, April 24, 2008, http://www.sd-commission.org.uk/data/files/publications/Herman_Daly_thinkpiece.pdf

62. Smith, Richard (2010) "Beyond Growth or Beyond Capitalism?", real-world economics review, issue no. 53, 26 June 2010, pp. 28-42, http://www.paecon.net/PAEReview/issue53/Smith53.pdf

63. Hawken, Paul, Amory and L. Hunter Lovins (1999), "Natural Capitalism: Creating the Next Industrial Revolution", Little, Brown and Company, Boston.

64. Hawken, Paul (1993), "Ecological Commerce", HarperCollins, New York.

65. Rogers, Heather (2009), "The greening of capitalism?", Issue #70, International Socialist Review, Presented in Northeast Socialist Conference, New York City, October 2009, http://isreview.org/issue/70/greening-capitalism

66. Samuelson, P (1954), "The pure theory of public expenditure", Review of Economics and Statistics 36, November, 1954, pp387-389.

67. "Carbon Emission Trading", Wikipedia, http://en.wikipedia.org/wiki/Carbon_emission_trading

68. IMF (March 2008). "Fiscal Implications of Climate Change". Fiscal Affairs Department, International Monetary Fund, March 8, 2013.

69. "Our Common Future: Report of the World Commission on Environment and Development", "Chapter 2: Towards Sustainable Development", United Nations, 2A/42/427, http://www.un-documents.net/ocf-02.htm

70. "Green Economy", http://en.wikipedia.org/wiki/Green_economy

71. "Sustainable development", This graph is licensed under the Creative Commons Attribution-Share Alike 3.0 Unported license and created on original 09 March 2006 by Johann Dréo at Wikipedia. http://en.wikipedia.org/wiki/File:Sustainable_development.svg Wikipedia grants permission to copy, distribute and/or modify this document under the terms of the GNU Free Documentation License, Version 1.2, Retrieved on, Retrieved on May 9, 2014

72. World Wide Fund for Nature (2012) "Living Planet Report 2012", Gland, Switzerland, http://www.wwf.or.jp/activities/lib/lpr/WWF_LPRsm_2012.pdf

73. Rotering, Frank (2009), "Needs and Limits: A New Economics for Sustainable Well-Being", ISBN 0978345924, 9780978345921.

74. Reinhardt, F. (1999) 'Market failure and the environmental policies of firms: economic rationales for 'beyond compliance' behavior.' Journal of Industrial Ecology 3(1), 9-21.

75. Gramsci, A. (1932-1934) Some Theoretical and Practical Aspects of Economism, http://www.marxists.org/archive/gramsci/editions/reader/q13-18.htm

76. Carson, R. (1962) Silent Spring, Houghton Mifflin.

77. Schick, Gerhard (2010), "Greening Capitalism is Not Enough", Triple Crisis, May 27, 2010, http://triplecrisis.com/greening-capitalism-is-not-enough/

78. Smith Richard (2011), "Green capitalism: the god that failed", real-world economics review, issue no. 56, 11 March 2011, pp. 112-144, http://www.paecon.net/PAEReview/issue56/Smith57.pdf

79. McKibben, Bill (2011), "Eaarth: Making a Life on a Tough New Planet", Griffin, New York.

80. "Green Washing", http://en.wikipedia.org/wiki/Greenwashing

81. Climate Change 1995: Economic and Social Dimensions of Climate Change, Contribution of Working Group III, Intergovernmental Panel on Climate Change (IPCC), Cambridge University Press, New York, 1997. http://www.ipcc.ch/ipccreports/sar/wg_III/ipcc_sar_wg_III_full_report.pdf

82. Hawken, Paul (1993), "Ecological Commerce", HarperCollins, New York.

83. The image is taken from the report, "Synthesis and Assessment Product 5.2: Best practice approaches for characterizing, communicating, and incorporating scientific uncertainty in decision making," page 11. This report is freely available and can be downloaded from http://www.ipcc-wg2.gov/njlite_download.php?id=5805 This image is in the public domain because it contains materials that originally came from the U.S. National Oceanic and Atmospheric Administration. This version is copied from http://commons.wikimedia.org/wiki/File:Stabilizing_the_atmospheric_concentration_of_carbon_dioxide_at_a_constant_level_would_require_emissions_to_be_effectively_eliminated_(vertical).png

84. Helm, Dieter (2005), "Economic Instruments and Environmental Policy", The Economic and Social Review, Vol. 36, No. 3. & presented in Nineteenth Annual Conference, Irish Economic Association, Kilkenny, May 6-8, 2005. http://www.dieterhelm.co.uk/sites/default/files/EconomicInst_EnvrnmntlPolicy.pdf

85. Heinberg, Richard (2011), "The End of Growth: Adapting to our New Economic Reality", New Society Publishers, Canada. Chapter 4.

86. Oppenheimer, M. and A. Petsonk (2004), "Article 2 of the UN Framework Convention on Climate Change (UNFCCC): Historical Origins, Recent Interpretations, http://www.princeton.edu/step/people/faculty/michael-oppenheimer/recent-publications/Article-2-of-the-UN-Framework-Convention-on-Climate-Change.pdf

87. "Kyoto Protocol", http://en.wikipedia.org/wiki/Kyoto_Protocol

88. "Global Warming: Challenges, Opportunities and a Message of 'Be Prepared'", Green Evolution: Managing the Risks, Reaping the Benefits, March 2010, Initiative for Global Environmental Leadership (IGEL), Whatron, University of Pennsylvania,http://knowledge.wharton.upenn.edu/papers/download/030310_green_evolution_ss.pdf

89. "Clinton Hails Global Warming Pact: But early Senate ratification is unlikely", All Politics (CNN). 11 December 1997, http://www.cnn.com/ALLPOLITICS/1997/12/11/kyoto/

90. Dessai, S. (December 2001), "The climate regime from The Hague to Marrakech: Saving or sinking the Kyoto Protocol?", Tyndall Centre Working Paper 12, Norwich, UK http://www.tyndall.ac.uk/content/climate-regime-hague-marrakech-saving-or-sinking-kyoto-protocol

91. "China now no. 1 in CO2 emissions; USA in second position", PBL Netherlands Environmental Assessment Agency, http://www.pbl.nl/en/dossiers/Climatechange/moreinfo/Chinanowno1inCO2emissionsUSAinsecondposition

92. Lynas Mark (2008), "Six Degrees", National Georgraphic, New York, pp. 269-70.

93. Hansen, James (2010), "Storms of My Grandchildren: The Truth About the Coming Climate Catastrophe and Our Last Chance to Save Humanity", Bloomsbury, New York, pp. 182-83, and p. 206, p.213.

94. "Canada pulls out of Kyoto protocol". The Guardian. 13 December 2011, http://www.theguardian.com/environment/2011/dec/13/canada-pulls-out-kyoto-protocol Retrieved on: May 17, 2014.

95. David Ljunggren and Randall Palmer (13 13 December 2011). "Canada to pull out of Kyoto protocol". Reuters. Financial Post.

96. "Cap and Trade", Fact Sheet1, Carbon Trade Watch, http://www.carbontradewatch.org/factsheets/fact-sheet-1-cap-and-trade.html

97. "Collapse of Chicago Climate Exchange Means a Strategy Shift on Global Warming", Politics, Fox News, November 9, 2010, http://www.foxnews.com/politics/2010/11/09/collapse-chicago-climate-exchange-means-strategy-shift-global-warming-curbs/#ixzz2ejUrPiYC

98. Kanter, James and Mouawad, Jad (2010), "Money and lobbyists hurt European efforts to curb gases," New York Times, December 11, 2010

99. Lohmann, Larry (2009), "Uncertainty Markets and Carbon Markets. Variations on Polanyian Themes", New Political Economy, August 2009, http://www.thecornerhouse.org.uk/sites/thecornerhouse.org.uk/files/NPE2high.pdf

100. Bohm, Steffen et al (), "Greening Capitalism? A Marxist Critique of Carbon Markets", Organization Studies November 2012 vol. 33 no. 11 1617-1638, http://oss.sagepub.com/content/33/11/1617

101. Mouawad, Jad (2009), "Not so green after all: alternative fuel still a dalliance for oil giants" New York Times April 8, 2009.

102. "Imminent EU proposals to clamp down on fridge gas scam", By Andrew Willis, November 24, 2010, China-EU Relation, Euro Observer, http://euobserver.com/china/31347

103. "Carbon-Credits System Tarnished by WikiLeaks Revelation", By Quirin Schiermeier and Nature magazine, Scientific American, September 27, 2011, http://www.scientificamerican.com/article.cfm?id=carbon-credits-system-tarnished-wikileaks

104. Smith, Kevin (2007)"The Carbon Neutral Myth: Offset Indulgences for Your Climate Sins",Carbon Trade Watch,Transnational Institute, The Netherlands, February, 2007, http://www.carbontradewatch.org/publications/the-carbon-neutral-myth.html

105. "Carbon Offsets", Fact Sheet2, Carbon Trade Watch, http://www.carbontradewatch.org/downloads/publications/factsheet02-offsets.pdf

106. "Jim Hansen's arguments for a carbon tax in Storms, p. 215ff. For Al Gore's arguments see his Our Choice (Emanus, PA: Rodale, 2009), pp. 342-45 & p. 210.

107. Pigou, A.C. "II, Chapter IX: Divergences Between Marginal Social Net Product and Marginal Private Net Product" in The Economics of Welfare (1932).

108. "Carbon Tax", http://en.wikipedia.org/wiki/Carbon_tax

109. Krugman, Paul (2009), "The conscience of a liberal: Unhelpful Hansen", New York Times, December 7, 2009, http://krugman.blogs.nytimes.com/2009/12/07/unhelpful-hansen/?_r=0

110. "Green New Deal", Wikipedia, http://en.wikipedia.org/wiki/Green_New_Deal

111. Tienhaara, Kyla. (2009), "A Tale of Two Crises: What the Global Financial Crisis Means for the Global Environmental Crisis", Global Governance Working Paper No 37. Amsterdam et al.: The Global Governance Project. Available at http://www.glogov.org/images/doc/WP37.pdf

112. Cooper, George (2008), "The Origin of Financial Crises: Central Banks, Credit Bubbles, and the Efficient Market Fallacy", Vintage.

113. Yohe, G.W., et al. (2007). "20.6 Global and aggregate impacts". In M.L. Parry et al.,. Perspectives on climate change and sustainability. Climate Change 2007: Impacts, Adaptation and Vulnerability. Contribution of Working Group II to the Fourth Assessment Report of the IPCC. Cambridge University Press. http://www.ipcc.ch/publications_and_data/ar4/wg2/en/ch20s20-7.html

114. UNEP (2009a) Global Green New Deal, Policy Brief, Nairobi.

115. "A Green New Deal: Joined-up policies to solve the triple crunch of the credit crisis, climate change and high oil prices, Green New deal Group, http://dnwssx4l7gl7s.cloudfront.net/nefoundation/default/page/-/files/A_Green_New_Deal_1.pdf

116. Asici, Ahmet Atıl et el. (2012), "Green New Deal: A Green Way out of the Crisis?", Environmental Policy and Governance, Volume 22, Issue 5, 295–306(2012), http://onlinelibrary.wiley.com/doi/10.1002/eet.1594/pdf Retrieved on, May 21, 2014.

117. Ki-moon, Ban and Gore, Al "Green growth is essential to any stimulus" Financial Times, 16 Feb 2009, http://www.ft.com/cms/s/0/0fa98852-fc45-11dd-aed8-000077b07658.html#axzz2wPLp99cf Retrieved on: March 19, 2014.

118. "How China is Battling the Economic Crisis", San Francisco Sentinel, 23 May 2009.

119. "China's Emissions a Wild Card as G-20 Weighs Global Stimulus", The New York Times, 12 March 2009.

120. "Global Financial Crisis to Slow Climate Progress: Rudd", The Australian, 27 March 2009.

121. "Climate Scientists Living in Pollyanna World: Senator", Sydney Morning Herald, 16 April 2009.

122. Green New Deal Group (2008) A Green New Deal: Joined-up Policies to Solve the Triple Crunch of the Credit Crisis, Climate Change and High Oil Prices, London.

123. Vedeld, Trond (2011): Grønn økonomi og Rio 20+. "Business as usual" eller nytt paradigme? http://www.nibr.no/filer/2011-118.pdf (NIBR Notat 2011:118); Vedeld, Trond (2012): Developing Countries say no to green economy, yes to sustainable development (NIBR International Blog 31.01.12) http://blog.nibrinternational.no/#post48

124. "US Energy Information Administration", Annual Energy Outlook 2012, DOE/EIA-0383(2012), June 2012, http://www.eia.gov/forecasts/aeo/pdf/0383(2012).pdf

125. Helm, Dieter (2005), "Economic Instruments and Environmental Policy", The Economic and Social Review, Vol. 36, No. 3. & presented in Nineteenth Annual Conference, Irish Economic Association, Kilkenny, May 6-8, 2005. http://www.dieterhelm.co.uk/sites/default/files/EconomicInst_EnvrnmntlPolicy.pdf

126. Rogers, Deborah (2013) "Shale and Wall Street: Was the Decline in Natural Gas Prices Orchestrated?" Energy Policy Forum, February 2013, http://shalebubble.org/wall-street/

127. Heinberg, Richard (2013), "Snake Oil: How Fracking's False Promise of Plenty Imperils Our Future", Post Carbon Institute, Santa Rosa. pp. 96-107.

128. "Renewable Power Generation and Capacity as a Proportion of Change in Global Power Supply", This graph is prepared by Wikipedia, dedicated to the public domain and made available under the Creative Commons CC0 1.0 Universal Public Domain Dedication. http://commons.wikimedia.org/wiki/File:RE-CapChangeShare-Eng.png Data Source: data source: Global Trends in Renewable Energy Investment 2011, Bloomberg New Energy Finance, Frankfurt School, UNEP SEFI, Figure 24, http://www.unep.org/Renewable_Energy_Investment/ Retrieved on May 14, 2014.

129. Heinberg, Richard (2015), "Our Renewable Future", Post Carbon Institute, January 21, 2015, http://www.postcarbon.org/our-renewable-future-essay/ Retrieved on January 31, 2015.

130. REN21 (2014). "Renewables 2014 Global Status Report", http://www.ren21.net/portals/0/documents/resources/gsr/2014/gsr2014_full%20repo rt_low%20res.pdf Retrieved on January 14, 2015.

131. "List of countries by electricity production from renewable sources", http://en.wikipedia.org/wiki/List_of_countries_by_electricity_production_from_rene wable_sources

132. "Hydrogen Fuel", Wikipedia, http://en.wikipedia.org/wiki/Hydrogen_fuel

133. Zehner, Ozzie (2012). Green Illusion, Lincoln and London: University of Nebraska Press. pp. 1–169, 331–42.

134. "Toyota Is Bringing In The Future With A New Fuel Cell Car", by Stefano Pozzebon, Business Insider, November 18, 2014, http://www.businessinsider.com/toyota-launches-mirai-hydrogen-car-2014-11#ixzz3RYEc2MSB

135. "Tokyo is spending over $300 million to promote 'hydrogen fuel' — here's what that means", by Jonathan Fisher, 10 February, 2015, Business Insider, http://www.businessinsider.com/tokyo-and-hydrogen-fuel-in-2020-olympics-2015-2#ixzz3RYE3aJLO

136. Heinberg, Richard (2015), "Afterburn: Society Beyond Fossil Fuels", New Society Publishers, Canada, January 2015, page-103-116.

137. Inman, Mason (2013), "Behind the Numbers on Energy Return on Investment", Scientific American, March 19, 2013, http://www.scientificamerican.com/article/eroi-behind-numbers-energy-return-investment/, Retrieved on July 2, 2015.

138. Aspray, Tom (2011), "Uranium Shortage Can't Be Ignored", Forbes, July 26, 2011, http://www.forbes.com/sites/tomaspray/2011/07/26/uranium-shortage-cant-be-ignored/ Retrieved on July 2, 2015

139. "High-level radioactive waste management", Wikipedia, https://en.wikipedia.org/wiki/High-level_radioactive_waste_management, Retrieved on July 2, 2015.

140. "The dream that failed", The Economist, March 10, 2012, http://www.economist.com/node/21549936, Retrieved on July 2, 2015.

141. "Pandora's False Promises", http://www.beyondnuclear.org/pandoras-false-promises/ Retrieved on July 4, 2015.

142. Biello, David (2010), "Are New Types of Reactors Needed for the U.S. Nuclear Renaissance?", Scientific American, February 19, 2010, http://www.scientificamerican.com/article/are-new-types-of-reactors-needed-for-nuclear-renaissance/ Retrieved on July 4, 2015.

143. Heinberg, Richard (2015), "Afterburn: Society Beyond Fossil Fuels", New Society Publishers, Canada, January 2015.

144. "Solar Power", Wikipedia, https://en.wikipedia.org/wiki/Solar_power

145. "EROEI of at least 10:1 to Sustain Civilization", Energyskeptic, April 13, 2014, http://energyskeptic.com/2014/eroei-of-at-least-101-to-sustain-civilization/ Retrieved on August 2, 2015.

146. "The Clean Power Plan Will Collide With The Incredibly Weird Physics Of The Electric Grid" by Mark P. Mills, August 7, 2015, http://www.forbes.com/sites/markpmills/2015/08/07/the-clean-power-plan-will-collide-with-the-incredibly-weird-physics-of-the-electric-grid/ Retrieved on August 11, 2015.

147. "The Clean Power Plan: A Climate Game Changer", Union of Concerned Scientists, August 7, 2015, http://www.ucsusa.org/our-work/global-warming/reduce-emissions/what-is-the-clean-power-plan#.VcmrIPlVhBc Retrieved on August 11, 2015.

148. "Why the U.S. Power Grid's Days Are Numbered" by Chris Martin, Mark Chediak and Ken Wells, August 22, 2013, http://www.bloomberg.com/bw/articles/2013-08-22/homegrown-green-energy-is-making-power-utilities-irrelevant Retrieved on August 11, 2015.

149. Smith, Richard (2011), "Green capitalism: the god that failed", real-world economics review, issue no. 56, 11 March 2011, pp. 112-144, http://www.paecon.net/PAEReview/issue56/Smith56.pdf Retrieved on May 31, 2014

150. "Nature™ Inc? Questioning the Market Panacea in Environmental Policy and Conservation", The Hague, The Netherlands, June 30-July 2011, http://brambuscher.files.wordpress.com/2011/01/conference-programme-19-april-2011.pdf Retrieved on May 31, 2014

151. Kovel, Joel (2002), "The Enemy of Nature: The End of Capitalism or the End of the World?", Second Edition, Zed Books, December 9, 2008.

152. Polin, Robert et al (2008) "Green Recovery: A Program to Create Good Jobs and Start Building a Low-Carbon Economy", Political Economy Research Institute, http://www.peri.umass.edu/green_recovery/ Retrieved on May 31, 2014

153. Aşıcı, Ahmet A. (2011), "Green Recovery from the Crisis, A Comparative Analysis of Green New Deal and Ecosocialism", 9th International Conference of the European Society for Ecological Economics: Advancing Ecological Economics: Theory and Practice, Boğaziçi University, Istanbul, June 14-17, 2011, http://www.esee2011.org/registration/fullpapers/esee2011_bd0cc8_1_1304867254_6010_2169.pdf Retrieved on May 31, 2014.

154. "Steady State Economy", Wikipedia, http://en.wikipedia.org/wiki/Steady_state_economy Retrieved on May 31, 2014.

155. Keynes, John Maynard (1936) "The General Theory of Employment, Interest, and Money", Createspace (Nov. 15, 2011), ISBN-10: 1467934925

156. Keynes, John Maynard (1930) "A Treatise on Money: The Pure Theory of Money and the Applied Theory of Money", Martino Fine Books (June 1 2011), ISBN-10: 1614270422

157. Rotering, Frank M (2010), "Needs and Limits: A New Economics for Sustainable Well-being" 3rd Edition, Lulu.

158. Haque, O. (2011) The New Capitalist Manifesto: Building a Disruptively Better Business, Harvard Business Press, Boston.

159. HSBC (2009) A Climate for Recovery: The Colour of Stimulus Goes Green, HSBC Global Research, London, http://www.euractiv.de/files/docs/HSBC_Green_New_Deal.pdf Retrieved on May 31, 2014.

160. "Green Investing 2011:Reducing the Cost of Financing", World economic Forum, http://www3.weforum.org/docs/WEF_IV_GreenInvesting_Report_2011.pdf Retrieved on May 31, 2014.

161. Zaman, Monowaruz (2012), "Greenhouse care economics: A Solution to the Capitalist's Dilemma", International Journal of Green Economics, Volume 6, Issue 2, 2012, page. 189-504.

162. Krugman, Paul (1999), "Money Can't Buy Happiness. Er, Can It?", The New York Times,June 1, 1999 http://www.nytimes.com/1999/06/01/opinion/money-can-t-buy-happiness-er-can-it.html Retrieved on May 31, 2014.

163. "Six Degrees Could Change the World", National Geographic Society, 2008, Washington D.C, http://channel.nationalgeographic.com/channel/videos/six-degrees/ Retrieved on May 31, 2014.

164. "Clear and Present Danger: Clearing-houses may add danger as well as efficiency", The Economist, April 7, 2012, Retrieved on January 1, 2014. http://www.economist.com/node/21552217

165. "Derivative   (finance)",   Wikipedia, http://en.wikipedia.org/wiki/Derivative_%28finance%29 Retrieved on May 31, 2014

166. Edenhoffer, Ottmar and Lord Nicholas Stern (2009) Towards a Global Green Recovery: Recommendations for Immediate G20 Action, G20 London Summit, Potsdam Institute for Climate Impact Research.

167. "Oil Prices Will Take 5 Years To Recover - IEA", by Geoffrey Smith, Fortune, November 10, 2015, http://fortune.com/2015/11/10/iea-low-oil-prices-outlook-2015/ Retrieved on November 24, 2015

168. "Best way to fight climate change? Stop fighting", By Ben Knight, Geekquinox Science   and   Weather,   September   17,   2015, https://ca.news.yahoo.com/blogs/geekquinox/best-way-to-fight-climate-change--stop-fighting-184902022.html Retrieved on November 24, 2015.

169. "Former FERC Chief Jon Wellinghoff Speaks Out on Grid Security and Distributed Generation" by Chip Register, Forbes, Energy, February 3, 2015, http://www.forbes.com/sites/chipregister1/2015/02/03/former-ferc-chief-jon-wellinghoff-speaks-out-on-grid-security-and-distributed-generation/ Retrieved on November 24, 2015.

170. Jonas Meckling, Nina Kelsey, Eric Biber, John Zysman. Winning coalitions for climate policy. Science, 2015 DOI: 10.1126/science.aab1336

171. "Solar Costs Will Fall Another 40% In 2 Years. Here's Why.", by Giles Parkinson, Reneweconomy, January 29th, 2015, http://reneweconomy.com.au/2015/why-solar-costs-will-fall-another-40-in-just-two-years-21235 Retrieved on November 25, 2015

172. "FERC Chair Jon Wellinghoff: Solar 'Is Going to Overtake Everything'", by Herman   K.   Trabish,   August   21,   2013, http://www.greentechmedia.com/articles/read/ferc-chair-wellinghoff-sees-a-solar-future-and-a-utility-of-the-future Retrieved on November 25, 2015

173. "How to beat the climate crisis? Start with carrots",Science Daily, September 10, 2015, http://www.sciencedaily.com/releases/2015/09/150910144052.htm Retrieved on November 25, 2015

174. "Explained in 90 Seconds: Why 1.5 Degrees Matters", by Time McDonnell, 10 December, 2015, http://www.motherjones.com/environment/2015/12/paris-climate-agreement-could-be-more-ambitious-anyone-expected Retrieved on December 13, 2015

175. Nations Approve Landmark Climate Accord in Paris, by Carol Davenport, 12 December, 2015, http://www.nytimes.com/2015/12/13/world/europe/climate-change-accord-paris.html Retrieved on December 13, 2015

176. Paris UN Climate Conference 2015: 5 things we learn on day 3", The Sydney Morning Herald, December 3, 2015, http://www.smh.com.au/environment/un-climate-conference/paris-un-climate-conference-2015-five-things-we-learnt-on-day-3-in-paris-20151202-gle039.html Retrieved on December 13, 2015

177. Heinberg, Richard (2014), Renewable Energy after COP21: Nine issues for climate leaders to think about the journey home, Post Carbon Institute, December 14, 2015, http://www.postcarbon.org/renewable-energy-after-cop21/ Retrieved on December 15, 2015

178. Kotzias, George A. MEMC Electronic. Calyon Securities, CLSA. August 19, 2008.

179. "SunEdison", Wikipedia, https://en.wikipedia.org/wiki/SunEdison Retrieved on February 15, 2016.

180. "50 Smartest Companies 2015". MIT Technology Review. 2015, https://www.technologyreview.com/lists/companies/2015/ Retrieved on February 15, 2016.

181. Shah, Jigar (2013), "Creating Climate Wealth: Unlocking the Impact Economy", ICOSA, p.31-p37

182. Ayre, James. "SunEdison Predicts New FBR Polysilicon Process/Facility Will Lead To $0.40/W Solar Modules". CleanTechnica.com. October 7, 2014, http://cleantechnica.com/2014/10/07/sunedison-predicts-new-fbr-polysilicon-processfacility-will-lead-400-wp-modules-us0-40w/ Retrieved on February 15, 2016.

183. Colthorpe, Andy. "SunEdison to sell remaining shares in semiconductor business for US$193 million". PV Tech. 25 June 2015.

184. "Automotive industry crisis of 2008–10" Wikipedia, , https://en.wikipedia.org/wiki/Automotive_industry_crisis_of_2008%E2%80%9310 Retrieved on February 13, 2016

185. "New Balance of Power" by Clifford Krauss, , New York Times, April 22, 2015, http://www.nytimes.com/2015/04/23/business/energy-environment/new-balance-of-power.html Retrieved on February 16, 2016

186. "SunEdison Inc. (SUNE) Interactive Stock Chart", http://www.nasdaq.com/symbol/sune/interactive-chart Retrieved on February 12, 2016.

187. SunEdison's Results Show the Flaws of New Business Model by Travis Hoium, The Motley Fool, November 14, 2015, http://www.fool.com/investing/general/2015/11/14/sunedisons-results-show-the-warts-of-new-business.aspx Retrieved on February 16, 2016.

188. Ausick, Paul. "SunEdison Spin-Off TerraForm Power Scores Hot IPO". 24/7 Wall Street. July 18, 2014, http://247wallst.com/energy-business/2014/07/18/sunedison-spin-off-terraform-power-scores-hot-ipo/ Retrieved on February 16, 2016.

189. "Addressing the Challenges of RE Manufacturing in India: Horizon 2032", Centre for Study of Science, Technology and Policy (CSTEP) and World Institute for Sustainable Energy (WISE), http://shaktifoundation.in/wp-content/uploads/2014/02/RE-Mfrg_-Final-Report_-2015.pdf, Retrieved on 22 March, 2016.

190. "Solar Water Heater". Dnaindia.com. 28 November 2009, http://www.dnaindia.com/bangalore/report-live-life-off-the-grid-or-tap-the-sunshine-in-your-backyard-1317492 Retrieved on March 22, 2016.

191. "Rajasthan ERC – Draft solar tariff order". Indian Power Sector.COM, 14 April 2015, http://indianpowersector.com/2015/04/rerc-draft-solar-tariff-order/ Retrieved on March 22, 2016.

192. Transparent solar cells could turn windows into generators, by By Lucas,Computerworld, December 19, 2013, http://www.computerworld.com/article/2487034/sustainable-it/sustainable-it-transparent-solar-cells-could-turn-windows-into-generators.html Retrieved on April 21, 2016

193. "Solar Power Windows Ready For Production", by Stephen Hanley, September 5th, 2015, Green Building Elements, Retrieved from http://planetsave.com/2015/09/05/solar-power-windows-ready-for-production/ on April 21, 2016

194. "Solar windows can power buildings" by By Lucas,Computerworld, September 4, 2015, http://www.computerworld.com/article/2980236/sustainable-it/solar-windows-poised-to-change-the-way-we-power-buildings.html Retrieved on April, 21, 2016

Chapter 8: Capitalists Biasing

1. Tienhaara, Kyla. (2009), "A Tale of Two Crises: What the Global Financial Crisis Means for the Global Environmental Crisis", Global Governance Working Paper No 37. Amsterdam et al.: The Global Governance Project. Available at www.-glogov.org.

2. Coudouel et al. (2002), Poverty Measurement and Analysis, in the PRSP Sourcebook, World Bank, Washington D.C, http://siteresources.worldbank.org/INTPRS1/Resources/383606-1205334112622/5467_chap1.pdf Retrieved on May 31, 2014

3. "Poverty headcount ratio, or poverty rate, based on new 2014 World Bank international benchmarks for select countries", This graph is created by M Tracy Hunter at Wikipedia, http://commons.wikimedia.org/wiki/File:2014_Poverty_rate_chart_Chad_Haiti_Nig eria_Bangladesh_Kenya_Indonesia_India_China_Brazil_based_on_World_Bank_ne w_2011_PPP_benchmarks.png Source: Data source for the chart: Laurence Chandy and Homi Kharas (2014), What Do New Price Data Mean for the Goal of Ending Extreme Poverty?, Brookings Institute, Washington DC, http://www.brookings.edu/blogs/up-front/posts/2014/05/05-data-extreme-poverty-chandy-kharas This file is licensed under the Creative Commons Attribution-Share Alike 3.0 Unported license. Retrieved on May 31, 2014

4. Donnan, Shawn (2014), "World Bank eyes biggest global poverty line increase in decades", The Financial Times, May 9, 2014, http://www.ft.com/intl/cms/s/0/091808e0-d6da-11e3-b95e-00144feabdc0.html?siteedition=intl#axzz39qhmCq3k Retrieved on May 31, 2014

5. John Burn-Murdoch and Steve Bernard, The Fragile Middle: millions face poverty as emerging economies slow, The Financial Times, http://www.ft.com/intl/cms/s/2/95fb1cca-c181-11e3-83af-00144feabdc0.html#axzz37H3xiJiA 13 April 2014

6. "Country Briefing: Multidimensional Poverty Index (MPI) At a Glance" Oxford Poverty and Human Development Initiative (OPHI), Oxford Dept of International Development, December 2011 http://www.ophi.org.uk/wp-content/uploads/India.pdf?cda6c1 Retrieved on May 31, 2014

7. Sumner (2004), Economic Well-being and Non-economic Well-being, A Review of the Meaning and Measurement of Poverty, ISBN 92-9190-617-4.

8. Gallagher, Robert (1992), "Rickshaws of Bangladesh", May 1, 1992, University Press Limited, Dhaka, Bangladesh.

9. Begum, Sharifa & Sen, Binayak (2005), "Pulling rickshaws in the city of Dhaka: a way out of poverty?", Environment and Urbanization 2005 17: 11, DOI: 10.1177/095624780501700202, http://eau.sagepub.com/content/17/2/11 Retrieved on May 31, 2014

10. Quigley, Carroll (1966), "Tragedy and Hope: A History of The World in Our Time", The Macmillan Company, New York, pp.176-179

11. National Crime Reports Bureau, ADSI Report Annual - 2012 Government of India, Page 242, Table 2.11, http://ncrb.nic.in/CD-ADSI-2012/ADSI2012.pdf Retrieved on May 31, 2014

12. "1.5 lakh farmers committed suicide between 1997 and 2005", Rediff News, November 22, 2007, http://specials.rediff.com/news/2007/nov/22sld1.htm Retrieved on May 31, 2014

13. Assadi, Muzaffar. 1998. "Farmer's Suicide –Signs of Distress in Rural Economy", Economic and :Political Weekly, 23 (14):747-48.

14. Bateman, Milford. 2010. Why Doesn't Microfinance Work? The Destructive Rise of Local Neoliberalism. London: Zed Books.

15. "Derivative (finance)", Wikipedia, http://en.wikipedia.org/wiki/Derivative_%28finance%29 Retrieved on May 31, 2014

16. Heinberg, Richard (2011), "The End of Growth: Adapting to our New Economic Reality", New Society Publishers, Canada. pp. 1-25.

17. Zaman, Monowaruz (2012), "Greenhouse care economics: A Solution to the Capitalist's Dilemma", International Journal of Green Economics, Volume 6, Issue 2, 2012, page. 189-504.

18. Smith, Richard (2010) "Beyond Growth or Beyond Capitalism?", real-world economics review, issue no. 53, 26 June 2010, pp. 28-42, http://www.paecon.net/PAEReview/issue53/Smith53.pdf Retrieved on May 31, 2014.

19. "Capitalism", Wikipedia, http://en.wikipedia.org/wiki/Capitalism Retrieved on May 31, 2014.

20. Pluta (2011) Joseph E., "Human Progress Amid Resistance to Change", FriesenPress, Victoria, BC, Canada, April, 2011.

21. Stiglitz, Joseph (2003), "Information and The Change in the Paradigm in Economics", The American Economists, Vol. 47, No.2 (Fall 2003), http://www0.gsb.columbia.edu/faculty/jstiglitz/download/2003_Information_and_th e_Change_in_the_Paradigm_in_Economics_Part_1_2.pdf Retrieved on May 31, 2014.

22. Coase, Ronald H. (1937). "The Nature of the Firm". Economica 4 (16): 386. doi:10.1111/j.1468-0335.1937.tb00002, http://onlinelibrary.wiley.com/doi/10.1111/j.1468-0335.1937.tb00002.x/abstract;jsessionid=16ABFD68B30F545D522E3781022E0356.f04t01 Retrieved on May 31, 2014.

23. Ross, Stephen (1973), "The Economic Theory of Agency: The Principal's Problem", VOL. 63 NO. 2 American Economic Association, May, 1973, p-134, http://www.aeaweb.org/aer/top20/63.2.134-139.pdf Retrieved on May 31, 2014.

24. Zaman, Monowaruz (2010). Economics of Information Biasing And Its Application for Poverty Alleviation, VDM Verlag Dr. Müller e.K., Germany.

25. Kunen, James (1968), "The Strawberry Statement; Notes of a College Revolutionary", Random House, New York.

26. Griffin, Edward (1982), "The Capitalist Conspiracy", Transcript, H.B. Patriots, California, http://www.scribd.com/doc/2557593/Edward-Griffin-The-Capitalist-Conspiracy-Original-Transcript, Retrieved on May 31, 2014

27. Stigler, George J. (1967), Imperfections in the Capital Market, Journal of Political Economy, LXXV, pp. 213–225.

28. Stiglitz, Joseph E. (2002) Information and the Change in the Paradigm in Economics, The American Economic Review, Vol. 92, No. 3 (Jun., 2002), pp. 460-501.

29. Stiglitz, Joseph E. (2000). The Contributions of the Economics of Information to Twentieth Century Economics, The Quarterly Journal of Economics, pp 1441-1478.

30. North, Douglass C., (1994). Economic Performance through Time, American Economic Review, Vol.84, No.3, pp-359-368.

31. Hodgson, Geoffrey M. (2006). What Are Institutions, Journal of Economic Issues, XL, p-1-24.

32. Sperry, Roger W. (1991). In Defense of Mentalism and Emergent Interaction. Journal of Mind and Behavior 12, no. 2, pp. 221–46.

33. Hodgson, Geoffery M. (2003). The Hidden Persuaders: Institutions and Individuals in Economic Theory. Cambridge Journal of Economics 27, no. 2: pp. 159–75.

34. North, Douglass C., (1990). Institutions, Institutional Change, and Economic Performance, New York: Cambridge University Press.

35. Daly, Herman E. (2008) "A Steady-State Economy", Sustainable Development Commission, UK, April 24, 2008, http://www.sd-commission.org.uk/data/files/publications/Herman_Daly_thinkpiece.pdf Retrieved on May 31, 2014.

36. Joel Bakan (2004), "The Corporation", Free Press, New York, pp. 34-35.

37. Arnott, Richard J. and Stiglitz, Joseph E., The Welfare Economics of Moral Hazard (April 1991). NBER Working Paper No. w3316. Available at SSRN: http://ssrn.com/abstract=227986 Retrieved on May 31, 2014.

38. Simon, Herbert A. (1982). Models of Bounded Rationality. Cambridge, MA: MIT Press.

39. "Conspiracy Theory", Wikipedia, http://en.wikipedia.org/wiki/Conspiracy_theory Retrieved on May 31, 2014.

40. Justin Fox, "Wall Streeters like conspiracy theories. Always have", Time Magazine, October 1, 2009, http://business.time.com/2009/10/01/wall-streeters-like-conspiracy-theories-always-have/#ixzz25oLYj4FF Retrieved on May 31, 2014.

41. Quigley, Carroll (1966), "Tragedy and Hope: A History of The World in Our Time", The Macmillan Company, New York.

42. Quigley, Carroll (1966), "Tragedy and Hope: A History of The World in Our Time", The Macmillan Company, New York, pp.324

43. Digby, William (1901), "Prosperous British India: A Revelation from Official Records", Paternoster Square, London.

44. Quigley, Carroll (1966), "Tragedy and Hope: A History of The World in Our Time", The Macmillan Company, New York, pp.51

45. Mullins, Eustace (1985), "The World Order: A Study in the Hegemony of Parasitism", Ezra Pound Institute of Civilization, Staunton, VA 24401, pp.9

46. Morton, Frederic (1998), "The Rothschilds: A Family Portrait ", Kodansha USA; Reprint edition (First Published January 1st, 1963), ISBN-10: 156836220X

47. Quigley, Carroll (1966), "Tragedy and Hope: A History of The World in Our Time", The Macmillan Company, New York, pp.129

48. Quigley, Carroll (1966), "Tragedy and Hope: A History of The World in Our Time", The Macmillan Company, New York, pp.128-135.

49. Thomas, Antony (1997). Rhodes: Race for Africa. St. Martin's Press. ISBN 978-0-312-16982-4.

50. Rotberg, Robert I. (1988). The Founder: Cecil Rhodes and the Pursuit of Power. Oxford University Press. ISBN 978-0-19-987920-5.

51. Ferguson, Niall (1999). The house of Rothschild: the world's banker, 1849-1999. Viking. ISBN 978-0-670-88794-1.

52. "Eye of Providence, The Great Seal of the United States. This is the legitimate Great Seal of United States One Dollar bill use", This work is in the public domain in the United States and identified as being free of known restrictions under copyright law, including all related and neighboring rights. Repository: Library of Congress Rare Book and Special Collections Division Washington, D.C. 20540 USA, http://www.loc.gov/pictures/item/2004676788/ or http://loc.gov/pictures/resource/cph.3a45703/ Reproduction Number: LC-USZ62-45509, Rights Advisory: No known restrictions on publication. Retrieved on from https://de.wikipedia.org/wiki/Datei:Dollarnote_siegel_hq.jpg on May 31, 2014.

53. "New World Order (conspiracy theory)", Wikipedia, http://en.wikipedia.org/wiki/New_World_Order_%28conspiracy_theory%29 Retrieved on May 31, 2014.

54. "Annuit cœptis", Wikipedia, http://en.wikipedia.org/wiki/Annuit_c%C5%93ptis Retrieved on May 31, 2014.

55. Lewis and Short, A Latin Dictionary: Founded on Andrews' Edition of Freund's Latin Dictionary: Revised, Enlarged, and in Great Part Rewritten by Charlton T. Lewis, Ph.D. and Charles Short, LL.D. The Clarendon Press, Oxford, 1879.

56. "Novus Ordo Seclorum – Origin and Meaning of the Motto Beneath the American Pyramid", http://www.greatseal.com/mottoes/seclorum.html Retrieved on May 31, 2014.

57. Griffin, G. Edward, "The Capitalist Conspiracy", Documentary, 1969, , http://www.youtube.com/watch?v=udWXFC2sWU8 Retrieved on May 31, 2014.

58. Quigley, Carroll (1966), "Tragedy and Hope: A History of The World in Our Time", The Macmillan Company, New York, pp.952.

59. Schultz, Duane P; Schultz, Sydney Ellen, A History of Modern Psychology, p. 128

60. Stover, John F. (1997). American Railroads (2nd ed.). Chicago: University of Chicago Press. pp. 245–252. ISBN 978-0-226-77658-3.

61. "Standard Oil", Wikipedia, http://en.wikipedia.org/wiki/Standard_Oil Retrieved on May 31, 2014.

62. Quigley, Carroll (1966), "Tragedy and Hope: A History of The World in Our Time", The Macmillan Company, New York, pp.72

63. Meyer Weinberg, ed. America's Economic Heritage (1983) 2: 350.

64. Brandeis, Louis D (1914). Other People's Money and How the Bankers Use It. ch. 2, Ed. Melvin I. Urofsky. (1995). ISBN 0-312-10314-X

65. Bruner, Robert F.; Carr, Sean D. (2007), The Panic of 1907: Lessons Learned from the Market's Perfect Storm, Hoboken, New Jersey: John Wiley & Sons, ISBN 978-0-470-15263-8, pp. 38-40, 103-107.

66. "Panic of 1907", Wikipedia, http://en.wikipedia.org/wiki/Panic_of_1907 Retrieved on May 31, 2014.

67. "Federal Reserve System", Wikipedia, http://en.wikipedia.org/wiki/Federal_Reserve_System Retrieved on May 31, 2014.

68. Link, Arthur Stanley (1972), "Woodrow Wilson and the Progressive Era, 1910–1917 standard political history of the era.

69. "Nelson W. Aldrich", Wikipedia, http://en.wikipedia.org/wiki/Nelson_W._Aldrich Retrieved on May 31, 2014.

70. Keleher, Robert (1997-03). "The Importance of the Federal Reserve". Joint Economic Committee. U.S. House of Representatives.

71. Quigley, Carroll (1966), "Tragedy and Hope: A History of The World in Our Time", The Macmillan Company, New York, pp.60-61.

72. Quigley, Carroll (1966), "Tragedy and Hope: A History of The World in Our Time", The Macmillan Company, New York, pp.93-94

73. Mullins, Eustace (1985), "The World Order: A Study in the Hegemony of Parasitism", Ezra Pound Institute of Civilization, Staunton, VA, pp.12-14.

74. For details on this, see "50 Years After", an interview with Alexander Kerensky, U.S. News and World Report, March 13, 1967, pp.67, 68. Also Papers Relating to

the Foreign Relations of the United States-1918, Russia, House of Representatives Document 1868 (U.S. Government Printing Office, 1931) Vol. 1. pp.374-376.

75. Quigley, Carroll (1966), "Tragedy and Hope: A History of The World in Our Time", The Macmillan Company, New York, pp.949-950

76. Hegel, Georg Wilhelm Friedrich (1874), The Logic. Encyclopaedia of the Philosophical Sciences. 2nd Edition. London: Oxford University Press.

77. Henderson, Dean (2010), "Big Oil & Their Bankers in the Persian Gulf: Four Horsemen, Eight Families & Their Global Intelligence, Narcotics & Terror Network", Createspace, ISBN-10: 1453757732, pp.345-348.

78. Heinberg, Richard (2013), "Snake Oil: How Big Energy's Misleading Promise of Plenty Imperils Our Future", Post Carbon Institute, Santa Rosa.

79. "The Price of Offshore Revisited: Press Release", Tax Justice Network, 19th July 2012, http://www.taxjustice.net/cms/upload/pdf/The_Price_of_Offshore_Revisited_Presser_120722.pdf Retrieved on May 31, 2014.

80. Shaxson, Nicholas (2011), "Treasure Islands: Tax Havens and the Men who Stole the World", Bodley Head. ISBN 978-1-84792-110-9.

81. "Clear and Present Danger; Centrally cleared derivatives.(clearing houses)". The Economist (Economist Newspaper Ltd.(subscription required)). 2012-04-12. Retrieved on 2013-05-10.

82. Heinberg, Richard (2015), "Our Renewable Future", Post Carbon Institute, January 21, 2015, http://www.postcarbon.org/our-renewable-future-essay/ Retrieved on January 31, 2015.

83. Heinberg, Richard (2015), "Afterburn: Society Beyond Fossil Fuels", New Society Publishers, Canada, January 2015.

84. Tainer, Joseph (1990), "The Collapse of Complex Societies", Cambridge University Press, ISBN-10: 052138673X, ISBN-13: 978-0521386739.

Chapter 9: A Switch Over Strategy (SoS)

1. "Collapse", a documentary film directed by Chris Smith, interview of author Michael Ruppert on his book "Confronting Collapse: The Crisis of Energy and Money in a Post Peak Oil World", https://www.youtube.com/watch?v=IVd-zAXACrU Retrieved 22 February, 2015.

2. Simmons, Matthew (2003), "Revealing Statements from a Bush Insider about Peak Oil and Natural Gas Depletion" From The Wilderness Publications, http://www.fromthewilderness.com/free/ww3/061203_simmons.html Retrieved on 15 September, 2014.

3. "1.2 Billion Vehicles On World's Roads Now, 2 Billion By 2035: Report", by John Voelcker, Green Car Reports, 29 July, 2014, http://www.greencarreports.com/news/1093560_1-2-billion-vehicles-on-worlds-roads-now-2-billion-by-2035-report Retrieved 24 February, 2015.

4. Martenson, Chris (2011). The Crash Course: The Unsustainable Future of Our Economy, Energy, and Environment. John Wily & Sons, Inc., New Jersey.

5. Tienhaara, Kyla. (2009), "A Tale of Two Crises: What the Global Financial Crisis Means for the Global Environmental Crisis", Global Governance Working Paper No 37.

6. Heinberg, Richard (2011), "The End of Growth: Adapting to our New Economic Reality", New Society Publishers, Canada. pp.231-259.

7. "Clear and Present Danger; Centrally cleared derivatives.(clearing houses)". The Economist, April 12, 2012. Retrieved 2013-05-10.

8. "National Debt of the United states", Wikipedia, http://en.wikipedia.org/wiki/National_debt_of_the_United_States Retrieved on 15 September, 2014.

9. "Four energy policies can keep the 2°C climate goal alive", International Energy Agency, 10 June, 2013,

http://www.iea.org/newsroomandevents/pressreleases/2013/june/four-energy-policies-can-keep-the-2c-climate-goal-alive.html Retrieved on 15 Sept., 2014.

10. Gilbert, Natasha (2010), "Balancing water supply and wildlife", Nature, Published online 29 September 2010, http://www.nature.com/news/2010/100929/full/news.2010.505.html Retrieved on 15 September, 2014.

11. Heinberg, Richard (2015), "Afterburn: Society Beyond Fossil Fuels", New Society Publishers, Canada, January 2015.

12. "Notwithstanding Significant Uncertainties, the U.S.-China Joint Announcement on Climate Change Is a Big Deal", by Tim Boersma, Brookings, November 13, 2014, http://www.brookings.edu/blogs/planetpolicy/posts/2014/11/13-us-china-joint-announcement-on-climate-change-boersma Retrieved 14 January, 2015

13. "China's Reality in the US-China Climate Change Deal", by Sara Hsu, The Diplomat, November 14, 2014, http://thediplomat.com/2014/11/chinas-reality-in-the-us-china-climate-change-deal/ Retrieved 14 January, 2015.

14. Daly, Herman E. (2008) "A Steady-State Economy", Sustainable Development Commission, UK, April 24, 2008, http://www.sd-commission.org.uk/data/files/publications/Herman_Daly_thinkpiece.pdf Retrieved 23 August, 2014.

15. Zaman, Monowaruz (2012). "Greenhouse Care Economics: A Solution to the Capitalist's Dilemma", International Journal of Green Economics, Volume 6, No 2, 2012

16. Smith, Richard (2010) "Beyond Growth or Beyond Capitalism?", real-world economics review, issue no. 53, 26 June 2010, pp. 28-42, http://www.paecon.net/PAEReview/issue53/Smith53.pdf 23 August, 2014

17. Keynes, John Maynard (1926), "The end of laissez-faire", This essay, which was published as a pamphlet by the Hogarth Press in July 1926. http://www.panarchy.org/keynes/laissezfaire.1926.html 15 September, 2014.

18. Zaman, Monowaruz (2010). Economics of Information Biasing And Its Application for Poverty Alleviation, VDM Verlag Dr. Müller e.K., Germany.

19. Heinberg, Richard (2015), "Our Renewable Future", Post Carbon Institute, January 21, 2015, http://www.postcarbon.org/our-renewable-future-essay/ Retrieved January 31, 2015.

20. Joel Bakan, "The Corporation," documentary movie, Big Picture Media Corporation, 2003.

21. Demick, Barbara (2010), "Nothing to Envy: Real Lives in North Korea (UK ed.)", Granta Publications. ISBN 978-1-84708-141-4.

22. Rubin, Jeff (2012), "The End of Growth", Random House Canada.

23. "Hundredth monkey effect", Wikipedia, http://en.wikipedia.org/wiki/Hundredth_monkey_effect Retrieved Jan 15, 2015.

24. Amundson, Ron (Summer 1985). Kendrick Frazier, ed. "The Hundredth Monkey Phenomenon". Skeptical Inquirer: 348–356.

25. Keyes, Ken (1984). "The Hundredth Monkey. Camarillo: DeVorss & Co. ISBN 0-942024-01-X.

26. "The Power of Community: How Cuba Survived Peak Oil", a documentary film directed by Faith Morgan, 2006, Community Solutions: The Arthur Morgan Institute for Community Solutions, https://www.youtube.com/watch?v=L2TzvnRo6_c, Retrieved 20 April, 2015.

27. Zittel, Werner & Schindler, Jorg (2007), "Coal:Resources and Future Production", EWG-Paper 1/07, Ottobrunn, Germany:Energy Watch Group.

28. Meadows, Donella H; Randers, Jorgen; Meadows, Dennis L.; Behrens, William W. "The Limits to growth: A report for the Club of Rome's Project on the Predicament of Mankind", Universe Books, 2nd edition February 18, 1974.

29. Heinberg, Richard (2011), "The End of Growth: Adapting to our New Economic Reality", New Society Publishers, Canada. pp.105-145.

30. "Youth anxiety on the rise amid changing climate", by Gayle Macdonald, May 01, 2014, http://www.theglobeandmail.com/life/health-and-fitness/health/youth-anxiety-on-the-rise-amid-changing-climate/article18372258/

31. Quadir, Iqbal (2003). Bottom-up Economics, Harvard Business Review, Issue August 2003.

32. Daly, Herman E. & Farley, Joshua (2003), "Ecological Economics: Principles And Applications", Island Press, pp.178-180.

33. "Are you Ready for Generation Z" by Anne Kingston, July 21, 2014, Maclean's, Toronto, Canada.

34. US Public Debt Per Capita:52.69K USD for Jan 2014, http://ycharts.com/indicators/us_per_capita_public_debt.

35. "China Soon to Have Almost as Many Drivers as U.S. Has People", by Rose Yu, Nov 28, 2014, The Wall Street Journal, http://blogs.wsj.com/chinarealtime/2014/11/28/china-soon-to-have-almost-as-many-drivers-as-u-s-has-people/ Retrieved 22 April, 2015.

36. "Generation X", Wikipedia, http://en.wikipedia.org/wiki/Generation_X Retrieved on 15 September, 2014.

37. Hubbert, M. King (1956). Nuclear Energy and the Fossil Fuels 'Drilling and Production Practice, American Petroleum Institute. San Antonio, Texas.

38. Latin, Howard A. (2012) Climate Change Policy Failures: Why Conventional Mitigation Approaches Cannot Succeed, World Scientific Publishing Company.

39. Tapscott, Don (2008), "Grown up Digital: How the Net Generation is Changing Your World", McGraw-Hill.

40. "Barack Obama's green plans could cripple America's economy", by By Richard Wellings, The Telegraph, 03 August, 2015, http://www.telegraph.co.uk/news/worldnews/barackobama/11780350/Barack-Obamas-green-plans-could-cripple-Americas-economy.html Retrieved on August 6, 2015.

41. University of California - Berkeley. "How to beat the climate crisis? Start with carrots: Researchers say promotion of clean energy helps build key political coalitions." ScienceDaily. 10 September 2015. www.sciencedaily.com/releases/2015/09/150910144052.htm Retrieved November 25, 2015.

42. Jin, Jianfang (2014), "The General Theory of Eco-Social Science", Author House, Bloomington, IN, USA

43. "Best way to fight climate change? Stop fighting", By Ben Knight, Geekquinox Science and Weather, September 17, 2015, https://ca.news.yahoo.com/blogs/geekquinox/best-way-to-fight-climate-change--stop-fighting-184902022.html Retrieved November 24, 2015.

44. Jonas Meckling, Nina Kelsey, Eric Biber, John Zysman. Winning coalitions for climate policy. Science, 2015 DOI: 10.1126/science.aab1336

45. "Fact Sheet: White House Announces Commitments to the American Business Act on Climate Pledge", October 19, 2015, https://www.whitehouse.gov/the-press-office/2015/10/19/fact-sheet-white-house-announces-commitments-american-business-act Retrieved November 27, 2015.

46. Dhara , Sagar (2015) "The challenge is deeper than technology", Bulletin of the Atomic Scientists, 20 November, 2015 http://thebulletin.org/technologys-role-climate-solution Retrieved December 12, 2015

47. Graph prepared by the author by using data from " CO2 time series 1990-2014 per capita for world countries". Netherlands Environmental Assessment Agency, http://edgar.jrc.ec.europa.eu/overview.php?v=CO2ts_pc1990-2014 Retrieved December 12, 2015

48. Burrow, Sharan, "Back to the Future: Our Journey to Zero Carbon, Zero Poverty World", Huff Post, 24, September, 2015, http://www.huffingtonpost.com/sharan-burrow/back-to-the-future---our_b_8187960.html Retrieved December 12, 2015.

49. Heinberg, Richard (2014), "Renewable Energy after COP21: Nine issues for climate leaders to think about the journey home", Post Carbon Institute, December 14, 2015,

http://www.postcarbon.org/renewable-energy-after-cop21/ Retrieved December 15, 2015

50. Heinberg, Richard (2015), "Our Renewable Future", Post Carbon Institute, January 21, 2015, http://www.postcarbon.org/our-renewable-future-essay/ Retrieved on January 31, 2015.

51. Kennedy, John F. (1963), "President Kennedy's Inaugural Address", January 20, 1961, Washington, D.C, John F. Kennedy Presidential Library and Museum, http://www.jfklibrary.org/Research/Research-Aids/Ready-Reference/JFK-Quotations/Inaugural-Address.aspx Retrieved on February 21, 2016.

52. "I have a dream...", Martin Luther King, Jr, Speech at the "march on Washington", https://www.archives.gov/press/exhibits/dream-speech.pdf Retrieved on February 21, 2016.

53. Commencement Address at American University, June 10, 1963, John F. Kennedy Presidential Library and Museum, http://www.jfklibrary.org/Asset-Viewer/BWC7I4C9QUmLG9J6I8oy8w.aspx Retrieved on February 22, 2016.

Chapter 10 Greenhouse Care Economics

1. "Climate Change 2007: The Physical Science Basis", Intergovernmental Panel on Climate Change, Geneva, http://www.ipcc.ch/publications_and_data/publications_ipcc_fourth_assessment_report_wg1_report_the_physical_science_basis.htm,

2. "IPCC: rapid carbon emission cuts vital to stop severe impact of climate change", by Damian Carrington, The Guardian, November 2, 2014, http://www.theguardian.com/environment/2014/nov/02/rapid-carbon-emission-cuts-severe-impact-climate-change-ipcc-report Retrieved on January 31, 2015.

3. Zaman, M. (2012), "Greenhouse care economics: a solution to the capitalist's dilemma", International Journal of Green Economics 2012 - Vol. 6, No.2 pp. 189 - 204.

4. "First Plantation", Painting by S.M. Sultan, Oil on Canvas, 107X144cm, 1975, Collection: Bangladesh Shilpakala Academy, Dhaka, Bangladesh, printed with permission from Bangladesh Shilpakala Academy.

5. Heinberg, Richard (2015), "Our Renewable Future", Post Carbon Institute, January 21, 2015, http://www.postcarbon.org/our-renewable-future-essay/ Retrieved January 31, 2015.

6. Martenson, Chris (2011), "The Crash Course: The Unsustainable Future of Our Economy, Energy, and Environment". John Wily & Sons, Inc., Hoboken, New Jersey.

7. "What the Cancer Industry doesn't want YOU to know", http://www.youtube.com/watch?v=7YFS5qlAzgc Retrieved on January 31, 2015.

8. "Cancer Facts & Figures 2007", American Cancer Society, http://www.cancer.org/research/cancerfactsstatistics/cancerfactsfigures2007/index Retrieved on January 31, 2015.

9. "Docs Say Stop Taking Multivitamins", Stampler, Laura (2013), TIME, December 17, 2013 http://healthland.time.com/2013/12/17/docs-say-stop-taking-multivitamins/ Retrieved on January 31, 2015.

10. "Sustainable Energy for All", United Nations, http://www.un.org/millenniumgoals/pdf/SEFA.pdf Retrieved on January 31, 2015.

11. "Remap 2030: A Renewable Energy Roadmap", International Renewable Energy Agency (IREA), June 2014, Abu Dhabi. www.irena.org/remap Retrieved on January 31, 2015.

12. "What exactly are green bonds?" by Caldecott, Ben, January 11, 2011, The Guardian, http://www.theguardian.com/environment/cif-green/2011/jan/11/what-are-green-bonds 10 January, 2015.

13. "Solar-powered roads: Coming to a highway near you?" by Teo Kermeliotis, CNN, 18 September, 2014, http://www.cnn.com/2014/05/12/tech/solar-powered-roads-coming-highway/ Retrieved 3 March, 2015.

14. "Solar Roadways passes $1.4 million in crowdfunding: Just short of the $56 trillion required, but not bad for a crazy idea", by Sebastian Anthony, 27 May, 2014, http://www.extremetech.com/extreme/183130-solar-roadways-passes-1-4-million-in-crowdfunding-just-short-of-the-56-trillion-required-but-not-bad-for-a-crazy-idea Retrieved 3 March, 2015.

15. "As solar panels pile up, China takes axe to polysilicon producers", By Charlie Zhu, Reuters, July 31, 2013, http://www.reuters.com/article/2013/07/31/us-china-solar-polysilicon-idUSBRE96U1CD20130731

16. "List of countries by electricity production from renewable sources", http://en.wikipedia.org/wiki/List_of_countries_by_electricity_production_from_renewable_sources

17. "Electricity sector in Bangladesh", Wikipedia, http://en.wikipedia.org/wiki/Electricity_sector_in_Bangladesh Retrieved on January 31, 2015.

18. "Renewable energy", Wikipedia, http://en.wikipedia.org/wiki/Renewable_energy Retrieved on January 31, 2015.

19. "IEA Key energy statistics 2010", http://www.iea.org/statistics/ Retrieved on January 31, 2015.

20. National Research Council (2010). "Electricity from Renewable Resources: Status, Prospects, and Impediments". National Academies of Science. p. 4.

21. Mark A. Delucchi and Mark Z. Jacobson (2011). "Providing all global energy with wind, water, and solar power, Part II: Reliability, system and transmission costs, and policies". Energy Policy 39. Elsevier Ltd. pp. 1170–1190, http://web.stanford.edu/group/efmh/jacobson/Articles/I/DJEnPolicyPt2.pdf Retrieved February 8, 2015.

22. "Can Graphene Oxide Filters Unlock Our Most Abundant Water Source?", by Jason Dorrieron, 11 March, 2014, Longevity, Singularity, http://singularityhub.com/2014/03/11/can-graphene-oxide-filters-unlock-our-most-abundant-water-source/ Retrieved 8 February, 2015.

23. John Wiseman et al (2013). "Post Carbon Pathways". University of Melbourne, April 2013, http://www.postcarbonpathways.net.au/wp-content/uploads/2013/05/Post-Carbon-Pathways-Report-2013_Final-V.pdf Retrieved 8 February, 2015.

24. Sen, Amartya (1981), "Poverty and Famines: An Essay on Entitlement and Deprivation", Oxford University Press,ISBN-10: 0198284632.

25. Zaman, M. (2001) 'Greenhouse care-a proposal of a new economic development model for the poorest people of an economy', Journal of Business Administration, Vol. 27, Nos. 3/4.

26. Quadir, Iqbal (2003). Bottom-up Economics, Harvard Business Review, Issue August 2003.

27. "Ralegan Siddhi", Wikipedia, http://en.wikipedia.org/wiki/Ralegan_Siddhi Retrieved on January 31, 2015.

28. "The Value of Natural Capital - Communities regenerate natural capital". World Bank Institute. Retrieved 10 November, 2013.

29. "Green Belt Movement", Wikipedia, http://en.wikipedia.org/wiki/Green_Belt_Movement Retrieved on January 31, 2015.

30. Rothschild, M. and Stiglitz, J. (1976) 'Equilibrium in competitive insurance markets: an essay on the economics of imperfect information', The Quarterly Journal of Economics, Vol. 90, pp.629–649.

31. Zaman, M. (2010) Economics of Information Biasing and Its Application for Poverty Alleviation, VDM Verlag Dr. Müller e.K., Germany.

32. Zaman, M. (2001) 'Greenhouse care-a proposal of a new economic development model for the poorest people of an economy', Journal of Business Administration, Vol. 27, Nos. 3/4.

33. Yunus, M. (2007) Creating a World without Poverty: Social Business and the Future of Capitalism, Public Affairs, New York.

34. "Remap 2030: A Renewable Energy Roadmap", International Renewable Energy Agency (IREA), June 2014, Abu Dhabi. www.irena.org/remap Retrieved on January 31, 2015.

35. "Is the Green Investment Bank paving the way for a Green Economy or a Political Facade?" by Laura Cloutman, January 03, 2013.

36. IEA (2012), "Technology Roadmap: Bioenergy for Heat and Power", OECD/IEA, Paris,   www.iea.org/publications/freepublications/publication/bioenergy.pdf. Retrieved on January 31, 2015.

37. "Green Investment Bank announces £11m investment in biomass plant" by Ilaria Bertini, October 1st, 2013, http://blueandgreentomorrow.com/2013/10/01/green-investment-bank-announces-11m-investment-in-biomass-plant/ Retrieved on January 31, 2015.

38. Lovins, Amory B., "Sowing Confusion About Renewable Energy", Forbes, 5 August, 2015, http://www.forbes.com/sites/amorylovins/2014/08/05/sowing-confusion-about-renewable-energy/ Retrieved on January 31, 2015.

39. "UK Green Investment Bank hires two offshore wind directors" by Tom Revell, July 26, 2014, Blue & Grreen, http://blueandgreentomorrow.com/2014/07/26/uk-green-investment-bank-hires-two-offshore-wind-directors/ Retrieved on January 31, 2015.

40. "The green investment bank: neither particularly green, nor a bank" The Guardian, 27 January 2011, http://www.theguardian.com/environment/blog/2011/jan/27/green-investment-bank Retrieved on January 31, 2015.

41. Heinberg, Richard (2011), "The End of Growth: Adapting to our New Economic Reality", New Society Publishers, Canada. pp. 231-266.

42. JAK Medlemsbank, Delårsrapport Januari – Augusti 2011, https://www.jak.se/sites/default/files/Del%c3%a5rsrapport%20aug%202011%20pdf-original.pdf Retrieved February 9, 2014.

43. Heinberg, Richard (2011), "The End of Growth: Adapting to our New Economic Reality", New Society Publishers, Canada, Chapter 6.

44. Susan Arterian Chang, "Moving Towards a Steady-State Economy," The Finance Professionals' Post, a publication of the New York Society of Security Analysts, posted April 12, 2010.

45. "Eco-Municipalities: Sweden   and   the   United   States," http://www.knowledgetemplates.com/sja/ecomunic.htm Retrieved Feb 9, 2014.

46. "Are you Ready for Generation Z" by Anne Kingston, July 21, 2014, Maclean's, Toronto, Canada.

47. "IPCC: rapid carbon emission cuts vital to stop severe impact of climate change", by Damian   Carrington,   The   Guardian,   November   2,   2014, http://www.theguardian.com/environment/2014/nov/02/rapid-carbon-emission-cuts-severe-impact-climate-change-ipcc-report Retrieved on January 31, 2015.

48. "3mn more families to come under renewable energy system", The Bangladesh Today,   November   6,   2014,   http://thebangladeshtoday.com/featured-page/2014/11/3mn-more-families-to-come-under-renewable-energy-system/ Retrieved on January 31, 2015.

49. "Bangladesh Organic Products Manufacturers Association (BOPMA)", http://www.bopma.org/ Retrieved on January 31, 2015.

50. "The Power of Community: How Cuba Survived Peak Oil", a documentary film directed by Faith Morgan, 2006, Community Solutions: The Arthur Morgan Institute for Community Solutions, https://www.youtube.com/watch?v=L2TzvnRo6_c, Retrieved 20 April, 2015.

51. "Permaculture", Wikipedia, http://en.wikipedia.org/wiki/Permaculture

52. King, FH (2004) "Farmers of Forty Centuries: Organic Farming in China, Korea, and Japan", Dover Publications, March 19 2004

53. Mollison, Bill (1997). Introduction to permaculture, Ten Speed Pr, Revised edition, ISBN-10: 0908228082.

54. Hemenway, Toby (2009). Gaia's Garden: A Guide to Home-Scale Permaculture. Chelsea Green Publishing. p. 5. ISBN 978-1-60358-029-8.

55. "USDA National Agroforestry Center (NAC)". Unl.edu, 01 August, 2011, http://nac.unl.edu/ Retrieved 23 April, 2015

56. David Graeber: anthropologist, anarchist, financial analyst, by Greg Downey, October 15, 2011, http://blogs.plos.org/neuroanthropology/2011/10/15/david-graeber-anthropologist-anarchist-financial-analyst/ Retrieved Aug 19, 2015

57. "Man continues to fight for forest he planted by hand over nearly four decades", by Kelly Putter, Yahoo News, 11 Nov, 2015, https://ca.news.yahoo.com/blogs/good-news/man-continues-to-fight-for-forest-he-planted-by-hand-over-nearly-four-decades-220941007.html

58. "5 Reasons Community-Scale Solar is a Multi GW Market Opportunity" by Kevin Brehm and Joseph Goodman, Rocky Mountain Institute, March 17th, 2016, http://cleantechnica.com/2016/03/17/5-reasons-why-community-scale-solar-is-a-multi-gw-market-opportunity/ Retrieved on March 20, 2016.

59. Kevin Anderson, "Duality in climate science," Nature Geoscience 8 (2015), pp. 898–900, http://www.nature.com/ngeo/journal/v8/n12/full/ngeo2559.html Retrieved on: December 14, 2015.

60. Heinberg, Richard (2014), Renewable Energy after COP21: Nine issues for climate leaders to think about the journey home, Post Carbon Institute, December 14, 2015, http://www.postcarbon.org/renewable-energy-after-cop21/ Retrieved on December 15, 2015.

INDEX

Kennedy 32-3, 37-8, 151-4, 199, 300, 543, 605, 623, 708, 748-9, 755, 820, 859
Kennedy, John F. 708, 749, 859
Kennet, Miriam 756, 825
Keynes, John Maynard 736, 754-5, 841, 855
Keynesian Economics 180, 190, 754, 772
Kinetic Market Energy (KME) 261, 263-4, 271, 276, 291, 308, 344, 348, 382, 408
Kinetic Money 233, 263
Kissinger, Henry 157
Korean War 143, 150, 741
Krugman, Paul 709, 759, 774, 777, 780, 787, 836, 842
Kyoto Protocol 23-4, 520-2, 645, 834

L

Laffer Curve 196-7, 298, 758, 775
League of Nations 123-4, 131, 736
Lenin, Vladimir 119, 121
Levelised Costs of Electricity (LCOE) 498
Lewisian turning point 385-8, 797-9
License Raj 391
The Limits to Growth 10, 21, 415, 665, 701, 807
London Stock Exchange 371, 583
Louisiana 88, 725

M

Maclean 642, 686, 818, 857, 864
Macroeconomics 738, 749, 756-7, 760, 775-6, 778
Maddison, Angus 704, 715
Magsaysay Award 553
Malthusian Catastrophe 468
Mangal Pandey 96
Manmohan Singh 389, 391, 397
Mao Zedong 149, 155, 375

Market Energy (ME) 259-61, 268-9, 291
Market Energy Loop (MEL) 18, 268, 272, 274, 278, 281, 284-5, 290, 309, 315, 317, 346, 549-50, 556, 637
Market Energy State (MES) 260, 262-3, 269-70, 274, 530, 581, 617
Market Skewness Factor (MSF) 270, 292
Marshall, Alfred 753
Marshall Plan 142-5, 742
Martenson, Chris 697, 772, 781, 807, 854, 860
Martin Luther 61, 640, 717, 859
Marx 45, 73, 103, 121, 160, 168-70, 172, 208, 219, 234, 308, 562, 608, 729, 750
Marx, Karl 729, 747, 750, 769
Maugeri, Leonardo 743, 819-20
McDonald 606
McKibben, Bill 833
McNamara, Robert 744
Medicaid 207, 327, 350, 362, 365
Medicare 207, 350, 362, 364-5, 444, 448, 786
Meiji 85, 106, 730
Mercantilism 561
Methodological Individualism 753
Middle East 2, 20, 28, 47, 49-50, 52, 117-18, 139, 143, 145, 202, 214, 305, 436-7, 734-5
Mill, John Stuart 167, 206
Milton Friedman 128, 186, 188, 194, 207, 302-3, 322, 324, 369, 576, 779
Ming Dynasty 55-6, 715
Minsky 18, 268, 278, 296, 310-14, 358, 528, 531, 539, 772, 776, 788
Minsky, Hyman 788
Minsky Moment 313-14, 531, 539, 776
M.I.T. x, 372, 633
MIT 495, 672, 742, 759, 844, 849
Moghul Empire 56

Y

Z

Printed in the United States
By Bookmasters